Approaching
ECONOMICS

ADRIAN PERRY

Vice-Principal, Shirecliffe College, Sheffield

Published in association with the
National Extension College

Stanley Thornes (Publishers) Ltd

Originally published in 1985 in association with the National Extension College
Reprinted 1986, 1987
Second edition 1988
Reprinted 1989

Reprinted 1990 by
Stanley Thornes (Publishers) Ltd
Old Station Drive
Leckhampton
CHELTENHAM GL53 0DN

Reprinted 1991

British Library Cataloguing in Publication Data

Perry, Adrian
    Approaching economics.
    1. Economics
    I. Title
    330   HB171

    ISBN 0 7487 0370 5

Printed and bound in Great Britain
at The Bath Press, Avon.

ACKNOWLEDGEMENTS

It would be impossible to acknowledge all the help and encouragement that I have received in preparing this book without writing another book almost as long. My main debt is to the students and staff I worked with at Abraham Moss Centre in Manchester and Wakefield District College. I must particularly mention John Herman and Allen Wright for their comments and advice. Cathy Waite of Park Lane College in Leeds was invaluable in updating the second edition of this book.

    This book started life as a Flexistudy course for the National Extension College. I would like to thank Tim Burton, the NEC courses editor, without whose patience and encouragement the book would not have been completed as well — or possibly at all.

The publishers wish to thank the following examining bodies who gave permission to print past examination questions:

Northern Ireland GCE Board, University of Oxford Delegacy of Local Examinations (OLE), Oxford and Cambridge Schools Examination Board, University of Cambridge Local Examinations Syndicate, The Welsh Joint Education Committee, Associated Examining Board, the Northern Universities Joint Matriculation Board and the University of London School Examinations Board.

The article on page 27 is printed by permission of *New Society*, that on page 28 and 370 by permission of the *Guardian*. The chart on page 53 is based, with permission, on work by Dr Jim Taylor of the University of Lancaster.

Adrian Perry
May 1988
                                       For Megan and Rachel

Contents

How to Use this Book

INTRODUCTION

'Approaching Economics' aims to introduce you to the study of economics — a subject with a long history, yet one that is being constantly updated in the light of current events and changing policies. You'll be helped in your use of the book if you look through this first section, which explains how the book is structured.

STUDY UNITS

'Approaching Economics' is divided into 29 study units — chapters, if you prefer — each devoted to a particular topic. Each unit starts with a brief introduction that reviews the ground to be covered.

In the unit's introduction you will find the **aims** — all the things you should learn from the unit, set out as a convenient checklist. You may sometimes find these a little off-putting, but they should make sense to you by the end of the unit.

Within each unit are a number of 'self-assessment questions' (**SAQs**). These questions aim to check your understanding of the material covered. Some are very short, and some will involve you in quite a bit of work (such as plotting a graph, for example).

I have prepared suggested answers for all the SAQs, and you can find these in the special **Review Section** at the back of each study unit. Again — avoid the obvious temptation of looking up the answers before making your own attempt. Also in the Review Section you'll find past examination questions on the topics covered in the unit, and suggestions for further reading.

STUDY ADVICE

There's further advice about studying economics in Unit 29, the **Study Guide**. It gives you some general tips about further reading, information about the shape of economics exams and how you might tackle them, and advice on preparing essays. Have a look at that before you start the course in earnest.

I hope you'll enjoy the course, and end up with a good exam result and a greater understanding of the economic events that lie behind so many of today's political and social questions.

1 Basic Economic Ideas

AIMS OF UNIT 1

In this unit I aim to start you on your study of the science of economics. When you have completed it you should be able to:

- explain what economists mean by 'the economic problem'
- draw a production possibility diagram and use it to explain the concept of 'opportunity cost'
- describe the main differences and similarities between a western 'market economy' and a state-planned system.

WHAT IS 'ECONOMICS'?

We all have some idea of the subject matter of economics. Every day the newspapers, TV and radio tell us about unemployment and rising prices, international trade and company profits, demands for higher pay and lower taxes. Economics is everywhere. Alfred Marshall, a great Victorian economist, put it like this:

> Economics is the study of man's actions in the ordinary business of life: it enquires how he gets his income, and how he uses it.

Let's use this definition as a start. How does man get his income? Either by producing **goods** — such as food, bricks, cars or clothes — or **services** — such as haircutting, banking, teaching or driving a lorry. Economists call goods and services **commodities**.

SAQ 1: *Write down a list of commodities you have produced — either at work or in your leisure time. When you have done this, divide them into goods and services.*

I have written my own answer at the end of this unit: compare your answers with it when you have finished. My answer includes a wide range of things, from producing goods such as potatoes to providing a service such as teaching: your list is probably just as varied.

Think for a moment why you have produced these commodities.

The reason we produce things is so that they can be consumed to satisfy wants. As Adam Smith (an economist of the eighteenth century) said, 'the end of production is consumption': food is grown to be eaten, clothes made to be worn, TV programmes made to be broadcast and enjoyed.

The factors of production

The total amount of commodities — goods and services — that are produced in one year is called the **national product** (or **national income**). To produce the national product, economic resources are used. It is usual to divide these resources up into three categories, called the **factors of production.**

The first factor is **land**: this includes all the natural resources we use in production — raw materials, land itself, minerals from quarries and mines, the produce of the sea. Goods, after all have to be made out of something. But raw materials do not turn into clothes, food, furniture and books all by themselves. They require work. So the second factor of production is **labour**: this includes all productive human effort, paid or unpaid, whether by hand or brain.

SAQ 2: *Which of the following commodities can be produced using just* land *and* labour?

bread	fruit	furniture
haircuts	books	aircraft

However a moment's thought will show you that very little can be produced using just natural resources and workers: just try to think of a list of commodities that can be produced using land and labour only. It's not easy: most production also requires the use of other goods that we have made ourselves — in other words, tools and machinery. Economists use the term **capital** to cover this third factor of production. Capital is not produced to satisfy wants directly — who wants a pneumatic drill or circular saw for its own sake? — but to help us produce more efficiently consumer goods that *do* satisfy our wants. Because capital is man-made we can only have more capital goods by producing them. Producing capital goods, like producing any commodity, requires the use of productive factors — land, labour and capital — that could have been used to make things that added directly to satisfaction. So making more capital goods usually means that we have to do without some consumer goods at the time. Capital can take many forms. Efficient production nowadays requires not only **producer goods** such as hammers, furnaces, looms and computers, but roads, schools and colleges, and hospitals. These things are known as **social capital**.

SAQ 3: *(a) Look around you and select a commodity that you can see (a table, perhaps, or a rug). Write down all the resources used in producing it. Then divide those resources into land, labour and capital.*
(b)   When discussing the problem of keeping down costs in education, a government official remarked 'there is little opportunity of substituting capital for labour in teaching'. Think about what he meant by this and then name an industry where labour has been replaced by capital in recent years. Do you agree that this is not possible in teaching?

(Some economics textbooks name a fourth factor of production. They argue that the existence of land, labour and capital by themselves is not enough to ensure the production of commodities: someone is needed to organise production, hiring the land, labour and capital that may be needed and taking the risk that production may not be profitable. This fourth factor they name **enterprise** or **entrepreneurship**. We shall return to this in later units.)

SCARCITY: THE ECONOMIC PROBLEM

Production uses up resources. The problems of economics arise because we do not have enough resources to produce everything we want. The factors of production are limited, and so the amount we can produce is also limited. But human wants tend to be limitless: even in countries with very high incomes, people are still able to spend all their incomes and want more! *Limited resources, unlimited wants* — that's the central problem of economics. It's so central that it has a special title: the problem of **scarcity**.

It's important to be clear about the concept of scarcity. When an economist says goods are scarce, he simply means that there are not enough available for everyone to freely take as much as they want.

SAQ 4: *Look at the following commodities. Which of them would be described as 'scarce' by an economist?*

bread	oil	furniture
holiday travel	paper	capital

Opportunity cost

The concept of scarcity means that in all areas of economic life, we are faced with a choice. Human wants cannot be satisfied fully: we can't have all the cars, houses, leisure, clothes, wine, education, new hospitals and so on, that we want. So if we choose to have one commodity, we have to do without another. You'll be familiar with this problem from your own experience, I'm sure. Choosing to buy some new clothes may mean cutting out some social events; paying for a birthday present stops you buying a new record you might like. The same problems of choice face the government. Expanding the army, for example, will involve cutting back on roads, or schools, or pensions (or reducing on our own, private, spending by raising taxes).

Cost measured in terms of what you have to give up to get something is called **opportunity cost**. To go back to the first example given above, the opportunity cost of decorating the house is the summer holiday you had to sacrifice to do it.

SAQ 5: *Opportunity cost, then, is a way of measuring costs by looking at the alternative(s) we could have chosen by using resources in a different way — the opportunity we gave up. So what might an economist see as the opportunity cost of*
(a)   having a child?
(b)   the Trident missile system?
(c)   national breast-cancer screening for women?
(d)   a college education?

PRODUCTION POSSIBILITY DIAGRAMS

Economists frequently use diagrams to illustrate or clarify their ideas. I mention the use of graphs in Unit 29. The important concept of opportunity cost can be illustrated on a diagram showing the different combinations of commodities that could be produced by using differently the nation's resources of land, labour and capital. Let's use an example that often causes disagreement about the use of our resources: the thorny choice between producing arms, or civilian goods.

The vertical axis (the one running up the page) measures the amount of arms produced. The horizontal axis (the one going across the page) measures the amount of civilian goods produced. The curved line from A to C shows all the combinations of arms and civilian goods that can be produced.

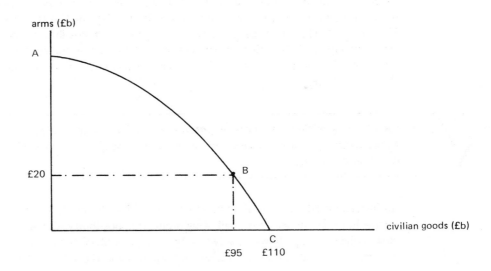

SAQ 6: *If we chose to produce the combination of goods shown by point C in the diagram, how many civilian goods would be produced? And how many arms?*

As you'll have discovered at position C, we would be producing £110 billion of civilian goods and no arms at all. So if a nation decides to produce arms in response to some threat, it must switch some of the factors of production away from making civilian goods to the business of making weapons. Look at point B, for example. We have gained £20 billion worth of weapons compared to point C – but only by giving up civilian goods. We now only produce £95 billion of civilian goods. The PP curve has illustrated the dilemmas that 'scarcity' force upon us. (In passing, you may wonder how the sacrifice of £15 billions of civilian goods gains £20 billion of military goods. It's to do with the idea of diminishing returns, to which I shall return in a later unit. Briefly, we assume that the resources switched from civilian to military production are those least suited to producing civilian goods and most suited to military. As a result, the gain in military production is greater than the loss of civilian commodities.)

SAQ 7: *To get the arms we want, we have had to give up £15 billion of civilian goods. What do we call this way of measuring the cost of arms production to society?*

This sort of diagram is called a **production possibility diagram**: it shows all the possible combinations of commodities that could be produced. It can be used to illustrate other ideas in economics. Take a look at the diagram below:

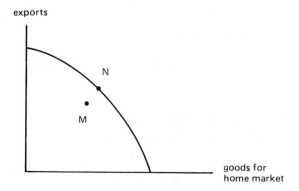

This time a different combination of commodities is shown: on the vertical axis, **exports** (goods and services produced for sale to foreigners) and on the horizontal axis those produced for the home market. You'll notice again the problem of opportunity cost. If all our resources are fully employed, then we cannot produce more exports without producing fewer goods for the home market. However, if some resources are unemployed, we will not be producing the maximum possible output, and will be at a position *inside* the production possibility line – such as point M. If we were to put the unemployed workers and idle machines to work, we could increase the output of goods for export *and* for the home market. In the diagram, this is shown by a move from point M to point N, where once again we are on the production possibility curve. At point N, resources are being fully used. Now that we have got to this 'frontier' on the production possibility line, output cannot be further increased unless we can somehow get a greater output from the resources that are available.

SAQ 8: *How might we get more output of commodities without using more factors of production? (Clue: When a factory produces more without employing any extra workers, we say that it has become more . . . what?)*

An increase in efficiency enables more commodities to be produced for both export markets and for the home consumer. In the following production possibility diagram, the economy has become more efficient. PP$_1$ shows what we were able to produce before our productive capacity was increased – and PP$_2$ shows the increase in output that is available now our productive capacity has grown. When a country has increased its ability to produce commodities, economists say that **economic growth** has occurred.

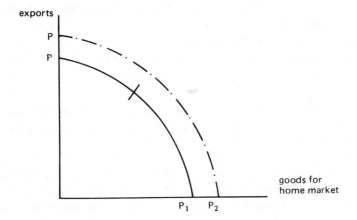

SAQ 9: *(a) Draw a production possibility diagram showing on the vertical axis government-produced goods (roads, education, health care, arms) and on the horizontal, goods for private consumption (consumer goods, food, clothes etc). Choose a point on the curve where society produces one-thirds government commodities and two-thirds commodities for private consumption. Label this point 'S'.*

Now suppose a government is elected whose policy is to cut taxation and government spending, switching the pattern of the economy towards the production of more commodities for private consumption. Where do you think the new position will be in relation to point S? Label such a possible point 'T'.

(b) In the text I suggested that to have more of one commodity society has to give up something else. See if you can explain these two cases which appear to contradict this. Illustrate with a diagram if you can.

(i) In the mid 1980s the UK could have produced more military goods without in any way reducing the output of other civilian goods.

(ii) Compared with 1960, when there was full employment, the residents of the Federal Republic of Germany are producing more goods for export and more goods for their own consumption.

(c) In 1974, the price of imported oil, upon which Britain was dependent, went up sharply. As a result, our standard of living fell. Why? (Clue: What was the opportunity cost of the extra exports we had to sell to pay for the oil?)

ECONOMIC SYSTEMS

Three key questions

Let's return now to scarcity, which I've said is the central problem of economics. The production possibility curve diagrams are just one way of showing the choices that scarcity force upon us. Opportunity cost is another. As a result of scarcity, three fundamental questions arise:

- **What** shall we produce? We cannot, after all, have everything, and so we have to decide which goods and services to produce and which ones to do without.
- **How** shall we produce? With many men and a few machines – or with little labour and much capital? And using which resources? When one method of producing is chosen, it involves an opportunity cost – the scarce resources are being used for one task rather than another.
- **For whom** shall we produce? If we cannot produce enough to satisfy everyone's wants, whose wants will be met, and whose will be left unsatisfied?

SAQ 10: *Many economic problems come down to a question of what, how and for whom to produce: maybe they all do. Which of the three questions, do you think was posed in the stories that followed these newspaper headlines?*

(a)   FEWER UNIVERSITY PLACES NEEDED, SAYS REPORT
(b)   MANNING DISPUTE DELAYS NEW STEELWORKS OPENING
(c)   BIG RISE IN PENSIONS DEMANDED BY UNION CONFERENCE
(d)   WESTERN NATIONS TO EXPAND COAL PRODUCTION TO REDUCE DEPENDENCE ON OIL
(e)   BANK PROFITS TOP £400m
(f)   WEST YORKSHIRE BUS SERVICE TO BE SUBSIDISED BY RATEPAYERS

All societies are faced with the problem of scarcity, and they all have to find a way to answer the three economic questions. Some sort of **economic system** must exist to resolve the problem of what to produce, how to produce and for whom to produce. In the past, these questions had traditional answers, and in the farmlands of Africa and Asia, crops are still grown and distributed according to age-old custom. But all over the world these **traditional economies** are being replaced (destroyed might be a better word) by systems that can cope better with our fast-changing times — either capitalist **market economies** or socialist **planned economies**. The rest of this unit takes a look at the different economic systems used in the world today. It's just a first look, though, because I want us to return to this topic later in the course when you have gained enough knowledge to make a fair comparison between the different economic systems.

The market system

This system, sometimes called the **price system**, is the one widely used in the West. Under a market system, people are relatively free to buy the goods they want with their incomes. If a good sells well, firms will continue to produce it. But if no-one buys the commodity, firms will stop making it, since in a market system firms seek to make profits from the sales of the commodities they sell. This forces firms to make only what consumers are prepared to buy: and so, it is argued, consumers (you and I) decide what society produces by the way we spend our money.

But if consumers decide *what* is to be produced, industry decides *how* to produce. Firms wishing to make the largest possible profit will employ the cheapest combination of factors that will get the job done. So in a market system, a production method gets chosen because it combines the factors of production at the lowest cost.

SAQ 11: *I've just explained how a market system decides* what *is produced and* how *to produce it. Earlier in this unit a third question was raised — for whom to produce; that is, who gets to enjoy the commodities that are produced? Explain how the market system resolves this question: what is it in such a system that decides who gets cars, bread, houses, shoes etc?*

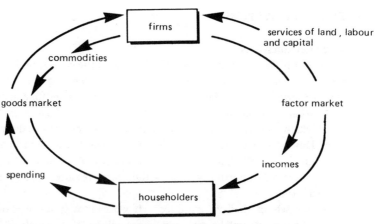

The circular flow of income

The diagram above shows how the market system works. Cover the right-hand side with your hand, and look at the left-hand side of the diagram. There, householders and firms interact in the buying and selling of the market place. Householders spend their money on commodities — goods and services — provided by the firms. If you now cover the left-hand side and look at the right-hand side of the diagram, you'll see that the householders obtained their incomes by providing the firms with the factors of production. For people this means selling their labour: but if you own natural resources or capital you can sell these to firms and get an income from doing so. Firms buy the services of the factors of production on the **factor markets** — the labour market (where people seek jobs and firms seek labour) being one factor market.

SAQ 12: *Now cover the bottom half of the diagram. Name the process going on in the top half, where the factors of production are being used up to make commodities.*

So a market system consists of firms trying to make the biggest possible profit by selling their goods and services; and householders trying to get the best deal they can from their incomes. The system's great advantage lies in the freedom it gives to householders. If they prefer tight jeans to baggy ones, or comics to culture, then that's what they get. The system is also very adaptable. When new products or opportunities occur, profit-seeking firms are eager to be first in on the new market.

However market systems do have disadvantages as well. The most obvious is the great gaps that exist between the living standards of different individuals in society. Those who have valuable skills or scarce resources to sell enjoy high incomes: those who haven't, don't. Many people find it unacceptable that an old or disabled person should have a very low income because they are not in demand on the factor markets. Another common problem in market economies is unemployment: there are periods when business is so bad that firms have to sack workers and stop producing commodities. We shall look at both the problem of earnings and the causes of unemployment in this course.

SAQ 13: *Education for most people in the UK is provided on a planned basis: that is, schools are built and teachers recruited by the state to meet a need for education projected by civil servants. Until recently, children were simply allocated to their local state school. This state school is paid for out of taxes and rates. Now, use your imagination to consider how things would work if education was run, not by the state, but by private firms in a market system.*
- *What would decide whether a school stayed open, or closed?*
- *What would decide the educational opportunities a child received?*
- *Can you think of any advantages of changing to such a system?*
- *What would be the disadvantages?*

Planned economies

The drawbacks of the market system have led the socialist states of Eastern Europe to try an entirely different way of running an economy. In these states, the government plans the production of commodities according to a fixed plan. Consumers get, and firms produce, what the plan says. Under a **planned economy** (also called a **command economy** or **collectivism** according to the textbook you happen to consult) a five- or ten-year plan is devised, and firms aim to fulfil this plan, not make a profit. The managers of firms have the responsibility of producing the amounts of goods laid down in the plan (so many yards of cloth, so many pairs of shoes) from the resources allocated to them by the planners. Productive resources are owned by the state, and no-one is allowed to employ anyone else.* In practice, however, the economies of Eastern Europe deviate from total planning. In Poland large parts of agriculture are in private ownership, although the State attempts to control the price at which agricultural goods are sold.

The planned economy has a number of advantages over the market system. For example, because the government can direct firms to employ available workers, there is little unemployment. However, like the market system, the planned economy also has disadvantages. Letting the government decide what is produced and who is to be employed and where gives the state great power. In a centrally planned society, publishers, trade unions, universities, TV and radio are all controlled by the state, limiting intellectual and political freedom. In addition, planned economies are often very inefficient. For example, if all a factory has to do to stay in business is produce its quota of 1000

*In fact there is an exception to this prohibition in the Soviet Union. Curiously enough for a socialist economy, the one category of private employee permitted is domestic servants.

shoes, who will care about style, price or quality?

SAQ 14: *All societies have to solve the problem of how to produce, but they have different economic systems. We've discussed planned economics and market economics, and mentioned the traditional economies under which many people of the Third World live. Explain how this will affect the decision of how to build a house in*
(a)   the USA
(b)   the Soviet Union
(c)   a village in West Africa.

The mixed economy

Well, then, which of these two systems do we use in Britain to decide what, how and for whom we shall produce? Look at this list of commodities and answer the question

SAQ 15: *Which economic mechanism – planning or market – decides who receives the following goods?*

cars	*jeans*
bread	*surgery*
primary schooling	*housing*

To get food, clothes or a car we have to buy from private traders who exist to make profits. But if we need education or health-care, we can use facilities planned and provided by the state. For example, the government ensures that enough school places exist for youngsters who are of school age, without any consideration of charging for entry or making a profit. In housing, we have both a planned and a market system. Tenancies of council houses are allocated on a planned basis, according to the needs or requirements of families that apply. But it is quite possible to go out and buy a house, and an increasing number of British families have done just that.

So in Britain there is a **mixed economy**. Some commodities are provided by profit-making firms via the market system, but other commodities are provided on a planned basis by the state. This means we have a 'middle way' between a pure market system and a strict planned economy. Note that, even in a mixed economy, private firms have to obey government controls on health and safety, pollution, monopoly and workers' rights. Furthermore, the less fortunate people in society are guaranteed an income high enough to survive – to provide some 'social security'.

In practice, all the world's economies are more or less mixed. The Soviet Union does not have a completely planned economy, for many peasants there grow crops on their own land and sell them for cash at local markets. Likewise, although the USA is usually regarded as an example of free-market capitalism, even there schemes exist to provide free or low-cost health care for the old and poor – and there is a nationwide system of government-supported schools and colleges.

Some economists believe that the two sorts of economic system will grow more and more alike in future. They claim that the market economies will become subject to more and more government control and planning, while planned economies will have to give greater freedom to managers and consumers. Signs of this tendency can already be seen. In western capitalist countries, governments take a large responsibility for the running of the economy, and if they make a mess of prices, incomes and the growth of the national product they get voted out of office. In the socialist countries, firms are increasingly being asked to make efficient use of resources and produce goods attractive to consumers. And in Hungary, industrial managers even have to achieve profit targets. However, you should be clear that the differences between market and planned economies are not the same as the difference between socialism and capitalism.

SAQ 16: *Look up the definition of capitalism and socialism in a good dictionary.*
*   *What is the essential difference?*
*   *Could a market system exist under socialism?*
*   *Could a planned economy exist under capitalism?*

REVIEW SECTION

First of all, make sure you have understood the key ideas introduced in this unit: we have covered a lot of ground, so check that you understand what is meant by:

commodities; the national product; the factors of production; capital; social capital; scarcity; opportunity cost; economic growth; the three key questions; market system; planned economy; mixed economy.

Further reading

You should be able to master these topics from this unit, but it would do no harm at all to do some further reading from the books recommended in Unit 29. If you would like to read a bit more about economic systems, I can recommend *Economic Systems* by Gregory Grossman (Prentice-Hall), which goes into the workings of the systems in some depth. Francis Dalton's book *Economic Systems and Society* (Penguin) will give you a broader insight into the politics of economics. Part 1 of *Readings in Economics – Book 1* by R. Rees and R.E. Baxter (Collins) contains some interesting extracts on scope and method of economics. But don't feel forced to read about economic systems yet: as I said in the unit, we will return to them in more detail later in the course.

Examination questions

Here are three essay questions that have been set on this basic topic in economics:

1. Define opportunity cost, and explain the importance of the concept.

(AEB 'A' level June 1982)

2. How does a market economy decide what to produce, how to produce and for whom to produce?

(Oxford and Cambridge 'A' level July 1984)

3. Explain the basis on which economists, in classifying economic systems, distinguish between 'market' and 'command' economies. On what basis, if any, is it possible to say which type of economy is superior?

(JMB 'A' level June 1987)

You'll be better placed to give a truly satisfactory answer to these questions a little later in the course: here are some questions which are not from past papers, but which will help you to explore some of the issues raised in Unit 1:

4. What are the economic problems of opportunity cost facing (a) the government and (b) you at the moment?

5. Since the late 1940s, the UK has had a state-planned national health service. However, in recent years there has been an expansion of private health care schemes. What do you feel are the advantages and disadvantages of such a trend?

Multiple choice questions

1. The fundamental purpose behind all production of commodities is to
(a) earn big profits
(b) increase exports
(c) fulfil state plans
(d) meet human wants
(e) use the factors of production

2. Which of the following is *not* an item of capital?
(a) a machine tool
(b) a power saw
(c) a wrist-watch
(d) a lorry
(e) a business computer

3. The economic problem is that
(a) two-thirds of the world are short of food
(b) there is a need for a price system
(c) resources are limited but human wants are not
(d) inflation exists in many economies
(e) exports seldom pay for imports

4. Capital, to an economist, means
(a) those goods which are used to aid production
(b) goods aimed at satisfying consumer wants
(c) the natural resources of the earth
(d) large amounts of money in the bank
(e) the products of labour

5. Land, labour and capital are
(a) divided into goods and services
(b) incorporated into every good offered for sale
(c) convenient categories into which to group productive resources
(d) present only in market economies.
(e) present only in planned economies.

6. Opportunity cost is a term which describes
(a) a bargain price for a productive factor
(b) costs related to optimum production levels
(c) variable costs
(d) short term costs
(e) none of the above

7. A man spends £250 on a new carpet. What is the opportunity cost to him of the carpet?
(a) £250
(b) the land, labour and capital used in making the carpet
(c) the other things he could have bought with £250
(d) the increased value of a better decorated house
(e) the reduction in his bank balance due to buying the carpet

8. Which if any of the following statements are correct?
(i) For planned economies, where unemployment is unknown, the problem of scarcity doesn't exist
(ii) For market economies, where advertising is used to persuade people to buy more goods, scarcity is not a problem
(iii) As resources are inadequate to meet all wants in both market and planned economies, scarcity is a problem

(a): (i) only   (b): (ii) only

(c): (iii) only   (d): none of them

ANSWERS TO EXERCISES

SAQ 1:   I haven't produced many goods in my life. I used to grow potatoes and cabbages in my garden, and I have worked on a farm producing more potatoes. I had a student job making filing cabinets, and another making sterilised egg for bakers. As far as services go, I have provided teaching, transported chemicals on a truck, helped with the Christmas post and written for a radio show.

SAQ 2:   None of them can! Bread requires bakery ovens, delivery vans and shops; fruit needs (at the very least) baskets for gathering; furniture needs hammers, saws, screwdrivers and glue-pots; haircuts need scissors, and so on. As I go on to explain in the text, very little can be produced without capital.

SAQ 3:   (a)   I picked the table I am writing on. It is made of wood, a natural resource that is clearly in the category of 'land'. The labour needed to cut and assemble it is obvious — also remember the labour needed to transport it to the shop and sell it. The capital equipment needed to produce the table includes saws, factories, vices, and hammers.
(b)   The industry that comes to my mind is car manufacture, in which automated production methods have meant that fewer men are needed to make a car than ever before. Some cars have even been advertised as being 'made by robots'. But many industries use even greater amounts of capital in proportion to the amount of human labour. The production of chemicals is an industry that involves the use of vast and expensive capital equipment and very few workers. Production techniques of this sort are described as **capital intensive**.
        As far as teaching goes, one could imagine a teaching method using TV, that allowed one teacher to deliver a lecture to thousands of students. Teaching machines and computer-assisted learning packages exist, too, which allow students to go through a learning programme at their own pace by pressing buttons when ready for the next section.

SAQ 4:   In the sense introduced above, they are all 'scarce'. This definition of scarcity is very broad. It means that all goods are scarce, apart from a few 'free goods' such as the air we breathe.

SAQ 5:   Opportunity cost looks at the opportunities you have given up by choosing to do something. Your answer may differ from mine on points of detail; but here's my list for comparison:

(a)   The opportunity cost of having a child for a family is all the the things they have given up. The major opportunity cost is the wife's income — the money she could have earned had she not raised a child. Compared with this, the costs of nappies and lolli-pops is not very great.

(b)   The opportunity cost of the Trident programme is what we could have had if we had chosen to spend the estimated £8,000 million in some other way, and used the specialist staff (and dollars) to do something different. This might mean alternative military spending (like stronger conventional forces), or other government programmes (better roads, schools or health care). Alternatively, government taxation or borrowing might have been correspondingly lower, in which case the opportunity cost was the consumer goods or savings that tax-payers might otherwise have been able to afford.

(c)   The opportunity cost of a breast-cancer screening programme (estimated cost £70 million a year) is the other things we could do with that money and resources. There are probably 'better buys' in health care for the money — better maternity care, perhaps, or health education on smoking and diet. This is the use of the concept of opportunity cost. When being asked to evaluate a scheme, economists do not ask 'Is this worth doing?' but (much better) 'Is this a better use of resources than any alterna-tive?'

(d)   The opportunity cost of going to college is mostly the income that could be earned by students if they didn't go to college. If we didn't send them to college, they would be out in the community producing commodities: so what we have foregone is their productive efforts. There are also the resources used directly in education: the college buildings and employees that could be used in alternative ways. In times of high youth unemployment the question of opportunity cost is given an extra twist. The savings on cutbacks in higher education have to be measured against the cost of social security to unemployed youngsters who would otherwise have gone on to higher education.

SAQ 6:   Answered in text

SAQ 7:   Opportunity cost

SAQ 8:   Greater efficiency, or productivity. A factory which produces more with the same number of workers is said to become more efficient (or productive).

SAQ 9:   (a)   The new point will be nearer the 'private goods' axis, showing the increase in private goods and the reduction in government commodities. How much nearer will depend on the size of the cuts in taxes and government spending.

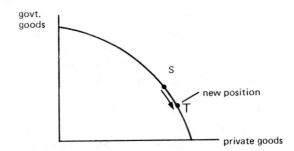

(b)
(i)   In 1980 the UK was deep in a slump — there were many unemployed workers, and so production of both military goods and civilian goods could be increased by putting them to work.
(ii)   Economic growth enabled the Germans to increase their production of all goods — exports and domestic goods. We'll look at the sources of economic growth in a unit soon.

(c)   The UK had to increase exports; as a result we could not produce as many goods for the home market, and our living standards fell.

SAQ 10:   (a)   *What* shall we produce? (Answer — fewer university places)
(b)   *How* shall we produce? (with many workers, or with few?) This is also a *for whom* question. Choosing a method of production that economises on labour will affect the amount of income earned by steelworkers, and may be aimed at raising profits.
(c)   *For whom:* the conference feels that more commodities should go to pensioners.
(d)   *How* shall we produce the energy needed for industry — but also a little bit of *for whom?* as the western nations wish to keep more of their own money!
(e)   *For whom*
(f)   A mix of all three. *What* to produce — subsidised public transport or whatever local ratepayers would have bought if their rates had been lower; *how* to provide mobility for the population of a large conurbation; *for whom?* also arises, for the beneficiaries of a cheap public transport policy are probably not the people who pay for it with high rates.

SAQ 11:   Under a market system households earn incomes from selling their labour (or land or capital) to firms. With these incomes, they choose the commodities they want. *For whom* then, are commodities produced? For those who (a) want them and (b) have earned enough to buy them.

SAQ 12:   Production

SAQ 13:   A school would stay open, or would shut, according to whether it could attract enough paying customers to make a profit. In this respect it would be no different from a sweetshop or the branch of a bank.

     The education a child received would depend very much on how willing her parent was to buy education. Advantages would include greater choice for parents and students. Furthermore, schools would have to provide an effective service or close down due to lack of custom. State control of the curriculum would be difficult, too and so political freedom would be encouraged.

     The disadvantages are that a child would suffer if his family wasn't rich enough or was unwilling to buy a place at a school.

SAQ 14:   In the USA, the method used would be the cheapest that produced the quality required. In the USSR, building enterprises would use resources allocated to them by the plan. In a country district of West Africa, houses would be built in the way that had always been used in the past.

SAQ 15:   Answered in the text

SAQ 16:   My dictionary (*Oxford Illustrated*) defines them as follows:
Capitalism: Economic system by which ownership of capital or wealth, the production and distribution of goods and services and the rewards of labour are entrusted to private enterprise.
Socialism: Political and economic principle that the community as a whole should have ownership and control of all means of production and distribution.

     So you can see that the essential difference concerns the *ownership* of property and the means (or 'factors' as we have called them) of production. Now the distinction between a planned and a market economy is more concerned with the system by which we decide the use of the means of production. So 'market socialism' is quite possible: nationalised firms would compete with one another, and would be allowed to go bust if they couldn't make profits. In some respects, this is what happens in Yugoslavia. Planned capitalism is also possible: private firms would do what the state plan said, and earn money from doing so. This happened in the Second World War in many countries — outstandingly in Nazi Germany.

2 The Standard of Living and Economic Growth

AIMS OF UNIT 2

This is the second unit on your economics course. In it, I try to cover quite a wide range of topics in order to launch you into the course, so you will need to keep notes as you go through: otherwise this unit will appear rather 'bitty' and disconnected. When you have completed the unit, you should be able to:

- define wealth, investment and economic growth
- explain what is meant by 'standard of living'
- list the factors that affect a country's standard of living
- review and evaluate some explanations for Britain's slow rate of economic growth.

LIVING STANDARDS

In Unit 1, you learned that economics is about the use of resources (which we grouped for convenience into three categories — land, labour and capital) to produce commodities (goods and services). A country which produces large amounts of high quality commodities for each member of its population will enjoy a high standard of living.

SAQ 1: *Economists define the standard of living as the material welfare of a community — measured in the amount of goods and services available to it per head. Look at the statistics below, which show the amounts of some named commodities that are consumed by an average citizen in each country in a recent year. Which country has the highest standard of living, and which the lowest?*

	Energy consumed per head (kg of coal equivalent)	Cars owned	Telephones	Population per doctor
		(per 1000 people)		
Switzerland	3752	267	586	601
Hong Kong	998	30	230	1642
Cameroun	97	6	4	26400

Of course, these figures don't give a complete picture of a country's prosperity. After all, a hot country will not need to consume as much energy to keep warm as a cold one; and fewer cars will be bought if the government can organise good public transport. If we wanted more accurately to compare the living standards of different countries, we would have to find out the value of *all* the goods and services made and consumed. You'll remember, I hope, that economists have a name for the value of the total amount of commodities produced in a country in a year.

SAQ 2: *Look back at the opening pages of Unit 1: what special name do economists give to the value of the total amount of commodities produced in a year?*

Actually working out the figure is a very complicated business called **national income accounting**, and it will take up most of the next unit. But without knowing anything about that, it will be evident to you that the citizens of Switzerland have a larger amount of goods and services available for their consumption than people who live in Cameroon. The differences in living standards between developed and developing nations is an important issue that is a cause of disagreement between the developed West and less developed parts of the world. Let's use what we already know of economics and how economies work to look at it more closely.

We have learned that goods and services are produced by combining the factors of production together. So the amount of goods and services that a country can produce will be affected firstly by the quantity of the factors of production it has, and secondly by the quality of those factors.

SAQ 3: *In the last sentence I referred to the quantity of a factor of production and the quality of a factor of production. Illustrate this idea by taking labour as the productive factor. What is meant by the quantity of labour? How might it be measured? What is meant by the quality of labour? Name some of the things that might lead you to describe one group of workers as being better in quality than another group.*

THE FACTORS OF PRODUCTION

Land: the gifts of nature
Let's go through the factors of production one by one and assess their importance in determining a country's standard of living, starting off with land. Remember, land in economic language doesn't just mean that part of our planet that isn't covered by water. It means all the gifts of nature, the natural resources that are available to be used in the process of production. So it includes raw materials, minerals, agriculture, fisheries, forests etc. A country that is well-endowed with abundant, high-quality natural resources will have a head start in providing high living standards for its people.

SAQ 4: *If we were to list the countries of the world in order of their wealth, the United Arab Emirates (UAE) would come out top and the country of Bhutan in the Himalayan mountains bottom. What is it about UAE's endowment of the factor land that gives it so high a living standard? What is it about Bhutan's land that keeps it so poor?*

Differences in natural resources can therefore explain some of the differences between rich and poor countries. But it cannot be the whole explanation — for countries like Brazil and Nigeria are rich in natural resources, yet cannot produce the standard of living of countries like Switzerland and Japan, who have few natural resources. So we must look beyond land, to differences in capital and labour to explain the ability of economies to give high living standards to their populations. Let's turn our attention next to the labour force.

Labour: the size and skills of the workforce
The size of the labour force is not the same as the size of population. For example, in 1979, the British population was 55.9 million, but only 26.4 million were in the workforce. Many people do not work because they are too young, or too old: it is unusual for someone in Britain to be a

member of the workforce before the age of 16, or after the age of 65.

Economists call the relation between the number of workers in a country and the total number of people the **dependency ratio**. A country with lots of children and old folk will have a high dependency ratio and vice versa.

SAQ 5: *Name the largest group of people who are aged between 16 and 65 but who are not economically active (no, it's not the unemployed). What measures could be taken to bring them into the labour force and so raise incomes and output?*

The dependency ratio measures the relationship between the size of the working population and the total population: its main use is to show the number of children and old people supported by the workforce. The **activity rate**, on the other hand, measures the proportion of adults that are part of the workforce and may be calculated as

$$\frac{\text{labour force}}{\text{16-64 yr. olds.}}$$

American economists refer to 'participation rates' rather than activity rates — but it's the same thing.

SAQ 6: *Look at this comparison of two countries: which will (other things being equal) enjoy higher living standards?*

	Dependency ratio	Activity rate
Country A	*Low*	*High*
Country B	*High*	*Low*

In fact, Britain's dependency ratio is subject to two conflicting trends at the moment. The dependency ratio is falling because of the sharp drop in the birth rate after the middle 1960s (meaning fewer dependent children) and the coming of age of the large age groups born between 1945 and 1965. However improved health care has increased the number of retired people in the community. On balance an ageing population is creating a higher dependency ratio. And although the activity rate rose in the 1950s and 1960s as more and more married women enter the workforce, this trend has now been reversed through the growth of male and female unemployment.

Now, the activity rate and the dependency ratio will affect the actual number of workers in a population. But the total amount of commodities will also be influenced by how much each worker produced. This is known as **labour productivity**. Here, the *quality* of the labour force will be important. A worker who is well-fed and free from disease will be more productive than one who is weak and ill. Education and training will also add to a worker's ability to produce commodities. And when considering a worker's effectiveness, we cannot ignore human factors such as enthusiasm and commitment. A person who sees him or herself as a member of a cooperative team doing a worthwhile job will be more productive than someone working half-heartedly. Changing attitudes could help us become richer through faster economic growth. This is why firms are keen to establish good working relations, and governments try to create incentives for harder work. But appeals to patriotism, or extra bonuses in the pay-packet can only do so much. The most important and crucial way that the output of a worker can be increased is by providing capital equipment. A factory which uses fork-life trucks, computers, power-tools and production-line robots will have higher output than one which is still in the screwdriver and trolley age.

SAQ 7: *What is meant by the term 'capital equipment.? The example I referred to in the text of a factory in manufacturing industry. But capital goods are also important in the industries that provide services — name some capital goods that would be useful (a) in an office (b) in a hairdresser.*

Capital
In order to raise the productivity of labour, we need more capital goods. Economists use the word

investment to cover spending on new capital goods. This may either be **gross investment**, a term which covers all the new capital goods bought and installed in a year, or **net investment** which counts only those capital goods which actually increase the total stock of capital (i.e. not counting money spent replacing machines that have worn out or broken down). Another way of describing investment is **capital formation.**

SAQ 8: *Economists use the word investment in a specialised way – to describe the amount of new capital created. What is the everyday use of the word investment? In what way is it different from the way that economists use the word? In what way is it similar?*

Now, as you learned in Unit 1, when capital goods are made they use up resources that could have been used to produce consumer goods that yielded more satisfaction at the time. I am sure that you can see the problem facing all societies trying to raise their output of commodities and therefore their living standards by increasing investment: the opportunity cost measured, for example, by the consumer goods we have had to give up.

SAQ 9: *In all societies, capital goods have to be produced by diverting resources away from producing other things – such as consumer goods. Why is this a particular problem in very poor countries? How might we in the developed countries help them avoid this dilemma?*

The problem of accumulating capital is crucial in raising a country from a low standard of living to a high one. If you have some knowledge of the economic history of Britain, you will know that the introduction of new machinery – steam engines, spinning jennies, steel furnaces and so on – transformed Britain from a farming country to the first industrial society. How did a poor agricultural society manage to accumulate such a wealth of capital goods?

Some historians, for example, have suggested that a society with very unequal incomes finds it easier to accumulate capital than a society with greater equality of incomes:

SAQ 10: *Why might a society with an unequal distribution of income find it easier to accumulate capital than one with the same average income spread more evenly?*

for the rich have a large surplus income with which to buy the required capital goods. Other historians have suggested that the frugal lifestyle of the nineteenth-century middle classes was a factor: far from spending their high incomes, Victorian capitalists ploughed their money back into the business. Max Weber, the German sociologist, spoke of a 'protestant ethic', a set of beliefs that valued hard work and thrift, and condemned idleness and pleasure.

This creates a dilemma for today's poorer countries, struggling to produce enough commodities to ensure that their people can have a decent standard of life. Should they allow an unfair distribution of incomes, hoping that the rich will invest their incomes in capital goods? And if this is not acceptable, and incomes are more equally distributed, where do they get the resources for the crucial capital goods they need when they could consume the whole national product without being well-fed or housed? Some societies have resorted to compulsion. This was true in the Soviet Union of the 1930s, when Stalin forced through a programme of industrialisation. The resources needed for this programme were ruthlessly grabbed by the state, and any opposition crushed.

Let's pause for a moment to summarise the work of the last three pages. Commodities are produced by combining the factors of production – land, labour and capital. Some societies are able to produce – and therefore consume – more commodities than others. This may be explained by differences in the amounts of the factors of production they have – what some economists call their 'factor endowments'. Societies that have generous natural resources, a skilled and healthy labour force and an ample stock of capital goods will find little difficulty in providing a decent standard of life for their inhabitants. By contrast, a country with poor soils, an underfed and unskilled labour force, and few tools or machines to aid production, will suffer a low level of output per head.

SAQ 11: *Look back at the countries cited in SAQ 1. Explain the difference between their living standards by contrasting their endowments of land, labour and capital.*

Enterprise

You may remember that in Unit 1 I referred to a fourth factor of production: entrepreneurship, or enterprise. An entrepreneur is someone who takes the risk of combining the factors of production to make commodities, i.e. buys the raw materials, maintains the capital equipment, hires the labour, and so on. A country that lacks entrepreneurial talent may still lag behind economically, despite having adequate supplies of land, labour and capital. Middle-Eastern countries are some-times said to suffer from a lack of entrepreneurs: although there is a long tradition of trading (that is, buying goods from one source and selling them somewhere else), few people are skilled in manufacturing commodities from local factors of production.

USING THE FACTORS EFFICIENTLY

Simply having enough of the factors of production — land, labour, capital and maybe enterprise — is not enough. The factors must also be used efficiently, not wastefully. This will happen if there is skilled management, and it will also be helped if the advances in knowledge acquired by scientists are applied to industry in the form of technical innovation. The skills and knowledge of the labour force will also need to be kept at a high level with well-organised programmes of training and education.

Specialisation

There is one technique above all, known to mankind for centuries, that increases the amount of commodities that can be produced from a given amount of productive resources. It is called **specialisation**, and operates when workers concentrate on just one or two productive tasks, rather than doing many tasks.

Imagine an economic system in which all the families are self-sufficient. They make all the commodities they need themselves. They grow their own food, weave their own cloth from their own animals' wool, build their own houses and furniture, collect fuel for their fires and so on. Because each household has to do everything, many find themselves doing things they are not very good at. 'Jack of all trades, master of none' goes the proverb; and it's true — to take just three examples, few people can mend a leak with the skill of a plumber, make crockery with the skill of a potter or set a broken leg with the skill of a surgeon. If, instead, the population *specialises* at what they are best at, the total output of commodities will rise. The man who is good at making shoes can do it all the time, raising the output of shoes; the builder does nothing but build; the farmer concentrates on producing food. A simple numerical example might illustrate the advantages of specialisation:

SAQ 12: *In this example, I'm going to take two men, Howard and Neil. In their society, the most important commodities are woollen cloth and wheat. With his land, Howard can produce 1000 kilos of wheat in a year; on the other hand, if he chose to produce just cloth, he can make 100 metres. Neil is less good at wheat production. In a year, he can produce just 500 kilos; on the other hand, if he specialised in producing cloth alone, he could make 300 metres. So*
- *Howard can make 1000 kilos of wheat or 100 metres of cloth*
- *Neil can make 500 kilos of wheat or 300 metres of cloth*

Now answer the following questions:
- *(a)   If each man spent half his year producing what and half producing cloth, how much would Howard produce of each? How much would Neil produce? If we added together their production, how much wheat and cloth would be made altogether?*
- *(b)   If the two men specialised in producing the commodity they were best at, which would Howard produce? Which would Neil produce? How much would each produce? If you add together their total production, how much extra wheat and cloth are produced compared with (a)?*
- *(c)   If Neil and Howard swap 300 kilos of wheat for 125 metres of cloth how much of each commodity does each man have? Are they better-off than when they were self-sufficient?*

21

There are great gains in production to be made from intelligent specialisation. And these gains do not just result from differences in the tastes or talents of workers. Look at the examples in the exercise you have just done. Neil is better at producing cloth, Howard at growing wheat. The reason could be due to the different land they farm: if Neil's farm is in a rainy area, he will have lush grass to feed his sheep — but the climate will not favour wheat growing. By contrast, Howard might be in a drier, flatter area that would suit the production of cereal crops. Where this happens, the country will gain if its various regions specialise in different products.

SAQ 13: *Does Britain have regions that specialise in different products? Which product does your own region specialise in producing. Name a product that is not made in your region of Britain.*

But specialisation isn't just a matter of different activities in different regions. In Britain specific industries are highly specialised. For example, different firms produce different parts of a car, and even within a firm that makes cars components, workers will have specialised tasks to do. Some have office jobs, ordering raw materials or calculating wages; others maintain the machinery; others perform different tasks in the manufacture of the actual product; still others package the finished article or transport the product away. Specialisation within a factory is known as **division of labour**. Here's a list of the reasons why specialisation and the division of labour raise output:

- Workers can stick to the task for which their strength or dexterity are best adapted. What is more, they can get better at these tasks by repeating them and gaining skill and experience.
- Time is saved because workers do not have to move from job to job or keep changing tools.
- Repetition enables a worker to use machinery in the most efficient way possible. Machines can be used more easily if we break a production process down into a number of simple operations, and this increases productivity.
- There is a saving because each worker only needs the tools for his particular job. Let's go back to Howard and Neil for a moment. If they are self-sufficient, they each need a plough and a weaver's loom. But if they specialise, Howard doesn't need weaving machinery and Neil can do without ploughs and seed-drills. No tools stand idle when specialisation is the rule.
- Simplified and mechanised work makes it easy for workers to leave one job and take up another. This is an important factor in today's changing economy. Many jobs are disappearing while others are being created, and unemployment can be alleviated if workers are able to move from one job to another easily. If workers move easily from job to job, economists say labour is **mobile**.

  Labour mobility has two aspects. If people can move easily between different occupations, we refer to a high degree of **occupational mobility** of labour. This would be present if workers from the declining cotton textile industry could move into jobs in North Sea oil installations. But this would also require the second type of labour mobility — **geographical mobility**, which refers to the ease with which labour can move from place to place. The textile industry is to be found in Greater Manchester, but the oil installations are off the east coast of Scotland.
- Specialisation makes it easier for managers to measure and estimate production, and so better organise production.

SAQ 14: *You have just read through a list of the advantages from specialisation. Now jot down what you see as the disadvantages of specialisation.*

Let's take a breather there, and look back over the ground we have covered. We have seen that a country can produce commodities abundantly if (a) it has plenty of land, labour and capital (particularly capital) and (b) if those factors are used efficiently. In a moment, this unit will move on to apply these ideas to Britain's disappointing performance over the past 30 years. But there are two more factors that should be mentioned first — factors that will also affect the standard of living a country can enjoy.

OTHER FACTORS AFFECTING LIVING STANDARDS

Relations with the rest of the world
Many countries have had their economic development held back because of exploitation by other,

stronger countries. Colonial conquest has plundered the wealth of countries and disrupted their social system. Some writers believe that this process is continuing in a hidden form in today's world. Dominant countries are still impoverishing other nations through multinational companies and political/financial manoeuvring. No survey of the economy of central America could ignore the role of the USA; no economic history of Ireland can ignore the importance of England.

But colonialism is only one way in which international relations affect living standards. Another way involves 'terms of trade': this is the name given to the relationship between the prices we get for the exports we sell, and the prices we have to pay for the imports we buy. For example, if we can import goods from the rest of the world cheaply, we will have a higher standard of living than if we have to pay a great deal for them. This is a topic we will look at more fully when we study international trade. But I expect you can see even now that a country that is faced with a sudden rise in the price of its imports will either have to import less, or export more to pay for the higher import bill. Either way, there will be fewer commodities available for consumption — and so there will be a fall in living standards.

SAQ 15: *Read this quotation from the Jamaican Deputy High Commissioner for Trade:*
'Ten years ago, it took three tons of Jamaican bananas to buy an Austin car. Now the island has to produce 11 tons per car.'

(a)   *Have the terms of trade changed in Jamaica's favour or not?*
(b)   *What will the result of this be for Jamaica's standard of living?*
(c)   *Have the terms of trade moved favourably or unfavourably for the sellers of Austin cars — that is, Britain?*

The terms of trade moved sharply against Britain when, in 1973-4 the price of oil shot up. At the time, Britain was an oil importer and so was forced to export more goods to pay for the same amount of oil.

Booms and slumps
In assessing the factors that affect the standard of living, we must look at one further factor — is the country actually using all its factors of production, or are some lying idle? We cannot, after all, produce the largest possible output of commodities if we let capital stand idle and labour be unemployed. This has been a recurring problem in modern economies — indeed, at one point in the 1930s, unemployment reached 20% of the population. In the 1980s the world economy is again facing problems of stagnating economic growth and world trade. This recession has driven rates of unemployment to over 10% in many industrialised nations and is causing poverty-related economic and political instability in the Third World. I will review the problems and causes of recessions in Units 4, 5 and 6.

SAQ 16: *We have now finished our first survey of the things that influence the standard of living of different nations. I asked you at the outset of this unit to take brief notes as you worked your way through. Now is a good time to compare your notes with the ones I have made at the back of this unit.*

BRITAIN'S ECONOMIC PERFORMANCE

The evidence
Disquiet has been expressed for some time at the slow rate at which Britain has been increasing its national product. The slower economic growth rate of Britain means that its inhabitants, once among the richest in Europe, are now no longer top of the league. If we arranged the countries of the world in a 'league table' with those with the highest incomes at the top and those with the lowest at the bottom, Britain would take these positions:

1960	7th
1964	10th
1968	13th
1972	15th
1976	19th

Its position is now in the middle twenties. The following charts from *The Economist* tell the same story: Britain's economy has been growing, but the faster growth rates of our European rivals means that they have overtaken us.

SAQ 17: *Look at the charts below. Which was the most powerful economy in Europe in 1950? Which country had the highest living standards? What changes took place between then and 1976?*

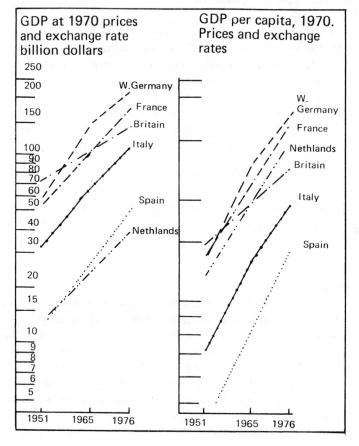

(GDP is one way of measuring national output. I will explain the relationship between the various measures of national output in the next unit.)

This slide from the position of being one of the most powerful economies in Europe to being a mere 'also-ran' is something that must concern many people — economists, politicians, even the man in the street. Slower economic growth will mean

- a slower growth in the amount of commodities we can consume, and therefore of our standard of living.
- a decline in the power and influence of Britain, for economic strength confers political power.
- greater conflict between different groups in society. People have come to expect a rising standard of living: if the national income doesn't rise, then individual incomes cannot rise — unless one person gains at the expense of someone else. In a society used to growth in living standards, this is a recipe for conflict.
- that the government will have difficulty finding the money for improved public services. When incomes are rising fast, the government gets more and more money from taxation: but if there is slow growth this doesn't happen. So we have to either pay higher taxes or put up with a lower standard of government services — old schools, long waits for medical care, low pensions.

Should we seek faster growth?

It's no wonder economists have been anxious to find out the causes of Britain's slower economic growth. Indeed, most of them would like to see Britain increasing its rate of growth, so that the national product rises fast each year. However, there are some commentators who claim that more economic growth is not desirable. They feel

- that advanced industrial countries already manufacture enough commodities to give everyone a decent standard of living. If we produced any more commodities, we would probably make wasteful luxuries — second cars, electric toothbrushes, a fifth TV channel.
- that a society that is intent on raising its output of commodities will ignore many of the things that make life worth living — cleanliness, peace and quiet, friendship, community feeling. More factories, motorways and airports will make life uglier, noisier and more hurried, and people will not enjoy being better off at all.
- that increased economic growth will destroy our planet. We will run out of the natural resources we need to live — oil, metals, fuels. What is more, increased pollution caused by industry will destroy the balance of nature.

Why have we had slow growth?

But, of course, Britain has not chosen slow growth deliberately: we wish to grow as fast as the Germans and Japanese, but have been unable to. I shall now go through some of the reasons for this. You should realise that this is an area where there are no definite answers and so opinions tend to differ, but I have tried to be as unbiassed as possible.

Explanation 1: Shifts in the labour force A possible explanation of Britain's slow growth in output is that Britain and her industrial rivals have different histories of economic development. Many countries, for example France, Japan and Italy, have until recently had a large proportion of their population working in the countryside on inefficient small farms. After the Second World War these workers drifted away from the land and moved to the towns: they left backward, family farms (where they were producing little) for higher-paid jobs in manufacturing industry (where their output per head was far higher). When a French peasant left his family farm, he probably did not cause its output to fall: there were already too many workers on the farm, and for much of the time he had been underemployed (i.e. there was not enough work to fill all his working days). But when he joined the workforce in, say, a Renault factory, he added considerably to output. So his switch from one sector (farming) to another (manufacturing industry) really boosted output in France. When the distinguished British economist Frank Paish looked at the difference between Britain and continental growth rates in 1968, he concluded that '. . . many continental countries still had a number of technologically backward sectors in their economies, offering great scope for technological improvement. The most important of these was farming, with a large number of peasant farmers each with a low output per head.'

SAQ 18: *The diagram below appeared in* The Economist *when that magazine looked at the comparative growth rates of European countries. The bar charts show how the number of workers employed in each sector changed.*

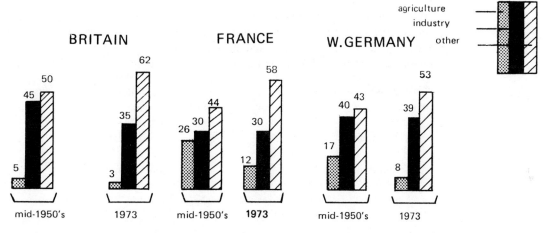

(diagram continued)

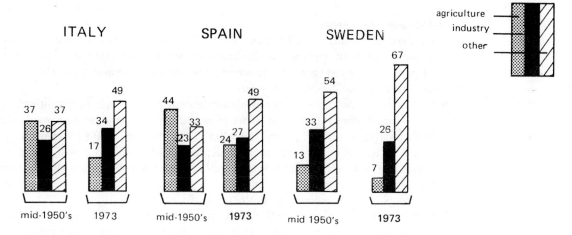

ITALY   SPAIN   SWEDEN

Let's use these as a bit of practice in interpreting diagrams.

(a)   *The key refers to agriculture, industry and 'other'. What activities are covered by 'other'? (That is, what jobs do people have outside manufacturing and farming?)*

(b)   *What trend is evident in the share of agriculture in employment?*

(c)   *Which country had the largest proportion of agricultural workers in the mid-1950s? How much had that proportion fallen by 1973?*

(d)   *Where had the agricultural workers gone?*

The crucial thing you must realise here is that compared to the other nations we have been looking at, Britain has a small and efficient agricultural sector: less than 3% of British workers are in agriculture. We cannot add to our manufacturing labour force by taking labour from inefficient farms into our factories.

This factor may account for the speed with which our industrial rivals caught up with Britain, but it cannot explain why they are now moving ahead of us. If our competitors got rid of an inefficient industry that Britain lost many years ago, this just brings them back on equal terms with us. But in fact other nations have moved ahead of Britain, so the typical German earns twice as much, and the French and Japanese half as much again as the typical British worker. We must look for other explanations to find out why the workforce of other countries has been so much more productive than that of Britain.

Explanation 2: Our low rate of investment   Earlier in this unit I stressed the importance of building up capital: if we wish to get more output from our labour force, then one of the most effective ways is to equip them with more machinery and better tools.

SAQ 19: *What word do economists use to describe the amount of new tools and machinery that we add to our stock of capital each year? (Refer back to p. 20 if you can't remember.)*

That's right — investment.

If we want to compare the investment records of different countries we can express their investment as a percentage of their national product. We can state what proportion of all the commodities made in a year are new tools and machinery. Below I have put two tables: the one on the left shows investment rates, the one on the right the change in incomes over the relevant period.

Gross fixed capital formation as a percentage of GDP		*Percentage increase in incomes in the same years*	
Japan	35	Japan	124
W Germany	27	Netherlands	57
France	26	France	55
Netherlands	25	W.Germany	46
Belgium	22	Belgium	46
Sweden	21	Italy	44
Italy	20	Sweden	35
Britain	18	USA	35
USA	17	Britain	23

SAQ 20: *What relationship exists between the two tables? Can you connect the two tables in a logical explanation?*

SAQ 21: *The graph below shows the relationship between the amount of productive investment undertaken by each country, and the change in output per person in that country.*
(a)   What relationship is there between investment and growth in output in this diagram?
(b)   Can investment explain why The Netherlands grows faster than Britain?
(c)   Can it explain why The Netherlands grows faster than W. Germany?

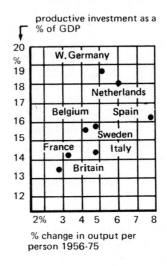

In summary then, Britain has a lower rate of investment than its competitors. As a result, British workers have had fewer items of capital equipment to help them produce goods and services. This must be at least part of the explanation of Britain's slow growth. Politicians from the left and the right wings of politics wish to increase our rate of investment in order to increase the efficiency of British industry. Right-wing politicians say that investment has been held back because firms have not been allowed to earn high enough profits to pay for the new capital goods, and because trade unions have the power to stop managers using the new machinery in the most effective and economical way. A left-winger would place the blame on the owners and managers of British industry, who have failed to invest for the past 30 years at least, and would argue that vigorous government action is needed to finance the necessary increase in investment.

Explanation 3:   Inefficiency in British industry Even when British firms *do* have the right amount of up-to-date investment, it still seems that it is not used as effectively as in the factories of our competitors. Spend a minute or two reading through these quotations:

Labour productivity is twice as high in the United States as it is here, and 50 per cent higher in West Germany and France, according to Pratten's findings. Between May 1972 and June 1973 he collected data from multinational firms which have plants in Britain and elsewhere, to discover whether there were any productivity differences and the reasons why.

Pratten found two economic causes for British low productivity — lack of long production runs and smaller volumes of output to meet a lower demand. But neither the old age of the factory nor antique machinery were rated as prime reasons for poor performance. Pratten reckons that when Britain is compared with West Germany and France better plant and machinery only accounts for 5 per cent of the productivity

difference.

Far more crucial — in his view — is what he calls the "behavioural differences." It is people's attitudes on the shopfloor and in the boardroom that provide the explanation. In case study after case study across every sector of industry, the same reasons for Britain's relatively poor productivity kept coming up — overmanning, absenteeism, lack of adaptability, resistance to new technology.

Take overmanning, for example. This is particularly true of the indirect workers — those who provide the back-up services for the production line. As Pratten writes, "It seems that in the UK the practice has been to allow more generous manning of many indirect functions — quality control, canteen services, production

control, office staff." Restrictive practices are often mentioned by the firms. The refusal of workers to interchange jobs is peculiarly British. Union leaders said they had little control over how workers on the shopfloor behaved while management claimed workers simply did not want to increase their productivity.

Pratten offers a few suggestions to improve this depressing picture, such as giving workers more security, providing more information to the shopfloor, creating better working conditions and breaking down the class barriers at work with the abolition of different status canteens. The union response to Pratten was negative, for it seems unions show no interest in labour productivity. (Is this really true?)

Review of *Labour Productivity Differentials Within International Companies*
by C. F. Pratten (*New Society*, August 1976)

Far and away the most striking difference in the pattern of manufacturing investment in Britain and in the other main industrial countries is in the additional output which new capital spending produces.

On the basis of calculations made in Whitehall, French and Japanese industry got almost exactly double the increase in manufacturing output for the same increase in capital stock as did British industry. German industry got over one and a half times as much. Italian and Swedish industry got half as much again. Even US industry got 20 per cent more.

A key difference between the economic performance of Britain and of other faster growing economies, in short, is not that they invest more, or indeed that they invest more in relation to their manufacturing output. It is that they use their capital stock better than we do.

Not only do British firms get less from their investment than their counterparts in other big industrial countries. They get less from their workers. Again on the basis of rough Whitehall estimates, the growth of output per employee in manufacturing between 1960 and 1973 in Britain was only a quarter of that in Japan.

Taking countries at more similar points in their industrial development to Britain, output per head in manufacturing still grew slightly faster in the US, a third faster in Germany and Italy, and half as fast again in France.

All the evidence suggests, in other words, that what British firms are really bad at is getting the best out of their investment and their manpower.

Why? Attempts to explain it by looking at the performance of different industrial sectors, firms with old plant and machinery and firms with new, do not produce convincing results. Wide differences in the efficiency with which firms use their capital stock and their labour appear to exist in the same industrial sector.

Two explanations suggest themselves. Both are virtually impossible to prove. One is that the crux of the problem is the attitude of British trade unions; the other, that it is the quality of British industrial management.

It may well be that the conservatism of British unions and the existence of several within one industry or firm has pushed companies into maintaining high manning levels and discouraged the most efficient use of capital equipment.

A company is never more vulnerable than when it has spent money on a new piece of machinery.

In Germany, the firms examined would put their employees onto long hours of overtime while the new plant was being run in. In Britain, one firm studied would not increase overtime, would use more manpower initially, and then would run down the number of jobs as the plant and work methods improved. That is hardly a way of encouraging maximum co-operation with new investment plans.

Article by Frances Cairncross in *The Guardian* 22 September 1975

'In fact one can argue that the UK needs better investment, rather than more of it. However, Professor Dudley's study of the engineering industry suggests that the possibilities of increasing output with the existing capital stock are immense. His results suggest that halving the gap between the efficiency of the less productive firms and the (average) would make it possible to increase output by 50 per cent. Similar results were found by the Central Policy Review Staff in their 1975 study of the motor industry. Identical plant had been installed in two factories in Britain and in Germany and in Belgium respectively; different firms were involved. In the one case manning levels were similar but UK output was only half that of the continental factory. In the other, output was similar but the UK factors had twice as many workers . . . It is clear that management inertia and inefficiency is at least as responsible as trade union obstructiveness. Why production engineering is held in such low esteem in the UK is a related but unanswerable question.'

From *Modern Economic Analysis* by David Gowland (Butterworth, 1979)

SAQ 22: *Jot down two or three sentences that all the three authors I have quoted would agree on.*

Inefficiency in labour

Finding out that we are using our capital stock in an inefficient way should be the start of our enquiries, not the end. Why are we using our capital equipment less efficiently? Two different explanations have been brought forward. The first one looks at the British trade union movement. Now, Britain does not (surprise, surprise) have a particularly bad record of losing time due to strikes. Look at this table, for example:

Working days lost for every 1000 workers
(Annual average between 1975 and 1985)

Netherlands	23
W. Germany	28
France	139
Denmark	181
UK	478
Ireland	669
Italy	981

Source: Eurostat 87

SAQ 23: *If a country lost 1000 working days for every 1000 employees, how many days on average would each employee be on strike each year? Which country in the table loses least time through strikes? Which country has the worst record for losing time through striking?*

But it isn't the time lost by strikers that worries economists – losing .49 of a day per worker per year (less than six hours a year) is insignificant when compared to time lost through sickness, public holidays, absenteeism or plain loafing. On the other hand, if outdated and inefficient work practices are maintained by trade unions, production is lost all year round. The two practices that get most condemnation are **overmanning** and **demarcation**.

Overmanning means having more workers on a job than is necessary. For example, when labour-saving machines are introduced, unions sometimes insist that the same number of workers is employed as before. By contrast, a country intent on raising its national product would prefer the workers who are no longer needed to transfer into new jobs and raise output there. Demarcation is rather different: strict demarcation exists when workers stick to doing just one task in a factory and are not allowed to do any other, since that is someone else's job – often that of a member of a different union. The popular press calls demarcation arguments 'who-does-what disputes'. They arise because in Britain, many unions are organised along craft lines; that is, all the people of one skill (painters, clerks, plumbers, draughtsmen or whatever) belong to the same union no matter what industry they work in. So in a shipyard, or motorworks, or chemical factory there will be members of many unions. When an industrial process is introduced which cuts across these unions because it doesn't fit neatly into any one of these jobs, disputes often arise.

SAQ 24: *Hunterston in Scotland is the site of a large dock specially built for unloading iron ore into the local steelworks. Which two groups of workers do you think were in dispute about who should staff the new enterprise?*

Management inefficiency

But while many writers have blamed the unions for the poor productivity record of British manufacturers, just as many have criticised British managers. It is significant that companies in Britain that are managed by Americans enjoy higher productivity and profitability than British-managed ones. This may be because

- British management is untrained. Few British managers have formally studied business methods: indeed management studies are comparatively new in British universities.
- British management fails to attract top talent. In Britain, a job as an industrial manager does not enjoy the high status is does abroad – certainly it is less attractive than a job in medicine, the law, higher education, broadcasting or the higher grades of the civil service. So private industry fails to get the cream of the workforce – it employs 70% of the whole workforce but just 30% of university graduates.

In fact, more than half of our university graduates – in many respects the most talented entrants into the labour force – went into government employment of one sort or another. This leads us to a further explanation for Britain's slow progress – the idea that the government has been taking too large a proportion of our national resources.

Explanation 4: Too much government spending In the late 1970s two economists from the University of Oxford, Walter Eltis and Robert Bacon, started a vigorous debate about the amount of public spending (that is spending by the government on commodities) in Britain. This is not the place to enter into a long section about government spending and its effects on the economy – we'll do that later in the course – but you may be interested in a simple survey of their views. You will already know that commodities are made using land, labour and capital. You have also met the idea of opportunity cost – that is, that resources used in the production of one commodity cannot be used at the same time for something else, so the production of one thing involves the sacrifice of something else. The people who criticise government for taking too great a share of our national resources point to the composition of the national output, and the use made of it. There are four basic ways of using the commodities that make up our national output:

- Private individuals can use them for their own use and pleasure (*consumption*)
- Firms can buy them and use them to expand and improve their business (*investment*)

- We can sell them to foreigners (in the form of *exports*) to gain money that enables us to buy what we want from abroad
- The government can use the commodities to provide public spending services (*government spending*)

Economists who share the views of Eltis and Bacon believe that when the government increases its share of the national product, it does so at the expense of exports and investment in industry.

SAQ 25: *What problems will occur if we reduce exports and investment in order to improve the standard of government services?*

Other explanations I have now given you four explanations of slow growth:
- Our foreign rivals have benefited from favourable shifts in the occupations of their labour force.
- Britain has failed to invest enough in new capital equipment
- British labour and management, for a variety of social and historical reasons, are less efficient than their competitors
- The government has grabbed too high a proportion of the factors of production.

But of course, these are not the only ones that economists put forward. But each does emphasise that the answer to the problem lies in considering the quality and amount of the factors of production and how efficiently they are combined. The simple idea that commodities are produced using the factors of production can be used in the real world to look at a country — Britain — that is not producing the amount of commodities that its government and population would like.

REVIEW SECTION

Review your knowledge of this unit by filling in the missing words in the following passage (answers are given on p. 34):

The British economy has been growing at a _____ rate than that of her competitors for the past 30 years or more. There are a number of reasons for this. Britain has not had a convenient source of _____ leaving _____ productivity employment in _____. What is more, we have not created enough new _____ goods to aid our workforce: that is to say, our overseas competitors have had higher rates of _____ than we have. But there is evidence to suggest that even when we do have adequate investment, we use it _____ effectively than our competitors. This may be because _____ insist on having too many workers to work the new machinery, a situation called over-_____. Also _____ disputes (or 'who-does-what' disputes) have stopped management from being able to use labour effectively. On the other hand, there is evidence that _____ is also to blame, as a result of being untrained and amateurish. Finally, there is the notion that too _____ a proportion of our national resources are being swallowed up by the _____, meaning that there is little left for vital _____ and _____.

Now jot down your understanding of the following terms that have come up in this unit, and then check them against a dictionary of economics (the Penguin one would do well). When you have arrived at a final definition, write them out as a glossary for this unit.

   dependency ratio; participation rate/activity rate; investment; capital formation; factor endowment; division of labour; specialisation; mobility of labour; standard of living; wealth.

Further reading
There is really no need for further reading if you feel happy with your understanding of this unit. However if you would like to look a little more deeply into the topics I have covered, there are many books you can use. Peter Donaldson's *A Question of Economics* is an inexpensive Penguin book which has a number of easy-to-read chapters on Britain's growth problem. If you are confident enough to dabble in something more academic, look at Prest and Coppock's *The UK Economy* (Weidenfeld and Nicolson) (latest edition). A useful popular treatment of Britain's

economic problems is contained in an article in *Controlling the Economy* (N. Wall), part of the Economics Briefs series from *The Economist* (Collins). An interesting article on measuring growth in the UK economy appeared in the Economic Review January 1987. In the May 1986 edition of the same publication there is an article on Britain's Growth, 1973–1984.

As far as the advantages and disadvantages of economic growth go, there are a number of books to recommend. The author who started the debate on whether economic growth was worth knocking ourselves out for was J.K. Galbraith in his classic book *The Affluent Society* (Penguin); and the idea that growth cancels itself out with greater noise, pollution and hurry is argued in *The Costs of Economic Growth* by E.J. Mishan (Penguin). The book that suggested that economic growth would be defeated by pollution, exhaustion of natural resources and ecological disaster was *The Limits to Growth* by Meadows, Meadows, Randers and Behrens (Pan). The case in favour of economic growth is argued by Wilfred Beckerman in a book called (not surprisingly) *In Defence of Economic Growth* (Cape).

Examination questions

Examination questions on the topic of economic growth fall into two groups. Firstly, examiners wish students to have considered the advantages and disadvantages of economic growth, and ask questions like:

1. Contrast the meaning of 'growth' and 'recovery' when applied to an economy. Discuss whether or not you regard economic growth as desirable.

    (JMB 'A' level June 1986)

For this you would have to look back at pages 24-5 of this unit, and to get really good marks you might feel the need to have a look at a couple of the further reading suggestions I have mentioned. Remember to define the terms 'economic growth' and 'recovery' in introducing your answer.

Examiners are also anxious to read intelligent discussions of Britain's industrial problems. A question such as

2. 'How do you account for Britain's poor economic performance during the post-war period?'
    (Associated Examining Board 'A' November 1982)

looks for students who know the meaning of economic growth, the facts of Britain's recent performance and the factors that might explain it. Whereas:

3. 'What reasons have been advanced for Britain's poor growth rate in recent years? To what extent is a slow growth rate an indicator of an inefficient economy?'
    (Joint Matriculation Board 'A' 1982)

asks you to combine both perspectives.

ANSWERS TO SAQs

SAQ 1:   Judging from the data, Switzerland has the highest living standards: more energy used, more cars etc. Cameroon (an African country near Nigeria) has the lowest of the three — and the number of people to each doctor (26 400) makes you realise that high standards of living are not just concerned with colour TVs and deep freezers but involve better standards in less tangible commodities such as health and education.

SAQ 2:   National income, or national product.

SAQ 3:   The quantity of labour can be measured by the number of workers — or to be more accurate, the number of hours worked in total. The quality of labour involves how good the labour force is at producing commodities: a labour force which is well-fed and healthy, well-educated and hardworking will be of high quality. So the things that would affect the quality of labour would include health, education, attitudes etc.

SAQ 4:   The UAE has enormous reserves of oil (remember that mineral resources are counted as *land*): Bhutan has poor soil and a hostile highland climate.

SAQ 5:   Married women. They could be brought into the labour force if nurseries were provided conveniently and at low cost: if part-time jobs could be created this would allow women to fulfil other commitments they may want to (such as picking up children from school); perhaps the best incentive would be well-paid and fulfilling employment. This implies that the jobs are available, which often isn't true: the reasons for this will be investigated in the next few units.

SAQ 6:   Country A. Here, few of the population are dependent on others to produce the commodities they need (the dependency ratio is low) and many of the adults are working (the activity rate is high).

SAQ 7:   Capital equipment refers to goods that are used in the process of producing other goods and services: they do not directly satisfy wants themselves.

Capital equipment (a) in an office might include typewriters, desks, filing cabinets, calculators, microprocessors etc. In (b) a hairdressing salon it would of course be the driers, tongs, scissors, but also the chairs, sinks, cash-till (etc. etc.).

SAQ 8:   In everyday language, investment means putting your cash to use to purchase any asset — from shoes or a suit to a building society account or a new house. Economists use the word strictly to mean spending on capital goods. But when people use the word investment to mean doing without something in order to get future benefits ('I look upon my evening class attendance as an investment — if I pass the exam, I'll get a promotion at work') they are coming quite close to the economic meaning. For in economics, investment entails sacrifice now but greater output in the future.

SAQ 9:   The problem in poor countries is that everything that they consume is a necessity — for example food, shelter or clothing. So giving up consumption goods for investment goods involves a real sacrifice. The only way to avoid this is overseas aid — a richer country providing the capital goods out of its much greater resources.

SAQ 10:   Because in an unequal society the rich would have a large surplus income with which to buy the required capital goods. Were income divided more equally, few would have the spare wealth to establish (for example) a factory or warehouse.

SAQ 11:   Switzerland has little in the way of natural resources, but this is compensated for by a well-trained and hardworking population and a very high stock of capital. The energy and industry of the population of Hong Kong is legendary — but they are not as highly skilled as the Swiss, nor have they the amount of capital. Cameroon lacks both capital (it has not been through an industrial revolution where capital starts to accumulate) and skilled manpower: as a result the standard of living is low, which makes it difficult to accumulate capital or pay for education and health programmes which will improve labour quality and productivity.

SAQ 12:   (a)   If Howard divided his time he would produce half his possible wheat output, and half the possible wool output — that is, 500 kilos of wheat and 50 metres of cloth. Neil, likewise, would produce 250 kilos of wheat and 150 metres of cloth. So, if they were self-sufficient, together they would produce just 750 kilos of what and 200 metres of cloth.

(b)   If they specialised, Howard would grow wheat and Neil would produce cloth. Howard could produce 1000 kilos of wheat and no cloth, and Neil would produce 300 metres of cloth and no wheat. Total output would now be 1000 kilos of wheat and 300 metres of cloth. This is a great increase over what happened under (a) above: There are now 250 more kilos of wheat and 100 more metres of cloth.

(c)   If they traded, Howard would end up with 700 kilos of wheat and 125 metres of cloth; Neil would have 300 kilos of wheat and 175 metres of cloth. Compared to (a), both men have gained through specialisation and trade.

SAQ 13:   Agricultural specialisation is determined by climatic and topographical variations, and the availability of markets. Sheep farming is concentrated in the wetter upland areas unsuitable for other types of agriculture, e.g. Mid-Wales and the Pennines. Cereal production is more profitable in the drier, flatter areas of East Anglia. Fruit growing and dairying are more cost-effective in the south and southwest of the country.

SAQ 14:   There are a number of disadvantages — and you might think of ones I haven't got. Specialisation may create simple, repetitive tasks which bore workers. It may also destroy crafts and skills that have been known for generations; remove the satisfaction of seeing the whole job through; make unemployment more likely as workers become very specialised on just one skill that may not be needed if demand changes.

SAQ 15:   (a)   The terms of trade have changed in an unfavourable way — Jamaica is having to export more commodities just to get the same amount of imported goods.

(b)   As a result, Jamaica must either export more goods or import less — either way she has fewer commodities for home consumption, and so her standard of living falls.

(c)   The terms of trade have moved to Britain's favour — we get more bananas for the same number of cars. (footnote: luckily Jamaica sold a lot of bauxite (aluminium ore) and tourism to make up the missing money)

SAQ 16:   My own notes are as follows:

<u>LIVING STANDARDS</u>

A country enjoys high living standards if it can produce a large amount of commodities per head: this is best mentioned in terms of national income per head.

This is affected by

I. <u>FACTORS OF PRODUCTION</u>

a. <u>LAND</u>
Amount and quality of national resources ~ compare oil-rich UAE with poor Bhutan

b. <u>LABOUR</u>
Not just quantity (which depends on activity rates and the dependency ratio as well as actual size of population!) but <u>quality</u> (health, attitudes, skills of workforce)

c. <u>CAPITAL</u>
Very important indeed! major task in development is accumulating capital (n.b. problems of opportunity cost - how to sacrifice consumption)

2. <u>THE EFFICIENCY THAT THE FACTORS OF PROD. ARE COMBINED</u>

a. <u>TECHNOLOGY</u>
b. <u>SPECIALISATION/DIVISION OF LABOUR</u> ~ personal, industrial, regional (n.b. disadvantages!)

3. <u>RELATIONS WITH THE REST OF THE WORLD</u>

a. <u>Imperialism and colonialism</u> can impoverish a country.

b. Terms of Trade: ie. our s.o.l will fall if we are asked to pay more for our imports.

4. <u>BOOMS AND SLUMPS</u>
We may not be employing all our resources due to a business recession.

You may have a different style of taking notes — ask for advice from your tutor if you're having problems. The above aren't perfect — but they're the sort of notes I'd take if this unit was a lecture.

SAQ17:   In 1950 (1951 actually) Britain had the highest national product in Europe; Sweden and Switzerland had the highest income per head. By 1976 France and Germany had overtaken Britain in total size of national product; what is more, Britain's income per head was below The Netherlands, Belgium, France and W. Germany — who we had been ahead of in 1951.

SAQ 18:   (a)   The activities covered by 'other' are service jobs such as teachers, hairdressers, banking, legal services and nurses.

(b)   The trend is that agriculture falls — from 37% to 17% in Italy, and from 44% to 24% in Spain; and the picture is repeated throughout Europe.

(c)   Spain: it fell from 44% of the workforce to 24%.

(d)   In fact, they went into service industries, for if you look at the bar charts, manufacturing employment did not increase much as a proportion of the workforce. This doesn't mean that the farmworkers *all* went into service industries — but for every person who moved from agriculture into manufacturing, one moved out of manufacturing into service industry.

SAQ 19:   Investment.

SAQ 20:   The countries that are at the top of the table of investment seem to be at the top of the table of growth in output; and vice versa. Look, for example, at Japan's very high investment rate — there 35% of all commodities produced are fed back for industry's use. This must surely be related to its meteoric growth rate. This could be due to the fact that it is easier to increase output when workers have got plenty of new capital machinery to help them in production.

SAQ 21:   The relationship seems to be that countries which invest a lot grow faster. The Netherlands grows faster than Britain and it invests more — 18% as against roughly 13%: these things may well be connected. However, The Netherlands has had a faster percentage increase in output than Germany even though it has invested less: so this cannot be explained by differences in investment, and we must look elsewhere for a reason (better training? More ample natural resources — e.g. natural gas?)

SAQ 22:   My own summary would be something like this:
There is plenty of evidence that even when the right capital equipment is installed in Britain, it does not add as much to output as it should do — or as it does in other countries. British industry appears to waste opportunities for higher output: a change of attitude and better management could raise output considerably without the need for massive new investment.

SAQ 23:   One day. Of the countries mentioned, The Netherlands loses least days per worker and Italy the most.

SAQ 24:   The dispute was between the dockers and the steelworkers: both had a good claim to do the job, and both had suffered unemployment recently.

SAQ 25:   Lower investment will make industry less efficient and slow our growth rate. David Smith estimated in the *National Westminster Bank Review* that a 1% rise in government consumption will reduce the growth rate by 2%. The reduction in exports will mean that we will earn less money from sales to foreigners, and so will be unable to buy as much of the goods as we wish to buy from them. More of this when we come to the units on international trade.

Review question: Missing words are: slower; labour; low; farming or agriculture; capital; investment; less, unions; manning; demarcation; management; great or high; government; investment and exports.

3 National Income Accounting

AIMS OF UNIT 3

This unit is a guide to the national income accounts: it aims to show you how the government puts together the figures that show how much wealth the country is producing. National income accounts are an important source of information for economists, politicians and businessmen. Whilst some students may find this section of the course boring, I don't. Furthermore, a student who has a good grasp of the concept of national income will collect plenty of marks in the exam, and will find it easier to follow the ideas of macro-economics in Units 4, 5 and 6. So there are a number of good reasons really to put in the work to master this topic.

When you have completed this unit you should be able to:
- define national income
- list and explain the three ways used to calculate it
- define transfer incomes, residual error, capital consumption and explain their significance in national income calculations
- distinguish between GDP, GNP and national income, and calculate them from appropriate figures
- explain the difference between current and constant price calculations, and between market price and factor cost figures
- explain three uses for the national income figures and outline the qualifications that must be borne in mind when using them

WHAT IS THE 'NATIONAL INCOME'?

Unit 2 of this course opened with a table showing the number of telephones, doctors and cars per 1000 of the population in three very different countries. I asked you to make an intelligent guess as to which was the richest country from that information. It wasn't difficult: the contrast in the prosperity of the different countries was enormous. The Swiss had 50 times as many doctors per head as the Camerounians.

However, if we want to compare countries that are not so startlingly different, simple figures of 'energy per head' or 'TV sets per person' will not tell us much. The quantities of particular commodities produced by different countries depend on differences in tastes and climate. Britain for example, buys more TV sets and less wine than other European countries, and this is due to our excellent TV stations on the one hand, and high tax on wine on the other. We cannot get an accurate idea of living standards by picking out individual commodities: instead we have to find out the

the value of *all* the commodities that are produced in a year.

In Britain — and in most countries of the world — such a calculation is made every year. Since 1941, the government's Statistical Service has collected estimates of **national income** and published them annually in a table of accounts known as *The UK National Accounts* (or *Blue Book*). National income is an estimate of the money-value of the total amount of goods and services produced in an economy over a given period of time. When we have got this national income figure, we can divide this amongst the total population to find out an average standard of living in pounds or dollars per head.

SAQ 1: *In 1986 the UK National Income was £277 771 million and the total population was 56.7 million. Using your calculator, work out our national income per head.*

Why do we collect national income figures?

The collection of national income figures enables us to make interesting comparisons between one country and another. We can check whether our own economic performance is as good as that of other comparable countries. National income calculations also enable us to pick out the countries that are so poor that they require aid from richer countries. And just as we judge how much tax a person should pay from his personal income, we can look at national income to see how much nations should pay into international bodies like the European Community (EC) or the World Bank. In the row about Britain's payments to the EC, Britain used national income figures to support her arguments for paying less.

SAQ 2: *Look at the figures in Tables 1 and 2, and write a paragraph putting forward Britain's case for paying less into the Common Market budget.*

Table 1: Who pays the budget, 1980

Net contributors (i.e., countries who pay in more than they get out of the Common Market)

	£ million
Britain	1 209
W. Germany	699
France	13

Net beneficiaries (i.e. countries who get more out of the Common Market budget than they pay in)

Luxembourg	195
Denmark	247
Netherlands	281
Ireland	342
Belgium	367
Italy	489

Table 2: National income per head

(Common Market average equals 100)

Denmark	143
W. Germany	136
Belgium	128
Luxembourg	125
Netherlands	123
France	116
Britain	72
Italy	60
Ireland	50

The figures can be used for other purposes than making international comparisons. They are just as useful as an indication of important trends in the economy. For example, the government wishes to know what proportion of our national income goes into investment, as opposed to exports; whether profits are rising or falling; whether consumption or government spending is taking a higher or lower share of the national output. Government policies are more likely to be successful if ministers have accurate information, so correct national income figures help us towards the goals we wish to achieve — stable prices, high investment, faster growth in incomes. This is the reason the government started to collect the figures, and why it continues to produce a large number of economic statistics every year.

SAQ 3: *The government are not the only people who are interested in full and up-to-date figures on the progress of the economy. Who else will want to know what is happening to incomes, output, investment and so on?*

The national income figures also enable us to estimate how living standards and the level of production have changed over a period of time. After allowing for rising prices, for example, the national income statistics tell us that incomes in Britain at the start of the eighties were 65% higher than in 1958.

How the figures are calculated

Actually adding up the value of all the commodities produced in an economy as big as Britain's — with over 26 million workers and an output running into hundreds of billions of pounds — is an enormously complicated job. To understand how it's done, we'll have to return to a diagram we met on page 10 of Unit 1.

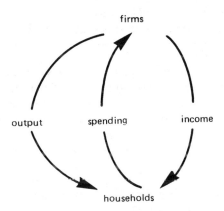

This simple model shows an economy at work. The firms are producing the commodities which I have labelled 'output'. They sell this output to households, whose spending is shown in the middle of the diagram; The amount people spend on commodities, labelled spending but more correctly called **national expenditure** is, of course, the same as the firms get for producing those commodities — the output or **national product**. And the money firms receive from making the national product is distributed in the form of wages, profits and rents. I have labelled this as 'income'.

SAQ 4: *When this diagram appeared in Unit 1, there was a fourth flow between households and firms. Firms receive the spending of households in return for the commodities they produce: what do they receive in return for the incomes they pay?*

The important thing to grasp when looking at the diagram is that income, output and expenditure are three ways of looking at the same thing. We should get the same result, whether we calculate the value of the goods and services produced or the money spent on buying them or the incomes received from making them. Perhaps this is easier to understand if we take it on the level of a small business:

Claybake Pottery makes 10 000 coffee mugs a week, which it sells for 50p per mug to a national chain store. Therefore the pottery makes £5000 worth of mugs (the value of its *output*) and the total spent on the coffee mugs by the chain store is also £5000. So in this example expenditure equals output. Most of the £5000, when received by the pottery, goes into paying the wages and salaries of the workers, although some is paid out to the suppliers of raw materials etc., and some goes to the owners of the pottery as profit. The incomes received for producing the mugs thus adds up to £5000. The value of expenditure equals the value of output equals the total of incomes – both in this example and in the whole economy.

Logically, then, the national product will come to the same figure, no matter whether we calculate it by adding together the value of everything produced, or the total amount of incomes earned, or the total of all spending. In the real world, life is a little more complicated, but the government does use these three basic ways to work out the figure. Let's look at them one by one.

The income method
We must include a wide range of incomes when we are working out what people receive in return for making the national product. We have to include the wages and salaries of all employees, the incomes of the self-employed and incomes from rent. There are the profits that firms earn, or the surpluses earned by nationalised industries.

SAQ 5: *Here are the figures that show incomes earned in 1986*

	£ million
Income from employment	209 445
Income from self-employment	34 340
Gross profits of companies	50 785
Gross surpluses of nationalised industries and government enterprises	8 287
Rent	22 497

(a)   what is the total of all incomes?
(b)   what is the share of profits in total incomes?

You'll notice that there are quite a few forms of income that I haven't included in this calculation. For example, there has been no mention of retirement pensions, student grants or social security payments. The reason is that we only include in national income calculations those incomes that people have received for making goods and services. The incomes I've just mentioned are not received for productive services: they have been transferred from the incomes of those who make commodities. Such incomes are called **transfer incomes**.

SAQ 6: *Rents are not counted as transfer incomes – why not? (clue: for what productive factor does rent represent payment?)*

A student grant, for example, is not earned income, but a transfer from the pockets of taxpayers. We can't count it twice over – once when earned by the taxpayers, twice when taken from them and given to students. Similarly, dividend payments on shareholdings have already been put down in the national income figures under gross profits from companies.

SAQ 7: *Here are three forms of transfer incomes that are not included in the national income figures.*
(a)   Where has the income been transferred from?
   (i)   retirement pension
   (ii)   unemployment benefit
   (iii) interest paid on your national savings account
(b)   Which of the following are transfer payments, and which are payments for productive services (think carefully).
   (i)   a farmworker's wages
   (ii)   a civil servant's wages
   (iii) child benefit payment
   (iv)   a landlord's income from rent
   (v)   interest earned on a loan to the government

The expenditure method

As I noted on pages 37-8 the income method is just one way of measuring the national income. We could also add up all the spending that takes place in the economy. Looked at this way, the national income is the total paid by final buyers for all the commodities produced in an economy in a given period of time. Perhaps I should explain the meaning of the term **final buyers**. Firms often buy goods from other firms and use them to manufacture other commodities, which they then sell to the public. For example, a builder buys bricks from a building merchant, who has bought them in turn from a brickworks. The house, when completed, is sold to a house-buyer. If we counted the value of the bricks when they were sold to the merchant, and then again when they were sold to the builder, and then again when sold as part of the house, we would be counting the same bricks three times over. So we only count them when sold to the final buyer.

The diagram on page 37 made it look as if householders are the only final buyers in an economy. But, of course, they aren't. In addition to their consumer spending, there is the day-to-day spending of central government and local councils. This is called **general government final consumption**.

When we have totted up private and public consumption, we must add on investment spending by firms. This takes two forms: it could be the fixed investment (or **fixed capital formation**) that Unit 2 explained was important for living standards and economic growth — factories, houses, machines, computers. On the other hand, firms have to hold stocks of goods and materials to carry on their business, and this is described as **capital formation in stocks**. This category is also used to include the value of work in progress but not yet finished.

What is more, many of the goods and services made in Britain are exported. We have to add these on to our figure if we are to get an accurate idea of the total amount of commodities made in Britain. Imports, of course, have to be excluded for the same reason. They are part of the output of other countries, and do not give rise to incomes in Britain.

SAQ 8:   *If I were to summarise the expenditure method of calculating the national income, I would say it involved adding up (a) consumers' expenditure, (b) general government final consumption, (c) fixed capital formation (d) value of the increase in stocks and works in progress, and (e) exports. (f), imports are deducted. Give an example of products in each of these categories.*

The residual error

The diagram on page 37 showed a neat and simple model of the economy. The expenditure on the commodities produced was the same as the incomes earned from making them — remember the pottery that made coffee mugs? So no matter how we measured output, we still got the same figure. But the real world is much more complicated, and though we *should* get the same figure when we add up the total of incomes and the total of spending, we never do. There are bound to be mistakes, unreported incomes and transactions, unintentional double-counting and so on.

The resulting difference between the income and the expenditure calculations is called the **residual error**. This error has to be put in somewhere, and as it happened it is presented as an item of income like this:

	Figure reached by the income method (£ million)	*Figure reached by the expenditure method (£ million)*
	326 049	319 089
Residual error	− 6 960	
	319 089	

You may feel that having an error of over £6000 million looks (in words of Oscar Wilde) like carelessness. While it should make you a little cynical about government statistics — which are often revised and adjusted when errors and omissions are discovered — it really isn't as bad as it first appears. It is, to look at it charitably, an error of just over 2% on an enormously complicated calculation.

SAQ 9:   *(a) What was the residual error in these years?*

	1983	1984	1985
Income-based estimate	£259 229 m	£280 129 m	£305 741 m
Expenditure-based estimate	£258 272 m	£275 395 m	£302 465 m

(b)   *One of the reasons given above for this error is 'unreported incomes': why might some incomes not be reported to the government?*

GROSS DOMESTIC PRODUCT

The figure we have now arrived at, either by adding together the value of all the incomes received for producing commodities or the value of all spending by final buyers, will show the total value of all the commodities made in a country in a year. This figure is called the **Gross Domestic Product**, or **GDP**. (The significance of the words 'Gross' and 'Domestic' will become clear in the next few pages.)

THE GROSS NATIONAL PRODUCT

The GDP, however, does not quite account for all incomes earned by British residents. Let me explain why. In this unit and the preceding one, I have made it clear that a country's standard of living depends on the goods and services it can produce. Generally speaking, a country cannot consume commodities that it hasn't produced: even if it imports goods, they have to be paid for by an equal export of commodities. Britain is lucky, however, because over the years it has built up a lot of overseas property: stocks and shares, land, factories and plantations. As a result, we receive income from this property each year, and this increases our national income. On the other hand, foreigners own property and shares in Britain, for which we have to make payments. If we add on to the GDP all the property income we get from overseas, and take off the property income we have to pay to foreigners, we arrive at a figure known as the **Gross National Product** (GNP). This is how it looked in 1986:

	£ million
GDP at factor cost	319 089
Net property income from abroad	4 686
Gross National Product at factor cost	323 775

SAQ 10: *Which of the following will increase the net amount of property income from abroad, and which will reduce it?*
(a)   *Interest paid by the Canadian Government on money lent to them by British residents.*
(b)   *Payments of profits by Vauxhall Motors to its parent company, General Motors in Detroit.*
(c)   *Rents on an office block in London owned by an Arab businessman who lived in Beirut.*
(d)   *Dividends paid to the British owner of shares in a Singapore electronics company.*

SAQ 11: *Here are the GDP figures (in £ million) for the named years, together with the net amount of property income from abroad, (a) Work out the GNP for the years in question.*

	1980	1983	1985
GDP	199 606	258 272	302 465
Net property income from abroad	−221	2 421	4 686

(b) What does the minus sign mean in 1980?

Market prices and factor cost

There's one more problem that we have to clear up before we can be happy that we have reached a figure that accurately reflects the value of all the commodities produced in a year. This is that the price of many of the things we buy includes tax. Taxes on goods we buy are called **expenditure taxes** to distinguish them from income taxes and other forms of tax. Cigarettes, cars, and alcoholic drinks are taxed at a particularly high rate, but most goods bear Value Added Tax (VAT) at a rate of 15%. So if we valued the GDP and GNP at the prices people actually paid, we would include a lots of tax money on top of the actual cost of production. It's a lot of money to include: in 1986, the British paid more than £60 000 million in such taxes. And it isn't only taxed goods that are sold at a price different to their real cost: some goods are subsidised. If we included these at the price they were sold, we would under-value them.

What I am saying is that the actual price people pay is often different from the real value of output, and different from the incomes received for producing the output. Taxes make the price artificially high, subsidies artificially low.

To compensate for this, the *National Income Blue Book* shows both GDP and GNP at **market prices** (that is, what people actually paid for it) and at **factor cost** (that is, the real cost after deducting indirect taxes and adding on the value of any subsidies). Here is the 1986 figure to give you an idea:

		£ million
	GDP at market prices	374 895
minus	taxes on spending	62 273
plus	subsidies	6 467
	GDP at factor cost	319 089

SAQ 12: *Here are the GDP figures for 1984 and 1985 at market prices and the figures for taxes and subsidies:*

	1984 (£ million)	1985
GDP at market prices	320 168	351 567
taxes on spending	52 496	56 812
subsidies	7 723	7 710

(a)   *Work out the GDP at factor cost*

(b)   *The GDP at factor cost in 1983 was £258 272 million – expenditure taxes of £49 113 million had been deducted and subsidies of £6 333 million added. So what was the original market prices GDP?*

(c)   *In 1980, the market prices GDP was £230 329 million and the factor cost GDP was £199 606 million. If Government subsidies were £5 718 million, how much was paid in expenditure taxes that year?*

Gross and net

We have now arrived at a figure for GDP. and GNP The GNP tells us how much income is received by British residents, and the GDP is a good estimate of the value of commodities produced in Britain. But in producing these commodities, some of the country's capital goods must have worn out. Others will have become outdated, or broken down. So we have to use some of the commodities we have made to replace the investment we have used up in producing the national product. As a result, we deduct from the GNP an estimate of **capital consumption** – that is, the capital we have consumed, or used up. Only after this deduction has been made do we have a figure that shows the net result of all the economic activity in the year in question. This we call the **net national product**, or sometimes net national income. This is the figure that economists are referring to when they speak loosely of the **national income**.

SAQ 13: *In 1986 the GNP came to £323 775 million. But during that year £46 004 million worth of capital goods were used up and had to be replaced. What, then, was the net national product for that year?*

Current and constant prices

Before leaving the maze of figures that make up the national income figures, we have to deal with one last complication – inflation. Look at these figures:

UK national income, 1976	£101 348 million
UK national income, 1986	£277 771 million

These statistics seem to show that we are nearly three times richer now than we were 10 years ago. Now, it is certainly true that average incomes have risen three times — but much of this increase is simply due to inflation. The 1976 national income seems so low because prices were so much lower then. Unless we allow for the effects of rising prices, it will be most difficult to really compare one year with another. That's why the *UK National Accounts* includes not just estimates of GNP and GDP at prices current in the years concerned but also estimates at prices that stay the same all the way through — what are called 'constant prices'. This is done by measuring the worth of the national product of all the years against one set of prices: say, those current in 1980. So, for example, the 1986 figures would be 'deflated' by a percentage representing the inflation between the two years. When this is done, we can make genuine comparisons between one year and another. Coming back to the figures just quoted, we can use the constant price figures to see things this way:

1976 UK national income (at 1980 prices)	£169 997 million
1986 UK national income (at 1980 prices)	£195 054 million

So we are not 274% richer — when the effects of inflation are taken into account, we are producing barely 15% more.

This is not the only time we have to make special allowance for inflation in the national income figures. When prices are rising, the stocks of raw materials and unsold goods that firms must have in order to run their business rise in their money value — and this rise in value appears on firms' balance sheets to swell the profits. But this is just an inflationary gain — no extra goods have been produced. The income method of calculation therefore takes off the inflationary rise in the value of stocks known as **stock appreciation**.

The output method

The diagram on page 37 of this unit showed three ways to work out the figure for the national product.

SAQ 14: *See if you can jot down the names of the three ways of calculating the national income.*

We've seen the details and complications of using the income and expenditure methods, the two main ways that are used to calculate the national income in Britain. Estimates of output are also made and may be used to gauge the accuracy of the other two calculations.

When adding up the output of all the various industries, we come to the same double counting problem we met in the expenditure method. For example, if we add up the output of tyre manufacturers and the output of car manufacturers, we will be counting a lot of tyres twice. So we have to add up only the value each industry adds to the things it buys in. Therefore the output method relies on calculating just the **value added**, which means counting the value of the output of the industry *minus* the cost of materials and services bought from other industries or imported.

SAQ 15: *Below is the record of one industry's contribution to the national product in the late 1970s. What happened to the value of its output? Can you hazard a guess as to what the industry is?*

	1975	1976	1977	1978	1979	1980
value of the output of industry X (£ million)	-30	521	1845	2488	5144	7649

We have now got to the end of the first half of this unit — the bit that explains how the national income is actually calculated. Before we go on to look at the problems that face us in interpreting the figures, it might be a good idea to go back and review your notes to see if you can briefly run through the procedures used in national income accounting. The next exercise is the grand finale to the section, and aims to test your overall understanding with an imaginary (and slightly simplified) national income table.

SAQ 16: *Work through these figures and answer the questions that follow. The figures are £000 million throughout.*

Column A			*Column B*	
Consumers' expenditure	28		Income from employment	27
General govt consumption	8		Income from self-employment	3
Gross fixed capital formation	8		Gross trading profits of companies	5
Rise in stocks (actual increase)	1		Gross trading surpluses of public corporations	2
	___			
Total domestic expenditure	45		Rent	3
				___
add exports	10		Total domestic income	40
minus imports	9		*less* stock appreciation	1
		(i)		
less taxes on expenditure	7		Residual error	
plus subsidies	2			___
	___			
		(ii)		

Add net property income from abroad	1	
	___	
	42	(iii)
Less capital consumption	3	
	___	
Net national product		(iv)

(a)   What is the figure at (i) called?

(b)   What is the figure at (ii) called?

(c)   Adding up the figures, how much did the figure at (i) come to? How much did the figure at (ii) come to?

(d)   What do we call the figure at (iii)?

(e)   What do you make the net national product (at iv)? Give another name for the net national product.

(f)   What is meant by the term 'stock appreciation'? Why is it deducted from the figures?

(g)   The national income accounts use two main methods of calculation. Which method is used in column A? Which method is used in column B?

(h)   Explain the difference between the figures at 'market prices' and at 'factor cost'.

(i)   What is 'property income from abroad'? What would it mean if this figure was negative (that is, minus £1 billion)? Why is the figure usually positive in the British national income?

(j)   What is 'capital consumption'? What do firms call it when they make an allowance for capital consumption in their own accounts?

SAQ 17: *Answer 'true' or 'false' to these statements.*

		True	False
(a)	The GNP should in theory be equal to the net national income.	☐	☐
(b)	The GNP may be calculated by adding up the total value of the output of each firm in the country.	☐	☐
(c)	Only earned incomes count towards the national income figures.	☐	☐
(d)	The national product calculations are made using tax returns.	☐	☐
(e)	There is very often a difference between the actual figures reached by using the income and expenditure methods of calculation.	☐	☐
(f)	If many people are borrowing money to buy goods, our national expenditure will be higher than our national income.	☐	☐
(g)	The national income figures were first published officially during Second World War to aid the direction of the wartime economy.	☐	☐

	True	False
(h) The increase in real production of commodities between two years is best discovered by comparing the GNP for the two years when they are valued at current prices.	☐	☐
(i) Britain's rate of increase in national income over the past 20 years has been roughly average for an advanced industrial nation.	☐	☐
(j) An increase in the national income doesn't necessarily mean that we are better off.	☐	☐

SHOULD WE BELIEVE THE NATIONAL INCOME FIGURES?

Having learned that careful estimates are made each year of our national output, most students are content to believe that these can be relied upon as a measure of our national welfare. They believe that a rising national income is to be welcomed as it shows we are getting 'better off'. In fact there are a number of reasons for believing that the national income figures are just a rough guide to our welfare, and that they should be viewed with some caution. The rest of this unit looks at the things we must bear in mind when using the national income figures.

Population size

An elementary but very important point is that the standard of living is measured by the national income per head: that is, how many commodities are available per member of the population. And just as the national income grows as the years go by, so does the size of population in many countries. If the national income goes up 2%, but the population rises by 3%, the country is worse off than before, not better off.

SAQ 18:   *Are there any countries in the world where population growth really could outstrip growth in national income?*

What sort of products. . .?

Some people would argue with the definition of standard of living that I have just given. They would point out that what matters in raising the living standards of the average man is the level of consumption per head rather than national income per head. For example, a rise in the national income could have come about through the production of more capital goods. These will probably raise living standards in the future – but most of us don't feel better off if there are more computers or machines in local factories, or if the government has opened a new airport or power station.

Similarly, the government might have stimulated output and created employment with a massive arms programme. However, this strategy does not provide goods for the domestic consumer, and although the GNP will rise the majority of people will have their spending power held down.

. . .and who gets them?

Further, the 'national income per head' that you worked out on the first page of this unit is just a notional figure – like the average married couple who have 1½ children and $\frac{5}{8}$ of a Ford Escort. In reality, the national income could be shared out in a very unequal way. It could go to a small, super-rich, elite, for example. When deciding whether to welcome a rise in the national income you should ask yourself who benefits.

This question is particularly interesting in relation to the economic development of poor countries, because many of the techniques that are advocated to increase the national income in those countries will not help the poor at all. For example, 'modern' techniques in farming often require large farms run by owners who can afford tractors and fertilisers. The poor peasant who holds a small plot of land for his family doesn't benefit – and may even have to sell up and become a propertyless labourer. So a rising national income in India, Mexico or Brazil may not trickle down to the most needy at all. Indeed, British economic historians still dispute whether the increased production that came about early in the industrial revolution benefited the whole population, or went in large profits to a small class of capitalists.

What about wealth?

Nor should we forget that the national income only measures the amount of commodities produced in a year. So it does not include all the goods we had when the year started. It does not tell us whether we have got two cars and three colour TVs each — only whether or not we have produced additional cars and colour TVs in the year in question. Any estimate of how well-off a country is must consider its wealth (the amount of its useful assets) as well as its income.

SAQ 19: *As a way of illustrating the fact that someone's standard of living is as much affected by what he or she has got as by what he or she earns, name three of your possessions that (a) add to your standard of living but (b) were not produced in the past 12 months.*

Changes in products

One factor that creates problems when we want to compare the national income of one year with that of another is that the commodities which make up the national income change. Take, for example, a car. In the 1950s, £600 would buy a middle-range family saloon car: today such a car would cost at least £4000. We could simply say that cars now cost seven times as much, but that's not quite true. Cars today are quieter, faster, safer, more reliable and have more accessories and features. Similar examples could be taken from a very wide range of commodities: record players, cooking stoves, fabrics, televisions. Indeed, some commodities are quite new: ballpoint pens, video recorders, calculators, non-iron fabrics, non-stick pans, soft contact lenses, antibiotic drugs, body-scanners, digital watches and so on. We find difficulties in comparing the amount of commodities made in one year with the next if the actual commodities are so different.

Unpaid work and unmarketed goods

One of the most problematical areas in national income accounting arises because generally only goods and services that are exchanged for money are included in the national income figures. So if a nurse looks after a frail old person, that is in the figures; if a son or daughter does, it isn't. If I dig my own garden, it doesn't appear as economic activity; but if I employ a gardener to do it, it does. The most glaring example of a useful activity that is simply not included in the national income is housework: all the cleaning, laundering, cooking and child-minding that would cost a fortune if it had to be bought on the open market.

SAQ 20: *(a)   Suppose a housewife who has previously stayed at home and looked after the house goes out to work for £50 per week. She hasn't the time to do the chores she used to do, so pays a neighbour £10 to do the housework for her.*
   (i)   How much will the recorded national income rise?
   (ii)   Is this rise an accurate measure of the increased work done?
(b)   Groucho Marx said he came from a village so poor that the inhabitants only made a living by taking in each others' washing.
   (i)   Would this village have a higher money income than a normal village?
   (ii)   Would it actually be any better off?

This problem runs through the calculations. Home-grown vegetables are not counted, but bought vegetables are: washing your car in your own driveway doesn't count, washing it in a commercial carwash does. Yet the output — a cabbage, or a clean car, is just the same both ways.

The problem becomes particularly acute in the countries of the Third World, where many people are self-sufficient — in other words, they grow their own food, build their own houses and make their own clothes. Few products are exchanged for money. Where the cash economy forms such a small part of the productive activity, estimates have to be made of the amount of commodities produced but not exchanged for money. Otherwise the national income figure will be much too small, and make the country appear much poorer — and its people's standard of living much lower — than is in fact the case. Thus in India about 80% of the population live in the rural areas and work on the land. They grow the food they consume. This means that agricultural production would be excluded from conventional national income accounting unless we make a careful estimate as an adjustment.

Pollution, congestion and noise

Just as some of the activities that benefit society — like raising children or cooking meals at home — don't count in the national income figures, some activities which may actually lower our well-being add to the national income. If, for example, the beautiful Snowdon region of North Wales was ripped up for mineral extraction, the national income might well rise (provided that the value of the minerals dug up was greater than the drop in tourism). Similarly, if a chemical works were to use a process that poisoned streams and killed local wildlife, the damage wouldn't show up on national income returns.

While much progress has been made in cleaning up polluted air and rivers, it is plain that increased output of commodities often means increased output of bad things. More cars means more congestion; a faster pace of business life means more ulcers and heart disease; more package holidays mean more noise, and more remote, tranquil places being ruined. Because we don't buy scenery, or put a money value on a peaceful life, we make it appear as if ICI building a potash mine in the middle of the North York Moors, or the Coal Board planning to dig up the Vale of Belvoir is pure economic gain. If we believe the national income figures, it *is*: but if we value wild places and tranquil beauty, it *isn't*.

Disproducts

But at least a polluting chemical works or an ugly coal mine is producing something useful: the fertilisers and fuel they produce do really add to the amount of useful commodities we can use. Some products are, however, harmful. Take cigarettes. If a cigarette factory opens and employs previously unemployed people, the national income will rise. Twenty or thirty years later, when the National Health Service takes on more nurses and opens more lung disease units, it will rise again. And when the victims of tobacco-related diseases have to be buried in new coffins and hearses, the national income will rise again. Yet wouldn't we be better off with no cigarettes, no need for medical treatment and no need for premature funerals?

The black economy

The national income figures are compiled, inevitably, from government statistics. Yet as you have seen earlier, there are a number of reasons why people may not let the government know of their economic activities. For example, they may wish to earn a second income (or even a first income) without paying any tax. They may want their business to be free of tiresome regulations on minimum wages or town planning. Their activities may even be criminal. For whatever reason, the plumber who asks for payment in cash only, or the motor mechanic who works at weekends to supplement his income are unlikely to find themselves in the official statistics.*

This unofficial economic activity is called the 'black economy'. We don't know how big it is, for obvious reasons, but we can make intelligent guesses using what American economist Edgar Feige calls 'the footprints left on the sand unwittingly by the irregular economy'. One technique used is to look at the differences between national income and expenditure figures; another is to look at the demand for high denomination banknotes (that is, £10 and £20 notes).

SAQ 21: *(a) Why should the demand for big banknotes give us a clue to the growth of the black economy?*

(b)   Between 1972 and 1978 consumers' expenditure went up by 244%, but the demand for high-value banknotes went up 470%. Could this indicate a growth in the black economy? Could it indicate anything different?

(c)   The national income accounts do have a figure that shows the difference between estimates of national income based on expenditure and based on income.

   (i)   What is it called?

   (ii) Would it be positive or negative if there was a lot of unreported income?

   (iii) Are the figures in SAQ 9 consistent with the theory that people don't report all their income?

In 1978 Sir William Pile, the former Chairman of the Board of Inland Revenue, estimated that the black economy might come to 7½% of the GNP. More recent estimates from the Central Statistical

*(Footnote: Of course, not all crime should be included in the GNP figures. Whilst a drug-peddler and a porno-graphic film-maker are producing goods, and a call-girl is providing a service, robbery and fraud are simply transfer incomes.)

Office have been lower, at around 3½% of GNP, but either estimate means that the government is losing thousands of millions of pounds' tax revenue each year — tax money that has to be taken instead from the law-abiding taxpayer. In 1984/5, £550 million was recovered from tax-dodgers in tax, penalties and interest: so just those who were caught contributed government revenue equal to half the PSBR.

Leisure

So far, I may have seemed to suggest that the national income statistics exaggerate the rise in our standard of living. But remember that present day societies enjoy much more leisure compared with those of the past. The national income figures will not indicate this benefit — for if workers have more holidays and a shorter working week, it will reduce the possible amount of commodities that can be produced. The following exercise may make this point clearer:

SAQ 22: *In 1950, Fred worked a 55-hour week for which he earned £5. Today, he works 40 hours and earns (at constant 1950 prices) £15. Is he*

(a)   *worse off?*
(b)   *twice as well off?*
(c)   *three times better off?*
(d)   *more than three times better off?*

Comparison of different countries, or different eras, must take into account the amount of leisure people enjoy in them. For example when comparing the GNP of Poland with that of Britain, we must remember that the six-day week is still usual in Poland. And when looking at our economic progress compared with the past, we cannot ignore the extra leisure we now enjoy. The American economist A. W. Sametz has calculated the value of the increased leisure-time, and came out with this table:

US National Product adjusted for leisure and other items between 1869 and 1966
(in billions of dollars and constant prices)

	GNP	Leisure	GNP + Leisure
1869-78	9.4	1.2	10.6
1929	97.0	60.0	157.0
1966	315.0	240.0	555.0

(quoted in Beckerman *In Defence of Economic Growth* p. 82)

If you do a little work with Sametz's figures, you will see that the actual GNP went up 33 times, but the value of GNP plus the extra leisure enjoyed went up a staggering 52 times.

International comparisons

If complications occur when using national income figures to work out what's going on inside a country, there are many, many more when using them to make international comparisons. Accounting procedures vary greatly between countries, and differing tastes and climates can make comparisons difficult. One major problem comes about because different countries have different currencies. Although exchange rates tell us how much of one currency we can buy with another, they can be misleading. For example, sometimes the rate of exchange does not reflect different costs of living. At the time of writing, you can get F11.40 or $1.20 for your tourist pound sterling: but most people find that they cannot buy a £'s worth of goods in France for F11.40, whereas they can get more than a £'s worth of goods for $1.20 in the USA.

Exchange rates can also fluctuate widely. In recent years, the £ sterling has gone as low against the US $ as £ = $1.08, and as high as £ = $2.40. We'd have to pick the right exchange rate — one that reflects the cost of living in the two countries — to get a really fair comparison of national prosperity from the national income accounts.

SUMMARY

There are a very considerable drawbacks in regarding the national income figures as a guide to welfare. Indeed, many of the things that make life really worth living – the peace and quiet of the countryside, the great satisfaction to be got out of a traditional craft – might be destroyed by economic development. Some things, like political liberty and religious freedom, a non-violent and caring society, cannot be valued in economic terms. However, the national income figures are the best guide to economic welfare that we have got – and they are an honest and useful estimate of the commodities we have produced and the incomes we have earned.

REVIEW SECTION

Further reading

On National Income Accounting, it's worthwhile getting hold of a copy of the most recent edition of *UK National Accounts* to look at the tables there, and the explanatory notes: it's expensive (the 1987 edition was £11.95), so a library might be the best bet. The HMSO publish *The National Accounts: A Short Guide* by Harold Copeman. Samuel Hay's book *National Income and Expenditure* (Heinemann) is recommended reading for a fuller knowledge of this topic, and the opening chapter of Prest and Coppock's *The UK Economy* (Weidenfeld and Nicolson) relates together the parts of the national income in a meaningful way. Wilfred Beckerman's book *In Defence of Economic Growth* (Cape) has a go at the people who claim that GNP figures overstate economic progress: it's quite readable for those new to economics. Have a look at page 22 of the *Economic Review* January 1985 which discusses the interpretation of National Income statistics.

Most standard textbooks have a chapter on national income accounting, although the figures and the particular details may not be all that up-to-date. If in doubt, believe this unit!

Examination questions

I explained at the beginning of the course that examining bodies use three ways of testing your knowledge and understanding: multiple choice questions, data response and essays. For this topic, the sort of multiple choice and data response items you've met in the Unit will be used to see if you can calculate the figures correctly. Essay questions are used to see whether you know of the drawbacks and problems involved in interpreting the figures, as is shown by the following:

1. What are the main conceptual and measurement problems involved in constructing national income accounts?

    (Northern Ireland GCE 'A' level June 1984)

2. What is the purpose and usefulness of national income accounts? Do conventional systems of national accounts achieve these objectives? How might such accounts be supplemented?

    (Oxford Local Delegacy 'S' level June 1984)

3. Discuss whether or not national income accounts provide a suitable measure of economic growth (a) over time and (b) between countries.

    (AEB 'A' level June 1983)

4. Discuss the problems which might arise in attempting to compare the standard of living in the United Kingdom with that in (a) Brazil and (b) the Soviet Union.

    (Oxford Local Delegacy 'A' level June 1986)

5. Evaluate the competing claims of the following measures to be indicators of a country's standard of living:

    (a) GNP at factor cost per head;

    (b) consumers' expenditure per head;

    (c) the stock of durable goods held by consumers.

    (Oxford Local Delegacy 'A' level June 1985)

6. By 1982 it had risen to £228.4 billion. To what extent does this increase indicate an improvement in the standard of living?

    (University of London 'A' level January 1986)

ANSWERS TO SAQs

SAQ 1:   I make it £4898.96p. This, of course, is the figure for every man, woman and child rather than the average income of each worker.

SAQ 2:   My paragraph would go something like this: The first table shows that Britain is by far the largest contributor to the EEC budget: we pay in twice as much as W.Germany, which is the next highest contributor, and most of the countries of the Community actually take more out than they pay in. This situation might be acceptable if Britain was by far the richest country in Europe, but it isn't. The second table shows that national income per head in Britain is just 72% of the Community average. It cannot be fair that Denmark, with a national income per head twice as high as Britain's, is taking money out of the EEC budget while Britain has to pay money in.

SAQ 3: The figures will also be useful and interesting to large companies, who wish to see trends and sales and investment; to unions preparing wage claims or economic forecasts; and to economists trying to see how their theories fit the facts in the real economy.

SAQ 4: Firms pay incomes in return for **factor services** – that is, the services of the factors of production. Wages are paid for labour, rent for the use of land, profits and interest for capital. The fourth flow is therefore factor services.

SAQ 5: I make it £305 354 million. (A number of minor adjustments actually make the final figure slightly different.) Gross profits are about 17% of this total.

SAQ 6: Rent is not a simple transfer of money from one individual to another – it is the payment for the use of a factor of production, land.

SAQ 7:
(a) Money paid to retirement pensioners has been financed from the taxed incomes of the working population; the same is true of unemployment benefit. The interest the government pays on its borrowing (for that is what national savings are) also comes from the taxpayers.

(b) Farmworkers' wages are, of course, payment for productive services growing food; a civil servant's wages are also payment for productive services – for the administration of the health service, or planning roads, or staffing prisons or whatever add to society's output of useful commodities; child benefit is a transfer; a landlord's income is in return for the service of using his flat or land; interest is a transfer from taxpayers.

SAQ 8: Obviously everyone has their own list, but here are some suggestions:
Consumers' expenditure: Spending on clothes, dining out, food, books, soap and toiletries etc.
General government final consumption: Spending on library books, hospital bed-sheets, petrol for police cars, rifles for the army, chalk for schools etc.
Fixed capital formation: New factories, business computers, machines, blast furnaces, shipyards, commercial vehicles, etc.
Value of the increase in stocks and work in progress: This could be any actual increase in the stocks firms hold: for example, if Ford have a stock of 30 000 cars at the end of the year compared with 20 000 at the beginning. If an oil-rig was half-completed, that would count as work-in-progress.
Exports include any good or service sold abroad, from whisky to Land Rovers.
Imports will therefore be any commodity bought from abroad: French apples, Japanese stereo equipment, German cars etc.

SAQ 9:
(a) The residual error was −£957 million in 1983, −£4734 million in 1984, and −£3276 million in 1985.

(b) The main reason for unreported incomes is probably tax evasion: if people reported their 'moonlighting' they would lose one-third of their income to the taxman.

SAQ 10: (a) and (d) result in payments of money into Britain, and therefore increase the net amount of property income from abroad; (b) and (c) involve us making payments outwards, and so reduce our receipts of property income from abroad.

SAQ 11: (a) GNP in 1980 was £199 384 million, in 1983 £260 693 million and in 1985 £305 865 million: remember, the way to get GNP from GDP is to add on the net amount of property income from abroad. (b) It means that we paid more out to foreigners that year as property income than we received.

SAQ 12:
(a) Requires you to add on subsidies and take off expenditure taxes. Thus, the 1984 GDP at factor cost comes to £275 395 million; and the 1985 GDP at factor cost is £302 465 million.

(b) Working back from the factor cost figure to find out what the GDP was at the prices people actually paid we have to take off subsidies (which made goods cheaper) and add on expenditure taxes (which made them dearer) to get £301 052 million.

(c) £36 441 million. If you add subsidies of £5 718 million on to the market price GDP, then the difference between that and the factor cost GDP must be the amount of expenditure taxes.

SAQ 13:   Net national product is GNP *minus* capital consumption. I make this £277 771 million.

SAQ 14:   Income, expenditure and output.

SAQ 15:   The industry in question is called 'Petroleum and natural gas': you should have spotted this from the very fast rise in value of output in the years quoted. Note that in 1975 there was a minus figure – showing that while it was being set up, the industry was costing more in new equipment than it was earning in sales of oil.

SAQ 16:   The answers are as follows:
(a)   GDP at market prices
(b)   GDP at factor cost
(c)   (i) £46 000 million, (ii) was £41 000 million
(d)   GNP at factor cost
(e)   The net national product (or national income, as it is known commonly) comes to £39 000 million.
(f)   Stock appreciation is the change in the value of stocks and work in progress due to inflation, rather than due to increase in the actual amount of stocks (which, of course, *is* counted). It is deducted because it is not an actual increase in production, just a paper increase in value.
(g)   Column A is the expenditure method, column B is the income method.
(h)   Market price calculations show the national product at the prices it was actually sold at. But this can be deceptive, for the figure is increased if the government taxes commodities, and reduced if it subsidises them. So to reach the real value of the goods, we must deduct the value of any taxes paid on commodities and add on the value of any subsidies. This calculation results in a figure called the 'factor cost' GNP or GDP.
(i)   Property income from abroad means incomes received by British residents from the ownership of assets abroad – like shares, land or companies. If this figure was negative, it would mean that we were paying more out to foreigners who owned assets (shares, companies) in Britain than we were receiving from the rest of the world. The reason Britain usually has a positive figure is due to all the investments we have made all over the world over the past decades.
(j)   Capital consumption is a measure of the amount of fixed capital that we have used up in the year. When prudent firms put aside money each year to cover the cost of replacing capital goods as they wear out: it appears in their accounts under **depreciation**.

SAQ 17:   (a)   False – net national income will take account of capital consumption.
(b)   False – this will give a greatly exaggerated picture, due to including products both sold and resold – a problem known as **double counting**. We must use the total of value-added by each firm.
(c)   True – that is, if you count rent and profits as earned incomes.
(d)   No – they use a survey of production by the government. It's the income method that uses tax returns.
(e)   True – this is why we have the residual error.
(f)   False – after all, you can only borrow from other people's incomes. In any case, expenditure is equal to income because all expenditure is received by someone!
(g)   True
(h)   No – this would be distorted by inflation. Constant price figures would be much better.
(i)   False – see Unit 2
(j)   True – see the following pages.

SAQ 18:   Yes. In Third World countries, the population growth can approach 3% or more each year. This wouldn't be a bad increase in GNP.

SAQ 19:   Everyone's list will be different. But, to take some examples from my own life, I have a five-year-old typewriter, three-year-old carpets, a two-year-old car and a fifty-year-old bed that are all contributing to my welfare, even though they weren't included in this year's national income. Consumer goods which give satisfaction over a long period of time – like washing machines, TV sets, furniture, cars – are called consumer durables, and pose quite a problem in national income accounting. There would be a very good case for arguing that consumer durables give services over a period of time, and so should be spread over a number of national income years.

SAQ 20:   (a)   (i)   The national income will rise £60 – the value of the two extra incomes.
(ii)   Now, £50 of that rise is genuine – the former housewife is producing com-

modities that were not produced before. But the £10 worth of work around the house, making beds and washing up, *was* going on before, and isn't an increase in our output of commodities. So the true rise of national income should be £50 only.

(b)   (i)   Yes.

       (ii)   No. Work it out — I'm no better off if I pay you £5 for washing my socks and receive £5 from you for washing yours.

SAQ 21:   (a)   Because people who are trying to avoid the taxman don't want a record of their income in their bank accounts: so they prefer to deal with cash rather than cheques. Big banknotes are more convenient for the cash economy.

       (b)   Yes it could — use of banknotes has grown faster than consumer spending would seem to warrant. On the other hand, when there is inflation (as there was between the years in question), we should expect the usage of higher value banknotes.

       (c)   It's called the residual error (remember?). If there was a lot of unreported income, then the spending estimate would be higher than the income estimate. So the residual error would have to be positive to 'top up' the artificially low figure reached through income-tax returns. In SAQ 9 all residual errors are negative — in each of those years, the income-based estimate was greater than the expenditure-based estimate; this is not consistent with the existence of a black economy. However, a careful examination of national income accounts (look at the 'Blue Book') will reveal some positive residual errors!

SAQ 22:   He's more than three times better off. He had three times higher income — plus an extra 15 hours of leisure.

4 An Introduction to Keynesian Economics

AIMS OF UNIT 4

When you have finished this unit, you should be able to

- explain why the national income can fall below the maximum output of the economy
- explain what a trade-cycle is
- sketch the circular flow of income, showing the place of savings and investment
- define the terms savings and investment and outline the factors that determine their size
- explain how changes in savings and investment affect the size of the national income
- explain the relation between consumption, savings, and income and show how the national income is determined by total spending.

STARTING MACRO-ECONOMICS

This unit aims to introduce you to the study of **macro-economics** — which is the name given to the study of the workings of the whole economy. You have already found out the factors that play a part in deciding the size of the potential national income, and in the last unit you learned how economists calculate national income. Countries that have high quality labour, plenty of capital goods, high levels of specialisation and can put their technical knowledge and education to good use — these societies can produce large amounts of commodities per head, and thus enjoy a high national income. I say they *can* produce these commodities, not that they do — for one of the problems with modern economies is that they often produce less than they could. Look at the following diagram, for example.

SAQ 1: *The following diagram shows both potential output — the output of manufactured goods we could have produced had we used our resources of land, labour and capital to the full (the broken line) and the actual output that was produced (the bold line).*

(a)   In what years were we producing our maximum output?

(b)   In what years were we further away from producing our maximum possible output?

(c)   What has happened to actual manufacturing output from 1955 to 1977?

Actual and potential output in manufacturing industry

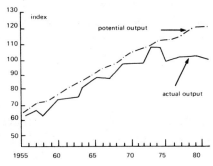

It is most important for economists to explain these changes in output and incomes, for they will have effects throughout the economy — on many people's lives, living standards and jobs. The next SAQ, for example, uses graph work to trace the relation between fluctuations in the size of the national income and unemployment.

SAQ 2: *I would like you now to plot two graphs on the graph paper on the right. On the top one, plot these changes in unemployment:*

1978	*−1.2%*
1979	*−8.1%*
1980	*+22.6%*
1981	*+58.3%*
1982	*+15.7%*

On the bottom scales, I would like you to plot these deviations from the trend in GDP. These figures show whether the GDP was growing faster, or slower than average in the years concerned.

1978	*+2.3%*
1979	*+1.4%*
1980	*−2.5%*
1981	*−1.6%*
1982	*+0.5%*

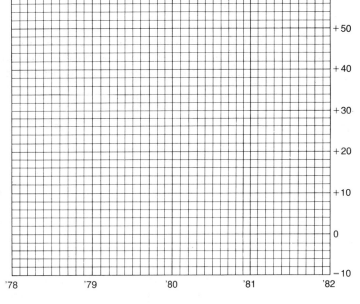

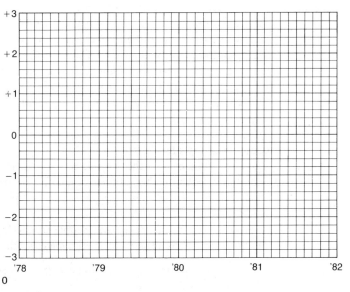

Now, taking each scale in turn, join together the points you have plotted to make two lines. What is the relationship between the changes in unemployment (top line) and changes in the GDP (bottom line?). Can you think of any good reason for this relationship?

THE TRADE CYCLE

Fluctuations in the level of output and employment have been noticed for many years. Back in the days of Queen Victoria, economists detected what they thought was a rhythmic regularity in trade and business. One year there was a boom: business was good, firms found it easy to sell the goods they made, and there was full employment. But just a few years later would come the slump, and, as businessmen found the going tougher, workers would lose their jobs. This process became known as the **trade cycle,** (or business cycle).

However, economists were unable to explain what was causing the slumps, or to tell governments what actions might be taken to avoid them. This was because economic theory at the time taught that a slump, caused by a drop in the sales of commodities throughout the economy, was impossible. The theory was known as Say's Law, after its originator, Jean-Baptiste Say (1767–1832), a French professor of economics. It went like this:

Say's Law

In Unit 1, I introduced you to the idea that in any economy two processes are at work: production (making commodities) and consumption (using them up). The units that consume are called households; the organisations that produce are named firms. We sketched a diagram like this:

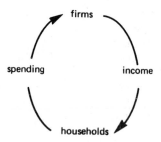

The picture is that firms produce commodities, and pay out incomes to the households. Every time a commodity is produced, an income is created. So a snappy version of Say's Law would be *supply creates its own demand.* There will always, therefore, be enough purchasing power around to buy up the output that is offered for sale: so a slump, when firms have to reduce output and sack workers because of bad trading conditions, seems impossible. For if income is always equivalent to output firms will always be able to sell their products. Of course, there might be a problem if consumers switched from buying one product to buying another: but for every job lost in the firms that made the unpopular product, a new job would be created in the new industry. A fall in the demand for one product will be balanced by a rise in demand for the other.

Criticism of Say's Law

The only problem with this elegant theory is that it doesn't fit the facts. Of course, national expenditure is equal to the national product. But anyone who draws from that the conclusion that total spending will always be high enough to give everyone a job can't have looked at the real world.

Karl Marx was one of the first people to develop a criticism of Say's Law. No short summary can do justice to his ideas, but a sketch might go like this:

> Incomes are paid out by firms to two types of people, workers and capitalists. Now, the workers will obviously spend their incomes, but will the capitalists spend the profits they receive on consumer goods? Perhaps not — instead, they will use their profits to buy more machinery to help their firm expand and succeed in business. So only a proportion of the incomes paid out by firms will be spent buying the commodities made by the firms. Sales will slump, workers be laid off and a depression will follow.

There is a germ of truth here, but only a small one. The money spent on buying new machinery will also create incomes and spending, because the firms and workers that make the steam engines, powered looms, the lorries and computers will be receiving money and spending it. In other words, investment spending creates just as much employment as spending on consumer goods.

SAQ 3: *If accumulating capital was the cause of unemployment, which countries in the world would have the highest rate of unemployment? Do they? (Think back to Unit 2)*

Marx did pinpoint an undoubted weakness in Say's Law, however: he was aware that the incomes do not simply flow round and round, from households to firms and back again. There are times when the incomes received by households are not spent on consumption – either saved, or taken in taxes by the government, or spent on imports that transfer the money from one country's circular flow into that of another. And firms do not sell only to British private consumers. They sell exports to foreigners; they make machinery and tools for other firms to buy as investment; and they sell a wide range of goods to the government. It is the effect of all these interruptions to the circular flow of income that John Maynard Keynes looked at when he developed his theory of employment in the 1930s.

KEYNES THE MAN

Keynes was born in 1883; his father lectured in logic at the University of Cambridge and his mother was one of the first women to study there. Keynes went to Eton, and on to Cambridge himself where he took a first-class degree in Mathematics even though (in a biographer's delightful phrase) his real interests were elsewhere. He took part in the competitive examination for entering the Civil Service, but came second due to a low mark in the economics paper. He complained that he evidently knew more about economics than the examiners: Keynes had many gifts, but modesty was not among them. The man who came first chose to work in the Treasury so Keynes had to settle for a job at the India Office. He later claimed that the only useful thing he did there in two years was to get a pedigree bull shipped to Bombay and he was glad to return to Cambridge to teach.

During the First World War, Keynes returned to the Civil Service but quit after taking part in the Peace Treaty negotiations in 1919. He felt that the demands that the victorious allies were making on Germany were unreasonable, and would lead to economic and political upheaval in Germany. He was right; and when the Second World War came around, he was again drafted into the Civil Service to help with the management of the wartime economy. His work was to earn him the title of Lord Keynes, and lead to the establishment of the International Monetary Fund and the World Bank. In his private life he was a man of great culture: he mixed with authors and artists, married a ballerina and was involved in setting up the Arts Council. Worn out by his work (and particularly disappointed by arduous negotiations with the Americans) he died in 1946.

The work for which Keynes is best remembered is the book he wrote in 1936, *The General Theory of Employment, Interest and Money*. This was written during the worst depression Britain has known, when unemployment reached as much as 20% of the labour force. Despite having passages of great wit and wisdom, 'The General Theory' is a difficult book for the layman to read. Indeed, economists still argue about what Keynes *really* believed. However, the outline of his attack on the economists who wrote before him (whom, he called the 'classical economists'), and of his own theory of national income determination are pretty clear. This is what I will now move on to consider.

SAQ 4: *What do we mean when we say one thing* determines *something else? What, then, does a theory of 'national income determination' describe?*

KEYNES' THEORY: SAVINGS AND INVESTMENT

I noted above that the circular flow of income does not just move smoothly round from firms to households and back from households to firms. There are a number of interruptions to the flow, and these are shown on the diagram over the page. Notice that there are at least three ways in which income can leak out. Firstly, there are *savings* — when households do not spend all their income, but put some aside as a reserve. In national income analysis, 'saving' just means not spending; it isn't therefore necessary to actually put money into the bank or insurance policy to 'save'. Then, there are *imports*. Spending on imported goods does not return to British firms, but flows into the circular flow of other countries. So when British consumers buy imported goods from Japan this creates greater output, employment and income in Japan but deflates the British economy. Lastly, there is *taxation*: we cannot spend money if the government takes it away from us! And so the amount that households spend on consumption is much lower than their total income.

Remember too that firms do not just make and sell consumer goods. They sell to other firms the machinery and tools they need (*investment*); they receive orders from foreigners, who buy British goods (*exports*); and they supply goods and services to the government. So the full picture of the circular flow would be as below.

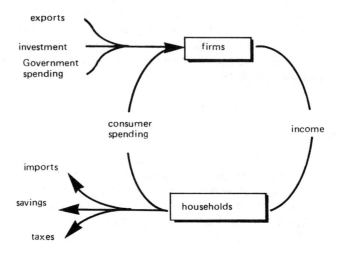

In order to keep the explanation and work in this unit nice and simple, I am going to ignore foreign trade and the activities of government for a moment. (I know that this is a bit artificial, but I promise you that I'll put them back in the next unit.) An economy without foreign trade is known as a **closed economy**.

SAQ 5: *If we consider a closed economy without taxes or government spending, we are left with just one 'leakage' and one 'injection' in the circular flow. Fill in their names on the diagram below, and explain what you mean by them.*

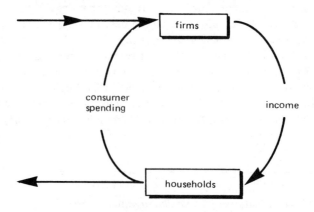

So now we have just savings and investment left. If you look at the bottom of the diagram in SAQ 5, you will see that income is either spent on consumer goods, or saved. Using the symbols C for consumer spending and S for savings, then,

$$\text{Income} = C + S$$

SAQ 6: *Fill in the missing figures in this list*
(a)   Income = 100, Consumption = 80, Savings = _____
(b)   Income = 600, Consumption = 550, Savings = _____
(c)   Income = 20, Savings = 1, Consumption = _____
(d)   C = 60, S = 20, Income = _____

Looking at the spending in the economy from the viewpoint of the firm, we can see that the total amount of spending in the economy is made up of consumption and investment spending. So, using I to stand for investment,

$$\text{Expenditure} = C + I$$

But we know that the diagram is a picture of the national economy, and we know from our work on national income accounting that the national expenditure is equal to the national income. But if

$$\text{Expenditure} = \text{Income}$$

then

$$C + I \text{ must be equal to } C + S$$

and if we now cancel C from both sides, we arrive at the conclusion that

$$S = I$$

Or, to put it into words, the amount households are putting aside as savings should be equal to the amount businesses are spending on investment. But it seems strange that savings must equal investment in order for the circular flow to make sense. The people who decide to save, and the people who take decisions on investment, are two quite different groups. On the one hand, there are households deciding what to put by for a rainy day, or paying the man from the Pru each time he calls; on the other hand, we find industrial managers working out the return from buying a new lorry or leasing a new factory. What mechanism can exist that brings the plans of these two differing groups into line? That's what I'm now going to look at: first of all, let's look at the factors that affect the amount of saving in society.

The propensity to save

People put money by for any number of reasons: to be able to buy something expensive (like a car or a holiday) in the future, to provide an income in old age, to provide a reserve of money to help with an unforeseen emergency. For many, saving is compulsory: teachers and local government officers, civil servants and employees of big companies have pension contributions taken off their salaries before they receive them.

But if we are looking for some overriding factor that influences how much we save, then we must surely come down to our level of income. People on low incomes find that they can save very little: in fact, people who suffer a fall in their income (say, when they lose their job) often cushion the blow by using up their past savings — what economists call **dis-saving**. But as income rises, people find that they can save more.

We can therefore sketch in a relationship between savings and income. The precise relationship between the two is called the 'propensity to save'. If we save one tenth of our income, then our propensity to save is ·1. As an example, here's a graph plotting the amount that an imaginary household saves on the vertical axis against the amount of income it receives, which is plotted on the horizontal axis: the savings line is labelled S.

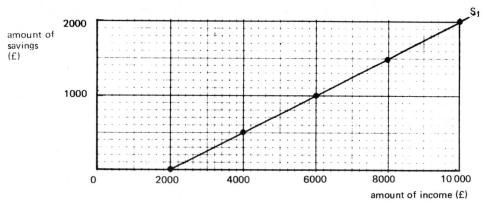

You can see that the amount saved rises as family income rises. If the income is just £2000 a year, then nothing is saved. But if income were to rise to £4000, they could save £500: and if income were to be £10 000 a year, they could afford to save £2000.

What I would like you to note here is the difference between the **average propensity to save (APS)** and the **marginal propensity to save (MPS)**. The APS measures the relationship between our total income and our total savings. Look at the example above. When the income is £6000, £1000 is saved: the APS is there $\frac{\text{savings}}{\text{income}}$, or $\frac{£1000}{£6000} = \frac{1}{6}$. But although we save one-sixth of our present income, if we were to get a rise of an extra £4000, savings would go up to £2000. A quarter of the extra income has been saved. It is not surprising that families are often able to save proportionately more from an increase in income: that's why we need a measure of the *extra* amount of savings that would follow from extra income. We have such a measure in the MPS, which is measured by the change in amount saved divided by change in total income.

So, to put it in easy-to-remember form:

$$\text{average propensity to save} = \frac{\text{total amount of savings}}{\text{total amount of income}}$$

$$\text{marginal propensity to save} = \frac{\text{change in amount saved}}{\text{change in total income}}$$

SAQ 7: *Work out the following:*
(a)   If I save £1000 out of an income of £5000, what is my APS?
(b)   If I save £400 out of an income of £2000, what is my APS?
(c)   If I consume £9000 out of an income of £10,000, what is my APS?
(d)   My APS is ·25 (or ¼), and I earn £8000. How much do I save?
(e)   My APS is ·2 (or ⅕), and I save £1500. How much do I earn?

And now, some examples to help you work out the idea of the marginal propensity to save:

SAQ 8: *Work out the following:*
(a)   If I save an extra £100 when my income goes up £300, what is my MPS?
(b)   If I save an extra £1000 when my income goes up £2000, what is my MPS?
(c)   When my income is £3000 a year, I save nothing: but when it goes up to £5000 a year, I can save £500. What is my MPS?
What is my APS when I am earning £5000?
(d)   Look at this table, which shows the amount that a household saves at various levels of income, and answer the questions underneath.

Income	£1000	£2000	£3000	£4000	£5000
Savings	£ –100	£ 0	£ 100	£ 200	£ 300

(i)   What is the APS when income is £4000?
(ii)   When income rises from £4000 to £5000, what is the MPS?
(iii) What is the APS when income is £2000?
(iv)   Savings are minus £100 when income is £1000. What is happening here? What do economists call this?
(v)   How much will the household be spending on consumption when its income is £3000?

So far, I have used the example of one household, or one person. But just as the amount of savings for a household varies directly with income, research has shown that the total amount of savings in a country is related to the national income: at a low level of national income the amount saved is low; but at a high level of national income, savings are much greater.

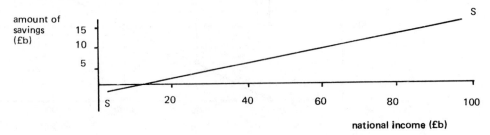

Shifts in savings

Although the size of a household or national income is the most important factor affecting the amount saved, there are other factors. I named some of these on page 58. What will happen, then, to the savings lines we have looked at if, for some reason, households decide to save more out of their incomes?

Let's do a worked example to find out. On the diagram below I have drawn the savings diagram from page 57. Once again you can see that nothing is saved when income is £2000; but when income rises to £4000, £500 is saved, when income is £6000 they save £1000 and so on. Now, let's suppose that the family whose income is shown in the diagram wanted to increase their savings — perhaps to take a long-promised trip to Australia, or maybe because worsening unemployment led them to build up a 'nest-egg' in case the breadwinner loses his or her job.

SAQ 9: *Plot this new, higher, level of savings onto the diagram below by drawing in a second line. Mark the new savings line S_2 to distinguish it from the original S line.*

Income	£2000	£4000	£6000	£8000
Savings	£ 500	£1000	£1500	£2000

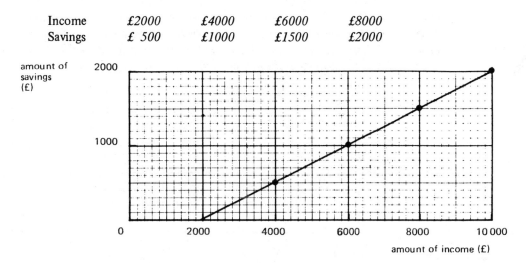

You will see that your new line, S_2, is higher than the original one. An increased propensity to save, then, will cause the S line to rise: to use economists' language, it will shift upwards. In the same way, there would be a downward movement in the savings line if households reduced their savings plans. Test your understanding of this by looking at this exercise.

SAQ 10: *Look at the diagram. It shows three savings lines. Which line illustrates the* lowest *propensity to save? Which one illustrates the* highest *propensity to save?*

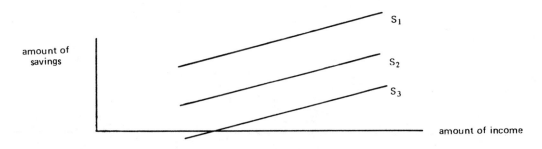

Investment *

Investment means expenditure on capital goods. Just as many things can affect a household's desire to save, many factors will influence a business person in deciding whether or not to invest — that is, buy new capital goods. Here's a list of some of the things that will influence the amount of investment planned by business:

● trends in sales. Does the business need fresh equipment to meet the orders it is getting?

---

*In national income analysis, we are dealing with the *net* national product. Therefore, the *investment* we speak of is *net* investment — that is, gross investment minus capital consumption.

- the cost of borrowing money. The managers of the firm may find that a planned project is not profitable when the money needed to get it off the ground has to be borrowed at high interest rates.
- new technology. For example new machinery with microprocessor control may offer a great advantage over present equipment.
- government policies. Grants and tax-reliefs have been used by governments of both parties to encourage investment; what's more, special help is available for firms wishing to move into new factories in the poorer regions of Britain.

What this all adds up to is one thing: the businessman will invest in new capital equipment if he expects to make a profit from doing so. Perhaps I should emphasise here that no project is certain to be profitable: what is needed to get new investment is the businessman's *expectation* that it will be profitable. Business confidence is as much a matter of mental outlook as scientific calculation; and it can be a brittle and unpredictable thing. Economic research has found that firms' investment plans fluctuate much more than the savings plans of households.

SAQ 11: *Look at the diagram below. It shows three possible levels of investment – decided, remember, by factors such as expected sales and the rate of interest. Which is the highest investment level? Which is the lowest? If businesses decided to invest more, which way would an investment line shift?*

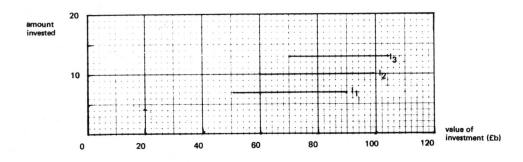

PUTTING THE JIG-SAW TOGETHER

We saw on page 57 that in any economy savings will be equal to investment, and have used the last few pages to look into the factors affecting saving and investment. What I am going to do now is put the two lines on to one graph, and see if I can explain the reasons why they equal one another.

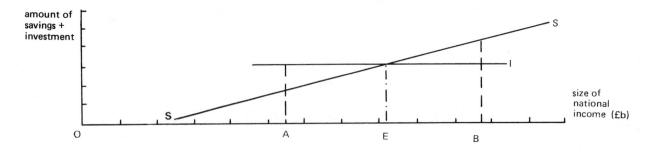

In this diagram I have plotted national income on the horizontal axis, and the amount of savings or investment on the vertical axis. The line marked SS is the one from the diagram on page 58, and shows that savings are determined by the amount of income and the propensity to save. The I line shows the amount of investment spending decided by business managers in line with their ideas about which investments will be profitable. You'll notice straight away that there is only one place where savings are equal to investment: at the level of national income marked OE. At the national income level OA, businesses are planning to invest more than households wish to save: and at income level OB, households wish to save more than firms are planning to invest. It will help you to understand why national income must be OE in size if I explain why it cannot be at OA or OB. To do this, I will use the circular flow of income diagram that we looked at before.

On the right is the start of a circular flow diagram. Firms are making £100 billion worth of commodities and paying out incomes – wages, salaries, rents, profits – to the same value.

When the households receive the income they put aside £10 billion as savings, and spend the rest – £90 billion. Looking at point A on the diagram above, we noted that firms' investment is higher than households' intended savings. So let's put an investment spending of £20 billion into the diagram. Can you see what is happening? Demand for the commodities firms are making is £110 billion, but firms have only produced £100 billion worth. Businesses will find that their stocks are running down, and when they are in this position – selling goods faster than they can make them – they will increase production and take on extra workers. Higher output, of course, means a higher national income. So, if households plan to save less than firms invest, the national income will be forced upward – and as it rises, so will savings.

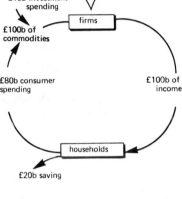

The next diagram shows the opposite situation. Here, we are at point B. The amount households are intending to save is greater than firms are planning to invest. As a result, the total demand for products – consumption spending plus investment spending – is less than the amount of products that firms are offering for sale.

We all know what happens when firms find they cannot sell all their output and stocks of unsold goods build up as a result. Firms reduce their production down to a level that will be saleable; down, in other words, to national income E, where savings are again equal to investment.

So the only place where national income will neither be pulled higher or pushed lower will be where savings are equal to investment – at point E on the diagram at the bottom of p. 60. National income is now said to be in **equilibrium**: no factors are at work to change its level. I'll give you a chance to work out a national income equilibrium by yourself:

SAQ 12: *On the graph, plot the following information about savings in an economy. The figures are in £000 million.*

Income	10	20	30	40	50	60
Savings	0	1	2	3	4	5

amount of savings and investment

amount of income

(a)   *Suppose that firms are investing £4 billion in the year we are studying. Draw in an investment line of 4.*

(b)   *At what level will the national income be in equilibrium? Why not at £30 billion? Why not at £60 billion?*

(c)   Optional question (if you've found this unit easy-going so far!): What is the MPS in this economy?

Important conclusion

Let's just pause before we go on to stress both the novelty of what Keynes had found out – and the importance. The national income was *not*, as the classical economists had thought, going to be always at its maximum, with the production of as many commodities as technically possible from the country's land, labour and capital. Instead, the national income in fact is going to stick at the level where the amount households plan to save is in line with businessmen's wish to invest. This *might* be at a happy state of full employment; on the other hand, it might not. There was no reason that Keynes could see why saving would always come to equal investment at a level of output and spending high enough to give everyone a job. In fact, the depression had shown him that it was perfectly possible for the national income to be in equilibrium well below the level needed for full employment.

Having found that the national income is in equilibrium where intended savings and investment are equal, let's look at what would happen if firms or households changed their plans, that is if there were changes in the level of savings and investment.

WHAT WILL HAPPEN TO NATIONAL INCOME IF MORE IS SAVED?

Here's a savings and investment diagram that shows national income to be in equilibrium at £150 billion. Now, what will happen if, for one of the reasons I outlined on page 57, households wish to increase their savings? We found out on page 59 that an increase in the propensity to save will show up on the diagram as an upward shift in the savings line.

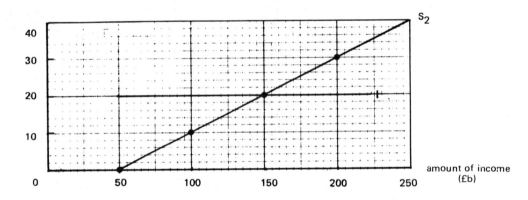

SAQ 13: *Draw this new, higher, savings line onto the diagram, and mark it S_2. Look at the diagram above and work out what has happened to the equilibrium national income.*

Income (£ billion)	50	100	150	200
New savings line (S_2)	10	20	30	40

A rise in the propensity to save (i.e. an upwards shift in the savings line) will lower the equilibrium national income.

Maybe this isn't such a surprising result. An increased desire by households to save can only mean one thing for firms – lower sales of commodities: after all, households can only raise their savings by spending less. As sales fall, firms produce fewer commodities, for there is no point making goods that cannot be sold. This cut-back in production will hit household incomes as unemployment mounts and overtime payments fall. This will again cut the demand for commodities. The national income will only come into equilibrium again where savings and investment are once more in balance. This is another illustration of the way in which changes in the level of the national income bring savings and investment into line.

But what you may find surprising is that the effect of an upward shift in the savings line is not to increase the total amount that people manage to save at all. Look at the diagram on p. 62 again. When the national income was £150 billion, the total amount saved was £20 billion: now the national income has fallen to £100 billion, the amount of savings is still only £20 billion. The increased desire to save has not resulted in any extra savings at all: it has been entirely cancelled out because of the drop in national income. This curious result is known as the **paradox of thrift**.

SAQ 14: *If you're not sure what the words 'paradox' or 'thrift' mean, look them up in a dictionary.*

Let's look at the paradox of thrift in more detail. Savings are a withdrawal from the circular flow. This means that expenditure declines and firms reduce output to adjust to declining demand for their products. Reduced output means fewer workers are required and unemployment grows. Growth in unemployment reduces the income of workers. The circular flow contracts and as savings are directly related to the size of income, a reduction in income will reduce the level of savings. What a surprise this must have been to the classical economists! They believed that the habit of thrift (making room for savings by modest consumption spending) was a thoroughly good thing. They thought that the extra savings would allow firms to invest more and increase efficiency and output: but we've found just the reverse. A desire to save more will cause a fall in demand, and a reduction in national income, and the amount the community manages to save will not rise. The perverse mechanism works like this:

> When national income is £150 billion, households desire to increase their savings (at present £20 billion) to one-fifth of their income (or £30 billion). But we know that national income is in equilibrium when savings are equal to investment – and investment has remained unchanged at £20 billion. So what happens instead is that national income falls until their savings are one-fifth of it: £20 billion, the same money amount as before.

You should now be able to work out the effects of a fall in the propensity to save. I have put this in the form of an exercise for you to do. First do the graph work, and then move on to the 'missing word' section.

SAQ 15: *On the graph below, plot the following line showing a reduced propensity to save:*

Income (£ billion):	40	60	80
New, lower savings line:	5	10	15

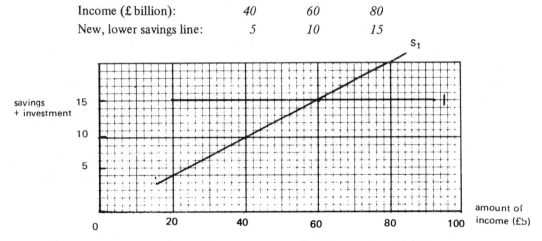

(a)   What was the original equilibrium national income?
(b)   What is the national income now that households have reduced their savings plans?
(c)   What has happened to the size of the national income? Why?
(d)   The actual amount saved is the same, despite the rise in the national income. Why?

Missing word exercise
A reduction in the propensity to save will be shown in a diagram by a shift _____ wards in the S line. The result of a fall in household's desire to save will be a _____ in the national income, for the fall in savings plans will be matched by a _____ in consumer spending. Firms will, therefore, experience an _____ in the sales of their products, and so will _____ output, causing a _____ in unemployment and a _____ in incomes. National income will _____ until, once again, _____ are equal to investment.

WHAT WILL HAPPEN TO NATIONAL INCOME IF INVESTMENT CHANGES?

Just as shifts in the S line can cause changes in the equilibrium level of the national income, so can shifts in investment spending. I'll go through this in the same way as I did when looking at shifts in savings — by using graphs to show the effect of a rise in investment and a fall in investment. I'll first of all take the case of a rise in investment spending.

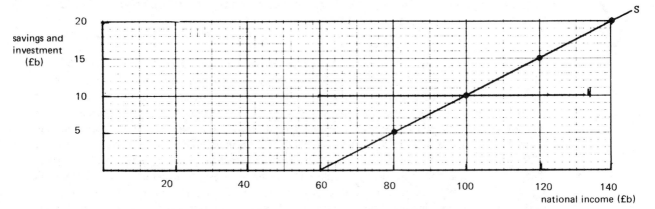

The diagram above shows the national income in equilibrium at £100 billion: here, firms are spending the same amount of money on new capital equipment as households wish to save. Let's see what happens if investment rises: draw on an I_2 line of £15 billion. The equilibrium national income has risen. If you don't like diagrams, you can still work this through mentally: an increase in orders for new machines, factories and so on will cause firms to produce more of these goods, creating higher incomes and more jobs. Once again, national income will be in equilibrium when it has risen enough to create extra savings, so that S = I when both are £15 billion. In the same way a reduction in investment spending will reduce the size of the national income. On the diagram below I have shown two investment lines. The one marked I_1 is the original high level of invest-

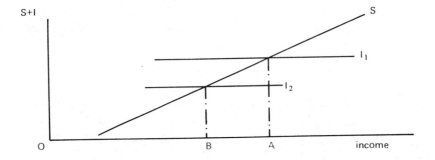

ment spending. The lower one, I_2 shows the reduced investment spending — caused perhaps by a drop in sales or a worsening of business confidence. Notice the equilibrium national income has moved from OA down to OB.

The investment multiplier

So a rise in investment will raise the level of equilibrium national income and jobs, and a fall in investment will reduce them. But modern research has shown that changes in investment cause a bigger change in national income than you would expect; for example, when investment rises by £1 million, national income rises by more than £1 million. Above, we used a diagram to see what would happen to a national income of £100 billion when investment rose from £10 billion to £15 billion. The thing to notice there is that equilibrium national income went up by £20 billion — that is, four times as much as the rise in investment. The investment has had an amplified effect on the size of the national income, an effect known as the **investment multiplier**.

> The investment multiplier records the effect on the size of the national income of a change in investment. If an increase in investment spending of £1 million raises the national income £3 million, then the multiplier is three — for the investment has pushed up national income by an amount three times itself.

SAQ 16: *Answer these questions about the investment multiplier.*
(a)   What is the value of the investment multiplier when
(i)   a rise in I of £5 million raises national income by £15 million?
(ii)   a fall in I of £20 million causes national income to fall by £60 million

(b)   How much will national income change if
(i)   investment rises £3 million and the multiplier is six?
(ii)   investment falls £6 million and the multiplier is two?

(c)   What is the change in investment that has caused the following?
(i)   an increase of £10 million in national income when the multiplier is five?
(ii)   a fall in national income of £35 million when the multiplier is seven?

What can account for this strange result? The answer is surprisingly simple: when investment spending rises, the people that receive the money spend it themselves in buying more commodities. Then the people who receive that spending spend it, and so on and on. The process does not continue forever, because of the propensity to save: each person who receives the extra income will save a little of it before he passes on the rest. Let's follow it round the circular flow diagram. At

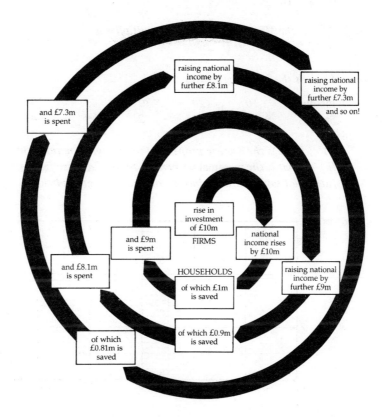

1, there is an initial increase investment of £10 million. This increases the incomes of households, who save 10% (I've picked a propensity to save of one tenth to make the calculation easier), and spend the rest on consumer goods. National income has by now risen firstly by £10 million (the extra investment) and by the £9 million rise in consumer spending that it caused. But this consumer spending will be received by someone, who will again save a little and spend the rest. Sticking to our MPS of one-tenth, the rise in national income is now £10 million + £9 million + £8.1 million. This extra £8.1 million is received by firms and paid out as salaries, wages, profits and rents: £0.8 million will be saved and the rest − about £7.3 million − will be spent. The rise of national income triggered off by that first bit of investment spending is now £10 million + £9 million + £8.1 million + £7.3 million. We can keep this calculation going for pages as the increased spending soaks its way through the economy: with every pair of hands it passes through, a little more is saved and a little less is passed on. So the process does not go on forever: it comes to a stop when *all* the increased investment spending has leaked away in savings, and once again the amount that households want to save is equal to the amounts that businesses wish to put into new machinery and stocks. But by the time that this has happened, the national income will have risen by a multiple of the original investment.

SAQ 17: *What will determine what that multiple will be: in other words, what will make the multiplier high or low?*

Well, it must have some connection with the marginal propensity to save. If the MPS is low, then little will leak away in savings each time the income goes round the circular flow: as a result, the process will go on for a long time. But if the MPS is high, the multiplier effect will be less: the investment spending will leak away quickly, and not give rise to so much spending and re-spending.

In fact, we can calculate the size of the multiplier if we know the MPS: mathematics tells us that the multiplier is equal to $\dfrac{1}{\text{MPS}}$. So if we divide the MPS into one, we can find out what the multiplier effect will be. If the MPS is one-fifth, the multiplier will be five (because one-fifth goes into one five times); if the MPS is ·1 or one tenth, the multiplier will be ten. Check your understanding of the investment multiplier before you move on.

SAQ 18:

(a)   What is the multiplier when the MPS is
    (i) ¼   *(ii)* ⅓   *(iii)* ½*

(b)   What is the MPS if the investment multiplier is
    (i) 2   (ii) 5   (iii) 2½

(c)   Look at the following figures

Income	10	20	30	40	50	60
Savings	0	1	2	3	4	5

    (i)   What is the average *propensity to save when national income is 20?*
    (ii)   What is the marginal *propensity to save in these figures?*
    (iii) Plot savings against income on the blank graph below.

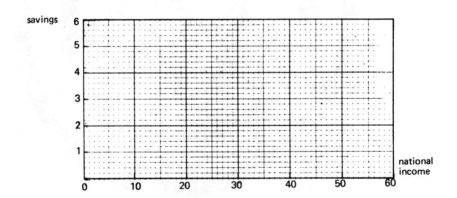

    (iv)   Draw on an investment level of 3. What is national income equilibrium?
    (v)   Work out the value of the investment multiplier firstly by calculating it from the MPS, and secondly by drawing on an investment line of 4 and seeing how much increased investment of 1 raises national income. Do the two methods agree?

ANOTHER WAY TO WORK OUT EQUILIBRIUM NATIONAL INCOME

So far we have worked out that the national income will be in equilibrium when households plan to save the same amount as firms willing to invest. It's the only way that the circular flow in the diagram (top of p. 67) will remain stable.

However, there is another way to work out where national income will settle. You should be able to remember from the unit on national income accounting that the national income is equal to the total expenditure in an economy: indeed, one of the ways of measuring the national income is to add up all the expenditure in an economy. So now we're going to calculate equilibrium by

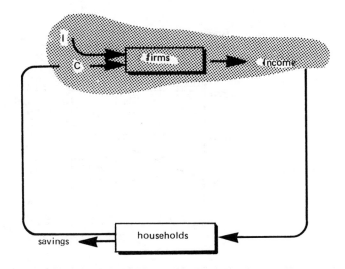

showing where total spending is equal to income, rather than by the S = I method we have used so far.

In our simplified model of the economy (remember, we've left out the effects of foreign trade and government taxes and spending) there are only two sources of expenditure — consumption (C) and investment (I). In the circular flow diagram above, I have shaded the area where C + I = national income. Let's turn to the things that determine how much consumption and investment will take place.

In fact, we have already worked out (on pages 59-60) that investment will be affected most of all by business profit expectations. So we can leave that aside for a moment and concentrate on what determines consumption.

Remember that consumption spending is the other side of the coin to savings. If we save a portion of our income, we cannot consume it: income = C + S. And, like savings, the size of consumption spending depends on income: as a person's, or a nation's income rises, more is spent on consumer goods. Exactly how much will be measured by the **marginal propensity to consume (MPC)**.

The marginal propensity to consume can be worked out like this:

$$\text{MPC} = \frac{\text{change in consumption spending}}{\text{change in total income}}$$

I hope that you have worked out that, once you know the marginal propensity to save it is pretty easy to get the marginal propensity to consume. If the MPS is ·2 (one fifth), the MPC is ·8 (four fifths): in other words, if income goes up £10, savings goes up £2 and consumption goes up by £8.

SAQ 19: *What is the MPC if*

(a)   the MPS is ·1?

(b)   the MPS is ·5?

(c)   when income rises £10, C rises by 7?

(d)   when income rises by £50, C rises by £40?

(e)   when income rises £80 million and savings go up £20 million?

(f)   when the multiplier is five? (Clue: work out first what the MPS is when the multiplier is ·5.)

Just as it is possible to plot the amount saved against income, it's also possible to plot the amount spent on consumption against income. This is what I've shown in the diagram (top of p. 68), which plots the income and spending of an imaginary person. You'll notice that at a very low level of income he is consuming an amount higher than his actual income: by borrowing, or living off past savings. As income gets bigger, a break-even point is reached where he spends all his income. At income levels higher than this, consumption is less than income. These things are easier to notice if we draw a line that joins together all the points where expenditure is equal to income. This is the line coming out of the origin at 45°: whenever the C line is above that, he's spending more than his income. But when the C line is below it, he's not spending all his income.

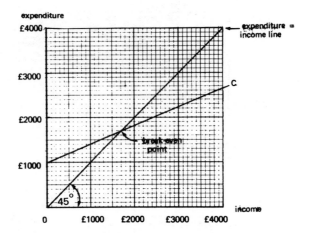

SAQ 20:

(a)   To the left of the break-even point, consumption is greater than income. What name do economists give to this situation? (Clue: – read page 57)

(b)   What is the average propensity to consume at the break-even point? (No need for calculation here)

(c)   To the right of the break-even point, the C line is below the 45° line. What determines the distances between the two lines at any one point?

I will now add to the amount of consumption the amount of investment spending, determined in the way I outlined on pages 59-60. The total amount of spending is now shown by the line marked C + I. It should be simple to see where the national income is in equilibrium: for where the C + I line crosses the 45° line, total expenditure will be equal to national income.

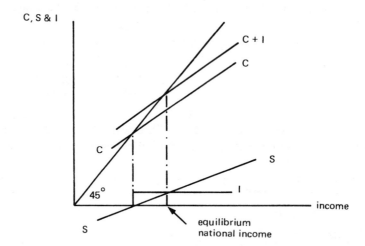

This is not a different theory of national income determination than the S = I method – it's a different way of explaining Keynes' theory. On the diagram above I have also put the S = I diagram. Notice that the national income equilibrium is the same by both methods; so is the break-even point, which is shown where the C line cuts the 45° line (i.e. where income equals spending) and where the S line cuts the horizontal axis (i.e. where savings are zero).

SAQ 21:

(a)   Fill in the blank spaces in this table, which shows consumption and investment in an economy.

Income	30	60	90	120	150
Savings	-10		10	20	
Consumption	40	60	80		120

(b)   Plot the savings line on the graph below and label it S. Where is the break-even point? Add an investment line of 20. Where is national income in equilibrium?

(c)   Plot consumption on the graph below, and label the line C. Now add on the investment spending of 20 to get a C + I line: this is done by putting the investment on top of the C line — I've marked the first two points to start you off. Where is national income equilibrium now?

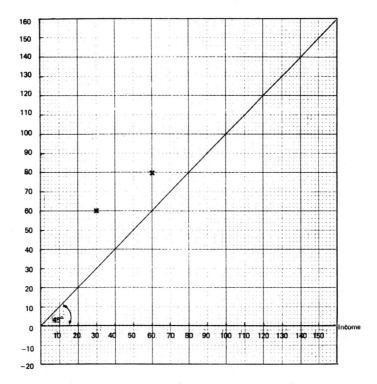

SUMMARY

This unit has introduced you to the idea that the size of the national income can change. Keynes showed that far from being always at its maximum, it can fall or rise under the influence of changes in investment, consumption and savings. This is important for a number of reasons. If national income is too low, then the output of commodities will be lower than it could be given from our resources. So we will have a standard of living lower than could have produced from our land, labour and capital. That's not all — you saw in SAQ 2 that when the national income falls (or even grows more slowly than usual) unemployment rises.

SAQ 22: *Why does unemployment rise when national income falls?*

In Unit 6 we will look at the ways that government may try to increase or decrease the size of the national income to maintain prosperity. But before we look at that, we must analyse more closely the effects on the national income of the factors we left out earlier — international trade and government activity — and at the relation between the national income and unemployment. This is the subject matter of Unit 5. I have also written an appendix to this unit on consumption and investment (see Appendix A pp 441-3): you may wish to leave this for the moment to keep things clear in your mind.

REVIEW SECTION

Glossary

I've introduced a lot of new terms in this unit, so here, for convenience, is a short glossary which will help you to remember some of the most important ones.

business cycle: see trade cycle.

circular flow of income: the cycle in which households obtain their incomes from firms, and spend them on the firms' products, so that the money returns to the firms who pay it out to households in rents, profits and wages. Households then spend these, and so on.

consumption: spending on commodities for immediate satisfaction of wants.

consumption function: the mathematical relationship between the amount of consumption spending and the things that determine its value – outstandingly, the level of income.

dissaving: when a consumer spends more than his or her income, the difference between his income and his spending must be covered by borrowing, or running down previously accumulated savings. This process is known as dissaving.

full capacity output: the output that would be produced by an economy if all the factors of production were to be fully employed.

investment: spending on capital goods; in macro-economics, it usually refers to net investment – that is, new capital formation (gross investment minus capital consumption).

investment multiplier: a measure of the effect on the size of the national income of a unit change in investment. If a rise of £1 million in investment leads to a £3 million rise in national income, then the investment multiplier is three (£3 million divided by £1 million).

propensity to consume: the proportion of an income that is spent on consumption. It is helpful to distinguish between the average propensity to consume (that is, the proportion of total income spent on consumption) and the marginal propensity to consume (the change in consumption spending resulting from a change in income).

propensity to save: the proportion of a given income that is saved. Be clear about the difference between the APS (the proportion of total income saved) and the MPS (the proportion of any change in income that is saved).

savings: in Keynesian theory, the amount of income not spent.

trade cycle: regular fluctuations in prosperity over the years, as periods of prosperity and full employment alternate with periods of high unemployment.

Suggested reading

You'll probably benefit from some background reading on this topic. It is dealt with in all good economics textbooks, so you might like to compare how it is covered in Richard Lipsey's *Introduction to Positive Economics* (Weidenfeld and Nicolson), Paul Samuelson's *Economics* (McGraw Hill) or Sir Alec Cairncross' *Introduction to Economics* (Butterworth). There are also a number of books which aim to simplify Keynesian thought for the wider audience: you might try *Keynes and After* by Michael Stewart (Pelican), *A Question of Economics* (especially chapter 3) by Peter Donaldson (Pelican) or *Keynes's General Theory: Fifty Years On* (Hobart paperback No. 24). See also C.P. & J. Sparkes *Savings and Investment* in the Economics Briefs series (Collins).

There are a number of biographies of Keynes in paperback. Roy Harrod's *The Life of J.M. Keynes* (Pelican) or Robert Skidelsky's *John Maynard Keynes* (Macmillan) are the fullest, but you have to be a Keynes freak to wade through them. Stewart's book or D.E. Moggridge's *Keynes* (Fontana Modern Masters) are shorter and more accessible. See also *Keynes and the Theory of Output and Employment* (*Economic Review* September '83 and November '83).

Essay questions

1. Distinguish between savings and investment. What are the likely effects of an increase in investment in a country with unemployed resources?

    (AEB 'A' June 1980)

2. Distinguish the equilibrium level of national income from the full employment level of national income. Why may they differ?

    (University of London 'A' January 1981)

Essay questions often ask you to combine your knowledge of different parts of the course. Here's one that will enable you to combine the simple Keynesian analysis from this Unit with some of the material about economic growth you met in Unit 2:

3. What will be the short term and long term effects of an increase in investment on both output and employment?

(Oxford Local 'A' June 1984)

Multiple choice:

1. Which of the following would *not* be the cause of a change in investment?
   (a)   a change in the rate of interest
   (b)   a change in expectations of profit in the future
   (c)   an expected fall in sales
   (d)   a rise in the propensity to save

2. Who is the idea that 'supply creates its own demand' associated with?
   (a) J. B. Say;   (b) Karl Marx;   (c) J. M. Keynes;   (d) Adam Smith

3. Which of the following does *not* represent a rise in investment?
   (a)   the purchase of a new lorry for ICI
   (b)   the purchase of a new house
   (c)   the purchase of new machinery for a textile firm
   (d)   the purchase of shares in ICI

4. In a closed economy without government spending, income is £80 million and saving is £20 million. So what is consumption?
   (a) 100;   (b) 120;   (c) 80;   (d) 60;

5. This question, and question 6 are based on the following data:

Net national product	Saving
200	20
210	22

   In this example, what is the average propensity to consume at 200?
   (a) 180;   (b) one-tenth;   (c) nine-tenths;   (d) four-fifths

6. What is the marginal propensity to save?
   (a) 2;   (b) one-fifth;   (c) one-tenth;   (d) $\frac{22}{210} = \cdot 1047619$

7. Which of the labelled points on this diagram shows the national income equilibrium after a rise in the propensity to save?

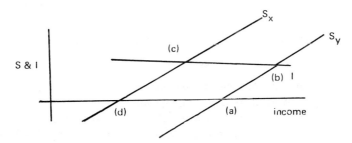

8.

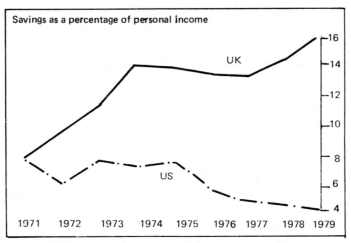

This chart shows the behaviour of savings in both the USA and Britain over the 1970s. Which of the following statements is true?

(a)   Household savings have tended to reduce national income in the USA but raised it in Britain.
(b)   Firms in Britain invested more than US firms.
(c)   The changes in saving would tend to depress national income in US and in Britain.
(d)   Savings habits would tend to reduce UK national income but raise USA national income.

9.   What is the MPC in this economy?

Income	20	40	60	80	100
C	21	37	53	69	75

(a) ·7;   (b) ·8;   (c) ·2;   (d) ·9;

10.   The paradox of thrift shows that
(a)   dis-saving always occurs at low income levels
(b)   a rise in savings will cause unemployment
(c)   saving must always equal investment
(d)   an increased desire to save may result in no increase in total savings.

11.   If the MPC is ·9, what will the multiplier be?
(a) 9;   (b) 1;   (c) 10;   (d) $\frac{1}{.9} = 1.1$

12.   If the multiplier is 5, what must be the amount saved out of an increase of national income of 30?
(a) 6;   (b) 5;   (c) 150;   (d) four-fifths

Questions 13 and 14 relate to this diagram

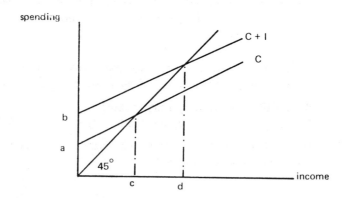

13.   Where will the national income be in equilibrium?

14.   Where will savings be zero?

15.   When is national income in equilibrium?
(a)   when there is full employment
(b)   when desired saving equals desired investment
(c)   when the average propensity to consume is equal to one
(d)   when the APS and the APC total one.

16.   If the national income is at present £100 billion, but the national income required for full employment is £120 billion (and the multiplier is 2), then to get full employment, how much must investment rise?
(a) £60 billion;   (b) £240 billion;   (c) £20 billion;   (d) £10 billion.

This is the answer code for questions 17–20:

(a) $\dfrac{\text{total savings}}{\text{total income}}$

(b) $\dfrac{\text{total spending on consumption}}{\text{total amount of income}}$

(c) $\dfrac{\text{change in national income}}{\text{change in investment}}$

(d) $\dfrac{\text{change in amount saved}}{\text{change in total income}}$

Which of these answers represents:

17.   The multiplier;   18. the APS;   19. the MPS;   20. the same as $\dfrac{1}{\text{MPS}}$?

ANSWERS TO SAQs

SAQ 1:   (a) We came nearest to producing maximum output in 1973/4; the mid and late 60s also show high levels of output relative to potential. (b) There were a number of years when actual output fell short of our potential — 1958–9, 1962–3, the early seventies. But the greatest distance between potential and actual output is shown in the diagram to occur in the period after 1975. (c) It rose from 1955 to 1974 — not smoothly, but in a series of steps. After 1974, manufacturing output fell, a fall that has been continued in the years since 1980.

SAQ 2:   You should see that the two lines move in opposite directions. When the national income grows more slowly than the trend (in 1980 and 1981), unemployment goes up — but when national income (GDP) moves faster than the trend, as in 1978 and 1979, unemployment drops, (but notice that although GDP recovers in 1982 unemployment still increases — albeit at a slower rate). There is a good reason for this: the GDP is, after all, the total amount of commodities made in a year — and if we make more commodities we need more workers. The demand for labour is a *derived* demand: derived from the demand for commodities.

SAQ 3:   If machinery put men out of jobs, then those countries which Unit 2 showed to have a high rate of investment (Japan, W.Germany) would have the worst unemployment problems. They haven't.

SAQ 4:   When something determines something else, it decides, fixes or settles it. A theory of national income determination, then, is a theory that looks for the things that decide what size the national income is going to be.

SAQ 5:   In this simplified model, the only injection is investment, and the only leakage is saving.

SAQ 6:   (a) 20;   (b) 50;   (c) 19   (d) 80.

SAQ 7:   (a) $\frac{1}{5}$ or ·2   (b) again, $\frac{1}{5}$ or ·2   (c) $\frac{1}{10}$ or ·1   (d) £2000 ($\frac{1}{4}$ of £8000);   (e) 7500 (one fifth of £7500 is £1500)

SAQ 8:   (a) one third, or ·33ʹ   (b) one half, or ·5   (c) one quarter, or ·25 — a quarter of the *extra* income is saved   (d) (i) one-twentieth, or ·05;   (ii) one tenth, or ·1 — income changes £1000, savings changes £100.   (iii) zero — this is the break-even point where nothing is saved or . . . (iv) dis-saved! What is happening is that families are spending more than their income by running down savings, and failing to renew clothes, household goods etc.   (v) I make £3000 minus £100 = £2900.

SAQ 9:   answered in text

SAQ 10: S_3 is the lowest, S_1 the highest propensity to save.

SAQ 11: I_3 is the highest investment level, I_1 is the lowest. So an increase in investment is shown by a shift upwards in the I line.

SAQ 12:   (b) National income is in equilibrium at £50 billion, where S and I are 4. It cannot be at £30 billion, because there households are planning to save less than firms are willing to invest — sales are booming, and business stocks are running down, and so firms will be increasing output and therefore national income. At £60 billion, households wish to save more than firms are willing to invest — stocks of unsold goods are building up, and so firms will cut back output and jobs. The only place where national income is in equilibrium is where intended saving equals intended investment. (c) $\frac{1}{10}$: when income rises by 10 (e.g. from 20 to 30), savings rise by 1 (e.g. from 1 to 2). Note that the MPS differs from the APS here, because nothing is saved when income is 10.

SAQ 13:   Your savings line should appear as follows:

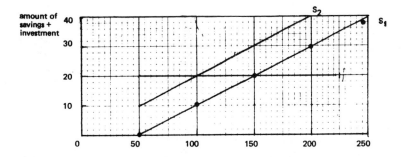

Because of the change in savings plans, the equilibrium level of the national income has changed: you'll find that it has fallen from £150 billion to £100 billion.

SAQ 14:   A paradox is an apparently absurd statement ('The wisest fool'; 'cruel to be kind'); thrift is the habit of making room for savings by frugal living.

SAQ 15:
(a)   The original national income equilibrium was £60 billion.

(b)   National income has risen to £80 billion, where intended savings once again equal intended investment.

(c)   The national income has risen, because the reduced propensity to save has increased consumer spending, and encouraged firms to expand output.

(d)   The amount of savings is always equal to the amount invested: what has happened is that income has risen so that the lower propensity to save at the higher income produces the same amount of savings as before.

Missing words: down; rise; rise; increase; raise; drop; fall; rise; savings.

SAQ 16:
(a)   i) 3   ii) 3 – the multiplier works downwards, too.

(b)   i) £3 million x 6 = £18 million;   ii) £6 million x 2 = £12 million

(c)   i) £2 million (which multiplied by five gives £10 million);   ii) £5 million

SAQ 17:   Answered in text

SAQ 18:
(a)   i) 4;   ii) 3;   iii) 2

(b)   i) ·5 or a half;   ii) ·2 or one-fifth;   iii) ·4 or two-fifths

(c)   i) one twentieth or ·05;   ii) one tenth of any increase in income is saved – so the MPS is one tenth, or ·1.   iii) is an exercise for you to do;   iv) S = I at a national income of 40.   v) You can work out that the multiplier is ten either by working out $\dfrac{1}{MPS}$ or by raising I one and seeing the national income go up ten.

SAQ 19:
(a)   ·9;   (b) ·5;   (c) ·7;   (d) ·8;   (e) ·75 (¾);   (f) four-fifths

SAQ 20:
(a)   dis-saving;

(b)   1 (total income is the same as total consumption spending, isn't it?)

(c)   The distance between the two lines represents saving (it is, after all, Y – C, which = S)

SAQ 21:
(a)   The savings line reads –10, *0*, 10, 20, *30*. The missing figure in the consumption line is 100.

(b)   is a plotting exercise: you should get an equilibrium where S = I at national income 120.

(c)   Again, you should find national income equilibrium where C + I = Income at 120.

SAQ 22:   The reason is that the number of workers required in an economy depends on the number of commodities demanded: if total demand is too low to buy up all the commodities that a country *could* produce, then firms will not need all the available workers.

5 Employment, Unemployment and the National Income

AIMS OF UNIT 5

When you have completed this unit you should be able to:

- explain what economists mean by withdrawals and injections and show how these can affect national income
- explain what is meant by aggregate demand
- show how the level of national income is determined in an economy that has foreign trade and government spending
- link changes in income and output to changes in the level of employment, prices and the balance of payments
- explain what is meant by an inflationary gap and a deflationary gap, by insufficient aggregate demand and excess aggregate demand
- define cyclical unemployment and distinguish it from other forms of unemployment
- discuss recent trends in unemployment using the ideas introduced in this unit.

INTRODUCTION

In the last unit I started to describe macro-economics by taking a simple view of the circular flow of income. Income was paid out by firms in the form of wages, salaries, rents and profits to consumers; and their spending flowed back to firms (see diagram at top of next page). I took into account only two interruptions to this circular flow:

- savings: the income households retain and do not pass on as consumption spending
- investment: the purchase by firms of additional factories, machinery and equipment for their businesses, and the additions to their stocks of goods.

I then showed how the national income will only be in equilibrium when what households wished to save was in line with what firms wanted to invest. And then I looked at the effects that changes in household spending and business investment would have on the size of the national income. In the diagram (top of next page), for example, the equilibrium size of national income is £200 billion, for that is the value of total spending by consumers and firms (C + I).

In fact, the real world is quite a bit more complicated than the one described in the diagrams (top of page 76): for these diagrams have left out two big influences on the modern economy. Firstly, there is no reference to *trade* with foreign countries. Secondly, I haven't put in anything about the *taxation* and *spending* of governments. If we wish to use any model to help us understand and predict what happens in our turbulent economy, we'll have to include these complications.

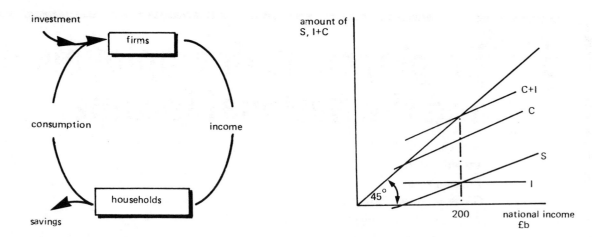

That is what I am going to do in the first half of this unit — show how national income equilibrium is reached when we include the effects of government and international trade. Let's start with trade.

FOREIGN TRADE

International trade affects the circular flow of income in two ways. Firstly, when we buy commodities from abroad (imports) we have to pay for them. As a result, income flows out of the British circular flow of income and into the circular flow of another country. Imports are labelled M, because we have already used I for investment. But the opposite happens when we sell commodities (exports) to foreigners. When this occurs, part of the foreigners' income will find its way to Britain. This flow is labelled X, because E is already used for expenditure. Because we have used I for investment, we are a little stuck for a symbol for income — as a result, economists have used the letter Y to symbolise net national product.

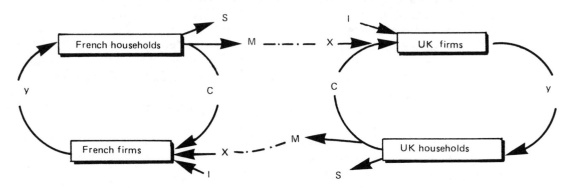

Foreign trade is shown on these diagrams. On the right is the British economy, and on the left is the economy of another country — say France.

SAQ 1: *Cover up the French circular flow with your hand, and look at the effect of imports and exports on the British economy. Which is a withdrawal or leakage? Which is an injection?*

So imports and exports will also have an influence on the size of the national income. Precisely what that influence is, you'll see in a moment. Let's take a while, though, to discuss the factors that influence the amount of importing and exporting that we do.

What determines the amount of imports that we buy?

Maybe the best way to approach this is to ask what decides the amount of imports that we, as individuals, buy. Some factors come straight to mind: whether there is a British substitute; the price; the quality and design; delivery times, and so on. However, the over-riding factor that determines how much we spend on imports is the size of our income. If our income is high, we will spend more on imports than if we have a low income. When our incomes rise, we spend more — and that will include more German cars, French wines, Japanese stereos and American jeans. This is true of a country, as a whole, too.

SAQ 2:   *Look at the diagram on the right carefully and explain*

(a)   what is meant by GDP
(b)   what happened to imports and GDP in 1973
(c)   what happened to imports and GDP in 1975
(d)   what connection the chart indicates between GDP and imports.

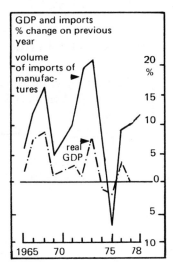

The conclusion you should have drawn from this exercise is that imports are a function of national income (using the word 'function' in the way described in the last unit). We can now draw a diagram linking M to Y: it looks something like the savings diagrams you drew in Unit 4. If a country is very poor — say at a national income OA, it can afford to buy very little from the rest of the

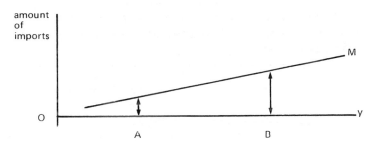

world. But as its national income rises, say to OB, so does spending on imports. You can regard this line, if you like, as the 'import function' — or, if you prefer, as showing our propensity to import. If we were to decide to spend more out of our national income on imports (that is to say, raise our propensity to import), then the M line would rise. A drop in the propensity to import, on the other hand, will be shown by a shift downwards in the M line.

SAQ 3:   *Which way would these changes shift the M line?*
(a)   imported goods getting cheaper   *fall/rise*
(b)   British goods improving in quality   *fall/rise*
(c)   an energetic 'Buy British' campaign   *fall/rise*
(d)   a report showing that Japanese cars are more reliable than British cars   *fall/rise*
(e)   a successful anti-inflation policy which makes British goods cheaper relative
       to imported goods.   *fall/rise*

What affects our exports?
If the level of imports depends on the size of the British national income, what will be the main influence on the sales of exports? Logically speaking, it must be the size of the national incomes of our customers. If the countries we sell to have booming economies and a fast growth in their national incomes, our export sales will rise swiftly. But if they are stuck in a recession, we will find

it harder to sell exports. The size of our exports, then, will not be a function of the national income. Like investment spending it will be determined independently: mostly by the size of other countries' national incomes but also by the prices of British goods relative to foreign goods, by quality and design, salesmanship and advertising, and so on.

Having looked at how international trade fits into the circular flow, let's complete the picture by slotting in the activities of government.

GOVERNMENT AND THE ECONOMY

Each year the Chancellor of the Exchequer prepares his budget, in which he works out his plans for the economy in the coming year. The budget outlines how much the government intends to collect through taxation and how much it intends to spend. So, as with foreign trade, the government affects the amount of spending in the economy in two ways. When it levies taxes on individuals and companies, it takes spending power out of the circular flow of income. And the higher

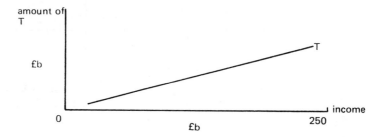

our income the more tax we pay. As a result, we can sketch the relationship between total tax paid and income that I've shown by line T in the diagram above. As people's incomes rise, the government gets more and more tax revenue — not just from income tax, but also from VAT and the other indirect taxes that we pay when we spend our incomes. But if national income falls, then tax receipts also fall as people earn less money and spend less in the shops.

SAQ 4: *I've explained that the T line shows the relationship between the total amount of tax we pay and the national income. What would be shown by a shift upwards in the T line? What might be the cause of this?*

Although the government reduces the amount of spending in the economy by taxation, it adds to the amount of spending when it uses that tax money to buy commodities. Government spending runs into billions of pounds. Some of this money will be spent on goods and services, from typewriters and filing cabinets to helicopters and antibiotic drugs, from rifles and blackboards to telephone exchanges and motorways. But millions of pounds are also spent on the wages of over five million government employees and on the benefit payments of the social security system. The amount of government spending that goes on is a political decision: elections decide whether we have in power a party that believes in expanding government spending, or one that believes in cutting back the role of government. So government spending depends not on the national income size, but on political and social beliefs.

WITHDRAWALS AND INJECTIONS

We can now draw a more realistic picture of the circular flow of income, including the influences of international trade and government and using Y as our symbol for income. This is what it looks like:

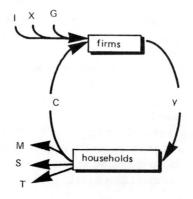

SAQ 5: *Write down which flows in the diagram each of the initials represents.*

Withdrawals

Notice that there are now three leakages (or withdrawals) that take spending out of the circular flow and away from British firms: S, M, and T. All of these things depend on the size of the national income. Indeed, we can put them all together in one line that indicates how the total

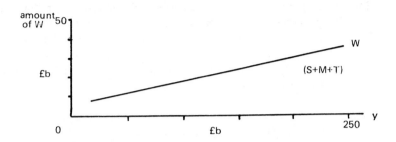

amount of withdrawals will vary with income. Note that at a low level of national income, the amount of withdrawals (W) is low: savings are small, we can't afford many imported goods and we are not liable for much tax. But as Y rises, all three withdrawals increase.

The W line will shift up or down according to changes in saving habits, tax rates or our propensity to import. For example, a shift upwards would indicate a rise in withdrawals — more saving, or higher taxes. On the other hand, a downward shift would show that our propensity to import or save had fallen.

SAQ 6: *How would the following events shift the withdrawals line?*

(a)	*an increased propensity to save*	*up / down / no effect*
(b)	*a cut in income tax*	*up / down / no effect*
(c)	*a rise in the price of imports*	*up / down / no effect*
(d)	*a rise in VAT*	*up / down / no effect*
(e)	*a rise in investment*	*up / down / no effect*
(f)	*a rise in the marginal propensity to consume*	*up / down / no effect*

Injections

Just as we can add up savings, taxation and imports to get a combined withdrawals line, so we can add together all the injections that add to demand for commodities — investment, government spending and exports. The thing that I have stressed about these injections (J) is that they do not depend on the size of the national income in the way that S, M and T do. They have a different origin: investment depends on business confidence and the rate of interest; exports depend on the buying patterns of foreigners; government spending depends on politics. To use an economists' term, injections are 'autonomous spending'. They are independent of the size of Y, and if we add them together into one line, it has to be a level one, like that in the diagram below:

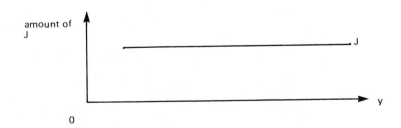

Now that we have drawn both the injections line and the withdrawals line, we can put the two together to find national income equilibrium:

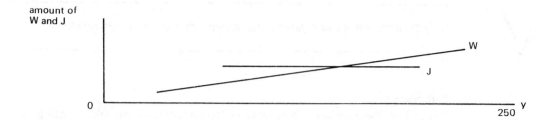

This diagram shows the whole picture. National income will be found where W is equal to J: that is, where S + M + T = I + G + X. You can work this out using the same logic as when we found that S = I. When there is a rise in withdrawals, firms find that their sales fall. At first, they allow stocks to build up, unsure as to whether the fall in demand for their products is just something temporary. But they cannot forever go on increasing their stocks of unsold goods, and they soon decide to reduce output. This has the effect of reducing the national income and also reducing the number of workers required. The national income falls to a new equilibrium where, once again, withdrawals are equal to injections.

SAQ 7: *Now see if you can follow through this logic by filling in the words in this passage:*

If, on the other hand, there is a rise in injections (perhaps due to a _____ in government spending, or a _____ in exports) firms will experience a _____ in demand: their stocks will _____ _____ and so they will decide to _____ output, taking on extra workers and causing a _____ in the national income. As the national income _____, there is a _____ in the amount of savings, and people find that they are paying a _____ amount in taxation. In the end, the national income rises until all the increase in _____ has leaked away in withdrawals and once again _____ are equal to

_____ .

Let's now look at the effect of changes in withdrawals and injections on the size of the national income. On the diagram below I have shown two different injection lines. Equilibrium is where W = J.

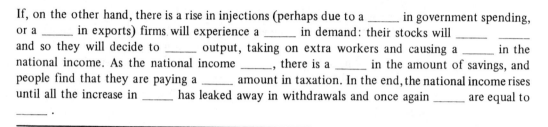

If there is a rise in injections (say, caused by an increase in government spending) J will rise to J_2, and the national income will be at a higher level, Y_2. So *a rise in injections (investment, government spending or exports) causes a rise in the national income*. If, by contrast, injections were to fall then national income would also fall. You can do this in the diagram above by working back from J_2 to the original J line.

The diagram below shows the effect of a shift or change in withdrawals. I have shown two

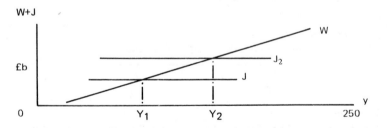

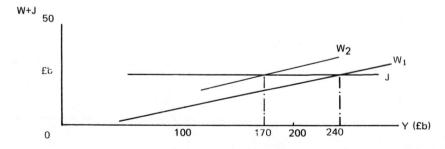

withdrawals lines: W_1 shows a lower propensity to withdraw than W_2. The national income would be £240 billion where W_1 crosses J. Now, suppose that the amount of withdrawals rose to W_2: this might be due to

- an increased propensity to save
- an increased propensity to import
- the government raising taxes

or some combination of all three. In this case, you can see that the national income would fall to £170 billion. So *a rise in the withdrawals line reduces the level of national income.*
This is best put into a table:

A shift upward in injections *or* A shift downwards in withdrawals	will tend to raise national income
A shift upward in withdrawals *or* A fall in injections	will tend to reduce national income

SAQ 8: *How will the following events affect the level of the British national income?*
(a)   a fall in the MPS
(b)   a fall in exports
(c)   a rise in income tax
(d)   a recession or slump in the USA
(e)   a fall in the value of the £ sterling that makes our imports dearer and our exports cheaper.
(f)   widespread cuts in government spending.

HELLO AGAIN TO THE MULTIPLIER

I hope you realise that a rise in government spending or exports will have the same sort of multiplier effect as a rise in investment. (You'll recall this idea from Unit 4.) Let's imagine that the government pays a civil engineering firm to extend the runway of an airport. That firm will pay out the money it receives to its suppliers, its workers and its shareholders: they will save some, pay tax on some and spend a little on imports, but the rest they will spend on British goods and therefore someone else will receive a rise in income. This person or firm will spend a portion and so on. So in this case there's a **government spending multiplier**. In the same way, economists refer to the **foreign trade multiplier** when assessing the effect of change in exports or imports on the size of the national income. However, this is a more complicated multiplier than the one we met in the last unit. There the multiplier worked through a simple process of spending and saving. When an investment impulse was sent through the economy, it carried on until it had all melted away in savings, like this:

The simple multiplier

New I	$=$	More C	$=$	More C	$=$	More C	$=$	More C	and so on
		more S		more S		more S		more S	

We found that the value of the investment multiplier was equal in value to $\frac{1}{MPS}$. However, such a multiplier calculation ignored the fact that the extra incomes created would be taxed, and that some of the extra spending would be on imported goods. Now that we have to take the effects of taxes and imports into account, we have a real multiplier that will work like this:

The real-world multiplier

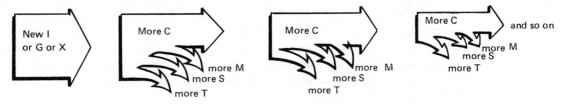

You can see from the diagram that the amount leaking away at each stage is higher than when we simply counted savings. For now, we recognise that when people receive or spend an income, they must pay tax — and that isn't passed on to the next person in the multiplier queue. We see, also, that people spend a portion of their income on imported goods: that will also be income that isn't passed on to British residents. The real world multiplier will therefore be found from this formula:

$$\frac{1}{MPS + \text{marginal propensity to import} + \text{tax rate}}$$

This makes real world multipliers much smaller than the enormous ones we dealt with in Unit 4. There, we found that with a marginal propensity to consume that was around ·8 or ·9 of income, the multiplier would be as high as five or ten. This isn't accurate. Let's work out the multiplier taking imports and taxes into account as well as savings. You saw in the Review Section of Unit 4 — Question 8 — that saving in Britain has risen to 16% of income — so let's say that the propensity to save will be at least 10% or, better ·1 of income.

The lowest realistic level for the tax rate is ·3 (or 30%). We spend at least 20% of our income on imports, too. So in real life the proportion that leaks away at each stage of the multiplier process must be at least ·1 + ·3 + ·2, which adds up to ·6. The sum $\frac{1}{·6}$ gives a multiplier of 1.66. Research tends to confirm this modest figure — the multiplier in most European economies lies between 1.3 and 2 only. Thus the multiplier is determined by the marginal propensity to 'leak' rather than the marginal propensity to save.

SAQ 9: *(a) What would be the value of the multiplier if the MPS was ·2, the tax rate was ·2 and the propensity to import was ·1?*
(b) What would happen to the value of the multiplier if
   (i)   there was an increase in income tax
   (ii) there was a drop in the proportion of our income spent on imports?

AND HELLO AGAIN TO THE 45° LINE

You used two methods in Unit 4 to find out how national income was determined: the second involved adding up all the expenditure in the economy and seeing where it equalled income — for you knew that national income is equal to national expenditure. When you used this method, you had to be content with just two categories of expenditure — consumption and investment — and you arrived at a diagram like the one below. But as you learned in Unit 4, total demand in the

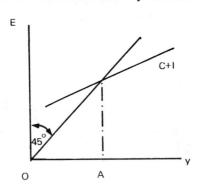

economy is made up of *four* components: in addition to consumption and investment there is also government spending and the effects of foreign trade. To include the effect of government spending, you just have to add 'G' to C + I. And to include the effect of foreign trade you must add on the income gained when foreigners buy our exports, and subtract the money that leaves the flow when we spend our income on imports. To show this we write X – M. The total amount of spending in the economy is now C + I + G + (X – M). Economists have a term for this: **aggregate monetary demand** (AMD) or more often just aggregate demand. This diagram is not much different from the C + I diagram you met in Unit 4, since the addition of G and X – M simply shifts the aggregate demand line upwards in the way that adding in the I line did. Once again, national income can be found where expenditure equals income. You can find this point by drawing on a 45° line (see Unit 4, pp. 68–9) where total expenditure (E) equals income (Y), and seeing where this is crossed by the aggregate demand line.

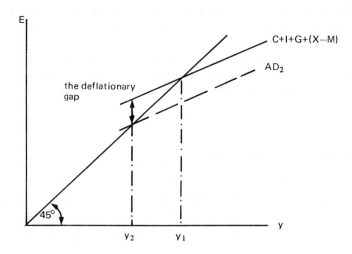

Why the level of aggregate demand is important

Suppose then the level of aggregate demand is high enough to give full employment. What happens if there is then a fall in aggregate demand? This might result from a fall in government spending, or a rise in the propensity to save or import — and in this case, aggregate demand would perhaps fall to the level marked AD₂ on the diagram. Firms would have fewer orders and would reduce output, laying off workers. Then the multiplier effect would work in reverse, as the unemployed workers cut back on their spending. The term we give to such a shortfall between the aggregate demand needed for full employment and the actual level of aggregate demand is **the deflationary gap**. I've labelled this gap in the above diagram.

In the case I've just outlined, the cause of unemployment is deficient aggregate demand. As economic activity slackens (for the reasons Keynes discovered, and which I've explained in this unit) the economy moves into a recession or (worse) a depression. This process would be familiar to the Victorians — it's the downswing of the trade cycle — and so the form of unemployment that is associated with it is called **cyclical unemployment**. It is sometimes also called **Keynesian unemployment** after the economist who first analysed its causes.

SAQ 10: *Cyclical unemployment would be worsened by three of the following events. Pick out which ones*

(a)   A fall in the MPS
(b)   A rise in the propensity to import
(c)   A rise in the interest rate
(d)   A cut in VAT
(e)   A cut in government spending
(f)   A fall in the value of the £ sterling abroad.

At this point, look back at SAQ 2 in Unit 4. You noticed there, I hope, a sharp relationship between changes in GDP and changes in employment. Now you can see both *why* this relation exists

- because the amount of jobs in Britain is closely related to the total amount of spending in Britain — by consumers, firms, government and foreigners. (Employment, then, is a function of aggregate demand.)

and *how* the GDP might fall below full-employment level

- because withdrawals — savings, taxes, imports — are too high, or injections — investments, government spending, exports — are too low.

THE GDP AND UNEMPLOYMENT

If the explanation I have just given you was the whole picture, there would be a very close relationship indeed between changes in GDP and employment. But although a relationship clearly exists, it isn't often as simple as the one you drew at the beginning of Unit 4. There are a number of reasons for this. If employers wish to produce more, they don't have to take on more workers: increased output can often be obtained by better use of the existing labour force, or by asking them to work overtime for premium payments. In the same way, employers are sometimes reluctant to shed labour when demand for their products falls. This isn't just due to opposition from the workers and their unions. It might equally be that employers are not willing to let workers go until they are sure that the fall in demand is permanent, for it can be very expensive to fire and re-hire workers.

The fact that employers can often respond to a change in the demand for their products without immediately hiring or firing workers puts a time-lag into the relationship between changes in GDP and employment: a change in output won't affect the numbers out of work until some time later.

OTHER CAUSES OF UNEMPLOYMENT

Although aggregate demand does influence levels of employment, there are good reasons to believe that it would be quite impossible to reach zero unemployment, no matter how high aggregate demand was. This is because there are some forms of unemployment that would occur in the most frenzied business boom. I'll now go on to list, and briefly analyse these forms.

Frictional unemployment

Each year about 4 million people out of our total workforce of 26 million move from one job to another — that is, over 300 000 each month. They may spend a few days or weeks unemployed before starting their new job: even if there are exactly the same number of jobs as workers, it would take job-searchers a while to find out about vacancies, secure interviews and so on. This form of unemployment is called **frictional unemployment** and it is likely that any economic system that is changing and developing will at any given time have a number of people frictionally unemployed. This type of unemployment isn't a serious problem, and many of the frictionally unemployed do not even go on to the unemployment register — after all, someone who leaves a job voluntarily is not eligible for unemployment benefit for six weeks.

SAQ 11: *In what ways might the government reduce the numbers of people who are frictionally unemployed?*

Casual unemployment

Some industries work on the basis of hiring workers for a given task, rather than as permanent employees. Construction workers, for example, are familiar with periods of unemployment between one contract and the next. Similarly, actors are often out of work when their play finishes its run. One particular form of casual unemployment affects trades that suffer from a seasonal variation in demand: this is called **seasonal unemployment**. For example, hotel workers and seaside landladies may sign on as unemployed when the holiday season is over. And people who work in the open — such as builders — are sometimes without work because of poor weather. An unemployment peak in 1963, for example, coincided with a particularly severe winter.

Because of the influence of seasonal factors, unemployment rises in the winter and comes down in the summer. This is why the unemployment figures that are usually quoted in the press and in economic journals are the 'seasonally adjusted' figures — that is, the picture after allowance has been made for seasonal trends.

Structural unemployment

Perhaps the most serious and worrying form of unemployment — leaving aside that caused in a slump by deficient aggregate demand — is unemployment caused by changes in the structure of demand in the economy — so-called **structural unemployment**. These changes in demand could be caused by many factors — changes in technology, in tastes and fashions, in the ability of foreign industries to compete, exhaustion or depletion of mineral resources like coal or iron ore. Such factors will cause some industries to decline and others to grow up as time passes. In Britain, for example, we have seen shipbuilding, cotton textiles and motorcycle manufacturing lose their importance in the economy, while oil production, financial and banking services, and electronics have grown. In theory, this is no problem — the people who used to work in the declining industry should switch to working in one of the expanding industries.

SAQ 12: *Why do you think workers who have lost their jobs in declining industries don't move into expanding industries.*

In practice there are two reasons why this doesn't happen. Firstly, workers may have the wrong skills for the new jobs. It's not much consolation to an unemployed shipyard boilermaker to know that he could easily get a job if he could write in shorthand, or program a computer.

Secondly, new industries may be set up in a different part of the country to those that are declining. Britain's older industries are localised — that is, they are to be found overwhelmingly in one or two of the nation's regions. The troubled cotton textile industry, for example, is situated in Lancashire and Greater Manchester. So workers who have lost their jobs in a cotton mill will find themselves hundreds of miles away from the booming North Sea oil industry or the London-based financial and banking sector. Moving is not only expensive and difficult — it means that people will have to uproot themselves from family and friends.

SAQ 13: *If structural unemployment is caused by workers having the wrong skills, or living in the wrong places, what measures could a government take that would contribute to its reduction?*

So even at high levels of aggregate demand, there will always be some people who are, for frictional or structural reasons, out of work. There will also be a number of people who might be considered 'unemployable'. This is not meant to be a term of abuse, for the 'workshy' are probably just a small proportion of this category. We must also include the severely disabled and chronically sick, the demoralised and a number of workers coming up to retirement age (whom employers are reluctant to employ and train for a matter of a year or two). The numbers in this category will not vary greatly from one year to the next and it is extremely unlikely that it could ever cause a large rise in unemployment.

SAQ 14: *Put these unemployed workers into the categories we have just discussed: i.e. are they frictionally, casually or structurally unemployed, or is their joblessness due to deficient aggregate demand (cyclical unemployment)?*

(a)   Closure of Welsh coal-mine makes 300 redundant.
(b)   London secretary leaves one job on 14th February and starts a better job on 21st February.
(c)   Landscape gardening contractor finds it impossible, because of the weather, to work between November and March.
(d)   Increase in the MPS causes a slump in the sales of the products of a number of industries.
(e)   Because wearing hats has gone out of fashion, a milliner loses her job.
(f)   A self-employed painter is unemployed between finishing painting a school and starting a contract to paint some fencing for the local council.
(g)   A slump causes unemployment in a wide range of industries.
(h)   A rock group find themselves with a fortnight's break between gigs.
(i)   Durham steelworkers lose their jobs when BSC Consett closes.

In summary then:

cyclical unemployment	occurs when there are fewer vacancies than unemployed. This is caused by too low a level of aggregate monetary demand.
frictional unemployment	occurs when there are vacancies, and the unemployed can fill them.
seasonal unemployment	occurs when specific industries suffer a seasonal drop in demand.
structural unemployment	occurs when there are vacancies, but the unemployed have the wrong skills in the wrong places and are thus unable to fill them.

It follows from this that we should talk of 'full employment' not when there is no unemployment (which will probably never happen) but when the number of unemployed people is about the same as the number of unfilled job vacancies. It is no consolation to workers to know that they are not cyclically unemployed, just structurally unemployed – but it does matter to governments.

As you have learned from the self-assessment questions, different types of unemployment need to be remedied by different policies. Frictional unemployment must be reduced through a more efficient job market – better notification of vacancies, better matching of applicants to jobs, speedier recruitment procedures. Structural unemployment, by contrast, will not be reduced by such policies – it will require retraining programmes to give workers up-to-date skills, and it will also respond to measures that will help workers move around the country or encourage firms to move into the depressed areas. But neither a more efficient job *nor* retraining programmes will help workers if, due to cyclical unemployment, the jobs simply aren't there for them. In that situation only a rise in aggregate monetary demand will help matters.

HOW ACCURATE ARE THE UNEMPLOYMENT FIGURES?

If cyclical unemployment is present whenever the number of vacancies is less than the number of unemployed, then Britain has suffered severe cyclical unemployment for at least the past ten years. This conclusion, however, does depend on the accuracy of the official unemployment and vacancy figures collected and published by the Department of Employment. This is where we take a trip into economic and political controversy. Some writers – mainly Conservatives – believe that the official figures are an exaggeration. They claim that the figures overstate the numbers available for work, and underestimate the real number of vacancies, making the unemployment problem seem much worse than in fact it is. On the other hand, there is some reason to believe that the unemployment figures might actually underestimate those available for work. Let's look at each of these arguments in turn.

'*The unemployment figures are an exaggeration*' The argument that the unemployment statistics overstate the problem has been voiced most vigorously by the Centre for Policy Studies (CPS) – an independent right-wing study group established by Sir Keith Joseph. They put forward these views:

- The frictionally unemployed are not really a problem – any flexible economy will have people leaving and taking up jobs. Of those signing on as unemployed on any one day, half will get a job inside two weeks and up to two-thirds inside a month. One cannot speak of an army of unemployed if more than half 'desert to the enemy' (i.e. the employed) each month.
- The unemployment figures include not only some people who have (to use the official phrase) a 'somewhat unenthusiastic attitude to work', but also some people who in fact have jobs in the unofficial 'black' economy but who are fraudulently drawing unemployment benefit anyway.
- The figures include a large number of people – maybe 50–60 000 – who have actually retired on a pension from their firm. They only continue to register as unemployed because by 'signing on' they can collect benefit and avoid paying national insurance contributions.
- The figures include a number of people who are in practice unemployable – say, an unskilled manual worker over the age of 50 in a depressed area.
- Most vacancies are not notified to the Department of Employment. It is estimated by the CPS that the actual number of vacancies is about three times higher than those reported to government Jobcentres. Employers find that it is easier to recruit through local papers, or through the grapevine – and in some cases, they may not want applicants from the ranks of the unemployed at all.

'*The unemployment figures understate the problem*' The economists who argue against these views do so firstly because they believe that many of the above arguments are untrue or misleading, and secondly because they believe that there are a number of people who are genuinely seeking work who do not register. They agree that the vacancy figures probably *are* an underestimate of the number of unfilled jobs, but the other arguments are as follows:

- Frictional unemployment generally is *not* included in the official figures, for the unemployment figures come from a count on one day of each month of those registered as unemployed. Someone who signs on to the unemployment register and finds a job before the next count will not appear in the figures as 'unemployed' at all. Further, research has shown that quite a few of the frictionally unemployed, though they find work quickly enough, have a number of bouts of unemployment in a year, bouts that add up in total to a serious loss of income. Indeed, just because someone is conveniently categorised as 'frictionally unemployed' doesn't mean that there is no hardship in unemployment – being without a wage packet for four weeks is no fun.

- Some workers certainly are demoralised and unenthusiastic about work – this is caused by the unemployment situation and the apparent hopelessness of getting a job. We should also be very careful about branding people as 'unenthusiastic'. Take the result of a recent study: social security officials were asked which claimants were not very enthusiastic about work, and which were keen to seek employment. When a follow-up survey was carried out some time later, it was discovered that the 'unenthusiastic' claimants had actually been more successful than the 'keen' ones in getting jobs. Reliable evidence for fraudulent claiming is difficult to obtain, for obvious reasons. On the one hand, people will be wary of admitting their criminal acts to researchers; on the other, the popular press delights in highlighting a single case as if it is proof of widespread 'scroungers'. When a researcher from Middlesex Polytechnic looked at 50 unemployed Glasgow families, he found that only one in five had any form of extra income from 'unofficial' jobs, and this income was within the limits allowed by social security regulations.
- While there are indeed a number of occupational pensioners, many of them are still actively seeking work. Only one-third have an income from their pension alone that would be adequate to live on.
- It is a mistake to label the long-term unemployed as unemployable: they are unemployed for a long time because there are few jobs, not because of personal inadequacy. The evidence for this is that the numbers of those unemployed for more than a year varies with the level of aggregate demand: in 1956, about 10% of the unemployed had been out of work for more than a year – in the eighties it is nearer 25%.

There are further reasons for disbelieving the arguments that unemployment figures are an overestimate. For example some workers who are seeking work do not register as unemployed at Jobcentres and Employment Exchanges. The British unemployment statistics only register such 'signers on'. Yet the main reason why people sign on is to obtain benefit: if you are not eligible for benefit, there is little point in registering. So workers who want to find a job but are ineligible for benefit often don't sign on. The largest proportion of these are married women – either those working as a housewife or wanting to re-enter the labour force after a period raising a family. Additionally, working women were until recently able to pay a reduced national insurance contribution that did not entitle them to receive unemployment benefit.

SAQ 15: *In the USA, the government collects the unemployment statistics in a different way to that used by the British government, there a door-to-door survey is taken (a bit like our census) in which people are asked whether or not they are unemployed. Will this tend to show a bigger or smaller figure than the British method for a given amount of actual unemployment?*

WHAT ACCOUNTS FOR THE RECENT RISES IN UNEMPLOYMENT?

The diagram below shows the average annual number of people who have registered as unemployed, between 1961 and 1986. How can we use the information about the causes of unemployment and the

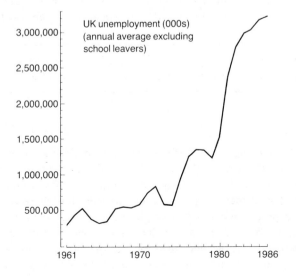

accuracy of the unemployment and vacancy figures to understand the history of unemployment?

Looking at the chart (p. 87), you'll see that in 1961 unemployment was very low. There was a recession in 1962 and 1963, but unemployment fell again to low levels in 1965; after the business cycle from 1961-6 unemployment rose and did not come down to previous levels. The recession of the early seventies was ended by a brief boom in 1973 and 1974, but then there was another step-up in the number unemployed. What we see when we look at the figures, then, is a series of booms and slumps — or 'business cycles' — with two shifts up — in the late 1960s and the mid-1970s. In 1980 there was a sudden acceleration in the numbers of unemployed from the already very high level. The numbers doubled from 1.5 million in 1980 to over 3 million by the end of 1986. What might account for these changes?

The late 1960s

Between 1966 and 1971 unemployment rose from 300 000 to over 600 000. Some of this increase can be explained by using Keynes' model of the economy — for during these years, governments made determined attempts to beat our continual inflation and balance of payments problems by raising taxation and holding down government spending. The increase in withdrawals (in this case taxation) and reduction in injections (government spending) would reduce the level of aggregate demand and thus employment. However, the rise in unemployment which then occurred cannot simply be explained by a fall in aggregate monetary demand — for example, the number of vacancies didn't fall anywhere near as sharply as the amount of unemployment rose. What this means is that something has happened to change the relationship between national income and unemployment, raising the numbers of people who register as unemployed at a given pressure of aggregate demand. There have been a number of attempts to explain this, along these lines:

- There was an increased incentive for the unemployed to register. So, though, there were no more people actually job-hunting, unemployment appeared to rise when those who in the past had not registered now decided to sign on. There is, for example, some evidence that married women, who in previous recessions just 'dropped out' of the labour force, now registered as unemployed.
- **Labour hoarding** fell. Labour hoarding is the name given to the situation when firms hang on to workers even when they cannot use them fully — mostly, because firms are expecting a future upturn in business that will enable them to put the workers back to productive tasks. Labour was scarce in the 1950s and 1960s, and a firm thought long and hard before releasing workers they might shortly need — particularly skilled workers. But the difficult trading conditions of the sixties made firms shed the labour they were hoarding.
- There were increases and improvements in welfare and redundancy payments in the 1960s that affected the numbers unemployed. Social security benefits for the average family came to half take-home pay in the early sixties; by the early seventies, they had risen to three-quarters of take-home pay. Further, redundancy payments legislation meant that workers who lost their job at a firm they had been serving for many years received lump sums in compensation. Even if one doesn't believe in 'scroungers' preferring idleness on the dole to real work, it is evident that improved benefits will (a) make it more worthwhile to register; (b) enable workers to spend a longer period searching for employment; (c) give job-seekers the opportunity to reject unattractive or ill-paid jobs. The result of the improved social security payments was, some economists believe, to make the level of unemployment about 100 000 or 200 000 higher than it would have been had the improvements not been made.

SAQ 16: *What is frictional unemployment? (no, don't look). Explain how improved unemployment pay might raise frictional unemployment. Is this a bad thing?*

The mid-1970s

After a brief boom in the early seventies, we noticed another step-up in unemployment — from 600 000 in 1974 to 1 400 000 in 1978-9. This was the result of the rise in oil prices that followed the Arab-Israeli war of 1973 and the continuous upward adjustment in prices that OPEC have maintained since then. This raised unemployment for two reasons. The main reason was that many of the oil producers who received the vastly increased oil revenues had very small populations. They did not need to spend their increased earnings on buying food or other goods from the rest of the world — they had enough already, as they were already very high-income countries. So they did not spend their oil receipts, but saved them. Money went out of the world's circular flow of income, when the oil-importers paid for their oil, but it did not come back as exports. The oil price rise can therefore be seen as a rise in the world's propensity to save — and a shift upwards in world savings had the same effect on the world economy as simple Keynesian economics says that a shift upwards in savings has on the economy of an individual nation: incomes fell and unemployment rose. The other effect of the rise in oil prices was to raise unemployment by putting up firms' costs: firms found that they could no longer profitably employ as many people now that they were paying out so much more in energy and raw material costs.

SAQ 17: *The chart below shows the changes in unemployment in Britain (unbroken line) and the world (broken line) in the years of the 'oil shock'.*

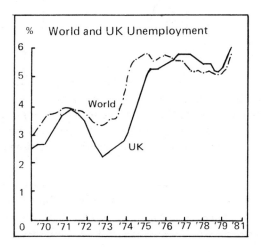

(a)   If rising oil prices, which affect all countries, were a cause of unemployment, would world unemployment also rise after the 1973-74 oil crisis? Does it?

(b)   By 1980, Britain was self-sufficient in oil. Does this mean that an increase in the price of oil no longer causes unemployment problems in Britain?

The late 1970s and early 1980s

By the early 1980s, a sequence of events had occurred, all of which contributed to rising unemployment by causing a drop in injections to, and a rise in withdrawals from, the circular flow (see page 78):

- a world slump, partly due to oil price rises, reduced British export sales
- cuts in government spending and rises in taxation which occurred as governments attempted to get their finances straight
- a drop in investment caused by a decline in business confidence
- increased import penetration into Britain. The rise in imports was a withdrawal from the circular flow, which gave rising unemployment a further twist
- the election of governments — particularly in the UK — who gave the attack on inflation a much higher priority than reducing unemployment.

EXCESS DEMAND

So, you have now seen the consequences of low levels of aggregate demand and national income. Employment depends on the level of output, and the level of output depends on the level of demand. Firms do not produce commodities unless they are likely to be able to sell them — and when demand is low, they therefore produce less. But the question I am going to pose in this concluding section of the unit is just the opposite: What problems are caused when national income is at a very high level in relation to the country's productive potential (i.e. the amount it can produce)?

On the following diagram, OE represents the national income necessary to secure full employment. The level of demand is shown — consumption(C) plus injections (J). Because all our resources of labour and capital are employed, the actual amount of commodities produced (what we call the *real* national income) cannot be increased. But that doesn't mean that demand cannot rise! Let's take an example.

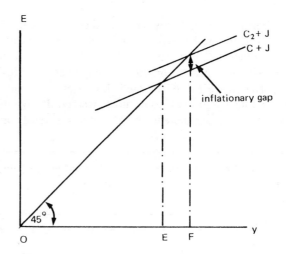

I am going to assume that households decide to save less. This will cause the amount of aggregate demand to rise due to an increase in consumer spending. We'll make this new aggregate demand line $C_2 + J$. At this point, the spending plans of consumers (C), firms (I), government (G) and foreigners cannot all be fulfilled — the economy is not capable, as we have seen, of producing enough commodities to satisfy total demand. So a rise in aggregate demand cannot result in an increase in output.

SAQ 18: *What do you think will happen when firms find their goods are easy to sell — when order books are full, unemployment very low and customers eager to buy?*

What happens is this: firms compete for skilled labour, which drives up wage rates and therefore costs, and they bid eagerly for raw materials and components, pushing up their prices and raising costs once again. You'll remember that when aggregate demand was too low I spoke of a 'deflationary gap'. By contrast, in the diagram above there is an **inflationary gap** which shows the excess demand in the economy. This **excess demand** gives the name to the form of inflation that is caused by too high a level of aggregate demand — **demand inflation.**

So, to put things simply, when aggregate demand is too low, there are problems of unemployment: and when it is too high, there is worsening inflation. In simple Keynesian economics we can regard unemployment and inflation as opposites. This next exercise takes a look at unemployment and inflation during ten years of the fifties and sixties to see if this is true in the real world.

SAQ 19: *Plot the unemployment figures against the scale on the right of the diagram. (Notice that the scales are 'inverted' — that is, turned upside down so that the lowest unemployment percentage comes near the top.) Then plot the figures for changes in retail prices on the left-hand scale.*

Year	Unemployment	Change in retail prices (%)
1961	1.3	3.4
1962	1.8	2.6
1963	2.2	2.1
1964	1.6	3.3
1965	1.3	4.8
1966	1.4	3.9
1967	2.2	2.5

(a)   *What relationship is there between the change in retail prices and the unemployment rate in the years plotted?*

(b)   *Is this consistent with the theory insufficient aggregate demand causes unemployment and excess aggregate demand causes inflation?*

(c)   *The last year quoted is 1967, when unemployment was 2.2% and the rate of inflation under 3%. What has happened to the rates of unemployment and inflation over the years between then and now? What problems does this cause for the economist who believes in demand inflation?*

THE PHILLIPS CURVE

Clearly, we shall have to look further into the problems of inflation, for it is hard to believe that in recent years inflation has been caused by aggregate demand being too high (and unemployment therefore 'too low'). But although in the eighties we still have inflation despite substantial unemployment, we must be clear that it has never been possible to have a level of national income that was high enough to achieve full employment, but not so high as to aggravate inflation: even in the comparatively tranquil years of 1957-67 that you have just plotted, whenever unemployment went down, inflation rose. The government had therefore to choose between these objectives: a rise in aggregate demand would cause unemployment to fall, and would raise output and living standards – but it would also cause prices to nudge upwards. In 1958, the economist A. W. H. Phillips put this idea into a simple and very influential diagram – shown below. The horizontal axis represents

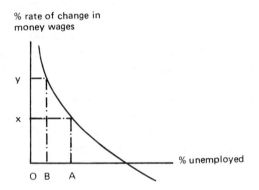

the percentage unemployment rate; the vertical axis represents the percentage change in wage rates – a reasonable measure of inflation, since rising wage rates are soon passed on to the customer in the form of higher prices. Phillips found that in the period he studied, 1862-1957, there was an inverse relationship between the two factors – just as our theory has predicted. In years when unemployment was high, wages and prices rose hardly at all: in fact, in some years of deep depression, they actually fell. By contrast, in booming years of full employment, wages and prices rose quickly. The line traced by plotting the various years was christened the **Phillips curve**. The steepness of the Phillips curve as it approaches the vertical axis shows that, the closer we get to zero unemployment, the greater the pace of inflation. When unemployment is OA, inflation is OX; but if we wish to reduce unemployment to OB, we will have to tolerate inflation at OY.

What has happened to the Phillips Curve?

When Professor Phillips wrote his famous article, the levels of both unemployment and inflation were lower than at present. Indeed, he calculated that an unemployment rate of about 5% would be enough to reduce the rate of increase in wages to nothing. But in the more turbulent days of the 1970s, when unemployment did indeed rise to 5% (in 1976), wages were still rising at the rate of over 10%. So the simple curve drawn by Phillips in the 1950s no longer holds, and we must try to explain why. There are two explanations:

- The Phillips curve is still there, but it has moved to the right, as shown on the diagram on the next page. In other words, there is still a relationship between unemployment and inflation, but a much greater degree of unemployment is necessary to achieve a drop in inflation. The reason for the higher levels of unemployment might be due to any of the factors I have discussed on page 88 – higher welfare payments, a drop in labour hoarding, a rise in registration of unemployment. Alternatively, you could think of the shift as being due to

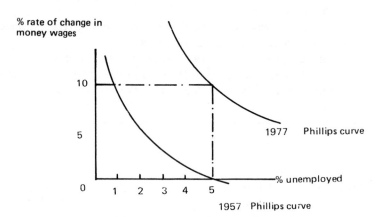

higher inflation at any given level of unemployment — because workers have come to expect and anticipate inflation, and are demanding higher money wage rises to cover anticipated and past rises in prices.

● The second explanation is that what has happened in the past ten years or so has not been demand inflation at all. According to this theory, inflation can be caused by a number of factors — certainly demand could be one thing, but so could others, like rises in the price of fuel or raw materials, or trade unions pushing up the cost of labour. Therefore, there are two different sorts of inflation — cost-push inflation and demand-pull. Cost-push inflation (sometimes just called cost inflation) is the result of increases in costs, and can happen at any level of aggregate demand: demand inflation, on the other hand, must be the result of high levels of aggregate demand. In fact, I'll be having a really close look at inflation, its causes, the problems it leads to and possible cures, in a separate unit later in the course.

SAQ 20: *In 1975 the unemployment rate rose from 2½% to nearly 4%, and inflation rose from 16% to 24%. In 1955 unemployment was 1% and the inflation rate 4½%. In which one of these years was cost inflation present? In which one was demand inflation the danger?*

SUMMARY

In this unit I have tried to extend the simple Keynesian ideas used in Unit 4 so that they can start to shed light on real-world problems, like unemployment and inflation. At the start, the withdrawals and injections model was completed with the addition of government spending, taxation, exports and imports: we then found that the national income is in equilibrium where withdrawals are equal to injections. Further, we defined aggregate monetary demand to include all the components of spending — and drew a new 45° diagram to show how equilibrium is reached with this method. Then we explored the problems that occur when aggregate monetary demand is too high or too low.

When aggregate monetary demand is too low, it causes cyclical (or demand-deficient, or Keynesian — the name varies according to taste) unemployment. This is not, I explained, the only cause of unemployment. There are also frictional and structural reasons for joblessness. What this means is that some people will still be seeking jobs even when there is a high level of aggregate demand leading to a full-employment national income. Indeed, the unemployment figures themselves are not an entirely trustworthy way to find out how many people there are who are looking for a job but unable to find one. These two factors mean that changes in unemployment cannot be simply explained as being always the result of deficient aggregate demand.

I then moved to consider the problems of the inflationary gap — where the level of demand exceeds the amount needed to assure full employment. When this happens, prices rise and imports are sucked in. So the government has to select some level of aggregate demand that most nearly meets its objectives of full employment and stable prices. As the researches of A. W. H. Phillips showed, this is not an easy task, for there is no happy balancing point where we can have jobs for all and zero inflation. In real life, a little less of the one means a little more of the other: reducing inflation has an opportunity cost in terms of high unemployment. What is more, whereas in the

1950s inflation would disappear if unemployment rose to 2% or so, nowadays inflation still persists at 10% or 12% unemployment. It's as if the 'cost' of buying lower inflation with unemployment has risen steeply over the past fifteen years or so. Levels of unemployment are now so high that reducing demand to lower inflation would mean accepting appallingly high unemployment.

REVIEW SECTION

Further reading

The Economics Brief by N. Wall, *Controlling the Economy*, contains excellent articles on unemployment. A broad-ranging look at the problem of unemployment, and possible policies, that will be excellent background for this unit and the next is *Unemployment and Employment Policy in the UK* by K.W. Glaister (Longman Economic Studies). The official view is found in *Economic Progress Report*, October 1987 – 'Trends In Unemployment'.

Examination questions

1. Explain the relationship between the consumption function and the multiplier in a closed economy without government. In what way will the multiplier be different in a closed economy without government. In what way will the multiplier be different if government and foreign trade are introduced into the model?

    (Northern Ireland 'A' level 1984)

2. Examine the effects of a rise in consumers' expenditure upon national income, investment and savings.

    (Oxford Local Delegacy 'A' level June 1985)

3. Distinguish between voluntary and involuntary unemployment. Discuss the policies that a government might adopt for the reduction of each type of unemployment.

    (AEB 'A' level June 1986)

4. Explain why, in your view, economists make such extensive use of the concept of equilibrium in formulating their theories. Discuss whether or not you regard the existence of unemployment as a sign that the national economy is in disequilibrium.

    (JMB 'A' level June 1987)

5. In the 1980s, both national output and the level of unemployment have risen in the United Kingdom. Examine the possible economic explanations of this phenomenon.

    (AEB 'A' level June 1987)

ANSWERS TO SAQs

SAQ 1:   Imports are a leakage, taking income out of the British circular flow whereas exports are an injection, bringing income into the country.

SAQ 2:   (a)   GDP stands for Gross Domestic Product – and it is an estimate of the money value of all the goods and services produced in an economy.

(b)   In 1973 there was a boom in the British economy: this resulted in a sharp rise in both GDP and imports

(c)   In 1975 there was a sharp drop in both imports and GDP.

(d)   The chart indicates that imports vary directly with GDP – i.e. that imports are a function of income.

SAQ 3:   (a)   If imported goods get cheaper, the M line would rise showing that at any level of income we would import more.

(b)   If British goods improved in quality, fewer imports woud be bought: the M line would fall.

(c)   fall – patriotic consumers would shift their spending in favour of home produced goods

(d)   rise — as well-informed car buyers foresook British cars for Japanese ones

(e)   fall — such a policy would make imported commodities less competitive in relation to British goods

SAQ 4:   A shift upwards in the T line would mean that we were paying more in taxes at each income level — that is to say, a rise in the tax rate would have taken place (say, VAT up, or a rise in the rate of income tax).

SAQ 5:   A (Savings), M (Imports), T (Taxes), X (Exports), I (Investment), G (Government spending)

SAQ 6:   (a) up; (b) down; (c) down (provided we bought less after the rise in price: if we kept on buying them at the higher price, the W line would actually go up); (d) up; (e) no effect — it's an injection; (f) fall (it's the MPC!)

SAQ 7:   The missing words are: rise, rise, rise; run down/be reduced; increase/raise; rise; rises; rise/increase; greater; injections; withdrawals; injections.

SAQ 8:   (a) rise; (b) fall; (c) fall; (d) fall (as our exports fall); (e) rise (if exports rise and imports fall — as they generally do when this happens); (f) fall

SAQ 9:   (a)   The total propensity to withdraw is ·5, and so the multiplier is 2.

(b)   In (i) (an increase in income tax) the amount withdrawn at each stage of the multiplier would rise, and so the value of the multiplier would fall. In (ii) if our propensity to import fell, the multiplier would rise because more of the spending was kept in the circular flow.

SAQ 10:   The answers are (b) more spending on foreign goods would cause income to leak out of the British circular flow; (c) which would reduce business investment and maybe also raise saving; and (e) reduced government spending means fewer jobs unless counteracted by equal tax cuts.

SAQ 11:   The obvious way is a more efficient labour market — better job notification, computer matching of vacancies and job-seekers etc. A more severe way would be to withdraw the unemployment benefit, which would speed people's job search.

SAQ 12:   Answered in text

SAQ 13:   If workers have the wrong skills, then a retraining programme is called for. If they are living in the wrong places, we have two alternatives: either move the workers to the work with relocation grants, or through housing policies that make it easier to swap council homes or find rented accommodation. Or move work to the workers by giving firms grants and allowances for setting up in depressed regions — or by simply refusing them permission to set up or extend factories in the prosperous areas. When the government attempts to influence the location of industry for this reason, we speak of regional policy. We will be looking at it again later in the course.

SAQ 14:   (a) Structural, (b) frictional; (c) seasonal; (d) cyclical; (e) structural (change in the structure of demand for clothing: it happened to my sister!); (f) casual; (g) cyclical again; (h) casual; (i) structural — but this is an interesting case, for if the steelworks closed due to the worldwide fall in demand for steel as a result of the recession (rather than as a result of changes in technology and increased foreign competition) the unemployment is cyclical, isn't it?

SAQ 15:   The figures will be higher, because you will pick up *all* the unemployed, not just those eligible for benefit. US figures must be compared with British figures bearing this distortion in mind — their better methods of collecting unemployment statistics makes their problem appear bigger than ours.

SAQ 16:   Frictional unemployment is explained on page 88. If unemployment pay is higher, people can spend longer looking for a job. If each frictionally unemployed worker spends ten days rather than five looking for work, the frictional unemployment will appear to double. This isn't necessarily a bad thing if it means workers have more time to pick the job which is right for them rather than grab the first vacancy that comes along due to shortage of cash.

SAQ 17:   (a)   If rising oil prices were the cause of unemployment, then they would affect the other oil importers as well as Britain — and you can see on the chart that the British rise in unemployment is paralleled by similar rises in the rest of the world.

(b)   Britain will still be affected by rising oil prices because (i) other countries will be in a recession and thus able to buy fewer of our exports; (ii) even though it comes from British fields, its high cost will make production costs high — enabling employers to profitably employ fewer people; (iii) if we are the only industrialised country self-sufficient in oil, then foreigners will feel that the £ sterling is a safe currency to hold, and thus buy sterling. This will push up its value, and make our exports dearer and imports more expensive.

SAQ 18:   When incomes are rising, unemployment is low, and increased demand cannot be met by raised output, prices are likely to rise.

SAQ 19:   (a)   The two lines should move together — as unemployment drops, inflation rises.

                (b)   Yes — high demand causes a drop in unemployment and an increase in inflation.

                (c)   In the 1970s, both unemployment *and* inflation were rising — this poses great problems for someone who says they are opposites, and that we can have one or the other but not both.

SAQ 20:   Cost inflation in 1975, demand inflation in 1955.

6 Fiscal Policy

AIMS OF UNIT 6

When you have completed this unit you should be able to:

- explain how Chancellors can try to close deflationary and inflationary gaps by the use of fiscal policy
- describe the problems involved in using fiscal policy accurately to adjust the level of aggregate demand
- explain what is meant by the national debt and discuss whether or not it is a burden to the economy
- define the following: balanced budget effect, built-in stabilisers, gilt-edged stock and fiscal drag.

Much of this unit explains the way in which Keynesian economic theory can be used to expand output and employment. This is a central part of most economics syllabuses. Remember that, though Keynesian ideas were accepted by governments throughout the past thirty years, there has recently been a 'monetarist' challenge from those who would not agree that governments can expand the economy and create jobs. We'll look at this rival view later in the course.

INTRODUCTION

In Units 4 and 5 I used the Keynesian theory of macroeconomics to explain why aggregate demand and thus the level of the national income might fluctuate in size. Changes in national income are caused by changes in the withdrawals from and injections into the circular flow of income. For example, a rise in the propensity to save would reduce national income; similarly, a rise in exports would increase it. But the equilibrium of national income that is reached in this way need not, you should remember, be at the happy point of full employment. Units 4 and 5 showed what could happen as a result of changes in the level of national income. Too low a level of demand pulls down national income, raising unemployment and slowing economic growth. On the other hand, too high a level of demand causes inflation, and 'sucks in' imports, worsening our balance of payments (that is, the accounts which show our transactions with other countries). Check your understanding of the causes and effects of changes in aggregate demand and national income with the following checklist:

SAQ 1: *The list in the left-hand column below shows a range of economic events. The right-hand column suggests a number of possible consequences of these events. All of these suggestions may be right, or just some of them, or none. Underline the consequences in the right-hand column that would be caused by the events in the left-hand column.*

(a)	*a rise in the propensity to save*	*unemployment up / unemployment down*
(b)	*a rise in investment*	*growth slows / prices fall / jobs increase*
(c)	*a cut in income tax*	*employment up / down*
(d)	*a reduction in government spending*	*faster inflation / slower inflation*
(e)	*an increase in motorway building*	*balance of trade improves) worsens*
(f)	*a new arms race*	*employment up / growth slows / growth quickens*
(g)	*New Zealand cuts British car imports*	*inflation slows / growth rises*
(h)	*fall in the popularity of Honda cars*	*employment falls / rises*
(i)	*a lower rate of interest*	*faster growth / fuller employment*

So any one of a number of events could alter the level of aggregate demand in Britain — and that would affect jobs, incomes and economic stability. You can see, then, that achieving the right level of demand is vital for our prosperity. Plainly, the country would be better off if it could in some way choose a level of demand and reduced inflation and unemployment to the lowest levels possible. But can we *choose* a level of demand in this way? After reading Units 4 and 5, you may be thinking that the level of national income is something out of our control — determined by things like 'business confidence' and 'the world's demand for British exports' that are as difficult to predict as they are to control. But there is one component of aggregate demand that we can alter and control if we wish: amount of money withdrawn or injected by government. What I aim to do in this unit is explain how modern governments use their powers of taxation and spending in order to influence the level of aggregate demand. Each year the government raises and spends large sums of money: its taxation and spending plans are outlined each spring in the budget. Using the budget to influence the level of aggregate demand is known as **fiscal policy.**

FISCAL POLICY: THE THEORY

Bridging the deflationary gap

Let's look first of all at the contribution that governments can make to closing a deflationary gap. You'll remember from Unit 5 that a deflationary gap results when the amount of aggregate demand in the economy falls short of the amount needed for full employment. I'll use the diagram below to explain this again. In this economy, the level of aggregate demand (consumption plus

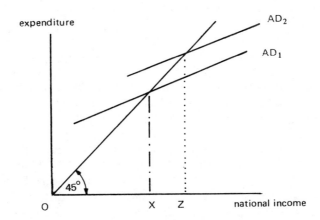

injections) is shown as AD_1. With total spending at this level, you'll see that national income equilibrium is reached at OX. However, this is not a high enough level to give everyone a job: full employment national income would have to be OZ for that to be achieved. To put it another way, demand would have to rise to AD_2.

A government policy of increasing demand (**reflation**) can be implemented in two ways. The most obvious is to raise government spending. This increased government spending would raise national income in the same way as any other rise in injections. Firstly, new jobs would be created in the industries that received the government contracts — more workers taken on in shipyards, civil engineering contractors, hospitals or local government; and then there would be multiplier effects as the newly employed people spend their incomes. Raising welfare benefits would have the same effect as a rise in direct government spending; for example, when the retired or disabled have a higher income, they increase their spending and thus expand the economy.

But raising its spending is not the only way in which a government can expand demand: the same result can be achieved by reductions in taxation. A cut in income tax would leave more money in people's pockets. Spending would rise and the rise in demand would encourage firms to take on extra employees.

SAQ 2: *(a) Explain how a cut in VAT would also raise the level of aggregate demand in an economy.*
(b)   I have explained that the government can reduce the numbers unemployed by either cutting taxes or raising government spending. What sort of commodities will the newly employed workers be making if the government decided to (i) increase demand by cutting taxes £500 million or (ii) by raising spending by £500 million.

So the government can raise demand either through lower taxes or through higher government spending. A doubly effective policy would involve both raising government spending and reducing taxation. This would boost demand in two ways, and firms would find that their sales both to the government and to private consumers were on the increase.

If you are alert you will at this point be asking where the money has come from for the reduced taxes and higher government spending. For if we find the money to reduce taxation by cutting government spending, there will be little effect on the total level of demand in the country: the increase in consumer spending will be matched by cuts in government spending, and so rather than expand output and employment firms will just switch from producing government orders to producing consumer goods.

The logic also applies the other way round. Let's suppose the government is worried about high levels of unemployment and decides to start some new job-creating projects. If it raised the money for these programmes from new taxes, then consumer spending would fall and the desire for a rise in aggregate demand (that is total spending — private and public) would be frustrated.* The newly created government jobs would be matched by a drop in employment in the firms making consumer goods. What the government has to do to operate an effective fiscal policy is to increase its spending *without* raising taxes. This means that the government's budget will no longer balance, for the amount spent will be greater than the amount taken in taxes. When this happens, we speak of a **deficit budget** and the excess spending is termed **deficit spending**. In order to bridge the gap between the amount spent and the amount brought in by taxation, the government must borrow. It was Keynes who made the breakthrough that justified deficit spending by governments to create jobs in a depression.

The government can borrow from many sources, but mostly it borrows from savers in Britain. Some savers lend their money directly to the government: for example, anyone who pays money into a National Savings Bank account or buys a Premium Bond is lending money to the government. But probably more money is borrowed by the government in an indirect way: for example, the managers of pension funds, insurance companies, and banks lend money to the government in exchange for stocks. Government stocks are **gilt-edged securities** (or just plain gilts) because they guarantee that the investor will be paid his interest. Over the years, the government has borrowed enormous sums of money in this way. The total amount that the government owes is called the **National Debt**. In March 1982 it came to £118 600 million. At the end of this unit there is a short appendix on the National Debt for you to study: it has been taken out of the main unit so that you can focus more clearly on the main point — that governments since the days of Keynes have been willing to spend very much more than they received in tax revenues in order to 'top up' the level of aggregate demand and reduce unemployment.

*In fact an equal increase in government spending and taxation does slightly expand the economy: see the discussion of the balanced budget effect later in this unit.

SAQ 3: *During the First World War, the British government borrowed enormous sums from the public and spent them on armaments. When the war ended, the budget was trimmed and taxes raised to pay back the money that had been lent. What effect would you expect this policy to have had (a) in the war years and (b) in the post war years when taxes were raised and government spending cut back?*

'Sound finance'

When Keynes first advised governments to spend more than they received in taxation, conventional economists and politicians were shocked. They had always felt that a government should balance its books, making sure that all expenditure was covered by taxation. This was called **sound finance** or 'Gladstonian finance' after the great Victorian Chancellor and Prime Minister, and was advocated by all Chancellors until Keynes' time.

Comparison was made with the family budget: if a family was unwise to spend more than it was earning, so was a government. But this analogy was false. Unlike an individual family, the British government had been borrowing millions for centuries; and unlike a family, governments can print money.

In the 1930s, when Keynes was advocating deficit spending to pull the economy out of the slump, politicians' attempts to balance the government budget were making matters worse. They found great difficulty in achieving a balance between government revenues and spending — because in a slump, the budget tends to go automatically into a deficit. There are two reasons for this.
Firstly, falling incomes and rising unemployment mean that the government gets less income in the form of corporation tax, income tax and taxes on spending such as VAT. Secondly, the government finds itself paying out more — particularly in welfare benefits like unemployment pay, free school meals, rate and rent rebates and so on. Faced with a budget that was going into deficit in this way, a pre-Keynsian Chancellor would know his duty. Taxes would be raised and expenditure cut in order to get the budget back into balance.

SAQ 4: *This exercise takes the form of a case study, which looks at the financial crisis of 1931. Don't be put off by the choice of an example from 50 years ago — it is a neat example of what 'balancing the budget' will do in a slump.*

In 1931 a government report showed that the government was spending £120 million more than it was receiving in taxes: as a result, the Labour Cabinet discussed economies that could be made in government spending. There was disagreement on a plan to cut unemployment pay by 10%, because there were 2¾ million unemployed and the dole was very low anyway. Unable to persuade his Cabinet, the Prime Minister dismissed them and formed a coalition with the Conservatives and Liberals, and a few of his colleagues who agreed with him. In the resulting budget, income tax was raised, surtax was raised, tax on beer went up, teachers' pay was cut by 15% and pay in the forces and the civil service was reduced. Unemployment pay was cut from 17 shillings (85p) to 15 shillings and threepence (76p) per week.

(a)   What would a Keynesian Chancellor see as the major problem in 1931?
(b)   What would be the effect of the measures described in the passage on the level of aggregate demand and unemployment

So the cuts that were inflicted in Britain and in other countries in the inter-war slump caused harm not just by reducing the living standards of the poor and weakening the defence forces of the democracies; they were also bad economics.

One controversial feature of the Thatcher government was that it appeared to be returning to the attitude that the size of government borrowing was more important than the numbers of unemployed. But even that government, which was heavily criticised for its conservative approach to the budget, ran budget deficits of between £8 and £10 billion.

The balanced budget effect

We now know that ironically a balanced budget tends to expand the economy: it is not the neutral, non-interfering financial rule that it was once thought to be. When the budget is balanced — and government spending and tax revenues are equal — the government is in fact adding to aggregate monetary demand. This is because some of the money that the government is taking from tax-payers and spending would otherwise have been saved. It may be easier to explain with an example. Suppose the government wishes to spend £10 billion in the coming financial year, and it therefore sets out its tax rates to get £10 billion. As a result consumer incomes will fall £10 billion. But remember that households would have saved some of the money that is now lost in tax: if the propensity to save was ·1, they would have saved £1 billion and spent £9 billion on consumption. So the effect of this government budget is to add £10 billion to spending in public expenditure, and reduce consumer spending by £9 billion (that £10 billion taken in tax minus the £1 billion that would have been saved). The net result is that total spending – aggregate demand – is £1 billion higher than it was before, owing to the government spending funds that would otherwise have been saved. This is known as the **balanced budget effect**.

A similar effect occurs when the government redistributes income between groups having different propensities to consume. Suppose, for example, a radical government decided to increase taxation on the rich by a large amount and transfer that money to the poor in the form of higher welfare benefits. You may think that this won't have any effect on employment or output, but it will. If the richer people have a low propensity to consume, and the poor have a high one, then more of the transferred money will be spent after the tax change than before.

SAQ 5: *Check your understanding of the 'balanced budget effect' by ticking true or false beside the following statements*

(a) When the government raises taxes and government spending by an equal amount, it has no effect on the level of aggregate demand.   *true / false*

(b) When the government cuts taxes and government spending by the same amount, it tends to raise unemployment (other things being equal).   *true / false*

(c) If the government wishes to increase its own spending without increasing the level of aggregate demand, it will have to raise rather more in taxation than it intends to spend.   *true / false*

(d) If the government wishes to cut government spending but keep the same level of aggregate demand, it will have to cut taxes by a greater amount than the planned fall in government spending.   *true / false*

(e) The balanced budget effect suggests that if a government is taking in exactly the same amount in taxation as it is spending on public services, it is having an expansionary effect on the economy.   *true / false*

(f) In the 1979 Budget, the government reduced income tax (particularly on high income earners) very considerably by raising the money instead from indirect taxes like VAT. Overall, then, the changes had no effect on aggregate demand.   *true / false*

Closing the inflationary gap

So far I have described only one sort of macroeconomic problem – too low a level of aggregate demand leading to low output and high unemployment. I have shown that the correct thing for governments to do in that situation would be to cut taxes and increase public spending. However, you'll remember in Unit 5 that too high a level of aggregate demand can cause economic problems too.

SAQ 6: *Low output and high unemployment result from too low a level of aggregate monetary demand. What, then, are the problems associated with too high a level?*

But what if the government is more worried about inflation and the balance of payments, and wishes to reduce demand? Can Keynesian fiscal policy be of help here? Let's look at another diagram.

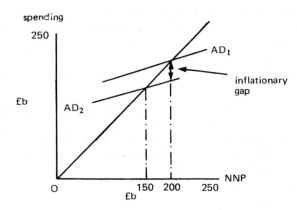

In this diagram aggregate demand is shown by line AD_1: this gives an equilibrium national income of £200 billion. But full employment national income is £150 billion. The level of demand is higher than necessary to achieve full employment, and so prices and imports are being dragged up. Here we have the inflationary gap introduced in the previous unit, and the problem for the government is not to raise the level of aggregate demand but on the contrary to reduce it. Again, either taxation or government spending may be used. The government can *either*

• raise taxes to lower people's disposable incomes thus reducing consumer spending

or

• reduce its own spending itself in order to reduce the level of demand directly.

A government that was really keen to reduce the level of demand would do as Chancellor Roy Jenkins did in 1969 – raise taxation and cut spending so sharply that the government ended up receiving more in taxes than it was spending – in other words, running a **surplus budget**. In these circumstances, the government is able to repay government stocks as they become due, reducing the size of the National Debt. In practice, though governments rarely start off with a balanced budget – throughout the 1970s, for example, the budget was in substantial deficit. When this happens, a government can still lower the level of demand by reducing the size of the anticipated deficit with tax increases or spending cuts.

SAQ 7: *The data below refer to a hypothetical economy.*

Income (000 million)	10	20	30	40	50
Consumption	15	20	25	30	35
Injections	5	5	5	5	5

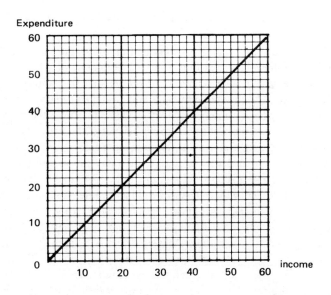

Plot this data onto the blank graph: firstly plot consumption against income, and then add the injections on by plotting a point £5 billion higher.

Now answer the following questions:

(a)   What is equilibrium national income here?

(b)   Suppose that full employment national income was 40: do we have an inflationary or a deflationary gap?

(c)   If full employment national income was 40, would the government wish to add to demand, or reduce it? By how much would national income have to change to reach full-employment national income?

(d)   Calculate the value of the MPC in this economy. When you have done so, use it to calculate the value of the multiplier.

(e)   Now that you have worked out the amount that national income has to change, and the value of the multiplier, what budget deficit or surplus would you recommend, were you Chancellor of the Exchequer?

(f)   Are there any reasons why a Chancellor might decide not to reflate the economy right up to full employment?

So following the revolution in economic thinking brought about by Keynes, governments now have the ability to adjust the level of taxation and government spending so as to make sure that there is the right level of aggregate demand in the economy. Fiscal policy allows governments to add to aggregate demand by running a deficit or reduce aggregate demand by having a budget surplus. A Keynesian Chancellor does not simply attempt to find enough money for the government's services: nowadays the Budget will be used to 'manage the economy'.

How much surplus or deficit?

But saying that when there is sustained and widespread unemployment, the government should run a deficit is not very helpful. The Chancellor will have to come to a decision as to precisely how much the budget should add to, or take away from, aggregate monetary demand. He therefore has to make what is known as a **budget judgement** as to the size of the budget deficit or surplus that should be aimed for. There is a rule which can help him here.

I explained on page 99 that when an economy goes into a slump, the government budget goes into deficit (look back over that page if you can't remember why government receipts go down, and government spending up, in a slump). When there is a boom the opposite occurs: the government budget goes into surplus. There are two reasons for this. Firstly, the amount of tax paid increases when people's incomes rise, since people spend on consumer goods, petrol and drink. Secondly, some items of government spending fall.

 SAQ 8: *Why do you think this is?*

It follows logically from this that a combination of tax rates and government spending programmes designed to ensure a balanced budget at full employment will cause a *deficit* if aggregate demand falls below the desired level, and a *surplus* if demand rises above the desired level. Now, this is just what is required – such a policy would add to demand when unemployment and growth need a boost, and cut aggregate monetary demand when inflation and payments problems threaten. So if a government aims at a budget that would balance *if* there were full employment, it will be guiding the economy in the right direction: this is called a **full employment balanced budget policy**.

If the government had such a budget, then any fall in demand would create a deficit. Receipts from income tax and VAT would fall, unemployment and welfare benefits would rise. This would cause a budget deficit, which in turn would add to demand (because it means the amount injected in G is greater than that withdrawn as T) counteracting the drop in private spending. For this reason the tax system and welfare payments are called **built-in stabilisers** (or automatic stabilisers) by some economists. While the stabilising effect will rarely be enough to put the economy automatically on the right path again, it is a useful check against the fluctuations that occur in a free-enterprise economy. Built-in stabilisers wouldn't just slow down a slump, either – for when incomes rose too fast due to the presence of an inflationary gap, taxes would automatically take out an increasing slice of earnings.

That may be a good thing if the increase in earning and spending is simply due to inflation. The tax system will bite into the inflationary gain, and take the heat out of the economy. However, if the higher incomes are due to economic growth, then the tax system will slow down a rise in spending that is in fact beneficial – since it buys all the new goods that are being produced. This situation, in which a tax system takes an ever bigger slice of people's incomes, is called *fiscal drag*. Fiscal drag isn't merely a problem because it reduces aggregate demand and so slows down economic growth. It can also create unfairness in the tax system by making low paid people pay more tax than intended. During a period of inflation fiscal drag will pull into the tax system people who were never meant to pay tax at all. An example might help make this complex topic clearer:

> In April, the Chancellor decides that the single person's tax allowance should be £1500 – that is, Ms X can earn £30 a week without paying tax. But during the year, prices rise by 20%, and Ms X wins a 20% pay rise. Is she as well off as before? No, because she has to pay tax on her rise. 30% of £6 is £1.80, so Ms X's take-home pay is now £34.20, yet she needs £36 to maintain the same living standards as last year.

Because of fiscal drag chancellors raise personal allowances each year: when Sir Geoffrey Howe raised tax allowances in his 1979 budget, more than 1.3 million people were taken out of the 'tax net'. In fact, the House of Commons passed an amendment to the 1977 budget that required the Chancellor to raise tax allowance thresholds in line with inflation each year – or if not, to explain why to Parliament. (This was called the 'Rooker-Wise' amendment after two Labour MPs – Geoff Rooker and Audrey Wise – who voted with the Opposition to bring this law in.)

Summary

So that's the theory of fiscal policy. Before moving on to look at the real world problems, I suggest you look back and check what you've learned so far in this unit.

SAQ 9: *Fill in the blanks in this passage:*

> Following the writings of _____ governments nowadays use their budget not only to raise money to provide _____ _____ but also to influence the level of _____ _____. If there is too low a level of _____ _____, there will be widespread unemployment. In order to attack this problem, the government should reduce _____ and raise _____ _____. This will result in a budget _____, and the government will have to bridge the gap between tax revenues and public spending by _____ (which will raise the National _____). If, by contrast, the government is more worried about the rate of inflation or the state of the _____ of _____, they will seek to reduce the level of _____ _____ by running a _____ budget.
>
> To an extent, the budget brings about these changes automatically: when aggregate demand falls, for example, the budget tends to go into _____ : some economists believe that this forms a built-in _____ . The practice of using the Budget the budget to level of total demand is called _____ policy.

THE PROBLEMS OF FISCAL POLICY

You may have read the last few pages with an increasing sense of unease – even bafflement. If the government can choose precisely the right level of demand – one that will secure full employment without inflation – what has been going on for the past 10 or 15 years? Why have many industial countries suffered from high unemployment?

The answers to these questions will come out in the next four or five units. For the first 20 to 30 years after Keynes wrote – from the beginning of the Second World War to the early 1970s – it seemed as if he had revealed the key to economic prosperity: unemployment stayed below 2%, and throughout the industrialised West there was a sustained boom: in Britain, economic growth increased annually by 2.5% and in Japan the figure reached almost 10%. It seemed that governments could receive a substantial measure of credit for this prosperity – downturns in western economies were remedied by fiscal policy with budget deficits making good deficiencies in aggregate demand. However, there were always a number of problems associated with fiscal policy, and these problems, triggered off by the oil crisis of 1973, came increasingly to the fore as the 1970s progressed. In this section I'm going to review these problems; at the end you'll be able to decide whether or not you agree with what James Callaghan told the Labour Party conference when he was Prime Minister – that we were no longer in an age where the government could spend its way out of a recession.

Conflicting objectives

One of the major problems of fiscal policy is that it is not possible to achieve simultaneously all the targets that governments want to achieve. The government has four macroeconomic goals:

- stable prices
- full employment
- a secure balance of payments
- fast economic growth.

The problem is that two of these will be best achieved by creating very high pressure of demand in an economy, but two of them will respond best to a low level of aggregate demand. More specifically, full employment and a fast rate of growth depend on a high level of demand, but a higher level of demand causes inflation and balance of payments troubles.

One important relationship has been that between unemployment and inflation. Throughout the postwar period, and very acutely in the 1970s and early 1980s, governments knew that a determined reflation of demand, that would reduce unemployment, might increase inflation. So they were faced with the dilemma: is it worth reducing unemployment by x% if it means having an inflation rise of y%? Chancellors of both political parties accepted higher unemployment for fear that inflation would be caused by increases in aggregate monetary demand.

SAQ 10: *What is the name given to the diagram that shows the 'trade-off' between unemployment and inflation?*
Why is it given this name? (Look back to Unit 5 p. 92 if you can't remember.)

As you saw in Unit 5, the problem with the unemployment/inflation trade-off is that in recent years increasingly large doses of unemployment seem to have been necessary in order to achieve reductions in inflation. Adding to aggregate demand through a generous budget ('expansionary' fiscal policy) might be an attractive policy in 1959, when inflation was less than 1% but what Chancellor would increase the level of demand in 1980, when inflation was around 20%? The unit on inflation looks at this knotty problem again.

The conflict between inflation and unemployment was not the only one that prevented Chancellors reflating. Another clash is that between economic growth and a secure balance of payments. Whenever the British economy has experienced a spurt in its rate of growth, the balance of payments has gone into the red.

Economic growth causes a rise in imports for two main reasons. Firstly, when manufacturers start to produce more they need more raw materials and components to make into finished goods — and much of this is imported. Secondly, the higher incomes that people earn in a boom (with lower unemployment and more overtime and premium payments) lead to increased purchases of imported consumer goods — cars, stereos, clothes, wine, and foreign holidays. Governments of both parties have brought in deflationary budgets to try to 'cure' a balance of payments problem: higher taxes and cuts in government spending reduce demand and therefore imports; but one problem has been solved by causing another — slow growth and mounting unemployment.

SAQ 11: *I've just explained how economic expansion can worsen the Balance of Payments. Using this explanation, account for the very large surplus on foreign trade in 1980, when unemployment was high and the British economy wasn't expanding.*

In fact, several determined attempts to increase Britain's rate of economic growth by reflation have failed because of the inflation and balance of payments deficit they caused. Reginald Maudling attempted a 'dash for growth' in the early 1960s, which came to an end when a record balance of payments deficit resulted in his party losing the 1964 election. The incoming Labour administration tried again in the mid-1960s, but despite a commitment to expansion at a rate of 4% a year under a National Plan which attempted to co-ordinate output, investment, earnings and exports. The attempt was 'blown off course' (Harold Wilson's phrase) by a mounting balance of payments deficit in 1967. The last attempt by a Chancellor to expand the economy with a reflationary budget aimed at fast growth was made by Anthony Barber in 1972. Alarmed by unemployment approaching the million mark (!) he cut taxation and increased government spending in true Keynesian style. This vigorous (and possibly foolhardy) attempt to 'get Britain moving' was abandoned amid rising inflation, a disastrous worsening of the Balance of Payments, the oil crisis and the miners' strike.

Problems of forecasting

If one set of problems result from the difficulties of simultaneously achieving each of the governments macroeconomic objectives, a second set of problems concerns forecasting. When I asked you to prepare a budget judgement in SAQ 6, I gave you firm figures and a graph-based diagram. The Chancellor has a task which is many times more complex. Firstly, he (or she) has to forecast what is likely to happen to the economy in the coming year or two if he does nothing. This will involve judging the state of the economy using all the sources of information available: economic statistics, comments from business and labour leaders, discussion with foreign finance ministers and international bankers about the world economy. The Chancellor, of course, has a great deal of help in making his predictions about the future course of the economy. The civil servants in the Treasury prepare a forecast several times a year about the country's progress; indeed, under the 1975 Industry Act they were required to publish their forecast twice yearly. This forecast is prepared using a computer.

The computer program, known as the 'Treasury model', takes in all the available statistics about trends in wages, imports, taxation, interest rates and so on and analyses them to produce predictions as to what will happen. The model is complex and highly mathematical: more than 500 equations and 1000 variables. It is not secret – since 1975 it has been possible to buy copies of the programme, and many firms, banks and universities have done so. This doesn't mean that they agree with the model, for economists will disagree about how an economy works. Some think that more importance should be given to changes in the amount of money: others would give greater importance to the behaviour of large firms or the demands of organised labour.

But even if the Treasury model was a perfect representation of how the economy behaves, it could still be overtaken by events. For example, it would take a remarkable computer to predict the next outbreak of fighting in the Middle East and its effect on oil prices; or, to take another example, to predict the results of an election in the USA or Germany, which will affect prospects for British exports.

SAQ 12:   *Which of the following could be predicted by a good computer model of the economy?*
(a)   the effect of the previous budget on unemployment
(b)   the amount of refund granted to Britain from the EEC budget
(c)   broad trends in British export sales
(d)   whether Datsun will establish a new plant in Britain
(e)   a US president vetoes a gas pipeline contract with the Soviet Union that would have created jobs for British steelmen.
(f)   fluctuations in interest rates

But the problem of forecasting is worse than this. The Chancellor is not just guessing about what will happen in the future – he's guessing about what is happening now. He and his Treasury team do not have any statistics on what is happening at the moment the budget is being prepared, because economic statistics (like other statistics) can only refer to what has happened in the past – what happened last year, or last quarter. Economic statistics are often revised, too: the first estimate of the amount of imports in a given quarter, or the change in bank loans in a given month are frequently found to be inaccurate. So the Chancellor is forming a view about the future from what happened in the past. Perhaps Sir Alec Cairncross, who worked in the Treasury for many years as as Economic Adviser, put it best when he compared economic management to steering a fast car using only the rear-view mirror. (Or, as Harold Macmillan said when Prime Minister, running the country on last year's railway timetables.)

The budget timetable

The way in which problems of forecasting and timing arise can best be illustrated by considering the timetable of each budget. Budget Day is usually on a Tuesday in March or April, but the Chancellor will have been working on it for much of the preceding three or four months. He will have consulted many groups – like the trade unions and businessmen, as well as smaller pressure groups that want more help for small businesses, housing or the disabled, or higher taxes on alcohol, dog-licences and so on. The basic outline of the budget will have been decided in February and March (relying, remember, on forecasts made from statistics that, at the latest, refer to the last quarter of the previous year). After the budget has been presented to the House of Commons, there will be parliamentary debates and investigations, so that the Finance Act – the law that brings the budget proposals into effect – will not be passed until the end of July. At this point, civil servants in tax, social security and other offices can start changing tax codes, benefit rates and so on. Households won't see any change in their circumstances for a time, and even when the lower (or higher) taxes and benefits get through to their pockets, they may not go straight out and spend it.

So shops and manufacturers may not perceive any change in sales and orders until the end of the year, and they will wait until they can be sure that this change is permanent before laying off or taking on workers. Most economists would stretch this chain of events further, and say that a budget will not affect the economy until a year or 18 months later.

What is more, the Chancellor may not influence the economy in the way he wants to. If he increases taxation in order to reduce consumer spending, households may reduce their savings to keep up the same living standards. Similarly, when Mr Barber cut taxes to reduce unemployment, much of the extra income was spent on imports that worsened the Balance of Payments rather than cutting the dole queues.

SAQ 13: *The diagram below shows the behaviour of actual and predicted unemployment in an imaginary economy. The solid line on the left shows the actual figures available to the Chancellor when his budget was prepared, the solid line shows the prediction about the future course of unemployment he received from his advisers, and the broken line shows what actually happened to unemployment in the year in question.*

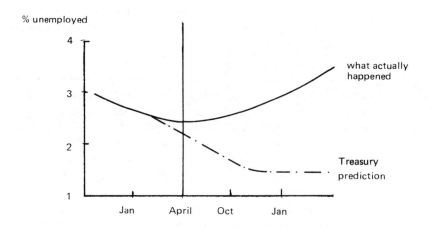

(a)   Why does the Treasury prediction start before Budget Day?
(b)   What does the Treasury predict about the future course of unemployment?
(c)   What sort of budget would be introduced as a result of this prediction?
(d)   Would a budget prepared in line with the Treasury prediction be the right one, in the light of what actually happened?

Given the difficulties of fitting fiscal policy to what is happening in the economy, it is hardly surprising that governments have sometimes worsened the movements in aggregate demand, rather than improved them. Perhaps we would not want to go as far as economists who have alleged that fiscal policy has actually made the economy *more*, rather than less, unstable: but it is clear that there have been occasions when budgets have exaggerated a boom or deepened a slump. The 1972 expansion, which I've already mentioned, occurred when economy was recovering by itself, and this caused a particularly sharp boom with consequential problems of inflation and payments deficits.

Problems of timing and impact

Even if the government are taking the correct decision on whether or not to expand the economy, they may have problems with timing; and the measures taken may affect some areas of the economy much more harshly than others. Let's look now at the problems.

It is very difficult to stop or start some spending programmes: once a programme of home improvement grants has been started, or the foundations for a motorway dug, the government is usually committed to the expenditure. There are some examples of government programmes cancelled as part of fiscal policy, of course: the Channel tunnel is one, and the raising of the school leaving age from 15 to 16 was postponed during the economic problems of the mid-1960s. But on the whole, Chancellors have used tax changes rather than spending changes to achieve their fiscal aims.

SAQ 14: *In altering the level of aggregate demand, why are taxes regarded as more flexible than changes in public spending?*

One way, though, in which governments and local councils have achieved cuts in public spending is by reductions in capital spending: that is, spending on new building and equipment. A local council finds it less painful to cancel a planned new swimming bath rather than sack two or three hundred workers. Yet all this apparently compassionate decision does is to transfer unemployment away from the council employees and on to the workers who earn their living building swimming baths (or schools, or hospitals, or whatever).

I've already mentioned civil engineering contractors as one group who suffer during a fiscal policy 'stop' period. But there are others, particularly in the production of consumer durables such as cars, fridges, TVs etc. This is because these manufacturers make items that we can choose not to replace if our income falls. When increasing taxes, or tougher bank lending rules, cut spending, it is the consumer durable industries that are hardest hit. We still need to buy bread, clothes and pay the rent: but we can do without a new stereo or carpet. So when aggregate demand drops by a few per cent, car sales drop dramatically. Similarly, when demand expands, spending on consumer durables goes up fast. Conversely, we spend no more on food and rent when our incomes rise — but we spend much more on new fridges, cars, records and so on.

The massive fluctuations in demand for consumer durables have caused great problems in the industries that produce them, in the following way:

- *new investment* No sensible firm is going to build and equip a new factory if next year they are going to be unable to sell the products of the existing plant.
- *labour relations* No worthwhile union leader will negotiate labour-saving work methods and new automation agreements if the effect is to throw workers out of jobs as soon as the present boom is over.
- *imports* Firms unable to produce enough (through insufficient investment) to meet demand at the peak of the boom will have problems with imports. Consumers will be unwilling to wait five or six months for the British car when a new French or German one is available immediately.

    Fiscal policy alternately expanding the economy to cut unemployment and contracting it to fight inflation is a process that has become known as 'stop-go'.

IMPROVING FISCAL POLICY

Mini-budgets

Governments have come to recognise that there is a lot of truth in the criticisms of fiscal policy. They now know that their forecasting and timing can go wrong. As a result, they no longer rely on on the once-a-year budget in April, but introduce financial and economic measures when the need is felt. Such packages of economic measures are called **mini-budgets.** Strictly speaking, a budget is a set of measures that requires legislation in a Finance Act, whereas a mini-budget does not. In recent years, very important and substantial changes of economic policy have been made in the months of November, July and December.

The regulator

Another aid to the Chancellor in more flexibly dealing with the economy is the *regulator*. This is the name given to his power to alter certain indirect taxes as and when he wishes: for example, VAT, tobacco, alcohol and petrol taxes.

I have shown in the last few pages that the Chancellor is not completely free to achieve a full-employment level of aggregate demand. There are problems of *conflicting objectives*, meaning that he cannot at the same time achieve all the desired goals. There are problems of *forecasting* — in understanding what is happening to the economy and therefore what the government needs to do to achieve high and stable levels of demand. And there are problems of *timing*, so that often the government is doing the right thing at the wrong time. All of these criticisms of fiscal policy have been known for some time; but the final problem I shall describe emerged in the seventies, when the deepening recession in Britain and the world caused British governments to run ever larger budget deficits. The problem relates to the effects on the rest of the economy of government having to borrow massive sums of money. Let's go into this in more detail.

Financing problems

You saw in the early pages of this unit that governments attempt to maintain the level of employment, output and incomes during a slump by adding to the level of aggregate demand. Keynesian macroeconomic theory encourages them to do this by spending more than they receive in taxation. The result is a gap between receipts and expenditure that has to be financed somehow: even the government has to pay its bills.

The government can get the money from two sources. It can borrow it from savers, in the way I described on page 101; or it can print more money. The objection to financing the deficit by printing money is obvious — the creation of billions of extra pounds to add to the amount of money in circulation will clearly result in inflation. But what's wrong with government borrowing?

To understand this, you have to realise that government borrowing in the past ten years or so has been massive; in 1975, it came to nearly 10% of the total national income. When this happens, financiers worry that the government is cornering the market in savings, leaving none left over for industry to use for investment. Industry cannot really compete with government for funds, because the government can afford to pay whatever rate of interest is needed. Whereas private firms have to earn profits to pay interest, the government has the simpler task of putting taxes up a little — or even raising another loan to obtain the money.

SAQ 15: *A friend tells you that the government should cut its borrowing so that private industry has more funds to invest. How would you answer her, bearing in mind what you know about (a) the effect on income and employment of a reduction in public spending and (b) the factors that make a businessman invest (see Unit 4)?*

This is the end of the main business of this unit — looking at the opportunities and problems that occur when we use the government budget to influence the level of aggregate demand. At the end of the unit you'll find suggestions for further reading and examples of examination questions, together with an assignment for you to send to your tutor. But before you get round to that, here is the promised supplementary work on the National Debt.

THE NATIONAL DEBT

What is the National Debt?

The National Debt is the debt owed by a government to people or to institutions (such as banks or insurance companies) either within its borders or abroad. The amount owed to British residents is known as the **internal debt**; that portion owed to foreigners is called the **external debt**. By far the largest part of the National Debt is internal. Only about 10% of the National Debt is external. So the National Debt is, to use the old phrase, something that we collectively owe to ourselves individually.

Economists generally think of the National Debt as originating in 1694, when a group of Scots merchants gained the privilege of setting up (paradoxically) the Bank of England in return for lending the government of the day just over £1 million to finance the latest war. Until the last 30 years or so, the history of the National Debt has been the history of Britain's wars: traditionally, British governments have preferred to finance wars out of borrowing rather than taxes. However, the use of Keynesian policies since the Second World War has resulted in a considerable rise in the size of the National Debt — in 1945, the National Debt was less than £25 billion, but today it is nearly £120 billion.

Why do governments borrow?

Governments have borrowed to pay for wars and to implement Keynesian policies. But they have also borrowed to pay for capital spending. It makes good sense to spread the cost of a new airport or hospital over a period of years, so that all the people who benefit from them pay for them. After all, when firms buy new premises or equipment, or individuals buy a new house or car, they too spread the payments over a period of time.

The total amount that all branches of government have to borrow in a year — central government, local government and nationalised industries — is called the **Public Sector Borrowing Requirement**. This is more conveniently known by its initials as the **PSBR**. Note that because it includes the borrowing of local councils and nationalised industries, the PSBR is a wider term than 'budget deficit'.

The make-up of the National Debt

As the diagram below shows, a part of the National Debt is in the form of National Savings and Premium Bonds: these are aimed at small savers and sold through Post Offices. The rest of the

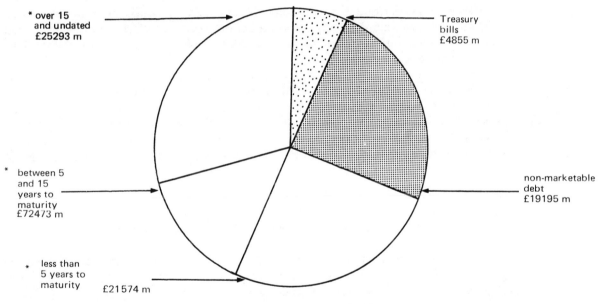

* over 15 and undated £25293 m

Treasury bills £4855 m

* between 5 and 15 years to maturity £72473 m

non-marketable debt £19195 m

* less than 5 years to maturity   £21574 m

*marketable debt £59340 m

National Debt is made up of financial assets that can be bought and sold, and so it is known as the **marketable debt**. The marketable debt is made up of two parts. First there is a certain amount made up of short-term borrowing: the government sells stocks that have to be repaid at the end of three months. These stocks are called **Treasury Bills**, and do not yield any interest. The financial advantage of buying them is that they are sold below face value, so by holding them until they are repaid buyers gain the difference between the purchase price and the price at which they are redeemed. The part of the National Debt that is made up of Treasury Bills is called the **floating debt** and is nowadays not very significant.

Second, the vast majority of the National Debt is 'funded' in the form of government stock — gilts — with a variety of periods to run until they have to be repaid (or, to use the technical term, until they *mature*). Some stocks, which are undated, the government never intends to repay, while others are coming up to be repaid shortly. It is one of the jobs of the Bank of England to make sure that there isn't a time when it has to repay a giant chunk of the National Debt all at once. To this end, it will repay some stocks before they mature, or raise a further loan to repay an old loan. One problem with this is that interest rates are higher now than when money was borrowed 20 or

30 years ago, and so 'retiring' an old issue with money gained from a new issue can be expensive: it might mean replacing a 3% stock with a 10% stock.

Who owns the National Debt?

This question is best answered with a table showing holders of the National Debt:

Insurance companies	23.3%
Pension funds	13.0%
Banks	7.6%
Overseas	10.7%
Individuals and private trusts	23.6%

This doesn't add up to 100% because I have left out a number of smaller holders such as building societies and unit trusts.

Is the National Debt a burden?

Concern is sometimes expressed about the size of the National Debt, and some politicians talk of the terrible debt we are leaving for our children to clear up (and there are still some people who leave their money in their will to the government to help with the National Debt). Let's look at the extent to which these fears are justified.

The external debt clearly is a burden. In paying interest to foreigners, or finally paying the debt off, we are transferring some of our income abroad. What's more, the payment of interest to foreigners worsens our balance of payments as money flows out of the country. But the 'burden' of an internal debt is much less clear.

For a start, to talk of passing a debt on to one's children is fallacious: the National Debt will not have to be repaid as a bank overdraft might have to be repaid by a family. In fact, one could argue that the internal debt involves no burden at all. Paying interest to holders of Government stock simply involves taking money from one British taxpayer and giving it to another one — robbing Peter to pay Paul. Given the fact that the sort of people who own holdings of government stock are likely to be taxpayers, even high taxpayers, we might even be robbing Paul to pay Paul. While this extreme argument should stop you losing sleep over the National Debt, there are some problems left:

- If we have to keep taxes high to meet payments on the National Debt, there might be a disincentive effect — taxpayers working less hard as the tax system leaves them with little reward.
- Interest payments form a significant portion of government spending — £10.4 billion out of £95.7 billion in 1981. This means that taxes are higher than they would otherwise need to be or that public spending in other directions will be lower.
- Paying interest on the National Debt involves redistributing income between British residents. Money is taken from the broad mass of taxpayers and paid to those who hold government stock. This is probably 'regressive' — that is, it probably takes income from low to middle-income earners and gives it to the richer people.
- People often argue that when the government borrows, it takes savings that would be better used by private industry. This assumes two things — firstly that the savings would indeed be used in investment rather than lying idle and causing a slump; and secondly that any use to which the government would put the funds they borrow — hospital building, welfare payments, roads, industrial training — is inherently less worthwhile than anything private industry would do with the money.

So whatever the 'burden' of National Debt that would be left by a government intent on reflating the economy by traditional Keynesian methods — cutting the taxes, raising government spending — it has to be measured against the real and known burden of a slump, with its unemployment and lost production. And in fact, the National Debt today is, compared to the National Income, at its lowest point for years. This is due to the fact that inflation and economic growth have caused the National Income to grow much faster than the National Debt.

At the end of the Second World War, the National Debt was three times as big as the National Income. Today it is about half the size of the National Income.

SAQ 16: *The average taxpayer has gained because inflation has reduced the value of the National Debt compared to National Income. Who do you think has lost as a result of this change?*

REVIEW SECTION

In this review section I give some suggestions for further reading, and then go on to look at a range of examination questions on fiscal policy and the National Debt.

Suggested reading

In a sense the best sources for information about economic management and fiscal policy are the serious newspapers and journals in the months before a budget. Your local library should stock back-copies of *The Economist* which will show all the options open to a Chancellor before the budget, and what the economic analysts make of it all after the budget. The Pelican books by Michael Stewart and Peter Donaldson that I have been recommending to you in the previous two units will again prove useful, as will *Control of the Economy* by Derek Lee — one of the inexpensive Heinemann range of *Studies in the British Economy*. If you find this level a little too basic for you, then by all means look at something a little more expert. *The UK Economy* by Prest and Coppock (Weidenfeld and Nicolson) is a university textbook which is regularly updated. This means that it will have an up-to-date discussion of the problems of fiscal policy, complete with figures. *The Economics of Modern Britain* by John Black (Martin Robertson, 2nd edn) has a rigorous, if somewhat mathematical treatment of fiscal policy, and also has an informative chapter on Government Debt. In fact, almost all economics textbooks have chapters on fiscal policy if you would like a second opinion on it: again, my advice is to try the books by Paul Samuelson or Richard Lipsey mentioned in Unit 29.

The classic review of the workings of British economic policy are Dow *The Management of the British Economy 1945-60* and Cohen *British Economic Policy 1960-69*. As far as the National Debt goes, try to find E. J. Mishan's little Penguin book *21 Popular Economic Fallacies*, which has a chapter discussing whether or not the National Debt is a burden. If you want up-to-date figures on the National Debt, how much it is and who holds it, *The Bank of England Quarterly Bulletin* publishes information every year in its December issue. Remember that this is an expensive publication, so again a library is your best bet.

Examination questions

Fiscal policy is a favourite topic for examiners, who are anxious that students should recognise modern budgets as much more than simply a way of raising money for the government. Here are some specimen essay questions:

1. 'Increases in public expenditure lead to lower unemployment and eventually to a reduction in public expenditure; public expenditure cuts lead to higher unemployment and to increased public expenditure.' Critically discuss this statement.

    (AEB 'A' level June 1985)

2. Define the term 'budget deficit' and explain how such deficits may arise. Discuss the possible effects on the international economy of a large budget deficit such as that experienced by the USA in recent years.

    (JMB 'A' level June 1986)

3. Explain fully what you understand by the National Debt and distinguish the main forms of debt issued by central government. Critically assess the view that the size of the National Debt is important.

    (Associated Examining Board 'A' 1981)

and a data response question:

4. 'The optimal policy for the government on arriving in office is to deflate in order to bring inflation down, then around mid-term to stimulate the economy to bring unemployment down and raise real incomes in time for the election, leaving their successors (or themselves) to cope with the rise in inflation that is the lagged result of the policy. Such models then imply that we observe a Boom–Election–Slump–Boom–Election cycle.' (Source: P. Minford & D. Peel, 'Is the Government's Strategy on Course?', *Lloyds Bank Review*, April 1981.)

    (a) Explain the meaning of 'deflate in order to bring inflation down'.
    (b) Why might stimulating the economy cause a 'rise in inflation that is the lagged result of the policy'?   (University of London 'A' June 1983)

A perennially popular question is this:

5.   Discuss the view that the government should aim at a balanced economy rather than a balanced budget.

You'd have to make clear in answering this question not only what you understand by a balanced budget, but also the characteristics of a balanced economy in terms of unemployment, the rate of growth, foreign trade and inflation. A question like

6.   Explain why the objective of full employment might be difficult for a government to achieve.

(Associated Examining Board 'A' June 1980)

can also concern itself with material from the Unit. Whilst a good answer would obviously bring in problems such as structural unemployment from Unit 5, it should also include notes about the problems governments face in implementing an expansionary fiscal policy. A more ambitious question for those wishing to discuss the opposition to Keynes found on the political right is:

7.   How does fiscal policy operate to influence demand in the economy? Contrast the role of fiscal policy under Margaret Thatcher's government with its role under previous governments.

(Northern Universities JMB 'A' 1982)

ANSWERS TO SAQs

SAQ 1:   These are all relatively simple checks on what you have learned in Units 4 and 5. Cuts in withdrawals or increases in injections will raise aggregate demand and thus improve employment and the growth rate, while worsening inflation and the balance of payments; and vice versa. So, the answers are: (a) unemployment up; (b) jobs increase; (c) employment up; (d) slower inflation; (e) balance of trade worsens (as demand grows from the extra incomes: of course, in the long run improving the country's roads might make us more efficient and thus cut imports); (f) employment up and quicker growth; (g) inflation slows (as we no longer earn export incomes from New Zealand); (h) employment rises; (i) faster growth and fuller employment (if you believe that a fall in the rate of interest will raise industrial investment).

SAQ 2:   (a)   A cut in VAT means that people pay lower prices for many goods in the shops — and so they have money left over to spend on other goods. Even if you are cynical and believe that shops will not reduce prices when VAT is cut, we still get an increase in demand as profits, and thus dividends and investment rise.

   (b)   If demand is increased by cuts in taxes, more consumer goods will be made, as households increase their consumption spending. If the reflation of demand is achieved by a rise in public spending, then public goods will be made (i.e. new roads, dams, classes etc.)

SAQ 3:   This policy expanded the economy vigorously in the war years, causing high employment but fast inflation. At the end of the war the government policy of raising taxes and cutting government spending lowered the level of aggregate demand and so raised unemployment and deflated the economy, leading to a speedy reduction in inflation.

SAQ 4:   (a) Most Keynesians would see unemployment as the main problem, rather than the budget deficit. (b) The measures proposed would raise withdrawals and reduce injections (T up, G down): this lowers aggregate demand and raises unemployment.

   A modern Keynesian Chancellor would not worry about the deficit — indeed he/she might even go into a bigger deficit by spending more to reduce unemployment.

   Some countries did engage in deficit spending in the 1930s. The outstanding examples of countries that spent their way out of the slump were the USA (where Roosevelt's New Deal policy involved an expansion of government spending) and Hitler's Germany (there's nothing like an arms race to raise employment and incomes.)

SAQ 5:   (a)   false: as we have just seen in the text, the effect is to increase aggregate monetary demand, because some of the income spent by he government (after being taken in taxes) would not have been spent by the taxpayers who earned it: it would have been saved.

   (b)   true: because the reduction in aggregate monetary demand caused by lower G will not be completely compensated by a rise in C, as some of the increased take-home pay created by the tax cuts will be saved.

(c)   true: taxes would have to be raised so that the reduction in private spending was exactly equal to the increase in government spending.

(d)   true: because some of the money returned by cuts in taxation will be saved, the government will have room to cut taxes by more than they have reduced government spending.

(e)   true. If you can't see why, read back over pages 99-100.

(f)   false — if the changes switched money from the poor to the rich, the country's average propensity to consume would fall, lowering the level of aggregate demand.

SAQ 6:   Inflation and Balance of Payments problems. Demand inflation occurs when the level of aggregate demand is too high to be satisfied by increased output, as all the country's economic resources are already fully employed. To get round this problem, traders import more goods to meet shortages and provide lower priced competition for British goods, swelling the import bill and worsening our Balance of Payments.

SAQ 7:   (a) Equilibrium is where C + J = Income, which when I drew it was at national income £30 billion. (b) There is a deflationary gap. (c) The government would wish to add to demand. The national income has to go up £10 billion to give everyone a chance of a job. (d) The MPC is ·5: half of any increase in income is spent. So the multiplier is 2 (did you remember this from Unit 4? Well done). (e) We want the national income to go up £10 billion, the multiplier is 2 so that a budget deficit of £5 billion will do the trick; (f) Yes — we learned in the last unit that the closer you get to full employment, the more problems you get with inflation and the balance of payments. So it might be prudent not to reflate right up to £40 billion.

SAQ 8:   Because demand-related spending on unemployment and welfare payments fall off as incomes rise.

SAQ 9:   Keynes; public services; aggregate demand; aggregate demand; taxation; government spending; deficit; borrowing; Debt; balance; payments; aggregate demand; surplus; deficit; stabiliser; fiscal. (Don't get anxious if you have a slightly different answer — you'll know in your bones whether you've got the right idea.)

SAQ 10:   It's called the Phillips curve, after the man who discovered it and published in a famous article in 1959.

SAQ 11:   When aggregate monetary demand is low, the balance of payments often improves. As you saw in Unit 5 (p. 78) imports vary with national income, so a low national income will reduce spending on imports: not just by cutting consumer spending, but also by reducing industry's demand for foreign produced raw materials and components.

SAQ 12:   A good computer program should give reasonably accurate information about (a), (c) and (f). The other decisions are more personal and political, and although they will affect British prosperity, they will be much less easy to predict. Indeed, even (f) will be affected by international considerations — for example, if we reduce interest rates while US interest rates remain high, money might flow from Britain to the USA.

SAQ 13:   (a)   Because statistics are not absolutely up-to-date and so the Chancellor will rely to some extent on predictive techniques to know where he is when he makes his budget decisions.

(b)   The Treasury predict a steady drop in unemployment until the autumn, when it flattens out at about 1½%.

(c)   This is a very low level of unemployment, and would raise the problems that come from overfull employment and too high a level of demand — inflation and balance of payments troubles. So the Chancellor would certainly not expand the economy: he would probably raise taxes and cut spending in order to restrain total demand.

(d)   What actually happened was that unemployment was rising very sharply; so any budget which reduced AMD would worsen the underlying trend in employment.

SAQ 14:   Taxes can be changed so much quicker than public spending programmes.

SAQ 15:   My answer would go along these lines. 'If the government cut back on public spending, this would reduce the level of demand. Firms would experience falling demand and would be laying off workers. So I think that it's pretty unlikely that firms would raise their investment spending in that climate. In my view, the way to higher investment is to maintain a high level of demand so that businessmen can have confidence that their capital spending will pay off in better sales'

SAQ 16:   The losers have been the people who own the government stock — who have seen the real value of the stocks and bonds they hold fall. Any rejoicing we may indulge in when inflation reduces the burden of the National Debt must be tempered by the knowledge that someone's savings have been eroded.

7 Money and Banking

AIMS OF UNIT 7

This unit aims to lay the foundations for your study of the economics of money. When you have completed it you should be able to:

- define 'money' and make clear what this means in modern Britain
- list the components of the money supply in order of their importance
- distinguish between the two main measures of money, M_1 and M_3
- define 'liquidity' and list assets in order of their liquidity
- explain why money is a more efficient means of exchange than bartering
- list the three functions of money
- show the importance of the PSBR in expanding the money supply
- explain what is meant by a 'discount house' and show how they make profits
- explain the process by which bank money originates and show the importance of the 're-serve requirement' in this process

INTRODUCTION

In the last few units that you have studied I looked at how the economy worked by investigating the total amount of spending that was going on. The approach I used was Keynesian: I looked at all the different groups who make spending decisions — consumers, firms, foreigners, governments — and analysed how they would take these decisions. In recent years, though, an alternative way of looking at how the economy operates has become popular. This new approach looks at information about the amount of money in an economy (the **money supply**) to see how it affects prices and the national income. There are some economists who believe that this **monetary** approach gives a more accurate idea of what is going to happen in the economy than the Keynesian theories which have dominated postwar economics. This unit introduces you to monetary economics. It asks what money is, why we have it and where it comes from. In future units you will move on from this base to look at the way in which changes in the supply of money affect the economy, and consider how the government can control the amount of money.

WHAT IS MONEY?

Economists define money as **whatever is generally acceptable in payment for goods and services or**

in settling debts. This is a definition that concentrates on what money *does*, rather than what money *is*: it says that when anything does the job described — that is, circulates in exchange for commodities — then it is money. What this means is that money can take different forms in different eras and different countries. And it does: in the past, iron bars, shells, even cows have been used as money. But what does money consist of in modern-day Britain? Just what is, to take our definition, 'generally acceptable in payment'?

Coins and notes *are* generally acceptable and they must therefore be included in any definition of the total amount of money in Britain. But while most of our day-to-day transactions take place using cash, larger transactions do not. It would be exceptional to buy a TV or stereo with cash, and to pay for a car or a house with cash would probably arouse suspicions. These large value transactions — many others for smaller amounts — are carried out with cheques. The question then arises — are cheques money?

Think for a moment what you are offering a trader when you pay for an item by cheque. It is not so much the coloured, oblong piece of paper that interests the shopkeeper — no-one will accept a cheque unless it is 'good' for the amount stated. What this means is that the cheque must be backed up by real money; its purpose is to tell your bank to transfer that money from your bank account to that of the trader.

It's important to be clear about the nature of this 'bank money': it does not exist in the form of piles of notes and coin in the vaults of the bank. Banks do, of course, keep a small balance of cash in their tills for customers to draw out, but the 'money' in most customers' accounts exists simply as entries in the bank's books. Nowadays, this means a computerised file: so the money in our bank accounts is nothing more than an item on the bank's magnetic tape or disk memory. But although it has no physical existence at all, it is still generally acceptable as payment. Let's return to the trader who you were paying by cheque a moment ago. He will be quite happy if your cheque results in your account being debited by the named amount, and his account being similarly credited. He won't insist that pound notes be taken out of one safe-box and put in another!

In summary, then, money in Britain is made up of coins, notes and money in current accounts.

SAQ 1: *On May 19 1982 the amount of money in Britain was £34,709 million. But only £10,466 million consisted of cash in the form of notes. What accounts for the difference? If the government wanted to reduce the amount of money and so issued less coins and notes, what would happen?*

Wider definitions of money

Of course, people do not just put their money into the current account of banks. There are other ways of storing money. For example a deposit account pays interest to customers; in exchange for this advantage they have to give notice that they wish to withdraw their money although, in practice, this is often waived. Further, the line that separates **demand deposits** (current accounts, that is) and **time deposits** (deposit accounts) is getting increasingly blurred: a number of institutions pay interest on current accounts, or link current and deposit accounts and automatically transfer money between them when the current account goes above or below certain sums. So the question we need to answer is this — should we include deposit accounts in our definition of money?

Official statisticians get around this problem by having more than one definition of money: M_1 includes only coins, notes and current accounts (it was M_1 that you measured in exercise 1); on the other hand, there is a broader definition of money that includes time deposits, called M_3. In March 1984 the government introduced a new (and their preferred) definition of money — M_0; this includes notes and coins in circulation with the public, money in the tills of the commercial banks and their operational deposits with the Bank of England. Although M_0 is a very narrow definition of money it forms the 'wide' monetary base of the government's Medium Term Financial Strategy. In the 1987 budget the government abandoned all other money supply targets in favour of M_0. Many economists believe that this has marked the end of the 'monetarist experiment' in the UK and that the government is returning to demand management.

SAQ 2: *Here are the figures of cash and bank deposits on 21 February 1979. Work out M_1 and M_3.*

Notes and coin in circulation	*£ 8 594 million*
Current accounts	*£16 725 million*
Deposit accounts	*£24 952 million*

(In passing, there is another complication. What you have just worked out is sterling M_3. If we are to get a full idea of all the money owned by people in Britain we would have to add on the bank accounts that some UK residents hold in foreign currencies: in the example above, that would make M_3 nearly £5 000 million higher than sterling M_3.)

Wider still and wider . . .

When newsreaders or politicians talk about the amount of money, they are referring either to M_0 or M_3. However, you should be clear that there are many other ways of holding wealth beside bank accounts. Building society accounts have grown apace recently, in response not only to the increased desire for home ownership, but also to the fact that such accounts offer a tax-paid interest rate and can be drawn upon, from almost any branch, on Saturdays. Today, building societies hold more money than bank deposit accounts. Should this be added to our money stock? And what about Post Office accounts, or credit card limits?

This is a difficult one. If we stick to our definition of money — that it must be generally acceptable in payment for goods and services — then this method of payment cannot be included. But if we think of money loosely as 'spending power people can lay their hands on', we must bear in mind all these easily accessible ways to get money. The government recognises this in their measure of **private sector liquidity**, a statistic that includes not just money but also National Savings Bank and building society accounts.

The fact is that there are many ways to hold wealth. They range from cash in the hand to jewellery, from houses to shares in major companies. All of these assets are to some extent **liquid** — that is, they can be turned into money. If we arranged all the ways of holding wealth in order of their liquidity, — the ease with which they can be converted to money — then some things at one end of the spectrum would be money and some things at the other end would plainly not be money. Where the line is drawn between money, 'near-money' and 'non-money' is as much a matter of taste as science.

SAQ 3:

(a)   *Arrange the following list of assets in order of liquidity. Write them on a list under one another, with the most liquid at the top. Draw a line to divide those assets which are money from those which aren't.*

coins	*stocks and shares*
jewels	*current accounts*
land	*premium bonds*

(b)   *Which is your most liquid asset? Which is your least liquid?*

WHY DO WE HAVE MONEY?

Now that I've defined money, let's see why we need money at all. The need for something that is generally acceptable in exchange for goods and services' is not felt in a society where people are self-sufficient. If we all produced our own clothes, vegetables, houses, shoes, furniture, tools and so on, we would have no need of money, since we would not need to exchange goods at all. This is the reason why so few primitive societies have a developed monetary system. But specialisation as you saw in Unit 2, results in higher living standards. When people specialise, they produce more of their commodity than they actually need for their own purposes, and aim to exchange the surplus they have made for the goods they haven't got. In the example in Unit 2, Neil and Howard swapped their surplus cloth and wheat and thus increased their living standards. This direct exchange of goods is called **barter**. Bartering still goes on today, sometimes even in international deals between companies and countries*, but it is a very clumsy way for individuals to do business. It suffers in practice from four decisive drawbacks:

- To barter successfully, not only has person A got to want what person B has got — person B must want what person A has got. This problem is called the **mutual coincidence of wants**.
- Some products do not easily divide up into tradeable sizes. Half a hammer, one-tenth of a cow, two-fifths of a sailing dinghy are not much use: so how does anyone who produces them buy something inexpensive (a newspaper, a box of matches)?
- Under a system of barter, it is difficult to work out what anything is worth. Suppose for a moment you have taken your wheat to market, and have received three offers: one person

*as for example in the recent deal in which the Soviet Union swapped millions of cubic metres of gas for W. German help setting up modern factories.

117

offers 12 lbs of toffee, someone else a box of nails, a third person offers a frozen chicken. Which is the best price?

- There is the sheer clumsiness of carrying goods around. What's more, some goods depreciate as time passes. A farmer trying to swap his cream for something else on a warm day would have only a few hours to complete his trade.

Looking at all these disadvantages, it is no surprise that most societies develop a monetary system. There are no first-hand reports of the birth of money, but it almost certainly started with a commodity that became used not only for the satisfaction it gave but also as money. For example, conch shells would be used not just as a beautiful object but also as a 'coin' that passed from hand to hand. A commodity used in this way is termed **commodity money**. However, the problem with commodity money is that it is difficult to divide into smaller denominations, and as in the case of shells, tends to vary in quality. For this reason the most acceptable form of commodity money soon became precious metal. Not only are gold and silver scarce and of consistent quality; they can easily be melted into larger or smaller value lumps: half an ounce is plainly worth just half as much as one ounce. The only problem that remains is that of trust: is this lump of silver I am being offered really silver, and really one whole ounce?

The way to get around this is to have the lumps of metal minted – that is, melted down, cast and stamped at one trusted and controlled factory. Coins originated as pieces of precious metal that had been stamped with the monarch's mark to assure citizens that they were of the right weight and purity.

Valuable coins, however, need safekeeping. By the 17th century wealthy people were using the services of the craftsmen who had experience of storing valued objects: goldsmiths. When gold coins were deposited at the goldsmith-banker, a receipt was issued promising to pay the coins out whenever the depositor wanted them. This was an early form of the banknote, and although many such notes were made out to specific individuals, notes which promised simply to 'pay the bearer on demand' became popular. These meant that the holder of the gold deposit did not have to return to the goldsmith-banker every time he wanted to buy something of value: provided the goldsmith was known and trusted, the notes could be exchanged for goods and services. These notes still survive in museums as examples of the first paper money.

While the goldsmiths' notes were circulating, their gold coins lay unused in the vaults. This money gradually came to be used as loans to business and individuals; and there was no need for the gold to actually leave the premises – the loans could be in the form of bank-notes like the ones already circulating. However, this expansion of banking was a bit risky. What would happen, for example, if the public lost confidence in one banker and all presented their notes for payment at once? The banker could not honour all the obligations, and would go broke. It became clear that the power to issue notes was best restricted to a few large, sound banks, and gradually the number of note-issuing banks was whittled down. The Bank Charter Act of 1844 effectively limited the power to issue banknotes in England to the Bank of England, although the last commercial bank to issue its own notes didn't disappear till the 1920s.

The 1844 Act also permitted the Bank of England to issue more notes than it had gold. This was called the **fiduciary issue,** and allowed just £14 million to be printed: nowadays, there is no connection between gold and the value of a bank-note. The Bank of England is free to issue notes as it wishes, and it does so to fit in with people's convenience.

SAQ 4: *I have just claimed that the issue of notes and coin these days is made to suit the convenience of the public. Look at these statistics, from the* Bank of England Quarterly Bulletin, *showing notes and coins in circulation with the public, in £million. What trends can you see in them? (What you should look for is the times of year when people seem to be needing to hold their wealth in cash.)*

	1976	1977	1978
Jan	5538	6315	7217
Feb	5654	6369	7371
Mar	5749	6447	7513
Apr	5905	6540	7543
May	5898	6603	7693
Jun	6009	6735	7814
Jul	6269	6957	8186
Aug	6261	6936	8130
Sep	6256	6946	8160
Oct	6241	6939	8184
Nov	6271	7004	8258
Dec	6462	7525	8682

Other functions of money

So far, I have concentrated on the advantages that money offers as a **means of exchange**. By inserting money into the trading process, we can avoid the clumsiness of barter. However, money has other functions besides this obvious one:

- It can be used to reckon up values and accounts, and to compare incomes and prices. In this respect, money is being used as a measuring unit, like a metre or a litre; economists call this function being a **unit of account**.
- It can act as a way of storing the value of your wealth: you can trade the commodity you produce today, receive money and maybe not spend it until sometime later. Barter, on the other hand, requires you to obtain some other commodity at the same moment as you part with your own.* With money, the decision as to what you obtain in exchange for your commodity can be deferred. In this way it acts as a **store of wealth** (or sometimes, **store of value**).

SAQ 5: *Which of these three functions will money perform less well when prices are rising? Why? What might people use instead?*

WHERE DOES MONEY COME FROM?

Cash — that is, coins and notes — comes from the government. When the High Street banks want more cash for their customers (that is, when the customers wish to hold more of their wealth in the form of cash and less in the form of bank accounts), they buy it from the Bank of England. As you have seen, the government's practice has been to supply cash as the public demands it — and Christmas and holiday times are examples of periods when there is an increased demand for cash. But cash is not the major part of Britain's money supply: most of what we call money is in the form of bank accounts — computer entries with no physical existence at all. How did this money come into existence?

The best way to explain this would be to imagine someone receiving £1000 in cash. Now, cash is inconvenient in some ways. Large sums are bulky to carry or store, and it is easily lost or stolen. So when most people receive such a large sum they pay it into a bank account for safekeeping.

What banks do with deposits

But banks are not just safe stores for depositors; they also lend money to business and individuals who wish to borrow. Indeed, banks keep the amount of cash in their tills to a minimum, for **till-money** is lying idle and earning no profits. Banks have two considerations in mind when deciding what to do with the money that is deposited with them — liquidity and profitability. A bank which lent out nothing, keeping all the cash that was paid in safely in the vaults would never be caught short of funds — but would be most unprofitable. It would fail to earn the revenue it needed to pay the costs of running the business and providing services for customers. On the other hand, a bank which went all out for profit and invested all its deposits in loans to customers might well come a cropper when depositors came to draw out their money.

In practice, bankers work out a prudent mix of loans and reserves. Very little of a bank's assets are held as cash — less than 2%. However, a further proportion is held in easily cashed form. For example, the High Street banks find it convenient to hold accounts at the Bank of England. Moreover, they can lend money in London on the understanding that it will be returned whenever they ask for it: this is known as **money-at-call** and is lent to the discount houses (this is explained in greater detail in an appendix to this unit). A further proportion of the money deposited with banks is used to buy stocks, shares and gilt-edged stocks, which offer a higher return than money-at-call. The most profitable business for a bank, though, is **advances to customers** — lending at interest to industry and private individuals.

---

*This is where Say's Law, which you met in Unit 4, comes from. In a barter economy, every supply does indeed create its own demand: when you go to market with a pig, you are wanting commodities to the value of one pig!

SAQ 6: *Look at the diagram below, which arranges the assets of banks in order of their profitability and liquidity. Fill in each of the blank boxes with one of these words: illiquid, very liquid, unprofitable, very profitable.*

| (a) | – – – – – – LIQUIDITY – – – – – – | (c) |

| Cash in tills | Money at call | Stocks, shares and gilts | Advances to customers |

| (b) | – – – – – – PROFITABILITY – – – – – – | (d) |

How banks increase the money supply

Let's assume that the banks simply hold one tenth of the money that is deposited with them as a reserve, and decide that they can lend the rest. Now, back to the fortunate person we mentioned above who has received £1000 and deposited it in a bank account. The bank holds on to £100 as its one-tenth reserve and the rest, £900 can be lent. If it is lent, then it will be spent and probably the person who receives the £900 will pay it into a bank account. Suppose, for example, the money is lent to someone to buy building materials for a house extension. In this case, the borrower will visit a builders' merchant or DIY shop, and pay the owner a cheque for £900. This cheque will be paid into the shopkeeper's bank account and (important !!) this adds to the amount of money. The additional £900 that is added to the bank account increases the amount of money in current accounts in Britain. But the process doesn't stop there. The builders' merchant's bank now has an extra £900. If it, too, keeps the same proportion in reserve as the first bank, it will keep one-tenth as a precaution and lend the rest out. So someone will be able to borrow £810; this will be spent and paid into another bank account, adding further to the additional bank account money that has been created. The bank which receives this deposit will retain one tenth (£81) and lend the rest. This extra lending of £729 will be spent, and paid back into the banking system by the person who receives it. One-tenth will be retained (nearly £73) and the rest — £656 — lent on.

This process goes on until all the new cash deposited in the system is sucked away as reserves. But while the process goes on, all the payments into the bank accounts add to the amount of money in the economy. So as a result of this deposit of £1000, the amount of bank accounts has risen by

£1000 + £900 + £810 + £729 + £656 + £591 + £532 + £479 + £431, and so on.

SAQ 7: *When you were learning macroeconomics, you studied a very similar effect where an increase in investment spending caused a chain of new spending through the economy*
(a)   What was the name of that effect?
(b)   How long did it go on?
(c)   What formula was used to calculate the final effect on the size of the national income of a change in injections?

While you are very welcome to sit down and pass an idle hour working out the total increase in money caused by an initial increase in cash deposited (it's easy enough with a calculator and the back of an envelope), there is a simpler way. Just as the value of the investment multiplier could be obtained from the value of the marginal propensity to save, we can work out the **credit creation multiplier** from the bank's propensity to hold reserves. The amount of money created by a new deposit of cash will be

$$\frac{\text{amount of}}{\text{new cash deposited}} \quad X \quad \frac{1}{\text{fraction held as reserve}}$$

I'll use this formula to work through the example we used in the text. The amount of fresh cash deposited was £1000; the portion kept as reserves by the banks was one tenth. Let's work this out:

$$£1000 \times \frac{1}{\text{one tenth}} = £1000 \times 10.$$

So in this case, the effect of the whole series of transactions will be to raise the amount of bank money by £10000 — the initial £1000 and then a chain of credit creation that came to another £9000.

SAQ 8: *By how much would an initial deposit of cash be multiplied if the banks held back the following proportion of money deposited as a reserve?*
(a) ¼; (b) ⅛; (c) ½; (d) one-fifth; (e) 5%

You can see from working through these examples that the size of the reserve requirement held by banks determines their power to create fresh credit (just as the size of the MPS affected the value of the investment multiplier). If the banks decided not to lend anything at all, they would not create any new money. On the other hand, if they felt no obligation to hold any reserve requirement at all, the process of credit creation could go on endlessly.

Summary

Now let's review what we have learned so far in this unit. The amount of money in Britain is made up of coin, notes and bank accounts: bank account money is created by the workings of the credit creation multiplier, whereby a reserve ratio of one-tenth allows an initial deposit to be multiplied by ten, a reserve ratio of one-fifth by five, and so on.

Credit contraction At this point it is important to realise that a withdrawal of cash from the banking system can cause a multiple contraction of deposits in the same way that a deposit of cash could cause a multiple expansion. Take the following example, assuming as we did earlier in the unit that banks feel they must keep one tenth of all their deposits in liquid form:

Anybank plc

Assets:	liquid reserves	£1 million	*Liabilities:*	Deposits	£10 million
	loans to customers	£9 million			

Now, if a large customer withdrew £100 000 (£·1 million) from an account, the bank would have to pay from its most liquid assets. It cannot, after all, call in overdrafts or business loans overnight. If the money was taken from the liquid reserves (say, by calling back money-at-call), the picture would be as follows:

Assets:	liquid reserves	£·9 million	*Liabilities:*	Deposits	£9.9 million
	loans to customers	£9 million			

(£·1 million has been taken off both sides — the customer's account and the liquid reserves)

The problem now is that the bank is short on reserves, which now form less than the desired 10% of deposits. In order to restore the ratio between liquid reserves and liabilities, the bank will have to reduce its lending. It will achieve this by allowing liabilities to fall to £9 million and slimming loans to customers down to £8·1 million. The end result is that the withdrawal of £·1 million has reduced total deposits by £1 million — showing just the same credit creation multiplier as if £·1 million had been paid in.*

So, to return to the man on page 120. If the £1000 he deposited in his bank had just been withdrawn from another bank, the effect on the banking system as a whole would be zero. The expansion of credit caused by his new deposit would be exactly matched by his withdrawal. In fact, withdrawals and deposits go on all the time, shifting money between banks but not in any sense creating fresh deposits. This leads us on to a fundamental question: what is the origin of increases in the supply of money? Where does that initial fuel come from that powers the whole process?

*This is a simplified version of a process that, like credit creation, would in practice involve a number of banks adjusting their advances to keep their liquid reserve ratios.

THE SOURCES OF A RISE IN THE AMOUNT OF MONEY IN BRITAIN

The amount of money in Britain can rise in either of two ways: through an increase in the Public Sector Borrowing Requirement or through an increase in bank lending. Let's look at the PSBR first.

SAQ 9: *Look through Unit 6 and answer these questions:*
(a)   What is the PSBR?
(b)   How does it differ from the budget deficit?
(c)   Why might the public sector have a borrowing requirement?

It is important to realise that a PSBR, no matter how large, does not automatically involve an increase in the amount of money in the economy. If the government can obtain the money by borrowing from private citizens, insurance companies, or anybody outside the banks, there is no monetary expansion. Let's suppose, for example, that I buy a government gilt-edged stock for £1000. I write a cheque out to the government, and £1000 is deducted from my account and added to the government's. In exchange, I get a piece of paper saying that the government owes me £1000, will pay it back in a given year, and will pay me interest until then. The effect of all this is to *transfer* money (from me to the government), rather than create it. A PSBR financed entirely by the sale of bonds to private individuals and companies that aren't banks (what is known as the **non-bank sector**) will not raise the money supply.

But if the government is unable to sell stock to the non-bank sector, they must either finance their activities with newly printed money or borrow from the banks. The way in which issuing currency adds to the amount of money in circulation is obvious: it actually increases the amount of coins and notes. The effect of borrowing from banks needs a closer look.

How banks multiply the PSBR

Let's once again take some simple figures as a way of showing the effect on the amount of money of funding the PSBR through the banks.

Let's say the government wishes to borrow some money — £200 million to cover the deficit of a nationalised industry. If it is unable to sell stocks to the non-bank sector (perhaps because the interest rate is too low, or the public expect government stocks to fall in price), it will be forced to borrow from the banks — we'll assume, by selling £200 million in Treasury Bills to the banks. The banks pay for these bills by writing a cheque drawn on their account at the Bank of England.

Despite having written a cheque for £200 million, the banking system still has enough liquid reserves to support its loan: Treasury Bills are easy to sell and the banks will regard them as a fair substitute for their reduced Bank of England account. However, when the nationalised industry spends the extra £200 million in wages or payments to suppliers, the people who receive this money pay it into their bank accounts. The banks now have all their original deposits (they've even got their cash back) *plus* an extra £200 million. The results of financing the PSBR through the banks is an increase in the amount in the economy.

The banks now have an extra source of money, which enables them to expand their lending to the private sector. That £200 million, which they lent to the government and now have back, has refuelled the credit-creation machine.

SAQ 10: *With a reserve ratio of $\frac{1}{8}$, and an extra £200 million to replenish the credit-creating powers of the banking system, how much new money will be created (if the credit-creation chain goes on to its theoretical maximum)?*

Other sources of expanded credit

A rise in bank lending to private firms and individuals can come from other places than a rise in the PSBR. For example, banks do not always lend up to their theoretical maximum limit; nor do firms always use their overdraft facilities to the limit. If business needs to borrow more (to buy raw materials and components when the economic climate is improving, perhaps, or to withstand a crisis that leaves them short of cash), they may draw on their credit facilities; and when the money they spend finds its way back to the banks, a new credit creation system might start.

A further source of deposits is the rest of the world: if there is an inflow of funds into British banks, that too could act as a base for expanded credit.

SAQ 11: *Suppose the government runs a PSBR of £8 billion, and finances it in the following manner*

	£ billion
New coin and notes circulating with the public	*1*
Borrowing from the non-bank sector	*6*
Borrowing from banks	*1*

Given a reserve asset ratio of 12½%, by how much will the money supply increase?

A note for the curious

If you're very perceptive you may have followed all the reasons why selling Treasury Bills to the banking system is likely to raise the amount of money in the economy, but may wonder why the government does not sell assets which are less liquid. For example, if the government sold long-dated gilts, it would reduce the banks' reserves and thus would not permit them to expand credit. This logic is fine as far as it goes, and you may find that this is the explanation given in older text-books on this topic, which stress the nature of the assets the government sell to the banks.

However, in the real world, the banks can borrow funds for a short while that will enable them to maintain their desired reserve ratios. Mind you, if all the major banks were seeking to borrow short-term cash, then interest rates in these money-markets would rise sharply. A government wishing to restrain the credit-creating powers of the banks could (and does) use this as a method of control (See next unit).

THE DISCOUNT MARKET

The discount market is made up of 11 **discount houses** – privately owned financial companies based in London. It is probably easiest for an outsider to think of discount houses as a sort of bank, for they do take money from one source and use it to make investments. However, the nature of their business is very distinctive in two ways. Firstly, they borrow the money they use at very short notice. Secondly, their business consists almost entirely of **discounting bills**. Let's look at each of these in turn.

Discount houses

Discount market

Liabilities on 16 January, 1980
Total: £4528 million
of which   £3969 million was borrowed at call or overnight
and   £4126 million came from the British banks.

The chart above, showing liabilities of the London discount houses tells much of the story. They borrow at very short notice from the other banks. Note that 87% of the borrowed funds are 'at call' and over 90% come from the British banks. The convenience of this market to the banks must be obvious – they can lend money and earn a small rate of interest even though they can have it back whenever they like. How do the discount houses make money? To answer this I need to explain more about discount bills.

More about bills

A 'bill' is an IOU – a document that shows that the firm or government named owes a stated sum of money and will pay it on the date indicated, usually three months after being issued. The main point to grasp is that a bill which promises to pay you £5000 in three months is not worth £5000 today. After all, if you had £5000 you could invest it at interest for that period of time: buying the bill for face value would mean that you would receive no interest from the borrower who issued it. In fact, bills are **discounted** – that is to say, bought at a price less than the amount that will be redeemed on the day it matures. If a discount house bought a bill with a maturity value of £5000 for £4850 three months before it matures, then the earnings on the bill will be £150 for three months (3% over three months, roughly an annual rate of 12%.) Bills are being bought and sold each day – this is, after all, what goes on in the discount market – and the nearer that a bill gets to its maturity date, the closer the market price gets to the maturity value. Buying the £5000 bill the day before it matures would cost you (at 12% per annum) £4995. So the discount houses can make money either by using the banks' funds that are loaned to them to buy bills and sell them again, or to buy them and hold them till maturity.

The discount houses have traditionally bought up all the unsold Treasury Bills that the government issues. They do this by making a bid each week for the number of bills the government wish to sell to them. However, the main form of bill that the discount houses trade in today is commercial – that is, bills issued by companies rather than the government. In January 1980, £2648 million of the discount houses assets were invested in such bills, and only £334 million in British and Northern Ireland Treasury Bills.

So the system looks like this: the major British banks always have substantial funds available to be lent for short periods of time. They lend them 'at call' or at very short notice to the London discount houses, who use the money to buy bills. This enables them to make a profit, the banks to earn a little money on what would otherwise be useless funds, and the issuers of bills (government and companies) to have a source of finance for short term needs. So far, so good.

SAQ 12: *Can you foresee any problems that might arise in this system – where banks lend large sums of cash 'at-call' and the discount houses use the money to buy bills from government and industry?*

A considerable danger is that when the banks run short of cash, they will all come to the discount houses for their money-at-call: the discount houses will be hopelessly lost, having urgently to sell millions of pounds worth of bills. But this problem has been foreseen, and when the discount houses run short, the Bank of England is prepared to loan them money against the security of the bills that the discount houses hold. When the Bank of England lends the discount houses money in this way, it is known as the **lender of last resort**. The Bank of England thus supports the banking system, enabling the banks to loan their funds out with the assurance that help will be given in an emergency. However, the Bank of England does charge a rate of interest for lending to the discount houses and this is usually higher than the profit that discount houses are making from holding bills. So if they go to the Bank of England for help, it will cost them dearly. This knowledge acts to restrain the banking system: more of this in the coming unit on monetary policy.

The Bank of England's chosen rate of interest used to be known as the **minimum lending rate** (MLR) or earlier, as the **bank rate**. Until recently the Bank of England would make a public pronouncement that it was changing the minimum lending rate. The commercial banks, building societies would then follow the lead set by the Bank of England. This practice of formally changing the minimum lending rate has now been discontinued. However it still happens on an unofficial level. The Bank of England varies the rate of interest it charges to financial institutions borrowing from it. This in turn then influences the base rates of the commercial banks and eventually the rates of interest charged to borrowers and interest paid to lenders.

SAQ 13: *How might the Bank of England's interest rate affect the rate of interest a housebuyer is charged by a building society?*

REVIEW SECTION

Although short this unit has been a pretty complicated one and has introduced you to some difficult ideas. Look through these true-false questions, and tick the answer you think is correct: then compare it with the answers at the end of the unit to see how well you've done.

SAQ 14:

(a)	*In a modern economy, the term 'money' is used to cover cash and bank deposits*	*true/false*
(b)	*Under no circumstances would a credit card account serve as money*	*true/false*
(c)	*Wealth and money are the same thing*	*true/false*
(d)	*Money is anything which is generally acceptable in payment for goods and services and in settlement of debt*	*true/false*
(e)	*Deposit accounts are considered money because they earn interest*	*true/false*
(f)	*Whatever is used as money should have inherent value*	*true/false*
(g)	*The value of money is fixed by the Bank of England*	*true/false*
(h)	*The largest part of the money in Britain is cash*	*true/false*
(i)	*The Bank of England may only issue a banknote if it has an equivalent value of gold in its vaults*	*true/false*
(j)	*Bank accounts are not considered money as they only consist of computer records and have no real existence*	*true/false*
(k)	*A banking system may hold money lent by depositors, but it will never create money*	*true/false*
(l)	*Credit creation occurs because banks are able to lend out more than is deposited with them because it is unlikely that all creditors will claim their money at once.*	*true/false*
(m)	*If a bank experiences a fall in its till-money, it will have to reduce the total amount of loans it has advanced*	*true/false*
(n)	*The credit-creation power of a banking system is based on the assumption that people will prefer to use cheques rather than cash*	*true/false*
(o)	*Notes issued by the Bank of England derive their value from the fact that they are acceptable by the community in exchange for goods and services.*	*true/false*
(p)	*One of the functions of discount houses is to lend money to industry for long-term projects.*	*true/false*
(q)	*A bank's most lucrative asset is often its most liquid.*	*true/false*
(r)	*A Treasury Bill is most valuable when first issued.*	*true/false*
(s)	*A rise in the PSBR will automatically raise the amount of money*	*true/false*
(t)	*Sales of assets to the banking system are a less satisfactory way of financing a PSBR than sales to the general public*	*true/false*
(u)	*If banks can multiply any injection of new cash by eight, it shows there is an 8% reserve ratio*	*true/false*
(v)	*Gilts is a term used to describe the shares of the top industrial companies (ICI, Marks and Spencer etc.)*	*true/false*
(w)	*In British monetary statistics, M_1 is bigger than M_3*	*true/false*

Further reading

In this unit I have covered two main topics — the definitions and origins of money, and how the British monetary system operates. The first topic will be dealt with by any good textbook — look at the ones recommended earlier. The problem with the second topic is that the picture is constantly changing, and (for example) many textbooks will contain descriptions of how the system worked before the changes in October 1981. These changes are best described in the *Bank of England Quarterly Journal* in March and June 1982, and the background to the changes are described in *Economics* Spring 1982 edition.

Nevertheless, you'll gain from some extra reading. As always, Prest's *The UK Economy* (Weidenfeld and Nicolson — seek most up-to-date edition) is excellent, giving a broad and detailed account of the UK monetary system. David Gowland has written a witty and well-informed account of money today in a chapter of *Modern Economic Analysis*, but you won't get much from it until you have mastered the basics in this unit and the next.

A fuller account of financial markets is to be found in Vivian Anthony's *Banks and Markets* (Heinemann Educational). A good up-to-date coverage of this topic is contained in the Economics Briefs series by N. Wall, *Money & Banking* (Collins).

Examination questions

Most of the examination essay titles that are asked require you to bring in information that will be explained in the next two units — on monetary policy, monetarism, and inflation. Nevertheless, you may wish to turn over in your mind the way you would approach :

Holding money always involves foregoing interest and is therefore irrational.

(University of London, June 1980)

ANSWERS TO SAQs

SAQ 1:   The difference was made up of money in current accounts. If the government stopped producing coin and notes, people would still have to buy for their day-to-day needs, and we would see a massive growth in the use of cheques. Alternatives to coins as small change are common in some countries, where a shortage of loose change has led to the use of chewing-gum or sweets as a form of small change.

SAQ 2: M_1 consists of cash plus current accounts; I make this £25 319 million. M_3 also includes deposit accounts, and so comes to £50 271 million.

SAQ 3:   My list would look like this:

First, coins — they are absolutely liquid

Second, current accounts, which can be turned into cash by simply turning up at the bank and writing a cheque for the money

Third, stocks and shares — these can be sold very quickly on the London Stock Exchange

Fourth, Premium Bonds may be cashed in, but give the Post Office a while to work it out!

Fifth, jewels — which can be sold at auctions or to jewel merchants

Last, land, which takes a while to sell because legal processes can take six weeks even if a buyer is found immediately.

At this point I confess that I have never sold jewellery or owned a Premium Bond, so there may be a way of selling them quickly that I don't know of. As far as your own assets are concerned, I hope you have a little cash — that is probably your most liquid asset. The most *illiquid* asset will vary according to your circumstances and your sense of humour. For most people it might be a car or a house; however, many people have a pension entitlement that is definitely an asset but is just not transferable (you can't sell the right to your retirement pension to anyone else at all).

SAQ 4:   All I wanted to show in the very daunting table was the way that people need more cash at Christmas and during the summer holiday season: see if you can find the little jumps in the supply of cash each July and December.

SAQ 5:   During inflation, money is losing its value: a pound today is worth less than a pound ten years ago. So when this happens money is not a very good **store of wealth**. What happens is that people tend to hold their wealth in other forms — such as shares, land and houses, gold, postage stamps, works of art.

SAQ 6:   (a) liquid;   (b) unprofitable;   (c) illiquid;   (d) very profitable.

SAQ 7:   (a)   The multiplier effect.

(b)   It went on until all the initial increase in injections leaked away in withdrawals (or, in the simple investment multiplier, when all the investment leaked away in savings).

(c)   The effect could be measured using this formula:

$$\frac{1}{MPS}$$

in the oversimplified investment multiplier, or more properly:

$$\frac{1}{\text{marginal propensity to withdraw}}$$

if we take into account all leakages.

SAQ 8:   (a) I'll give the working for this example: the credit-creation multiplier will expand the amount of money by $\frac{1}{\text{one quarter}}$, which comes to 4.   (b) 8;   (c) 2;   (d) 5;   (e) 20.

SAQ 9: The PSBR is the combined deficit of the public sector (it is not just the budget deficit but includes the borrowing needs of local councils and nationalised industries). The borrowing requirement, however, usually originates in a budget deficit, which is a consequence of using fiscal policy to expand the level of aggregate demand. The public sector also needs to raise money for long-term projects which are best spread over a number of years.

SAQ 10: £1 600 million — that is, eight times £200 million.

SAQ 11: Firstly, the money supply will go up by £1 billion due to the extra notes and coins circulating with the public: but these are needed for transactions and will not be deposited in a bank so they cannot form the basis of a credit-creation chain. However, the £1 billion borrowed from the banks would be multiplied in the way I've described. So the total increase in money will be £1 billion (cash) plus £8 billion (multiplied bank borrowing) = £9 billion.

SAQ 12: Answered in text.

SAQ 13: Because the financial system is competitive, building societies compete to attract savers. If the government (in their stocks) or the banks (in their deposit accounts) are offering higher interest rates, money will ebb away from the building societies. So they are forced to keep their rate of interest in line.

SAQ 14: (a) true

(b) false: it's quite possible to envisage a society which used credit cards as a generally accepted way to settle debts — indeed, many people believe that the use of computer terminals in shops will bring this in very shortly. Note that it is the actual account which is acceptable, not the piece of plastic.

(c) false. Wealth includes all useful assets, human and non-human: land, quarries, jewels, paintings, shares etc. Strictly speaking money is only the stuff that circulates in exchange for commodities. Note, however, that it is common to use the term 'money' to mean wealth in everyday speech, as for example, 'She's got plenty of money'.

(d) true

(e) false: the reason they are included in *some* definitions of money supply is that they can be used very speedily in settling debts or buying goods.

(f) false again: the money that circulates in the UK is intrinsically worthless paper and base metal.

(g) false: money is worth whatever it can buy, and has fallen in value steeply over the past 40 years. If only the Bank of England could fix the value!

(h) false: see exercise 1.

(i) false. This stopped years ago, and all the note issue is now fiduciary.

(j) false. As long as you accept payment that increases your bank balance, it's money.

(k) false: see text

(l) Read this carefully and you will see that it is false. Banks never lend out more than they have in deposits — if they did, they would pretty soon go out of business. What happens is that, out of the amount that has been deposited, some is loaned and some kept back as a reserve.

(m) false: till money is used to conduct everyday business and so cannot serve as a reserve to fall back on.

(n) false: you could go through the whole credit-creation process described in the early part of this unit without ever using a cheque. Credit creation rests fundamentally on the fact that every time the banks allow a loan, and that money is spent and comes back to them, they are creating a deposit.

(o) true

(p) false: they deal in very short-term borrowing. Even if they held all bills to maturity, it would just come to three months' loan.

(q) false: it's the other way round. The most liquid of all — till-money — earns no profit at all, whereas the least liquid — advances to customers — is the most profitable.

(r) false: it is most valuable on the day it matures

(s) false: not if it is funded by selling government stock to the public and non-bank sector

(t) true: sales to the banking system can be multiplied and add to the amount of money in circulation.

(u)   false: it shows a *one-eighth* ratio — that is, 12½%.

(v)   false: it is a term for government stocks. The slang term for the top industrial shares is 'blue chips'.

(w)   false again: M_3 is larger because it contains deposit accounts.

8 Controversy in the Theory of Money

AIMS OF UNIT 8

When you have completed this unit, you should be able to:
- explain what is meant by the demand for money
- define the term 'liquidity preference' and give three reasons why people might prefer to hold their wealth in liquid form
- state the relationship between rates of interest and the price of securities such as stocks and bonds
- show how the rate of interest is determined by the supply of, and demand for, money
- explain the 'quantity theory' and use it to relate changes in money supply to price changes
- evaluate Keynesian and monetarist views

INTRODUCTION

In Unit 7 I looked at what we mean by the word 'money', showed where money came from and explained how a rise in borrowing by the government or by private individuals could lead to an increase in the amount of money in circulation. In recent years, governments of various political persuasions both in Britain and abroad have taken tough measures to keep the supply of money under control. Why should they worry so much about the amount of money?

In this unit I try to explain how a rise in the amount of money will affect the economy. However, as I expect you're aware, this is a controversial area of economics. In the one hand, an influential group of modern economists says that controlling the supply of money is the most important contribution that a government can make to the stability of the economy. This group, popularly known as **monetarists** have their inspiration in the work of Milton Friedman and his colleagues at the University of Chicago. On the other hand, for the 30 years or so following the publication of Keynes' *General Theory*, British economists tended to downgrade the influence of money. In this unit I explore this 'extreme Keynesian' view and contrast it with the monetarist position.

The topics I discuss may at first sight appear a little dry. However, they are of crucial importance in deciding how to manage an economy, and if you can master the work in this unit you will be well on the way to understanding one of the most active controversies in modern economics. It will also enable you to approach the forthcoming unit on the inflation with greater confidence.

Before going forward, let's briefly review what you learned about money in Unit 7.

SAQ 1:
(a)   What is money?
(b)   Name three components of the British money supply. Which is the most important?
(c)   What is 'near-money'?
(d)   Why do people want money?

THE DEMAND FOR MONEY

You may have been surprised by that last question. The answer seems obvious: people want money in order to buy all sorts of good things — holidays, clothes, drink, a decent house. But looking at the question in this way reveals that people don't actually want *money* at all: they want to get rid of it by spending it on commodities that they *do* want. Money *of itself* is useless, it seems. Unlike shares or property, it yields no income; unlike fine wines or a new car, it can yield no satisfaction. Marooned on a desert island with just a million five-pound notes, we would quickly starve to death.

And yet there is, as you saw in Unit 7, an enormous stock of money in existence in Britain.

SAQ 2: *Look at the figures in SAQ 1, Unit 7, and work out how much money is held per head of the British population; remember, there are about 56.7 million people in Britain.*

Remember that all that money is held by someone — a person, a family, a firm. So perhaps the question 'Why is there a demand for money?' is not so stupid after all: it is merely enquiring why people find it helpful to hold on to money, rather than use it to purchase commodities which give satisfaction.

The answer must be that money is 'liquid'; it can be turned into other forms of wealth without loss or delay. We all need 'liquidity' to some extent, as Keynes appreciated. He called our desire to hold wealth in the form of money rather than in other assets our **liquidity preference**, and outlined three main motives for holding money:

The transactions motive

Firstly, there is the simple need to hold money to finance day-to-day purchases. Households tend to receive their income at fixed intervals — typically a week or a month. They need money to look after the transactions that they carry out between paydays. This **transactions demand** for money depends on a number of factors. If the economy has high prices and a high level of income, more money is needed for daily commerce than in a poorer economy with lower prices. Again, a firm requires more money if it has to wait for a long time between buying raw materials and components, and receiving money from sales.

The precautionary motive

Secondly, money is also held as a precaution; that is to say, in case it is needed for some unforeseen emergency (or bargain). The reason that money is more useful than other forms of wealth (precious stones, shares, land) is that it is immediately accessible. If we held our wealth in the form of, say, shares, we would be inconvenienced if we suddenly needed funds when prices on the Stock Exchange were low. So people want money to keep in their **precautionary balances** — that is, the places where money is kept for a 'rainy day'.

So far I have covered two reasons to hold wealth in the form of money rather than in the form of other assets — for daily transactions, and as a precaution against uncertainty. The demand for money from these two motives depends on many things: how cautious we are, how often incomes are paid, the level of prices, the size of real incomes.

SAQ 3: *Will the demand for money fall or rise in the following circumstances? Briefly explain your answers.*

(a)   Inflation raises prices and incomes
(b)   Changes in employment practices lead to more people getting paid monthly rather than weekly.
(c)   A slump cuts real incomes and throws people out of work.

The speculative motive

The third and last reason for staying liquid rather than buying commodities or assets is speculative — in other words, it might be the best way to make a quick profit. In order to understand this, imagine a rich individual or financial institution (such as a bank or an insurance company) trying to make a profit by buying and selling shares and bonds. The alternative to holding financial assets in the form of shares and bonds is holding cash. What advantage can be gained by choosing to hold cash?

To understand this, we have to go into technicalities a little, and in particular find out the relationship between the price of shares and bonds on the one hand, and the rate of interest on the other.

SAQ 4:   *Before moving into the next section of this unit, look up the following in a dictionary of economics*
(a)   shares
(b)   bonds
(c)   the rate of interest

Right. Let's start by considering a bond which was sold for £100 and pays £5 each year: a 5% return. Now, assume that the rate of interest goes up to 10%. What this means is that new loans being raised are paying £10 per year for each £100 borrowed. Who now will want to buy an asset that pays only £5 per £100? Investors will buy the new bond at 10% and there will be no demand for the 5% bond. Its price will therefore fall — but how far? Well, it will fall to £50.

SAQ 5:   *To understand why the price falls to £50, first work out the rate of interest when the bond that pays only £5 per year falls to £50. Then answer the following questions:*
(a)   Why won't the bond fall any further in price?
(b)   What would cause a rise in bond prices?

So, to recap, when interest rates rise, the price of bonds falls; when interest rates fall, bonds rise in price. You can probably work out for yourself why the bond we started off with, offering £5 on £100, would rise in price to £200 if the rate of interest ever fell to 2½%. The important thing to grasp is that bond prices move the opposite way to interest rates. Profits can be made by holding bonds when interest rates fall: the bonds that were worth £100 yesterday rise in price to, say £110. On the other hand speculators will make losses if they are holding bonds when interest rates rise.

This explains why the speculative demand for money is dependent on the rate of interest. If the rate of interest is high, it's likely that it will fall in the future. This causes a rise in bond prices. So at high interest rates, the demand for money is low. The profit-conscious investor will hold bonds rather than money. But when interest rates are low, investors will expect a rise in interest rates. When interest rates go up, bond prices go down, involving those who hold them in a loss. In these circumstances, people will prefer to 'stay liquid'; the demand for money will be high. The diagram below shows the relationship in graphic form. When interest rates are high (say, 20%) demand for

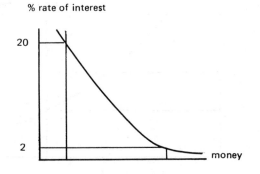

money is low. But when the rate of interest is low, the demand for money is high (as the diagram shows when the rate of interest is as low as 2%).

In fact, at very low interest rates the curve will become a horizontal line. Bond prices can only get cheaper, and the yield on funds invested is so low that there is no real reason for holding bonds and shares, rather than money.

Summary

To summarise the unit so far: when economists investigate the demand for money, they ask why people should want to hold cash rather than some other asset. They follow Keynes in picking out three reasons: a transactions motive, a precautionary motive and a speculative motive. While both the first two are relatively unaffected by the rate of interest (though if interest rates are really high we will be anxious to keep as much of our wealth in interest-bearing assets rather than in cash or current accounts), the speculative demand will be very sensitive to interest rate changes. So the *total demand* for money will be as shown in the diagram below. This adds the transactions, precautionary and speculative demands for money together. The curve $d_{p,t}$ shows the precautionary and transactions demand — not very sensitive to interest rates. But when we add on the speculative

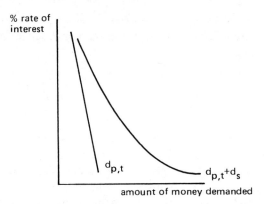

demand to get total demand for money ($d_s + d_{p,t}$) we see that it is heavily dependent upon interest rates. As a further way of understanding this, let's use the important concept of opportunity cost which I introduced in Unit 1.

SAQ 6:

(a)   *What is meant by the term 'opportunity cost'?*
(b)   *What is the opportunity cost of holding your wealth in the form of money rather than in financial assets like shares or bonds?*
(c)   *Is the opportunity cost higher or lower if the rate of interest is high?*

THE SUPPLY OF MONEY

You can read off from the graphs above how much money people want to hold at various rates of interest. But what will that rate of interest *be*? To find out, I must go back over some ground covered in the last unit and include on the diagram the supply of money. The supply of money, you'll recall, is the total amount of money in the economy; and it comes from two sources — either the government or the banks. On the graph below I've indicated the amount of money that exists in the economy as a result of the processes described in the last unit.

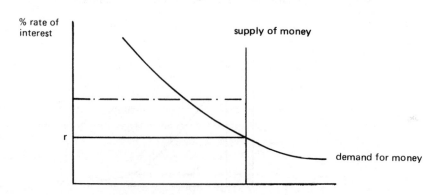

There is only one place where the supply of money and the demand for money are equal — on this diagram, at the rate of interest I have called 'r'. If the interest rate were higher — say the percentage illustrated on the diagram by the dashed line — more money exists than people want for their transactions, precautionary and speculative purposes. As a result, they will transfer their funds into interest-bearing form. If they move into buying shares and bonds, the prices of shares and bonds will rise. The £100 bond, yielding 5%, which I talked of earlier, will go up in price to £110 or £120. Now, a £120 bond paying £5 per year is no longer a 5% investment — it is hardly more than 4%. So the increased demand for such assets will reduce the rate of interest down to the level shown as 'r' in the diagram.

To test your understanding of this difficult concept, look at the reverse position — if the rate of interest were to be less than r.

SAQ 7: *Look at the diagram below, which shows the demand for, and the supply of money; then answer the questions that follow.*

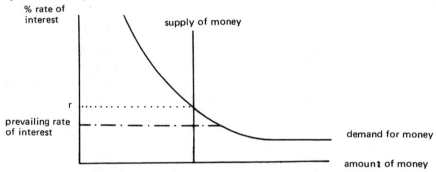

(a)   *In this situation, are people holding all the money they wish to hold?*
(b)   *If people want quickly to raise their money balances (their holdings of cash, or their current accounts), how can they do this?*
(c)   *What will this do to the price of assets such as bonds and shares?*
(d)   *What effect does this have on the rate of interest?*

So the rate of interest is determined by the interaction between the demand for money and the supply of money. The rate of interest ensures that these two forces are kept in balance; if there is an imbalance, caused either by an excess supply or excess demand for money, the rate of interest will change to even things up again.

You can see this mechanism in action by considering what will happen when the supply of money is increased or reduced. On the diagram below, an increase in the supply of money from m to **M**

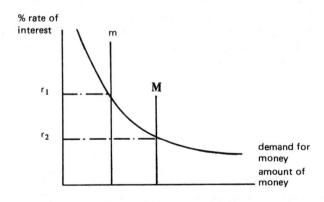

will reduce the rate of interest from r_1 to r_2. Note, though, that the government can choose to have a certain interest rate, *or* a certain money supply — it cannot fix both. It cannot have both m and r_2. A lower rate of interest demands a larger supply of money; likewise, a reduction in the money supply will cause a rise in interest rates.

This is a most important discovery, and it leads on to a most important question for governments. If they cannot control both interest rates and the money supply, which one should they control? The answer to this question will depend on the effects that changes in interest rates or the money supply have on the economy; this is where we step straight into controversy. For while some economists feel that we must control the money supply, whatever that means for interest rates, others are sufficiently concerned by the effects that high interest rates have on industry and and family budgets to aim to keep interest rates low by changing the supply of money.

This difference of opinion originates from differing views on the economy. Economists who believe that the main thing is to control the money supply do so because they believe that attempting to keep interest rates down by increasing the supply of money will lead to ever-increasing inflation. I'll examine this view later in the unit. However, those who wish to see interest rates stabilised are sceptical about explanations of inflation that depend so much on changes on the money supply: they are inclined to worry more about how trade unions push up wage rates, or how international trade spreads inflation around the world. Moreover they are concerned that a policy that involves high interest rates and strict limits on the amount of money will cause damage to industry and employment.

HOW DO INTEREST RATES AFFECT THE ECONOMY?

To get into this question, we must do a little revision. The first diagram below plots the hypothesis that increasing the supply of money drives down the rate of interest. This is accomplished, you will recall, by the buying and selling of securities. An increase in the supply of money increases demand for shares and bonds, causing their price to rise. The higher price reduces the percentage yield of a security.

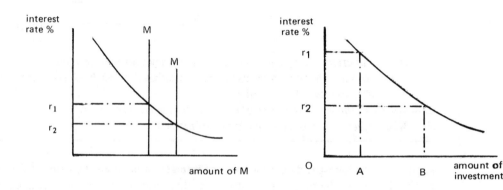

But when the rate of interest falls, investment rises. This is because in any economy there is a range of possible investments, each yielding a different rate of return. If interest rates are high many of these investments are not worth undertaking. A reduction in the interest rate makes a larger number of investments profitable. This is shown on the second diagram.

National Income came into equilibrium where savings equals investments. The diagram below shows two rates of investment. I_1 shows a low rate of investment that is the result of high interest rates. I_2 shows the greater amount of investment brought about by having a lower rate of interest, as shown in the previous diagram.

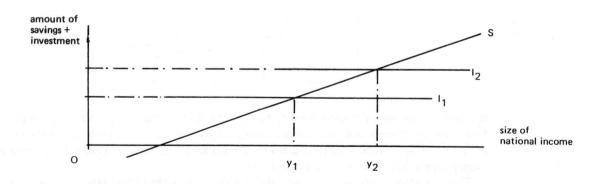

SAQ 8: *Write a short paragraph explaining how an increase in the supply of money will affect employment and the size of the national income. Make sure that you explain how raising the money supply will affect interest rates; how a fall in interest rates will affect the amount invested; and how a rise in investment will affect output and employment.*

Caution on interest rates

Now you've worked your way through this exercise, you may wonder what all the monetary fuss is about. If an increase in the supply of money reduces interest rates, raises investment and output, and cuts unemployment, then let's have more of it! This, indeed, can be seen as a not-too-unfair caricature of British economic policy from the forties to the sixties. Throughout this period, under the influence of the Keynesian thinking you have just worked through, government policy was to keep interest rates low to stimulate investment and employment.

In fact, the policy is open to criticism on a number of grounds. In the first place, interest rates are just one of the factors affecting investment. As I pointed out in Unit 4, business expectations are just as important – probably more so. In a booming business climate, where firms have full order books and are anxious to expand, an extra percentage point or two on the interest rate won't cause them to cancel a new machine or postpone opening a new factory. Large firms, after all, may be able to set the prices of their products a little higher in order to recoup the money needed to pay the higher interest charges. And just as high interest rates may not restrain investment spending in a boom, very low interest rates will not increase investment spending in a slump. Why should a businessman borrow money to expand his firm when he finds it difficult even to sell the output his present workforce and machines are making? Remember, interest rates were low throughout the slump of the 1930s – 2% being normal. Even this rate could not stimulate additional investment.*

There is an additional reason to believe that expanding the supply of money will be ineffective in a slump. I hinted at it on page 134. At very low rates of interest, there is no opportunity cost involved in keeping money in liquid form. As a result, the demand-for-money line is horizontal – the community are prepared to hold any increased money supply in liquid form, rather than buying financial assets and driving the rate of interest down to zero. Why buy financial assets when the return is so low as hardly to compensate you for 'parting with liquidity' (i.e. tying up your wealth in a non-spendable form)? When this situation has been reached, there is said to be a **liquidity trap**.

CRITICISMS OF THE KEYNESIAN VIEW

You learnt earlier that the government could choose to determine interest rates or the supply of money, but not both; and I explained that there were economists who advocated both courses. There are reasons for scepticism about the importance of interest rate controls, as you have just seen. But those who want to concentrate on controlling the amount of money – the monetarists – see this as a relatively minor part of their criticisms. More importantly, they feel

- that increasing the money supply will soon lead to increasing inflation.
- that when inflation occurs, interest rates have to rise to compensate lenders for the loss in value of money, and so
- that any reduction in interest rates which might result from government increasing the supply of money is purely temporary.

Now, in this unit so far I have taken a view which might be described as 'orthodox Keynesian'. I have argued that increases in the money supply affect the rate of interest through the purchase and sale of bonds and shares; that the resulting changes in the rate of interest have their effect in changes in investment and therefore in output and jobs. If the dissenting, 'monetarist', view I have just outlined is true, then a government policy which places much greater emphasis on keeping interest rates low than in controlling the money supply is harmful to the economy.

We now move to look at the **quantity theory of money**. This is a theory that connects the quantity of money (the money supply, that is) to the level of prices in an economy. It has long been known to economists, but has recently become a central idea in economic debate.

---

*which caused Keynes to toy with the idea of negative interest rates (i.e., if you borrow money now you pay back *less* next year!).

THE QUANTITY THEORY OF MONEY: MONEY AND PRICES

The relationship between the amount of money in circulation and the level of prices has interested economists for hundreds of years. What we now know as the **quantity theory** of money was first developed in the seventeenth century. Early economists asked what would happen if the supply of money rose more swiftly than the amount of trade. This was far from being merely an intellectual speculation. Discoveries of gold in the New World had vastly increased the amount of gold coinage in circulation in Europe. These discoveries had been associated with a period of prolonged and marked inflation. So the quantity theory connected two things that experience showed to be intimately linked: the amount of money, and the level of prices. A simple version would go like this: if there are 100 goods to be sold, and the public have 100 gold pieces to buy them, the average price will be one gold piece per article. Double the amount of gold pieces in circulation, the theory goes, and prices will double; goods will now fetch on average two gold pieces each. To put this into a simple equation:

**average prices are equal to the amount of money,
divided by the amount of transactions going on.**

This looks rather cumbersome, so I'll use some shorthand. Using P to stand for the level of prices, M to stand for the amount of money and T for the volume of transactions, the simple quantity theory would be as follows:

$$P = \frac{M}{T}$$

SAQ 9: $P = \frac{M}{T}$ *is an equation that relates the price level to the amount of money and the number of transactions. I'm sure that when at school you learned to manipulate equations like this: see if you can switch the formula around to show what*
(a)   money is equal to
(b)   the number of transactions is equal to
(c)   PT is the total value of sales in the economy. Look at it carefully and see if you can explain why.

Now, there is a deficiency in this simple version of the quantity theory. M = PT must mean that the total amount of money in an economy is equal to the total value of all the transactions — and that just isn't true. In 1979, for example, the expenditure-based figure for GDP was £163 647 million, while sterling M_3 at the year's end was just £55 620 million. One of the characteristics of money is that it can be used again and again — in 1979, it appears that the average unit of money (and remember here we're talking mostly about money in bank accounts, not use of coins each day) turned over about three times.

So we must have some measure of how intensively money is used to make the quantity theory at all workable. After all, a vast increase in the supply of money might lead people to keep bigger cash balances, keep a larger sum in their wallets and handbags — make the money do less work. Likewise, a sharp decline in the money supply will probably encourage people to use money more quickly. Imagine, for example, what would happen if a firm that prints bank notes were to go on strike just before Christmas. Isn't it likely that we would make our cash work harder, digging out any notes we might have put in piggy-banks, and using cheques wherever possible? We must have some measure of how quickly money is used to make any sense of the quantity theory: money not spent will have no effect on prices, but spending a limited money supply faster than normal will put pressure on prices.

This measure is to be found in the idea of the **velocity** of money, sometimes called the **velocity of circulation**. There are various measures of this, but the one I shall use is the *income* velocity of circulation — that is to say, the national income divided by the amount of money.

SAQ 10: *Using the figures mentioned in the text above — GDP of £163 647 million and sterling M_3 of £55 620 million — work out the income velocity of circulation in 1979.*

Now we have a measure of how quickly money is used, we can tighten up the quantity theory considerably. This is what Irving Fisher, a celebrated American economist, did earlier this century. His quantity theory went as follows:

$$P = \frac{MV}{T}$$

To put this in words, which is the way some people prefer it, the level of prices is equal to the amount of money times the velocity of money (V) divided by the volume of transactions that went on. The conclusion from this is that a rise in prices may be caused by one of three things:

- an increase in the supply of money
- an increase in the velocity of circulation
- a decline in the volume of transactions

If the quantity theory is correct, we now have a very powerful equation – one that can be used to predict the level of inflation. To take an example, if we know that the velocity is 2 the money is 50 and the volume of transaction is 10, then we come to

$$P = \frac{50 \times 2}{10} = \frac{100}{10} = 10$$

So, with information about money supply and transactions, we can predict the level of prices.

SAQ 11: *Now try your hand with these figures. I have chosen imaginary examples in order to keep the maths at a fairly simple level. In each row, one figure is missing; fill it in using Fisher's quantity theory.*

	M	V	P	T
(a)		4	10	10
(b)	20		10	10
(c)	100	8	10	
(d)	10	10		20
(e)		6	12	50
(f)	8000		240	100
(g)	100	7		350
(h)	40	5	20	

SAQ 12: *Now attempt these questions, which aim to drill you in your understanding of the quantity theory.*

(a)   *Starting from* $P = \frac{MV}{T}$, *find the equations for M, V and T. What does MV equal?*

(b)   *What three things could result from a rise in M?*

(c)   *What would happen to P if V fell? If there is a fall in the value of V, what, in plain English, are households and firms doing?*

(d)   *Use the quantity theory to find out the three things that could cause a rise in P. For a rise in P to be caused by a rise in M, what must we assume about V and T?*

Now that you have worked through some exercises on the quantity theory, you will probably have formed your own view on its strong and weak points. One of its more attractive arguments is the idea that a rise in the money supply will be spent. Remember, the Keynesian orthodoxy says that when individuals and institutions find themselves with excess money balances, they will buy financial assets; but why should they not buy other things? In the quantity theory, excess money balances spill out onto the market for goods and services, and are not confined to the markets for financial assets like bonds. Similarly, an attempt to recharge depleted money balances might be accomplished, not by selling financial assets (as in SAQ 7(b)) but by reductions in spending.

The problem of velocity

The drawback of the theory is that in taking account of changes in the velocity of circulation it has lost much of its usefulness. This may seem a strange charge to make: how can adding a more realistic component to a theory reduce its power? To answer this, I will have to take you on a brief excursion into the philosophy of science.

What makes a theory scientific is the ease with which we can test whether or not it is true. A theory that says that two elements combine in given proportions to make a certain compound can be tried out in a laboratory to see whether what happens is in line with the predictions of the theory. Often, the best way of finding out how true a theory is, is to make predictions from it: Mendelayev's work on the periodic table of elements, for example, predicted the discovery of elements unknown at the time of his work. Similarly, Einstein's work on relativity was impressively supported by astronomical observations that occurred just as predicted. The defining characteristic of a scientific theory is that it is capable of being disproved. As it stands, the quantity theory cannot make predictions, and cannot be disproved.

I'll take an example to explain this curious fact. The quantity theory appears to say that a rise in the supply of money will raise prices. However, this is only true if the velocity of circulation doesn't change. If the velocity drops when the money supply rises, there will be no effect on prices at all; indeed, a big enough drop could cause prices to fall as a result of an increase in the money supply. Do this example to see what I mean

SAQ 13: *Use the quantity theory to find the value of P if M = 20, V = 3 and T = 12. If M rises to 40, what will happen to P (a) if V remains unchanged (b) if V drops to 1.5 (c) if V drops to 1?*

Is velocity stable?

So without some specification of how V behaves, the theory cannot say whether a rise in the quantity of money will cause prices to rise, fall, or stay just as they are. It's as if Newton's physics said that an apple that detached itself from a tree could go down, but on the other hand it could go upwards, or alternatively it could stay where it was in mid-air. Of course, monetary theory is not this vacuous in reality; considerable research has been done on the velocity of circulation, and monetarists believe that this research shows velocity to be predictable. Certainly, it is rather unstable from month to month, but over a longer period of time a stable picture emerges. Let's see if we can throw some light on this by looking at some statistics from the 1970s — a period of considerable turbulence in British monetary affairs.

SAQ 14: *This information is taken from the Annual Abstract of Statistics, and shows National Income and Money supply (M₃) from 1969 to 1976*

	Money supply (£ million)	National income (£ million)
1969	16 596	39 885
1970	18 175	43 809
1971	20 541	49 298
1972	26 245	55 259
1973	33 430	64 321
1974	37 633	73 977
1975	40 573	93 078
1976	45 125	108 080

(a) *For each year, divide money supply into national income to get the income velocity of circulation.*

(b) *Plot the income velocity that you have found on the graph below.*

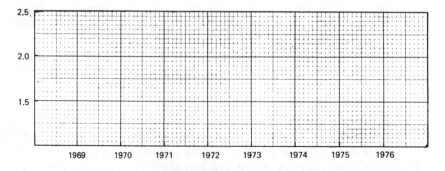

This example shows a reasonably stable velocity of circulation until 1972 and 1973. In these years there was a very considerable increase in the supply of money, and as a result the velocity dropped — from the 2.4 of the earlier years way down to 1.9. This can be seen as a period when people and institutions had larger money balances than they wanted, with the result that they needed to make their money work less hard. However, excess money balances (as we all know to our cost) tend to get spent. When this has happened, the velocity figure returned to the earlier average value.

This experience illustrates monetarist ideas about velocity. They believe that velocity will be reasonably stable in the long run — say, over a four or five year period — but that it can be disturbed temporarily. If, for example, the money supply rises much faster than normally for a while, velocity will fall. However, after a lag (the lag which showed up in SAQ 14 and to which I'll return) during which excess money balances are run down, velocity returns to normal. However, you must remember that the money supply which is now circulating at the same velocity as before is larger than the earlier money supply.

SAQ 15: *Suppose that M rises very sharply one year, but that for 18 months or two years after this rise, V falls to compensate. What will happen to prices (a) in that first 18 months or so and (b) after the two years?*

Money and output

So I have disposed of one objection to the quantity theory — that it is meaningless because changes in velocity could completely cancel out any effect of any change in money supply. Most economists would nowadays agree that it is possible to predict the behaviour of V with some accuracy, although they would probably prefer to talk of a 'stable demand for money function'. But we are still left with one more variable to look at — T. T stands for the real transactions in an economy — the goods and services that are bought and sold. Isn't it possible, you may ask, that a rise in M might stimulate output so that rather than raising P it caused an increase in T? Suppose the economy is in a state of slump: resources are underused and unemployment is high. An increase in money supply, caused by higher state spending or an increase in bank lending, would increase aggregate demand. Firms would take on extra workers and put into use idle factories and machinery. The rise in M therefore leads to more T, not higher P.

SAQ 16: *Go back to the figures in exercise 13, where M = 20, V = 3 and T = 12. What was the value of P that you worked out there? Suppose that M rises to 30, but the resulting increase in aggregate demand raises T to 18. What happens to P?*

We have come across another source of dispute here between monetarists and Keynesians. Monetarists would deny that increases in the money supply will do anything to raise output except in the short term. Going back to our previous point about velocity and lags, they argue that the increase in money supply will feed through into prices in the end, and when that happens any temporary increase in employment and output will be choked off by higher wages and costs. But rather than continue to present what monetarists believe in passing comments, I think it's time to move into a new section completely devoted to the views, and the critics of:

THE NEW MONETARISM

The story so far

Keynesians have tended to approach money as just one way among many of holding wealth; traditional Keynesian theory asserts that money affects the economy most powerfully through its effect on interest rates. Over the past 15 years or so, though, there has been a determined academic counter-attack by a group of economists who believe that money is an important, and direct, influence on the economy. In America, Milton Friedman has led a group of economists (many educated at the University of Chicago) who have brought the quantity theory back into respectability. In Britain, their work has been taken up by academic economists (major bastions at present include the University of Liverpool and the London Business School), by controversialists like the

Institute of Economic Affairs, and by politicians such as Sir Keith Joseph.

(In passing, there is no necessary connection between monetarism and right-wing politics; monetary economics must remain scientific investigation based upon hard evidence about the behaviour of the supply of money, the national income etc. Precisely why most monetarists are right-wing remains an interesting topic for discussion. I have my own theories, but must record the rebuke of a great friend who informs me that the central banks of the Communist countries retain a firm control of the money supply that would gain the approval of Ronald Reagan or Enoch Powell.)

What monetarists believe

Monetarists' views have rather greater complexity than is generally admitted. In order to grasp them fully, you must be clear in your mind about the difference between 'real' things, and 'money' things. Let's take the national income as an example. The real national income consists of all the goods and services produced in a given economy in a given period of time. The money national income is the money value of all those goods and services — and so the money national income could go up (due to inflation) whilst the real national income stayed the same, or even fell.

SAQ 17: *Explain the difference between money wages and real wages. How could it be possible for a worker to have a rise in real wages even though her money wages fell?*

Fine. Now that we've got that out of the way, we can look at the two central planks of monetarist belief:

- They believe that in determining things measured in money, such as prices, the money national income, and money wages, the determining factor is the amount of money. To put it baldly, an increase in the quantity of money will lead to an increase in the money national income. What is more, money works directly to alter prices and wages, not through the Keynesian mechanism of interest rates. An expansion of the money supply through rising bank credit encourages weak business management, with firms giving in more easily to inflationary wage demands. On the other hand, restrictions on credit encourage 'realistic' wage settlements, curbing inflation and making firms more competitive in both home and foreign markets.
- But though the quantity of money will affect 'money things', it will not affect real things, like the real national income, real wages, the rate of unemployment. The level of the real national income is decided by the things we looked at in Unit 2 — the quality and amount of the land, labour and capital available, and the skill with which they are combined. Real wages will depend on the productivity of the workforce — how many commodities they can produce each week. Most controversially, monetarists believe that the rate of unemployment is not determined by the level of aggregate demand (as you learned in Unit 5), but by structural factors — how skilled the labour force is, how easy it is to find out about and move to vacancies, what barriers trade unions erect to interfere with the labour market and so on. Once you have taken account of all these forces, there will be a 'natural rate of unemployment' that cannot be reduced by fiscal or monetary expansion (except briefly at the cost of added inflation).

Now, Keynesians have always stressed the importance of adjusting the level of aggregate demand to ensure high levels of employment and income. Monetarists, convinced that these policies are inflationary and counter-productive, reject the demand-side policies of the Keynesians with an emphasis on the 'supply-side'. By making workers more mobile and motivated, the firms more dynamic, commodities will be produced efficiently, on time and at the right price.

The main policy advice that comes out of monetarism is, therefore, 'don't tinker with the money supply'. What must be assured is a small increase in money supply each year — just enough to provide finance for the additional output of the economy. Keeping the increase in the supply of money at a steady 2% or 3% per year is known as the **fixed throttle** approach. Any other policy will be, to use Friedman's analogy, throwing a spanner in the works. Too fast a rise in the supply of money will cause inflation, and a sharp reduction will cause a slump.

The backing for monetarism

It is important to remember that the policy recommendations of monetarism are not the strange beliefs of some modern cult-religion. They are statements arising out of social scientific enquiry, and so they should be tested to see if they explain the world. How do these statements stand up to the scrutiny of researchers?

The central proposition of monetarism is that the money supply determines the level of the money national income some period later (after the famous lag); so researchers have usually investigated how money supply has correlated with national income in the past. In the United States, some very impressive results have come out of these investigations. Friedman has almost rewritten American monetary history. Perhaps the most celebrated finding was that of himself and Anna Schwartz — that the Great Depression of the 1930s can be explained, in monetarist style, by a severe contraction in the quantity of money at the beginning of the decade caused by the collapse of large numbers of small banks.

In Britain, the evidence has not been as impressive. However, the monetarist explanation has gained ground, probably because of the greater explanatory value of monetarism in a world where inflation and unemployment are both rising. By the late 1970s, even a Labour Prime Minister (James Callaghan) was warning his party conference that it was no longer possible for a government to spend its way out of a recession. He was soon replaced by the Conservative administration of Margaret Thatcher, a government for whom control of the money supply and a rejection of Keynesian budgetary policies were central beliefs. By 1981, the Chancellor of the Exchequer, Sir Geoffrey Howe, was actually raising taxation in order to achieve his monetary targets, despite the evidence of 2½ million unemployed that would have led a Keynesian to a 'giveaway' budget policy.

What's wrong with monetarism?

The battle against the ideas of the new monetarists has been joined by a number of economists. They make two sorts of objection. On the one hand, there are academic objections which pick at the logic or evidence of monetarism; and on the other hand, there are critics who acknowledge the logic of monetary control but shudder at its costs. It is difficult to be fair to both sides while presenting views with the vigour they deserve, but here goes:

What do monetarists mean by money?

As you found out in the previous study unit, money is defined as whatever is acceptable in exchange for goods and services. Following this definition, I led you through a long discussion concerned to find out what this actually might include in today's world. You can pick a very tight definition or a very loose one that might include a wide range of near-money, including such things as building-society accounts, credit cards, and national savings deposits. Which one are the monetarists worried about? This isn't a small point — there have been a number of recent years when M_1 and M_3 have behaved very differently. Should we be worried after a year in which M_1 has risen gently but M_3 has risen fast?

In answer to this query, monetarists generally emphasise that they have a very strict definition of money. They reject the broad Keynesian sweep represented by the Radcliffe Committee, which concerned itself with the general level of liquidity in the economy. Monetarists see a very sharp division between what is money, and what isn't. They would choose M_1 as the indicator to watch; indeed, some would be even tighter than this and concentrate on coins, notes and deposits of the commercial banks at the central bank (what is known as **high-powered money**).

Is the statistical evidence for monetarism convincing?

I have just said monetarism is based on the idea that money national income is determined by the money supply a period previously; I also noted that this appears to have been supported by at least some research evidence. The money national income does appear to go up 18 months to two years after a rise in the money supply. Doesn't this show that monetarism is right?

Many people have their doubts. You can prove anything with statistics, or, in the more thorny prose of Professor Cramp (see readings at end) 'there is no difficulty in adducing support from statistical data for any mildly plausible theory'. . .'Strong relationships have been shown to exist between the number of storks in Lapland and the Swedish birth rate, or . . . the incidence of dysentry in Scotland and the British inflation rate. One has to rely on theory to reject even these absurdities. However, even when there is some genuine relationship between the variables there are still problems. For example, purchases of wedding rings precede marriages, but it would be foolish to conclude that the act of purchasing a wedding ring causes a wedding. Yet this is the sort of deduction that has been made by monetarists.' (Gowland, *Modern Economic Analysis 1*)

The wedding ring example is useful, for there, event B (buying the ring) and event C (the wedding) are caused by unnoticed event A (the forming of a caring relationship between a man and a woman). We could be seeing an analogous process with the money supply and the national income. Some economic event could cause both the rising money supply and rising money national income. For example, were the government to run a budget deficit, or ease credit restrictions, or were there to be a balance of payments surplus leading to an inflow of money: in each of these cases money supply might rise, and the subsequent rise in national income occur. Yet in each case the change in national income can be explained by orthodox Keynesian theory.

SAQ 18: *Explain how a rise in money supply causes an increase in money national income by (a) monetarist and (b) Keynesian theories. Would it be possible to look at economic statistics of the period and distinguish which explanation was true? (Clue: what would happen to investment under Keynesian and monetarist ideas?)*

What is the evidence for a stable velocity of circulation?
When the monetarist revival first occurred, the obvious line of attack upon it was to stress the velocity problem (see p. 139-141 of this unit). The quantity theory, it was pointed out, was meaningless because V could vary infinitely, robbing the theory of any predictive value. Few economists would now take this ultra-Keynesian line: the existence of a stable demand for money is regarded by most as firmly established.

But a second objection then occurs. The stable velocity that appears in monetarist literature has referred to years in which the governments have not been monetarists and have been prepared to allow the creation of enough money to buy the money national income: in these cases the velocity has had no need to vary. But if the government curbed the money supply too sharply that it affected industry and the banks severely, velocity might be much more unpredictable.

SAQ 19: *This is an extract from an article by Malcolm Crawford of the* Sunday Times. *Read through it and answer the questions at the end.*

> For the UK at least (velocity) has proved fairly unstable in the short run — which casts some doubt on the usefulness of the money supply in predicting expenditure. For example, the velocity fell 9% in 1973. Had the 1972 velocity been maintained the increase in the money supply in 1973 would have been accompanied by a growth in total expenditure of 27%. Even with output up 6% that would have meant prices rising by over 20%. Fortunately they did not rise by anywhere near that much. The velocity does seem to have a fair amount of 'give' in it when the supply of money grows abnormally fast or slowly.

(a)   Is there anything a monetarist would find to disagree with in the article?
(b)   Is there anything a monetarist might wish to add to the conclusions in the article?

Does any increase in the money supply have the same effect, however it occurs?
Monetarist literature appears to say that any given increase in the money supply will have the same effect on prices — no matter what it is spent on or who receives it. This seems unlikely when we consider that a rise in the money supply could be the result of
  • government increasing borrowing to pay higher wages to its employees
  • increased sales of exports, or foreign money flooding into London
  • government and banks making money available to modernise industry
and it could end up in the hands of
  • consumers
  • industrialists
  • the banks.

An analysis of the effects of an increase in the money supply must surely take into account how that money will be used.

Will the pains of monetary restraint be too severe?

Monetarists say, you will remember, that a sharp rise in the money supply will in the short run raise output and reduce interest rates, but in the longer term will simply raise prices without any addition to real national income. They follow that logic the other way, too: monetary restraint (that is, increasing the money supply less than the rate of inflation) will, they argue, lead to unpleasant short-term consequences (falling output, rising unemployment), but after the lag, prices will stabilise. In the new stable and predictable economic climate, business will recover.

This is an attractive idea, in line with the British belief that if the medicine is unpleasant, it must be doing you good. Non-monetarists, however, express the gravest doubts about the economics of the 'short sharp shock'. Ervin Miller's article (quoted in the readings at the end of this article) draws attention to the costs of monetary restraint; and Lord Lever, a respected financial adviser to several Labour governments, believes that the impact of monetary restraint is on jobs and output, not on prices. This certainly seemed to be the consequence of the 'Thatcher experiment'.

SAQ 20: *Suppose for a moment that the monetary explanation of inflation is wrong, and that rising prices are in fact caused by trade unions and monopolistic firms pushing up wages and prices. Use Fisher's theory to work out what would happen under these circumstances if government kept a tight hold on the amount of M. (Clue: what will happen to T if M and V are kept stable while P goes up?)*

SAQ 21: *Over the past few pages I have outlined a number of criticisms of monetarism. Among them has been the view that*

(a)   Monetarism is impractical because changes in V will render monetary control ineffective.

(b)   Monetarism is undesirable because its costs in lost output and jobs are greater than any benefit to be gained from lower inflation.

Are these views compatible?

What if we already have high inflation?

The monetarist rule is that the amount of money in the economy should be increased in line with the rise in the ability of the economy to produce commodities — that is, 2% or 3% per year. If there is no inflation, this makes a lot of sense. But what should our policy be if prices are rising at a rate of 10% or 15% per year?

Let's look at this problem through monetarist eyes. To raise the money supply by an amount equal to or bigger than the amount of inflation would enable the inflation to continue indefinitely — it would build the inflation into the system forever. So that's out. On the other hand, sticking to the 'fixed throttle', raising the money supply by 2% or 3% only, would be to invite disaster. In the short term, velocity might rise to keep the economy ticking over, but after a lag output and employment would contract sharply. So the best policy would be what is called 'winding down' — that is, reducing the money supply just a little each year. So the government would set money supply targets — say, 12% to 14% in year 1, 10% to 12% in year 2, 8% to 10% in year 3 and so on. By the time the 'proper' rate of increase in the money supply is reached, inflation will have also wound down, and employers, unions and consumers will have got used to life at zero inflation.

Let's be clear, though: throughout this winding down, there will not be a big enough money supply to buy up full employment output (as a Keynesian might see it), and people and institutions will be attempting to rebuild their money balances by cutting costs and spending (as a monetarist might see it). This means above-normal unemployment and below-normal growth throughout the time.

MONETARY POLICY

Let's review where we have got to before looking at monetary policy. If a government cannot finance its borrowing by sales of gilts to the non-bank sector, it may release funds into the banking system that are then multiplied by the operation of the credit-creation multiplier: I covered this ground in Unit 7. If the money supply grows too fast, it can worsen inflation; this is the prediction of the quantity theory of money (in Unit 8). Inflation needs to be avoided for the reasons outlined at the beginning of this unit. That's why governments nowadays set monetary targets each year, targets that show the amount of increase in the money supply that will be permitted. The next section of this unit describes the action they can take to bring money supply under control — the weapons of **monetary policy**.

SAQ 22: *Monetary policy is the part of economic policy that regulates the amount of money in the economy. Name two other policies that might be used against inflation (Clue: what would be best for dealing with demand-pull inflation? With cost push inflation?)*

Control through PSBR

The most obvious way of controlling the supply of money would be to keep the size of the PSBR down. If the government were to reduce its spending or raise taxes, then the amount that would have to be borrowed (and maybe financed through the banking system) would be reduced. Indeed, both Labour (1976) and Conservative (1979) governments have reduced the PSBR for monetary reasons. This is a relative innovation: until the mid-1970s, governments took political decisions about the desired level of public spending, and then chose the levels of taxation and borrowing that would give it the income it needed. The PSBR reflected the Keynesian 'budget judgement' rather than any worry about monetary expansion.

Remember, though, that a high PSBR does not automatically contribute to monetary growth: provided that it is funded completely through the non-bank sector, it will not increase the amount of money at all.

SAQ 23: *How might the government ensure that it is able to sell all the gilt-edged stocks it wishes to the non-bank sector?*

Control through interest rates

The most obvious way to make sure that gilts can be sold is to give them an attractive rate of interest. This will attract investors, and may even draw in funds from abroad, to fund the government deficit. But higher interest rates have a further effect: in making people less willing to borrow and more willing to save, it will reduce bank lending to the private sector by cutting the demand for loans. It is important to note here what I pointed out earlier – that the government can either choose its interest rate target or its monetary target. Once it decides to stick within a given money supply, then it must raise interest rates to whatever level is required to sell the appropriate amount of gilts and choke off the required amount of bank lending.

SAQ 24: *High interest rates will be successful in reducing the money supply, then. But what disadvantages might such interest rates bring*
(a)   to industry?
(b)   to the average family?

Acting on the banking system's reserves   So governments can reduce monetary expansion by restraining their own spending or by raising interest rates. Either of these policies will prevent the banks from starting the credit-creation process that was described in Unit 7. But even if the banks do get their hands on some new deposits, the government can still act to reduce their power to expand credit. Remember the importance of the banks' reserves of cash and easily-cashed assets? They were the foundation upon which the credit-creation process was built: if the government were able to draw some of these liquid reserves from the banks, then they would be forced to reduce their lending by a multiple of the amount withdrawn. If you can't remember how this works, check back over Unit 7, particularly pp. 119-21.

The government can reduce the liquid holdings of the banks in three main ways:

(a)   *Open-market operations*   The first way is to use the market in government securities – gilts and Treasury Bills. If the government were to wish to reduce the supply of money then it could enter the market as a seller of government stock. If the public (and this includes the insurance companies and pension funds as well as individuals) buy the gilts, then they write cheques in favour of the government, drawn upon their accounts at the banks. When the banks have to pay the cheques, they find that their liquid funds are reduced. As a result, they will be forced to reduce the loans that they have extended.

SAQ 25:   *Explain how the government might expand the money supply by the use of open-market operations. Start with them entering the open market for government securities as a buyer.*

(b)   *Special Deposits* The second way of reducing the liquid reserves of banks is startlingly direct: the Bank of England can force banks to deposit a given amount with them in a blocked account that cannot be counted as part of liquid reserves. Following such a directive, the banks find themselves short of cash, and have to restrain their lending as outlined before.

(c)   *Funding* If the government were to alter the type of security it sold to the public and banks so that it sold more long-term gilts and fewer short-term securities, then it would be indulging in what is known as **funding**. The effect is to reduce the number of assets that financial institutions can regard as liquid, and once again has a restraining effect on the money supply.

Direct controls   If the government finds that, after trimming the PSBR and acting on the bank's reserves, it still needs further ways to reduce monetary expansion, then it might use direct controls. These have taken many forms. In the 1950s and 1960s, banks were instructed not to increase their lending by more than a certain percentage from one year to the next: alternatively, they were requested to ensure that lending was directed towards favoured customers (like exporters, manufacturers or farmers) and away from loans for consumers or property deals. A more recent form of direct control was the **corset** – a Bank of England measure that automatically drew in extra Special Deposits from banks that exceeded a modest rate of growth of deposits. Such direct controls fell out of favour (the corset was abolished in 1980) because they were so easy to avoid.

Is it possible to control the money supply?

From your reading of Unit 7, the control of money supply must have seemed simplicity itself: through control of the PSBR, and sales of debt to the non-bank sector, the government is able to limit the amount of money. In practice, however, monetary control can be very tricky for two reasons:

- firstly, when the government tightens up on the money supply and bank lending, firms find it difficult to sell their goods and need to increase their own overdrafts to get by – which tends to drive up the money supply.
- secondly, government restrictions on the lending of the major banks will not cut borrowing – they will encourage borrowers to go elsewhere for their loans. In the 1970s a number of unreliable small banks (**secondary banks**) grew up for this reason. More recently, Bank of England attempts to reduce bank deposits led to a lively market in loans between large companies that cut out the banks altogether.

These problems are a consequence of the complexity of the financial system. Any attempt to restrict it at one point may simply shift the activity to another point. This is why economists have compared monetary policy to squeezing a balloon – push it in in one place and it will bulge out elsewhere.

Nor must the government risk 'popping the balloon'. It has no wish to put intolerable strains on the financial system. A strict and severe monetary squeeze, sucking money out of the system, might cause the failure of some major financial institution. The consequences of the collapse of, say, a major bank would be incalculable: just such an event precipitated the European financial collapse of 1929. So when the financial system is under pressure, the Bank of England moves in to support it. In the mid-1970s, for example, it led a considerable rescue operation aimed at saving the secondary banks that had been hit so hard by the collapse of the property boom. Such a policy is forced upon any responsible government, but it does place the financial authorities in a considerable quandary. When, as happened recently, the Bank of England effectively lends money to banks that are caught short of cash by a strict monetary policy, you might well wonder what the point of it all is.

SAQ 26: *Control of the money supply is also made more difficult because the drop in sales, output and employment caused by a tight monetary policy will raise the PSBR.*
(a)   Why does the PSBR rise in a slump?
(b)   What effect will this have on the money supply?

There is an Appendix on the attempt by Sir John Hicks and Alvin Hansen to reconcile monetary and Keynesian ideas about how the economy works on pages 443-4. I've kept it separate because it doesn't fit easily into the flow of the unit, but it still represents an important chunk of work and you would do well to go through it and try to grasp the idea it contains.

REVIEW SECTION

Further reading

Many of the references given in the previous unit are equally good for this one. Lively accounts of the arguments among economists are to be found in *The Guardian Guide to the Economy* by Frances Cairncross and Phil Keeley and in *A Question of Economics* by Peter Donaldson. 'The bumpy path of monetarism' (*Economist*, 14th November 1982) gives an insight into the practical application of theory to the real world. See also *Economics* Spring 1982.

The Institute of Economic Affairs was a leading force in introducing the British public to the monetarist revival in the USA. They have published a number of pamphlets arguing the monetarist corner — see if your library has got *Monetary Correction* by Milton Friedman (IEA Occasional Paper 41) or *Too Much Money* by Wood and Gordon (IEA Hobart Paper 68). Two sources that are also more suited to the confident student are David Gowland's *Modern Economic Analysis* (especially Chapter 5) and Keith Hartley's *Problems of Economic Policy* (p. 63 on).

See the Economics Briefs mentioned in the previous Unit. The article 'The Money Supply and the PSBR' in the *Economic Review*, May 1987, looks at the interdependence of monetary and fiscal policy, and *Lloyds Bank Review,* October 1987, has a useful article by Christopher Dow entitled 'A Critique of Monetary Policy'.

Examination questions

There are a large number of questions for which you will find an understanding of monetary theory useful — but a good number will have to wait until I've dealt with monetary policy and inflation in forthcoming units. As far as essay topics specifically on this unit are concerned, they break down into the detailed ones such as

1. Distinguish the methods by which the Bank of England may seek to control the money supply.
    (Associated Examining Board June 1980)

2. Explain briefly what is meant by the money supply. Why might a government seek to control the rate of growth of the money supply?
    (AEB 'A' level June 1987)

or questions that take a broader look at the significance of the monetarist views, like

3. How likely is it that a 10% increase in the money supply will lead to a 10% increase in prices?

This question — popular with examiners — gives you the chance to reveal your understanding of the quantity theory; mention the velocity problem, but show that you have been told about recent monetarist work here. Remember to open your essay by clearing the ground with a definition of the money supply. I think that the wording of the question invites you to give alternative views of the effects of a rise in money supply — such as the Keynesian one (i.e. money supply rises — interest rates fall — investment rises — NI rises, causing inflation *only* if excess demand is present, as shown on the Phillips curve).

ANSWERS TO SAQs

SAQ 1: (a) Money is whatever is generally acceptable in payment for goods and services and in settlement of debt

   (b) Coins, notes and bank accounts — by far the largest component of which is money in bank accounts

   (c) Close substitutes for money, such as Treasury Bills, National Savings accounts, building society accounts, credit card facilities etc.

   (d) See following discussion in the text

SAQ 2: I make it about £1 037.09 for each man, woman and child (!)

SAQ 3: (a) If inflation raises prices and incomes we will need more money — not just for the transactions motive (remember when £1 was enough for a good evening out?) but also for precautionary motives. When prices are high, we need more money to repair the roof leak or replace the car's silencer.

(b) In practice, it requires a larger supply of money: to meet his paybill, the employer will need four times as much money (though less often). Another way to look at it is to consider the wage earner who is paid, say, £100 per week and spends it all. If paid weekly, his average holding of money is £50 — £100 on payday, nothing six days later. If his firm switches to pay him monthly, his average money needs will be £200-£400 on the 1st of the month, zero on the last day of the month.

(c) A smaller amount will be needed — incomes are lower and fewer transactions need to be financed. In summary, the day-to-day demand for money depends on the level of prices, the level of activity of the economy, and the institutional arrangements for payment.

SAQ 4: I'll let you rely on your dictionary here. The thing I would like you to notice is that although economists talk about 'the rate of interest', there are in reality many rates of interest. If lending is very short term (such as the overnight loans of the London money markets), the rate of interest can be very low. Longer term loans earn higher rates of interest — indeed, many building societies have a range of rates of interest that relate to different length loans. There is also a difference of interest rates according to the safety of the loan: whereas lending to the government is pretty safe, lending to a troubled company isn't and you may expect an extra payment to be made to you to cover the risk that you are taking in lending to a 'dodgy' customer. Inflation can complicate matters too. When prices are rising at 10%, an interest rate of 10% is not very attractive — all it does is maintain the value of your money without giving you any payment for lending it to someone: the 'real' rate of interest (using the term real to mean what it can buy in actual commodities) is zero. In fact, the real rate of interest has sometimes been negative in recent years, as interest rates have failed to keep up with inflation.

SAQ 5: The yield is 10% (if you bought two at £50, you would spend £100 and get £10 for it. At the price of £50, the yield on this bond is the same as the £100 bond that offered 10%.)

(a) Because it is now just as attractive as the £100 bond that pays £10. If it fell in price to £49 it would be a better buy than the £100 bond and investors would buy it until the price went back up to £50.

(c) A fall in interest rates. A fall to 2½% would double the price of a 5% investment. So when interest rates change there are profits and losses to be made by buying and selling bonds. Now can you see why rumours of changes in interest rates result in activity in the market for gilt-edged stock?

SAQ 6: (a) Opportunity cost is cost measured in terms of what you have given up to obtain the commodity you chose.

(b) The opportunity cost of holding your wealth in the form of money is the rate of interest or profits you could have earned by investing it in shares and bonds.

(c) The opportunity cost is higher as the rate of interest rises, since you are giving up more earnings by staying liquid. Note also that the opportunity cost will be affected by inflation: staying liquid during a fast inflation is an expensive business.

SAQ 7: (a) No — the demand for money exceeds the supply of it

(b) By selling financial assets such as shares and bonds. (If you said that people would replenish their money balances by spending less on commodities, hold on for a few pages — you may be monetarist!)

(c) This will drive down the price of stocks and bonds.

(d) This will drive up interest rates.

SAQ 8: I hope your paragraph will be something like this:

"An increase in the money supply will release money into the economy that will be surplus to the requirements of firms and individuals; they will use the money to buy financial assets. The higher price of stocks and bonds caused will result in lower interest rates, making a number of previously unprofitable projects worthwhile. The new investment — extra machines, factories and so on — will raise employment through the economy via the multiplier effect as well as the initial effect of the orders. So a rise in money supply will raise income and employment via the effect on interest rates."

SAQ 9: (a) M = PT (I multiplied through by T)

(b) $T = \dfrac{M}{P}$

(c)   PT is the total value of sales because it is the number of transactions times the average price of those transactions. If an economy, for example, produced only 500 tons of wheat at £10 per ton, total output would be valued at 500 x £10 (T x P) = £5000.

SAQ 10:   I make it 2.94 — by dividing M into GDP.

SAQ 11:   These are my answers — use the example in the text as a work-through if you have problems. (a) M = 25   (b) V = 5   (c) T = 80   (d) P = 5   (e) M = 100   (f) V = 3   (g) P = 2   (h) T = 10. You can make the calculation easier by converting the quantity theory equation into MV = PT and then working out what P, T, V and M equal (see next SAQ).

SAQ 12:   (a) $M = \dfrac{PT}{V}$; $V = \dfrac{PT}{M}$; $T = \dfrac{MV}{P}$;   MV = PT

(b)   a rise in P or a rise in T or a fall in V (or a combination of the three)

(c)   P would fall. A reduction in V shows firms and households using money less intensively, preferring to hold larger money balances for a given level of income or prices.

(d)   P could rise due to a rise in M, a rise in V or a fall in T. For a rise in P to be caused by a rise in M, V must not fall, and T must not rise by the same rate as M rose.

SAQ 13:   (a)   P starts out at 5 (MV is 60, divided by T) If M rises to 40 and V remains unchanged, prices will double — work it out yourself.

(b)   If V drops to 1.5, though, prices stay the same (again, 60 divided by 12) and if

(c)   velocity falls to 1, prices in fact fall (40 divided by 12 = 3.3)

SAQ 14:   I make the income velocity 1969 — 2.4; 1970 — 2.41; 1971 — 2.4; 1972 — 2.1; 1973 — 1.9; 1974 — 1.97; 1975 — 2.29; 1976 — 2.4. Double check your graph against these figures to make sure it's correct.

SAQ 15:   (a)   in the first 18 months, prices do not rise as fast as money supply has increased but

(b)   when the temporary fall in V has worked its way out of the system, prices have risen by the full amount of the rise in M.

SAQ 16:   P remains unchanged. The extra money supply has caused an equivalent rise in output.

SAQ 17:   When economists speak of money wages, they are referring to the amount that someone gets paid in money — say £80 per week, £9 000 per year or whatever. The *real* wage of a worker, by contrast, is measured by the amount of commodities that can be bought with the money wage. So we have to take into account the level of prices as well as the money wage. For example, rising prices could cancel out an increase in money wages. If prices went up 10% while money wages rose by only 5% real wages have fallen.

In the example quoted in the exercise, it would be possible for a worker to have a rising real wage with a falling money wage only if prices were falling faster than the money wage.

By the way, try not to confuse money wages with disposable income (that is, the amount an income receiver has left after deductions like tax, social security contributions etc.). Your money income refers to your gross pay or salary, and so would not be affected by changes in taxation.

SAQ 18:   Monetarist explanation: An increase in the amount of money will cause people and institutions to hold larger balances of money than they want. They will therefore run down their money balances (i.e. increase their spending) causing increased demand and thus increased prices.

Keynesian explanation: If the money supply rises above the amount needed to finance transactions, people will use their spare cash to buy shares and bonds, driving down the price of these assets. This is the same as a fall in interest rates, and the easier and cheaper borrowing encourages firms to increase their investment spending. This raises aggregate demand and thus National Income.

How to distinguish: a Keynesian would see investment as the main part of the extra demand, but a monetarist wouldn't. So, if the Keynesian explanation is right, investment will rise as a proportion of the national income following an expansion of the money supply. In practice this is difficult to observe, due to the many other things that cause investment to fluctuate.

SAQ 19:   The only thing that a monetarist might jib at is in the opening sentence: monetarists would claim that the money supply *is* useful for predicting expenditure, though not in the short term mentioned in the article. But a monetarist would go on to claim that the amount of 'give' in the velocity of money mentioned in the article is just a short-term phenomenon. In a while (say, 18 months to two years) velocity will return to normal and the larger money supply will cause rising prices. He/she would argue that this is just what happened after the expansion of the money supply in 1972-3 — inflation rose sharply in 1974-5.

SAQ 20:   If P goes up, and M and V aren't altered, then T must go down. To put it into plain English, a given amount of money can buy fewer goods if prices rise. Demand for goods (and thus sales) will fall, and unemployment results.

SAQ 21:   No. If V can vary to allow any amount of M to buy up PT, then changes in the supply of money will not have any effect on the level of prices or the size of the real national income.

SAQ 22:   Fiscal policy involves using the budget to reduce the pressure of demand inflation. Prices and Incomes policy is the method preferred for dealing with cost inflation.

SAQ 23:   Answered in text.

SAQ 24:   (a)   High interest rates would raise the cost of borrowing to industry, and would in particular reduce the level of new investment: *see* the MEC diagram in Unit 4.

(b)   Higher interest rates would increase the cost of consumer credit, but the most important effect might well be to raise mortgage payments as the high interest rates were transmitted to building society loans.

SAQ 25:   The Bank of England would purchase government securities on the open market, paying for them with cheques drawn against the government's accounts. Those who sold the securities to the government would deposit their cheques with their banks, who would thus have some increased deposits to base the credit-creation process upon.

SAQ 26:   (a)   The PSBR rises in a slump because the lower economic activity results in less tax revenue (incomes and sales fall) and because welfare-related government spending (particularly unemployment benefit) rises (See Unit 6 page 102).

(b)   The higher PSBR will have no monetary effect if it is financed by sales of gilt edged stocks to the non-bank sector. It is inevitable, however, that with a larger PSBR, this will prove more difficult.

9 Inflation

AIMS OF UNIT 9

In this unit I'll be pulling together a number of strands from different parts of the course — Keynesian macroeconomics, monetarism, trade unions, and so on. I'll attempt to use these strands to shed some light on the controversy that surrounds the problem of inflation. You should take outline notes as you go through the unit, and when you have completed it you should be able to:

- define the term 'inflation'
- give at least four reasons why inflation has disadvantages
- explain why 'price freezes' are rarely used
- describe the 'excess demand' explanation of inflation, using material recalled from previous units
- explain how fiscal policy may be used to reduce excess demand
- explain why demand-pull explanations of inflation fell out of favour and give an account of cost-push ideas
- define 'incomes policy', and give an account of how it is supposed to work
- outline the monetarist explanation of inflation, using an amended Phillips curve diagram to explain how governments cause increased inflation by attempts to maintain overfull employment.
- criticise the monetarist view.

WHAT DOES 'INFLATION' MEAN?

Inflation refers to a general rise in prices. When prices rise, a given sum of money buys less — so you can look at inflation either as a process in which the cost of living is rising, or as one in which the value of money is falling. Inflation can be measured in a number of ways: the most well-known measure in this country is the *Retail Price Index (the RPI)*. But however inflation is measured, there's no denying that it has been with us for many years: prices have been rising throughout the post-war period. Of course inflation doesn't necessarily make us worse off. Throughout most of the past forty years money incomes have risen faster than prices; as a result, there has been a rise in real incomes despite the presence of inflation. This has led some people to say that we shouldn't worry too much about inflation. Indeed, it has been claimed that gentle inflation — say, 2% or 3% on prices each year — is good for the economy. It encourages investment, for when businessmen come to sell their products, they will receive more money than they paid for the machinery, raw materials or in wages. This is a short-sighted view, though, for inflation can have some disturbing effects on an economy.

WHAT'S WRONG WITH INFLATION?

The first problem with inflation is that a gentle, 'acceptable' pace of inflation can get worse, accelerating into a faster rate and finally into a very high level of inflation that can make money useless.

High rates of inflation are known as *hyperinflation*, and though experiences of hyperinflation are rare (and generally follow a social catastrophe, such as military defeat) they are sufficiently unpleasant to be remembered and avoided. 'We used to go to the shop with money in our pocket and return with goods in our baskets', remembered one hyperinflation victim, 'but now we go with money in our baskets and come back with a few things in our pockets'. When this happens, people will no longer trust money and may return to the clumsy and inefficient method of barter discussed in an earlier unit.

Then there is the problem that inflation redistributes income and wealth in a haphazard way. Those who can adjust their incomes quickly can keep up with an inflation – but those who depend on fixed incomes are the losers. A particular problem occurs when borrowing and lending take place during inflation. Borrowers will be able to repay the amount borrowed in devalued currency, which is grossly unfair to those who have saved their income and lent it. This has led to the conventional view that inflation reduces savings.

SAQ 1: *(a) How could a government ensure that savers and lenders do not lose during an inflationary period?*
(b)   Have savings fallen during the recent period of inflation in Britain? Can you explain this?

A third problem results from inflation in an economy like Britain's which engages in international trade to buy its food, raw materials and other imports. We can only pay for these imported goods by selling our exports, and if the price of our exports rises faster than those of our competitors, we will lose our customers. International trade is a very competitive business. To take one example, a foreign buyer wishing to re-equip his fleet of commercial vehicles can choose from German, Swedish, Italian, French and Japanese lorries as well as British ones. If our prices have been pushed up by inflation, we will lose the business. What's more, British buyers may find imported goods becoming more attractive, further worsening our balance of payments with the world.

We shall see when we look at the topic of overseas trade that when we have difficulty selling our exports and buy too many imports, the exchange rate of the pound (that is, the amount of foreign currency we can buy with £1) tends to fall. This makes imported food and fuels more expensive and increases the inflation that started the problem in the first place.

Perhaps the worst effect of inflation is the disruption and uncertainty that it causes. Persistent inflation constantly alters relative real wages and real prices, making it difficult to make rational decisions about how to spend money, how to plan for the future, which career to enter and so on. Let's take the example of a 20% inflation: even if a group of workers got an annual 20% rise, the uncertainty and unpleasantness would still be there. Graph 9.1 shows the behaviour of the workers' real wages during the year: at their highest after their annual wage increase, then falling

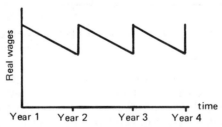

Graph 9.1 Real wage behaviour

throughout the year until the day just before receiving their next annual rise, when the standard of living will have fallen by one-fifth. There's no wonder that militancy and sheer bloody-mindedness increase in wage disputes during fast inflation! Milton Friedman draws our attention to the behaviour of a group of ambulancemen who refused to go to the help of the sick during a wage dispute – an attitude they would never have adopted in a stable-price economy.

The last disadvantage of inflation is the comparatively minor inconvenience of having to visit the bank more often and having to carry more cash.

Why not a price-freeze?

If inflation has these disadvantages, we must look for ways to bring it under control and avoid its costs. The most obvious policy, and one that is often advocated by the layman, is a *price-freeze*; that is, a law, or other binding agreement, that prices shall not be raised at all.

There are several objections to this simple idea in practice. Firstly, it's doubtful whether a 100% freeze on prices is possible. For example, the 1972 attempt at a sixth-month price-freeze was defeated by rises in the price of imported goods. We cannot order foreigners to keep their prices steady.

SAQ 2: *Suppose that a government ignored the problem of imported goods and passed a law forbidding price rises in the UK. How might this affect UK firms?*

The second objection to a price-freeze is more complicated. It concerns the role of prices in a market economy. The prices of goods act as signals. A high price limits the number of buyers; and it tells firms which goods are in demand from consumers. Without the rationing and signalling of a price system, firms and consumers have no information on which to act. Scarce goods sell out quickly and queues become the norm; unwanted goods accumulate in unsold piles. Generally, a black market starts (selling goods at their 'real' prices). But if the freeze is vigorously enforced — as it was in postwar Germany by the occupying British and American forces, or by different methods in Idi Amin's Uganda — the economy comes to a halt.

Even if a price-freeze were possible, it would make more sense to deal with the causes of inflation, rather than the symptoms. Doctors try to relieve the pain of appendicitis, by removing the cause rather than by using painkillers. Similarly, economists want to cure inflation by removing its causes. To do this, of course, they need an accurate understanding of the causes of inflation, and here once again there is controversy. You have already met two differing views — the Keynesian view that inflation is the product of excess aggregate demand, and the monetarist view that inflation is caused by the money supply rising faster than the increase in output. I shall also be reviewing the concept of **cost-push inflation** where prices go up due to rises in costs unconnected with the pressure of demand.

DEMAND-PULL INFLATION

In Keynesian macroeconomics the size of the national income is determined by aggregate demand — that is, the total spending of individuals and families, firms, local and national government and foreign buyers. If aggregate demand falls below a certain point (full-employment national income), there is not enough demand to buy up all the goods being produced and cyclical unemployment occurs. But, more relevant to the present topic, if aggregate demand increases when resources are fully employed, the extra orders and spending cannot raise output and employment, only prices. When inflation is caused in this way, it is called 'demand-pull' inflation (see Unit 5, pp. 89-92).

SAQ 3: *(a) If inflation was caused by high levels of aggregate demand, what would be the relationship between inflation and cyclical unemployment? (b) If demand was very high indeed, would unemployment approach zero? Why, or why not? (c) Reproduce and name the diagram that plots the alleged relationship between unemployment and inflation (look back to Unit 5, pp. 89-92, if you want to check this).*

Now, the idea that prices could be pulled up by excess demand seems logical enough, but we must again remember that 'scientific' theories stand or fall by the evidence. What evidence was there for **demand-pull** inflation?

There are two main pieces of evidence. Firstly, the Phillips relation appeared to be confirmed by research: economists have looked through the statistics right back into the Victorian period, and found that there was a consistent relationship between unemployment and inflation in most of the years studied. Indeed, you have done a small exercise like this yourself in Unit 5, plotting unemployment and inflation through the 1950s and 1960s.

The second piece of evidence for demand-pull theories was found in the phenomenon of **wage drift**. Wage-drift refers to the difference between the increases in wage rates that are agreed by unions and employers in national negotiations, and the increase in workers' actual earnings that follow. For example, if the engineering workers are awarded a 6% rise in year X, but the figures show that in that year earnings in engineering rose 9%, then wage-drift of 3% has happened. There are a number of reasons why earnings might rise more quickly than wage rates: increased overtime, for example, or premium and bonus payments for extra output. But employers have often been found to be paying wage rates well above the union minimum. In the boom of the 1950s and 1960s, an employer who offered only minimum wage rates would very soon find him or herself short of workers — particularly those with scarce skills. The significance of this is that if costs are rising because workers are getting paid above the union rates, inflation cannot be caused by unions pushing up wages and costs. It is excess demand, causing shortages of labour and a competitive bidding up of wages, that is to blame. Higher prices then result because firms pass on their higher labour costs to the consumer.

SAQ 4: *(a)   What would wage-drift be in these cases?*

	Change in wage-rates	Change in earnings	Wage-drift
Year 1	*10%*	*12%*	....
Year 2	*8%*	*12%*	....
Year 3	*6%*	*7%*	....

(b)   Could wage-drift ever be negative? Give an example, and explain why it might happen.

Fighting demand-pull inflation: fiscal policy

The correct remedy for inflation caused by too high a level of demand would be a fiscal policy aimed at reducing demand to a level that does not cause rising prices. The government can achieve this in one of two ways. It can *increase taxation*, so that consumers and firms are left with less money to spend, or, alternatively, it can *reduce its own spending*. A doubly effective policy would combine the two, coupling rises in taxes with cuts in government spending. The problem with reducing government spending, as we have seen, is that it is difficult to alter in the short-term and so in general the Chancellor has used increases in taxation to 'damp-down' the economy.

The obvious drawback to this policy is the resulting unemployment and lost production. Clearly, the government is solving one problem by creating another: the costs of high unemployment are as great as those of high inflation, and what is worse, they are spread very unevenly. Unskilled workers and depressed regions will bear the brunt of the fall in sales and jobs, for an average national unemployment figure of, say, 10%, will mean 20% or 30% in the blackspots of Liverpool, the North, and South Wales — worse for the disabled and the black. You will also have seen (Unit 6, p. 107) in our discussions of fiscal policy, how government action to reduce the level of demand might actually work against the long-term good health of the economy. Firms won't expand, nor unions agree to more efficient work practices, if a slump in jobs and sales is just around the corner.

THE DEATH OF THE PHILLIPS CURVE?

So fiscal policies had their critics even before the 1970s. But the simple demand-pull explanation of inflation was finally buried by the evidence of a decade in which both unemployment and inflation rose by leaps and bounds. The conventional Keynesian view that we can have either unemployment *or* inflation but not both is difficult to maintain in a country with rising unemployment *and* double-figure inflation. Look at this table:

	Actual rate of wage inflation	*Rate of wage inflation predicted by Phillips curve*
1967	7.8	2.1
1968	5.3	1.8
1969	7.3	1.8
1970	13.6	1.6
1971	11.9	0.9

(*source:* Saunders *The Current Inflation: an academic view* 'The Bankers' Magazine' May 1973)

SAQ 5: *How do you predict the rate of inflation from the Phillips curve? Was the estimate made during the years 1967-71 too high or too low? In which year was the error greatest?*

With the apparent disappearance of the Phillips curve, economists had to look elsewhere for an explanation of inflation, and they found it in the idea of 'cost-push' inflation. Cost-push (sometimes called simply 'cost inflation') results from increases in production costs that might happen even when demand is low. These rising costs might be caused by a number of factors — increased raw material or energy prices, for example — but the main attention of economists looking at cost-push theories of inflation has been directed at the way trade union action pushes up money wages and thus labour costs. This is how cost inflation happens:

A number of well-organised workers in industry A push for and obtain an excessive wage increase (i.e. a rise in money wages greater than their increase in output)

This rise is viewed by other workers in industries B, C and D as the going rate — no union will easily settle for less. As a result the higher wages and labour costs spread

The inflation rate rises: workers find that their increased money-wages have been 'eroded by rises in the cost-of-living', and so . . .

Firms are faced with increased costs of production. Because firms fix their prices to cover costs, plus a mark-up for overheads and profit, prices are increased in line with wages

This is a 'spiral' effect, and gets worse the longer the spiral climbs upwards. The inflation is accompanied by increasing industrial unrest (as groups are obliged to 'run to stay in the same place') and by a decrease in our ability to compete with cheaper foreign goods both in the UK and in the export markets.

I am sure that this is a familiar story. However, it is important to realise the difficulties such an explanation causes for a clear-thinking social scientist. Inflation is not something that is either 'on' or 'off', like a light-switch; it varies very greatly in intensity. In some years, inflation is negligible — as in 1959, when the recorded inflation rate was almost zero. At other times, the rate of inflation can gallop along; in 1975, prices rose by nearly 25% in one year. No economist can be happy attributing variations in the rate of inflation, which was 40 times higher in 1975 than it was in 1959, to 'greed' or 'strong and well-organised unions'. Unions were just as well-organised in 1959 as in 1975, and it is probable (but difficult to confirm) that people were as greedy. To provide a convincing argument in favour of cost-push inflation we must explain why unions have become tougher in wage bargaining in recent years.

Why have unions become more militant?

Two main explanations have been put forward, both of which assert that people have increasingly come to distinguish between the real wage and the money wage. Whereas a worker in the 50s might welcome a £1 a week increase as a real indication of being better-off, today's more sophisticated (and inflation-experienced) worker will take into account inflation and taxes and know how little such an increase actually means. He or she sees through the 'money illusion'.

The first explanation of increased union militancy can be called the **frustrations hypothesis**. This suggests that workers expect an annual increase not just in their money incomes, but in their real incomes. This was no problem in the 1950s and early 1960s — economic growth meant that the national income increased by a regular 2% or 3%, and so there were enough commodities to ensure a rise in real incomes. However, during the 70s and 80s the rate of economic growth in Western economies slowed down dramatically, and even stopped in some years. The extra 'real income' was not there to satisfy the demands of wage-earners, and so increases in money wages could only lead to higher prices. The advantage of this theory is that it explains the international nature of inflation: prices did indeed shoot up all over Western Europe and in the United States. The problem is that it assumes that people — particularly wage and salary earners — have accurate ideas about the movements of their real incomes.

SAQ 6: *What information do you need to work out the change in your real income between this year and last?*

The second explanation for greater worker militancy was put forward in a book called *Do Trade Unions Cause Inflation?* by Jackson, Turner and Wilkinson. (Cambridge University Press, 1972). They pointed out that in the late 60s, a combination of higher inflation and rising government spending brought a large number of wage earners into the tax-paying bracket, with immediate effects on the size of their take-home pay. In the immediate postwar years in Britain, you needed to earn a lot more than the average wage to pay tax; nowadays, tax becomes payable at less than half average earnings. In fact, even someone receiving welfare benefits such as the Family Income Supplement can be liable for tax.

Of course, this increasing tax burden has been paralleled by better government services — leisure, education, health, welfare services are very much better than they were in the immediate postwar period. Harold Wilson was fond of pointing out that the tax paid by workers bought them this wide range of government services, and could be thought of as part of a worker's standard of living. He called it the **social wage**. Having a good school for my daughters raises my quality of life quite as much as having a good living-room carpet. However, workers rarely recognise that taxation provides this social wage, and as a result there is a tendency to frame pay demands in terms of post-tax incomes — what is more popularly known as **take-home pay**. So if income taxation was set at a rate of 30%, and the rate of inflation was 10%, workers would fight to obtain a rise of 13% to keep post-tax income in line with inflation. If granted, such a rise adds to inflation.

How do we cure cost-push?

If the actions of trade unions are genuinely the cause of inflation, then governments can attack inflation in one of two ways — either by confronting and defeating the trade unions, or by persuading them to join in a cooperative attempt to reduce inflation.

Curbing the unions. An example of the first type of policy would be for the government to reduce trade-union power. Such a policy would include outlawing the 'closed shop', restricting the rights of pickets, restricting the ability of unions to involve firms and workers not involved in the dispute in question, or insisting on a secret postal ballot conducted by neutral observers for each pay settlement or proposed action. These actions could be reinforced by a determination to 'stand up to the unions' in some visible way — as in the busmen's strike in 1958, the postal strike of 1971, the civil servants' dispute in 1980 or the miners' strike in 1984.

The disadvantages of such a policy are clear: the number of working days lost through strikes rises and the industrial atmosphere becomes embittered. What's more, the policy doesn't work against real industrial strength. It may be easy enough to pick off the firemen, postal workers or hospital cleaners, but power-station workers, miners or water workers are more formidable opponents.

INCOMES POLICIES

As a result of the disadvantages just outlined, governments have more frequently tried a cooperative approach, involving workers and unions in an **incomes policy**. The idea is this. Unions, employers and the government get together and agree that the **wage-price spiral** is self-defeating. They agree to a rate of growth of money incomes that will not add to inflation, and after the pay restraint has worked through into lower costs and prices, inflation is seen to fall.

SAQ 7: *What will determine the rate at which money wages may rise without increasing inflation? In other words, what factors might allow us to pay ourselves more next year than this?*

The theory sounds so attractive that it seems strange that we don't have a permanent incomes policy in operation, limiting inflationary rises and sharing out the national income in a rational way. However, in practice incomes policies often fail because of the practical problems of implementing them. Here are a few of the problems:

(a)   If during a period of pay restraint prices continue to rise (due, as we noted earlier, to rising import prices), the public support that is essential to the success of the policy evaporates.

(b)   What happens to non-wage incomes, like profits and dividends? It is plainly unfair to hold down wages without holding down these other sources of income. Many radical writers see incomes policies as a way to hold down workers' incomes to the benfit of capitalists (see, for example, Miliband's *The State in Capitalist Society* pp. 74-5). It is no answer to put a limit on dividends: forbidding firms from paying out earnings to shareholders simply stores up profits in the firm's bank account, causing a rise in share prices.

Similarly self-employed workers — not just craftsmen but also professional workers — are not affected by the restrictions of an incomes policy.

(c)   It is in practice very difficult to police the policy and enforce obedience. In 1973, for example, the agreed wage limit was 6% but in the event earnings rose by 13%. This has the effect of penalising the groups of workers who have settled within the rules.

(d)   The figure used to decide what is a reasonable non-inflationary rise is the rate of growth of productivity (see SAQ 7 above). However, the national average growth in productivity disguises wide variations from industry to industry. Some groups of workers, particularly those who can use large amounts of capital equipment (steelmen, power station workers) might increase their output per head by 20% or more – does this entitle them to a 20% rise? On the other hand, the productivity of some workers has actually fallen. For example, class sizes in many schools are smaller than they were 10 or 15 years ago – does this mean that school-teachers must expect a cut in their salaries? If we tie wages to a national *average* productivity figure, in effect those groups who achieve great increases in output per head are being asked to hold back so that those whose productivity is static or falling can be given a rise.

(e)   Should the pay limit be fixed as a percentage (say, 5%) or as a fixed sum (say £5 per week)? The problem with percentage rises is that they give much more to the highly paid than to those on low incomes. But a fixed-sum rise alters differentials between skilled and unskilled workers.

This opens up an enormous area of discussion. Should everyone get the same wage rise, or should 'special cases' be singled out for individual treatment? To take some examples, if we decide that low-paid local authority manual workers, or nurses, or miners at the coalface, deserve above-average rises, precisely who is to get the below-average rises?

(f)   Incomes policies interfere with the free working of a market economy and with wage negotiation. It will therefore distort wages and earnings, making them differ from what workers could otherwise earn, and what employers would otherwise pay. This distortion gets progressively worse the longer the policy operates and ultimately causes pressures that lead to a collapse of the policy in a 'wages explosion' or 'winter of discontent'.

A particularly serious and unjust distortion can occur if one group of workers find themselves cut off by the introduction of a pay policy. Suppose a particular group of workers received its annual pay award in November: if a pay policy were to be introduced in October, they would find themselves disadvantaged in relation to workers who settled earlier in the year.

Are incomes policies effective?

Finding out whether incomes policies actually work is not as easy as you might think. It isn't enough simply to see what happens to inflation when a policy is introduced. Economists must make an estimate of what inflation *would* have been, had there been no incomes policy. So even if inflation rises after a policy is introduced, this doesn't necessarily show that the policy has been ineffective: it may have reduced inflation below what it would otherwise have been.

Calculating what inflation would have been had events been different involves some use of the Phillips curve. Researchers look at how great inflation was in the previous years when the level of aggregate demand was equal to that in the year in question: comparing what are called **policy-on** years with **policy-off** ones. It's a hazardous technique, made more difficult by the fact that the many years of incomes policy have clouded our view of how inflation behaves in a **policy-off** period. Between 1961 and 1979, for example, there were only two periods without any form of incomes policy – 1963-4 and 1969-72. Nevertheless, calculations have been made of income policy effectiveness. It seems that incomes policies have had little effect on inflation. However, there are three periods in which incomes policies do appear to have reduced inflation below expected levels:

● in 1948-50, the voluntary wage standstill introduced by Sir Stafford Cripps (with TUC support) caused exceptionally low increases in wages and prices.

● In 1966, Harold Wilson brought in a legally enforceable six-month pay freeze, and followed it with six months of 'severe restraint'. It worked, reducing inflation to 3% by April 1967.

● In 1975-6, the incoming Labour government abandoned the looseness of their 'Social Contract' (an understanding on pay and other items of economic policy with the TUC that had been unsuccessful in reducing prices or wage increases), and imposed a tighter incomes policy that achieved a remarkable reduction in inflation.

An inflation tax?

So, looking back, it seems that incomes policies can be effective for short 'crisis' periods during which wage earners will agree to restraint. The problem occurs when trying to extend the policy over a longer period, when 'voluntary restraint' breaks down. This has led to the idea that we could use the tax system permanently to enforce an incomes policy. Such an **inflation-tax** would eliminate many of the policing problems. Two forms of inflation tax proposals exist. One aims to tax away from a given income-tax payer any excess of earnings increase over the nationally agreed norm. This causes problems in cases where earnings rise due to more overtime worked, or promotion. So the alternative – to tax firms whose wages bill rises by more than a given per capita percentage – is the more practicable alternative.

THE REBIRTH OF MONETARY EXPLANATIONS OF INFLATION

So far I have given two contrasting explanations of the rising level of prices: one concentrates on the high level of demand, the other on pressures on costs. A common-sense view of postwar in-flation (taking the size of unemployment as a guide) would say that demand inflation was behind the price rises of the postwar world up to the late 1960s and early 1970s, at which point cost-push inflation became the problem. In recent years, however, there has been a revival of monetary theories of inflation. Monetarists assert that demand-pull and cost-push are, in reality, early and late versions of the same disease – inflation caused by excessive rises in the supply of money.

It might be a good idea at this point to review your understanding of the quantity theory of money (Unit 8, pp. 136–9). Check your learning by answering the following questions:

SAQ 8: *(a) What is the quantity theory? (b) What is the relation between money supply and prices, other things being equal? (c) What determines whether a rise in the money supply is exces-sive, or acceptable? (d) Why shouldn't rises in money supply be swallowed up by reductions in velocity, with people holding larger money balances?*

The ideas of the new monetarists can best be explained by starting from graph 9.2 below.

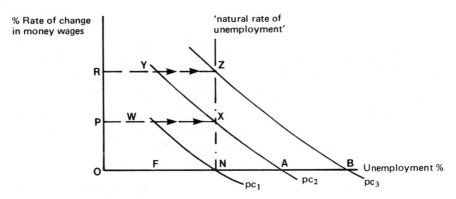

Graph 9.2 The 'expectations-augmented' Phillips Curve

Here, the rate of unemployment is ON, and the rate of inflation is zero. The level of unemploy-ment is at the 'natural rate of unemployment', set by factors such as the skills of the workforce, labour mobility, difficulty of finding out about vacancies, and so on. Monetarists see this natural rate of unemployment, then, as being determined by structural factors in the economy rather than by the pressure of demand. But suppose for a moment that the government did not agree with them, and decided that ON was an intolerable level of unemployment; it might then decide to ex-pand the economy by Keynesian measures, such as a bigger budget deficit, paid for by borrowing, which might in turn raise the money supply.

This, say the monetarists, would have a short-term effect in reducing unemployment to OF. But increased demand doesn't just reduce unemployment, it raises prices: this is shown on a Phillips curve. I've drawn a Phillips curve (marked pc_1) passing through point N. The extra surge of spending I've described pushes us out along the Phillips curve to point W. However, the argument continues, it wouldn't end there. The extra money supply raises prices and money wages after a short lag; and so the manufacturers who took on extra workers will find that extra demand has also raised their costs and wages. The workers who were persuaded by higher wages to take other-wise uncongenial jobs find that inflation has reduced the value of their wages back to the level at which they were previously unwilling to take those jobs. They therefore quit their jobs. As a result, unemployment returns to ON again; but we now have inflation of OP%.

SAQ 9: *Suppose a Keynesian Chancellor interprets the rise in unemployment from OF to ON as cyclical unemployment, caused by a deflationary gap,*
(a)   What will he do in his next Budget?
(b)   What is the name given to using a Budget this way?

I'll assume that the Chancellor decides on a boost to aggregate demand. The economy will now move out on a new Phillips Curve to point Y, associated with a higher rate of inflation OR%. Soon firms and workers will see through this new inflationary expansion and unemployment will return to its natural rate, ON at position Z. The effect of Keynesian policies has not been to reduce un-employment at all but simply to increase the rate of inflation from zero to OR.

The Phillips curve relationship between unemployment and inflation is, according to the monetarists, a purely temporary one. In the long-term, increases in money spending will not reduce unemployment below the natural level. If an unexpected surge of (inflationary) demand takes place, in the short run firms will indeed take on extra workers and workers accept more jobs: but anticipated inflation will not have this effect, merely causing firms to mark-up prices and unions to expect bigger wage rises. It follows that the government can only reduce unemployment below ON − the natural level − in the long run by letting inflation run higher than expected. But such a 'runaway' inflation would eventually have to be curbed. To use the symbols from Fisher's quantity theory that you met in Unit 8, the extra M will leak away entirely in higher P, leaving T and V unchanged except in the very short term.

SAQ 10: *Check back now on your understanding of the monetarist position. What do they say would happen following a sharp increase in the money supply, to*
(a)   T − that is, the amount of transactions in the economy?
(b)   V − the income velocity of money?
(c)   Does it follow that no attempt to reduce unemployment below the present natural rate will be successful?

The flaw in the Phillips curve

Now consider the vertical axis of the Phillips curve diagram. This is usually drawn to chart changes in money wages, while the horizontal axis charts percentage unemployment. Friedman has pointed out that this isn't really comparing like with like. We should compare real unemployment with changes in *real* wages − changes in money wages over and above the inflation rate. An increase in the supply of any commodity requires (other things being equal) the offer of a higher real price. So an increase in the real price of labour (i.e. the real wage rate) is needed to persuade unemployed members of the workforce to take up vacancies that were previously unfilled. A mere money-increase won't work − unless people are unused to inflation and confuse a rise in money wages with a rise in real wages. Such a confusion is common in economies without a history of inflation, and is called the **money illusion**. However, such an illusion will not survive long in an economy like ours. You may like to compare this diagram with the one on p. 92 of Vol. 1, where we puzzled over the apparent shifts in the Phillips curve.

MONETARIST REMEDIES FOR INFLATION

Let's return to the diagram on p. 157 for a look at a monetarist's ideas for reducing inflation. They argue that if the government had reached point Z (largely through its own stupidity or that of its predecessors), there is only one way of returning to stable prices. This involves sliding down the Phillips curve until inflation is zero; but in the process, unemployment has gone up to OB. The following extract from the *Midland Bank Review* (November 1974) puts the theory neatly. Read through it and answer the questions at the end.

> The plan of campaign is somewhat as follows. At some stage in the process of continually increasing wages and prices, the authorities decide to use their powers of credit control to restrict the growth of the money supply to a rate below the current rate of growth of output in money terms. The inertia of the inflation continues to push prices and wages up as before. But as the authorities are now restricting the amount of credit available, individuals and businesses experience liquidity problems; interest rates rise and the level of real demand falls. If prices are kept at the higher level, output is adjusted downwards and redundancies begin. Alternatively, to restore demand, the last price rise is cancelled; but the squeezing of profit margins (or rise in real wages) causes labour to be laid off. As unemployment rises above its normal level, the bargaining power of labour is undermined and the growth of money wages checked.
>
> Taken so far, the problem of inflation has merely been replaced by a problem of unemployment. It appears that, if the rate of inflation is to be kept permanently at a lower level, the rate of unemployment must also be kept permanently at a higher level − you cannot bring both ends of the seesaw to the ground. But some claim that you can, and envisage a second phase of the counter-inflationary plans as follows. The lower rate of growth of prices achieved in the first phase modifies the future rate of growth of prices which wage earners expect and which those who bargain on their behalf enter into their money wage claims at any given rate of unemployment. The reduced rate of increase of money wages feeds through costs to a further decrease in the rate of increase in prices, which in turn reduces the expected rate of increase in prices which enters the next round of money wage claims. In this way the growth rates of money wages and of prices are wound progressively downwards

at the going rate of unemployment. Once the rate of increase of prices has fallen below the rate of increase of the money supply which the authorities originally decided to permit, the purchasing power of the money stock in the hands of the public will begin to rise and the economy will experience an increase in demand which will restore full employment at the lower rate of inflation. In the end, the victory over inflation is won with some wounded but no dead.

Two features of this plan of campaign against inflation need to be noted. The first is that it does not involve merely a risk of unemployment; unemployment of an abnormal size is a necessary element in the strategy, although at the end of the day it may be possible to re-move it. But the second point is that the possibility of removing it comes to hand only after a period during which the expectations of wage-earners concerning the future rate of infla-tion have been gradually modified by experience and reflected in the size of money wage claims which are submitted in any given state of the labour market. As many Monetarists realise, it would be optimistic to suppose that this period of adjustment in expectations would be 'as an evening gone'.

SAQ 11: *(a) Who are 'the authorities'?*
(b)   What is a 'liquidity problem'?
(c)   Put into economists' terms the expression 'you cannot bring both ends of the seesaw to the ground'.
(d)   Using the diagram on p. 157, describe the path that the economy takes if it follows the advice contained in the second half of this extract. Start at point Z.
(e)   What would a monetarist mean by 'unemployment of an abnormal size'?
(f)   While most monetarists believe that incomes policies have no role to play in the control of inflation, there are some who think that such policies could be useful in the strategy out-lined above. How would they fit in?
(g)   Explain how high unemployment reduces the bargaining power of labour.

The increased acceptance of monetarist ideas, and the election of Mrs Thatcher and Ronald Reagan, both of whom are committed to using the mechanisms of monetary policy I've described, makes it important to consider criticisms of the monetarist analysis.

You should be clear at the start that no-one denies that excessive increases in the money supply *can* cause inflation: for example, inflation in Tudor times was undoubtedly caused by discoveries of gold in the New World, and 'printing-press' inflations followed the First World War in some European countries. Nor does anyone dispute that rising prices have been accompanied by a steady growth in the quantity of money throughout the postwar period. What the argument is about is this: is the increase in money supply the *cause* of the rising prices?

The monetarists maintain that the government causes inflation through increased supply of money, and then Trade Unions push and strike to keep their members' incomes in line. Cost-pushers say that unions (and other forces) push up prices and then the government, reluctant to allow interest rates to go high enough to affect investment or employment, allow the money supply to expand to make way for the higher price level. They ask how an excessive money supply can raise prices other than through the mechanism of excess demand, and ask what evidence there is for excess demand in the 1970s and 1980s, with their high rates of unemployment and low rates of vacancies.

(In this connection, you may wish to ponder the monetarist view of a labour market in which large numbers of unemployed people are withholding their labour until the real wage rate rises. While there are certainly a few menial jobs that remain unfilled even in a slump, the view seems at odds with the real world of unemployment).

Further, the fact that incomes policies have been successful when they have received the support and acceptance of the workforce seems evidence for some form of social or cost-push explanation.

REVIEW SECTION

Here is a summary of this unit, with some words missed out. Go through it, pencilling in the missing words. (Answers on p. 163)

Inflation describes a situation in which prices are . . . . leading to a . . . . in the value of money. Since the war, wages have on the whole risen more . . . . than prices, yet infla-tion still has a number of disadvantages, for example:

(a)   . . . .

(b)   . . . .

(c) . . . .

(d) . . . .

Given that a price freeze is impractical because of (a) the difficulty of holding down the prices of . . . . goods and (b) the role of prices in a . . . . economy, we must try to remove the causes rather than the symptoms of inflation. The explanation of inflation that seemed to fit the experience of the 1940s to 1960s was that rising prices were an inevitable consequence of running an economy with high levels of employment and aggregate demand: this sort of inflation is called . . . . -. . . . . inflation, and fits neatly into the . . . . economic theory. The evidence that inflation was caused this way was to be found in the relation between . . . . and . . . . charted on the . . . . ; and secondly, in the fact that earnings frequently raced ahead of wage rates, a phenomenon known as . . . . If too much spending does indeed cause inflation, then the correct medicine for the chancellor to give is a . . . . budget, ... taxes and . . . . government spending.

However, a large number of economists believe in the 1970s we were experiencing a different form of inflation, a . . . . -. . . . . inflation. This is the result of pressures on production costs caused by unions or import prices or energy prices. This re-evaluation of the causes of inflation has come about because from 19. . onwards there were high levels of both . . . . and . . . . , undermining the basis of the . . . . relation.

The correct way to counter this sort of inflation would be either to take a tough line and confront . . . . power or try a more conciliatory approach with a . . . . and . . . . policy. In recent years, the views of American economists from the University of . . . . have said that the first two theories of inflation are wrong and that, in the words of Milton . . . . , 'inflation is always and everywhere a . . . . phenomenon'. They believe that there is no way to reduce unemployment below its natural level by expanding demand, and that government attempts to do so by expanding the . . . . of . . . . will merely cause a rise in . . . . If this is true then the correct policy measure would be for the government to . . . . less . . . . There is in fact quite a strong correlation between the supply of . . . . and the level of . . . . , but whether this relationship is one of causation is more controversial.

Further reading

Inflation is a complex topic, and is one where theories can collapse in a short time as they are disproved by events — 'in economics, the questions remain the same; it's just that the answers change'. There are also different schools of thought and strongly held views. So try to do a range of reading, covering more than one viewpoint.

General texts: You might start with Peter Donaldson's lively and readable Pelican book *A Question of Economics* (Chapter 4, especially). A more specialised book that shouldn't pose too many problems for an 'A' level Economics student is *Inflation* by Trevithick another Pelican book. Two articles from *Economic Review* will also supplement the work of the last few units: 'The Phillips Curve: Current Problems' (Michael Sumner, March 1987) and 'Monetary Control in the UK' (Michael Artis, November 1984). Inflation in the UK is also well covered in *Controlling the Economy* by N. Wall (Collins, Economics Briefs series).

Biassed work: Friedman can sometimes write material that is accessible to the non-expert, and you should not feel put off by the fact that he is a 'big name'. You might try, for a start, *Unemployment and Inflation*, an Institute for Economic Affairs Occasional Paper (No. 44). It also contains some valuable notes, putting Friedman's views in a British perspective, by Prof. D. Laidler. Brian Griffiths' book *Inflation* (Weidenfeld and Nicholson) is also written from a monetarist viewpoint. On the cost-push side, try to get hold of *Do Trade Unions Cause Inflation?* by Jackson, Turner and Wilkinson (Cambridge University Press).

The real world: Accounts of inflation in the real world are best found in magazines such as the *Economist.* Prest and Coppock's tireless *The UK Economy* will always repay study, but make sure that you have the latest edition. Also recommended is Keith Hartley's *Problems of Economic Policy* (Allen and Unwin – especially ch. 5). Two thoughtful Bank Review articles have surveyed the costs and problems of inflation. See if you can find *How important is it to defeat inflation?* by Roger Bootle (Three Banks Review, Dec. 1981) and *Why do governments worry about inflation?* by Hughes and Tomlinson (NatWest Bank Review, May 1982). A further useful contribution to the debate about the costs of inflation is to be found in *Economic Review* for September 1983. Ivor Pearce puts the view that inflation is a great danger in 'What's wrong with inflation?', and Frank Hahn discusses 'Does inflation matter?' in a more reassuring style.

These recommended texts will only be available in their totality to a lucky student who has access to a well-stocked library. You may find that your local library has only a few of them – or that they offer alternative books not mentioned here.

Examination questions

1. What are the main causes of inflation? What factors do you consider to have been most important in bringing down the level of inflation in recent years?

    (Northern Ireland GCE 'A' level June 1984)

2. Outline briefly the main differences between Keynesian and Monetarist approaches to monetary policy. In 1986 the money supply (Sterling M_3) grew by about 18% whereas price inflation was about 3%. What are the implications of this for Government policy to control inflation?

    (JMB 'A' level June 1987)

3. 'Inflation is caused by excess demand and sustained by expectations.' Discuss.

    (AEB 'A' level June 1987)

4. (a) Explain and interpret the diagram below.

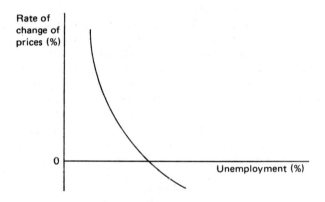

(b) In the light of the following figures, comment on the Phillips curve and the British experience during the period 1971-76.

Year	Rate of change of Retail Price Index (%)	Unemployment (%)
1971	9.5	3.4
1972	6.8	3.7
1973	8.3	2.6
1974	15.9	2.6
1975	24.2	4.0
1976	15.7	5.4

(University of London 'A' June 1983)

5. 'Inflation is always and everywhere a monetary phenomenon'. Discuss.

    (University of London 'A' June 1983)

ANSWERS TO SAQs

SAQ 1:   (a)   The government could attempt this in two ways. It could pass a law that insists that contracts have a cost-of-living adjustment built into them so ensuring that borrowing is paid back at its true value: this measure is sometimes called **indexation** and I discuss it in the appendix on the Price Index at the end of this unit. Alternatively, the government could allow interest rates to rise high enough to compensate lenders for the lost value of their money.

(b)   If you look at the data in Unit 4, you'll see that savings haven't fallen. No-one can quite explain this, but one popular view is that the increased uncertainty of today's world has made people more anxious to build up some reserves in case some unexpected and expensive event – like losing one's job – occurs. We must also remember that interest rates have risen in recent years, so that savers are not completely losing out; and there has been aggressive marketing of many savings institutions (life-insurance salesmen, building-society advertisements).

SAQ 2:   In this case, the firms would find that their receipts were being held down while their costs rose – particularly if they were in an industry depending on imported raw materials or components. So firms would either go bust as their profits collapsed, or would leave the industry and no longer supply the commodities they had previously made.

SAQ 3:   (a)   The relation would be an inverse one -- the higher the level of aggregate demand, then the higher the rate of inflation and the lower the rate of unemployment.

(b)   Unemployment would not reach zero, due to structural and frictional factors.

(c)   The diagram I wanted you to draw is the Phillips curve, as shown on p. 91 of Unit 5.

SAQ 4:   (a)   In year 1, wage drift is $12 - 10 = 2\%$; in year 2 it is 4%, and in year 3, 1%.

(b)   Wage-drift might be negative if the change in earnings was less than the change in wage-rates (say, when rates went up 5% but earnings went up just 3%). This might happen when the economy was in a recession, with overtime and bonus payments falling. Employers might then find that unemployment was so high that they no longer needed to offer high wages to attract labour.

SAQ 5:   The Phillips curve allows you to predict inflation from the level of unemployment. The estimate made in the years in the example were too low – as you can see, in the year of 1967, wages rose 7.8% when they were expected to go up just 2.1% – an error of 5.7%. The worst error was in 1970, when the inflation estimate was out by 11%.

SAQ 6:   You need a statement of your earnings, and of tax deducted. You also need accurate information about the behaviour of retail prices, ideally calculated month by month. And if you are at my level of mental arithmetic, a calculator or slide rule would also come in handy.

As Peter Wiles remarked, this shows that it is extremely difficult to obtain information about changes in real wages, and tends to cast doubt on theories that require workers to have a sophisticated knowledge of real wage movements.

SAQ 7:   The rate of productivity. If we can produce 5% more goods, then we can take home 5% more pay without it increasing production costs.

SAQ 8:   (a)   The quantity theory relates changes in money supply to changes in the price level as follows: $MV = PT$, where M is the quantity of money, V the velocity of circulation, T the number of transactions and P the average price.

(b)   If you hold V and T steady, a rise in M causes a rise in P.

(c)   Money supply may rise in line with real national income – that is, enough to finance the purchase of the commodities that are produced in an expanding economy. Money supply might even be allowed to rise if there is evidence that firms and households want to hold larger money balances. Anything in excess of the amount needed for increased trade or money balances is excessive, although monetarists would allow that when inflation is going on, it would be wise to wind the increase in money supply back to the level of the rise in real national income only gradually.

(d)   It could be. The evidence from previous units is that, on the whole, it doesn't happen – see Unit 8, pp. 138-40.

SAQ 9:   (a)   In order to reduce unemployment and 'reflate' the economy, aggregate demand will be expanded through cuts in taxation and increases in government spending.

(b)   Using the government budget to adjust the level of demand rather than merely to raise revenue for government spending is known as fiscal policy.

SAQ 10:   (a)   We have seen that monetarists believe that economic activity and employment (and therefore T – the real number of transactions) would rise briefly but then fall back.

(b)   V would drop initially but would return to a stable value after a while.

(c)   No. Monetarists certainly argue that monetary expansion will not be effective, and will ultimately lead to inflation. But reforms in the labour market – such as quicker notification of vacancies, better arrangements for retraining and labour mobility – would be effective in reducing the natural rate of unemployment to a lower level.

SAQ 11:   (a)   The authorities are the arms of government that control the money supply – the Bank of England and the Treasury. They might restrict the supply of credit by any of the measures of monetary policy described in this unit.

(b)   A shortage of liquid resources – cash, if you like a more down-to-earth term than money balances.

(c)   The government can either achieve low rates of inflation or low rates of unemployment, but never both.

(d)   The economy slides from Z to B as the monetary squeeze goes on. If you believe the second part of the extract, the decline in inflationary expectations permits progress from B back to N as time passes.

(e)   Unemployment above the 'normal rate of unemployment' that is determined by the structure of the labour market.

(f)   The maverick monetarists who believe that incomes policy might have a role point out that an incomes policy might lead people to expect some improvement in the level of inflation, and might thus assist in the winding down of inflationary expectations.

(g)   There are some who would argue that it doesn't — that the workers who are pushing up wages are not necessarily the ones threatened by unemployment in the marginal industries. Nevertheless, if there is a high rate of unemployment, employers will not have to bid up wages to obtain scarce labour; unions might decide to settle for low pay-rises in order to increase employment in struggling industries, and their members might become less willing to support action that imperils the health of their firm.

Review Section
rising, fall, quickly;
it makes it more difficult to sell exports;
it hits savers, and benefits borrowers in an arbitrary manner;
it might escalate to hyper-inflation;
it increases social uncertainty and discontent;
imported; market (or free-enterprise); demand(-)pull. Keynesian; inflation (*or* changes in money-wages); Phillips Curve; wage-drift; deflationary (*or* surplus);
cost(-)push; (19)67: inflation; unemployment; Phillips;
union; prices; incomes; Chicago, Friedman; monetary; supply; money; prices; print; money; money; inflation.

10 Supply

AIMS OF UNIT 10

This unit starts you on the study of microeconomics, and is rather different from the work you've done so far. After working through this unit you should be able to:
- define the term 'supply'
- explain why the quantities that firms supply vary according to the price they receive
- depict (on the supply curve) the relationship between the quantity supplied and price
- list the factors that might cause a rise or fall in supply, resulting in a shift in the supply curve
- explain what is meant by supply elasticity and, in calculating its value, explain what is meant by an elastic, unit elastic and inelastic supply curve
- point out the difference between the objects of macroeconomic and microeconomic analysis
- define the term 'market'

INTRODUCTION

We are about to go down a new path in economics. Much of the course till now has concerned macroeconomics – ideas about what happens to prices, employment and output in the whole economy. Microeconomics looks instead at the individual components that make up an economy. For example, it aims to explain changes in the prices of particular commodities rather than the national rate of inflation; the output of selected industries rather than the behaviour of GNP; employment and wages in individual occupations rather than total employment. However, micro- and macro-economic analysis should not be viewed as separate and unrelated parts of the course, for there are some problems which require insights from both.

SAQ 1: *Which of the following questions is the concern of microeconomic analysis, and which macroeconomics?*
(a)   national unemployment
(b)   employment in the textile industry
(c)   changes in average wage rates
(d)   why doctors earn more than nurses
(e)   what factors may cause a fall in national output
(f)   why a slump in housebuilding may take place.

MARKETS, SUPPLY AND DEMAND

In Britain, some commodities (education, policing, health care) are provided by the government. However, most of our economy is not regulated by the state, but works through the interaction of producers and consumers in **markets**. The concept of a market is central to microeconomics. Everyone recognises the everyday meaning of the word — a place where traders set up stalls and buyers go to look at and buy the commodities on offer. But terms like 'stock market' or 'housing market' that appear in our newspapers indicate a broader meaning. Economists follow this wider conception of a market by using the word to mean any situation in which sellers are in contact with buyers of a commodity. A market need not, then, be a particular place or building.

Let's take as an example the 'foreign exchange market'. Dollars, francs and marks are bought and sold over telephone and telex links that connect banks and firms in many countries, making it very much a worldwide market. Similarly, the market for housing in your area will consist not of a single building but of the complex of estate agents, lawyers, local papers, building societies and even newsagents' windows that connect buyers and sellers.

SAQ 2: *List some commodities for which there is a worldwide market, and some for which the market is very local.*

The prices and quantities of commodities traded in markets depend on the wishes of the buyers and sellers who are doing the trading. For any given commodity sellers wish to receive a high price, but equally, buyers seek the lowest ones. That much is obvious: but microeconomic analysis looks in turn at the behaviour of the buyers and the sellers — firms and households — to see if a more subtle picture can be drawn.

In this unit, we'll begin our study of microeconomics by looking at *supply*: the willingness of firms to offer commodities for sale. Then, in Unit 11, we'll look at demand: how much consumers are able to buy, and at what price.

SUPPLY

Economists define, supply as *the amount of a commodity that firms are able and willing to sell in a given time at a given range of prices.* The last few words of that definition are important: the amount that a firm supplies to the market will depend crucially on the price that it receives. The higher the price fetched by a commodity, the more of it the firms will be willing to supply.

We can illustrate this by taking as an example the supply of a product that is reasonably simple to produce — wheat. The amount of wheat supplied to the UK market will depend on the price it fetches. No European farmer is able profitably to produce wheat at a very low price — only a few imports from low-cost Australian or American producers are available. At a somewhat higher price, wheat production in the UK becomes worthwhile for a few highly efficient farmers in eastern England. As the price rises still further, to present levels, wheat can profitably be supplied by farmers in the Midlands and north of England; and it pays existing producers to use more fertilisers or more workers to get additional output from existing fields. Were the price to go even higher, additional supplies of (admittedly high-cost) wheat would become available from smallholdings and highland farms. The rising price would then encourage existing producers to produce more wheat, and marginal producers to enter the market. This is illustrated on the graph on the right which shows more and more being supplied as the price goes higher. The line that connects these points, showing how much is supplied at each price, is called the **supply**

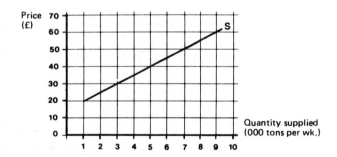

Graph 10.1 The supply curve

curve. (Note that a supply 'curve' can be a straight line. For the sake of simplicity I've used straight lines for most of this unit.)

SAQ 3: *(a) The date overleaf relates the price and quantity of tomatoes supplied to a wholesale market. Presented like this, such data is known as a **supply schedule**. Use the information on the supply schedule to plot a supply curve on the blank graph.*

No. of boxes supplied	400	500	600	700	800
Price (£)	10	12	14	16	18

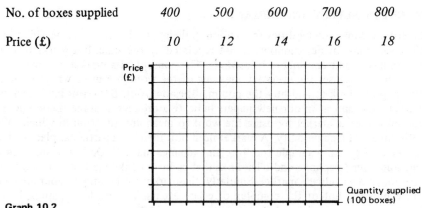

Graph 10.2

(b)   Explain why more oil will be supplied to the UK market as the price goes higher. Answer by using the paragraph in which I explained how this works with regard to wheat, changing the examples used as appropriate.

How changes in price affect the amount firms supply

We've seen that as prices rise, we can expect the quantity supplied to rise. But it's useful to know by precisely how much supplies will increase in response to higher prices — or how much they'll fall away if prices collapse. Look at the supply curve below, for example:

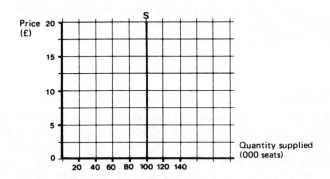

Graph 10.3

Here the amount that is supplied is completely unresponsive to price. No matter how high the price goes, no more will be supplied. This graph applies to a stadium with a fixed capacity: no matter how much spectators are prepared to pay for a ticket to a major sports event, the supply of tickets is fixed. When, as here, the amount that is supplied does not increase at all when price rises, economists describe supply as totally **inelastic**. Such cases are rare, for generally if consumers are prepared to pay more, firms will find some way to provide larger supplies of a commodity.

Let's suppose that, in the stadium we've just discussed, it is possible to erect additional seats in temporary stands. Erecting the new seats will be an additional expense, an expense that promoters can only meet profitably by selling tickets at a higher price. Nevertheless, the ability to provide additional tickets if the price is higher means that the supply curve is no longer vertical. Looking at the curve in graph 10.4 we see that when tickets are sold at £5 each it is only profitable to provide standard accommodation in the stadium for 100 000. But if the public is prepared to pay £10 per

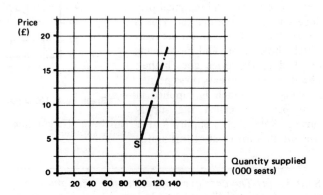

Graph 10.4

ticket an additional 10 000 seats can be made available in temporary stands. Indeed, if people were prepared to pay even more, it might be possible profitably to provide a relayed TV coverage of the events to specially hired cinemas or cable TV outlets, providing yet more seats. However, prices have already had to double to get just a few extra seats. Supply is still rather unresponsive to price changes — still inelastic, even if not as completely inelastic as in graph 10.3.

We can measure the extent to which price changes will affect supplies using this formula:

$$\text{elasticity of supply} = \frac{\text{percentage change in quantity supplied}}{\text{percentage change in price}}$$

In the example I used above and showed in graph 10.4 when ticket prices are increased by 100% — from £5 to £10 — the number of seats that promoters are prepared to supply goes up from 100 000 to 110 000, i.e. 10%. So elasticity of supply here is $\frac{10}{100}$: one-tenth or a number value of ·1. The reason that the calculation comes to less than one is because the percentage change in quantity supplied is less than the percentage change in price. Supply is termed inelastic with respect to price whenever this is true. If the percentage change in price is matched by an equivalent percentage change in supplies (e.g. a 1% rise in price increases quantity supplied by 1%), we speak of **unit elasticity**.

SAQ 4: *Work out the number value of elasticity of supply in these examples:*

	Percentage change in price	Percentage change in quantity supplied
(a)	8	2
(b)	10	5
(c)	12	8
(d)	5	25
(e)	2	2

In which of these examples is supply inelastic with respect to price? In which is it unit elastic?

In (d) above, the number of elasticity of supply is 5: because the percentage change in quantity supplied is greater than the percentage change in price that caused it, the elasticity calculation gives us a figure greater than one. Where this occurs, supply is said to be **elastic**. The next graph illustrates (d), where a 5% change in price caused supplies to vary by 25%. You can see that supply

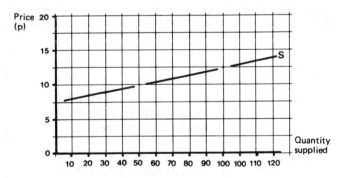

Graph 10.5

is much more responsive to price — much more *elastic* — than in graph 10.4. On any given graph, the steeper the supply curve, the less elastic it is. Be wary, though, of reading too much into the slopes, of supply curves, as changes in the scales of a graph can steepen or flatten the apparent slope of a curve.

SAQ 5: *(a) Work out the elasticity of supply in each of the examples below. Put the number value in the first column, and in the second write E, I, or U according to whether supply is elastic, inelastic or unit elastic with respect to price.*

	Percentage change in price	Percentage change in quantity supplied	Supply elasticity	E / U / I
(i)	10	20		
(ii)	6	2		
(iii)	1	3		
(iv)	7	7		

(b)   Which of these two curves is the most elastic?

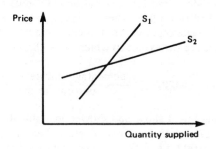

Graph 10.6

Perfect elasticity

The supply curve I've depicted in graph 10.7 is a curious one. It stretches horizontally across the page, meaning that supply is totally elastic. Let me explain what this means, taking an example from, say, the supply of potatoes. Where the supply curve is horizontal, anyone who can pay the

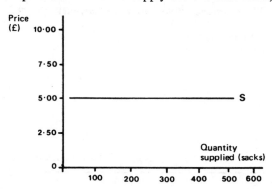

Graph 10.7

asking price — in this case, £5 for a 50 kg sack — can buy as much as they wish. That's the going price, and there are no shortages. This is another extreme case — perfect elasticity — and is as rare as the example of the totally inelastic supply in graph 10.3.

SAQ 6: *Fill in the summary table below to check your knowledge of supply elasticity.*

Term	Description	Number value
(a)	Consumers may buy an infinite amount at the present.price, but nothing at a lower price	Infinity
Elastic	A change in price will cause a proportionately greater change in quantity supplied	*(b)*
(c)	A given percentage change in price will bring about a matching change in quantity supplied	One
Inelastic	*(d)*	Between one and zero
(e)	Quantity supplied does not change, no matter how much price changes	Zero

---

What factors affect elasticity of supply? In practice, elasticity of supply depends a great deal on time-lags. Alfred Marshall, the distinguished Cambridge economist I mentioned in Unit 1, distinguished three periods when dealing with the response of firms to changes in price: the short term, the medium term and the long term. In the very short term, the supply of almost anything is fixed. To take Marshall's example, if we all decided that we desperately wanted fish today, the shops would be taken by surprise and sell out their stocks. In the medium term, though, we could get more fish by bringing into use underused boats or paying fishermen more to work longer shifts and make more frequent trips. In the long term (say, four to five years), more fishing boats could be built, and more school-leavers trained to become fishermen. This example nicely illustrates why questions of supply elasticities really boil down to questions of time-lags.

The concept of time-lags relates to a real world problem of supply inelasticity which has worried successive Chancellors of the Exchequer. If the government were to decide to expand the economy how long would it take before firms got going with increased production? (*SAQ 7*) If UK firms were slow to respond to an upturn in demand, then the additional demand would either raise prices (as consumers compete for scarce supplies) or, more likely, increase imports (as consumers impatiently turn to foreign suppliers).

SAQ 7: *How and why might the government expand the economy?*

FACTORS THAT AFFECT SUPPLY

The price of the commodity
We have already seen that usually firms will supply more of a commodity the higher the price that is offered, and that we can show the relationship between price and quantity supplied on the supply curve. Exactly how much extra will be supplied if price rises — or how much less if it falls — is measured by the elasticity of supply. However, firms' willingness to offer a commodity for sale is affected by a number of other factors — factors that might cause them to offer more or less for sale at a given range of prices.

Costs of production
Firms' willingness to supply will be affected by production costs. The costs of production can be looked at under two headings — the cost of the factors of production (*SAQ 8*) and the efficiency with which they are combined. If production costs fall, firms are able to supply a product more cheaply: so a greater quantity can be supplied at a given range of prices. This is most likely to result from improvements in production technology. If costs rise — for example, due to higher energy prices or wage rates — less can be supplied within the same price range.

SAQ 8: *What are the factors of production?*

Prices of other commodities
The supply of one commodity is often directly influenced by the price of another. For example, if the price of milk rises some farmers will be tempted to use their fields for pasturing dairy cows rather than producing wheat. In this case a rise in the price of milk will cause a fall in the supply of wheat. The general rule is that the supply of one commodity falls if the price of the other rises. This is only likely to be important where resources can be switched reasonably easily between the production of two commodities, and where this is so, we speak of **competitive supply**.

There have been times (in the mid-1970s) when lucrative House Improvement Grant work attracted so many craftsmen that the new housing programme suffered: the supply of skilled labour between new and renovated housing was competitive. However most commodities are not connected this closely. And in direct contrast, there are commodities which are produced as part of the production process that makes something else — oil, plastics and petrol, for example, or beef and hides. Where this happens, we speak of **joint supply**. In this case, a rise in the price of one commodity will raise the supply of the other.

SAQ 9: *Which of the following would cause a rise in the supply of eggs?*
(a)   more efficient hen-houses
(b)   more expensive feed for hens
(c)   falling beef prices
(d)   increased profits for potato producers
(e)   higher prices for chicken meat

The attitude of firms
We have talked so far as if suppliers of commodities were only seeking the biggest profit or the highest wages — yet we know that this isn't so. A farmer may produce beef cattle because of family

tradition; a talented woman may stay in a low-paid NHS job from a sense of social worth; a film company may turn down a lucrative project that they consider to be in poor taste. Attitudes, then, will affect the supplies of a commodity.

SAQ 10: *There is considerable over-supply in the market for actors and actresses, despite the fact that pay is usually poor and periods of unemployment long. Why do you think there is this high level of supply?*

Unpredictable production problems

There's little to say about this final factor, except to cite examples. A manufacturing firm may be affected by technical problems or a labour dispute; or a farmer may find that disease or weather reduce supplies.

SHIFTS IN SUPPLY

Let's look at the way that changes in the factors I've outlined above will affect supplies of a commodity. When the price of a commodity rises, then larger amounts will be supplied; we can read this off on a supply curve, as in the graph 10.8. Here, a rise in price from 60p to 80p has increased

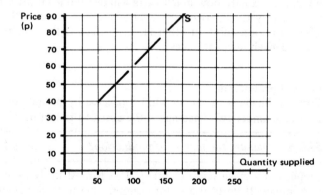

Graph 10.8

the quantity from 100 to 150 (*SAQ 11*). The supply curve itself shown that more will be supplied at a higher price and less at a lower. Changes in the other factors that affect supply, though, mean that more or less is supplied at *each* price. Here are the factors, for example, that could cause a rise in supply:

SAQ 11: *What is the price elasticity of supply here?*

- lower production costs
- lower prices for goods in competitive supply
- higher prices for commodities in joint supply
- positive changes in the attitudes of suppliers
- unexpectedly good production conditions (e.g. a bumper harvest)

We illustrate what happens when these conditions occur by shifting the supply curve. In the curve in graph 10.9, for example, I have shown a shift from s_1 to s_2. You can see that more is supplied at each price: whereas only q_1 was supplied at price p_1, now q_2 is supplied.

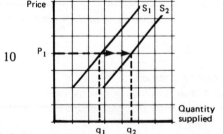

Graph 10.9 A rise in supply

Graph 10.10
A fall in supply

The reverse movement — a fall in supply causing the supply curve to shift leftwards — means that less is being supplied at each price than previously. I've shown this in graph 10.10.

SAQ 12: *List the reasons that might have caused the fall in supply shown in graph 10.10.*

Let's summarise where we have got to. A rise in supply means that more is supplied along a whole range of prices, and is shown by a movement of the supply curve to the right. A fall in supply means that less is offered for sale at each price – in other words, the curve shifts to the left. But a simple change in the price of the commodity will not alter the position of the supply curve; you simply go up or down the curve to read off the consequent change in quantity supplied. The curve itself traces the relationship between price and quantity supplied.

SAQ 13: *Questions (i) to (vi) below refer to shifts in the supply curve. Use the following answer code to indicate how, other things being equal, the supply curve will shift in the circumstances.*

- *(a)   The curve will shift to the right.*
- *(b)   The curve will shift to the left.*
- *(c)   There will be no change in the position of the curve.*
- *(d)   There is not enough information to make a judgement.*

- *(i)   How will a rise in the price of lamb shift the supply curve for beef?*
- *(ii)   How will a rise in the price of lamb shift the supply curve for lamb?*
- *(iii)   How will a fall in oil prices alter the supply curve for plastics?*
- *(iv)   How would a change in business opinions against whaling shift the supply curve for whale-meat products?*
- *(v)   How will a change in ideas about UK economic policy shift the supply curve for sterling?*
- *(vi)   How would higher grants for engineering students affect the supply of skilled engineers?*

Effects of taxation and subsidies

Sometimes a government may wish to encourage or discourage the production of a commodity. It can use taxes and subsidies for this purpose. When firms have to pay a tax on each unit of a commodity made and sold, the effect is very much the same as a rise in costs. For example, when a tobacco firm is asked for a 40p tax for each packet of cigarettes sold, it will get the money in by raising the price to the customer. As a result, the supply curve shifts upwards by 40p: what used to be offered for sale at 60p now costs £1.

SAQ 14: *(a) Plot the following supply curve on the blank graph and mark it s_1.*

Price (£)	*1*	*2*	*3*	*4*
Quantity supplied	*1000*	*2000*	*3000*	*4000*

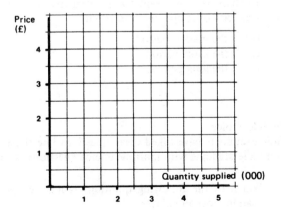

Graph 10.11

(b) Now draw a new supply curve resulting from a 50p tax on the commodity. You do this by raising each price by 50p, so that you are plotting the amount that firms were previously willing to offer at £1 against a price of £1.50.

If, on the other hand, government wishes to encourage the output of a commodity by subsidy, the supply curve moves downwards. The effect is similar to a reduction in costs.

APPENDIX: THE STRANGE CASE OF THE DOWNWARD-SLOPING SUPPLY CURVE

While the vast majority of commodities exhibit an upward-sloping supply curve, it is possible to find some downward-sloping supply curves: that is, a situation where more is supplied as the price goes down *or* less as the price goes up. An example of the first case occurs in colonial economies where growers of commodities such as coffee, sugar and tea are forced by lower prices to increase output so that more can be sold to keep up living standards.

As an example of the second case we can take the case of real wages. Over the past fifty years, real wages have been rising, yet hours worked have been falling. So, despite a rise in the price of labour per hour, hours of work supplied have fallen. (Note though, that the supply curve for particular *sorts* of labour is still upward-sloping. Although a general increase in wages may cause workers to take longer holidays and work a shorter week, a rise in the wages of one industry will still attract more workers by drawing them away from other industries.)

REVIEW SECTION

Summary

This has been a brief unit to start your study of microeconomic analysis. You've learned that in order to try to understand how individual markets work economists look at how consumers and firms interact. Starting by looking at firms, I showed how the amount firms would offer for sale varies with price: the term *supply* was used to describe the amounts that would be offered at a range of prices. I used the idea of *supply elasticity* to show how economists measure the relationship between price and quantity supplied. I then introduced other factors that could affect supply – such as production costs – and showed how a rise or fall in supply would follow a change in these factors. Finally, I used shifts in supply curves to illustrate changes in supply – a fall in supply moving the supply curves leftwards, and a rise being indicated by a rightward shift.

Further reading

You will find that almost every economics textbook introduces you to the supply curve: check, for example, with the texts mentioned in Unit 29, or with G. Hewitt *Economics of the Market* (Fontana) Chapter 2. We shall be returning to the supply curve in later units to see how the upward sloping line is derived.

Examination questions

1. 'The supply of the factors of production are more likely to be inelastic than elastic.' Discuss.

(AEB 'A' June 1985)

2. Explain why it is thought that more of a product is normally supplied at a higher price per period. What are the factors which govern elasticity of supply?

(University of London 'A' January 1982)

3. Explain what is meant by the elasticity of supply. What factors are likely to influence the elasticity of supply of fresh fish in

    (a)   the market period
    (b)   the short period
    (c)   the long period.

(Northern Ireland GCE 'A' 1984)

Multiple choice

While examiners have asked essay questions like those above about supply it is more usual to test your understanding with multiple choice questions as follows:

1. Which of the following questions is most properly the concern of macroeconomics rather than microeconomics?
    (a)   a sharp rise in vegetable prices
    (b)   a shortage of maths teachers
    (c)   a rise in the Retail Price Index
    (d)   a surplus of dairy produce in the EEC

2. Which of the following is necessary for the existence of a market?
    (a)   a well-known building or meeting-place
    (b)   a fixed price for the commodity traded

(c)   telephone or telex links
(d)   contact between buyers and sellers

3.   Some communities use the hot water that comes from the cooling of power stations to provide central heating for nearby districts. In this case, electricity and heating are in a situation of
(a)   joint supply
(b)   competitive supply
(c)   joint demand
(d)   inelastic supply

4.   If a fall in price of 10% results in supplies falling by 5%, supply is said to be
(a)   perfectly inelastic
(b)   inelastic
(c)   unit elastic
(d)   elastic

5.   If doubling of the price of a commodity results in no extra supplies, then supply is said to be
(a)   elastic
(b)   inelastic
(c)   unit elastic
(d)   perfectly inelastic

6.   The supply of divers to North-Sea oil companies is likely to be
(a)   inelastic — no matter how good the pay, adverse work conditions will deter employees
(b)   elastic — an increase in wage rates will attract at least some workers from other industries
(c)   elastic in the short run, but inelastic in the long run as firms employ all the qualified workers
(d)   inelastic in the short run, but more elastic in the long run as more workers attracted by high pay train as divers

7.   In the diagram below, (a), (b), (c) and (d) are all supply curves. Which of them is of unit elasticity?

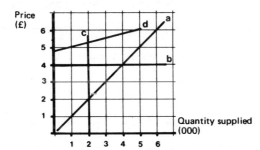

Graph 10.12

8.   We speak of an increase in supply when
(a)   more is supplied at higher prices
(b)   more is supplied at lower prices
(c)   more is supplied at all prices
(d)   the supply curve shifts leftwards

9.   An increase in supply might result from
(a)   increased energy costs
(b)   increases in the price of rival commodities
(c)   increased wage costs
(d)   changes in producer attitudes

10.   A totally inelastic supply curve will
(a)   slope upwards at 45°
(b)   go vertically upwards
(c)   be absolutely horizontal
(d)   slope downwards to the right

11.   Which of the following commodities are produced via the market mechanism?
(a)   defence   (b)   policing
(c)   street lighting   (d)   newspapers

12. Which of the following commodities are in competitive supply?
(a) wheat and straw
(b) bacon and pig's liver
(c) nurses' and lorry-drivers' labour
(d) cars and lorries

Questions 13-19 use the diagrams below, which refer to the supply curves for a particular commodity, as answer keys. They can be used once, more than once, or not at all.

(a)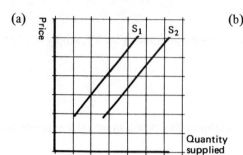

(b)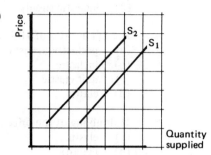

(c)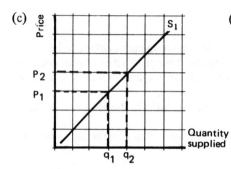

(d)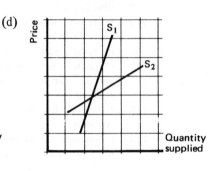

Graphs 10.13-10.17

In which of these diagrams:
13. does a movement from s_1 to s_2 show the result of a rise in production costs?

14. does s_1 indicate supply in the short term, but s_2 show a longer-term supply curve?

15. does a movement from s_1 to s_2 show the result of poor weather conditions on the supply of an agricultural commodity?

16. is the result of a higher price on supplies shown?

17. does a movement from s_1 to s_2 show the effect of improved production methods?

18. does a movement from s_1 to s_2 show the effect of additional taxation on the commodity in question?

19. is a supply curve of unit elasticity shown?

20. Which of the following is *not* a valid reason for the supply curve to slope upwards?
(a) In the short-run, producing additional units can involve higher production costs (such as overtime payments to staff)
(b) When the price of a commodity rises, firms will enter the newly profitable market
(c) When the price of a commodity falls, some firms will find themselves unable to produce the commodity profitably.
(d) Producing large amounts of a commodity is always more expensive for a firm than producing smaller quantities.

ANSWERS TO SAQs

SAQ 1: Questions (a), (c) and (e) deal with matters that affect the whole economy: that makes them macroeconomic in scope. Because questions (b) and (d) look at individual markets (textiles, and NHS workers) they are the concern of microeconomics. Question (f) might profit from both microeconomic analysis (where factors peculiar to the building industry are important) and also from macroeconomic analysis (if, for example, the fall in house-construction is part of a general slump in output and incomes).

SAQ 2:   You will have your own list for this. Examples for which the market is local might include fish and chips, or hairdressing. Worldwide markets exist in commodities such as cocoa, coffee, tin, rubber, oil etc.

SAQ 3:   (a) is a reasonably simple plotting task. My own answer to section (b) goes as follows: 'If oil fetched a very low price, it would only be profitable to produce it in the low-cost, easy fields of the Middle East. At a somewhat higher price, more supplies become profitable as smaller oil fields are exploited and it becomes economic to refine poorer quality oils. As the price gets even higher, offshore fields become profitable; and were the price to go even higher, it would become possible to obtain additional supplies from converting coal to oil. So the higher the price, the more supplies will be forthcoming.'

SAQ 4:   (a) .25 (inelastic); (b) .5 (inelastic); (c) .66 (inelastic); (d) 5 (elastic); (e) 1 (unit elastic).

SAQ 5:   (a) (i) 2, E (ii) .33, I (iii) 3, E (iv) 1, U; (b) s_2: the shallower of two curves on a given diagram will be the more elastic. Remember my warning, though, about judging elasticity from apparent slopes. It all depends on the scales!

SAQ 6:   (a) perfectly elastic; (b) greater than one; (c) unit elastic; (d) a given percentage change in price will cause a lower than proportionate change in quantity supplied; (e) perfectly inelastic.

SAQ 7:   They might expand demand in order to cut unemployment and increase output and incomes, using either fiscal (tax and spending) or monetary (money and credit) policy.

SAQ 8:   Land, labour and capital.

SAQ 9:   (a) would, by lowering production costs; (b) wouldn't, as costs would rise; (c) might, if disgruntled beef-producers switched to producing eggs instead; (d) might reduce egg supplies if farmers moved away from egg production into potatoes; (e) would increase egg production if chicken meat were to be jointly supplied with eggs.

SAQ 10: Because actors and actresses are attracted by the non-monetary rewards of the job (artistic expression, fame) and also because there is a long-shot that comes off for the few who enjoy high status and incomes.

SAQ 11: Price has gone up 33%, quantity supplied by 50%. Elasticity therefore works out to 1.5.

SAQ 12: The reasons are the opposite of the ones a paragraph or so earlier that resulted in a rise in supply.

SAQ 13: (i), (b) — beef farmers may switch to lamb production; (ii) (c) — as the relationship between lamb prices and supplies are already shown on the supply curve; (iii) (a) — as production costs fall (iv) (b) — caused by an unfavourable change in producer attitudes; (v) (d) — a trick question: the nature of the change is not specified; (vi) (a) — as talented youngsters who are choosing between, say, engineering and pure science courses are attracted by the better-supported course.

SAQ 14: Is a plotting task: you should have two parallel lines, one 50p above the other. Mark the taxed supply curve s_t.

11 Demand

AIMS OF UNIT 11

This unit complements Unit 10 and aims to cover the topic of demand. At the end of it, you should be able to:

- define the term 'demand'
- distinguish between market and household demand
- plot a demand curve
- use both the idea of marginal utility and indifference curves to explain why the demand curve slopes downwards
- define price elasticity of demand, calculate its value, and explain its importance
- explain what is meant by income elasticity of demand
- list the factors that will affect demand and show how a rise or fall in demand will shift the demand curve

INTRODUCTION

A wit once remarked that any parrot could become an economist as long as it was taught two words — supply and demand. Like most witticisms, there's something in this: in Unit 10 I explained how in order to understand markets we need to look in turn at the behaviour of sellers (supply) and of buyers (demand). I then went on to define and analyse supply. We'll now go a stage further and look at demand, so that in Unit 12 we can tackle the market mechanism as a whole.

DEMAND

Economists define demand as *the amount of a commodity that consumers are willing and able to purchase in a given period of time at a given range of prices*. There are two important things to note about this definition. Firstly, the definition makes it clear that, for demand to exist, consumers must be able to pay for the commodity: we are dealing, in other words, with *effective* demand. Merely to want or need something does not create a demand in a market unless that want is backed by money. Secondly, the definition speaks of 'a given range of prices'. The amount of a commodity that will be bought depends on the price at which it is offered. In general, more will be bought at a lower price than at a higher price.

Demand curves

Economists depict the relationship between price and quantity demanded on a demand curve. As in the unit on supply, we'll plot the price on the vertical axis and quantity on the horizontal (though this time, it's quantity demanded rather than quantity supplied). Let's suppose that when the price is £2, 300 units are demanded; at £3, 250 and at £4 just 200. Notice how the fact that more is demanded the lower the price causes the demand curve to slope downwards to the right:

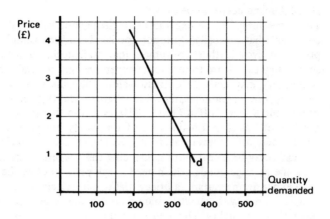

Graph 11.1

SAQ 1: *Now plot the figures below which show the expected sales of petrol from a hypothetical motorway filling station each day*

Price (£)	1.50	1.75	2.00	2.25	2.50
galls demanded	7000	4000	2000	1250	750

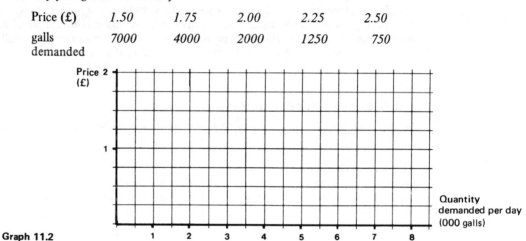

Graph 11.2

You'll notice a difference in gradient between this demand curve and the previous one (even bearing in mind my cautionary words about making judgements from slope gradients in Unit 10). In graph 11.1, demand is not very responsive to price. When prices double (from £2 to £4), sales hold up remarkably well, falling by just one-third. In the graph that you plotted in SAQ 1, a comparatively small change in price (£1.75 to £2.00) halved sales. As with supply curves, such differences between demand curves reflect different responsiveness to price changes: and here, too, we measure this in terms of elasticity — this time, elasticity of demand. We'll look into this in more detail later in the unit.

Demand curves and total expenditure

It is possible from the demand curve to measure what total expenditure will be on a commodity,

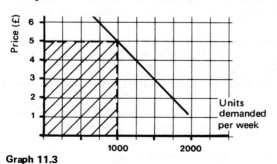

Graph 11.3

total expenditure being the total sales of a commodity multiplied by the price at which it is sold. In the graph on the left, we see that 1000 units of a commodity are sold at a price of £5. If firms chose to sell at this price, they would receive £5 x 1000 = £5000 in sales revenues. This is illustrated by the shaded rectangle on the graph, which has a base of 1000 units and a height of £5. The area of any rectangle is base times height, and so the area of this rectangle represents the £5000 that would be spent on the good in question in the time and at the price specified.

SAQ 2: *Look back to graph 11.1. How much would firms receive in sales revenues if the price were £4? Draw and shade in the rectangle that represents this sum.*

Do all demand curves slope down?

There are alleged to be exceptions to the general rule of downward sloping demand curves. One concerns what are called 'inferior goods'. Take the example of very cheap cotton shirts. If their price falls even further, consumers may well decide that instead of having a wardrobe of cheap shirts, they can afford to buy some expensive ones instead. Thus, in this case a fall in the price of a commodity may actually decrease sales. This case is, however, quite exceptional, and you may well, like most economists, regard it as rather doubtful. Inferior goods are sometimes called 'Giffen goods'. Sir Robert Giffen (1837-1910) observed that the poor bought more bread as its price rose, not less: it was such a major part of the family budget that a rise in its price meant that a poor family could afford less meat, fruit, biscuits, etc., and so had to fill up with bread.

There may be a few more convincing cases where demand actually increases with price. There are some prestige goods, which need a high price to show the status people must have to buy them — an expensive restaurant, a pricey night-club, certain brands of jeans. And as people have come to associate price with quality, manufacturers are sometimes happy to keep prices high to retain a reputation for quality. The management of products as diverse as Kerrygold butter and Turtle Car-wax have revived company fortunes through an awareness that the public associates premium prices with higher quality. Indeed, perfume manufacturers sought legal help in 1981 to stop their products being sold too cheaply in supermarkets.

Finally, speculation may have an effect. Sometimes when the price of a commodity rises sharply (whether it's gold, shares in a particular company or a widely traded raw material) people rush to buy on the expectation that the price will rise higher still. But this, like the Giffen case, is an exception to the rule. For the vast majority of commodities (what are called **normal goods**) a rise in price will reduce the quantity of that commodity that is demanded.

FACTORS THAT AFFECT DEMAND

We can now go on to list the things that will affect demand for a given commodity.

The price of the commodity

We've already worked out that at a low price, sales will be greater than at a high price. This is the relationship depicted on the demand curve, which enables us to read off the quantities that would be demanded at a given range of prices.

The consumer's income

We would expect that, as consumer incomes rose, so would the quantities of a commodity that would be demanded at a given range of prices: in other words, a rise in demand would take place. A fall in incomes would, by contrast, reduce demand. The amount consumers are free to spend is reduced by income tax and national insurance payments: it would be more accurate to say that demand for a commodity will vary with disposable income. Consumers' ability to afford a commodity — particularly an expensive one such as furniture, hi-fi or a car — will also vary with the cost and availability of credit and hire-purchase arrangements.

The extent to which demand for a commodity changes as a result of a change in income is termed the **income elasticity of demand,** and is measured in the percentage increase in demand for that commodity when the consumer's income goes up 1%. Income elasticities vary widely. Some commodities exhibit very low income elasticities: if your income rose from £5000 to £10 000, you'd probably spend very little more on potatoes or matches. Other goods, though, have high income elasticities of demand: video-recorders, or foreign holidays are examples.

SAQ 3: *(a) Could income elasticity of demand ever be negative? What would this mean, and for which products would such a value be likely?*
(b) What other form of demand elasticity is there besides income elasticity: what is the difference between them?

The price of other commodities

There are two cases to consider here, as shown on next page:

(a) *Complementary goods*; that is, goods which are consumed together. In this case, when demand for one rises, so does demand for the other. For example the demand for gas central-heating fitments is affected by the price of gas: if gas is cheaper than competing fuels, we may expect a higher demand for gas central-heating equipment than if it were more expensive.

(b) *Substitutes* such as butter and margarine, oil and coal, cotton and nylon. These goods are competitive, and we would expect a fall in the price of one good to cause a drop in the demand for its rival. For example, when butter was subsidised by the 1974-9 Labour Government, margarine sales slumped.

SAQ 4: *Graph 11.2 depicted the demand for petrol at a motorway filling station. Name some complements and substitutes that would affect demand for petrol at that station. Aim to find four or five items.*

The effects that changes in the price of one commodity can have on the quantity of another commodity that is demanded can be measured using an idea known as the **cross-elasticity of demand**. This involves using the following formulae:

$$\text{cross elasticity of demand} = \frac{\text{percentage change in quantity of commodity 1}}{\text{percentage change in the price of commodity 2}}$$

Cross elasticities can be negative or positive. If the two commodities we are considering are substitutes, we would expect the cross-elasticity to be positive: an increase in the price of electricity should lead to an increase in the demand for gas. But the reverse will be true in the case of complements. A rise in the price of electricity will probably reduce the number of electric cookers demanded, and as the magnitudes move in opposite directions, the cross-elasticity of demand will be negative.

The tastes and preferences of the consumer
These are clearly important to the understanding of demand. The rise in demand for casual clothes during the past twenty years (and the associated decline in demand for more formal business-wear, like suits) was a result of changing attitudes and styles of life rather than changes in price or incomes.

SAQ 5: *How might a firm make consumer attitudes towards its product more favourable?*

The four factors I've just outlined — price, incomes, tastes and the prices of other commodities — would all affect an individual's demand for a commodity. Any market, though, is made up of many individuals: the market demand curve is therefore made up of all the individual demand curves added together. The following exercise shows you how.

SAQ 6: *The figures below show the quantities of a commodity that would be demanded by three major consumers in a market. Use this information to discover the total quantity demanded at each price, and plot this market demand curve on the blank graph provided.*

Price (£)	20	30	40	50
Quantity demanded by consumer 1	30	25	15	10
Quantity demanded by consumer 2	20	10	7	5
Quantity demanded by consumer 3	10	5	3	–
	—	—	—	—
Total quantity demanded				

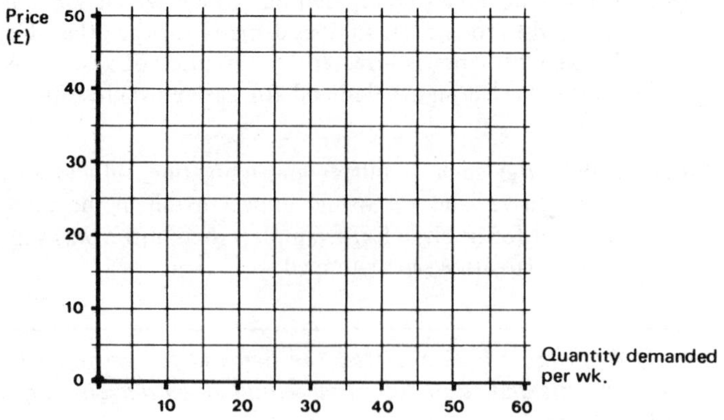

Price 50
(£)

Graph 11.4

When you realise that market demand is the sum of all the individual demands of the various households, then you'll understand that market demand will not just depend on the four factors I've mentioned so far. Also important will be:

Number of consumers
The larger the number of consumers, the greater the demand. A growth in population raises demand for most commodities. Some commodities, of course, depend for their sales on the proportion of a particular age-group among the population. A rising population caused by people living longer will increase the demand for medical services: a decline in the birth rate will adversely affect the demand for baby-wear. (Both trends have been evident in recent years.)

The distribution of the national income among the population
In a country where the distribution of the national income is very unequal, demand for luxury goods will be higher than in a country where the same average level of income is spread more equally.

SAQ 7:   *Assess how the following factors will affect the demand for middle-priced houses for sale, using the column on the right to indicate whether they will cause demand to rise (R), fall (F), or remain unchanged (U).*

R / F / U

(a)   A rise in consumer incomes

(b)   Mortgages becoming more difficult to obtain

(c)   Higher rents for council housing

(d)   A rise in the proportion of 25-45 year olds in the population

(e)   Abolishing tax concessions on house-purchase to finance higher retirement pensions

---

SHIFTS IN DEMAND
The effects of an increase or decrease in the price of a commodity on the quantity of that commodity that is demanded are shown on the demand curve itself. But changes in the other factors affecting demand will increase or decrease the amounts that would be demanded at given prices. We've seen that a rise in incomes would raise demand, for example. On the other hand, demand for a commodity would fall if a substitute became cheaper. Such rises and falls in demand will cause shifts in the demand curve.

An increase in demand can be depicted as a shift of the whole demand curve to the right, from d_1 to d_2 (graph 11.5). Notice that with a rise in demand, more is demanded at each price: 35 instead of 30 at £1, 25 instead of 20 at £2, 15 instead of 10 at £3.

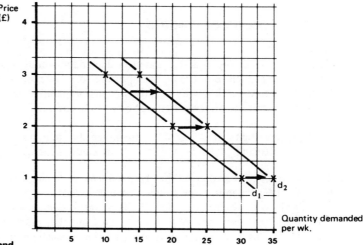

Graph 11.5
An increase in demand

Such an increase in demand might be caused by:

- increased consumer incomes
- cheaper complementary goods
- higher-priced substitutes
- more favourable consumer attitudes
- a growth in the number of consumers
- a favourable change in the distribution of the national income

A fall in demand, illustrated in graph 11.6 can result from:

- a fall in consumer incomes
- higher-priced complements
- cheaper substitutes
- adverse changes in consumer attitudes
- a decline in the number of consumers
- an adverse change in the distribution of national income

Such a fall would result in a shift of the demand curve leftwards, as in graph 11.6 in which curve d_2 connects the smaller quantities that would be demanded at the range of prices shown.

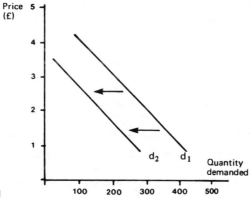

Graph 11.6 A fall in demand

SAQ 8: *In this exercise, I want you to say whether the events described in (a) to (g) will, other things being equal, shift the demand curve for oil to the right (R), left (L) or not at all (N). Put your answers in the column on the right.*

R / L / N

(a)   A successful advertising campaign by the coal industry, advo-advocating a return to 'real fires' at home

(b)   Increased car sales

(c)   A recession in industrial countries

(d)   Discovery of new oil deposits in the Irish Sea

(e)   A successful national insulation campaign

(f)   Cheaper gas

(g)   A rise in oil prices (careful !)

PRICE ELASTICITY OF DEMAND

What is it?

So far we have simply said that quantity demanded will depend on price: as price rises, we expect less to be demanded. But it is often important to know more than this: firms and governments will be most interested to know by exactly *how much* quantity demanded will fall if prices rise. Economists measure in the price elasticity of demand, using the following formula:

$$\text{price elasticity of demand} = \frac{\text{percentage change in quantity demanded}}{\text{percentage change in price}}$$

The terminology is similar to that I introduced in dealing with elasticity of supply in the previous unit. If a 1% change in price causes demand to change by exactly 1%, then demand is said to be unit elastic with respect to price. If the quantity demanded is more responsive to price changes than this, then a price change of 1% will cause quantity damanded to change by an amount greater than 1%. In this case, we speak of demand that is elastic with regard to price. If a price change of 1% causes quantity demanded to change by less than 1%, demand is price inelastic.

SAQ 9: *Work out the value of price elasticity of demand in these examples, and say in which of them is demand elastic, unit elastic or inelastic with regard to price.*

	Percentage change in price	Percentage change in quantity demanded	Value	E / U / I
(a)	*5*	*1*		
(b)	*10*	*50*		
(c)	*1*	*3*		
(d)	*20*	*20*		
(e)	*50*	*–*		

In the last example in SAQ 9, demand is completely inelastic: despite a considerable price change, there is no change at all in the quantity demanded. This extreme case is shown in graph 11.7 below, in which the demand curve is vertical. Graph 11.8 shows quite the opposite – a demand curve that

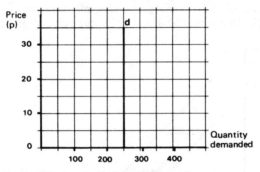

Graph 11.7 A perfectly inelastic demand curve

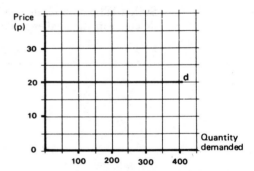

Graph 11.8 A perfectly elastic demand curve

is perfectly (or infinitely) elastic. Here an infinite amount is demanded at one price (20p), but nothing at all is demanded at the next highest price. Below I've included a table which summarises the range of conditions of price elasticity of demand (ignore the final column for the moment).

	Term	*Value*	*Change in total spending caused by a price rise*
Quantity demanded does not vary at all as price is varied	Perfectly inelastic	Zero	
Quantity demanded varies, but by a smaller percentage than price	Inelastic	Less than one	
Quantity demanded changes by the same percentage as price	Unit elastic	One	
Quantity demanded changes by a greater percentage than price	Elastic	More than one	
Quantity demanded is infinite at one price, but none will be bought if there is a rise in price	Perfectly elastic	Infinity	

Problems in calculating price elasticity of demand

Two problems occur in attempting to calculate price elasticity of demand. The first is that changes in price and quantity demanded will be in opposite directions: when price goes up, we would expect quantity demanded to go down. I am sure that you can remember enough basic maths from school to recall that dividing a positive number into a negative one — or negative into positive — results in a negative answer. So, in your answers to SAQ 9, you should have put minus ·2, minus five and so on. In practice, most economics books (and teachers) get round this by simply ignoring the minus sign and speak of elasticities of two, ·5 and so on.

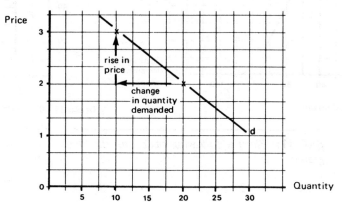

Graph 11.5(a)

The second problem is a tougher nut altogether. I can best explain it by reproducing the original curve from graph 11.5. There, when price rose from £2 to £3, quantity demanded dropped from 20 to 10. Now, working out the price elasticity of demand from this data results in unit elasticity: a price rise of 50% has resulted in a fall in quantity demanded of 50%. But let's now drop the price back from £3 to £2 (which, coming down, is a reduction of one-third): there is a consequent rise in quantity demanded of 100% as sales go up from 10 to 20. Price elasticity of demand is now $\frac{100}{33 \cdot 3}$ or 3. But this is ridiculous: we're measuring the same curve and should surely get the same result both times. It's a mathematical poser that results from the fact that a given quantity or sum of money (in this case, 10 units and £1) are a smaller proportion of a larger number than of a smaller one.

SAQ 10: *To illustrate this little puzzle, jot down your weekly income on a bit of paper. Then reduce it by 50%. Finally add on 50% of the reduced figure. Do you get back to your original income? Why, or why not?*

There are a number of ways round this problem. One way involves taking a mid-point halfway between the two values and working out the elasticity using them as a reference point. The mid-points in our example are £2.50 and 15 units. The change in quantity demanded is 10 (66% of 15 units) and the change in price is £1 (40% of £2.50), and so the revised value of price elasticity of demand comes out at 1.65. In fact, though, estimates of price elasticity of demand are unlikely to be very accurate when analysing the effects of price changes as big as 40%: a much more satisfactory approach would be to measure the effect in quantity demanded of very small changes in price. Students who are familiar with calculus will know of its techniques for measuring very small changes in the gradients of curves.

Another way round the problem is to look at what happens to total spending on the commodity (that is, the sales revenue of firms who sell it) as price changes. If a fall in price of 1% raises sales by more than 1% (if, that is, demand is elastic) then consumer spending on the commodity will be higher after the price change than before. If, on the other hand, demand is inelastic with regard to price, a 1% price cut would cause quantity demanded to rise by less than 1%, resulting in total spending on the commodity being less than before.

Let's go through this with the aid of some graphs, and armed with the knowledge from earlier in this unit that we can tell from rectangles drawn under demand curves how much is spent on the product at each price. In graph 11.9, demand is inelastic. As a result, raising the price (from 60p to 80p) by a certain percentage reduces quantity sold, but not by the same percentage. Look at the graph: as quantity demanded falls from 50 to 40, £6 of revenue is lost (10 units that would have been sold at 60p — the rectangle C). But as 40 units are sold at the higher price, an additional 40 x 20p comes in — as shown by rectangle B. This extra £8 outweighs the lost £6, and shows that where demand is inelastic, a price rise increases total revenue. Revenues were A + C, and are now higher at A + B.

The opposite is true in graph 11.10. Here, reducing the price would raise revenue quite considerably. At price 80p, revenue is 20 x 80p (= £16, shown as rectangles D and E): at the lower price of 60p, sales are 60 and revenues rise to £36 (rectangles E + F).

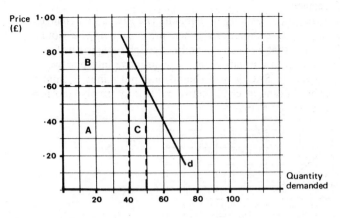

Graph 11.9 Inelastic demand

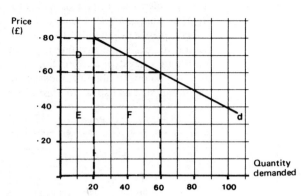

Graph 11.10 Elastic demand

SAQ 11: *Plot the following figures on the blank graph:*

Price	20	40	60	80
Q.d.	60	30	20	15

Mark on the graph rectangles of total revenue when price is 80p and when price is 60p. What happens to total spending on the commodity as price varies. Why?

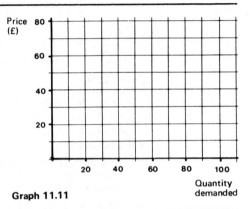

Graph 11.11

SAQ 12: *(a) Go back to the table summarising price elasticity of demand on p. 35 and fill in the final column with the behaviour of total spending as a result of prices rising in differing elasticities. (b) The diagrams above indicate that the steeper a demand curve, the more inelastic it is. What precautions should we take before coming to such a conclusion?*

Factors affecting elasticity of demand

We need to ask why consumers of one product should react to a price cut by buying much more than before, when the demand for another product is much less affected by such a change. What factors, in other words, cause demand to be elastic or inelastic with regard to price?

Availability of substitutes If no substitute is available for a given product consumers will be obliged to keep buying after a price rise. The availability of a substitute will depend on time in some cases: no-one with a coal-fired boiler will switch to gas immediately coal rises in price, but as time passes those purchasing new heating systems will avoid the higher-priced fuel. However, products for which there are plenty of substitutes available may be expected to have a high elasticity of demand. If butter is pricey, we switch to margarine; if it is cheap, we use it instead of lard or cooking oil.

Price of commodity relative to total expenditure. A doubling of the price of, say, elastic bands or a packet of spice is unlikely to affect the quantity demanded very much, as these products form too small a proportion of household spending to cause consumers to react. On the other hand if potatoes double in price demand is likely to drop.

Income. Demand for cars is likely to be highly elastic for marginal purchasers (those just able, or just unable, to afford to run one). For those whose incomes mean that they can easily afford a car, or never afford one, price changes will have little effect: demand would therefore be highly inelastic.

Need. A note of caution here: while you may think that if a commodity is essential, it will have a low price elasticity of demand, in practice such a judgement is of little use. Some people regard their ski-ing holiday as an essential! However, it *is* clear that some products (such as petrol, cigarettes or beer) continue to be bought even when prices rise, as people seem to make cuts in their spending elsewhere to pay for them. The reason, incidentally, that the Chancellor of the Exchequer increases taxes on such goods is precisely because of their price inelasticity: no extra tax revenue will come in unless people continue to buy the product after the price has been raised by taxation.

Frequency of purchase. Demand for consumer durables – washing machines, cars, TVs – can fluctuate sharply. When incomes fall, new purchases are postponed: we make our car, or record player, last another year or so. On the other hand when new purchases are favourable – due, perhaps, to less stringent HP regulations or a rumoured rise in VAT – demand soars. On the other hand, if we have to buy a product every week, there is no chance to defer purchase when the price rises nor any prospect of 'rushing to buy' when the price comes down.

SAQ 13: *(a) Look at the following list of commodities, and put them into two categories – products likely to have a high price elasticity of demand, and those likely to have a low price elasticity of demand.*

> *Soap;* Pear's *soap; matches; appendicitis operations;* Anchor *butter; narcotic drugs; toothpaste; British exports.*

(b) Taxation on cigarettes is sometimes justified on the grounds that it not only raises money for the government, it also discourages the consumption of a dangerous commodity by raising the price. Comment on this statement, using the concept of price elasticity in your answer. (Aim to write between six and ten lines.)

Who cares about elasticity?

Perhaps this question has already occurred to you. The answer is that knowledge of the value of elasticity of demand is important to businessmen and governments, and for a number of reasons:

- Businesses wish to know the effects that changes in price will have upon their sales. Raising prices when demand is inelastic will increase the firm's revenues; but doing so when demand is price elastic might be disastrous.
- Governments will wish to estimate the yield of a prospective indirect tax: to make an intelligent guess will require an idea of the way sales will react to the increased price. It does no good, as Chancellor Healey found in 1978, to raise the tax on spirits if people then stop buying them. This example is a valuable reminder that we cannot say that the entire demand curve for a given product is inelastic. The price can be pushed high enough to deter even the keenest consumer.
- State agricultural policies have to grapple with the problem of selling unexpectedly large or small harvests. Knowledge of the elasticity of demand for farm products enables us to guess what will be the effect of such fluctuations on prices and farm incomes. If demand for (say) wheat is highly inelastic, then we know that additional supplies can only be sold if the price plummets, drastically affecting farmers' living standards. This information would help governments to decide whether or not to buy up or destroy surplus production.
- Elasticity of demand matters when assessing the effects of a fall in the international value of the £ sterling. Commentators tell us that such a drop is good for exporters, as it reduces the price of British exports when priced in foreign currencies: but will this drop in price persuade foreigners to buy enough additional British exports to earn the money to pay for the imports we wish to buy from them? This is a topic we shall have to go into again when we look at Britain's balance of payments later in the course: nevertheless, I hope that you are noticing that concepts that are introduced early on in our microeconomics course are useful in planning government policy and business strategies.

SAQ 14: *(a) Distinguish carefully between price elasticity of demand, income elasticity of demand and cross-elasticity of demand. Jot down the formulae used to calculate each.*
(b) Fill in the missing words in this paragraph:

> *The theory of demand states that a change in the price of a commodity will be followed by a change in the . . . . of that commodity. Price elasticity of demand measures precisely how great will be the responsiveness of quantity demanded to changes in . . . . The demand for a commodity is said to be price-elastic when the change in quantity demanded is . . . . than the percentage change in price. In this case, cutting the price of a commodity will lead to a . . . . in the amount of money spent on the good. But if a change in the price causes a . . . . than proportionate change in quantity demanded, demand is said to be inelastic with regard to price. When the percentage change in price is exactly matched by the change in quantity demanded, economists refer to . . . . elasticity of price.*

This concludes much of the work of this unit: the demand curve, factors affecting demand and the shifts in demand curves that they cause, demand elasticity. It's important for you fully to understand this topic in order to make a success of the next unit, on price theory. You can test your knowledge with the multiple choice items I have included in the review section. But before we get to that, let's spend some time on a pretty basic question:

WHY DO DEMAND CURVES SLOPE DOWN?

On the first page of this unit, I stated that 'in general, more will be bought at a lower than at a higher price'. This may appear to be self-evident: but then, so did a flat earth. What theories can we find to justify the crucial idea that quantity demanded is inversely related to price, and that consequently demand curves slope downwards to the right?

Marginal utility

One tool that can help us with this topic was developed by Alfred Marshall, who put forward the idea of **diminishing marginal utility**. By *utility*, he meant the amount of satisfaction, or usefulness, obtained from consuming a commodity. *Marginal* utility refers to the amount of utility gained from consuming one more unit of the commodity. And the idea of *diminishing* marginal utility is that, the more of a commodity we consume, the less utility we get from each additional unit consumed. Although our total satisfaction or utility rises with additional units consumed, the addition

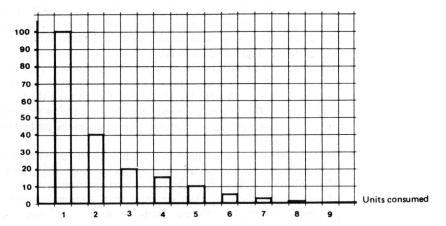

Graph 11.12 Marginal utility

to satisfaction from each extra unit is smaller and smaller. I'll try to explain this using a hypothetical example from graph 11.12, which depicts the marginal utility gained from the possession of pairs of shoes. To have one pair of shoes is essential in a country like Britain: a consumer who has no shoes will gain enormous utility from obtaining a first pair (column 1). Most of us find a second pair of shoes very useful, though they do not add as greatly to utility as did the first pair. A third pair (column 3) would provide an alternative style or colour, a fourth might be slippers or sports shoes, and so on. But each additional pair will add less to utility than the pair before, until a point is reached where additional pairs of shoes do not add to utility at all (which happens after we've got eight pairs in the example above). This is what's meant by diminishing marginal utility, and it's said to be true of almost all products.

If we attach a money value to the utility obtained (with the first pair of shoes giving £100 worth of utility, the next £40 and so on), we can use the idea to derive a downward sloping demand curve. If only the first pair bought gives £100 of utility, then only one pair would be bought by our hypothetical consumer at a price of £100; if price were £40 per pair, two pairs would be bought — the first (worth £100 to the consumer) and the second (worth £40). If the price were £5, you can see that six pairs would be bought.

SAQ 15: *(a) How many shoes would the consumer whose marginal utility is shown in 11.12 demand if the price were £10?*
(b) How many shoes would be demanded if they were given away free (i.e. if price were zero)?

Consumer surplus

Let's suppose that the price of shoes in our example is £15. Despite this, the consumer still gets £100 of utility from the first pair of shoes consumed. In this case, the consumer has got £85 of utility 'free'. This difference between the amount that a consumer would, if pushed, be prepared to pay for the commodity and the amount that actually is paid is called **consumer surplus**, and alerts us to the fact that the satisfaction and use of a commodity often outweighs the money spent on it by consumers. Graph 11.13 illustrates the idea of consumer surplus (MU = marginal utility).

Here, the price is 20p, and the number of units consumed is 3. Consumer surplus (shaded area) is 30p for the first article, 20p for the second, 10p for the third.

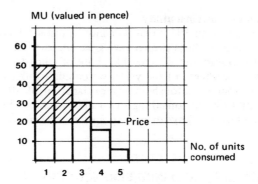

Graph 11.13 Consumer surplus

SAQ 16: *Why doesn't this purchaser consume four units of the commodity?*

Consumer equilibrium

Economists say that a consumer is in equilibrium if no change in his or her pattern of spending will increase the total amount of utility gained from the available budget. For consumers to be in such a position, they must obtain the maximum possible value for money (or, in our terms, utility per £). This will be where

$$\frac{\text{MU of last unit of commodity 1 purchased}}{\text{price of commodity 1}} = \frac{\text{MU from commodity 2}}{\text{price of commodity 2}} = \frac{\text{MU from commodity 3}}{\text{price of commodity 3}}$$

and so on.

However, if the last pound spent on (say) clothes gives more satisfaction than if spent on (say) a cinema ticket, consumers can gain by buying fewer cinema tickets and more clothes. This pushes us down the clothes MU scale and edges us back up the cinema ticket MU scale, so that ultimately the ratio of MU to price is once more equal. Here, equal satisfaction is gained from the last £ spent on each commodity and so no improvement in utility can be made by reallocation of expenditure.

Marginal utility and public policy

You may well have understood the arguments of the last few paragraphs but still felt that MU theory is far removed from everyday economic problems. Yet MU can be used to shed light on such policy issues as income redistribution and pricing of public services, as the two examples that follow will show.

Redistribution of income It is possible to show through MU that a progressive tax and social security system (that is, one which takes money from the rich and gives it to the poor) adds to the total utility of society. The argument runs as follows: if you reduce the income of a rich individual you make it impossible for that individual to buy commodities that may yield a very low MU (a tenth pair of shoes, a third car, a holiday cottage abroad). Transferring the cash to a poorer person enables that individual to buy commodities much higher up the MU scale (a second pair of shoes, a first car, the first holiday for years).

Pricing Another principle that can be drawn from MU is that it is wasteful to provide commodities free. If, for example, water is supplied to households for a block charge (so that in effect additional gallons can be consumed free of charge) people will consume it right up to the point of zero marginal utility: that is, when consuming water gives virtually no use or satisfaction to the consumer. On the other hand a meter system which charged consumers realistic prices per gallon would cut low-utility water usage.

SAQ 17:   *Do you think that this argument against providing commodities free of charge applies to these situations:*
(a)   The UK road system, where a motorist (provided that a block road tax has been paid) may use as many additional miles of road as wished without additional charge.
(b)   The National Health Service, where a patient suffering from an operable condition may receive surgical treatment without charge.

Criticisms of marginal utility

The problem with MU is that it cannot be tested: if a consumer claimed to get greater utility from a fourth pair of shoes (which gave great pleasure from, say, ski-ing) than from the first pair (used for the necessary but disagreeable chore of going to work to earn enough for the winter holiday that is the highlight of the year), we couldn't prove her wrong. The reason I have chosen hypothetical examples throughout my explanation of MU, after all, is because real examples do not exist: utility is not something that can be measured in practice. This drawback has led economists to seek alternative ways to analyse consumer behaviour. One such involves the use of

BUDGET LINES AND INDIFFERENCE CURVES

Budget lines

These plot all the possible combinations of two products that a consumer could purchase from a given budget. Graph 11.14 gives an example. Here, I've taken a consumer with £40 to spend on sweaters and shirts. If shirts cost £5 and sweaters £10, then our consumer could buy

| 8 shirts and no sweaters | *or* | 6 shirts and 1 sweater | *or* | 5 shirts and 2 sweaters | *or* | 2 shirts and 3 sweaters | *or* 4 sweaters |

I've placed these combinations on the budget line in graph 11.14. The gradient of the budget line will reflect the ratio between the prices of the two goods chosen. So a change in the relative prices

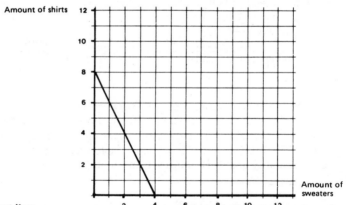

Graph 11.14   Budget lines

will change the slope. On the other hand, a change in the consumer's budget will shift the budget line to the right in the case of an increase (showing that more of both commodities can be bought), or to the left in the case of a fall (showing a reduction in the quantities of both commodities that can be bought).

SAQ 18:   *(a) Plot on graph 11.14 the new budget line that would follow if sweaters fell in price to £5, while shirt prices remained unchanged at £5. Label this line BL_2.*
(b) Now assume that the consumer is able to allocate £60 for the purchase of shirts and sweaters (at price £5 each). List the combinations of shirts and sweaters that can now be purchased, and plot them on the graph as BL_3.

Indifference curves

These show the combinations of two commodities that consumers regard as equally satisfactory: combinations between which, so to say, they are indifferent. In graph 11.15 I've again taken sweaters and shirts as the example. IC_1 shows that this consumer regards having six shirts and five sweaters (position A) or five shirts and six sweaters (position B) as equally satisfactory, though position C (four shirts and eight sweaters) indicates that as our consumer gives up more shirts, then he will need increasing numbers of sweaters to feel equally well-off. When he possesses eight shirts and four sweaters, he'll happily give up two shirts for an additional sweater; then he has six shirts and five sweaters, and would give up only one shirt to get an additional sweater; he then has five shirts and six sweaters and would need to be 'bribed' with two sweaters to give up one more shirt. This changing rate at which a consumer will be willing to forsake one commodity for another is known as the **marginal rate of substitution.**

I've put a second indifference curve on 11.15. Here a consumer values two sweaters and four shirts equally to four shirts and two sweaters, and to eight sweaters and one shirt. The level of satisfaction shown by IC_2, though, is lower than IC_1. Plainly, having four shirts and eight sweaters is preferable to having one shirt and eight sweaters. So an indifference curve to the left of the original one shows a lower level of satisfaction; an indifference curve to the right would show a higher level.

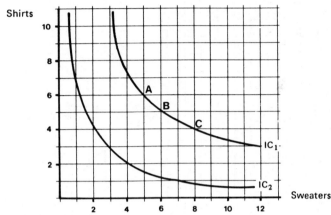

Graph 11.15 Indifference curves

SAQ 19: *Look at the various budget lines in 11.16 below. Starting with the bold budget line each time, which budget line indicates*

(a)   a rise in the consumer's available budget?
(b)   a fall in the price of commodity A?
(c)   a rise in the price of commodity A?
(d)   a rise in the price of commodity B?
(e)   a fall in the consumer's available budget?

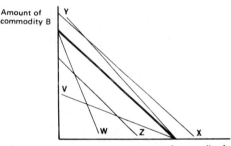

Graph 11.16

CONSUMER EQUILIBRIUM REVISITED

Now look at graph 11.17, which combines both budget lines and indifference curves. The consumer will be in equilibrium at point X. There, the consumer is on the highest indifference curve that can be reached with the amount of money available: the higher levels of satisfaction represented by IC_3 are not attainable within his present budget. IC_1 of course is attainable, and the consumer could spend his budget on the quantities shown by points Y and Z: but to do so would involve lower levels of satisfaction than point X.

Having seen that consumer equilibrium is to be found where the consumer's budget line touches the highest possible indifference curve, let's look again at the factors that affect demand.

Price of the commodity itself
In graph 11.18, we see the equilibrium of the consumer both before (BL_1) and after (BL_2) the price of commodity X has fallen. The reduction in price allows the consumer to move up to a new position of equilibrium on a higher indifference curve – IC_2. The quantity of commodity X that is demanded has risen from two units to five, showing us that (as suspected) a reduction in the price of a good will raise the quantity demanded.

Prices of other commodities

SAQ 20: *So are commodities X and Y complements or substitutes for each other?*

Note that in graph 11.18, a reduction in the price of commodity X has reduced the consumption of commodity Y from 3 to 2.5 units.

Changes in incomes

Graph 11.19 shows three budget lines. Let's start with BL_2, where consumer equilibrium is at X. Note how a rise in the budget line to BL_3 enables the consumer to attain a higher indifference curve and a new equilibrium at Z, at which the quantities of both commodities demanded have risen. A fall in the budget line to BL_1 reduces quantity demanded for both.

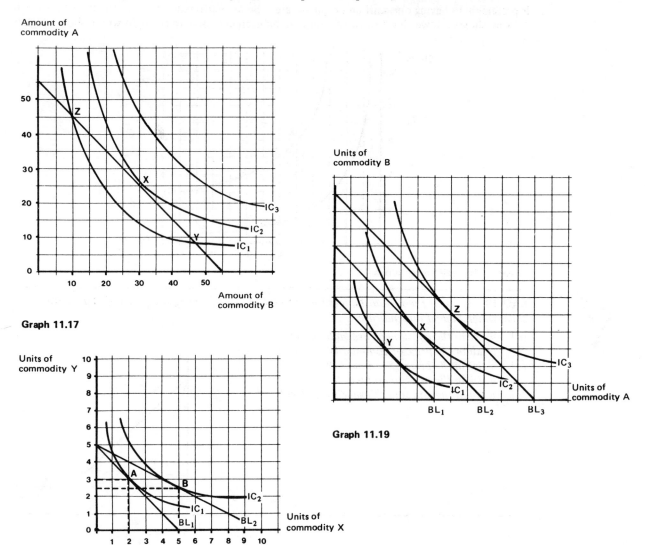

Graph 11.17

Graph 11.18

Graph 11.19

REVIEW SECTION

The further work on marginal utility and indifference curves finishes this unit. Look back at the learning objectives that I set out in the introduction, and check through them to ensure that you feel happy that you have covered them. You might be helped in this by looking at some of the essays that have been asked by examiners on this very topic: jot down outline answers to one or two, and you'll soon realise how effective your learning has been. As promised, I've also put in a twenty-item multiple choice test for you to use in checking your knowledge — it follows the suggestions for further reading in a moment.

Further reading

Extra reading on this topic can serve three purposes. Firstly, there is the important function of simply reinforcing the learning of the main points made in this unit — the demand curve, shifts in demand, the factors that affect demand, demand elasticities, consumer equilibrium. You can get this from any of the textbooks mentioned in the *Study Guide*. Secondly, you might find it interesting and useful to see how demand actually fits into the real world. I can wholeheartedly recommend Ralph Turvey's book *Demand and Supply* (Allen and Unwin). It's an Open University recommended book, too, so you should find that it is available in most public libraries: look especially at Chapter 1 for the moment. The *Economist* booklet called 'The Uncommon Market' also used real-world statistics and examples to flesh out the arid bones of demand theory. Look especially at *Getting and Spending* on pp. 30-1. Lastly, if you are interested in how a noted social commentator looks at marginal utility, seek out J. K. Galbraith's book *The Affluent Society*, and have a read through Chapter 10.

Examination questions

1. 'The demand for a commodity will usually be greater the lower the price, other things unchanged.' Explain why this is so, and discuss the significance of 'other things unchanged'.
    (AEB 1981)

2. Explain briefly how, according to any theory of consumer behaviour with which you are familiar, consumers allocate their incomes on different items of expenditure. How, if at all, is it possible to reconcile the existence of advertising with this theory?
    (JMB 'A' level June 1987)

3. Using either (a) indifference analysis or (b) utility theory, explain why the demand for goods is downward sloping. Why might some demand curves be upward sloping?
    (Northern Ireland GCE 'A' 1983)

4. Why might the imposition of a further duty on tobacco reduce the revenue the government obtains from duty on tobacco?
    (University of London 'A' January 1983)

5. Given below are the daily utility functions for three cold drinks for a man arriving at a desert oasis with a budget of £28.

	DRINK A	DRINK B	DRINK C
Price	£2	£4	£6
Quantity	*Total utility*	*Total utility*	*Total utility*
1	8	8	14
2	14	13¼	27
3	18	18¼	39
4	21	23	49
5	22	27½	55
6	24	31¾	60
7	25	35¾	62

Assuming that holding money has no utility for him and that he seeks to maximise his satisfaction, answer the following:
(a) On his first visit the only drink for sale is B. How many drinks does he buy, and why?
(b) In the circumstances of (a), calculate the consumer's surplus.
(c) On the return visit, with another £28, all the drinks are available. How will he now allocate his budget between the three drinks?
(d) What is unlikely about the total utility figures for drink A?
    (University of London January 1980)

6. Evaluate the usefulness of utility theory.
    (Oxford and Cambridge 'S' level July 1984)

MULTIPLE CHOICE CHECKLIST (Answers at end of SAQ answer section)

Questions 1 – 3 use this answer code:

(a) $\dfrac{\text{change in consumer spending}}{\text{change in consumer income}}$

(b) $\dfrac{\text{proportionate change in quantity demanded}}{\text{proportionate change in price}}$

(c) $\dfrac{\text{proportionate change in quantity demanded}}{\text{proportionate change in income}}$

(d) $\dfrac{\text{proportionate change in quantity demanded of one commodity}}{\text{proportionate change in price of another commodity}}$

Which of these formulae refer to
1.   Income elasticity of demand?
2.   Cross elasticity of demand?
3.   Price elasticity of demand?

4.   For some goods, price elasticity of demand is positive. We call these goods
   (a)   normal goods
   (b)   free goods
   (c)   economic goods
   (d)   inferior goods

5.   A fall in demand for frozen vegetables can be attributed to
   (a)   rising incomes
   (b)   falling prices for frozen vegetables
   (c)   cheaper refrigerators
   (d)   cheaper fresh vegetables

6.   Increased petrol prices may be expected to cause the demand curve for Jaguar Cars to
   (a)   shift to the right
   (b)   shift to the left
   (c)   become more elastic
   (d)   remain unchanged

7.   Increased prices will cause the demand curve for petrol to
   (a)   shift to the right
   (b)   shift to the left
   (c)   remain unchanged
   (d)   become more inelastic

8.   Which of the following will shift the demand curve for double-glazing to the left?
   (a)   an exceptionally cold winter
   (b)   rumours of unsatisfactory and expensive double-glazing installation
   (c)   increases in the price of both gas and electricity
   (d)   a rise in consumer incomes

9.   Which of the following events would affect the market demand for carpets, rather than the individual household's demand?
   (a)   cuts in income tax
   (b)   a successful advertising campaign for carpets
   (c)   cheaper floor-tiling
   (d)   a rise in population

Questions 10–15 use the following code to answer questions about price elasticity of demand:
   (a)   perfectly elastic   (b)   elastic
   (c)   unit elastic   (d)   inelastic
   (e)   perfectly inelastic

Select the correct term for demand for the commodity in each of these examples:
10.   When price is cut, household spending on this commodity falls

11.   When price rises 10%, revenue received by firms rises

12.   When price rises 10%, quantity demanded falls by 18%

13. A further education college increases its evening-class fees, but finds that just as many students enrol as previously

14. Over-production of wheat causes farmers' incomes to fall

15. A cut in bus fares leaves total fare revenue the same as before

16. Which of the following commodities is likely to have the lowest price elasticity of demand?
    (a) *Double Diamond* light ale
    (b) light ale
    (c) beer
    (d) alcoholic drink

17. Consumer surplus is an idea that suggests that
    (a) more will be demanded at lower than at higher prices
    (b) no change in spending can be made that will increase consumer welfare
    (c) consumers often get more value from a good than is represented by the price
    (d) in a market system, the allocation of resources is decided by the interaction of buyers and sellers

18. As more and more units of a commodity are consumed by a household, the total amount of utility gained from that commodity will
    (a) diminish
    (b) rise, but by successively smaller amounts
    (c) rise steeply
    (d) remain unchanged

19. Which of the following statements about indifference curves is not true?
    (a) They connect points of equal utility to the consumer
    (b) The point on a given indifference curve furthest from the origin indicates the point of greatest consumer satisfaction
    (c) Of two indifference curves plotted on the same scales, the most rightward one shows the highest level of utility
    (d) Indifference curve analysis can be used to derive predictions about the effect on quantity demanded of changes in consumer incomes

20. Look at this graph, and answer the question that follows on p. 46.

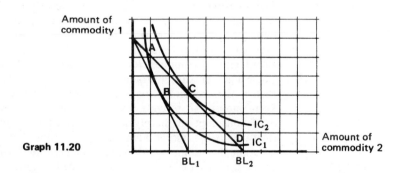

Graph 11.20

Which of the movements described above indicate the effect of a reduction in the price of commodity 2 on consumer equilibrium?
    (a) a movement from point B to point C
    (b) a movement from point C to point B
    (c) a movement from point A to point C
    (d) a movement from point B to point D.

ANSWERS TO SAQs

SAQ 1:   This is a simple plotting, which should give you a downward sloping demand curve.

SAQ 2:   At price £4, 200 units are demanded: your rectangle should be £4 x 200.

SAQ 3:   (a)   Income elasticity of demand would be negative if we spent less on a good as our income rose. Such goods would be genuinely inferior goods — bread, potatoes, cheap electrical goods. It would probably be more accurate to think of inferior goods as those goods for which less is bought when income goes up than the price-elasticity idea of goods for which more is bought as price rises;

      (b)   Price-elasticity, which measures how quantity demanded changes when price is altered.

SAQ 4:   Complements? The only one I can think of is the price of cars (others like AA subscriptions, car maintenance costs, batteries and tyres etc. seem too small to be a real influence): substitutes might be diesel fuel for diesel-engined cars, coach and rail fares.

SAQ 5:   Advertising and marketing are the main ways that firms attempt to influence consumer attitudes.

SAQ 6:   My totals are (respectively) 60, 40, 25 and 15: the plotting is pretty simple.

SAQ 7:   (a) rise; (b) fall; (c) rise (higher rents will force some consumers to the market for buying houses); (d) rise; (e) fall — this switch in the distribution of income is away from house-buyers towards those who have their own houses already.

SAQ 8:   (a) Left (more popular substitute); (b) right (more popular complement); (c) left; (d) no effect — this would affect supply rather than demand, unless consumers worried about oil supplies running out are reassured by announcements of new supplies and so order oil-fired equipment; (e) left (less oil needed for a given home temperature); (f) left (cheaper substitute); (g) no effect — remember that the demand curve itself shows the relationship between price and quantity demanded, so it doesn't need to shift when price changes.

SAQ 9:   (a) ·2; I; (b) 5, E; (c) 3, E; (d)1, U; (e) 0, I (perfectly inelastic, in fact).

SAQ 10:   You don't, because 50% of a low figure is less than 50% of a high figure.

SAQ 11:   Total spending remains the same as the curve is of unit elasticity.

SAQ 12:   (a)   Your columns should read: perfectly inelastic — revenue goes up by the same percentage as price; inelastic — revenue goes up as a result of a price rise; unit elastic — revenue remains unchanged as price rises; elastic — revenue falls as a result of a rise in price; perfectly elastic — revenue falls to zero when price is increased.

      (b)   You must ensure that the scales on the slopes you are comparing are the same at the very least. There are a number of reasons to be wary of using apparent slopes as guides to elasticity, but this is the main one.

SAQ 13:   (a)   The important thing here is to look for substitutes. There are few substitutes for soap, matches (which also form a very small proportion of household spending, making them price inelastic), appendicitis operations, drugs or toothpaste. However, good substitutes exist for branded butter and soap (other brands) and for British exports (supplies from other industrialised countries).

      (b)   These arguments are contradictory. If one wishes to use taxation to raise revenue, then it is important to have a low price elasticity of demand (i.e. people must keep smoking to provide government revenues); but if taxation is aimed to reduce consumption sharply in order to improve the health of the population, then it must be pushed high enough to reduce the number of smokers and thus government revenues — i.e. it must be raised until demand is price elastic.

SAQ 14:   (a)   Check through the text for this: basically, these concepts are to measure the effect on demand for a commodity of (price elasticity) a change in its price; (cross elasticity) a change in another commodity's price; (income elasticity) a change in consumer incomes.

      (b)   Quantity demanded (amount sold is OK); price; greater; rise; less; unit.

SAQ 15:   (a)   Five — the sixth pair is not worth this price.

      (b)   Eight.

SAQ 16:   Because the fourth unit only yields MU of 16p, as against a price of 20p. A rational consumer would gain by keeping the money in his or her purse.

SAQ 17:   This is a matter of opinion, of course. (a) seems to me to be valid: because roads may be 'consumed' by motorists without a charge-per-mile, they are consumed up to the point of zero utility. A metering system would make people cut out unnecessary journeys and duplicated journeys and reduce their use of road space, helping to cut traffic congestion by eliminating consumers who do not value their journey very highly. Indeed, it is technologically possible to charge more for rush-hour use of roads, which might keep them free for essential business users in much the same way as the high phone charges in weekday mornings do for phones. The argument in (b) seems altogether weaker: it is difficult to think of anyone making a 'trivial' or 'wasteful' use of a surgical operation! GPs, though, complain of abuse of free consultations from time to time; the problem here is one of income distribution — a rich hypochondriac would still be able to waste a doctor's time, even if the fee were high enough to deter a genuinely sick poorer individual.

SAQ 18:   Your diagram should look like this:

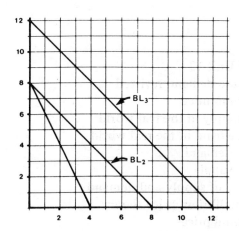

Graph 11.21

SAQ 19:   (a) X; (b) Y; (c) V; (d) W; (e) Z.

SAQ 20:   Substitutes: otherwise a fall in the price of one good would have increased demand for the other.

Multiple choice checklist answers

1c; 2d; 3b; 4d — when price rises people buy more, so the value of price elasticity will be positive; 5d; 6b; 7c — this relationship is shown on the actual curve; 8b — a leftward shift is a fall in demand, all the others tending to raise it; 9d; 10d (or e); 11d (or e); 12b; 13e; 14d (if demand were elastic, higher wheat production would all be sold, raising farmers' incomes); 15c; 16d (the key is to look at the availability of substitutes); 17c; 18b (*total* utility is what you're asked; the fact that marginal utility diminishes means that successively smaller amounts of utility are added to a growing total); 19b (all points are of equal utility); 20a.

12 Equilibrium price

AIMS OF UNIT 12

In the last two units we've been looking at the behaviour of consumers and firms in competitive markets. The aim of this work has been to prepare you for this unit, in which I hope to explain how prices are formed in such markets. When you've worked through this unit, you should be able to:

- explain the markets for which supply and demand analysis is helpful
- explain what is meant by equilibrium price, and indicate the point of equilibrium price and quantity on a supply and demand diagram
- plot supply and demand curves onto a graph from data
- define, and explain the effects of, excess supply and excess demand
- list the effects on equilibrium price and quantity of shifts in demand and supply, explaining how such effects may depend on differing elasticities of demand and supply
- explain problems caused by interventions into competitive markets, and list the ways that might be used to minimise these problems.

A word of warning

Before using supply and demand to explain the prices commodities fetch, let's be clear that the theory does not apply to *all* markets. We are looking in this unit at markets where a number of firms compete to sell a competitive commodity. Where several firms are competing, they cannot freely choose a price for their product, but have to take the reigning market price, which might even fluctuate from day to day. There are many examples of such markets:

- agricultural markets – meat, milk, vegetables, cereals
- raw materials for industry; metal ores for copper, iron, aluminium and many others
- precious metals
- the markets for stocks, shares and government bonds
- international currency markets.

It is characteristic of firms in these markets that they are **price-takers** and cannot dictate their selling price. In some markets, however, firms are **price-makers**. In these markets – such as newspapers, cigarettes, many manufactured goods and branded goods generally – firms decide their own selling price, often by working out production costs and adding a mark-up to cover overheads and profit. We will not be studying these price-makers until a little later in the course.

The fact that supply and demand analysis is most properly applied to competitive markets with many small firms is sometimes presented as an anti-climax, almost as if it was irrelevant to the fixed-price markets for the products of big firms. But this isn't true: the market forces of supply and demand are in fact very pervasive. For example, although the price of cars is carefully planned and announced by the makers, market forces affect it in two ways:

- Competitive markets will determine the price of the metal, rubber, glass, plastics and other commodities used in a car. Changes in the international value of the £ (determined by supply and demand on the international currency markets) will affect the prices of components and supplies bought from abroad.
- The 'list-price' is often a fiction. If a car is selling poorly, handsome discounts or trade-in offers are made available to prospective buyers: but no such discounts are available on popular or desirable cars.

Remember, too, that almost all second-hand markets are competitive, so that the forces of supply and demand will affect us when we buy a house, second-hand car, books or furnishing.

SAQ 1: *For which of the following is the use of supply and demand analysis most appropriate?*
(a)   bus fares
(b)   lamb prices
(c)   fish prices
(d)   the price of Mars *bars*
(e)   Habitat furniture prices
(f)   land prices

SUPPLY AND DEMAND REVISITED

In Units 10 and 11 we saw that while firms react to higher prices by producing more, consumers are deterred from buying and react to higher prices by demanding less of a commodity. The relationships between price on the one hand, and the quantities demanded and supplied on the other, are illustrated on (respectively) the demand and supply curves. SAQ 2 checks your knowledge of supply and demand before you go on any further.

SAQ 2: *(a)   Define supply and demand (try it without looking back).*
(b)   List at least four factors that would shift the supply curve for paper to the right. What name is given to such a shift?
(c)   List six factors that would shift the demand for lead to the left. What does such a shift indicate?

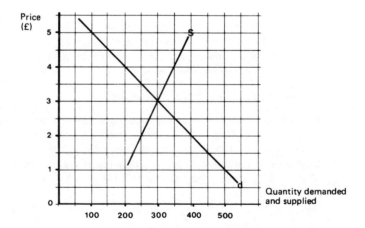

Graph 12.1

Graph 12.1 shows both supply *and* demand curves. As before, I've plotted price against quantity (quantity demanded in the case of the demand curve, quantity supplied on the supply curve). Look carefully at the graph. At any price higher than the one indicated by the crossing of the supply and demand curves, the amount that firms are willing to supply will be greater than the amount demanded by consumers. For example, if the price were £4, 200 units would be demanded and 400 supplied. The unsold surplus left on the market – in this case, 200 units – is called **excess supply**. When excess supply exists, it will tend to reduce prices.

Similarly, at any price below the intersection of the supply and demand curves, the amount demanded will exceed the amount supplied. Look what would happen in graph 12.1 if price were £2: 350 units would be demanded but only 250 supplied. In this case there is **excess demand** (of 100 units) indicating that, at that price, consumers wish to buy more than firms can profitably supply. As a result of the shortages, the price will tend to rise.

EQUILIBRIUM PRICE

From these observations, we can see that there is only one price which is subject neither to upward nor downward pressure. This is where the supply and demand curves cross – for, at that price, the amount demanded and the amount supplied are exactly the same. The market is 'cleared', and no unsatisfied customers are left looking for the product at the going price. In graph 12.1 this point of balance is to be found where the price is £3 and the quantity is 300 units. Economists call this point **equilibrium**, and refer to the **equilibrium price** and **equilibrium quantity** found there.

This is the most important point in your course: you've learned that in a market where competition is sufficiently lively to prevent one big firm setting the price itself, the market forces of supply and demand automatically produce a price that clears the market of all the commodities produced without surplus or shortage.

SAQ 3: *Plot the following supply and demand curves on the blank graph:*

Quantity supplied	0	100	200	300	400
Price (£)	0.50p	1.00	1.50	2.00	2.50
Quantity demanded	250	200	150	100	50

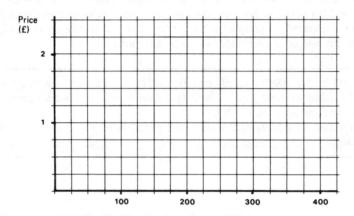

Graph 12.2

(a)   How great is excess supply when price is £2?
(b)   How great is excess demand when price is £1?
(c)   What is equilibrium price and quantity in this case?

EXCESS SUPPLY IN THE REAL WORLD

In many markets, the forces of supply and demand do indeed act together to form an equilibrium price. However, there may be reasons why governments and their agencies wish to intervene in the workings of a competitive market. They may seek to reduce prices below market levels in order to help poorer consumers, or perhaps they may wish to raise the market price in an attempt to ensure that producers get a decent income. Let's look first of all at the latter case, where government seeks to maintain a high price in order to help producer firms. An example might be the agreement between governments to maintain high airline prices to help the finances of their (often nationalised) airlines. In the graph on the left (12.3), I've drawn an imaginary demand curve for air trips to Paris from London. The supply curve illustrates the airline's willingness to provide seats at a range of prices. If government agencies fix the price at £80 per flight, you can see that many more seats will be provided than the public wishes to buy at that higher price.

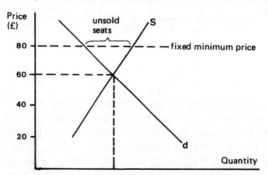

Graph 12.3 Minimum price laws

SAQ 4: *What is the name economists give to the situation, where more is supplied than is demanded?*

The result will be half-empty planes, according to our theory of equilibrium price. In fact, this is seen to occur in reality.

A more celebrated case of excess supply is to be found in the Common Agricultural Policy of the EEC. The officials of the EEC fix food prices at levels higher than would be the case if there was a free market in agricultural goods in an attempt to make sure that European farmers obtain decent incomes. But at the higher price, more is supplied than is demanded (just as in graph 12.3). This results in the production of large unsold surpluses, such as the celebrated beef, butter and skimmed milk 'mountains'. When this occurs, the government can try to retrieve the situation in a number of ways:

- It can buy up the surplus at the fixed price and stockpile (or destroy) the surplus.
- It can 'dump' the surplus – 'dumping' is a term used for the practice of selling one's surpluses cheaply (even below cost) outside your main market.
- It could establish a quota system which would restrict the amount of a commodity any firm could produce. No farmer, for example, would be allowed to produce more than a certain amount of beef. This system has been used to control sugar-beet production in the UK; and in the USA, farmers have been paid to keep land fallow, not growing wheat.*
- It could use the surplus for social purposes. Beef tokens, for example, were sent to Social Security claimants at one stage to encourage them to buy low-cost meat to reduce the stockpile.
- It could attempt to shift the demand curve to the right by methods such as advertising.

SAQ 5: *Which of the above methods have been used to help deal with the butter surpluses of the EEC? (Don't worry if you aren't sure of the answer to this.)*

Despite the additional methods that governments use in an attempt to hold price above equilibrium, there are often ways to obtain the commodity at below the official price. For example, at the time of writing it is possible to obtain low-priced airline tickets from unofficial dealers ('bucket-shops'). Such practices tend to break down the official price and encourage a move towards equilibrium.

Case study on price fixing
In 1982-3, the demand for oil from the OPEC countries had fallen due to a recession in industrial consumer countries, and to increases in supplies from non-OPEC sources (like the North Sea). This fall in demand would normally mean lower prices. The oil producers, however, wished to keep the price of their product at previous levels, and tried to achieve this by agreeing production quotas among members. This was found to be very difficult, however, as some oil producers were willing to sell (and customers, naturally enough, to buy) at the new equilibrium price.

Minimum wage laws
So far we've used the concept of excess supply to look at two well-known problems – the EEC's agricultural surpluses, and at the behaviour of oil prices. However, economists have also used the concept to analyse labour markets. In this use of supply and demand, the supply curve shows the amount of labour that would be offered at various wage-rates: obviously, the higher the wages the more employees will be attracted to a particular occupation, and so the supply curve slopes upwards. The demand curve shows the employers' demand for workers – downward sloping because fewer workers can be profitably employed at high wages than at lower ones.

Now, in some industries in Britain, and more widely in other countries of the world, there are minimum wage laws. It is a legal offence to employ a worker in some industries (catering, hairdressing, some textile trades, for example) at wage rates lower than the minimum agreed by the wages councils.

The use of equilibrium price theory suggests that such laws are misconceived. If, it is argued, it is illegal to employ people at a wage rate below the minimum wage (*see* graph 12.4), then there will be an excess supply of labour. Workers wishing to supply their labour at the existing wage rate will be unable to find a job, and unemployment will occur in the industry in question. If wages were allowed to fall to equilibrium (W_e on the graph), the numbers employed will rise and there will no longer be unemployment in the industry. Everyone who wants to work at the going wage will be able to be employed.

---

*which led to humourist Art Buchwald's request for government subsidy on account of all the wheat he had failed to grow.

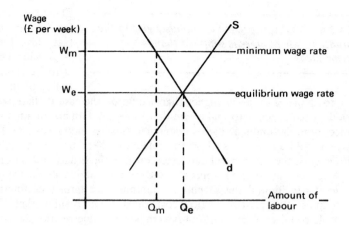

Graph 12.4 Minimum wage legislation

SAQ 6: *Equilibrium price theory, then, appears to condemn minimum wages laws which set legal earnings above equilibrium. Would this be true of laws which set the minimum wage at, or below, equilibrium?*

We'll look more closely into the economics of wages later in the course, and will return to the question of whether wage-cuts will increase employment. Certainly, the experience of minimum-wage laws in the USA suggests that they can indeed have just the effect predicted by price theory. However, it is dangerous to draw similar conclusions for a whole economy. Widespread wage-cuts would reduce aggregate demand, and so their effect in improving a national unemployment problem is dubious and controversial.

EXCESS DEMAND IN THE REAL WORLD

Just as there are examples in the real world of excess supply, caused by maintaining prices above market equilibrium, so too there are examples of excess demand. In this case, far from trying to keep the price artificially high, the authorities try to keep it below equilibrium – often to protect low income families from the problems of high prices. An example can be found in the Fair Rent system in Britain, where government-backed Rent Tribunals can decide that a landlord has set the level of rent too high, and that it should be reduced. Instructions to assessors ask them to ignore 'scarcity value', and as a result, rents (particularly for unfurnished property) are far lower than they would be under an unrestricted market.

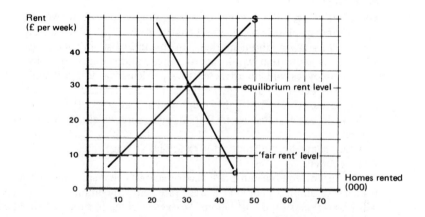

Graph 12.5 Maximum price laws

Look at graph 12.5, which illustrates the supply and demand for rented accommodation. You'll see that the equilibrium rent is £30 per week, but that the rent tribunal has stipulated a 'fair rent' of only £10 per week. At that price, very little accommodation is supplied (and what is supplied is often of the poor quality implied by that rent).

SAQ 7: *Look at graph 12.5 and answer these questions:*
(a)   How much accommodation is offered for rent at the fair rent level?
(b)   How great is excess demand for rented accommodation at that rent?
(c)   How much accommodation would be offered were the government to allow rents to rise to the equilibrium rent?
(d)   At equilibrium, have all the people who wanted rented accommodation at the fair rent price now got it? Why, or why not?

In practice, price controls are often ineffective. The problem with fixing maximum price below equilibrium is that, at that price, there will be less supplied to the market than the market wants — and so unsatisfied consumers will exist. With such consumers able and willing to pay a higher price than the one prevailing in the market, and firms willing to sell, a 'black market' starts up.

In order to avoid a black market, one (or a mixture) of the following measures may be used to allocate the scarce supplies of the commodity:

* *First-come, first-served:* in this case, consumers will have to queue or join a waiting-list to get any supplies. In Eastern Europe, where price control is the rule, queueing is commonplace. In Britain, one of the main distinctions between state-provided and market-provided health care is the presence or absence of waiting lists.
* *Rationing:* where this is used, the government can issue coupons that allow each family a limited amount of the product. This was used extensively in the UK between 1940 and 1950 to allocate scarce supplies of imported food.
* *Suppliers' preferences:* Alternatively, in the absence of official systems, the commodity will be allocated as the seller wishes. An example of this is the way that some garages serve only regular customers when short of petrol during an oil crisis.

SAQ 8: *The graph below shows the demand and supply for seats at the Centre Court for the first day of Wimbledon Tennis Championships.*

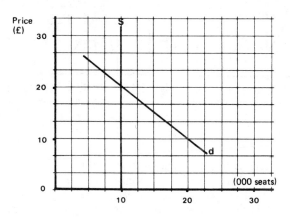

Graph 12.6

(a)   10 000 seats are supplied, no matter what the price.
So how would you describe the supply curve?
(b)   If the Wimbledon Club decided to fix prices at £10 per seat what problems might ensue?
(c)   How might the problems occurring in (b) be avoided?

Excess supply, excess demand and prices

The existence of shortages and surpluses is not the only problem with excess supply and excess demand situations. An additional drawback is the interference with the signals that prices give. Let me explain: if prices are kept high in an industry where there is already a surplus (say, dairy farming) then additional investment and higher output will be encouraged. By contrast, a falsely low price will discourage production of the commodity for which excess demand exists: just look at the lack of rented unfurnished flats or houses. This 'low price, low investment' problem is very acute in planned economies where many commodities (particularly food) are subsidised.

SHIFTS IN DEMAND

The theory of price determination by supply and demand can also give us predictions as to what will happen to equilibrium price and quantity when demand shifts. On the left here (graph 12.7)

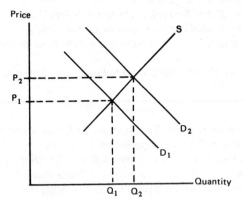

we see the market position for a commodity. The equilibrium price p_1 is reached where the supply curve s_1 and the demand curve d_1 cross. If there was a rise in demand — caused perhaps by rising incomes or increased popularity for the product — the demand curve would move to the right, from d_1 to d_2.

We can read off the result from the graph. At the former equilibrium price, p_1, there is now excess demand. In a competitive market, the price would rise. The point at which quantity supplied and quantity demanded are once again in balance is at price p_2. Equilibrium quantity, too, has risen. So

Graph 12.7

the market system has worked, providing increased supplies when more is demanded: but at the cost of higher prices.

So an increase in demand will cause a rise in the equilibrium price and quantity. Precisely how much equilibrium price and quantity will rise depends crucially on the elasticity of supply. On the two graphs below I have drawn the same shift in demand. In graph 12.8 demand is highly elastic. As a result, the shift in demand causes a substantial rise in equilibrium quantity but only a minor rise in price. If the supply curve is inelastic, however, a rise in demand will cause a proportionately

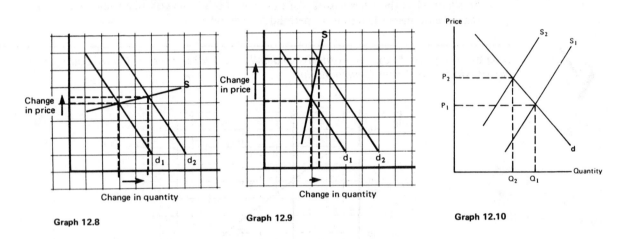

Graph 12.8   **Graph 12.9**   **Graph 12.10**

greater increase in price than quantity. Remember, though, that supply elasticities often depend on time: suppliers can respond to changes in price in the long term much more than they can in the short term (*see* Unit 10 pp. 168-9). As a result, it is conventional to distinguish between **momentary equilibrium** (the equilibrium price and quantity reached immediately, with a very inelastic short-run supply curve); **medium term equilibrium** (with a slightly more elastic supply curve making case); and **long-term equilibrium** (where supply has had enough time to make a full response to the price change).

SAQ 9: *In what ways will the equilibrium price and quantity reached in the long run differ from that reached in momentary equilibrium?*

Falls in demand

Just as a rise in demand will cause a rise in price and quantity at equilibrium, a fall in demand will result in a reduction in both the market price and the quantity traded. (Look back at graph 12.7, if you wish, and imagine a move back from d_2 to d_1.) And here, too, the effect will depend to some extent on supply elasticities. A drop in demand in graph 12.8 will result in a big reduction in equilibrium quantity but a minor fall in price: by contrast, a move from d_2 to d_1 in graph 12.9 would cause a much greater drop in price than in quantity.

SHIFTS IN SUPPLY

In graph 12.10, I've shifted the supply curve rather than the demand curve. We see a situation in which supply has fallen from s_1 to s_2. This might be due to an increase in the cost of production, or perhaps to a poor harvest.

The effect of a fall in supply is to raise price – in this case, from p_1 to p_2. But look how equilibrium quantity has fallen as well – from q_1 to q_2. An increase in supply would reverse this chain of events. If supply were to move back from s_2 to s_1, equilibrium price would fall and the quantity traded would rise. (*SAQ 10*)

SAQ 10: *List four reasons why the supply of a commodity might rise.*

Once again, elasticities will determine precisely how much of the change in supply will fall upon price, and how much upon equilibrium quantity. This time, though, it will be the price elasticity of demand that will be important. Look at graphs 12.11 and 12.12 to check how a shift in supply will affect price and quantity when demand is respectively price elastic and price inelastic.

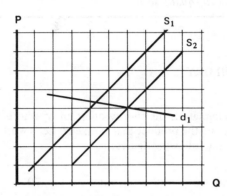
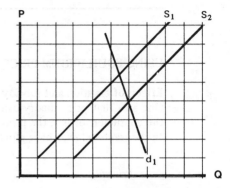

Graph 12.11 Elastic demand and shifting supply   **Graph 12.12 Inelastic demand and shifting supply**

SAQ 11: *Assuming that the axes in 12.11 and 12.12 are plotted equally, say in which graph demand is most elastic with respect to price, and write a brief paragraph explaining how the effects of shifts in supply on equilibrium quantity and price vary according to price elasticity of demand. Draw in the changes in price and quantity on graphs 12.11 and 12.12.*

THE 'LAWS' OF SUPPLY AND DEMAND

We can now make the following predictions about the effects on equilibrium price and quantity of shifts in demand and supply in a competitive market:

	Effect on price	*Effect on quantity*
A rise in demand	RISE	RISE
A fall in demand	FALL	FALL
A rise in supply	FALL	RISE
A fall in supply	RISE	FALL

These are often referred to as the 'laws of supply and demand'. They are not in fact unshakeable laws, but they do appear to fit the facts on the majority of occasions.

SAQ 12: *Put in the right-hand columns the effects the following events would have on the price of houses sold in a given village:*

rise / fall in price

(a)   *higher real incomes*
(b)   *better transport to the village*
(c)   *announcement of airport being built nearby*
(d)   *local shortages of rented accommodation*
(e)   *rise in the mortgage rate*

SAQ 13: *What would be the effect on the equilibrium quantity of coffee in a competitive market of the following events*

rise/fall in quantity

(a)   improved strains of coffee leading to increased production
*(b)   quota agreements between producers to restrict
        production*
(c)   rises in tea prices
(d)   medical report blaming coffee for health problems

SAQ 14: *Explain, using diagrams if you wish, why car number plate AP 1 is more valuable than END 552T, even though they are both equally scarce.*

USING EQUILIBRIUM PRICE THEORY

Effects of taxation and subsidy

One area that price theory can illuminate is the thorny question of who pays indirect taxes. Is it the consumer, or is it the producer of the product that is taxed? Let's work through an example. In the graph below, I have plotted the following figures:

Price (£)	.40	.50	.60	.70
Quantity supplied	100	250	400	550
Quantity demanded	300	250	200	150

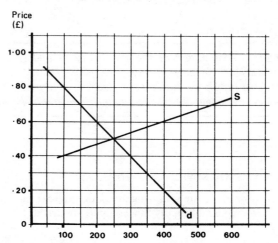

Graph 12.13
Taxes and price

Equilibrium price is 50p, and the equilibrium quantity is 300 units.

Now, let's suppose that a tax of 10p per article is put on this commodity. If you look back at your work on supply, you'll know that this has the effect of moving the supply curve upwards by 10p. The amount that firms formerly were prepared to supply at 40p will cost 50p and so on. Plot this supply curve on graph 12.13:

Price (£)	.40	.50	.60	.70
Quantity supplied	–	100	250	400

The effect is very similar to a fall in supply: the supply curve moves to the left. Read off the new equilibrium price. I make it about 58p. So the consumer is paying 8p extra compared with the former price, and the firms are forced to find the extra 2p to pay the government's tax. So long as the demand curve slopes downwards, any indirect tax will be paid partly by consumers and partly by firms. So one can think of a real life tax (say the National Insurance surcharge on employers) partly raising prices to consumers, and partly increasing employers' costs. The actual distribution of the tax between consumer and producer will depend on the price elasticity of demand for the commodity in question. A simple sketch will show you that the more inelastic the demand curve, the greater the proportion of the tax that will be paid by consumers. At the extremes, if the demand curve was perfectly inelastic (*SAQ 15*) all the tax would be paid by the consumer, but if the

SAQ 15: *What would the inelastic demand curve look like?*

SAQ 16: *What would the elastic demand curve look like?*

demand curve were perfectly elastic (*SAQ 16*) the whole burden of the tax would fall upon the firm.

So much for taxes. *Subsidies* will work the other way. In this case the suppliers are prepared to put more on the market at a given price. Use graph 12.13 again, working back from s_2 to s_1. Going down like this is the equivalent of receiving a 10p subsidy, or a cut of 10p in tax per unit. How much does price fall? Not, you may be surprised to note, by 10p. It will depend again on the price elasticity of demand. In this graph it's about 8p, but it would be less if demand were more elastic.

Taxes and subsidies in graphs;
It is possible to read off from a supply and demand graph the revenues raised by an indirect tax and the cost of a subsidy. Graph 12.14 shows two prices. Price OA was the equilibrium price

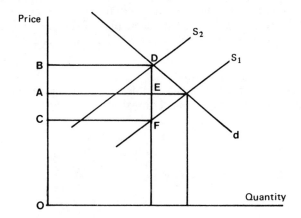

Graph 12.14

before the imposition of the tax: it is found where demand curve d crosses supply curve s_1. When the tax is imposed, the supply curve shifts up to s_2, and so a new equilibrium price is found at OB. The size of the tax is shown by the upward shift in the supply curve – FD or CB. You can see that AB of the tax is paid by the consumer in the form of higher prices and AC – the balance – is paid by firms. Rectangle CBDF shows the government's total tax take from the new tax. Of that total, ABDE is the total tax paid by consumers and CAEF the amount borne by firms.

SAQ 17: *Look at graph 12.15 below, which illustrates the beneficiaries of a subsidy scheme that, by helping firms with their costs, shifts the supply curve from s_1 to s_2.*

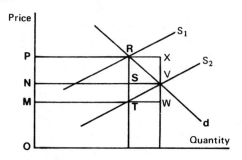

Graph 12.15

(a)   What was the price before the subsidy was put on?
(b)   How big was the subsidy per unit?
(c)   What is the price after the subsidy has been introduced?
(d)   Which rectangle shows the gain to firms from the new subsidy?
(e)   Which shows total government spending on the subsidy?

SAQ 18: *Farmers claim that subsidies lower the price of food to the consumer without increasing farm incomes: consumers see agricultural subsidies disappearing into farmers' pockets without reducing prices. Who is right? (Assume demand for food is inelastic with respect to price.)*

AGRICULTURAL PRICES

SAQ 18 has looked at the prices of agricultural commodities. We'll finish this unit by using equilibrium price theory to look at the way the prices of farm products are affected by shifts in supply and demand. There are a number of special factors that we will look at that make the analysis of agricultural prices a particularly challenging area of equilibrium price theory. These factors are:

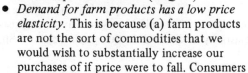

- *The market is genuinely competitive.* In the supply of many agricultural goods, many small firms compete to sell to a large number of retailers and wholesalers — a very good example of a competitive market. (*SAQ 19*)
- *Demand for farm products has a low price elasticity.* This is because (a) farm products are not the sort of commodities that we would wish to substantially increase our purchases of if price were to fall. Consumers

SAQ 19:   *Are farmers therefore price-makers or price-takers?*

don't buy much more tea, sugar, peas or potatoes as they get cheaper, and (b) many foods are inexpensive enough to form a comparatively small part of today's household budget. Few households are nowadays embarrassed by a rise in egg, milk or bread prices.

- *It is difficult to tailor output to demand.* In manufacturing, factory output can be adjusted to rising or falling demand within days or weeks. But weather and pests can have unpredictable effects on farm yields. Even if this were no problem, for most products output can be adjusted only with some difficulty: a crop once planted is a fixed investment.

Inelastic supply and demand

The effect of inelastic supply and demand curves is to exaggerate the changes in price caused by shifts in supply and demand. Look at graph 12.16: you can see there that a comparatively small

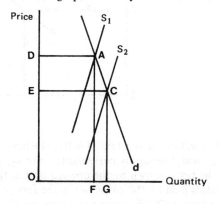

Graph 12.16

increase in supply — from s_1 to s_2 (the result, perhaps, of an unexpectedly good harvest) — causes a massive price-fall. Price in the previous year was OD: it is now OE. The effect on farm incomes is catastrophic. When price was OD, farmers earned the income shown by the rectangle ODAF. Now, they receive just OECG — which represents a substantial fall in earnings. Sometimes, the price falls so low that it is insufficient to cover picking and marketing: this is when crops are ploughed-in or burnt. A more likely result, though, is for farmers to gain what they can by selling at whatever price is available.

An unpredictable shortfall in supply will have an equally drastic effect in the opposite direction: prices will rise sharply as consumers compete for scarce stocks. In the 1976-7 potato shortage, prices rose very steeply. And we shall learn when we come to study the economics of the Third World that similar sharp fluctuations in export earnings occur as a result of shifts in the supply and demand for products like copper, coffee, sugar, sisal, tin and so on.

Cobweb theory

To make matters worse, use of equilibrium price theory suggests that agricultural prices will fluctuate wildly for some years after a shortage or glut. Look at graph 12.17. You can see, I hope, the equilibrium point pretty easily. But let's suppose that (although farmers plan to produce the equilibrium quantity) unforeseen problems reduce the crop to Q_2 instead. Now, for the duration of this particular season supply is inelastic at that quantity, and the price which that limited output will fetch is P_2. This is where life starts to get complicated. Farmers will now be planning the next season's output with this abnormally high price in mind. The

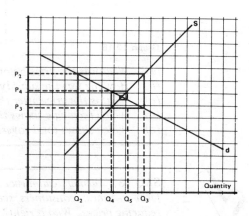

Graph 12.17   A converging cobweb

supply curve tells us how much farmers will produce at $P_2:Q_3$. But when this quantity is produced in the next season, it cannot be sold. The graph shows that the market can absorb this quantity if price falls to P_3. But when P_3 is the market price, farmers will only wish to produce – just read it off from the supply curve – Q_4. This is a quantity below the equilibrium quantity, and as a result, price rises to P_4: at this price, farmers plan to produce Q_5 and so on. The market, as you can see, eventually returns to equilibrium, but only after several seasons of instability in which price and quantity chase each other in the characteristic 'cobweb' pattern that gives this concept its pet name. Oscillations of this sort have in fact been observed in agricultural markets – most famously in the North American pork market, hence its other name, the 'Hog Cycle'.

You may be surprised to learn that the cobweb we've just looked at in graph 12.17 is the best-behaved of a rather rowdy family. Graph 12.18 shows an *oscillating* cobweb – where prices ebb and flow from high to low without ever reaching equilibrium. And the cobweb in 12.19 goes right off the rails – it's a *diverging* cobweb in which any disturbance will get ever further away from equilibrium until nothing is produced at all.

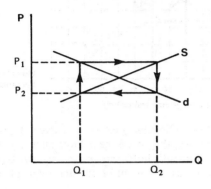

Graph 12.18 Oscillating cobweb

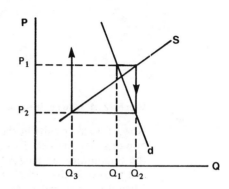

Graph 12.19 Diverging cobwebs

Now, this last example seems pretty unlikely and draws attention to the flaws of cobweb ideas (farmers don't rely on one year's price alone, and they do learn from their mistakes). Nevertheless, cobwebs show that there are times, even in theory, where the free play of supply and demand will not achieve an automatic and painless coordination of sellers and buyers.

Now that you've seen the problems caused to producers of food and primary products by fluctuating prices, you're probably more favourably inclined to government action to stabilise prices than when I introduced you to the butter mountain earlier. One measure that may be used by governments is **buffer stock**: a reserve of the commodity that is purchased and stored when there is a surplus in order to be sold when there is a shortage.

How buffer stocks might work

A simple buffer-scheme. One way to intervene in the market would be to buy up any surpluses for the buffer stock warehouses when the price fell below a certain 'floor', and to sell from stored stock when shortages occurred. This apparently sensible scheme has a decisive drawback: it guarantees farmers a fixed market for any quantity produced. This open-ended guarantee will encourage over-production, as additional output will always bring in more money for producers.

A more sophisticated scheme. We can get round this by looking more closely at the government's aims when it decides to enter the market for agricultural products. These are not really to ensure a high and stable price as much as to ensure a stable level of farm incomes, making sure that producers' living standards do not see-saw with each harvest. One way to approach this is to consider a demand curve of unit elasticity.

SAQ 20: *What does this mean?*

It is a characteristic of such a curve that firms' total revenue remains the same at all prices, for a given percentage cut in price is matched by an exactly similar percentage increase in sales.

SAQ 21: *The figures below correspond to graph 12.20. Work out total revenue at all prices.*

£	6	5	4	3	2	1
Quantity demanded	10	12	15	20	30	60

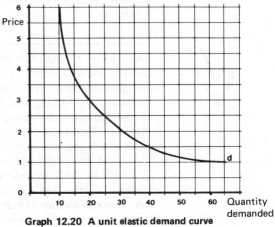

Graph 12.20 A unit elastic demand curve

207

If the demand for agricultural products were unit elastic, then, we'd have no problems. No matter how wildly prices moved, farm incomes would remain stable. So it makes sense for the government to try to make demand unit elastic. On graph 12.21 I suggest a way of doing this. d_1 is the actual demand curve for the product in question: you can see that it is pretty inelastic with regard to price. d_2, by contrast, represents the 'ideal' of unit elasticity that will ensure stable farm incomes.

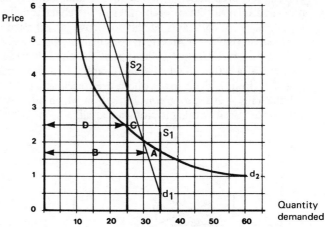

Graph 12.21 Using unit elastic demand curve to help agricultural policy

Now, if a glut results in the production of (say) 35 units (shown by curve s_1), price would fall to 50p in a free market. To stabilise farm incomes, the government buys quantity A. Total sales of the commodity are now A (sales to the government's buffer stock agency) *plus* B (sales to the normal market at that price); together they bring us to a point on the unit demand curve as planned. Quantity A is stored. (*SAQ 22*)

In years of shortage the reverse occurs. Consider what might happen if supply fell to 25 (curve s_2). Without intervention, price would rise to £3.50 or so. But if the government does not wish to see such an exaggerated increase in

SAQ 22:   *What has happened to farm incomes?*

prices and farm incomes it will sell quantity C from its buffer stock. Supply is now quantity D (25, sold by the farmers) *plus* quantity C (sold by the government from its warehouses and coldstores). The price falls back to £2.50.

SAQ 23: *Suppose such a buffer stock were established for a commodity, with the aim of buying in years of glut and selling in years of shortage. What chance has the scheme of paying for itself (i.e. will selling in one year cover the cost of buying in another)?*

The advantage of such a scheme is that it doesn't offer the same one-way promise of a simple buffer scheme: if we adopt the 'unit elastic' idea, then overproduction still brings down prices (if not quite so drastically as under the free market).

REVIEW SECTION

This completes the material for this unit. You may wish now to check your knowledge by running through the learning objectives that I set you in the introduction. See if this missing word exercise is helpful:

SAQ 24: *In a competitive market (that is, where firms are too small to be price-. . . . . . .) price and quantity are determined by the forces of . . . . and . . . . . . There is a point where the supply and demand curves cross. Above this point, ... is greater than . . . . and so excess . . . . exists, which will tend to force the price . . . . At any price below the intersection of the curves, by contrast, quantity supplied is . . . . than quantity demanded, leading to a situation of excess . . . . which exerts . . . . pressures on price. As a result, price tends to a point where quantity supplied and quantity demanded are equal, a point known to economists as . . . . A rise in demand will tend to . . . . equilibrium price, whereas a rise in supply (shown by a shift in the supply curve to the . . . .) will . . . . it. The effect of shifts in supply and demand on price and . . . . will depend crucially on the price . . . . of the two curves, which can cause real problems in managing agricultural markets.*

As a further check on your progress, I've included an assignment to submit to your tutor at the end of this unit. It *is* an important topic and so I'd like you to take some care over the assignment, which consists of a few short-answer questions and an essay.

Further reading

Again, this is a topic which you will find in most economic textbooks — look first for extra help at the ones recommended in the Study Guide, or to G. Hewitt *Economics of the Market* Chapters 2 and 3. Once again, I can highly recommend Ralph Turvey's book *Demand and Supply* for the way it brings the real world to the dry world of graphs and curves.

Examination questions

Much of the examination of your knowledge of this subject will take the form of multiple-choice questions (looking to find out how easily you can shift curves and find new equilibria) or data-response questions, such as:

1. Below is an extract from the *Guardian* that appeared in 1981. Explain what has happened with the aid of graphs:

PAY LAW LEADS TO SACKINGS

A Government decision to set a minimum wage for workers has backfired for thousands of people in Zimbabwe with wholesale redundancies being reported. Officials of the ruling party of the Prime Minister, Mr Robert Mugabe, said yesterday that in the Salisbury area alone more than 5,000 workers were dismissed. Worst hit were the domestic servants and farm workers for whom the minimum has been set at £22 per month: employees in the industrial and commercial sectors had also been dismissed.

2. Describe briefly the conditions (or determinants) of demand and supply. Explain why and how price changes may occur when the conditions of demand and supply

   (a)   change
   (b)   are constant

   (AEB 'A' level June 1985)

3. What factors would be likely to cause a fall in the prices of:

   (a)   coffee
   (b)   oil
   (c)   personal computers

   (Oxford Local Delegacy 'A' June 1986)

4. How might the price mechanism be expected to resolve the problem of the approaching exhaustion of a non-renewable natural resource? Examine the case for government intervention in such a situation.

   (AEB 'A' June 1986)

5. 'Price increases when demand rises or supply falls.' 'A rise in price cuts demand but raises supply.' Discuss.

   (Oxford Local Delegacy 'A' June 1985)

6. The prices of houses in the United Kingdom increase in sudden short-lived booms, rather than gradually. Why?

   (University of London June 1980)

7. Discuss the factors which determine the extent of any change in the price of a particular good following an increase in the demand for that good.

   (AEB 'A' June 1986)

8. Explain why the prices of agricultural products tend to fluctuate more than those of manufactured products.

   (AEB 'A' November 1986)

Notice how each of these essays applies the use of supply-and-demand analysis to a particular market or situation: it really is important for you to become 'at home' with this area of the syllabus.

ANSWERS TO SAQs

SAQ 1:   We're looking here for competitive markets where no firm is big enough to fix the prices: this means that the analysis is most appropriate to (b), (c), and (f).

SAQ 2:   (a)   Look this up in the units concerned;   (b) it's a rise in demand and could be caused by a fall in production costs, a fall in the price of competitive commodities, higher prices for a commodity in joint supply, favourable changes in firms' attitudes, or unexpectedly good production conditions;   (c) a fall in demand (that's what a shitt to to the left shows) might be caused by a fall in consumer incomes, rising prices of complements, cheaper complements, unfavourable changes in consumer preferences, a fall in the size of the market or an unfavourable change in the distribution of the national income.

SAQ 3:   (a) 200 units;   (b) 100 units;   (c) I make it about £1.33 and 166 units.

SAQ 4:   Excess supply.

SAQ 5:   Almost all of them. The famous 'butter mountain' is a result of buying and stockpiling surpluses; 'dumping' is represented by the subsidised sales of butter to Russia; quotas were introduced to dairy farmers (amid protests) in 1984; social use of surpluses are shown in the provision of intervention butter to old people's homes and hospitals; and butter is advertised aggressively.

SAQ 6:   No: there is no objection to such laws — except that they are a waste of time. An equilibrium minimum wage obliges employers to pay what they would be happy to pay anyway, and a minimum below equilibrium is not effective, as the market wage is higher anyway.

SAQ 7:   (a) Just 10 000 homes;   (b) excess demand is 30 000 homes;   (c) 30 000 homes   (d) no, 40 000 homes were demanded at £10 per week, but there are just 30 000 provided at the equilibrium level as 10 000 households have been priced out of the market. Remember that demand refers to want backed by purchasing power: a homeless family with no money cannot indicate 'demand' for housing in a market system.

SAQ 8:   (a) totally inelastic, (b) excess demand of 10 000 seats exists: therefore price will not allocate the seats and some other method has to be chosen such as (c) a ballot for tickets, a queue, a system that distributes tickets as a reward for faithful service to junior tennis, a rationing system that only gives people tickets every other year — some way of replacing the allocative function of price. Black markets can still occur, of course, if those who receive tickets through 'official' channels wish to resell.

SAQ 9:   If supply is more elastic in the long than in the short term, then in the long term price will be lower and equilibrium quantity higher than in momentary equilibrium.

SAQ 10:   *See* SAQ 2b.

SAQ 11:   Graph 12.11 shows how a given shift in supply will affect price and quantity where demand is elastic with respect to price. Here, a rise in demand reduces price a little but has a bigger effect in raising quantity. By contrast, when demand is more inelastic (*see* graph 12.12) a rise in supply will reduce price sharply whilst raising the equilibrium quantity by a comparatively small amount.

SAQ 12:   (a) rise;   (b) rise;   (c) fall — demand for houses falls *and* supply increases with residents being more eager to sell; (d) rise — substitute good, of course; (e) fall.

SAQ 13:   (a) rise;   (b) fall — if effective;   (c) rise — increased demand for coffee as a substitute becomes dearer;   (d) fall as demand falls.

SAQ 14:   There is only one of each, so supply is equally inelastic. But demand for a plate corresponding to common initials will exceed demand even for the plate of an author and economist.

SAQ 15:   It would be vertical.

SAQ 16:   It would be horizontal.

SAQ 17:   (a) OP — where s_1 and d intersect; (b) RT (or PM — same thing), that is, the amount the supply curve moves down shows the unit subsidy; (c) ON, where the new supply curve s_2 crosses the demand curve; (d) NVWM: the price has only come down from OP to ON, and so NM is the amount per unit that firms get to retain; (e) the total cost is MPXW-MW (the subsidy per unit) multiplied by MW (the number of units sold at the new, lower price).

SAQ 18:   If the demand curve for food is downwards sloping, the benefits of subsidies will be split between producer and consumer. The more inelastic the demand curve, the greater the benefit to the consumer and the less to the producer. If demand were perfectly inelastic (unlikely) the full amount of subsidy would go to consumers in cheaper prices.

SAQ 19:   Price-takers.

SAQ 20:   *See* following sentence.

SAQ 21:   Total revenue is 60 at all prices, confirming that the curve is of unit elasticity.

SAQ 22:   They remain unchanged — see previous SAQ answer.

SAQ 23:   In theory, very good. When there is a glut, prices will be much lower than when there is a shortage: so a successful scheme should be in the happy position of buying cheap and selling dear.

SAQ 24:   Makers, supply and demand: quantity supplied; quantity demanded; supply; downwards; less; demand; upwards; equilibrium; raise; right; reduce, quantity; elasticity.

13 The competitive firm

AIMS OF UNIT 13

When you have worked your way through this unit, you should be able to:
- list the important assumptions necessary for the existence of perfect competition
- reproduce the cost curves of a competitive firm and explain their shape
- explain what is meant by the equilibrium of the perfectly competitive firm, explain why it occurs where marginal cost is equal to marginal revenue and indicate the point on a diagram
- link the supply curve to the marginal cost curve of the competitive firm
- define 'normal profit' and show why the long-run equilibrium of a competitive industry will be found where firms make only normal profit.

At the end there are some multiple choice items for you to use in checking your understanding. There are also the usual self-assessment questions and answers.

INTRODUCTION

Unit 12 covered a great deal of ground in showing how free markets work. We saw that, in markets where the forces of supply and demand determine price and quantity, an equilibrium was reached which cleared the market, leaving no surplus or shortage. Supply and demand analysis is very revealing, and is a tool economists often use to analyse the behaviour of commodity, factor and financial markets. It does leave a number of important questions unanswered, though. Is production in such markets undertaken efficiently, with low costs being passed on to the consumer in low prices? In the absence of government regulation, will firms earn high profits that exploit the consumer? Why do some firms keep going although making a loss? How do firms arrive at their production decisions? The purpose of this unit is to answer these questions. If you fully understand the work in this unit you'll have a foundation for the study of Units 14, 15 and 16, which look at more profound questions about our society: Why do giant firms merge? Should the trend to bigger firms worry us? What can be done to protect consumers against powerful companies? Is nationalisation the answer — and what problems are associated with nationalised industry? So this unit forms not just a continuation of our study of markets — it's the start of that area of economics known as 'the theory of the firm'.

To have a single, all-embracing theory of the firm would be impossible. Firms, after all, come in many shapes and sizes: partnerships and limited companies, banks and sweetshops, cooperatives and family firms. Some firms earn bigger incomes than whole countries; others fail to make enough for one person to live off. In order to start, then, we shall have to make some generalisations about the way firms behave and the conditions they work under. This unit is concerned with the behaviour of firms working in 'perfect competition'. The important features of a market which is perfectly competitive are:

1. The unit of production is small: indeed, a perfectly competitive industry is made up of many small firms such that no single firm supplies more than a very small share of the market. The firms are so small in relation to the market as a whole that they can increase or decrease the level of their output without any effect on the price the commodity fetches on the market. What's more, firms are too small to affect the prices of the factors of production they buy. The example of agriculture comes to mind here: no matter how much an individual farm expands or contracts its milk production, it is too small to produce a glut or shortage that would alter equilibrium price.

SAQ 1: *Based on the information in paragraph 1 above, draw a curve that shows the demand for the product of a perfectly competitive firm. What name is given to such a curve?*

2. Products are homogenous: and because of this, consumers do not have any 'brand loyalty' to one firm in preference to another. The products of all firms are perfect substitutes for each other.

SAQ 2: *What is the distinction between firms that are price-makers and those that are price-takers? Where there are many firms producing a virtually identical product, will an individual firm be a price-maker or a price-taker?*

3. Firms can enter or leave the industry at will — no trade secrets, patents or technical reason can prevent a new firm from starting up. One of the major barriers that prevent the entry of firms into attractive and profitable areas is the need for large-scale production. For example, to be able to produce competitively, a new steel mill would have to possess an annual output of hundreds of thousands of tonnes. This prevents small firms setting up rival production. This is the reason why perfect competition cannot exist where the economies of large-scale production are present. (We'll return to economies of large-scale production in the next unit.)

4. Firms and customers have the fullest information upon which to base their decisions. For example, they know what other firms are charging, how profitable other lines of business are, the prices of different methods of production.

The last major assumption we shall make is:

5. Firms aim to maximise their profit.

You may feel that this is the most obvious and uncontroversial of all the assumptions we have been forced to make. However, people who have made careful studies of firms have found other forms of behaviour. Some firms seem to be keen to maximise their growth or sales. In these instances firms will undertake risky and possibly unprofitable business in order to expand their share of the market, or enter new markets. Other firms may not aim to maximise anything, but try to balance the interests of workers, managers, shareholders and customers. This is plainly something we'll have to look at later in the course: but for the moment we have a set of simplifying assumptions that will allow us to continue. A little later in the unit I'll discuss the assumptions of perfect competition, and ask whether they are so unrealistic as to make any theory drawn from them valueless.

EFFICIENCY AND THE FIRM

Firms use the factors of production — land, labour and capital. Their business is to combine these factors together to make commodities. Firms will make the greatest profit if they manage to keep their use of the factors of production to a minimum — that is to say, if they are efficient in their use of them. Take a look at these figures:

	Units of land	Units of labour	Units of capital
Method A	10	8	3
Method B	10	6	2

If we ask which of these methods is the most efficient in its use of resources the obvious answer is method B: it uses less labour and capital than method A, without needing any more land. Method B, then, is technically more efficient than method A. But in real life things are rarely so clear-cut. Firms usually face a variety of production methods that use varying amounts of productive factors. Look now at these figures:

	Units of land	Units of labour	Units of capital
Method X	10	10	10
Method Y	20	5	15
Method Z	5	20	15

Which of these methods is the most efficient? Method X uses less land than method Y, but it requires more labour. Method Z uses less land than either X or Y, but more labour than either. It's impossible for a firm to pick the right method without knowing what it will have to pay for its inputs — without knowing, that is, the factor prices. Do this exercise for yourself:

SAQ 3: *Which of the above methods of production would be the cheapest given the following factor prices?*
(a)   land = 2,   labour = 1,   capital = 1
(b)   land = 5,   labour = 1,   capital = 2
(c)   land = 1,   labour = 5,   capital = 2

You can see that for each set of prices there is a cheapest combination of factors. The cheapest method will change as factor prices change.

Technical versus economic efficiency

It's important to be clear here that when discussing 'efficiency' we mean economic, rather than technical efficiency. Technical efficiency involves the use of the minimum physical inputs to get a given output. Economic efficiency, by contrast, concerns the cheapest way to get a given output. Let's take an example. The most technically efficient car engine might very well be an expensive racing version that squeezes the maximum amount of power out of a gallon of petrol. Production car engines, on the other hand, are less powerful — even, less efficient in a technical sense — than the racing or laboratory models that require to be tuned each day by specialists and require expensive labour and skilled assembly. Yet these engines make more economic sense to the firms that produce them and the individuals that buy them.

COMBINING THE FACTORS AT LOWEST COST

We've now established that firms will select the cheapest set of inputs to achieve a given output. When the price of the factors of production changes, firms will alter the production method used — *see* SAQ 3 above for an example. Efficient management of production will tend to use cheaper factors in place of those whose price has risen. This is the **principle of substitution** which states that when factor prices change, relatively less of the dearer and more of the cheaper will be used.

SAQ 4: *So what will be the response of a profit-maximising firm to:*
(a)   a rise in oil prices
(b)   a rise in wages?

Optimum factor combination

It follows from what I have said that for any given set of factor prices there will be a combination of land, labour and capital that will result in production at lowest cost. This is known as the **optimum factor combination**. The further firms move away from this optimum combination, the higher will the cost of production become.

   This might be easiest to explain with an example. Suppose that a firm finds that, at present prices, its optimum combination of factors is ten units each of land, labour and capital. If the firm wishes to expand production, it will be best to keep the factors in these equal proportions. Alternatively, if it wants to cut back and produce less, it will be wise to reduce factor inputs equally. The problem is that this is rarely possible in real life. Land cannot be bought instantly, and it takes time to build new factories and install new capital equipment. Some factors can be varied more easily, of course: additional labour can be obtained with overtime working, for example. But the supply of other factors is, at least in the short run, fixed. Even if all factors could be instantly increased in exactly the right proportions, there is still likely to be a problem of using less suitable workers or less accessible land. This idea is illustrated on graph 13.1, which shows what happens as we move away from the point of optimum factor combination – point Y on the graph. At point Y, average cost (AC) per unit of production is at its very lowest. If we try to increase produc-

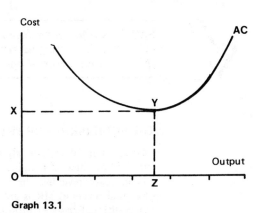

Graph 13.1

tion from quantity OZ, costs will rise because we cannot increase all factors in the right proportions: remember, as some factors are fixed in the short-run, changes in output will involve moving away from that optimum combination of factors that assures lowest-cost production. From point Y onwards, output can only be increased by additional units of variable factors (workers to a factory, fertilisers to a field, etc.) that will result in increasing average cost. The further we get away from the optimum factor combination, the higher will costs become.

SAQ 5: *Look at graph 13.1 and say how much average cost will be at point Y. How can we calculate the firm's total cost of producing quantity OZ from the diagram?*

Marginal cost

If we are concerned with the behaviour of the profit-maximising firm we need to know more than simply the behaviour of the average cost curve. In deciding whether or not to offer additional units for sale the firm will be concerned not with the average cost of all the units that have been produced so far, but with the additional cost of the extra units being considered. Because the addition to total costs resulting from the production of one more unit is such an important idea, it has a name – **marginal cost**. For example, if the cost of producing 11 units is £50, and the cost of producing 12 units is £55, then the marginal cost of the twelfth unit is £5 – that is £55, minus £50.

SAQ 6: *Calculate average cost and marginal cost from the following figures:*

Output	1	2	3	4	5	6	7
Total cost	30	50	66	80	110	150	210
Average cost							
Marginal cost							

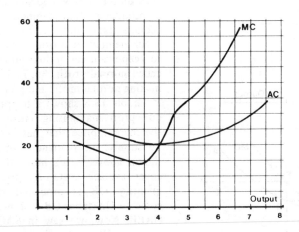

Graph 13.2

When this data is plotted, it appears like the graph on the left (13.2). The MC (marginal cost) curve is below the AC (average cost) curve at the start, but rises to cut through the AC curve at the AC curve's lowest point, and rises steeply thereafter. The mathematics of this are pretty simple. Whenever MC is below AC (that is, an additional unit of output is costing less than the average of all previous units) then average cost will be falling. But if MC is above AC, each additional unit is costing more than average and so the average cost of production is rising the more that is produced. This explains why the MC curve cuts the AC curve at the lowest point.

Marginal revenue

At this point we have to bring in one more concept – **marginal revenue**. The marginal revenue of a unit of production is the addition to total revenues resulting from the sale of the extra unit.

Now, for a firm in perfect competition – which, remember, can sell all it wants at the present price – marginal revenue will be equal to the market price. Each additional unit will be sold at the going price in the market.

> **SAQ 7:** *A firm can produce 100 units and receive sales revenues of £700, or 101 units for £707.*
> (a)   *What is the marginal revenue from the production of the 101st unit?*
> (b)   *What is the market price in this competitive market?*

THE EQUILIBRIUM OF THE FIRM

Bearing in mind the steeply rising marginal cost curve, we now have a clue as to how much the firm will produce. If marginal cost is less than marginal revenue, then producing one more unit will add more to revenues than it wll to costs: as a result it will create additional profit. So where (marginal revenue) MR is greater than MC, the firm will produce additional units. But as soon as the additional costs of producing an extra unit exceed the income that the sale of that unit will bring in, firms will cease expanding production. To produce where MC is greater than MR would involve the firm in a loss. Look at this in graph 13.3. Here, I have drawn the steeply rising MC curve from graph 13.2 along with a marginal revenue line: remember, for a firm that can sell anything it can produce at the market price (P), marginal revenue must be equal to that market price. Now, at point OA, MR is more than MC, so the firm will increase output to gain more profits. However, at OC, MC is greater than MR and so producing at that point would involve putting BC units on the market at a loss. The firm's equilibrium will be at point B for when MR is equal to MC the firm will have wrung every penny of profit that is pos-

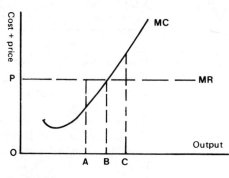

Graph 13.3

sible from this market; additional units, where MC exceeds MR, will make losses. So we can state the following principle: **the profit maximising firm will be in equilibrium where marginal revenue is equal to marginal cost.**

Profits . . .

If we add to the MC/MR graph the information about average costs we can see the amount of profit or loss that the firm makes. Look at graph 13.4: the firm will be maximising profits where MR = MC. On this graph that's at point E. You may think that the firm is making no profit at all

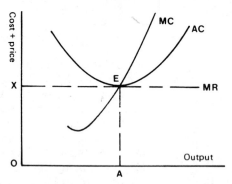

Graph 13.4

here, as the price OX is apparently just enough to cover the cost of production. However, firms must make profits to survive in a private enterprise market economy: if they didn't, they would shut down or switch to producing other commodities. That's why economists include in production costs a small element of profit – the profit needed to keep resources in their present use. This is called **normal profit**. So, in 13.4, the firm is making normal profit and no more.

Graph 13.5 shows a happier picture for our profit-maximising entrepreneur. Here, the market price that has been determined by supply and demand is higher than that shown above – it's more than enough to cover average costs. As price is OA and quantity OB is produced total revenues come to OA times OB – shown by rectangle OAEB. Now, we saw in SAQ 7 that total costs are shown by the rectangle under the AC curve. The average cost of produc-ing OB is OC and so total costs are OCDB. This leaves AEDC as profit – and, let's be clear, this is over and above the normal

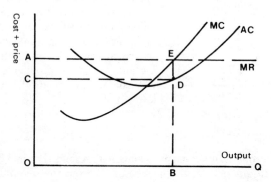

Graph 13.5

profit that has been included in the production costs OCDB. When firms earn an amount above normal profit we refer to excess profit or **supernormal profit**.

SAQ 8: *Shade in the area of excess profit in graph 13.5, and label it supernormal profit.*

. . . and losses

Graph 13.6 shows a firm that is making a loss. Equilibrium is still where MR=MC, but at this level of output, average cost is OB. The price – OA – is not high enough to cover costs, and so the hatched rectangle represents the amount that the firm is losing. The question that probably springs to mind is this: Why should the firm continue to produce goods when it is making a loss by doing so? The answer is complex.

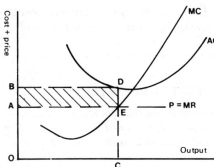

Graph 13.6

Firstly, we must remind ourselves that costs can be divided into fixed costs and variable costs. Fixed costs are those that do not vary with the level of production – they have to be paid, whether the firm produces nil units or a million. Examples include rent, rates, interest payments on outstanding loans, etc. Other costs vary according to how much is produced – wages, salaries, raw material costs, bills for fuel and light.

Now, in the long run, a firm will remain viable only if its revenues cover its costs (including normal profits): for this to occur, price must equal average cost. This makes the lowest point of the average cost curve the break-even point: if price falls below here, production is unprofitable. In the short-run, however, the firm may be prepared to continue in production and make a loss *provided* it can meet the variable costs of output. For they would have to pay the fixed costs even if they shut down. If continued production can pay all the variable costs and make some contribution to the fixed costs, the firm will be making a smaller loss than would be the cost if it ceased production altogether.

A numerical example might make this clearer. Suppose a civil engineering firm is considering a contract to build a stretch of motorway for £5m. If its fixed costs are £1m, and the variable costs of the contract are £4.5m, it can only take on the contract at a loss of £0.5m. Yet, with no other business in prospect, failure to get the contract will mean that the firm makes an annual loss of £1m – the still-payable fixed costs. Getting the contract will reduce that prospective loss.

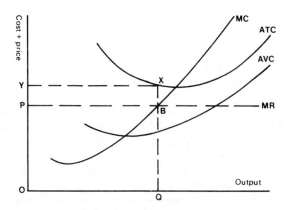

Graph 13.7

This idea is shown in the rather formidable graph above. Let's go through it bit by bit. The average cost curve now has its proper name – ATC for average total cost. Total cost is made up of fixed and variable costs, and it's the variable costs that interest us this time: they are shown by the AVC (for average variable cost) curve. At price P, equilibrium is at point B where MR = MC. The firm makes a loss shown by the rectangle YXBP, because the cost of producing OQ is OYXQ whereas the total revenue is only OPBQ. But at equilibrium output, all variable costs are covered (OP exceeds average variable cost) and so some money is left over after meeting variable costs to meet some of the fixed costs. If, however, the price falls below AVC, not even variable costs are covered. At that point a firm would shut down.

SAQ 9:
(a)   The break-even and shut-down points are not marked on graph 13.7. Put them on.
(b)   The liner Queen Elizabeth 2 *was built by John Brown, the Clydeside shipbuilders, at a loss. Why did they tender for the contract at a price that wouldn't give them any profit?*
(c)   We've seen that a firm would hang on in an industry as long as they were covering variable costs. How long would they hang on? Is there any other reason for a firm to stay in an industry while experiencing losses?

SAQ 10:   *Earlier in the unit we assumed that all firms studied were profit-maximisers, yet here we have firms making losses. How must we modify our assumptions about firms' behaviour to take this on board?*

THE SUPPLY CURVE REVISITED

We are now going to use the two ideas we've just worked through — that is, equilibrium of the firm where MR = MC and the knowledge that for a short time the firm will be willing to produce as long as variable costs are covered — to return to an old friend. Look at graph 13.8 below:

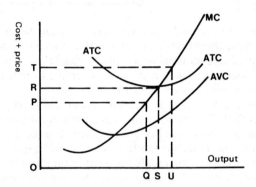

Graph 13.8

If price were OP, then the firm would produce where MR = MC — that is to say, quantity OQ. Were price to rise to OR, OS would be produced. At the higher price OT, it would be profitable to produce additional output — OU. Putting this onto a schedule would lead us to something like this:

Price	OP	OR	OT
Quantity supplied	OQ	OS	OU

This looks remarkably like the supply schedule of the sort we met in SAQs 3 and 4 of Unit 10 — and in fact it is. **The supply curve of a perfectly competitive firm is that firm's marginal cost curve (above its average variable cost curve).**

SAQ 11: *(a) Why isn't the MC curve below the AVC curve part of the firm's supply curve?*
(b)   We have learned that the rising MC curve shows one firm's supply curve: but the market supply curve used in supply and demand analysis shows the amounts all firms in the industry are prepared to supply. So how can we arrive at this market supply curve from the MC curves of individual firms?

THE LONG-RUN EQUILIBRIUM OF THE PERFECTLY COMPETITIVE FIRM

So far, we have seen that the firm is in equilibrium where MR = MC, for that's where profits are maximised or losses are minimised. We have seen that this point could be reached where the firm was making supernormal profits, where it was making just normal profits or even where it was sustaining a short-term loss.

Graph 13.9 shows a firm that is making a profit greater than the normal profit that is included in the calculation of costs that forms the AC curve, i.e. it is earning supernormal profits. In the graph, the market price is £5 and the quantity produced is 100. At this output, costs are well below £5 — nearer £3.50. The firm is thus making an excess profit of £1.50 over the level of profits normal in the economy. (*SAQ 12*)

SAQ 12: *Shade in the area of excess profit.*

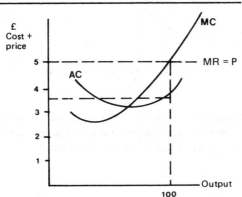

Graph 13.9

Now this excess profit is fine for the firms producing in this industry. But other firms will look with envy at the profits these firms are earning. Now remember our assumptions from the beginning of this unit — that there is perfect information, and free entry and exit of firms to each industry. Put these together, and you'll see that firms will move into producing this product that promises such high profits. The effect of a rush of firms into the industry can be illustrated on the supply-and-demand graph (13.10). With the increased production brought about by the new producers, the supply curve has moved to the right (from s_1 to s_2). As a result, more is supplied but price has been forced downwards.

This leads economists to conclude that supernormal profits will be a temporary phenomenon in a competitive industry. Rivals will enter the industry and force down the price. For how long will firms continue to enter the industry? Well, just as long as it offers above-average rewards. As soon as the profit rate here is down to normal level, there is no incentive for firms to switch into this line of business. The profit rate has been competed back to normal.

The exact opposite can be seen in graph 13.11. In this case the price is too low to allow profits to be made. As a result, firms will drift out of the industry, either closing down or turning to the output of other commodities. The absence of profit can deter firms just as strongly as profits can attract them. But as firms leave, supply falls. Remember that the market supply curve is made up by summing horizontally all the individual supply curves in the industry — so as firms leave the industry and less is supplied at each price, the market supply curve will shift to the left. This causes price to rise, enabling the surviving firms to gain a normal profit as price recovers.

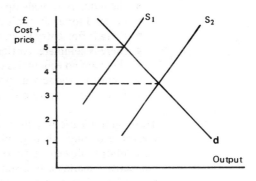

Graph 13.10

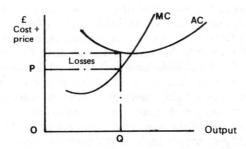

Graph 13.11

SAQ 13: *At what point will firms stop quitting the industry and decide to stay?*

The conclusion of all this is that, if an industry is earning supernormal profits, firms will enter that industry and compete the profits down to a normal level. Similarly, if an industry is making losses, firms will leave and cause the situation to right itself. The only long-run equilibrium position for a firm in a competitive industry is therefore shown in graph 13.12. Neither excess profits nor losses are being made, and note also that production is taking place using the optimum factor combina-

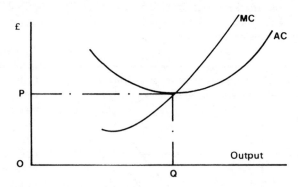

Graph 13.12

tion. Thus, production is at the lowest cost, using the most economically efficient combination of factors. If this is true, it is a very powerful argument in favour of the free market, for it seems as if the market needs no intervention to assure efficient low-cost production.

A SIDELIGHT ON ECONOMIC MODELS

The comforting conclusion we have just arrived at rests crucially on the assumptions that we have already made:

- the industry is made up of many very small firms
- demand for each firm's products is perfectly elastic
- there is free entry to and exit from the industry
- there is complete, costless information
- there are no economies of large-scale production
- identical products are produced by each firm
- firms aim to maximise profits.

These simplifications were made in order to clarify the main point at issue: what happens in a market economy when firms combine the factors of production to make a commodity. The assumptions allowed us to reach important — and striking — conclusions about the workings of competitive markets. In a similar way, when we looked at the behaviour of consumers in Unit 11, we used the idea of a rational consumer with information about all commodities and prices, allocating a budget so as to maximise utility per penny. And in Unit 4, we were able to start a very illuminating look at the operation of the economy with a simple Keynesian circular flow lacking foreign trade, taxes or government spending.

All these theories used simplifying assumptions in order to make some sense amid the complexities of the modern world. When economists construct a theory from such a stripped-down skeleton of the real world, they speak of an **economic model**. Simplified models are used in other sciences, of course: physicists' calculations of motion start with bodies moving in a vacuum, ignoring problems of friction and wind-resistance; and in chemical equations, all chemicals are pure.

However, the problem with the economic model that you have just been studying — the theory of the perfectly competitive firm — is not that it is an over-simple version of reality. We could live with that. The problem is that hardly any markets correspond to the assumptions. Perhaps we can except a few — the Stock Market, agriculture, the market for foreign currencies — but most of the UK GNP is made by big firms, not small ones; economies of large-scale production *do* exist; products tend to be differentiated, not identical; a substantial government sector that doesn't maximise profits exists; and so on. The result is that the theory is so unrealistic that 'it is hard to see its relevance in a highly developed capitalist economy' (Curwen — *see* refs at end). Indeed, the assumptions needed to make perfect competition work in the textbook manner are so restrictive that they have led the economist Oskar Lange to put forward the eccentric but logical view that they could only happen under government direction in a socialist society!

The obvious step forward is to take a more realistic view that includes the possibility of large firms growing up to dominate markets. This is the subject of Unit 14.

REVIEW SECTION

This unit has launched you on your study of the theory of the firm, with the simplified world of the firm in perfect competition. Now check through the learning objectives at the beginning of this unit and make sure that you are happy that you can do all the things asked there. One way that you can check your understanding is to do the multiple choice checklist I've included below as SAQ 14. There is no assignment to hand in to your tutor this time round, but have a look at the essay questions below and outline your answer to one on a side of paper.

SAQ 14: *Answer these multiple-choice items to check your knowledge of Unit 13*

1. A small farmer is closer to being a perfect competitor than Ford Motors because
   (a) a small business is more likely to keep close control on costs
   (b) Ford Motors employs people, whereas it is a characteristic of perfect competition that firms are owner-managed
   (c) a small farmer is much more likely to face a downward sloping demand curve
   (d) Fords supply a substantial part of the UK market for motor cars.

2. The statement that 'it is absurd for India to build highways in this day and age using just workers, spades and baskets' is
   (a) correct – much greater efficiency would come from the use of mechanical diggers
   (b) incorrect – because we cannot tell what makes economic sense without a knowledge of relative factor prices
   (c) correct – economic development involves the replacement of labour with increased capital goods
   (d) incorrect – it must be cheaper for a country with abundant labour to use cheap labour rather than expensive capital.

3. Look at the following table, and state which method is technically inefficient

	Units of capital	Labour	Land
(a)	6	200	50
(b)	10	250	70
(c)	10	150	50
(d)	40	70	60

4. The principle of substitution suggests that increasing use of capital would be the result of
   (a) a cut in interest rates
   (b) a fall in real wages
   (c) cheaper raw materials
   (d) increasing business confidence.

5. The U-shape of the average-cost curve indicates
   (a) that small firms find it difficult to finance expansion
   (b) that optimum factor combination is maintained at all outputs
   (c) that beyond a certain point, diminishing returns sets in
   (d) the fact that in the long-run costs rise with output.

6. What is the average cost of production at 400 units in this example?

Quantity produced	100	200	300	400	500
Fixed costs	100	100	100	100	100
Variable costs	200	300	350	700	1400

   (a) £400
   (b) £0.25p
   (c) £350
   (d) £2

7. What is the marginal cost of the fifteenth unit in this example?

Quantity produced	13	14	15	16	17
Total cost (£)	550	590	640	700	770

   (a) £50
   (b) £640
   (c) £42.66p
   (d) £60

8. This graph shows the cost and revenue conditions of a firm in perfect competition. What would be its profit maximising output?

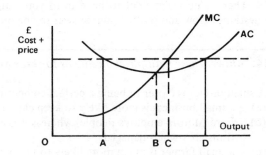

Graph 13.13 **The long run equilibrium of the firm in perfect competition**

(a) OA   (b) OB   (c) OC   (d) OD

9. The perfectly competitive firm is in equilibrium where marginal cost is equal to marginal revenue because
    (a)   this is where there is the optimum factor combination
    (b)   production cannot be expanded further in the short-run
    (c)   no other position offers higher profits
    (d)   at this point, the final unit produced earns most profit.

10.   In which of the points on the graph below is the firm making no profit of any sort?

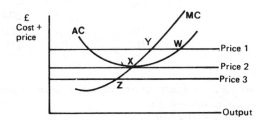

Graph 13.14

(a) X, Y and Z   (b) W, X and Z   (c) Z alone   (d) W and Z only

11.   Which rectangle in the graph below shows the contribution to fixed costs made by producing at a loss when price is OC and average costs OA?

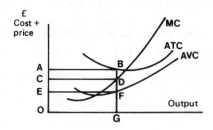

Graph 13.15

(a) ABDC   (b) CDFE   (c) ABFE   (d) ABGO

12.   Which points on this curve connect the beginning and the end of this firm's supply curve?

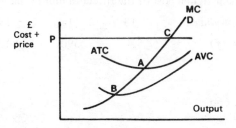

Graph 13.16

(a) AD   (b) AC   (c) BD   (d) BC

13.   Which of the following is not an example of an economic model?
  (a)   Keynesian macroeconomics
  (b)   the theory of consumer equilibrium
  (c)   supply and demand determination of price
  (d)   national income accounting.

Questions 14-20 use the following:

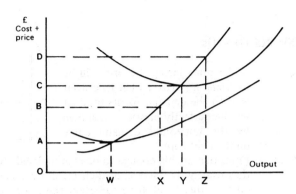

Graph 13.7 Loss making equilibrium — in the short run

14.   Below which price would it pay the firm to close down rather than continue production?

15.   At which price could excess profits be made?

16.   What quantity will be produced at that price?

17.   At which price will only normal profits be made?

18.   Which price would pay the firm to produce in the short term, but not in the longer term?

19.   Which of these prices is likely to persist for more than a short period of time?

20.   Which of the prices shown will be associated with an influx of firms to the industry?

Further reading
Look first at your textbook of choice — all the ones mentioned in the Study Guide have clear and well-presented chapters on this fundamental topic. If you strike lucky with your local library, you may find the following excellent books that will serve you well over the next few units:

  P. J. Curwen, *Theory of the Firm*, Macmillan
  Gordon Hewitt, *Economics of the Market*, Fontana

Examination questions
Again, this is a topic which lends itself to multiple-choice testing rather more than to essay questions. Nevertheless, the following essays may give you cause for thought:

1.   Why do we sometimes see firms continuing to produce even though they are making losses?
  (Oxford Local Delegacy 'A' June 1984)

2.   Explain and illustrate the nature of equilibrium for a firm in perfect competition in the short run and in the long run.
  (Northern Ireland GCE 'A' June 1983 and University of London June 1982)

3.   How is the market supply curve in perfect competition derived for the short run and also the long run?
  (Oxford and Cambridge 'A' July 1984)

4.   How will the introduction of a sales tax affect production, prices and profits in a perfectly competitive industry in the short and in the long run?
  (Oxford Local Delegacy 'A' June 1985)

5.   What are the main characteristics of a perfect market? Assuming that perfect competition exists, describe and explain the conditions necessary for equilibrium of the firm and industry.

The Joint Matriculation Board has recently shown interest in the idea of economic models, and has asked students to consider the characteristics of economic models with reference to particular examples — say, consumer behaviour or the theory of the firm. This is something that gives you scope for an excellent individual answer if you give the matter some thought, and some background reading.

ANSWERS TO SAQs

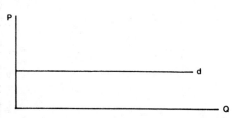

SAQ 1:   If the price facing the firm will be the same no matter what its output is, then the demand for its product will be perfectly elastic — as shown by the horizontal demand curve on the right here.

SAQ 2:   Firms that are big enough to be able to decide their own prices are called price-makers: they usually fix the level of their prices by a mark-up on production costs. Price-takers, on the other hand, have to accept the price that the market decides — very much as you or I have to accept the price we get from selling our sterling for foreign currency prior to a holiday abroad. So the firms we will be discussing are price-takers.

SAQ 3:   (a)   Method X, which costs 40; Y = 60; Z = 45.
(b)   Method Z costs 75; X now costs 80 and Y 135.
(c)   Method Y costs 75; X costs 80 and Z 135.

SAQ 4:   (a) To economise on oil by substituting other factors (more economical machines, more double-glazing and insulation in factories, etc.) (b) To use less labour, which can be replaced by more capital.

SAQ 5:   Average cost at point Y is OX (read off from the AC curve). The cost of producing OZ is OX times OZ, which equals OXYZ.

SAQ 6:   Average cost works out to 30, 25, 22, 20, 22, 25, 30 and marginal cost to 20, 16, 14, 30, 40, 60.

SAQ 7:   (a)   The addition to total costs is £7 — so that's the marginal cost.
(b)   If an extra unit is sold for £7, then that's the market price here.

SAQ 8:   The excess profit is shown by AEDC.

SAQ 9:   (a)   The break-even point is where the MC curve cuts the ATC curve; the shut-down point is where the MC curve cuts the AVC curve.
(b)   Because getting the contract at a price that covered variable costs and yielded some contribution to fixed costs was better than not getting any work at all, and suffering the full extent of the fixed costs. I presume that there must have been fierce competition for the contract to push the firm to this extent.
(c)   The time would depend on how long it took to be rid of the long-term contracts on rent, rates and interest payments. If these costs can be sloughed off, then it makes sense to get out of the industry. Another factor that would be important is financing: who would be providing the finance for these losses, and when would they pull the plug? The reason a firm might stay on apart from the AVC argument is in the case of optimism about the future (or even incomplete information about the future).

SAQ 10:   We must now add that they would be loss-minimisers if profit maximising was not possible.

SAQ 11:   (a)   Because firms will not supply when price falls that far — it would involve them in deeper losses than actually shutting down.
(b)   The market supply curve is obtained by adding together all the supply curves of the individual firms: it represents the total amount that would be offered for sale on that market from all producers.

SAQ 12:   It's the rectangle between the lines at £3.50 and £5.

SAQ 13:   When price has risen sufficiently for them to earn normal profit again.

SAQ 14:   1d, 2b, 3b, 4a, 5c, 6d, 7a, 8c, 9c, 10c, 11b, 12c, 13d, 14 — OA, 15 — OD, 16 OZ, 17 OC, 18 OB, 19 OC, 20 OD.

14 Big business

AIMS OF UNIT 14

This unit takes the theory of the firm one step beyond the world of perfect competition described in Unit 13, and looks at the factors that lead to the growth of large firms, and how this might affect our theory. When you've finished this unit, you should be able to:

- explain what is meant by constant, decreasing and increasing returns to scale and link them to the long-run average cost curve
- distinguish between diseconomies of scale and decreasing returns
- define economies of scale and list five reasons why a large firm might produce more cheaply than a small firm
- list four types of merger and explain why firms might wish to merge
- define monopoly and list the reasons why it might occur
- explain the disadvantages of monopoly, using diagrams showing monopoly equilibrium where MR = MC
- outline the possible advantages to monopoly
- describe the UK government's competition policy, explaining the provisions of the 1973 Fair Trading Act, the 1976 Restrictive Practices Act and the 1980 Competition Act.

INTRODUCTION

In Unit 13 we concentrated on short-run cost curves. We analysed the behaviour of costs when it is not possible to alter the quantities of all productive factors; when, for example, increasing quantities of a variable factor are added to a fixed factor. In this situation, attempts to increase the volume of production will cause sharp increases in the average cost of production as we depart from the optimum factor combination and move into a phase of diminishing returns. This is what caused the steeply rising marginal cost curve in the graphs of Unit 13.

It is, however, important to realise that productive factors are only 'fixed' in the short run. In the longer view, it is possible to buy (or sell off) even the factors that were regarded as fixed in Unit 13 — such as premises and machinery. So there is no reason why, given a little time, the entrepreneur wishing to increase (or decrease) output may not increase (or decrease) all factor inputs in proportion. In other words, the U-shaped average cost curve in the last unit was a **short-run average cost curve**.

What will a **long-run average cost curve** look like? There are three possibilities: it could slope down, indicating lower long-run costs as the scale of production increases; slope upwards, showing increasing costs; or be horizontal, showing that costs are unchanged. I'll spend the next few pages looking at each of these possibilities.

LONG-RUN AVERAGE COSTS

Constant costs

Let's take the last possibility first. Graph 14.1 shows the short-run cost curves of three firms in the same industry.

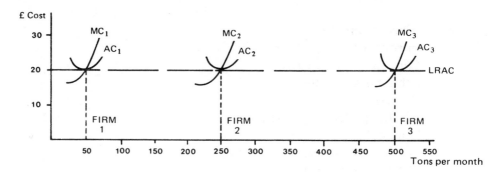

Graph 14.1   Constant returns to scale

Firm 1 is the smallest, producing only 50 tons a month. Firm 3, by contrast, is a large unit with an output of 500 tons per month, while Firm 2 falls somewhere between them in its scale of production. You'll notice, however, that the average cost of production is unaffected by the size of the firm. In the long-run, when all factor inputs can be changed in proportion, average costs are constant whether the firm is large or small.

In such an industry, we speak of **constant returns to scale**. The long-run average cost curve, which envelops all the short-run average cost curves, is horizontal, and so there appears to be no optimum or 'right' sized firm. I've marked in the long-run average cost (LRAC) curve on the graph. In real life, a number of industries exist in which firms of various sizes compete apparently on level terms — clothes manufacturing, for example, or retail newsagents.

SAQ 1: *(a)   Name one national retail newsagent chain, a local chain with more than one shop, and a one shop business. What factors would make it easier to run a chain of shops rather than just one? What factors would make it more difficult?*

(b)   Name another industry that, in your view, is typified by both big and small firms.

Increasing costs

The second possibility I mentioned in the Introduction is illustrated in the graph 14.2: **decreasing returns to scale**. In this industry, large firms have higher costs than small ones. Notice how Firm 3 has higher short-run average costs (SRAC) than the smaller Firm 1. So here, the optimum-sized firm would be small. Where this is true, we speak of **diseconomies of scale**. The diseconomies of scale can be seen from the rising LRAC curve of graph 14.2.

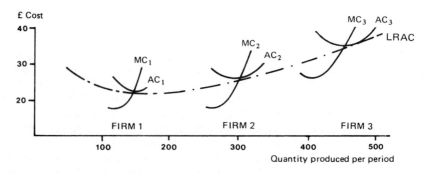

Graph 14.2   Decreasing returns to scale

SAQ 2: *What will happen to big firms in an industry with a rising LRAC curve? Could conditions of perfect competition exist in the industry?*

In reality there are a number of industries where the small firm predominates: fish-and-chip shops and hairdressing are examples. These small firms survive for a number of reasons. One we have just discussed — because there are no economies of scale to be gained from growing any bigger, they are at their optimum size. In this case, it makes sense to stay small. It is easier to exert managerial control over small businesses — the owner is often on the spot to avoid problems before they arise, to notice any waste, to assess what's going wrong and what's going right with the business. This intimate personal control is lost as an enterprise gets bigger — we have all experienced the inefficiency and anonymity of the big business — and sometimes the loss of personal control can add so much to costs that any technical advantage from large-scale production is lost. Where this is true, economists speak of **managerial diseconomies of scale**.

Other firms stay small because they deal in a specialised market (e.g. Morgan sports cars) or work in a field where personal service and distinctive craftsmanship is important (e.g. bespoke tailors). Alternatively, a firm may be small because it is at an early stage in its development — even Marks and Spencer started as a market stall.

Even if scale economies do exist, a firm can only be as big as its market. Adam Smith put this in a nutshell: 'specialisation is limited by the extent of the market'. This is why firms that serve a local market only (a fish-and-chip shop, a night-club) remain small. The same is true for specialist manufacturing firms. If a firm is only catering for a limited market with a small output, there will be few opportunities for the economies of a large-scale firm — for example, for workers to specialise on one task all day (painting undercoat, drilling a particular hole, fitting handles in a furniture factory, etc.). Similarly, it would not be worth installing large and expensive items of capital equipment unless they can be used continuously, which means producing a large output. And what applies to specialised equipment applies equally to specialised staff, like accountants, lawyers, personnel officers, research scientists and so on. These are not worth employing unless a substantial output is to be produced.

SAQ 3: *Suggest what the difference is between diminishing returns and diseconomies of scale.*

Lower long-run costs

We now come to the third possibility I mentioned in the introduction. There are many industries where larger firms seem able to operate at lower cost than smaller ones, and such an industry is illustrated in graph 14.3:

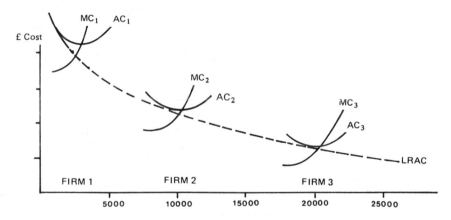

Graph 14.3 Scale economies

This is the case of increasing returns to scale. Where production is cheaper in large volumes and large firms, economists speak of **economies of scale**, or, more simply, **scale economies**. The Firm 3 that produces 1000 units has higher costs than the Firm 2 that produces 10 000 units, which is itself less competitive than the giant Firm 1 which produces 20 000 units. In other words, the LRAC is falling.

SAQ 4: *(a) Name three industries that, in your view, are subject to economies of scale. What will be true of the size of firms in those industries?*
(b) Suppose that the LRAC slopes downwards continuously to the right — what does this mean, and what will be the likely number of firms in the industry?

What shape will the LRAC curve have in practice?

It is conventional to assume that, in any industry, there will be a smallness of size that is so low that economic production is not possible, and also there will be a size so large that production is clumsy and uneconomic. The LRAC curve will therefore look like that in graph 14.4 − falling initially as the firm grows in size but ultimately rising as scale diseconomies set in. Note that there

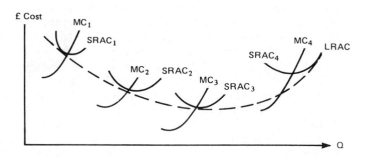

Graph 14.4 The LRAC curve

are no precise scales on the axes, for the precise shape of the curve will vary from industry to industry. For this reason, the optimum size of firm will vary from industry to industry, and might even change within an industry as technology changes.

SAQ 5: *(a) Which firm in 14.4 is at the optimum size?*
(b)   In the middle years of this century, the motor-car industry changed from being a craft-based industry where skilled workers built each car individually to one in which unskilled workers built cars on production lines. What happened to the optimum firm size as a result?

Economists have been anxious to confirm from real-life examples whether this is all true. It is, after all, quite important to discover whether the increased importance of large firms in our economy is a contribution to lower costs and higher living standards, or whether it is likely to lead to impersonal and inefficient production. P. J. Curwen (see references at end) described three research techniques which have been used to shed light on this area of the subject.

One way involves actually going into operating firms and obtaining accounting information about how much it costs to produce commodities; another involves calculating how much different levels of output would hypothetically cost given information about the costs of machines, raw materials etc; a third takes a look at the size of firms in the industry, sees how big are the ones that are surviving and doing well, and takes them to be 'optimally sized'. The conclusion of these studies tends to the same view − that in many industries, the long-run average cost curve is falling. Curwen quotes the economist Peter Wiles (1961):

> The long-run average cost curve descends like the left-hand branch of a capital U, swiftly at first and then more gently. Decreasing costs with size are almost universal. But the U seldom turns up again. Sharply increasing costs with size are practically un-known, and even slight increases are rare. 60% of the examples obey what we may call the law of L-shaped costs. Another 31% show a slight increase of costs in the largest size class (but) most are well within the (researchers' usual) margin of error.

SAQ 6: *Sketch the LRAC that Wiles describes. Which diagram in this unit does it most resemble?*

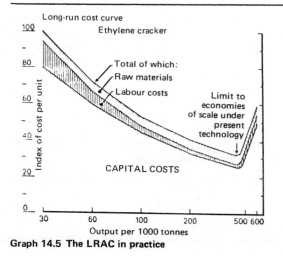

Graph 14.5 The LRAC in practice

The LRAC curve in graph 14.5 is based on actual figures from the petrochemical industry. Note how the larger the plant is, the cheaper will be production until we get to quite extraordinarily large sizes where special machinery bigger than anything previously known has to be designed, installed and used.

The question we now need to answer is: Why is large-scale production so much cheaper than small-scale production? What factors contribute to the scale economies shown in the falling LRAC curve that we've observed in theory and in fact?

ECONOMIES OF SCALE

If costs fall as the size of a firm rises, then internal economies of scale exist.* These can be divided into five main headings:

1. *Technical economies* exist when costs fall with larger size due for technical and engineering reasons. For example, a large steelworks is more efficient than a small one because it offers the chance of integrating all the processes of production into a system in which transport and energy costs are minimised. A modern steelworks will combine an iron-ore dock, a blast-furnace, a steel furnace and rolling mill. Large dimensions often yield economies: for example, a 40-tonne lorry will not need 20 times as much fuel, or crew, as a two-tonne lorry. There are sometimes straight mathematical reasons for such economies — doubling the dimensions of a pressure-vessel or oil-tanker more than doubles the holding capacity.

Large firms can use large, efficient machines and can utilise the division of labour more fully. A large car-plant, for example, can employ a worker simply to put on car-door handles all day, thus losing no time changing tools or doing an unfamiliar task. The recent introduction of expensive robots can only be justified by very large production runs.

SAQ 7: *Check back to p. 22 of Unit 2 to look at the other advantages offered by the division of labour, and at the disadvantages.*

Technical economies will cause plants to be large, rather than firms. The remaining forms of scale economies also account for the growth of big firms that own a large number of individual plants.

2. *Managerial economies* result from the way that larger firms can employ specialised managers. For example, a large company can employ its own lawyers, advertising staff, computer experts and accountants. What is more, there are opportunities for delegation of responsibility: in a large enterprise, top management can concentrate on the important and demanding tasks while passing to subordinates jobs that, while valuable, don't require their skills.

3. *Marketing economies* result from cost-cutting in buying inputs (such as raw materials) and selling output. The obvious example here is to be found in the bulk-buying power of the large retail chains such as Asda, Tesco or Sainsbury's who can buy so cheaply that their price to the consumer is sometimes lower than the wholesale price that is charged to the small shopkeeper.

Advertising is another important example of marketing economies of scale. One hoarding costs the same, whether for a national or local company; and when a single TV advertisement costs thousands of pounds to show, let alone make, only firms with a mass-produced, nationally sold product find it worthwhile. What is more, a firm with a range of products may find that advertising one line creates interest in another: the soup advertisement that tells us about Heinz Oxtail also presents us with the brand name of beans, ketchup and so on.

SAQ 8: *Another marketing economy is alleged to flow from economies in the administration of sales. How might these emerge?*

4. *Financial economies* refer to the way that large enterprises find it easier to raise funds than their smaller rivals. A firm which already has a substantial business can finance expansion out of **retained profits**: this method is not available to a newcomer to the industry. What is more, when a firm is large and well-known it acquires a reputation for reliability among banks and investors. Pension funds and insurance companies (**institutional investors**) prefer the security of a large, known firm. In particular, the facilities of the Stock Exchange's capital market are more readily available to a large company. To sell a substantial issue of new shares (a **launch**) involves a large fixed cost that isn't worthwhile for a small company.

5. *Risk-bearing economies* 'Don't put all your eggs in one basket' goes the proverb; yet many small enterprises have no choice but to specialise in one product, or a narrow product range. They are thus very vulnerable to a switch in demand. A larger firm can not only produce a broad spread of products, but can supply a wide range of markets.

SAQ 9: *Using the example of a large civil engineering contractor, explain why presence in a number of countries makes the earnings of the firm less vulnerable.*

*We shall see a second type of scale economy, 'external' economies of scale, in Unit 18.

One industry where it is essential to spread risks across a number of ventures is film-making. Many, perhaps most, films make a loss: yet the profit from one 'blockbuster' is able to repay losses on ten other films. So the studio that has a steady output of films has an advantage over an independent producing a 'one-off', despite the undoubted presence of some managerial diseconomies in the larger corporations.

SAQ 10: *In an increasing number of education authorities in Britain, sixth-form teaching is being concentrated in sixth-form colleges or brought into colleges of further education to make 'tertiary colleges'. One of the reasons for this is that economies of scale are thought to exist when students from a large number of schools are grouped together for their sixth-form studies.*
(a)   Suggest how each type of scale economy might apply to a sixth-form or tertiary college.
(b)   What diseconomies of scale might result from grouping courses into a single large institution?

MERGERS

Where internal economies of scale exist, large firms will be more efficient than small ones. These efficient large units can emerge in two ways:
- through internal growth, as the firm expands its share of the market
- through take-over and merger, as the firm joins with rivals to form a single unit.

I'm going to look at the second of these ways in this section. However, it needs to be said at the outset that scale economies are not the only reason for which firms merge. Firms can enjoy greater security in the market by joining up, and may even end up with monopoly advantages that can be exploited at the expense of consumers. Even being free of the need to compete is a motivation: 'the greatest monopoly profit is quiet life' said the economist W. J. Baumol. One reason that managers may be keen on mergers is that in merging they increase the size of their departments or sections, thus acquiring more perks and higher incomes without the tiresome need for better performance that would be required to achieve the same goal by internal growth. We'll look in the next unit at the modifications of economic theory needed in a world where managers rather than owners take decisions.

Mergers can take one of four forms:

1.   *Horizontal integration* is the simplest kind of merger, where two firms making the same product join together. An example of a large, horizontally integrated concern is the General Electric Company, which has been built up by taking over Associated Electrical Industries and English Electric, themselves formed from a number of electrical engineering concerns. When horizontal integration occurs, technical economies of scale become possible as larger machines and more opportunities for the division of labour become available.

Another, more controversial way of cutting costs from a horizontal merger is to eliminate spare capacity. Thus, three factories working at two-thirds capacity can be merged: two factories are then given the orders necessary to work fully, while the third factory is closed and sold off. Although this procedure plainly makes much economic sense, the consequences in local unemployment can be drastic.

2.   *Vertical integration* involves buying up the firm before or after you in the chain of production. Brook Bond, for example, own a number of tea plantations. Another tea firm, Lyons, have a history both of backward vertical integration (buying up tea merchants and coffee suppliers) but also of forward vertical integration (they once owned a chain of Lyons restaurants, and still retain a stake in hotels). This form of integration enables firms to have greater certainty in supplies, and to achieve improvements in quality control. The dangers for the public are that when a firm takes over a supplier or market outlet, the choice for consumers becomes more limited.

SAQ 11:   *50% of petrol filling stations are owned by large oil companies, and nearly all the remainder have long-term contracts with those companies. What form of integration is involved here?*

3.   *Lateral integration* describes the situation when two firms making similar but not identical products merge. An example can be found in BL formed from British Motor Holdings (making family cars) and Leyland Motors (making trucks and buses). The economics here are likely to be more of a financial and marketing kind than technical: indeed, production is undertaken by separate divisions of the company.

4.   *The conglomerate merger* has been particularly in vogue in recent years. This is the term for a combination of two essentially dissimilar firms. The advantage of conglomerate merger is that the resources of money and expertise from the whole group are available to individual sections, and the combined enterprise is less vulnerable to fluctuations in the market for a particular product. The public might feel less enthusiastic, however, for a trend that offers greater monopoly power without any pay-off in the form of low-cost mass-production. There are a number of examples of conglomerate companies at the moment, though it is likely that any printed details here will be out of date before publication: regard this list as 'specimens':

Trafalgar House owns civil engineering and building companies, the Ritz hotel, the *Daily Express* and the *Star* as well as the Cunard liner and holiday company.

Thorn/EMI Angus Steakhouses, HMV records, hospital equipment, household electrical goods, the Blackpool Tower, Thames TV, ABC cinemas, fire protection equipment, squash courts.

Sears Holdings: William Hill bookmakers, Dale Martin wrestling, Freeman, Hardy and Willis shoe shops, Mappin and Webb jewellers.

SAQ 12: *Using the beer-brewing industry as an example, give examples of all four types of merger. If you can quote from real-world cases, which exist in abundance, do so!*

WHITHER PERFECT COMPETITION?

In the first half of this unit we have seen that there are good reasons to believe that the LRAC will be downward-sloping — that is, for costs to fall as enterprises get bigger. This offers lower costs to consumers, but means that the world analysed in Unit 13 is unlikely to exist in very many industries. Small firms, owned by an entrepreneur and vigorously competing in a market where they are each individually insignificant, will become the exception rather than the rule. This suggests that we should look again at our theory of the firm, and face up to the possibility of industries being dominated by a few firms — or even just one. When a firm achieves such a dominant position the term **monopoly** is used. We shall now look at monopoly — what it means, why it occurs, its advantages and disadvantages and what governments can do about it.

MONOPOLY

What is monopoly?

Monopoly literally means 'one seller' — the extreme opposite of perfect competition. Such a situation is pretty rare, but the analysis I'll show you is just as valid when applied to a group of firms acting together to fix prices (a **cartel**) and also gives useful insights about markets of just two or three firms. Monopoly can be measured in one of two ways:

- Firstly, by the market share — the percentage of the market supplied by one seller. Pure monopoly would occur when one firm had 100% of the market. British monopoly laws are alerted at a lower level — when one firm has 25% of a market: according to the economist Prais this occurs in some 700 product markets. Market share can also be expressed in the form 'X firms control Y% of the market': what is known as a **concentration ratio**. For example, the state of competition in brewing can be assessed in the light of the knowledge that six firms produce 70% of British beer. Concentration ratios can be deceptive, though. They may underestimate the degree of monopoly in one locality: to stick with the beer example, there are areas of East Anglia where only one brand is available from a town's pubs. On the other hand, where imports are an important feature of a market, concentration ratios may overstate the degree of monopoly.

SAQ 13: *So does the bald statement that 93.6% of British cars are produced by four firms understate or exaggerate the market dominance of Ford, Vauxhall, BL and Talbot?*

- Secondly, we can make use of the idea of normal profit that was introduced in Unit 13. The argument is that the presence of excess or supernormal profits must indicate that the industry is in some degree monopolistic. This can be confirmed if we look at firms such as IBM, Polaroid, British Gas, Xerox. An international comparison might interest you: the 'big four' UK banks make profits about three times as great as the more numerous and competitive US banks.

SAQ 14: *What is 'normal profit'? Can supernormal profit exist under perfect competition? Can it persist under perfect competition?*

Why do monopolies occur?

There are a number of reasons for the absence of competitors in an industry: the reasons given below form a list of 'barriers to entry' that prevent other firms entering the monopolised market.

1. *Scale economies* We have already looked at the advantages of large firms when the LRAC curve is falling. To compete effectively, a newcomer to the industry would have to produce on a massive scale (known as the **threshold**).

SAQ 15: *Look back at graph 14.5 and say what the threshold level is in that industry.*

Prais' work (which I mentioned above) leads economists to the conclusion that financial and marketing economies are more important than technical ones.

2. *Patents and copyrights* One way to maintain a monopoly is to hold the patent or copyright to it, which prevents other people legally making the same product. Governments realise that patents and copyrights confer monopoly power, but believe that this will be compensated by the technical and artistic invention that they reward. So although at any one time competition might be the most efficient way of producing commodities, through time patents improve the economy. This argument is most controversial in the case of the drug companies, whose patent rights permit them high profits on new drugs as a reward for research and development.

SAQ 16: *To test your understanding of how copyright laws contribute to economic welfare over a span of time, explain why*
(a) bootlegged copying of videos is good for the consumer in the short run but
(b) needs to be stopped.

3. *Unfair trading* involves business practices that aim to destroy competition. Examples are legion and include: solicitors making it difficult for house-buyers to do their own conveyancing; LRC Industries (the 'Durex' firm) financing anti-pill research and publicity; large oil companies giving subsidies to their petrol stations when hard-pressed by competitors; British Oxygen setting up subsidised 'fighting companies' to put rivals out of business.
4. *Geographical isolation* can create the conditions for a 'local monopoly': examples include the village grocery store that is able to charge high prices because it is a bus-ride away from competing supermarkets.
5. *Control of a natural resource* occurs in the case of the South African diamond company De Beers, whose ownership of the Kimberley mine gives them the power to control the world market in diamonds. OPEC enjoyed its greatest successes when it presented a united front of world oil producers, and its power was eroded by the development of non-OPEC suppliers.
6. *Statutory monopolies* are set up by the law of the land (i.e. by statute). For example, any attempt to run an unlicensed radio or postal service is illegal. There are often social justifications of such monopolies (who would deliver the mail to the Outer Hebrides if Private Posts Ltd. were creaming off the lucrative inter-London market?). Again, in some industries the economies of scale are so pronounced that competition would be wasteful: rival gas firms or water boards would just raise costs and create twice as many roadworks! Such industries are called **natural monopolies**.

SAQ 17: *Name two other natural monopolies.*

THE FORMAL ANALYSIS OF MONOPOLY

The monopolist's demand curve

The demand curve for the products of a firm in a perfectly competitive industry is horizontal (or perfectly elastic). This is because the firm is so small that no matter how much it expands or reduces its output, the total production in the industry is hardly affected at all. This will not be true for the monopolist. Because a monopoly firm is producing *all* the product that is made, it faces the market demand curve. Let's suppose that this demand curve is as shown in graph 14.6 on the right. The graph plots this demand curve:

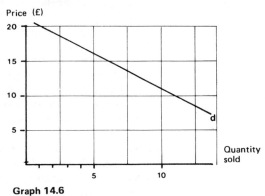

Graph 14.6

Price (£)	20	19	18	17	16
Quantity sold	1	2	3	4	5

So the monopolist has the choice of producing one unit and selling it for £20, or two units that can be sold for £19, or three units for £18 and so on. Which price and output will be chosen? Well, we learned in the last unit that a profit-maximising firm will produce where its marginal revenue is equal to its marginal cost (check back if you've forgotten why – it's an important concept). Let's work out the marginal revenue from the demand curve above. MR, remember, is the addition to total revenue coming from the sale of one more unit, so I'll have to work out total revenue (TR) first by multiplying price by quantity demanded.

Price (£)	20	19	18	17	16
Quantity sold	1	2	3	4	5
TR	20	38	54	68	80
MR		18	16	14	12

Important point: Note how MR is no longer equal to price. For example, although the second unit is sold for £19, its marginal revenue is £38 – £20: just £18. This is because, in lowering the price to £19, we have sold one more unit (gaining £19) but lost £1 in selling the first unit for £19 when it could have been sold at £20. Therefore the monopolist's MR curve slopes downwards more steeply than the demand curve because as the monopolist firm drops the price to sell more, it loses the revenue that previously could have been gained on the first few units sold at a higher price.

SAQ 18: *Look at the figures below and complete the questions that follow:*

Price	12	11	10	9	8	7	6
Quantity sold	2	3	4	5	6	7	8
Total revenue	——	——	——	——	——	——	——
Marginal revenue	——	——	——	——	——	——	——

(a)   *Work out the total revenue for each level of output.*
(b)   *Work out the marginal revenue for each level of output.*
(c)   *Why does the marginal revenue decline so sharply?*
(d)   *What happens to total revenue when the price is cut from £7 to £6? Why?*

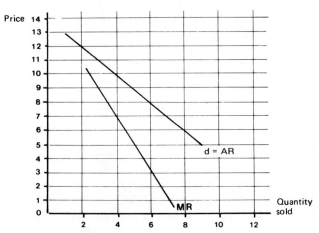

Graph 14.7 **Marginal revenue and average revenue**

I've plotted the demand curve and the marginal revenue curve from SAQ 18 in graph 14.7 above. It shows that characteristically steeply sloping MR curve of the monopolist. The price at which output is sold gives the average revenue (total revenue divided by quantity sold), so the demand curve can also be labelled the AR curve, showing as it does the average revenue at each level of output.

The monopolist's equilibrium

Let's now put what we've just learned of the MR and AR curves together with the cost conditions of the industry. Of course, while the MC and AC curves retain the characteristic shape first seen in Unit 13, they are now the cost curves of the whole industry.

Looking at graph 14.8 we can see that profit-maximising equilibrium is once again where MR is equal to MC: producing more will, after all, take the firm into an area where the additional production costs of units made will exceed the money brought in by their sale (look at the graph and note that MC exceeds MR to the right of equilibrium point E).

Having chosen quantity OX, our monopolist will sell that output at the highest price that the market will bear. If we read upwards from the equilibrium point to the demand curve, we see that the equilibrium quantity OX can be sold at a price of OB.

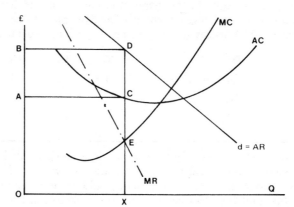

**Graph 14.8
Monopoly
equilibrium**

Now, were this industry under conditions of perfect competition, the equilibrium point in the market would be where the supply curve (= the rising MC curve, remember?) crossed the demand curve. But the monopolist doesn't have a supply curve, but simply sells OX at OB. It selects the most profitable output, and that is that. In fact, at this point the firm is making a supernormal profit. Total revenue (price times quantity) is represented by the rectangle OBDX, whereas total costs (AC times quantity) are shown by rectangle OACX. There is a supernormal profit of ABDE. Notice also that the equilibrium of the monopolist does *not* occur at the point of lowest average cost.

When economists assert that competitive conditions are to be preferred to monopoly they base what they say on the three conclusions of the analysis we've just gone through:

- A monopolised industry will produce fewer commodities, at a higher price, than a matching competitive one.
- A monopoly will earn supernormal profits.
- A monopoly will produce inefficiently (i.e. at a higher cost than is technically possible, as shown by the lowest point on the AC curve).

What is more, the monopolist's equilibrium is a long-term, stable one. Whereas supernormal profits in a competitive industry will attract entrants to compete prices and profits down, this will not happen in a monopoly industry.

SAQ 19: *Why not?*

SAQ 20: *In the early 1970s, the oil-exporting countries banded together to act in a united way in the output and pricing of their oil (i.e. they decided to act like a monopoly). Assuming that before this decision the oil market was pretty competitive, what would the theory of monopoly lead you to expect to happen to (a) the price and (b) the output of oil?*

X-inefficiency

The ideas I've introduced on the last page or so are the basis of the conventional criticism of monopoly. But there is another, more down-to-earth, reason to believe that monopolies will be inefficient. Up to now we have assumed that firms keep their costs down to an absolute minimum. This is fair enough in the competitive markets of Unit 13: the entrepreneur in charge of a business would know that, without a firm control of costs, the firm will be in trouble.

But why should the managers of a large powerful firm crack down on costs when a reasonable profit is being earned and no rivals threaten? Cost-cutting is a painful business, after all — doing without perks, making people work harder, keeping a sharp eye on all stages of production. It's much more likely that the monopolist will allow inefficiency to creep into the enterprise, in wasteful use of materials and labour, ambitious and costly capital programmes, fat expense accounts and management salaries. This source of inefficiency — which stems from the fact that the firm is no longer run by a profit-maximising entrepreneur, but by salaried managers — was first described by the economist Liebenstein in 1966. He called it **x-inefficiency**, 'x' standing for the unknown factor of waste. The presence of x-inefficiency has been confirmed by the success of management shake-ups in improving the efficiency and lowering the costs of large firms (e.g. Unilever in the 1970s; British Oxygen after 1980; the British Printing Corporation after Robert Maxwell's take-over).

SAQ 21: *Check back to the first few pages of this unit and find out the main reason for a rising LRAC. Does it fit in with the ideas in the previous paragraph?*

Adding together the conventional criticism of monopoly, derived from the MR = MC diagram, and Leibenstein's ideas on x-inefficiency, leads us to a wholly hostile view of monopoly. It wastes resources, lets costs rise, makes excess profits from consumers. It seems, then, that governments should take a very firm line against large firms: . . . or should they?

THE ADVANTAGES OF MONOPOLY

We should beware of over-simplification. Let's pause for a moment and take stock. I have shown that monopoly causes losses to society if costs remain unchanged when the market falls into the hands of one large producer: in graph 14.9, MC_1 shows the marginal cost curve of an industry. If the industry operates under perfect competition, then market equilibrium is reached at price OP, where the supply curve (= the MC curve) crosses the demand curve. Monopolising the industry will result in marginal revenue line MR and a new equilibrium with price at OS.

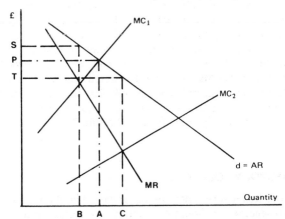

**Graph 14.9
Monopoly with
scale economies**.

SAQ 22: *What will be the difference to equilibrium quantity between the competitive and monopolist equilibrium?*

Scale economies

However, it is possible that the industry reached its monopoly position by economies of scale. If this were true, then costs would be lower in one big firm than if the industry were to be organised into many small firms. The curve MC_2 shows this lower price is OT. What has happened is simple to explain: the scale economies have cut costs by a greater amount than monopoly profits have added to them. The result is that, where scale economies are great enough, production under even a profit-maximising monopolist can result in a lower equilibrium price and a higher quantity produced.

Economists (like Knight in the US) have argued that monopolies achieve their superior market position by performing better on the market: by the survival of the fittest, if you like. Let's take a British example: in the UK, the detergent market is dominated by two companies (Unilever and Proctor and Gamble). This duopoly has attracted much adverse criticism — particularly of their wasteful advertising spending. But economist George Polanyi believes that the firms have reached their dominance because they have proved more efficient.

Innovation

Joseph Schumpeter, the distinguished Austrian economist, argued that monopolies are innovators, bringing forward new products via the research and development programmes that only monopoly profits can finance. The argument is that new products (ballpoint pens, artificial fibres, office dry-copiers, antibiotic drugs) were all initially produced by monopolies at what seemed like outrageous prices. As time passes, competition erodes the monopoly profit and competes prices down: we now throw away ballpoint pens and feed antibiotics to fatten up farm animals.

It must be said that the evidence for Schumpeter's belief is pretty slim. In 1979 The *Economist* reported American estimates that small firms' research programmes are much more effective than those of large firms — up to 24 times as many innovations per research dollar. O'Brien (*see* reference at end of this unit) argues that successful innovation is not related to size within an industry: indeed, big companies sometimes buy inventions from smaller firms (as revealed in the Monopolies Commission report on British Oxygen).

SAQ 3: *The 1964-70 Labour Government funded an Industrial Reorganisation Corporation in order to achieve more mergers. Having learned of the dangers of monopoly, can you justify such a policy?*

COUNTERVAILING POWER

So far I have discussed fairly clear-cut pro- and anti-monopoly views. However, the attitude of J. K. Galbraith — and many other modern writers on the firm — is less easy to categorise. Galbraith says that the economic system has changed so much that 'perfect competition' is no longer an option open to us. The market-place is dominated by big sellers and big buyers, who negotiate contracts with a keen eye to price and quality. For example, chain stores like Marks and Spencer exert firm control over their suppliers through their contracts and car manufacturers ignore the preferences of fleet-buyers at their peril. This new form of supply-and-demand has been dubbed **countervailing power** by Galbraith. He believes that the power of big buyers moderates any worries we might have about the emergence of dominant sellers.

Galbraith's ideas (expressed in *The New Industrial State*, 1967) owe much to the work of Professor Robin Marris. Marris has stated that the idea of the profit-maximising small entrepreneur is 'nineteenth-century'. He believes that we will come to 'a remarkably flexible and adaptable system by means of rivalry among a moderate number of large-scale independent organisations which continuously grow, form and reform'.

MONOPOLY POLICY

All this leaves government in a quandary. Should it break up monopolies to avoid excess profit and inefficiencies? Or should it encourage mergers, in order to achieve lower costs through scale economies, and new products through massive research programmes? A sensible policy might very well be to investigate each worrying market situation to analyse the costs and benefits of monopoly. Then we could allow the mergers or agreements that offer benefits to the public, but strike out those which on balance lead to disadvantages for the public. Such a policy towards monopoly is known as the pragmatic approach, and contrasts with the differing approach of the Americans to monopoly policy.

SAQ 24: *Look up the word 'pragmatic' in your dictionary. What does it mean? What is the opposite of a pragmatic policy?*

British monopoly policy (or, as it is sometimes known, 'competition policy') is covered in the main by three Acts of Parliament. GCE examiners will expect you to have a grasp of the legal measures available to governments in their treatment of monopolies, so here's a brief summary of those Acts:

Fair Trading Act 1973

This established the Office of Fair Trading, run by a powerful Director General of Fair Trading. The DGFT's job is to oversee and report on the state of competition in the economy. He (or the Minister of Trade) can refer monopoly situations (defined, as we've seen, as a market share of 25% or more) to the Monopolies and Mergers Commission (MMC), a government agency which has expert staff to evaluate mergers and monopolies. If the MMC finds that the market situation acts against the public interest, the Minister can make orders to correct the matter. In practice, governments have preferred to ask the DGFT to seek assurances from offending firms to end the practices complained of. The Minister additionally has powers to refer any *proposed* merger which would create a market share of 25% (or involving assets of over £15m) to the MMC.

Restrictive Practices Act 1976

This aims to hit not monopolies but **restrictive practices** – such as firms agreeing collectively to fix prices or selling conditions. Any agreement between two or more firms that might limit competition has to be registered with the DGFT, who must automatically refer such agreements to a Restrictive Practices Court. The RPC (consisting of five judges and ten other members picked for their commercial knowledge and experience) has a tough remit: it *must* disallow any agreement unless a good case is made on one of these grounds:

- essential to protect the safety of the public
- makes some other specific benefits available
- is a defence against someone else's restrictive practice
- protects the industry against an outside monopoly
- prevents persistent and serious local unemployment
- assists export earnings
- supports an agreement that has already been passed by the RPC
- doesn't materially affect competition.

These grounds are known as the **gateways**. *Additionally,* agreements must convince the RPC that the advantage under the gateway exceeds the cost of the restrictive practice to the public. This condition is known as the **tailpiece**, and was invoked (for example) when the RPC agreed that a textile-spinning agreement did safeguard local jobs, but that this benefit wasn't enough to justify interference with competition.

SAQ 5: *There is an agreement in the UK restricting the dispensing of medicines to qualified pharmacists only: which gateway does this come under?*

Competition Act 1980

This allows the DGFT and MMC to deal with a wide range of anti-competitive practices (even if the 25% market share is not reached). The DGFT can investigate and refer to the MMC almost any business practice which may distort or reduce competition. Public undertakings – such as water boards and transport authorities – were brought into the searchlight of monopoly legislation for the first time. The Act also allows the Trade Minister to refer any nationalised industry to the MMC for comments on its efficiency or possible monopoly abuses.

As with the Fair Trading Act 1973, the DGFT can accept undertakings from offenders; in fact the DGFT can investigate and obtain assurances without reference to the MMC – as happened in the case of ICI's dealings with the glass industry. As a last resort, the Minister can make orders to restore competition and strike out anti-competitive agreements.

DOES MONOPOLY POLICY WORK?

Much valuable work has been done by the MMC and the RPC, both in investigation and action – with the RPC perhaps the most effective.* There is a certain rationality in this, as **price rings** reduce choice and increase profits without any corresponding benefits from scale economies.

---

*Indeed, one explanation for the 'merger craze' of the 1960s and 1970s was that it was much easier to get a merger proposal past the MMC than a restrictive agreement past the RPC. Cooperating firms thus had an incentive to merge.

Hence the exam essay: 'Monopoly can sometimes be justified, but cartels never'. However, follow-up studies into particular markets revealed that commitments made to the government after monopoly investigations were often not honoured. More important, there is increasing evidence of rising concentration in UK industry, and the fact that industrial concentration has been increasing much faster in the UK than in other countries where the law is stricter (e.g. the US) must indicate a more relaxed approach to competition policy in the UK. Monopoly policy has failed to reduce the trend to larger firms.

Alternative policies on monopoly

There are, however, alternatives to the pragmatic UK monopoly policy. The most obvious one is a dogmatic monopoly policy — one that makes any monopoly position illegal, no matter what the justification. Other policies that would enhance the degree of competition in the economy might include:

- *encouragement of small firms* — particularly if they are handicapped by lack of access to finance: since the mid-1970s a substantial range of incentives has been made available to small firms
- *freer international trade:* there are very few global monopolies, and foreign giants are often better-placed to deal with UK giants than UK pygmies. Scale economies dictate that the UK has very few car, chemical, aircraft firms (etc.) — but international competition can keep them on their toes.
- *deregulation:* removing government controls and prohibitions in areas like coach travel and *NHS* contracts.

And if monopoly is inevitable, we might try:

- *nationalisation:* some people argue that if a monopoly is created, then it should be in public ownership. That way, the profits come to the exchequer, and monopoly abuses can be prevented by ministerial control. Unit 16 looks at nationalisation in more detail.
- *regulation:* the American phone system is not nationalised, but it is such a 'natural monopoly' that it offers private owners opportunities of exploitation. As a result, the US government imposes rules of behaviour they must follow. A similar approach to monopoly was used by the UK government in its dealings with railway companies before nationalisation.
- *tax:* if monopoly profits are to be made, the argument goes, let's grab a share of them for the public. An example is to be found in the 'excess rental' payable by ITV companies in the UK. Taxing away monopoly profits, though, doesn't answer the problem of monopoly fully.

SAQ 26: *Explain why a government would remain unhappy with a monopoly situation, even if all the excess profits were taxed away. Make use of the criticisms of monopoly on p. 234.*

REVIEW SECTION

Summary

In this unit, we have seen that once we start to consider the long-run cost curves of firms, there are good reasons to believe that larger-scale production would be cheaper than smaller-scale production. These economies of scale will lead to the growth of large companies. We've seen that a profit-maximising monopoly will restrict production to keep up prices and profits, to the detriment of the public. On the other hand, there may be some advantages in large firms — in cheap mass-production and product innovation. UK monopoly law investigates the advantages and disadvantages of monopolistic and other restrictive practices and judges whether they are in the public interest. However, the policy hasn't made an impact on the increasing concentration in the UK, and so other methods might well be considered.

I haven't had space in this unit to go as deeply into the topic as is desirable, and so please make sure you do some supplementary reading and get going with some research in your local library.

Further reading

All economics textbooks should have a discussion of scale economies and the problems of monopoly. You would certainly benefit from looking through the treatments in any of the textbooks recommended in the Study Guide. Start further reading with *Competition, Monopoly and Public Policy* by Neil Watts (Longman). A quite excellent magazine article is 'Mergers — Time to Turn the Tide' by O'Brien in *Lloyd's Bank Review* of October 1978: see if your library (or tutor) has a copy for you to consult. O'Brien's article also gives useful references for further reading. Sam Aaronovitch of the South Bank Polytechnic has taken a special interest in large firms and the growth of concentration — *see* his book *Big Business*, Macmillan, 1975. Galbraith's *New Industrial State* is available in paperback and is very readable. An account of EEC competition policy is in 'Three Banks Review' (December 1983).

Priest's *Manual of Applied Economics* discusses economies of scale in reality, and Curwen's *Theory of the Firm* (Chapter 12) gives a brief summary of research evidence. See also Hewitt *Economics of the Market* (Chapter 8), and *A Question of Economics* by Peter Donaldson (Penguin — especially Chapter 16).

An excellent source of information on this topic is Economic Briefs, *Monopoly* by Daniel Jeffreys (Collins).

Examination questions

Pick out two cases which have come before the Monopolies and Mergers Commission or Restrictive Practices Court (ideally, one from each). Give an account of the disadvantages to the public of the practices investigated; outline the defence that the firms put up; explain what the judgement of the Court or Commission was in each case. Useful sources include:

> *Problems of Economics Policy,* Hartley (relevant chapters)
> *Current Issues in Economic Policy,* Grant and Shaw (relevant chapters)
> *Monopoly and Restrictive Practices,* Stanlake (Ginn)
> *Monopoly,* Lee, Anthony & Skuse (Heinemann)
> *Case Studies in Monopoly,* Sandford

although other books will have details too. Use your local, school or college library fully, and don't be afraid to enlist the aid of the librarian. He or she might very well point you at Keesing's *Contemporary Archives* — a publication that sets out all the important news of the week in a filed ring-binder. As a result, Keesing's will enable you to refer to monopoly and restrictive practice cases that are too recent to get into the textbooks.

1. Are high profits the sign of monopoly?

(Oxford Local Delegacy 'A' June 1984)

2. Assess the extent to which (a) horizontal mergers, and (b) vertical mergers suppress competition and act against the public interest.

(Oxford Local Delegacy 'A' June 1985)

3. In what way might monopoly lead to a misallocation of resources? Consider the view that the costs incurred in the misallocation of resources under monopoly may well be outweighed by the benefits of large scale production.

(Northern Ireland GCE 'A' June 1984)

4. What criteria might be applied when assessing whether a merger between two firms was in the public interest?

(University of London 'A' June 1983)

5. Explain why a firm might seek to grow. Examine the advantages and disadvantages for the consumer of such growth.

(AEB 'A' November 1986)

6. Discuss the rationale for the main strands of competition policy in the United Kingdom.

(Oxford Local Delegacy 'S' June 1986)

7. Why might a firm's average cost curve be U-shaped (a) in the short run and (b) in the long run? Will a firm that sets price equal to marginal cost make greater or less than normal profits when its average costs are rising?

(Oxford Local Delegacy 'A' June 1986)

8. 'Costs determine price, demand determines quantity.' Discuss in relation to perfect competition and monopoly.

(Oxford Local Delegacy 'S' June 1985)

(*see also* essays in Review Section of the next unit)

ANSWERS TO SAQs

SAQ 1:   A national chain would be W. H. Smith or Menzies. Your local examples will vary according to where you live. A chain enables the employment of specialist staff (accountants, for example) that a small firm cannot afford; there may also be economies to be gained from bulk-buying. However, as the enterprise gets bigger it gets more difficult to manage; whereas a proprietor of a single shop can keep an eye on staff and stocks. There are a large number of industries in which small and large firms co-exist: for example, house building, record retailing, furniture manufacturing, publishing.

SAQ 2:   Big firms will experience higher costs, and will therefore be driven out by competition from the many more efficient smaller enterprises: such conditions would be helpful for the continuation of perfect competition, which you'll recall depends on the presence of many small firms.

SAQ 3:   Diminishing returns mean that rising costs occur when one factor is increased while all other factors remain constant; diseconomies of scale refer to increases in average costs that result from increasing the scale of production (e.g. even when *all* factors are increased in proportion).

SAQ 4:   A very large number of industries are subject to scale economies — chemicals, car manufacturing, steel, shipbuilding, aircraft manufacture, banking and so on, almost ad infinitum. We should expect that where scale economies exist, large firms will emerge to dominate the market as they can offer lower cost output than small er firms. At the extreme, if the LRAC slopes downwards continuously to the right, the larger the firm, the lower cost the production. Logically, we will end up with just one firm in that industry.

SAQ 5:   (a) Firm 3 — for it is at the lowest point of the LRAC curve, exploiting all possible scale economies without straying into the area of the rising LRAC when scale diseconomies set in. (b) The optimum firm size grew as the benefits from mass production became possible.

SAQ 6:   It looks like this: The nearest you'll get to it in this unit is the scale economies shown in 14.3 — though look, too, at 14.5.

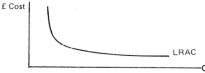

SAQ 7:   *see* Unit 2 for this.

SAQ 8:   Because administering a sale of 500 is no less costly than a sale of 5 000 000: the time it takes to talk to customers, send an invoice, make a salesperson's visit is in principle no different.

SAQ 9:   Because a recession (or cut in government spending) in one country might be compensated by a boom or increase in building activity in another. So a firm can avoid (say) a recession in the UK by landing a contract in (say) Nigeria or Hong Kong.

SAQ 10:   (a) *Technical:* large items of equipment (computers, libraries, sports halls, catering kitchens, laboratories) can be spread over more students; staff can specialise in (for example) geology without having to simultaneously prepare for other subjects they know less about and teach less well; students can be pooled so that instead of a number of very small classes in (say) German or RE spread through a number of sixth forms, one large viable group can be formed with the matching saving in staff costs. *Managerial:* specialist office tasks can be done by administrative staff; provision for reprographic and audiovisual learning aids can be developed by specialists; high salaries can be used to attract quality managers at Principal and Vice-Principal level, *Marketing:* economies can be made in the bulk-buying of paper and other stores; items like printed prospectuses and registers are cheaper when ordered in long runs. *Risk-bearing:* when the economy shifts, staff can be relocated away from courses in low demand to newer areas. (b) Diseconomies of scale might include managerial diseconomies — poor control of costs due to remoteness of control; poor morale as relationships are less warm; less personal care for students, who feel lost in a large, impersonal institution.

SAQ 11:   Vertical

SAQ 12:   *Horizontal:* one brewery takes over another (e.g. Watneys took over the Manchester brewery Wilson's, Courage took over the Berkshire brewery of my youth, Simonds). *Vertical:* breweries taking over pubs, in the much-criticised 'tied house' system that denies the public a choice of beers in most pubs. *Lateral:* taking over a similar line — as in the merger between Whitbread and Showerings (the Babycham people): most breweries have taken over wine merchants and developed their own brands of spirit. *Conglomerate* means breweries joining with an enterprise that is nothing to do with alcoholic drink. An example might be where Unilever took over Allied Breweries — though CAMRA fans may feel that there is a lateral connection between some modern beers and chemicals.

SAQ 13:   It exaggerates it. Foreign competitors ensure that the car market is much more competitive than the statistic makes it seem.

SAQ 14:   It is the level of profit necessary for continued production of a commodity. Supernormal profit can exist in the short-run under perfect competition — say, because of a rise in demand in a particular industry: it will not, however, persist, as new entrants will come in and compete away the profits until they are 'normal' once again.

SAQ 15:   It's about 500 000 tonnes.

SAQ 16:   (a) In the short run the increased supply brings down prices but (b) if allowed to continue, film producers will not get an adequate reward for their risky ventures and so production of new videos will slow dramatically.

SAQ 17:   Electricity, phones, postal services (though I only asked you to name two).

SAQ 18:   (a) Total revenue is price times quantity: 24, 33, 40, 45, 48, 49, 48; (b) marginal revenue is then 9, 7, 5, 3, 1, and -1; (c) because to sell additional units, the price must come down. This reduces the value of sales that could have been made at higher prices. (d) total revenue actually falls when you sell one more — because it earns more to sell seven units at £7 then to sell eight at £6. Marginal revenue is therefore negative.

SAQ 19:   Because there are the entry barriers listed on page 86: patents, scale economies, control of a natural resource, etc. So no-one can come in and compete the profits back to normal.

SAQ 20:   As in the graph, the monopolist's price will be higher *but* this requires their output to be lower. A monopolist cannot choose to sell as much as he likes at the going price: a price/output combination must be chosen.

SAQ 21:   Managerial diseconomies. Yes.

SAQ 22:   Monopoly output will be OB; competitive equilibrium quantity (where MC=s crosses the dd curve) will be OA, so the customer will get BA less of the commodity.

SAQ 23:   If the advantages to the economy of larger and more efficient firms is greater than the disadvantages of monopoly profits and exploitation, there is much to be said for encouraging mergers.

SAQ 24:   A pragmatic approach is one that judges events by their practical effects. The contrast is with a dogmatic approach, which takes a rigid, theoretical stand. Thus a pragmatic policy on monopoly says 'monopoly is neither right nor wrong: let's judge each case on its merits'; the dogmatic attitude would be 'monopoly is always and everywhere bad'.

SAQ 25:   Check through the gateways and I think you'll see why this was justified on the grounds of public safety: plainly, we wish to have our medicines dispensed by someone with knowledge of the medical effects of dosages of drugs.

SAQ 26:   Because the trouble with monopolies is not just that they earn excess profits; they also produce inefficiently, and a monopoly tax won't correct this: only making price equal to marginal cost will (as we shall see later in the course). What is more, an excess profits tax is an invitation to x-inefficiency: why cut costs when all your efforts will swell the taxman's take? Wouldn't it be better to buy all the reps a better car?

15 Another look at firms

AIMS OF UNIT 15

At the end of this unit, you should be able to:

- explain the strengths and weaknesses of the 'perfect competition' and 'monopoly' theories of the firm
- define monopolistic competition and explain why such a market structure would lead to excess capacity
- say what is meant by 'cost-plus pricing' and 'price leadership'
- explain and evaluate the kinked demand-curve theory of oligopoly, making clear the markets to which it applies
- show how the divorce between ownership and control leads to alternative views of the firm's aims
- list these aims (other, that is, than profit-maximisation) and show how they lead to different behaviour by firms than under traditional theories
- contrast a number of models of the firm, showing differences in market share, control over price, management structure and economic aims.

INTRODUCTION

In the past two units we've looked at two contrasting market situations. Unit 13 took a look at perfectly competitive markets, with many small firms making identical products. The model we developed made a strong case for such unrestricted markets: it showed that they kept costs, profits and prices to a minimum. But Unit 14 introduced the idea that if the LRAC sloped downwards, large firms would enjoy lower costs and therefore be able to dominate markets. Analysing the market situation that results alerted us to the excess profits, inefficiency and high prices that would follow from a profit-maximising monopoly. In this unit, I'll try to show the relevance of these two markedly contrasting analyses, and introduce some alternative ways to look at firms.

HOW RELEVANT ARE THE THEORIES OF COMPETITION AND MONOPOLY?

At this point you should check back to the opening of Unit 13, where I explained the rather restrictive assumptions of perfect competition. You'll meet very few firms in your day-to-day life that fit them. Because of this, some economists have written off the theory as outdated.

SAQ 1: *Name an economist who holds this view.*

In my view this is an overreaction. Theories which deal with markets where no single seller can affect prices are highly relevant because

- many important financial and commodity markets operate via supply and demand (*see* Unit 12, p. 196)
- the small firm still has an important role in the economy (*see* Unit 14, p. 227)

Despite this, any attempt to construct a 'theory of the firm' must acknowledge that today it is the big firm that is the dominant economic unit. The growth of industrual concentration (*SAQ 2*) has been well documented. S.J.Prais has shown that the share of the largest 100 enterprises in manufacturing output has risen from 16% in 1909 to 41% in 1972. The Green Paper (*see* reference in previous unit) claimed that the five largest firms accounted for 90% or more of output in nearly one quarter of the UK product markets.

SAQ 2: *What is industrial concentration? How is it measured?*

Note, though, that although there is evidence of growing size, the UK has very few monopolies in the strictest sense.

SAQ 3: *What is meant by the expression 'monopoly' in its strictest sense? What is the looser, 'statutory' definition of monopoly?*

Firms which produce the whole amount of a commodity, and therefore face the market demand-curve are rare. Much more common is 'oligopoly' — a term referring to a market with 'few sellers'. It is, in any case, difficult to make precise judgements about the extent of monopoly, for much depends on how tightly we define the product under consideration. Johnny Walker have 100% of the market for Black Label whisky, for example — but this doesn't make them a monopolist. Other whiskies are close substitutes: and other spirits like rum, gin and brandy form less perfect substitutes. And if spirits become too pricey, consumers would switch to wines and beers.

In the next few pages, I'll try to adapt the traditional cost and revenue curve graphs we've met in Units 13 and 14 to the circumstances of markets with few sellers, or where firms have a monopoly of their own branded good despite the presence of close substitutes — to markets, that is, where **imperfect competition** exists.

MONOPOLISTIC COMPETITION

What does it mean?

Monopolistic competition is a term applied to a market situation in which there are a large number of producers (as in perfect competition), but where producers make goods which are slightly different from each other's. Thus, firms have a monopoly over their own product, though there are many close substitutes. An example would be the manufacture of jeans, where Levi, Brutus, Wrangler (etc. etc.) all supply similar but differentiated, casual wear. Because the products are not identical, demand for an individual firm's output will not be perfectly elastic. Raising the price of one brand of jeans would not lose all the firm's customers, because at least some of them would regard the product as good enough to be worth paying the extra. This is the concept of **brand loyalty** (you may already be familiar with it) and explains also why cutting the price of one brand of jeans will not get all the other firms' customers. If firms can raise their selling price without losing all their customers, the demand must be downward sloping; and firms facing downward sloping demand curves have more steeply sloping marginal revenue curves.

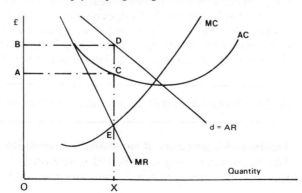

Graph 15.1
Short-run equilibrium in
monopolistic competition

Equilibrium: long-run and short-run
All of which leads us to the short-run equilibrium of the firm shown in graph 15.1. Equilibrium is at point F, where marginal revenue is equal to marginal cost. The firm therefore selects output OX,

SAQ 4: *Explain why a profit-maximising firm will be in equilibrium where MR = MC.*

The firm therefore selects output OX, which can be sold at a price of OB: as a result, an excess profit of ABDC is made.

You may at this stage wonder why we need a separate theory of monopolistic competition, for graph 15.1 is exactly the same as diagram 14.8 — the equilibrium of the monopolist. But there is a crucial distinction. The monopolist's equilibrium persists in the long run because effective barriers to entry exist: as a result, entrants cannot compete the excess profit away. (*SAQ 5*) But in monopolistic competition, entry barriers are much less effective — it is comparatively easy to set up a jeans-manufacturing operation (or make soap, or cough medicine, or open a pub, or launch a specialist magazine, etc.). The entry of new firms attracted by the excess profit in graph 15.1

SAQ 5: *As a reminder, list some of these entry barriers.*

will take away some of the custom of the existing firms (such as the one shown on the graph); in effect, the demand curve of each existing firm is shifted to the left. What is more, those demand curves will become more elastic as the products of new entrants weaken brand loyalties. New firms will continue to enter the industry — and push those demand curves to the left — for as long as the industry offers excess profits. This occurs when the equilibrium shown in graph 15.2 is achieved.

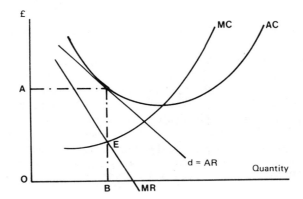

**Graph 15.2
Long-run
equilibrium in
monopolistic
competition**

In this graph, equilibrium is at OE, giving an equilibrium output at OB. The price at which the output sells is OA. There are two important things that must be noted about this equilibrium.

- *normal profits only are being made,* as price is equal to average cost at OA.
- the firm is producing a level of output lower than that required for the lowest cost production. Our theory predicts that *a monopolistically competitive industry will suffer chronic excess capacity*: that is, a large number of firms will all be underemployed.

So monopolistic competition gets the worst of all worlds. It has the inefficient resource allocation of monopoly, and the insecurity of competition. This insecurity is made greater by the possibility that even the equilibrium shown in graph 15.2 may not be stable. Aggressive newcomers, believing that their sharper management or newer equipment can cut costs lower than existing firms, will keep entering the industry and reducing the existing firms' market share. As a result, firms will not be able to cling on and will be forced out of business. What remedy is there for this?

Advertising One response to the situation would be to launch an advertising campaign. This offers two advantages to the entrepreneur. In establishing a clear 'brand image', it will make demand for his product more inelastic and thus insulated from the attractions of rivals; and in gaining extra custom, it will shift the firm's demand curve to the right. In the longer view, however, advertising is likely to attract retaliation from other producers, and this will raise costs: all the firms will have to maintain high advertising budgets to stay in the same place. Worse, advertising that raises profitability will attract new entrants and shift the demand curve to the left again.

SAQ 6: *Does advertising have a role under perfect competition?*

Problems with the theory of monopolistic competition
The theory was developed in the 1930s by Joan Robinson in Britain and by E. H. Chamberlin in the USA. It represented a welcome move towards reality, for unlike the perfectly competitive

model, it dealt with firms who could not sell all they wanted at the going price. A role for advertising, that pervading fact of modern economic life, was found in the theory. The predicted equilibrium — with low profits, excess capacity and marginal firms being edged out of the industry — seems to be realised in a number of sectors of the economy. Confirmation can be found, for example, in half-empty pubs and snack-bars.

SAQ 7: *Petrol stations can be seen as firms in monopolistic competition, selling a product slightly differentiated by brand and location. From your own observation, would you say that the model we have just looked at accurately describes conditions in that industry?*

However, the ideas of monopolistic competition are deficient in a number of ways. Firstly, the firms in the theory take no account of the behaviour of their rivals on the market when choosing price and output levels. Secondly, according to the theory we've just looked at, prices would fluctuate just as much as they would under conditions of perfect competition. If the firm's demand curve shifted to the left, prices would be reduced while if it moved right (in response perhaps to a successful advertising campaign) prices would be raised. But one of the characteristics of the market for branded manufactured goods is that the price does *not* fluctuate with demand: the term sometimes used is **sticky** prices. Even in severe recessions, the prices of cars, chocolate bars, shirts, records, etc., are not reduced. An accurate theory of the firm must explain why prices remain unchanged when demand and costs change: let's move on to consider one such theory.

OLIGOPOLY

Cost-plus pricing
To gain an insight into this phenomenon, economists have gone into industry with surveys and asked managers and accountants how they fix their prices. Economic theory suggests that firms would maximise their profits by charging 'what the market will bear' — by selecting the optimal combination of price and quantity from the demand curve that faces them. Research has found little evidence that managers act in this way. Prices are generally selected by a process known as **cost-plus** or **full-cost** pricing. This means managers work out average costs at the anticipated output: then add a mark-up to represent the desired profit level to make the price that is charged (indeed, most publishers price their books on roughly this principle). Thus, the price of manufactured goods is not reached by a market process as much as administered by managers of large firms.

Prices that are administered (i.e. decided by some sort of cost-plus pricing system) and sticky (i.e. unchanging in the face of changes in costs and demand) are particularly common in markets where there are few sellers — what are termed **oligopolistic** markets. When faced with just three or four rivals, a firm must take into account their likely reactions to any change of price or production level. What follows is an explanation of one model that incorporates both an administered price and consideration of the reactions of rivals.

The kinked demand curve
An oligopolist is faced with two demand curves: *see* graph 15.3. In this graph, OP is the present price.

SAQ 8: *How has that price been determined?*

At this price, the firm can sell output OQ. The demand curve AB shows what would happen

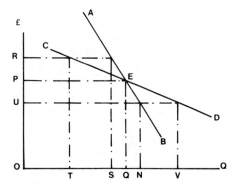

Graph 15.3

to the firm's sales if its prices were matched throughout the industry. For example, if the firm raised prices to OR, and so did every other firm in the industry, then it would sell quantity OS. Similarly, if throughout the industry price was cut to OU, the quantity that this firm would sell would be ON.

The demand curve CD illustrates what would happen to the sales of the firm if it acted alone in raising or lowering price. If it was the only one to raise prices to OR — while its rivals kept the price at OP — sales would fall to OT. In raising prices, the firm would lose all but the most faithful of customers. The reverse would be true of a unilateral reduction in price: the firm would pick up all but the most loyal of his competitors' customers. Cutting price to OU in this case would raise the quantity sold to OV.

SAQ 9: *Which demand curve is most elastic with respect to price — AB or CD?*

Which of the two demand curves will operate? Well, they both will. If the firm in graph 15.3 raises prices, its rivals will keep their prices at the original level to pick up its business: above price OP, curve CE will be the relevant one. If, however, the firm cuts prices in an attempt to pick up the customers of its rivals, then the rival firms will have to take up the challenge of the 'price war' and cut prices. In other words, curve EB will operate below price OP.

The oligopolist therefore faces a bent, or kinked, demand curve: in graph 15.3, it will be curve CEB. In graph 15.4 I have added the marginal revenue curves for the two demand curves: FG is the curve that shows the marginal revenue for demand curve CD, and HJ shows the marginal revenue if operating from curve AB. Again, if CE is the appropriate section of the demand curve above price OP, then MR curve FG must be the relevant one there; but below price OP, it is the MR curve related to demand curve AB that is effective — curve HJ. I have marked boldly the effective kinked MR curve. Note that there is a step as we move from MR curve FG down to MR curve HJ.

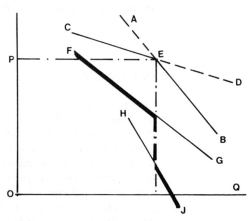

Graph 15.4

Oligopoly equilibrium

Within graph 15.4, changes in both cost and demand conditions can be shown not to alter profit-maximising firms' choice of selling price. In graph 15.5, we see that market price will be the same (where MR = MC) whether the MC curve shifts up to MC_2 or down to MC_3. In other words, the step between the MR curves — the **region of indeterminacy** — can accommodate a variety of MC curves.

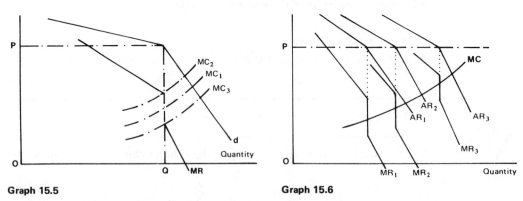

Graph 15.5   **Graph 15.6**

In graph 15.6, demand conditions have changed: I have shown three demand curves, marked AR_1, AR_2 and AR_3, and shown and numbered the three MR curves that result. You will see again that price will remain unchanged: the firm adjusts to changes in demand by increasing or decreasing equilibrium output.

This theory of oligopoly accounts for the observed behaviour of firms: selling at prices that do not fluctuate (apart from very infrequent 'price-wars') and adjusting quantity sold to changes in demand. As price competition is rare, rivalry between firms takes the form of advertising, packaging, special offers, after-sales services — even gimmicks like newspaper bingo or free entry to competitions. This behaviour is known as **non-price competition**, and is typical of oligopolistic markets.

SAQ 10: *Below I have laid out in table form the four kinds of market that we have looked at so far in the course. I have classified them according to the number of firms, differences in product, ease of entry and control over price. Checking through this and previous units, fill in the boxes I have left empty — it may be a good idea to do this in pencil first and check your answers with my suggestions at the end of this unit.*

	How many firms are there in the industry?	*How easy is it to enter the industry?*	*How different are the products of the firms?*	*How much control does an individual firm have over price?*
Perfect competition				
Monopolistic competition				Not much
Oligopoly		Difficult	Could be standardised or differentiated	
Monopoly			No real substitutes for the firm's product	

Problems with the theory of oligopoly

The theory of oligopoly is ingenious — maybe a little too ingenious. You may feel that industrial realities have been squeezed into the MR = MC model with an academic shoe-horn. Moreover, research has cast some doubt on the kinked demand-curve so central to the model. The main criticism has concentrated on the model's assertion that price cuts will be matched, but price rises will not. In practice, price rises are followed just as often, and as swiftly, as price cuts. This is so pronounced in some industries that it has been given a name — **price leadership**. Where price leadership exists, the price is set by the leading firm in the market and others follow: when a price rise is announced by the dominant firm, the remainder of the firms in the industry follow suit.

At the extreme, firms may engage in a form of collaboration, attempting to fix prices and output to achieve a 'joint profit-maximisation'.

SAQ 11: *What legal remedies are open to the government to stop firms getting together to fix prices and carve up the market?*

Indeed, oligopolies may not even want to force profits to their highest short-run level. The long-term interests of the company may be better-served by less aggressive behaviour that will avoid conflict with rivals, keep customers happy and avoid attracting the unwelcome attentions of either new entrants to the industry or the Director General of Fair Trading. But if we are to admit this possibility — that firms are not out to maximise their profits — then we must move away from the MC = MR models we have used so far and develop a new frame of reference. This is what I shall attempt in the remainder of this unit. I'll start by asking the question:

WHO IS IN CHARGE OF BRITISH INDUSTRY?

In our discussion of the firm up to this point, I have assumed that the owner-manager of the firm has taken the decisions on output and price.

SAQ 12: *What motivation has been uppermost in the mind of the entrepreneur in all our models of the firm so far?*

This was a valid idea in the Victorian world in which classical economics grew — most firms were small and would have gone under in the fierce competitive climate had not the owner-manager kept a firm eye on costs and profits. As Graham Bannock writes in his book *How to Survive the Slump*. (Pelican 1975).

> 'At first, joint stock companies were directed by persons who had major, often controlling, shareholdings. As the companies grew in size and issued more equity capital these shareholdings were diluted. Ownership and control of companies became separated, until today the typical Board of Directors that control and run the business are remunerated mainly by salary and own only a few per cent, at most, of the stock of their company. The shareholders are, increasingly, other companies — financial institutions such as insurance companies, unit trusts and pension funds — which hold the wealth of the ordinary citizen, who thus owns big business (at one or two removes) but has little control over it.'

Very few individuals now hold substantial proportions of the stock of individual companies. The Diamond Commission (into Income and Wealth in the UK) found only five shareholdings of more than 5% owned by individuals in the top 30 UK companies. In the past 30 years or so the pension funds, unit trusts and insurance companies (**institutional investors**) have amassed huge shareholdings as workers' pension contributions and insurance premiums have been funnelled towards them and invested on the Stock Market. Personal shareholders held nearly 70% of all shares in 1963: that proportion fell below 50% in the next ten years. The *Guardian* (31 July 1977) went further, with an estimate that the institutions now hold as much as two-thirds of all shares.

This has two startling implications:

- for democracy. It means that a small group of men — as few as 20 — control the bulk of savings flowing into industry. The investment manager of the Prudential, or the Post Office pension fund, is probably much more influential than your elected MP in deciding the future prosperity of the UK economy.
- for the theory of the firm, for we have just learned that the owners of UK industry do not take part in the running of the business. On the whole, institutional investors are content to leave the decisions about running the company to the managers, although they do sometimes make their voices heard when forced to do so by calamitous mismanagement in a firm.

An interesting survey of the issues surrounding the growth in **institutional investment** is given by Sir James Ball in *Lloyds Bank Review*, October 1984.

SAQ 13: *In the last unit we looked at the increasing concentration of UK industry: we now see that ownership of that industry is also being concentrated (into institutional hands). What connection is there between these two trends? (see Unit 14, p. 229)*

Let's now see how these changes in the control of industry affect our theory of the firm.

MANAGERIAL THEORIES OF THE FIRM

We have now learned that today there is a divorce between the ownership and control of UK industry. Firms are not run by owners any more, but by salaried managers. In these circumstances we must seek a theory of the firm that gives due weight to the values and priorities of these managers. We would not expect them, for example, to be profit maximisers. As J. K. Galbraith pointed out (with a smirk), if business decision makers really wanted to maximise their own profits, they would constantly have their hand in the till. In fact, the directors and senior managers of large companies are almost a by-word for integrity: Galbraith gave this paradox the title of 'the approved contradiction'.

This is not to say that managers will be indifferent to their own income and living standards: they will wish to maximise their own salaries and perks. Now, research evidence shows that the size of a manager's pay depends on the size of the company much more than on company profitability. Look at the table below, which relates the sales turnover of firms to the average salary of senior managers in those firms:

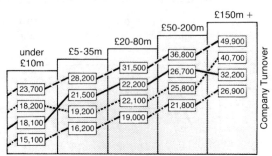

Source: PA Personnel Services, quoted from *The Sunday Times*, 13 September 1987

Baumol and sales-revenue maximisation

The economist W. J. Baumol used data of this sort to put forward (in 1959) the idea that managers will aim for maximum sales revenue in order to increase their salaries. This implies producing beyond the point where MR=MC. Graph 15.7 shows the conventional monopoly equilibrium, at E where MR=MC. Profits for the shareholders are maximised by producing output OA and selling it at price

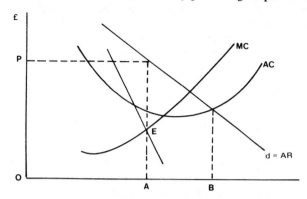

Graph 15.7

OP. But the firm could produce more without making a loss: for example, at output OB average revenue is equal to average cost and so normal profits only are being earned. Baumol realised that managers couldn't expand sales indefinitely: they had to earn enough profit to keep the shareholders satisfied and to keep up the value of the company's shares. For example, it is unlikely that managers would feel free to expand sales as far as OB. Nevertheless, Baumol's model would have firms producing more, and earning less profit, than conventional theories of the firm.

Advertising again

The strength of Baumol's analysis is that it explains the importance of advertising to the firm. Even though it may raise costs and eat into profits, advertising boosts sales revenues. Advertising also offers another benefit to the firm: it creates an entry barrier. New firms will find it difficult to enter the market for (say) detergents or chocolate bars because of brand loyalty generated through the advertising spending of existing firms.

SAQ 14: *Why are entry barriers advantageous to firms in an industry?*

Marris and growth-maximisation

An alternative approach to take account of managerial preferences was adopted by the economist Robin Marris. Marris feels that managers would be concerned to see their organisation grow fast. Being part of a fast-growing firm, or department within a firm, would enhance the manager's income and prestige, and would probably also pay off in additional perks – a larger car, a plusher office, more subordinates and a fancier job title*. As with Baumol's model of sales revenue maximisation, there is a constraint on the manager. Fast growth can be risky, as it involves using spare cash for acquisition of other companies or new investment projects. It is likely, therefore, that the manager will select the set of company policies that achieve the fastest growth that is compatible with financial security.

Marris's theory explains the diversification so evident in today's large companies. Growth by expanding the sales of one's existing products is likely to become increasingly difficult: the only way to achieve permanently growing demand is to diversify into new product areas by innovation or merger.

SAQ 15: *What name is given to a merger between two companies of differing industries? What scale economies are likely to be available from such a merger? Which scale economies are unlikely to become available?*

WHY MAXIMISE ANYTHING?

Baumol's revenue-maximising manager and Marris' growth-maximising executive seem as single-minded as the profit-maximising entrepreneur of traditional theory. Managers are likely in reality to aim at a number of goals: certainly they will wish to achieve adequate levels of profit, growth in

*So important do these perks appear to be for management behaviour that O. E. Williamson has developed a model that might fairly be termed 'perk maximisation'!

sales and market share. But they will also wish to maintain cordial relations with other departments inside the firm, and with customers; keep the trust of suppliers and creditors; even gain a measure of job-satisfaction from the quality of the product. Research has shown that managers do not, for example, aim to maximise short-run profits as they feel that to do so would be 'unfair' to customers.

We are now beginning to reach the edge of the subject of economics and move into politics and sociology in viewing the firm as a political entity (involving the exercise of power and authority, and bargaining between interest groups) or as a social system (with its own hierarchies, values and culture). At this point it might be best to look at the most complete statement of the managerial view of the firm, and make some comments in defence of the traditional theory of the firm.

CAN WE FORGET THE MARKET?

J. K. Galbraith (in his book, *The New Industrial State* 1967 — available in Pelican paperback) argued that the large, manager-run firm had grown so dominant in today's world that the market had been superseded. The interplay of buyer and seller existed, if at all, in the countervailing power I described in the last unit. The managers worked to ensure a secure and stable environment for their firms. Demand was manipulated by advertising and planned through market research, so that, far from consumers telling firms what to produce via their 'money votes' (look back at 'consumer sovereignty' in Unit 1), firms are able to tell consumers what to want (a reversal that Galbraith entitled 'the revised sequence'). The firms' capital needs are almost entirely met by retained profits, freeing them from dependence on banks or private investors. Business executives' manipulation extends, according to Galbraith, as far as political lobbying and the corruption of public officials. All this adds up to a new version of the planned economy, but here the planning of investment, employment, output and prices is done by the executives of large companies — even foreign companies — rather than by civil servants.

If this analysis is correct it means we have to rethink our old distinction between micro and macroeconomics. Perhaps we now have to consider a government's meso-economic policy, *meso* being the Greek word for 'in-between'. This was the force behind the 1974-78 Labour Government's ideas on industrial policy, which included the stillborn 'planning agreements' between large firms and government.

The return of the market

There are those, however, who would argue that the managerial writers, and especially Galbraith, have exaggerated the significance of the changes in the organisation of the economy in recent years. The attempt to reinstate the profit-maximising model uses these arguments:

1. *Cost-plus pricing is quite consistent with profit-maximising behaviour in a competitive market.* This is supported by the assertions that:
    *   firms rarely have an unchanging list price: they can adjust the stated price in line with market conditions — varying discounts, for example. The car market is a good example of this — only a mug pays the full list-price unless the car is in great demand.
    *   It doesn't matter that managers say they don't price to marginal cost: if they are attempting to make as much profit as possible (which, when pressed, most admit to), then they must be equating MR and MC even if they don't realise it. What is more, most managers operating a cost-plus pricing system pay special attention to variable costs of output, which are very near marginal costs.
    *   the mark-up chosen in cost-plus pricing varies with market conditions, illustrating the influence of demand on price.

2. *Advertising is an acceptable form of marketing.* It is not the inherently wasteful activity implied in the theory of monopolistic competition, nor the defensive barrier of oligopoly. This is because, in a changing economy with changing consumers, the perfect information and homogeneous products of perfect competition are not present.
    *   because ignorance of products and prices is present, advertising makes markets more perfect by providing information.
    *   because products change through time, advertising introduces consumers to new and improved commodities.
    *   by increasing the sales of a product, advertising makes available scale economies that lower unit costs.

SAQ 16: *Comment on the last sentence.*

3. *Managers are not a separate group with different interests and aims to the rest of the share-holders.* It is admitted that shareholders do not intervene in the day-to-day running of the firm, but this may well be because managers are doing the job that the shareholders want them to do: 'why keep a dog and bark yourself?' When managers fall down on their job, even institutional investors make their presence felt. There are a number of examples of where they have stepped in to shake up a problematical company (e.g. Burton's, Woolworths).

More profoundly, it is argued that managers share the same goals as shareholders. In his book *The Power Elite* (Penguin), for example, C. Wright Mills showed that in the USA, top managers were often top shareholders: this has become increasingly true as managers become entitled to 'stock options' as part of their 'remuneration package'. Ralph Miliband in *The State in Capitalist Society* (Quartet) has developed and extended this criticism with reference to more recent research into the relationship between managers and owners in Britain and Western Europe. Much of this work is summarised in Robin Blackburn's section in *Ideology in Social Science* (Fontana), where he argues that managers are significant shareholders, have the same class and educational background as the rest of the owners, and share the same ideas about the economic system. It is argued, therefore, that there is no need for an economic theory which seeks to discover differing, managerial, goals.

REVIEW SECTION

General summary

This unit has covered the topic of imperfect competition by taking, for a start, two well-known models — monopolistic competition and oligopoly. We then contrasted the four market forms we have studied, placing them on a spectrum from perfect competition to monopoly. Much of the discussion in this unit has been designed to fulfil the aims of, for example, the AEB's syllabus, which states:

> '. . . candidates will be expected to know the significance of the divorce of ownership and control'

and

> 'Candidates will be expected to carry out the formal analysis of prices and outputs with downwards sloping demand curves, and be aware of the objectives of firms under different market conditions, not necessarily assuming the maximisation of profit.'

Further reading

During the unit I've mentioned a number of books that are worth looking into further. Galbraith is probably the most accessible in that he is available in Penguin paperbacks, and he is a lively and interesting author. This *doesn't* make him right about everything! Heinemann Educational Books have a couple of useful titles — *Pricing in Practice* by Davies and Hughes, and *Advertising* by Savage. Any standard textbook will almost certainly have the formal analysis of oligopoly and monopolistic competition, but for a look at more modern theories, see Curwen (quoted in last unit), Gowland *Modern Economic Analysis 2* (Chapter 7), and 'The revolution in monopoly theory' in *Lloyds Bank Review*, July 1984. Look also at 'Pricing and competition in the private sector' by Barry Harrison (Longman Economic Studies) and 'Microeconomics: New Theories and Old' by Graham D. Fitzpatrick (Oxford).

Examination questions

1. Why does economics need a theory of oligopoly? Why is it so difficult to provide one?

    (Oxford Local Delegacy 'S' June 1986)

2. Describe the characteristics of an oligopolistic industry and examine the different explanations of oligopolistic price and output determination.

    (AEB 'A' June 1985)

3. Why are a firm's profits maximised where marginal cost equals marginal revenue? In what circumstances might a firm use criteria other than profit maximisation for determining the price of its product?

    (AEB 'A' November 1986)

4. 'The crucial difference between monopolistic competition and perfect competition is the existence in the former of product differentiation.' Briefly explain this statement. Discuss the implications of each market structure for the efficient allocation of resources.

    (AEB 'A' June 1987)

5. 'The classical theory of the firm relied heavily on the notion that firms are small, owner-managed organisations operating in highly competitive markets whose demand functions are

given and where only normal profits can be earned. If the firm did not therefore maximise profits it would fail to survive under those conditions. Setting aside the question as to whether this ever was a valid description . . . it is certainly far removed from the actual characteristics of firms in many branches of economic activity today. It is only when the main features of the organisation of modern corporations are taken into account that the questions of the goals of the firm and its decision processes can be effectively discussed.' (J.F. Pickering, *Industrial Structure and Market Conduct*, Martin Robertson, 1974.)

(a) Explain, within the context of classical theory, how profit maximisation is crucial for a firm's survival.

(b) What 'main features of modern corporations' would you consider the author had in mind when he questioned the adequacy of the traditional theory of the firm? Giving your reasons, state whether you would agree that such theory is now obsolete.

(University of London 'A' June 1980)

Finally in Unit 13 I discussed the characteristics of a model. Now that we've waded pretty deeply into the theory of the firm, you may wish to consider this question:

6. What is the purpose of an economic theory? Discuss, in the context of EITHER consumer demand theory OR the theory of the firm, whether or not it is necessary for a theory to be realistic in order to be useful.

(JMB 'A' June 1986)

ANSWERS TO SAQs

SAQ 1:   J. K. Galbraith is the man mentioned in the last unit — he feels that we now have an economy dominated by large buyers and sellers (*see* later in this unit).

SAQ 2:   The extent to which a market is dominated by a few firms: it's measured by concentration ratios, which show the market share of the largest five (or so) companies.

SAQ 3:   In its strictest sense, it means one seller. However, the UK law can take action when 25% of the market is in the hands of one producer.

SAQ 4:   Up to the point where MR = MC, producing additional units adds to the profit, as the revenue brought in from additional sales exceeds the cost of those sales. Beyond that point, additional revenues are less than costs and so more output would cut profits. MR = MC is essentially the equilibrium of a profit-maximiser.

SAQ 5:   Check back to the opening of Unit 14 for these.

SAQ 6:   No. There's no point if the firm can sell all its output at the going price.

SAQ 7:   In my view the model works well. It has been estimated that the petrol needs of UK motorists could be met by one-third of our present number of petrol stations, so the chronic excess capacity is there. So too is the 'pushing out' of the marginal firm by newcomers, and the hairline profits typical of monopolistic competition.

SAQ 8:   By cost-plus methods — adding up production costs, with a mark-up for overheads and profits.

SAQ 9:   CD — the shallower of two intersecting curves is always the more elastic.

SAQ 10:   Perfect competition: many firms; easy entry; identical products; no control over price (price-takers). Monopolistic competition: quite a few firms; moderately easy entry; differentiated products. Oligopoly: few firms; quite strong control over price. Monopoly: one firm; very difficult (entry barriers exist); firm can choose whatever combination of P and Q it likes.

SAQ 11:   *See* the last unit for the anti-monopoly acts. The relevant act here is that against restrictive trade practices.

SAQ 12:   Maximum profit (or minimal loss).

SAQ 13:   The managers of financial institutions prefer to invest in a large, known company. It is alleged that this encouraged the growth of giant companies while starving the new industries of funds.

SAQ 14:   Because they prevent other firms entering to compete profits away.

SAQ 15:   Conglomerate merger, which might lead to risk-bearing economies in particular, as well as the financial and managerial economies large companies claim. It is unlikely that technical economies will become available, as these come from producing more of the same thing.

SAQ 16:   Advertising will only lower unit costs if (a) the LRAC is downward-sloping and (b) the addition to one firm's sales is not achieved by reducing another firm's sales (and thus raising their unit costs) and (c) a situation in which all firms are advertising to stay in the same place doesn't occur (which would lead to no additional scale economies, just higher selling costs).

16 Nationalised industry

AIMS OF UNIT 16

There is vigorous political controversy about the nationalisation of industry. On the left of the political spectrum, there are those who believe that Britain's economic problems can only be solved by bringing more industries into public control. On the right, by contrast, some commentators wish to see nationalised industries returned to private ownership in order to increase efficiency and reduce the call on the taxpayer. This unit aims to give you the information needed to find your own views on this topic: at the end of the unit, you should be able to:

- assess the importance and contribution of nationalised industries to the UK economy
- define a nationalised industry, and list the major ones in the UK
- explain the political, economic and social reasons for nationalisation
- outline the objectives of the nationalised industries, and in particular detail the financial obligations required of them by modern government
- explain how the objectives of the nationalised industries often conflict, and give recent examples of such conflicts
- outline the drawbacks of nationalisation.

One note of caution: at the time of writing, many changes are being introduced, including the sale of some nationalised enterprises to private owners. In this area of economics, in particular, it pays to keep up to date with events.

WHAT IS A NATIONALISED INDUSTRY?

It is not easy to give a completely clear definition of a nationalised industry or public corporation. A brief explanation might say that industrial activity is nationalised if it is owned and controlled by the state. This would, however, lead to the inclusion of a number of bodies that no-one would regard as nationalised industries — from Newcastle Polytechnic to the SAS, from the Tower of London to the Royal Northern Hospital. To be more correct, then, we must say that a nationalised industry is not just (a) publicly owned but also:

(b)   run by a board appointed by the appropriate government minister
(c)   engaged primarily in industrial or other trading activities
(d)   dependent for survival on sales to industry or the public.

This will include (in the UK) quite a large range of firms — British Steel Corporation, the Central Electricity Generating Board and the National Coal Board, just to take some examples. Prior to the privatisation programme of the 1980s nationalised industries accounted for 11% of UK output, 8% of employment and 19% of fixed capital investment. The investment programme of British Telecommunications alone, for example, was responsible in some years for nearly 5% of UK investment.

SAQ 1: *The paragraph above states that it is difficult to provide a clear definition of a nationalised industry. While some firms are obviously nationalised, and others obviously not, there are enterprises that fall into a no-man's land halfway between the two. Using the definition above, which of the following categories does each firm given below fit into: nationalised industry, not a nationalised industry, or difficult to decide?*

(a)   British Oxygen Company
(b)   British Rail
(c)   British Broadcasting Corporation
(d)   Independent Broadcasting Authority
(e)   British Waterways Board
(f)   British Petroleum (BP)
(g)   The Bank of England
(h)   The National Westminster Bank

WHY WERE INDUSTRIES NATIONALISED?

Political reasons

In 1945, very little of British industry was under government control. Such national industrial activities as there were — like the Post Office, the Mint and the Royal Ordnance Factories — were run like government departments. However, that year saw the return of a Labour government, equipped for the first time with a Parliamentary majority that could put into effect the promise of Clause IV of the party's constitution:

> To secure for the workers by hand or by brain the full fruits of their industry and the most equitable distribution thereof that may be possible upon the basis of the common ownership of the means of production, distribution and exchange, and the best obtainable system of popular administration and control of each industry or service*

After all, the dictionary definition points out that socialism is 'the principle of social organisation that puts the means of production and distribution in the hands of the community' (*Chambers Twentieth Century Dictionary*). Socialists believe in public ownership because they believe that private ownership of industry is inefficient and unjust — inefficient because the cut-throat competition of the capitalist system makes for unemployment, conflict and waste; unjust because the owners of capital gain their power and wealth from the efforts of the working people. It was therefore *political motives* that were behind the start of nationalisation in many countries. Similarly, it is political judgements that have supported denationalisation and privatisation by those who see nationalised industry removing the edge to efficiency that only private ownership and competition can provide.

Socialists have also argued that it is necessary to obtain public ownership and control of the 'commanding heights of the economy' (Aneurin Bevan's phrase) in order to achieve effective national planning. This century, governments have increasingly been expected to take a positive role in the economy, working for full employment, regional development, a sound balance of payments, and so on. Socialists argue that this task is only possible when the major firms in the economy are under public control. Nationalisation serves this purpose in many countries of the Third World today: helping governments to plan the advance of an underdeveloped economy. In many cases, this gives the word nationalisation a double meaning, for it refers not just to the process of taking privately-owned industry into the public sector, but also to the purchase of a national industry from foreign owners.

*Several policies could fulfil the aspirations of Clause IV: the present style of nationalisation is not necessary. Alternative policies might be the establishment of cooperatives, worker-controlled small firms or municipal enterprises, for example. Problems with massive nationalised firms have increased interest in such alternatives as the Mondragon Cooperatives (in the Basque region of Spain) and the Scott-Bader Commonwealth, which encourage self-managed cooperatives in the UK.

SAQ 2: *What other methods does the government have to control economic variables like employment, regional development, economic growth? Are these methods adequate, or is there an argument for nationalisation even if they are used fully?*

Economic reasons

Moving from political to economic reasons, we come to **natural monopolies**. You'll remember from Unit 14 that in some industries scale economies are so pronounced that efficient and economic production requires just one enterprise over a region or even a whole country: examples include electricity supply and telephone system, where competition between rival companies would be wasteful and expensive.

The development of railways in Britain provides an example of the problems of competition in industries that would benefit from national planning. When British Railways took over the private railway companies, for example, there were five different railway lines between London and Exeter: and this example can be repeated for the London to Glasgow line, and others between major cities. What is more, some British cities have more than one main railway station, getting to the point (in London) of having rival stations built side-by-side. Countries which came later to railways did not suffer from this duplication. In Germany, for example, many towns have a 'Hauptbahnhof', or main railway station in the centre of town, taking all services.

It is of course possible to have a privately owned monopoly where scale economies make a national system of railways (or phones, or electricity, or gas) the most economic form of organisation. The government could arrange to control possible abuses through regulations on prices, services and profits. However, in practice, this is very difficult and opens opportunities for corruption. There is much, therefore, to be said for the view that if a monopoly must exist, it should be publicly rather than privately owned. Nationalisation can therefore be justified as a way *to avoid monopoly abuses.*

There is also the question of social costs to be taken into account. It may actually make sense to keep an unprofitable public transport service running where it lowers road building costs or reduces costly congestion. A private firm couldn't afford to take these genuine costs into account. A fuller account of the problem of externalities and social costs is to be found in Unit 18, pp. 284-5.

Historical reasons

While much of Britain's first wave of nationalisation followed the reasons we have given so far — that is, to advance socialism, to aid national economic planning, and to take natural monopolies under public control — we must not forget the historical circumstances in which this was happening. In 1945, the British economy, like the British people, was emerging exhausted from a lengthy and costly war. In some major industries — coal, railways — there had been little capital investment for six years as resources were diverted to the war effort, and as a result there was a desperate need for new investment. Because the industries concerned were declining industries that had a poor profit record, it was unlikely that private funds would be available to assist their reconstruction. If the government wished the industries to be kept alive it would have to use public money, and it did so. Nationalisation was therefore a way *to provide finance to reconstruct a troubled industry.* There is no doubt that this reasoning was also a factor behind the nationalisation of the steel industry in the 1960s, although it could be argued that in this case many of the industry's problems were caused by politicians.

Of course, a laissez-faire economist might very well argue that these industries should have been allowed to decline and die. Economic progress involves a gradual change in the pattern of industries, with newer industries replacing dying ones. It would be argued that a declining industry releases resources of land, labour and capital that are picked up by the newer industries; and that this desirable transfer of resources is unlikely to happen if the government steps in with cash hand-outs for the failures of the market system — what are called 'lame ducks'.

Social reasons

The trouble is that in the real world, transfers of resources from dying to growing industries are rarely as smooth as economics textbooks might make it appear. There are immobilities of labour, for example. It may make accounting sense to close down the pits that are making a loss, but such a policy will have a disastrous effect on mining communities. But a nationalised mining industry can stand the losses on some uneconomic pits, and can offer alternative jobs in expanding mines for workers from the pits that have to close. There is, therefore, a case for nationalisation for social reasons rather than economic ones. Let's look at some social problems that might be tackled in a more human way by a government-owned nationalised undertaking, rather than by a private profit-maximiser:

- Services (e.g. posts, railways, electricity) to remote communities will rarely be profitable, and yet these services form the basis of a full life.
- Industries such as steel, shipbuilding and coalmining are highly localised, and so a decline in employment (however economically inevitable) needs to be planned carefully and implemented gradually.
- Social factors are particularly relevant to power-supply industries. Low-income families may get into trouble with their fuel bills in a cold spell. A nationalised industry can follow guidelines that will minimise suffering to such people — as evidenced by the reluctance to disconnect pensioners in the winter quarter, for example, or frequent contacts with social workers about troubled cases.

SAQ 3: *Do you find these reasons valid? If so, are there ways to solve these problems without the use of nationalisation of industry?*

Nationalisation by accident

I cannot leave the reasons for nationalisation without mentioning nationalisation by accident. A large number of industries have come into the public sector as a result of chance. On the continent of Europe, for example, governments stepped in during the bank failures of the 1920s and 1930s and ended up owning firms that owed money to the banks. Austria has a large and assorted selection of publicly owned industries for this reason. In Germany, some industries are owned by the state because they were confiscated from Nazi supporters at the end of the Second World War. Equally curious nationalisations have occurred in Britain — the pubs in Carlisle fell into state control as part of a campaign against drunkenness, travel agents (like Thomas Cook's, since sold) and hotels came along with the purchase of the assets of the railway companies. The government has also come to the aid of companies that are so important to the economy that they cannot be allowed to collapse — like Rolls Royce, who in 1971 faced ruin when an aircraft engine contract went wrong, or BL, who in 1976 had to accept government control or disappear. Neither act was a carefully considered policy as much as a response to circumstances — indeed, Rolls Royce was nationalised by a Conservative Government. (In 1987 a Conservative government privatised Rolls Royce).

Other reasons for nationalisation

In addition to the reasons we have looked at thus far, there are a number of other justifications that have been put forward for nationalisation. It has been claimed that nationalising an industry can repair a troubled and stormy industrial relations atmosphere, or improve safety at work (in the coalmines, for example). Abroad, state monopolies have been created as a way of making money for the government: some countries have state alcohol monopolies, others monopolies in salt and tobacco. The match industry in France, Germany and Italy has been taken into state ownership for this reason.

Finally public money is often used to sponsor 'infant industries' — that is, industries which are passing through the first stage of their growth and so are unable to support themselves. This doesn't just apply to manufacturing industries in developing countries (like aircraft, steel and cars in India, for example) but also to new technology in advanced industrial countries. Britain, Japan and France are all giving government aid to sponsor budding microelectronic industries.

THE CHANGING OBJECTIVES OF NATIONALISED INDUSTRIES

The list of reasons for nationalisation we have gone through is pretty long, and in some cases contradictory. They are in any case much too broad to be of any use in guiding a manager in a nationalised industry who has to take decisions about output, investment and prices. Precisely how should nationalised industries be run? Should they act as profit-maximisers in order to make the maximum contribution they can to the national finances? Or perhaps aim to break even in an effort to give consumers a good deal and low prices? Or should they run as a social service, leaving commercial considerations aside in an effort to increase employment and equalise living standards? The problem is acute, and it faced those who were first put in charge of nationalised industries, for no-one, it seemed, had given much thought to how the industries were to be run after they had been nationalised.

The Acts of Parliament that brought the industries into public ownership were of little help: they asked the Boards of each enterprise to 'run an adequate service' and 'have regard to efficiency', but the only financial requirement was that they should aim to break even, taking one year with another.

SAQ 4: *If an industry is asked just to cover costs, does it set price equal to MC, AC, AVC or AFC?*

This soon proved to be a considerable problem. A firm aiming just to break even might fail to make any profits to reinvest in the business – indeed, unforeseen inflation will cause severe losses. The ability to 'take one year with another' gave managers little incentive to cut their losses: tough decisions could always be deferred for a year, or more. As a result, nationalised industry deficits became a considerable problem, and by 1961 the government moved to end the problem by insisting (in a White Paper, *The Financial and Economic Obligations of Nationalised Industries*):
- that industries should break even over five-year periods
- that prices should include an element for depreciation sufficient to replace capital equipment at realistic prices
- that when planning investment, target rates of return should be used.

The 1967 White Paper (*The Nationalised Industries: A Review of Economic and Financial Objectives*) went further. It required that investment in all projects be judged by a required rate of profit of 10% – about equal to profits in an average industry at the time. This was a reasonably sensible rule, for it is inefficient to allocate resources to nationalised industries if they then yield a smaller return to the community there than if they were used elsewhere.

Prices were to be set equal to **long-term marginal cost** – that is, variable cost plus a proportion of fixed costs to pay for capital. Nationalised industries were asked to avoid paying for loss-making services with profits from more successful areas: a practice known as **cross-subsidisation** that obscures the inefficient and more costly parts of the business. Alongside this hard-headed approach, there was a fair attitude to the vital 'social service' obligations of nationalised industries that I outlined earlier. It was decided that if a nationalised industry was asked to perform an unprofitable task for social reasons – for example, to keep open a railway line to a remote community – then such a service would be removed from the general accounts of the nationalised industry and paid for separately.

SAQ 5: *Time for a little revision about costing. First, explain what is meant by the terms 'marginal cost', 'fixed cost' and 'variable cost'. Then say how the long-term marginal cost I outlined above differs from the idea of marginal cost we dealt with in earlier units. How great will be the marginal cost of providing a rail trip from Glasgow to Edinburgh? Why?*

As you'll see a little later in this unit, the idea of marginal-cost pricing, although theoretically sound, has a number of practical difficulties. However, it wasn't the guidelines of the White Paper that caused the acute problems that were to strike nationalised industries in the 1970s; it was interference by politicians.

During the period 1971-5, prices were rising very fast in the UK, fast enough to alarm both the public and the government. As a contribution to the fight against inflation, the government of the day held down the prices of nationalised industries. But, as costs could not be contained, the policy caused these industries great losses. By 1975, the government was having to borrow £1.2 billions to cover their deficits – 1½% of national income. The situation plainly could not be allowed to continue, and so the decision was taken to allow the prices charged by nationalised industries to rise again. In 1976 they went up 40%, and by 1977 were once again covering costs.

SAQ 6: *In his successful 1970 election campaign, Edward Heath advocated restricting the prices of nationalised industries in order to reduce the rate of inflation. At first sight this policy seems most attractive, but think carefully and give three criticisms of such a policy. You might like to consider the following aspects of the problem:*
- *What is the effect on the government's borrowing requirement? What's wrong with that?*
- *Who benefits from keeping down the prices of nationalised industries? Who pays for it?*
- *What will consumers do with the money they save through cheaper nationalised industry prices?*
- *How will the policy affect morale and efficiency of nationalised industry?*

This episode played havoc with the finances of the nationalised industries and soured relationships between ministers and managements. As a result, the National Economic Development Office (NEDO) commissioned a study that reported in 1976. One recommendation of NEDO – that high-level 'Policy Councils' be established for each industry, to act as a buffer between ministers and managers and develop sensible long-term plans for the enterprises – was rejected by the government in its 1978 White Paper (*The Nationalised Industries*). However, the government did recognise the necessity of laying down some ground-rules for the running of nationalised industries, and presented the following ideas:

- Long-term corporate plans for each industry should be worked out between the industry and the appropriate ministry. These plans will not be interfered with by ministers, except in the most urgent of circumstances.
- Where a minister wants an industry to do something it does not wish to do, the minister will have powers to instruct it to do as he or she wishes, but only if the minister is prepared to pay the cost of the offending project.
- New ways to indicate good performance should be worked out and used. For example, a financial target should be devised, decided for each industry in accordance with its circumstances and set for three to five years. New investment should be judged by reference to a real rate of return of 5% (i.e. 5% more than inflation). And other indicators of good performance should be developed, because financial targets can be met by exploiting monopoly power. Such indicators might include (for example) international comparisons of price or productivity.
- More guidance on pricing policy. There was still a desire for marginal-cost pricing, but with the benefit of experience, the limitations of marginal costing were recognised (*see* sections on pricing policy pp. 259-61)

Cash limits

The control of the nationalised industries was reinforced by the introduction of an external financing limit (EFL). This is exactly what its name implies — a restriction on the industries' ability to borrow outside the organisation. It works like this:

Each year a nationalised industry needs money to pay its bills — for wages, raw materials, capital costs. Most of these costs are covered by money gained from selling commodities to the public. However, if expenditure is greater than sales revenues and the industry needs to raise more money (usually to finance an investment programme), it is given a cash limit that restricts its ability to raise external finance.

SAQ 7: *A nationalised industry estimates that its capital expenditure will be £500m, of which £300m will be covered by profits and depreciation allowances. What is its need for external financing? Suppose for a moment that the government allows this as the agreed EFL limit: could anything happen in the year concerned to make the limit inadequate?*

Occasionally an industry is given a 'negative cash limit': what do you think this means?

THE PROBLEMS OF A NATIONALISED INDUSTRY

The historical account of nationalised industries that I've just given highlights a number of the problems that have beset them. Let's go through them one by one.

Conflicting objectives

A nationalised industry cannot achieve all the objectives set for it at the same time. We have seen that in the mid-seventies, the aim of profitability and efficiency was defeated by the aim of aiding government economic policy against inflation. But there are many other examples: nationalised industry may wish to close down old plants (e.g. coalmines and steelworks) that are losing money, in order to cut costs and compete efficiently, but to do so would cause grave social problems in the areas concerned.

The government has sometimes intervened in the running of nationalised industries in order to help in the management of the economy. On the one hand, when they have considered that the level of total demand in the economy is too high, they have forced nationalised industries to cancel capital investment. And when demand has been judged too low, nationalised industries have been encouraged to order new equipment they don't yet need. For example, the Central Electricity Generating Board was once prevailed upon to order a new power station early to prevent unemployment in the construction industry.

Only declining industries are nationalised

Industries which are efficient, profitable and successful are not nationalised: it is only when an industry is felt to be 'failing the nation' that the government decides to take it into public ownership. As a result, the industries that end up being government-owned tend to be old and riddled with problems — coal, railways, shipbuilding, steel.* This may, in part, account for the disappointing record of nationalisation.

SAQ 8: *Think of a technically advanced industry that has been taken into public ownership. What has been the reason for nationalisation? How well has this industry performed?*

Lack of commercial discipline

A firm in the private sector has a number of spurs to efficiency that are not present in the case of a public monopoly. Bankruptcy is no threat to a nationalised undertaking — in more than 30 years, the government has not let a single nationalised industry go under. For example, when Laker Airways collapsed, it had smaller debts than British Airways. Furthermore, competition is less severe in some of the nationalised industries, such as electricity.

SAQ 9: *Some nationalised industry managers claim that, far from being monopolies insulated from competition, they are running industries that face vigorous competition. Look at the following nationalised industries and suggest the ways in which they face competition:*
(a)   British Steel
(b)   British Rail
(c)   Central Electricity Generating Board

The fact that the nationalised industries do not face the same commercial pressures as private sector companies has led to the search for other mechanisms of control I've outlined in this unit — profit targets and EFLs.

Political interference

Because the nationalised industries have been under the control of government ministers, they have often suffered from politically-motivated interference, often for reasons of vote-catching. Richard Marsh recounts a story of when he was Minister of Transport and proposed closing down a railway line in mid-Wales that carried very few passengers and lost a lot of money. Discussion on the matter stopped when it was pointed out that the line ran through some marginal constituencies, and closing the line would lose votes to the opposition. This sort of political interference is against the spirit of the original nationalisation plans. The idea then was that ministers would give broad guidance on policy, but would not interfere in the day-to-day running of the industry: in practice, the reverse has been true.

PRICING POLICY IN A NATIONALISED INDUSTRY

Introduction

To introduce the topic of pricing in a nationalised industry. I have reproduced the monopolist's equilibrium on graph 16.1 below. The profit-maximising position is where MR = MC, and you will know that for a monopolist the MR curve slopes down more steeply than the dd = AR curve.

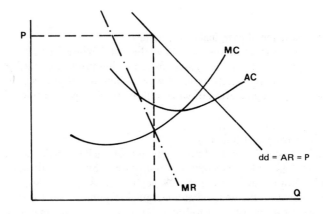

Graph 16.1

Remember, too, that nationalised industries are not allowed to diversify away from their basic purpose. So a declining industry has no alternative but to decline. Contrast this with the way that private companies diversify in order to avoid being stuck in a declining market (e.g. Imperial Group from tobacco into convenience foods, Rank from cinemas into office machinery).

So for a monopolised industry, output is set lower than in a competitive industry, and price higher.

However, now that we have taken the industry into public ownership, we can relax the assumption of profit-maximisation. The firm no longer seeks to make the greatest possible return; it wishes to achieve the best outcome for society as a whole. This is achieved where price is equal to marginal cost. In the monopoly diagram above, price (P) is greater than marginal cost. As a result, people who would be prepared to buy the good at a price that fully covers the cost of production are unable to do so. Let's look at the logic of this more closely.

The rationale of marginal cost pricing

First, two definitions which you need to be clear about:

The marginal cost of production measures the cost to society of the resources that have been used up in making the final unit of a commodity. It is therefore the opportunity cost of that unit.

The price of a commodity measures the resources that a buyer is prepared to give up in order to obtain that commodity, and so is the consumer's opportunity cost.

So, if price *exceeds* marginal cost, the consumer places a greater value on the last unit produced than society has to pay in producing that unit. So welfare would be increased if extra units were produced – the gain in consumer satisfaction would be greater than the cost to society in resources used. However, if price is *less than* marginal cost, consumers are valuing the last unit produced at a price lower than it is costing us to produce that good. This is a waste of resources, and it would make sense not to produce where price is less than marginal cost. Only at a position where marginal cost and price are equal are consumers valuing output at exactly the same value as producers: here, then, resources are being allocated rationally. This is the essential justification of pricing at marginal cost.

SAQ 10: *Look at graph 16.2 below. It shows the cost and demand conditions of a monopolised industry. Then answer the following questions:*
1. *Which points illustrate (a) the equilibrium of a profit-maximising monopolist (b) the equilibrium of an industry that has been instructed just to cover its costs (c) the equilibrium of an industry that has been instructed to set prices equal to marginal cost?*
2. *What is the relevance of questions (b) and (c) to nationalised industries over the past thirty years?*

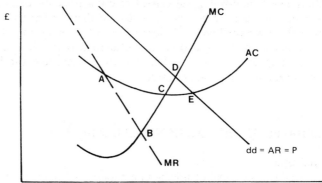

Graph 16.2

The problems of marginal cost pricing

You read earlier in the unit how the 1967 White Paper instructed nationalised industries to set their prices equal to marginal costs. Furthermore, the section we have just covered suggests that this is an economically rational way to behave. In practice, however, there are a number of drawbacks to the application of what appears to be a 'golden rule'. These are:

A decreasing cost industry

We have seen in Unit 14 how some industries have such enormous scale economies that their long-run average cost curve slopes down infinitely. Such an industry is depicted on graph 16.3. Note that MC is sloping down even more steeply than AC, a necessary condition for a falling LRAC. I have also drawn on the demand and marginal revenue curves for this large monopoly.

Were the industry to follow the way of the profit-maximising monopolist, it would be in equilibrium where MR = MC and make a generous profit. But in this position, it is able to produce extra units at a lower cost than the consumer is willing to pay: so, following our marginal cost logic, we instruct this industry to set price equal to marginal cost. This is at point E, where substantial losses are made.

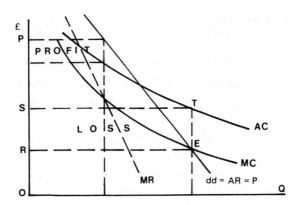

Graph 16.3

This is not a fictional case. Marginal costs in some nationalised industries are extremely low. Once a pipeline has been laid and a gasfield tapped, the cost of providing one extra unit of gas is very low; similarly, once a train has been provided, the cost of carrying one extra passenger is almost zero. It is very difficult to follow the economically rational pricing rule if it results in heavy losses for nationalised undertakings, if only because the volume of taxation needed to finance such a policy might well have economic effects that have to be calculated.

SAQ 11   *Some nationalised undertakings (such as electricity and water supply) have very large fixed costs and very small variable costs. What charging policy do telephone and gas bills have in common? How does it help to solve the problem outlined above?*

Market prices

Nationalised industries might very well be in competition with prices that are not set near their own marginal costs. British Steel has to compete on world markets with Japanese producers; BL Cars must sell cars in markets where there is also fierce international competition.

On the other hand, where it is possible to charge prices above marginal cost, nationalised industries will wish to do so in order to gain revenue. For example, charging high prices for businessmen's inter-city train journeys.

What is marginal cost?

While the concept of marginal cost seems crystal-clear in a textbook, it is often difficult to pin down in practice. Let's take an example:

Suppose I wish to buy a ticket from British Airways to fly to Amsterdam: the plane used on the trip has 130 seats, and I buy the last. The marginal cost of my trip is very small indeed, filling as I do the last seat of an airliner that is already bought, crewed and fuelled. But the next passenger to book a trip involves BA in putting on another plane — the marginal cost is enormous. So what is the marginal cost of a trip to Amsterdam?

This example explains why the government has been keen to develop an idea of what they term **long-run marginal cost**, under which charges for all passengers (or gas users, or train passengers, etc.) include not just the short-term marginal costs of the trip (a little extra fuel, another plastic dinner, a ticket to print and a suitcase to load) but also a contribution to capital costs. Such **a contribution to capital costs becomes easier to apportion when there is peak-loading on a system.**

PRIVATISATION

The policy of 'privatisation' involves the sale of public industry to private shareholders. Whilst there have been a number of examples of publicly owned industry being sold back to the private sector before 1979 (eg. the sale of Thomas Cook in the 1970s, and the denationalisation of the steel industry in the 1950s) privatisation was brought to the front of the political stage by the 1979 Thatcher government. That administration was impatient with the traditional government measures described above (like profit targets and pricing guidelines), which aimed to make nationalised industry behave as if it were subject to commercial disciplines. Why not, they asked, cut to the heart of the problem by making these industries into commercial enterprises?

Aims of privatisation

Privatisation can be justified as a reaction to what is perceived as a disappointing record of nationalised industry in terms of efficiency and profitability. But besides this negative reason, there are a number of positive arguments in favour of selling nationalised industry to private shareholders:

- Increased competition, which will benefit consumers.

- The money raised from the sale of the enterprises can be used to fund government deficits, making it less necessary to sell gilts.

- Placing shares of nationally known enterprises on the market can be used as a way of widening share ownership.

- Finally, there is the positive belief in the virtues of private enterprise as against state-run industry. Freed of bureaucratic controls, it is argued, the industries will be able to become more efficient and profitable.

The problems of privatisation

These advantages seem persuasive at first sight. However, further investigation makes the case for privatisation much less impressive. Those who are sceptical of the advantages of privatisation answer in the following way:

- Competition may be welcome, but it has nothing to do with privatisation. The intensity of competition depends on market conditions, not ownership (see SAQ 9). For example, Jaguar Cars were involved in a vigorously competitive market both before and after privatisation. On the other hand, British Telecom will inevitably be a near monopoly whether publicly or privately owned.

- Funding a government deficit via privatisation only makes sense if a good price can be had for nationalised assets. If not, then the government is giving up a stream of future earnings that could be used to finance spending or reduce borrowing in future years. The cost of restructuring British Airways, and the 'giveaway' share prices of Amersham International and British Telecom cast doubt on the economic wisdom of financing a deficit via assets sales.

- The launch of British Telecom did achieve an extension of share ownership, with an estimated 2 million shareholders. Other sales have been less impressive: and in any case, wider share ownership today is best represented in the pooled funds of insurance and pension funds.

- The argument of increased efficiency is evenly balanced. It must be remembered that at least some of the nationalised industries were taken into public ownership because they had collapsed under private ownership. Additionally, the idea of efficiency is not the same as profitability; privatised firms might well ignore the social costs of (eg) closing down public phone booths, or withdrawing bus services.

REVIEW SECTION

Further reading

For a sound basic introduction to this topic, see Peter Donaldson's *Guide to the British Economy* (ch. 5). Advanced level students will find a full and informative treatment of nationalised industry in Frank Livesey *A Textbook of Economics* (ch. 19), and for a superb but more difficult approach, see the section on nationalised industry in Prest and Coppock *The UK Economy*. Also recommended is Peston's chapter in Grant and Shaw (ed.) *Current Issues in Economic Policy*.

For further information on the pricing controversy, see Ray Rees' book *Public Enterprise Economics*; the classic articles are in the *Pelican Modern Economics Reader* 'Public enterprise' (ed. Turvey), but you may find these to be rather technical, and certainly above the standard needed for GCE study. *Nationalised Industry* by Reid and Allen (Pelican) and *Public Enterprise in Practice* by Pryke survey the track-record of the nationalised industries, but are getting a little dated now. For more information on the pricing problem, see *Pricing in Practice* by Davies and Hughes (Heinemann) or *Economics of the Market* by Hewitt (Fontana). A good general discussion on nationalised industries by Michael Webb is to be found in Gowland (ed.) *Modern Economic Analysis 1* (Butterworth).

The policy of privatisation is starting to be implemented in earnest at the time of writing, so look for some up-to-date material here. I can recommend the Economic Briefs *Monopoly* by Daniel Jeffreys, and units 8 and 9 of another in the Economics Briefs series *The Structure of Industry* by Stewart Hughes. See also *The Listener* (26 June 1986) with an article on 'Britain for Sale'.

Examination questions

1. Explain briefly, with the aid of cost and revenue curves, when it becomes uneconomic for a competitive private firm or plant to remain in business. Discuss whether or not the future of nationalised plants or firms should be governed by the same criteria.

(JMB 'A' June 1985)

2. What is meant by 'economic efficiency'? What effect, if any, is the privatisation of large sections of the public sector likely to exert on the efficiency of the economy?

(JMB 'A' June 1986)

3. Explain what is meant by marginal cost pricing and discuss the problems involved in applying it to nationalised industries.

(Associated Examining Board 'A' June 1982)

4. 'The divergence between private and social costs is the major reason for nationalisation of industry.' Explain the meaning of this statement and assess its validity.

(Northern Ireland GCE 'A' 1983)

5. Discuss the economic consequences of privatising nationalised undertakings.

(Oxford Local Delegacy 'S' June 1985)

or

Examine the general economic arguments for and against the privatisation of the United Kingdom's nationalised industries.

(AEB 'A' November 1986)

ANSWERS TO SAQs

SAQ 1:   (a) and (h) are privately owned companies, despite their grand titles. At present, British Rail and the British Waterways Board are nationalised as defined earlier in the unit: the Bank of England and the IBA are considered nationalised industries, though whether they 'engage primarily in trading activities' seems doubtful. BP is technically a private company, although the government until recently held a substantial minority shareholding — indeed, had a majority for many years. The BBC fulfils many of the criteria, but can the licence fee really be thought of as 'sales to the public'?

SAQ 2:   There are a number of other policies — fiscal policy, monetary policy, help with employment and training through subsidies to the unemployed or to depressed regions. Whether these are adequate is a matter of your point-of-view: certainly they failed to achieve satisfactory levels of employment throughout the seventies and early eighties, though whether a policy of widespread nationalisation would have helped is an open question.

SAQ 3:   Let's take this question in two parts. Are the reasons valid? Well, a free-market enthusiast would argue that services to remote communities should be charged at full-cost: if people aren't prepared to pay, then that shows that they find the services offered cost more than their own valuation of them (*see* discussion on pricing in Unit 18).

You may find this a chilling viewpoint, but on a more moderate level it can be argued that there are other ways besides nationalisation to meet the problems outlined — direct subsidies to private suppliers to help remote communities, special benefits to help poor families cope with high fuel bills, retraining and help with moving for those made unemployed by the decline of a traditional industry.

SAQ 4:   Price should be equal to average cost: in fact, as average cost in the usual theory includes an element of normal profit, price might even be set a little below average cost.

SAQ 5:   Marginal cost is the addition to total costs caused by the production of one more unit of output. Fixed costs are the costs that must be paid whatever the level of output — things like rent, rates, interest charges on past borrowing. Variable costs are the costs that vary with output, an idea very close to marginal cost. The way that LRMC as described above differs from the short-term marginal cost we've looked at earlier is that it includes an allowance for the fixed costs, particularly capital costs: remember, all costs are variable in the very long run. Now, the marginal cost of a rail trip to Glasgow can be almost zero (in the simple idea of marginal cost as the addition to BR's costs caused by one more passenger) or rather more, if you assume that passengers travelling to Glasgow involve BR in the longer view in buying rolling stock and keeping stations open.

SAQ 6:   ● The effect on borrowing is to increase it, unless the lower charges are met from taxes. This could either lead to an increase in the money supply (if it is financed by new money being created) and thus inflation, or to higher rates of interest if the money is funded from sales of more gilt edged stocks.

- The users of the nationalised industry output benefit: the taxpayer pays unless it is all covered by borrowing (see above).
- Spend it (or maybe have some) and add to pressure of demand elsewhere.
- It is likely that any individual working for an industry making a growing loss because of government restrictions will lose morale and make a less effective contribution. Certainly, the government will find it hard to justify new investment in a loss-making enterprise.

SAQ 7:   £200m. This could be made inadequate by any number of factors — inflation (= rising costs); a recession (= falling sales); strikes might also have an influence, as might increasing foreign competition. The negative EFL of an industry means that it is expected to raise all its investment funds from its profits *and* on top of that contribute to the Exchequer — almost a form of indirect taxation.

SAQ 8:   There have been a number: phones (a natural monopoly that made high profits through most of its nationalised years): British Aerospace (nationalised because of its monopoly position with defence contracts of the government, and because of the need for government funds in high technology) which has a mixed record as a profit earner: even Rolls-Royce Aeroengines (rescued as described elsewhere).

SAQ 9:   BSC competes with foreign steel producers and, in some product areas, with private steel firms; BR has only 8% of passenger miles, and competes with bus (12%) and cars (80%); the CEGB competes with gas, coal, paraffin, etc. in domestic heating.

SAQ 10:   (a) B (where MR = MC)   (b) E (where P = AC)   (c) D. The relevance is that the first statutes asked nationalised industries to break even (roughly, P = AC), whereas recent attempts have been made to get them to price at marginal cost (after the 1967 White Paper)

SAQ 11:   They have a fixed charge before starting to count units: this policy of a block charge makes a contribution to the massive fixed costs of connecting up and telephone exchanges and gas pipelines from the North Sea (etc. etc.) which are necessary whether the consumer is a heavy or light user of the commodity in question.

17 Industrial location and regional policy

AIMS OF UNIT 17

In this unit I look at industrial location and regional policy — if you like, the geography of economic activity. I examine where industry goes in a country, why it goes there and not anywhere else, and go on to look at the problems that are caused by the decline of industries upon which regions have become dependent.

When you have finished this unit, you should be able to:
- assess the influence on location decisions of raw materials, markets, energy costs, labour and space
- define external economies of scale, list the three of them and link the idea with 'industrial inertia' and 'geographical momentum'
- explain why the localisation of industry occurs, and measure the extent of localisation using a location quotient
- account for the decline of localised industry in the UK and relate it to the lower prosperity of the UK's outlying regions
- choose data that will show regional differences in prosperity
- explain and evaluate the options open to government when regional imbalances occur
- define regional policy and list the measures taken by government to redress regional differences in employment and income
- give some evidence of the effectiveness of regional policy.

INDUSTRIAL LOCATION

Economic theory usually considers that firms are run by entrepreneurs who must keep costs down to a minimum in order to maximise their profits. If this is true, then firms will be located in the place where production can be undertaken at its very cheapest — at what is known as the **least-cost location**. Of course, there will not be a single least-cost location for all industries — different technologies require different places, so that what is the right place for a publishing company will be wrong for a steelworks. Let's consider the factors that might influence location decisions by looking at a very simple idea of the process of making commodities from Unit 1:

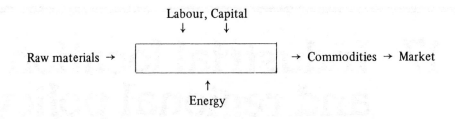

Raw materials → [   ] → Commodities → Market

Labour, Capital

Energy

SAQ 1: *What is going on in the box? What general name do we give to the resources that are combined in the act of making commodities?*

Going through the factors mentioned in the diagram, we see that raw materials are made into commodities using *labour, capital* and *energy*, and then taken to a *market*. We'll now go through these influences one by one to assess their importance for **industrial location**.

Raw materials

Some industries are closely tied to the source of their raw materials — you can't, for example, locate a coalmine or quarry in London. However, with the improvements in transport that have occurred over the past hundred years, the attraction of a plant sited near to raw materials is decreasing. But it is still a powerful pull if an industry uses a process that involves losing a lot of bulk in manufacture — such as sawmills, sugarbeet refining, brickyards. The factor which is really at work here, though, is not so much the 'attraction' of a site near to raw materials as the deterrent effect of the high transport costs. It would make no sense (for example) to take sugarbeet all the way to London or Manchester from the farmlands of East Anglia when the majority of the weight carried would be lost and thrown away in the process of manufacture. It follows that if a bulk-losing process forms the start of an integrated chain of processes, then the whole plant will be located near to the source of raw materials.

Where it is possible to concentrate or 'wash' the raw material so that not quite as much weight is lost in processing, the pull of raw material lessens. For example, the iron ores of Labrador come out of the ground only about 30% iron, but can be improved to 60% or better before shipment.

SAQ 2: *(a) The iron ores of Lincolnshire started to be exploited this century. They are not more than about 20% iron. Explain whether, in your view, the ore was shipped off to established steelworks, or whether steelworks were built nearby; give reasons for your guess.*

(b)   The following processes are carried on near the source of their raw material. What is the initial stage of the integrated production process, and why is that process attracted to the source of raw materials?
- *newsprint mills*
- *meat-canning*

Where raw materials are perishable, they must be processed at source. This is most obviously true of agricultural canning and freezing — so we find for example Bird's Eye Factories in East Anglia. Indeed, this has been taken to a logical conclusion in 'factory ships' that process and freeze fish while still at sea. A similar reason has pulled some industries to the ports that met the arrival of tropical products — such as the chocolate industry of Bristol and the (now defunct) cane sugar trade of Liverpool.

There are some areas of Britain whose industrial heritage is built almost completely on local raw materials. Teesside is a good example: the iron and steel industry was originally based on iron ores that were discovered in the nearby Cleveland Hills, and on Durham coal. The chemical industry used the tar, benzole and ammonia that are by-products of the coking process. What is more, the Stockton-Billingham area lies on deposits of salt and anhydrite, which go to make chlorides and caustic soda. So the heavy industries of this major industrial region owe their origin to local raw materials.

Markets

If raw materials are one end of the production process (the start), then the culmination comes when the good is presented at the market. Industry can be attracted to the market where the product is sold. This is particularly true where much weight is gained during processing. For example, soft-drink manufacturers add water to the ingredients brought to them, making the finished product much heavier than the bought-in materials (a **bulk-gaining** process). This means that it makes more sense for them to build local plants near to each market; the alternative would in effect be the transportation of large volumes of water around the country. To summarise, then:

- bulk-losing processes will be attracted to raw material sources
- bulk-gaining processes will be attracted to the market.

SAQ 3: *Let's use the example of the oil-refining industry to apply the principles just learned. When oil refineries were first built in any numbers, many of the products were wasted: few of today's plastic or pharmaceutical uses had been discovered. As a result, up to three quarters of the delivered tonnage was discarded, and only 25-30% refined into usable commodities. By contrast, today's oil refinery uses almost all the delivered oil.*

(a)   When were oil-refineries bulk-losing plants? When were they not bulk-losers?

(b)   Where do you expect oil refineries were located when so much crude oil was wasted? Where are they now?

(c)   (Question for detectives) How have ships used to transport petrochemicals altered as a result of this change?

Discussion of whether an industrial process involves gaining bulk or losing bulk is appropriate when we are talking about manufacturing industry. However, most of the jobs in today's economy are not in manufacturing — they are in service industry, in public administration and in financial services. This 'tertiary industry' will be strongly pulled to a market location.

Energy

In addition to raw materials and markets, successful production of commodities requires energy. Sources of energy were immobile during the early years of the industrial revolution. Plants had to be built where there was water-power (e.g. the textile factories on the Pennine flanks of northern England, or on the Fall Line in the USA), or later where there was coal. The pull of coal can be seen on any map of Great Britain: most of the major conurbations outside London are situated on coalfields.

Better transport, and then electricity, gradually freed industry from the need to site plants near deposits of coal. At first, though, there were considerable losses in transmission of electrical power, which caused electricity-using industries to cluster around power stations. However, regional differences in the cost of energy don't matter so much today, except for plants (like steel furnaces or power stations) which use large amounts of coal, and other heavy energy users. The prime example is the aluminium-smelting industry which is attracted to cheap electricity — as in Switzerland or Canada, where hydro-electricity is available.

Labour

Discussing the influence of labour on the location of industry might seem curious — can't labour move to the appropriate location for an industry? However, although labour is more geographically mobile than raw material deposits and the older sources of energy, it is more immobile than we sometimes assume. This can be seen from regional differences in unemployment and income.

SAQ 4: *Why do differences in unemployment rates between different regions indicate that labour is immobile?*

The crucial way in which labour affects location is through unit labour costs. Firms will be attracted to an area or country that assures them of low unit labour costs. This doesn't necessarily mean that firms wish to go where wage-rates are at their lowest. In many industries, a skilled and experienced labour force can keep costs far below the   levels that would be achieved by a low-wage workforce in the underdeveloped countries. Take the steel industry, for example: American steelworkers earn more than European ones, who in their turn earn more than Indian steelworkers, and yet in production costs US steel is cheaper than European, with Indian steel requiring subsidy and protection. But where processes use a great deal of labour of necessity (as in the assembly of electrical goods, or toys), or require little skill or training (e.g. cotton textiles), one might expect industries to be attracted to cheap labour.

So firms which require skilled workers will look for areas where the skills they require are available; but where there is no need for skills, a firm might locate where labour is cheap or near to its market.

SAQ 5:   *See if you can answer this question, based on the motor-car industry. When originally established, motor-car construction was a craft industry; but by the 1930s it had become a mass-production industry needing little skill from the workforce. Explain, then, why (a) the UK motor industry is strongly represented in the West Midlands (b) in the interwar period Fords built a factory in Dagenham on the north bank of the Thames estuary. (c) What changes in the location of the car industry could we expect in the future?*

Labour practices and attitudes affect unit labour costs. Surveys have shown (both in the USA and UK) that some businesses have regard for the labour-relations image of a region when choosing a site for a new plant. This has been a factor in the migration of industry to the American South (witness the growth of Atlanta to a major business community) and in the decline of Liverpool.

Space
Considerations of space have quite an effect on the location of the modern factory, which is flat and extensive compared to the tall, compact, buildings of the Victorian era. This architectural change can be traced to a number of factors: there is no longer any need to run a large number of machines off one steam engine (via belts and pulleys), and modern product-handling techniques like conveyors and fork-lift trucks require a flat and accessible layout.

The most obvious consequence of the space-using factory is the growth of the trading estate on by-passes and other outer-town locations. The old and abandoned factories are sometimes used for alternative activities: in Lancashire and Yorkshire, for example, former textile mills are used for mail-order firms and other stores-related uses. Sometimes, though, the inner city is abandoned (as at Pittsburgh and Sheffield, where the expansion of steel plants was too great to be fitted in the town centre). This has led to a shift in the prosperity of the conurbation, leaving decaying inner-city areas.

Where space is extremely important, industry is attracted to the flat and undeveloped land around river estuaries. Oil-refineries in the UK are on estuaries, as are some of the newer steel-works: and these industries attract a number of ancillary activities and firms. Some industries are attracted to remote and spacious sites on grounds of safety: munitions and fireworks, and now-adays nuclear power stations.

Industrial inertia
A number of industries are located in areas which appear to offer no local advantages. There are iron and steel plants in areas which no longer have local supplies of coal and ore; furniture works in places where the forest was cut down years ago; carpet looms in towns which nowadays import Australian wool to weave. This is because expensive plants cannot be moved, and it is often cheaper to renew and expand them than to move to a location that makes more sense in changed circumstances. Economists call this **industrial inertia** (geographers call it geographical momentum!).

EXTERNAL ECONOMIES OF SCALE

SAQ 6:   *In Unit 14, we looked at internal economies of scale. Without looking, see if you can list five types of internal scale economies.*

The reason that the word 'internal' is used is to point out that these are factors that lower costs of production *within* a firm. There are also *external* economies of scale, where economies result not from an individual firm getting bigger, but from an increase in the size of the whole industry. They might occur for three main reasons:
- because a large number of firms following a particular trade have settled in one area and thus derive mutual advantages. The local labour force become used to the skills and disciplines of the industry; the local college trains students in appropriate courses; local markets and advisory services are established; transport facilities relevant to the industry grow up. These are called **economies of concentration.**
- because in a large industry, it becomes worthwhile to set up trade magazines, forecasting and technical services, and industry associations set up information bureaux. These **economies of information** mean that firms save money by getting fuller information more cheaply.
- because when an industry is large, small firms grow up to provide specialist services and commodities. An example of this is to be found in the industrial West Midlands, where the motor industry uses many small firms to supply components or design services. When the produc-

tion process is broken down into small parts like this, creating a pool of specialists that benefit the industry, we speak of **economies of disintegration.**

External economies show us that it is not necessarily irrational for an industry to remain in position once its initial advantages — such as local raw materials — have gone.

Random locations

Besides industrial inertia, there are a number of location decisions that appear to have happened more or less randomly. The reason that BL Cars is so strongly centred on Oxford is that Alfred Morris started his first plant there, in his own home town: in the same way, Ford of America are the major employer of Dearborn, Michigan. The textile industry of Albany, N.Y. can be traced to a local parson who invented the collar-detachable shirt. The locations that occur as a result of personal choice do not disprove the idea that firms choose a least-cost location. Had any of the sites mentioned been profoundly unsuitable, then the firms would have gone out of business and Ford and Morris cars would simply be small entries in automotive history.

Government policy

Government policy is nowadays a very important factor in the location of industry. It is the influence of government on location decisions that this unit now goes on to discuss: why it happens, what form it takes, and how effective it has been. An industrialist looking for a site for a plant would today be wooed by a large number of governments and local authorities, each offering cost-saving deals in the form of low taxes, cheap land, ready-built factories and many other regional incentives. Anyone answering an examination question about factors affecting industrial location must mention the influence of government. But before we move forward to this topic, here's a project that will enable you to consolidate the knowledge already gained in this unit.

SAQ 7: *Using material from the economic geography books in your library, write brief notes on the location of three of the following UK industries. Concentrate on (a) where the industries are located and (b) the reasons they are in that location:*

car-making	*shipbuilding*	*printing*	*cotton textiles*
pottery	*wool textiles*	*brewing*	*iron and steel*

MEASURING LOCALISATION

We have seen in the previous pages that the location of industry, and thus employment, will depend on a number of factors. Because each region has different characteristics — different mineral deposits, nearness to transport, population, topography and so on — they will develop their own blend of industries. Typically, some regions will concentrate on the manufacture of one type of commodity or another so that regional specialisation will occur. It is possible to measure the extent of regional specialisation by the use of what economists call a **location quotient**. This is a useful, and simple, statistical tool that compares the extent to which a region's employment is concentrated in a given industry with the average for the country, and it is calculated as follows:

$$\text{location quotient} = \frac{\text{\% of region's workforce in the industry}}{\text{\% of the nation's workforce in the industry}}$$

Taking an example: suppose that 16% of the workers in Aberdeen work in the oil industry, compared with 2% nationally. The location quotient here is 8; this shows that the area in question has a strong concentration on oil production.

SAQ 8: *Work through these questions to test your understanding of location quotients:*
(a)   Suppose a region of the country has 12% of its workforce in car manufacture, as opposed to 3% nationally. What is its location quotient?
(b)   The North West region has a location quotient of 2.125 for cotton textiles. Put this into a simple sentence that the layman would understand.
(c)   What is meant by a location quotient of 1? What would be true if the North of England's location quotient for financial service industry was less than 1?

An alternative measure of regional specialisation is the **coefficient of localisation**. For each region, the percentage of the employment in that industry is calculated; then the percentage of the nation's workforce employed in the region in all industries is subtracted, as in this hypothetical example:

> A region has 12% of the nation's coalminers;
> it has 8% of the nation's total workforce.
> So the coefficient of localisation is +4.

You'll see that a plus coefficient shows that the region concentrates in a particular trade or industry, whereas a minus coefficient shows a lack of concentration. If we add together all the plus coefficients we will reach a measure of how specialised the region is in its industrial structure. A very high figure will show that there is a high degree of localisation, that is to say, that the region is heavily dependent on a few trades.

WHAT'S WRONG WITH LOCALISATION?

Concentration on one or two major industries is no bad thing if those industries are booming. Aberdeen doesn't complain, for example, of its over-dependence on the North Sea oil industry. But being dependent on a narrow range of industries causes great problems when those industries decline; when this happens, the coefficient of localisation becomes an indicator of the vulnerability of a region. Britain's regional problem stems from the decline of industries that were strongly localised.

REASONS FOR REGIONAL DECLINE

In Britain, regional decline started when foreign countries developed their own basic industries. This didn't just mean that these countries no longer bought Lancashire textiles, Welsh coal and Clydeside shipping: they also provided stiff new competition on world markets. The process was worsened by the exhaustion of some mineral resources — coal and iron seams ran out, causing costs to rise and plants to close. Both factors caused a decline in employment in traditional industry:

Decrease in employment in selected industries 1950-80

	000s	%
Textiles	554	57
Mining and quarrying	513	61
Shipbuilding	123	48
Agriculture, forestry, fishing	535	59

While traditional industries declined, a range of newer industries grew up away from the older industrial regions: motor vehicles, aircraft, electrics and electronics, consumer durables. These manufacturing industries were supplemented by office and service employment, financial and government administration. These activities were not tied to the traditional bases of coal and steel: with the growth of tertiary industry and the use of electrical power, more than 75% of industry is 'footloose' today. The result was that the older industrial areas not only saw the loss of their traditional jobs; they failed to share in the growth of alternative employment that was growing up.

As the declining regions had lower incomes and higher unemployment, the amount of spending on shops, dining out, leisure and service industry in recreation and housing was lower in its turn. This made the picture worse.

SAQ 9: *There is a name in macroeconomics for this process, where a fall in income causes a fall in spending which in itself causes another fall in income and another fall in spending and so on. What is it?*

So Britain had acquired a regional problem. The usual way to document this is to compare unemployment figures: figures in the North, Scotland and Wales are normally much higher than in the prosperous Southeast. However, a wide range of regional statistics can illustrate the phenomenon:

Unemployment by region, 1986

	%
UK	11.9
South East	8.7
North	17.1
Wales	14.5
Scotland	14.3
N. Ireland	18.8

Average income per household (1984–5)

UK	206.8
South East	248.0
North	170.4
Wales	187.1
Scotland	198.3

(In the South-East, 8% of households earned less than £50 per week in 84–85, in Northern Ireland, 14.5%

Education 1984–5

percentage leaving school with:

	no graded result		3 'A' levels	
	male	female	male	female
England	10.7	8.1	11.1	8.9
North	11.7	10.4	8.6	7.6
Wales	18.9	14.2	7.9	8.3
South East	10.4	7.6	12.8	10.1

These statistics are taken from *Regional Trends 1987*, and could go on for some pages: a roughly similar story of different living standards and life quality would be revealed by other tables, for example of

- children staying on at school
- days off work due to sickness
- percentage of households with fridges, colour TVs, telephones
- size of doctors' and dentists' lists
- death rates, both adult and child.

Your local library will probably have the latest copy of Regional Trends, and you will find it interesting to compare your own area with the national average in these terms.

We shall now go on to think about what options a government has, faced as it is with the knowledge that one citizen will enjoy a much higher quality of life than another depending on where he/she lives. But before we move on, test your learning of the last passage:

SAQ 10: *Briefly give four reasons why Britain has had a problem of declining regions. Try to do this exercise without looking back through the text.*

WHAT SHOULD GOVERNMENT DO ABOUT REGIONAL DISPARITIES?

A government faced with this problem has got three basic alternatives. Firstly, it could decide to do nothing. This seems to pose two problems, besides the basic injustice of condemning sizeable chunks of the country to poor living standards. It is a waste of economic resources, resources of labour and capital; and it is a policy likely to lead to the political defeat of the government , or at the very least political strains leading to demands for political independence. Having ruled out inaction, two policies remain. The government can either bring work to the workers, or try to move the spare workers to where the work is.

Bringing workers to the work

This seems to be the policy that fits in best with the ideas of a market economy. Firms, one might argue, should be allowed to choose their least-cost location, and workers encouraged to move away from the remote or disadvantageous places they now occupy. There are, in fact, a number of schemes that have aimed to move workers to areas where work is more plentiful. Cash help, for example, is available to pay for fares and relocation expenses. However, moving workers to the work has never been a major part of the government's regional policy for a number of reasons:

It doesn't work The first objection to such a policy is that migration hasn't solved the problem in the past. Although Britain has had regional differences in prosperity since the 1920s, labour migration has not evened things up — despite up to 50 000 workers moving every year. The name we give to this is **geographical immobility of labour**: workers prefer to stay near their home and amid a familiar environment, or perhaps cannot move because of problems of housing and education.

SAQ 11: *Suppose a policy of 'workers to the work' was energetically pursued in the UK. Which workers would be the ones who moved from depressed regions to the more prosperous areas? What effect would this have on the regions they left?*

Social capital Even if workers did move, it might not be a good idea for society. Firms locating in the Southeast might be choosing what is for themselves a least-cost location, while imposing costs on society as a whole — the old distinction between private costs and social costs. For example, increased emphasis on the Southeast would cause more pressure on our social capital: schools, roads, power stations, public transport, housing. In depressed areas, these facilities are underused. Further, there will be overcrowding in the richer areas: it makes little sense to have congestion, pollution and delays in one area when there are underused roads and factories elsewhere.

SAQ 12: *Using your own words, explain the social capital argument for regional balance, taking as your example airport facilities in Britain.*

Inflationary ripples Economists also argued that regional differences in unemployment can have inflationary effects. If there is a very high demand for skilled labour in one region, it can pull up wages as firms bid for scarce labour. With Britain's nationwide collective bargaining system, higher wage rates are set. Thus, inflation may ripple out from the 'over-heated' area where there is excess demand for labour.

Do firms choose least-cost locations anyway? Much of the foregoing argument has assumed that managers of firms choose the best location for their company, and therefore solid economic arguments must be used to suggest moving firms where they don't want to go. Research evidence, however, suggests that the location decisions of firms are by no means the pure economic 'least-cost' considerations beloved of textbooks. Managers look at relatively few alternatives, and select on often capricious grounds. The accessibility of a golf-course was thought important in one case: and in another, managers' families were so prejudiced against northern England that a number of promising locations were ruled out from the start.

If firms do not choose least-cost locations, then we need worry a little less about justifying government intervention in location decisions.

These are all arguments against moving workers to the work and in favour of alternative measures for ensuring a more even spread of prosperity through a policy of *bringing work to the workers*. This has formed the central idea of government regional policy for the past 50 years. We'll now go on to look at how governments have put this policy into operation.

REGIONAL POLICIES

A start is made

Regional policy started with the De-rating Act of 1929. In those days, unemployment benefit was paid out of money raised through local rates: as a result, areas of high unemployment had high rates which deterred firms from moving in. Then came the 1934 Special Areas Act. These acts were small by modern standards: by 1939, the legislation had found only 12 000 new jobs (3 000 in South Wales, for example, compared with 60 000 unemployed there); but they started the policy of defining certain areas (variously called 'Development Areas' or 'Areas for Expansion' or 'Assisted Areas') towards which industry would be directed. By 1984, 35% of the working population, fell within the assisted areas.

What are the policies used?

The actual areas and measures used to redress regional imbalance vary from government to government and year to year, and so there would be little point you learning what the present schemes involve. However, the following broad policies have been tried:

Physical controls   There are a number of ways in which the government has tried to actually restrict and direct the movement of firms. For example, firms wishing to establish plants of a certain size have to have an Industrial Development Certificate (IDC): such a permit is only issued if the proposed development is 'in accordance with the proper distribution of industry'. Recently, the issue of IDCs has had little effect and in 1980 the use of IDCs was formally abandoned by the government. The need for jobs in all parts of the country had made it difficult for a government to deny permission to expand even in the 'prosperous' regions of the country. However, there have been periods (such as the immediate postwar years) when IDCs were a purposeful and effective way of moving industry out. Office Development Controls have been tried, and a government-run Location of Offices Bureau has worked to sponsor moves of clerical and administrative jobs out of London.

One of the major forms of physical controls has been intervention by ministers. In the mid 1970s the Ford engine plant was located in Bridgend after considerable government encouragement (especially by the then Prime Minister James Callaghan). In the past, car plants have been encouraged in Liverpool and Scotland, steel works in Llanwern (S.Wales) and Ravenscraig (Scotland). The history of these politician-selected sites is sad.

Capital subsidies   Another way in which government has influenced location decisions is by offering capital subsidies.

SAQ 13:   *What does the word 'capital' mean in economics? What, therefore, will a capital subsidy do?*

Civil servants feel that the initial capital cost of setting up a factory is crucial in deciding a firm where to go: managers, it is felt, accept that running costs can be met in the normal way of business. Capital subsidies have included:
- Advance factories, built to stand ready for a user, and offered rent-free for several years, or for purchase at favourable rates.
- Subsidy on initial capital cost of building and machinery either by actually paying part of the cost (up to 15% in the worst areas), or by tax allowances (allowing higher profit to be made) or by interest relief (making commercial loans cheaper to firms in the assisted areas).

Labour subsidies have been used to correct the capital-bias of capital subsidies. Making capital cheaper to firms in development areas meant that firms which were heavy users of capital — such as chemicals, oil refineries etc. — were attracted.* As a result, relatively few jobs per £ were created: in the case of ICI Teesside (an enormous petrochemical complex built with government aid), a local MP calculates that it would have been cheaper to pension the workers off to the South of France than to create jobs at what it cost the taxpayer. In one case, the extra capital grants enabled a firm to install a computer-controlled system that made a number of supervisory workers redundant (!). There is another criticism of capital subsidies besides their cost: it is that the capital equipment bought might very well be made outside the development area, syphoning off regional aid to prosperous regions, or even abroad.

Labour subsidies are sometimes claimed to be self-financing, in that they actually pay for themselves in taking workers off the dole, and in the jobs created by the respending of the regional multiplier process. They do at least ensure that the money aimed at development areas is spent in development areas. Labour subsidies have included:
- mobility and retraining allowances through the Manpower Services Commission
- Temporary Employment Subsidies to keep workers in their jobs while their firm survives a difficult period
- a Regional Employment Premium, paid in the 1960s and early 1970s to employers in development areas: it gave employers a fixed sum per employee.
- service industry grants for each service industry job moved into a development area.

SAQ 14:   *Which of these measures stands most chance of being self-financing? Explain your answer.*

*In 1982-3, £92m of Britain's £690m 'automatic' regional grant aid was spent on one North Sea oil terminal in the Shetlands that created few local jobs and would probably have been built anyway.

Government example The government also works by example, moving out to the assisted areas activities that do not have to be located in London. It can be argued that Ministries do need to be near Parliament; however, offices further from the decision-making process certainly do not. In some countries, of course, whole new capitals have been built to create a better regional balance — Brasilia, for example. The UK hasn't gone anywhere near that far, but a number of government activities have moved out. Tax offices are found throughout the North, the Post Office Girobank is based in Bootle, Premium Bonds in Lytham St Anne's, the Department of Social Security in Newcastle-upon-Tyne. Such moves often attract the opposition of staff (as when the Royal Mint went to Llantrisant in South Wales) or of consumers (when the Company Records Office went to Cardiff). From time to time, opposition wins: plans to move the Ministry of Defence civil servants to the Northeast finally fell through after determined opposition. Of course, many government offices remain in London: the offices of the Forestry Commission (in Savile Row) and the National Coal Board (in Buckingham Palace Road) seem difficult to justify on grounds of regional balance.

Another feature of government support for less prosperous regions is in the provision of a better regional 'infrastructure' — roads, airports, ports, housing and so on. The EEC is active in improving infrastructure, and in offering retraining and relocation grants to workers from troubled industries. New Towns have also been used in development areas in an attempt to create lively and attractive growth areas away from the overcrowded Southeast.

How effective has regional policy been?

It is difficult to assess how effective regional policy has been. This is partly because the level of regional policy has varied so wildly (from 20% of start-up costs in 1952 to 50% in 1964), partly because it is difficult to know what would have happened to the regions had their been no regional policy.

There are also various technical problems with taking changes in unemployment as a measure of how successful regional policy has been (*see* Gowland's book, which I quote in the review section at the end of the next unit), although quite striking figures can be produced. The next SAQ, for example, is based on figures before and after determined attempts to right regional problems.

SAQ 15: *Look at these figures and answer the questions beneath.*

	Change in manufacturing employment 1965-75	Unemployment as % of UK	
		1965	1975
Southeast	− 2.4%	63	69
West Midlands	− 0.2%	48	99
Scotland	+ 0.1%	215	127
Wales	+ 0.6%	187	138
Northern	+ 0.7%	185	146

(a)   construct a bar graph to show the percentage changes in manufacturing employment between the regions

(b)   describe the changes, and explain why they might have occurred

Nevertheless, attempts have been made to assess the impact of regional policy — not surprisingly, considering the enormous sums of money that have been channelled this way (£.5b 1976-7). Some researchers have put the number of jobs created as high as 250,000, though a more conservative estimate might be less than half of this.

RECENT TRENDS IN REGIONAL POLICY

There have been a number of changes in regional policy in recent years, but there is no doubt that the biggest influence on the view of regional prosperity differences has been the problems with the national economy. It is little comfort to a region whose unemployment has doubled to know that elsewhere unemployment has trebled, and so they are relatively better placed. The rising tide of unemployment, even in hitherto prosperous areas like the industrial West Midlands, has reduced the government's interest in specifically regional problems.

In 1984 there was a considerable change in regional policy. It reflected two of the issues you've already met in this unit: the widening of unemployment problems to more areas, and unease about the cost-effectiveness of regional aid. Areas like the West Midlands were added to the assisted areas; at the other end of the scale the Special Development Areas — which covered parts of the country like Merseyside or Glasgow, and attracted specially high levels of help because of acute regional problems were abolished. There were now only two tiers of help: the 'inner tier' qualifying for the full range of relief and aid, and an 'outer tier' getting selective help only.

This was matched by an increased emphasis on selective aid rather than automatic help for firms in assisted areas. Research had shown, as we have seen, that regional aid was often an extremely costly way of creating jobs: one estimate put the cost at £35,000 per job, even allowing for multiplier effects. The 1984 changes made aid to many more projects conditional on satisfying efficiency criteria, like:

> a ceiling on the amount of assistance: £10,000 per net new job created in assisted areas. This also aimed to stop the encouragement inherent in the old grant system to switch from one assisted area to another.

> grants must be spent on new capacity, not replacing older machinery or buildings.

Whether the extra bureaucracy associated with making applications and satisfying civil servants as to these criteria will defeat the purpose of the new approach, only time will tell. One factor in the decision was a desire to make full call on the resources of the EEC's Regional Development Fund, an increasingly important body (particularly in areas of declining coal and steel industries).

One trend has certainly been the realisation that there are pockets of deprivation, unemployment and low living standards even within the 'prosperous' regions. This is particularly true of the **inner city** areas which have grown more desolate and unpleasant as both industry and middle-class residents have moved out. Look at these figures on infant mortality, for example:

	Deaths each year per 1000 live births
Bromley	9.7
Lambeth	17.7
Stockport	9.7
Manchester	18.5

(*Local Government Vital Statistics, 1979*)

Now there is no pattern of regional difference here — leafy Stockport (a borough which contains many pleasant commuter suburbs) has a mortality rate almost half that of inner-city Manchester. Employment and income are also lower in the inner-city. Government policies have therefore moved more to urban renewal than to regional balance. Under Labour, increased rate-support money was channelled to inner-city boroughs. The Tories, true to their free-market ethos, have encouraged small business and other employers in the inner city with the creation of 'enterprise zones', areas in which the usual town planning and other development and employment laws are moderated. In 1984 six 'free ports' (areas where goods can be imported free of all duties and taxes provided they are exported after processing) were designated in Belfast, Cardiff, Prestwick, Liverpool, Birmingham and Southampton.

REVIEW SECTION

Further reading

Many of the best books on industrial location are geography books like *The Geography of Manufacturing* by Alexandersson (Prentice-Hall), *Industrial Activity and Economic Geography* by Estall and Buchanan (Hutchinson), and *The Location of Manufacturing Industry* by John Bale (Oliver and Boyd).

Articles and books on regional policy get outdated quickly. Beware of this when reading Lee's *Regional Policy and the Location of Industry* (Heinemann), and the changes outlined in *Economics*, Spring 1986; useful and interesting chapters on the regional problem can be found in Donaldson *Economics of the Real World*, Livesey's *Textbook of Economics* Ch. 16, and Hartley's *Problems of Economic Policy* (Allen and Unwin). There are interesting *Case Studies in Regional Economics* (Heinemann) prepared by K. Button and D. Gillingwater. D.J. Storey grapples with the problems of 'Regional Policy in a Recession' in *NatWest Bank Review*, November 1983. The Pelican book *The Grass is Greener* (D. Smith) looks interestingly at regional differences, and the *Economist* article of 1 April 1978 looked at European regional problems. Prest and Coppock's *The UK Economy* is, as ever, good if written for undergraduates. There are very good articles in two of the Economics Briefs series: Unit 7 of *The Structure of Industry* by Stewart Hughes (Collins) and Unit 10 of *Controlling the Economy* by Nancy Wall.

Examination questions

The examiners can question you on this topic in a number of ways — in the multiple choice section, or in the data-response and essay sections. Here's an example of a data-response question on regional problems, for example:

1.

Gross domestic product per head of population
(United Kingdom = 100)

	1971	1975	1979
North	87.1	94.9	93.0
Yorkshire and Humberside	92.7	94.9	95.4
East Midlands	95.6	96.7	98.6
East Anglia	94.6	92.3	94.0
South East	113.8	112.8	113.4
South West	94.0	90.4	91.6
West Midlands	102.9	99.8	96.4
North West	96.3	96.2	95.9
Wales	88.0	89.9	88.4
Scotland	93.3	96.7	96.6
Northern Ireland	75.4	76.0	77.5

Source: *Regional Trends* 1981

(a) (i) Describe the regional variations in gross domestic product per head of population in 1979.
(3 marks)

(ii) Suggest causes for the regional variations you have described. *(4 marks)*

(b) To what extent was British regional policy successful in reducing regional disparity during the nineteen seventies?
(5 marks)

(AEB June 1983)

And here is a selection of essay-type questions:

2. Discuss the arguments for and against the free market approach to regional imbalance.
(Associated Examining Board 'A' June 1982)

3. Outline the influences which are chiefly responsible for the pattern of urban and regional unemployment in Britain. Does Economics give any guidance as to whether or not it is desirable or possible to do anything to change this pattern?
(JMB 'A' level 1985)

4. How would you explain the economic decline of inner city areas in the United Kingdom? Suggest possible remedies and discuss their economic implications.
(AEB 'A' level 1987)

5. Why does unemployment vary so widely between different regions of the United Kingdom? What implications follow for policy?
(Oxford Local Delegacy 'S' level 1985)

ANSWERS to SAQs

SAQ 1: Production; the factors of production.

SAQ 2: (a) The ore was processed locally, at places such as Scunthorpe — the reason being that the transportation of such ores would be wasteful, involving the moving of tons of waste. (b) Newsprint comes from woodpulp, and is associated with sawmills; it's attracted to the raw material end because so much bulk is lost in sawmills. Meat canning is found near slaughterhouses.

SAQ 3: (a) They were bulk losers originally; less so today. (b) They were based originally near the oilfields, whereas today they are located near markets (in the estuaries of rivers near major cities in industrial countries, for example. (c) In the twenties and thirties there were petrol tankers (taking finished products from the refinery to the market); today, oil tankers (taking unrefined raw material to the refinery). NB: Political matters can intrude here — an increasing number of petroleum exporting nations wish to carry on the lucrative refining themselves, which may bend the refineries back to the source of the raw material!

SAQ 4: Because, if labour was mobile it would move to ensure similar unemployment rates everywhere. If Durham had worse unemployment than Kent, people would move until the differential no longer existed.

SAQ 5:   (a) When the motor industry was a craft industry, it had to be located in the area which offered skilled engineering craftsmen — which initially meant the West Midlands, with its tradition of cycle building. When mass production methods reduced the skill input (b) the need was for cheap labour near the market — which made Dagenham, on the edge of London's East End, an attractive option. (c) In the future we may expect car making to migrate to countries with lower labour costs still.

SAQ 6:   Check back to Unit 14 if you've forgotten.

SAQ 7:   This is very much a research assignment to do if you have the time: you'll get most out of it if you use it as an opportunity to see whether the principles we've looked at over the past few pages actually work in practice.

SAQ 8:   (a) 4. (b) The proportion of workers with jobs in cotton textiles is more than twice the national average. (c) It means that the industry in question has the same proportion of the region's workforce as of the national workforce. If the northern region had a location quotient of less than one in financial services, proportionately fewer of the region's workers are in that employment compared to the national picture.

SAQ 9:   The multiplier. What we have seen here is that a regional multiplier exists.

SAQ 10:   Foreign competition; exhaustion of raw materials; growth of new industries elsewhere; regional multiplier exaggerating decline.

SAQ 11:   The more mobile — the young, the skilled with a good prospect of work, the lively and ambitious: this would mean that the region they left ended up with a less flexible and skilled workforce, adding to the problem.

SAQ 12:   'It makes no sense to build expensive new airports in the London region when regional airports in Manchester, Leeds and Bradford, East Midlands, Cardiff, etc. are underused. Far more sensible would be a policy to encourage economic activity away from London so that the expensive investments we have already made in regional airports are more fully used.'

SAQ 13:   Capital refers to the tools and machinery used in production — see Unit 1, p. 6 — and so a capital subsidy gives financial help in buying new machinery, factories, tools etc. Using the terminology we learned in consumer theory, a capital subsidy will have an income effect (it will lower a firm's costs, making any project or region so helped more attractive) and a substitution effect (making capital relatively cheaper in relation to labour, and thus encouraging the use of capital-intensive methods of production — see comments later in the unit).

SAQ 14:   TES and REP are likely to cover their own cost if they keep workers off the dole: remember the estimate of keeping a typical worker unemployed exceeds £5000 in lost output.

18 Looking at the market

AIMS OF UNIT 18

In this unit I discuss the workings of a market system in broad terms, and lay out an account of its advantages and disadvantages. By the time you have worked through it, you should be able to:

- say what is meant by 'consumer sovereignty'
- outline the political case for the market system
- explain the problems that have been encountered when governments have attempted to replace the market with centralised planning of the economy
- define the 'optimal allocation of resources' and show how it is reached in a competitive market economy
- list and outline six disadvantages of a market system
- distinguish between 'private costs' and 'social costs' using the concept of externalities; explain the problems that might arise from a divergence between private costs and social costs, and show three ways the problem might be overcome.

INTRODUCTION

Over the past eight units we have looked at the workings of the market in various guises — supply, demand, perfect competition, monopolies, pricing in nationalised industries, and so forth. We can now pick up the threads of a general discussion on economic systems that we started in Unit 1. There, we met the 'economic problem' of scarcity. (*SAQ 1*) Where scarcity exists, we have to use an economic system to resolve the three main economic questions:

SAQ 1: *Explain the meaning of the term 'scarcity' in economics.*

What is to be produced?
How is it to be produced?
Who is to receive the commodities when produced?

What to produce

In a market economy, consumers decide themselves what is produced through their purchases. If people wish to buy a product, producers will usually be able profitably to provide it. If demand increases, higher prices and profits in the industry concerned will attract resources from elsewhere in the economy to satisfy the need. We have seen the process at work in the competitive markets described in Unit 13 (on perfect competition). The following SAQ tests your memory of that process.

SAQ 2: *Fill in the missing words in this passage:*

If there is an increased desire for a commodity, then the demand curve for it will shift to the right*, causing a* ..... *in the price of the commodity: this will* ..... *the profits of the firms in that industry* above *the average (or '*normal*') level. When such* abnormal *profits are being made, firms will* enter *. . the industry, causing the industry supply-curve to shift to the* right*, driving the price down until the industry is in equilibrium where only* normal *profits are being made. Working in reverse, we would expect that, if demand for a product fell,* profit *would fall below the level necessary to keep firms in the industry. As a result, firms will* leave *the industry, bringing supply into line with demand once more.*

Note the role of profits and losses in this process: they act as economic signals, indicating to firms the changing preferences of consumers. The firms that make the largest profits are those which most accurately provide what the consumer desires. Recent business history provides an interesting example. In the 1970s there was a trend away from the business-suit towards more informal and casual clothes. Firms that were prepared to respond to this change in consumer preferences prospered: but Burtons, the High-Street tailor, was slow to follow the trend. As a result its profits fell and the value of its shares suffered, leading to a management shake-up and a drastic review of company policies. Burtons now sell a more lively and informal range of clothing, and have acquired other clothing chain stores to provide a more responsive service. This case shows how consumer preferences affect *what* is produced.

The idea that consumers dictate what is produced is known as **consumer sovereignty** or, more popularly, 'the consumer is king'.

How to produce
We also saw in Unit 13 how the price system tells firms *how* to produce: they combine the factors of production in order to achieve the lowest-cost output. If one factor becomes scarcer and more expensive than another, the entrepreneur switches to a production process that economises on the expensive factor and uses more of the cheaper one. This rational process — low-cost production, using scarce factors with the greatest economy — occurs not due to the public-spiritedness of the entrepreneur, but in order to make the largest profit.

SAQ 3: *Following the oil crisis of the mid-1970s, it made a lot of sense to develop and use passenger cars that were much more economical on fuel than the models that were then available. Explain carefully how, without much government planning or control, the workings of the market caused the development and introduction of such cars.*

Who to produce for
So the market system, with its signals of prices and profits, decides not only what is produced, but also how it is produced. More controversially, it decides who gets the commodities that are produced. The question 'who gets a new car?' is simply answered in a market economy: 'those who want a new car and can afford to buy one'. An individual's ability to afford something — their income — depends in a market system on the price they can get for their **factor services** — their land, labour or capital. Someone whose scarce factor services are in great demand, or who possesses considerable amounts of land or capital, will enjoy high earnings and be able to buy a wide range of commodities. Units 26 to 28 look into earnings and differentials more closely.

Within the constraints of their income consumers make their choice of commodity — and their purchases feed back to firms as a signal. Notice how the distribution of income affects not only the recipients of the goods that are produced, but also the composition of the output. As we saw in Unit 11, consumer demand depends upon the distribution of income. A country in which the national income goes predominantly to a rich elite will have a different pattern of demand — and therefore of output — to a country in which the same average income is distributed more evenly.

THE ADVANTAGES OF A MARKET SYSTEM

The rest of this unit contrasts the advantages and disadvantages of the market system. It is usual to

argue that the market system has three great advantages:
- It is a necessary condition of political freedom;
- It relieves the government of complex and time-consuming functions, allowing it to get on with its essential jobs;
- It is the most efficient form of economic organisation.

Let's appraise these arguments in turn.

Political freedom

The first point starts with the idea that there are fundamentally only two ways of organising an economy – through the market, or through central government planning. 'One is central direction involving the use of coercion – the technique of the army and the modern totalitarian state. The other is voluntary cooperation of individuals – the technique of the market-place' (*Capitalism and Freedom* by Milton Friedman, University of Chicago Press, 1962). The market is argued to confer greater personal freedom not only because it permits greater choice to consumers, but more importantly because it disperses power and influence throughout society, rather than concentrating it in the hands of an all-powerful central government:

> History has taught that, while it is not a sufficient condition, a system of economic freedom is a necessary condition for political freedom. Economic totalitarianism seems unable to coexist with political liberty. The greatest threat to individual liberty lies in the concentration of power. And, if economic power is allied to political power, concentration is almost inevitable. Conversely, if they are retained in different hands – if economic power is dispersed widely throughout society – political power is limited too. Private ownership acts as a check on the accumulation of power by government and thus safeguards the existence of personal liberties.
>
> (*Why Britain Needs a Social Market Economy* – Centre for Policy Studies, 1975)

The CPS pamphlet I've just quoted from goes on to argue that there is nowhere in the world that economic central planning allows political freedom, and believes this to be no coincidence. In this it echoes Friedman's views – 'I know of no example in time or place of a society that has been marked by a large measure of political freedom, and that has not also used something comparable to a free market to organise the bulk of economic activity' (Friedman, *op.cit* p. 9). 'The evidence suggests that every step towards replacing the market by administrative discretion takes us further down the road to political totalitarianism' (CPS). In a famous and influential book, Friedrich von Hayek described the path of increasing government regulation and intervention in the economy as 'The Road to Serfdom'.

The obvious response to this line is to answer that the freedom and independence conferred by private property is in practice confined to a few. However, some freedom is better than none. If the alternative to working for the government is working for a rich private company – well, that's better than no alternative at all. Freedom is indivisible: greater amounts of it are good for all. On a more practical level, choices exercised by the well-to-do may be argued to benefit all. For an example of this argument, look at the next SAQ:

SAQ 4: *In his pamphlet,* Participation without Politics *(IEA), Samuel Brittan takes the example of a poorly run school, and argues that the existence of alternative, private, education will help improve the quality of that school even if very few parents can afford to take advantage of it. How?*

Freeing the government for important tasks

The second point in favour of the government is that the market system takes care of a complex yet vital area of life – the production and distribution of commodities – leaving the machinery of government to concentrate on its really important tasks, the tasks that it alone can do like law and order, and defence. If we can relieve the government of problems that can be solved by the market system, 'they can be in a substantially better position to face up to the responsibilities which have to be theirs alone. . . the market sector (thus) fulfils the function of saving the state from itself' (Lomax, 'The Role of Markets' *NatWest Bank Review* May 1975). It is argued that when the government is asked to take responsibility for running the economy, decisions are taken on the basis of political prejudice and pressure-group activity: legislators are buried beneath a mass of lobbying on butter prices, jobs in shipbuilding, subsidies for microelectronics, and so on forever.

Economic arguments for the market

There is no doubt that the main argument put forward for the market is that it is the most efficient form of economic organisation:

. . . private enterprise nourishes a form of economic organisation — which is the market economy — which has proved itself the most powerful generator of material welfare that mankind has ever known. As Solzhenitsyn wrote in his *Letter to Soviet Leaders* (January 1974), '(Marx) was mistaken when he forecast that the proletariat would be endlessly oppressed and would never achieve anything in a bourgeois democracy; if only we could shower people with as much food, clothing and leisure as they have gained under capitalism.'

(*Why Britain Needs A Social Market Economy*, CPS)

The way such efficiency is said to be achieved is this: economic decisions are decentralised down to individuals who are in fact pursuing their own economic self-interest. For business decision-makers and consumers to act selfishly does not muck the system up: it actually helps make things work better. The logic stretches back to Adam Smith:

Every individual endeavours to employ his capital so that its produce may be of the greatest value. He generally neither intends to promote the public interest, nor knows how much he is promoting it. He intends only his own gain. And he is in this led by an invisible hand to promote an end which was no part of his intention. By pursuing his own interest he frequently promotes the interest of society more effectually than when he really intends to promote it.

(*Wealth of Nations*, 1776)

This is the central justification of the market system: that by harnessing self-interest, it actually manages to produce the commodities we desire. The alternative to a market system is a centrally-planned economy: but just imagine the amount of planning and organisation that would have to be undertaken to bring food, clothing, furniture, fuel and so on to a moderately sized conurbation — Leeds, say, or Bristol. Yet the price system ensures that the city is supplied without scarcity or shortage.

SAQ 5: *Explain how, under the market system, a surplus or shortage of a particular commodity would be corrected.*

The complexity of the task of economic organisation done by the market stands revealed the moment that we attempt to move away from a market system to a planned system, where very substantial inefficiencies crop up.

These inefficiencies have been amply documented in western analyses of Soviet-type economies. It has been suggested that under this system, planners have generally lacked adequate criteria for the allocation of resources of different sectors. The pricing mechanism has not been sufficiently sensitive to factors of supply and demand, so encouraging the accumulation of unwanted goods and acute shortages of goods in heavy demand. Given the range and multiplicity of economic decisions that must be taken in a complex industrial system, the extreme centralisation of decision-making has almost inevitably led to delays, waste and bureaucratic inefficiency. In the absence of an 'economically rational' pricing system, resource allocation seems frequently to be based on political criteria, while managerial authority has been subject to various forms of interference by local party officials. Again, the system of production bonuses has been subject to much abuse: managers have often succeeded in being set exceedingly low targets, thus ensuring generous bonuses for themselves when targets are exceeded. Similarly, managers have been able to earn high bonuses by manufacturing goods for which there is no demand but which are relatively simple to produce. The literature on socialist economies is replete with similar instances of waste and inefficiency encouraged by a highly centralised planning system.

(Frank Parkin, *Class Inequality and Political Order,* 1971)

As Parkin indicates, these problems of replacing market economies with planning are well-documented, and discussed frankly even by those sympathetic to the socialist states of Eastern Europe. Maurice Dobb, for example, in his book *Socialist Planning: some problems* (published by the Communist Party publishers, Lawrence and Wishart) draws attention to four main failings in planned systems:

(a)   When the target is expressed in quantity, such as tonnage of machinery or yardage of cloth, then there is an incentive to distort production so as to maximise output in those terms. 'If targets for weaving cloth are expressed in length, it 'pays' to produce narrow cloth of the simplest weave'. (*SAQ 6 overleaf*)

(b) There is no incentive to achieve a high quality of output – 1000 cars are 1000 cars, even if they drink oil and rust after a year.

(c) Long-term improvements and investments may be abandoned because of the short-term problems they cause to plan fulfilment. Innovation, in particular, is discouraged.

(d) Emphasis on plan-fulfilment makes people anxious to be allocated a lenient target, to under-state their real potentialities. Whence the saying, 'a wise director fulfils his plan 105%, but never 125%'.

SAQ 6: *So suggest why, at the time of writing there is a shortage of thin cabinet nails in Romania.*

Such has been the inefficiency of such central planning techniques, that ways have been sought to improve their effectiveness: decentralised decision making, the use of computers, even (particularly in Hungary) a modified version of the profit motive.

So, in sum, it is claimed that the market system helps political freedom, takes unnecessary tasks off the government's back, produces goods more efficiently, is responsive to change and re-spects consumer preferences. This is a formidable list of advantages, but it doesn't stop there.

Optimality

Given certain assumptions, it can be shown that the market system reaches the very best allocation of resources possible: an 'optimal' allocation of resources. Resources are said to be allocated in an optimal way when it is not possible to alter the allocation of resources without making someone worse off. Let's use a supply-and-demand graph to explain how free markets achieve such a rational allocation of resources.

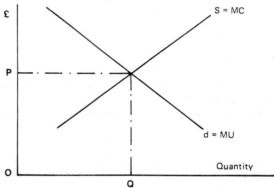

Graph 18.1

In graph 18.1, I have drawn conventional supply and demand curves. The supply curve is, of course, the rising marginal cost curve of all firms in the industry (check back to Unit 13 p. 218 if you can't quite remember why). At any given point on the curve we are shown the cost of pro-ducing the very last unit. The demand curve expresses consumers' marginal utility – that is to say, amount of satisfaction gained from consuming the last unit of the commodity. Now, look at graph 18.1: equilibrium price will be at OP, and equilibrium quantity will be OQ. Because this is the point where the supply curve (=MC) crosses the demand curve (=MU), then at this point the amount of utility (satisfaction/usefulness) gained from the last unit of the commodity produced is exactly equal to the costs to society of producing that unit. Making more of the commodity would mean producing units that added a greater amount to costs than they added to utility, which is wasteful.

SAQ 7: *If all markets were in equilibrium, and there was full employment,*
(a)   what would be the opportunity cost of producing more of the commodity shown in graph 18.1?
(b)   how would the relation between MU and MC in those markets be affected?

Producing some goods whose cost to society exceeds the benefit we get from them, while in other markets marginal utility exceeds marginal costs, is plainly not optimal. Welfare could be increased by switching resources from the market where MC exceeds MU to those where MU exceeds MC. This would happen automatically under a market system. This is another powerful argument for leaving most economic activity to the unrestricted interplay of supply and demand. (You may like to compare this point with the traditional criticism of monopoly from Unit 14.)

Of course, not all commodities can be supplied by private enterprise. There is a need for govern-ment to provide defence and to lay on a legal system that will ensure law and order. But the points that have been made over the past few pages make a strong case for the market system. No wonder that it exerts such a powerful influence on the thinking of most modern economists, and many writers on current affairs. The writings of Milton Friedman and his colleagues from the University of Chicago have fuelled the revival of interest in the market system; in this country, there has been the untiring work of the Institute for Economic Affairs, always eager to put forward market-based solutions to economic problems. And in the early 1980s, there has been an influential group of politicians at the heart of the Conservative Party — Margaret Thatcher, Sir Keith Joseph, Geoffrey Howe, and others — keen to provide free-market policies for Britain's economy.

THE DRAWBACKS OF A MARKET SYSTEM

However, the market is not without its critics. The attractive picture that I have presented so far in this unit, of an effective and democratic way to solve our economic problems, is contested on a number of major grounds. I'll look at the objections to the market in some detail, but briefly outlined the critics say:

- the inequality of wealth and income that result from a market economy make the claims about 'consumer freedom' and 'choice' empty;
- the real world rarely has the vigorous competition and free information necessary for the effective working of a market system;
- the true costs of producing a commodity are often not shown in the market price, causing pollution, congestion and danger to the public ;
- consumers are often ignorant of the true costs and benefits of products;
- equilibrium is rarely reached in a world of labour immobilities and inflexible prices;
- an unregulated market system will result in periodic booms and slumps, alternating unemployment with inflation.

Let's now look at each of these objections more closely.

Inequality of wealth and income

Consumer sovereignty asserts that purchasers select the commodities that are produced in a society by casting their 'money votes' for the product they wish for. Some advocates of the market have extended this idea with their talk of 'economic democracy', but

> . . . they never faced the fact that, whereas their idea of political democracy rested on the principle of 'one man, one vote' and was thus equalitarian in its foundations, their so-called economic liberalism rested on a very different and most unequal weighting of men according to their business drive, their efficiency as producers, their possession of property as a starting advantage, their unscrupulousness, or ruthlessness, or sheer luck.
>
> (G. D. H. Cole, *Socialist Economics*, 1950)

Market economies seem inevitably to generate differences in income and wealth that make substantial differences in living standards between rich and poor. Such differences seem to be more marked than differences in ability. It is a topic to which we shall return — yet even those who recognise the problem still stick to a belief in the market. Firstly, they believe that high incomes should continue to exist as a reward for ability and effort. Secondly, they feel that the market can be used to help the poor. In the words of the CPS pamphlet:

> Because successive governments have neglected the teachings of market economics, attempts to help the less fortunate have usually been misconceived and cost-ineffective, and have often done more harm than good.
>
> (CPS 'Why Britain Needs a Social Market Economy')

SAQ 8: *Suppose a government wished to help those on low incomes, but felt that the free market offered benefits of consumer choice and economic efficiency. What would be the best way to ensure that those on low incomes enjoyed access to decent education, housing and health care? In what way would this approach differ from present policies in the UK?*

Market imperfections

The second objection to the market system was that, in the real world, the conditions that the textbooks say are needed for the effective working of markets do not exist. We have seen in Units 14 and 15 that industry is increasingly dominated by large firms that can select price and output levels, and launch new products with expensive advertising campaigns. Consumers rarely have the fullest information about the commodities they buy. The full list of requirements for a free market was most cruelly exposed in an advanced text first published in 1957, J. V. Graaf's *Theoretical Welfare Economics*:

Graaff shows that economists had not really appreciated the long and restrictive list of assumptions necessary for the optimally efficient allocation of resources envisioned in the model of a competitive, free-market capitalism to be realised. He lists seventeen such assumptions which he has shown to be necessary: many of them are so restrictive that one must agree with Graaff that 'the measure of acceptance. . . (this theory) has won among professional economists, would be astonishing were not its pedigree so long and respectable. A few of Graaff's seventeen conditions will suffice to illustrate the point. The theory required (a) that any individual's welfare is identical with his preference ordering, i.e. that children, drug addicts, fiends, criminals and lunatics, always prefer that which is best for them; (b) that neither risk nor uncertainty is present; (c) that productivity is completely unaffected by the existing distribution of wealth; and (d) that all capital goods as well as consumer goods are infinitely divisible. These represent but four of Graaff's seventeen restrictive conditions which must obtain before the price/market system can achieve optimal economic efficiency. In the light of this, it is obvious that perfect competition could never . . . possibly be achieved.

(Hunt, 'Orthodox economic theory and capitalist ideology' from *A Critique of Economic Theory*, Penguin, 1972)

This doesn't mean that we should completely disregard the market system — after all, it may have fewer inefficiencies than the possible alternatives — but it does rather remove the aura of scientific validity. The market system can no longer be proved to lead to an optimal allocation of resources and thus maximum efficiency. In these circumstances, advocates of the market can only fall back on an idea of 'workable competition' in which, though perfect competition doesn't happen, a reasonably large number of firms compete to serve pretty well-protected consumers.

SAQ 9: *Explain why each of the following make a market more perfect:*
- *small-ads for second-hand cars*
- Which *magazine*
- *the Director General of Fair Trading*
- *Job Centres*

Social costs

The third criticism of market economics concerned the question of social costs. If we have a market system in which firms try to maximise profits, they may very well take decisions that are against the interests of society as a whole because the costs they have to pay (the **private costs**) differ from the real costs to society (**social costs**). Social costs, then, are made up of the private costs plus any external costs (**externalities**) like pollution, congestion, risk to health etc.

Let's take pollution. It may very well make financial sense for a firm to emit smoke into the atmosphere, rather than control effluent. Despite the fact that such emissions will cause nuisance to nearby residents and health problems to those with chest complaints, getting rid of pollutants in the form of smoke is free for the firm. Similarly, a firm may release poisonous waste into a river, killing fish and making the water unfit for swimming and boating.

In these cases, the production costs are being borne partly by the firm and the final consumer (via the price) but also to some extent by the residents and fishermen whose environment has been spoiled. As the production costs are not reflected fully in the firm's private costs, price is lower and production higher than would be the case under a realistic allocation of costs. I've shown this in graph 18.2.

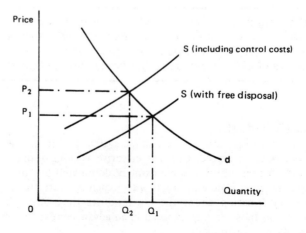

Graph 18.2

SAQ 10: *(a) Look back at the passage on optimal resource allocation on page 282 and explain why the quantity Q_2Q_1 should not be produced: make sure that you indicate the terms 'marginal utility' and 'marginal cost' in your answer.*
(b) Should there be no pollution at all under optimal resource allocation?

In today's Britain, the problem of externalities is met by law. Firms have to obey the legislation concerning clean air and water; developers have to obtain planning permission. Law is not, however, the only way to deal with externalities. I'll use the example of a noisy airport to show the four main approaches that could be used:

- taxation or subsidy: these would make the private costs to the airline equate with social costs: night flights, for example, might be heavily taxed;
- legal controls: the local council could simply ban all night flights, or all flights above a certain noise level;
- compensation: the airlines could compensate local residents for the lost sleep with payments for disturbance and double glazing;
- blackmail: the residents could pay the airlines to go away.

It's up an interesting little back-alley of economic theory that we learn that the last two of these possibilities is equally consistent with a market solution.

Just as products which confer costs on society that are not included in the price will tend to be overproduced, products which confer benefits on third parties will tend to be underproduced. Where social benefit exceeds private benefit, the government may well subsidise a commodity's consumption to increase usage. Examples include **merit goods** such as education (all society benefits from a well-educated labour force with imaginative and compassionate ideas), public health (it benefits me when you have an inoculation against an infectious disease), libraries (access to information benefits us, as does the development of a lively and literate public). One interesting example of external benefits is industrial training. Firms who train employees well have found in several countries that they can lose employees to other firms who can afford to pay more because they do not incur training costs. It was this problem that led to the establishment of the Industrial Training Boards in Britain.

Ignorance and paternalism
When the government encourages the production of merit goods (and I say more about these in the next unit) it could argue that it is correcting a fault in the market mechanism. However, when it is prohibiting the consumption of narcotic drugs or pornography it is replacing the preferences of the consumer with its own preferences — saying, if you like, 'we know better than you what is good for you.' Such government intervention means that a mixed economy produces more symphony concerts and sports halls, less drugs and prostitution than would be the case under a free market. Governments intervene to assure what they consider a more socially correct mixture of commodities: an instance of paternalism.

SAQ 11: *Alternatively, you could argue that forbidding the consumption of narcotic drugs is not paternalism: it is a case where social costs exceed private costs. What 'external' ill-effects might result from drug addiction?*

In passing, we should notice that not everyone is a 'consumer' in the sense of a person who makes decisions about consumption and expenditure. Humans are typically arranged into households, in which the head of household makes the major decision on consumption spending. With this in mind, a number of points can be made about the 'politics of the family'. Government support for education might be seen as representing the interests of a future generation (who at the moment have little money) against the interests of the present generation. Similarly, writers from the women's movement point out that 'consumer sovereignty' is often 'well-paid male head-of-household sovereignty'.

In the areas where the government makes choices on our behalf, it is itself acting as a consumer, making choices about the items of 'collective consumption' that society wishes to have. We shall look at the role of government in a mixed economy in more detail in Unit 19.

SAQ 12: *If most citizens cannot use the market to express their preferences in education, health care, the local environment, social welfare etc., how may they make their views heard?*

Disequilibria

Market systems work well in a textbook world where equilibrium is always reached. However, the real world is full of disequilibrium situations. We've looked at some disequilibrium situations in our course: take the 'cobweb' theorem that we looked at in Unit 12 as an example. This analyses the effect of a disturbance in a market caused by (for example) a temporary shortfall in supply.

SAQ 13: *Under what supply and demand conditions will the workings of a free market cause price and quantity to return to equilibrium? Under what conditions will the workings of the market not cause a return to equilibrium?*

You may, if you wish, regard the regional problems described in Unit 17 as a sign of disequilibrium. If demand for labour in Newcastle fell relative to demand for labour in London, a freely working market system would see (a) wages in Newcastle fall relative to London wages, raising local employment and (b) workers move to jobs in London. In practice wages are inflexible and labour immobile, and so the government is obliged to intervene.

Booms and slumps

In Units 4–6, you learned that a market system can experience periods of time when national income falls below its full potential – a slump, or recession – and also periods when problems are caused by an over-high level of demand. In these circumstances, governments compensate for the shortfall or excess in total demand through their taxation and spending.

SAQ 14: *(a) What problems are caused when the national income falls below its full potential; Which problems are associated with over-full demand?*
(b) What is the name given to the use of government budgetary policy to adjust the level of aggregate demand?

You may regard the macroeconomic problems that occur in market economies as another situation of disequilibrium. It could be argued that unemployment and lost output would not occur if prices and wages were flexible, for then the market system would in the long run work its way back to equilibrium in all markets – even the labour market. Keynes put this argument where it belongs with his famous remark that 'in the long run, we are all dead'.

As I was rather severe on planned economies earlier in this unit, I must now redress the balance by pointing out that overt unemployment is rare in Eastern European economies: indeed, chronic excess demand for labour is found in some countries. A government which aims to employ all its workforce can plan sufficient output to achieve that end: the question you have to consider is whether the very substantial inefficiencies of the planned system are sufficiently wasteful to outweigh the advantages of full employment and economic growth achieved.

REVIEW SECTION

Summary

It is difficult to summarise such a wide-ranging unit as this. What I have attempted to do is outline the workings of the market system, indicating its strong and weak points. Although it scores in flexibility and consumer choice, it does have considerable drawbacks in social injustice and economic stability. This is why many countries have mixed economies, with both public and private ownership of the means of production, and use of both market and planned systems in allocating different commodities. A number of economic and social commentators have seen a tendency for the planned and market economies to become more alike as the years pass, an idea that has been dubbed **convergence**:

> The contrast between command and market systems has, in the view of many observers, come to stand out less clearly in recent years. This is seen partly as a result of the growth of state ownership of industry in western societies, and of the tendency of governments to exercise their jurisdiction in the economy. Equally, and more controversially, the changes are also seen to be occurring in Eastern Europe – in particular, changes designed to reduce the role of central planning in favour of greater reliance on market forces and similar indices of economic rationality.
>
> (Parkin, *op.cit*, p. 168)

While J. K. Galbraith would not agree that the market system is breaking through in Eastern

Europe, he certainly puts forward the convergence view in his book *The New Industrial State* (1967, pp. 389-90).

> Convergence begins with modern large-scale production, with heavy requirements of capital, sophisticated technology and, as a prime consequence, elaborate organisation. These require control of prices and, so far as is possible, of what is bought at those prices. This is to say that planning must replace the market. In the Soviet-type economies, the control of prices is a function of the state . . . . With us, the management is accomplished less formally by the corporations, their advertising agencies, salesmen, dealers and retailers. But these are differences in methods rather than of purpose. Large-scale industrialism requires, in both cases, that the market and consumer sovereignty be extensively superseded.

If this is the case, then soon we shall be no longer contrasting market and planned systems, but concentrating instead on the issues raised in the management of a modern and complex mixed economy.

Further reading

Clearly, this is a unit that will raise strong views on both sides of the argument. For this reason, it is more than usually worthwhile to do some wider reading: start with a basic textbook, and if you can get them, the books from which I've quoted in the text. David Gowland's *Modern Economic Analysis 2* has an excellent chapter on the drawbacks of the price system that covers much of the ground that I have done here.

The best argued case for the free market is still *Capitalism and Freedom* by Milton Friedman — widely available in paperback. Making the same point from a British angle are *Participation without Politics* by Samuel Brittain (published by the Institute for Economic Affairs) and *Why Britain needs a Social Market Economy*, a punchily argued piece of 'Thatcherism' from the Centre for Policy Studies. On the other side of the fence, you may wish to look at Brian Sedgemoor's *The Case for Socialism* or Tony Benn's *Arguments for Socialism*. An excellent advanced but readable account of the problems and opportunities of a Socialist economy is *The Economics of Feasible Socialism* by Alec Nove (Allen and Unwin).

Penguin publish Peter Donaldson *A Question of Economics* – which I've tipped as worth buying before (see especially Chapter 11), and Francis Dalton's *Economic Systems and Society*. A set of articles from *The Economist* are reprinted in *Schools Briefs on Markets* edited by Peter Maunder (Economics Association) with a set of tasks and questions following each article.

Examination questions

1. Explain the basis on which economists, in classifying economic systems, distinguish between 'market' and 'command' economies. On what basis, if any, is it possible to say which type of economy is superior?

    (JMB 'A' June 1987)

2. Explain why a divergence between the private and social costs of road travel may result in congestion. Discuss the economic measures which might be employed to reduce road congestion.

    (AEB 'A' June 1987)

3. Define and distinguish public goods, merit goods, and private goods. Assess the economic case for individuals' financing the costs of vocational education from their own resources.

    (Oxford Local Delegacy June 1985)

4. Describe briefly what are externalities. How and why might taxes and subsidies be used to regulate externalities?

    (AEB 'A' November 1986)

5. Discuss the possible effects of advances in information technology on the efficiency of the economy. Consider how such changes are likely to affect the structure of employment in the UK.

    (JMB 'A' June 1987)

Having covered this unit, you might now be able to look with fresh eyes at some essay questions that have been printed in other units. You may feel that you are now in a better position to answer question 4 on page 263.

As far as data response questions go, I have prepared the following from an article in *The Times:*

PLANNING BECOMES A NIGHTMARE FOR MOSCOW

Article by Alec Nove, Professor of Economics at the University of Glasgow, from *The Times*
April 16th 1980.

Last year was outstandingly bad for the Soviet economy. Growth fell to an all time low of 1.9 per cent; the weather adversely affected the grain harvest; industrial production was well below expectations. Indeed, there was an absolute fall in output of such important products as coal, steel, cement, fertilizer and railway locomotives.

The pages of the Soviet press are filled with sharply critical articles. The railways cannot cope with freight movements: 'I saw with my own eyes at Lesosibirsk piles of good timber which have been awaiting transport for five years' (Pravda, January 7, 1980).

The investment programme is over-expanded and construction delays are growing, and meanwhile 'from year to year utterly hopeless plans are based upon equally utterly hopeless measures' (Pravda, February 26, 1980). Mr Brezhnev has complained that many consumer goods, such as needles, thread, toothbrushes and babies nappies, are unobtainable. Food shortages have grown worse.

The preliminary figures for the first quarter of 1980 are a notable improvement over the previous year. But it is clear that the five-year plan which ends in 1980 will not be fulfilled. Specialist journals and Pravda articles regularly discuss ways and means of achieving the necessary increase in efficiency and labour productivity.

A decree reforming national planning and management was issued in July 1979, but this did no more than to change the detailed formulation of plan-indicators, within a system still essentially centralized. Indeed, the effect of the changes that have been introduced is to make it, if anything, more centralized still.

Centralized planning is a source of both strength and weakness. It enables the political leadership to determine priorities, to direct to key sectors the best materials, and to attract to them the best labour and management (by its power over wages and salaries).

Since most incomes are paid out by the state, it has been possible to enforce an incomes policy. Thus in 1980 average wages will be 15 per cent above 1975 levels; this is actually less than the '16–18 per cent' promised in the original five-year plan document. In striking contrast to the West, trade unions do not demand higher wages in the Soviet Union and there is no unemployment; on the contrary, there is a serious shortage of labour.

Apart from the obvious case of armaments, centralized planning is most clearly effective in the field of energy. True, the Soviet Union does have an energy problem but its essence does not lie in the planning system but rather in geography and geology.

The more accessible sources are becoming exhausted, and reserves are to be found in remote areas, mainly in the frozen north of Siberia. Substantial investment is necessary to develop these regions, and this is one reason for the slowdown of Soviet growth.

However, long-term energy planning is not a sphere in which western capitalism has any advantages – high interest rates, inflation and uncertainty, together with political pressures, impede the emergence of a long-range energy policy.

In the Soviet Union a long-term energy plan is in operation. There has been a spectacular increase over the last 10 years in the output of oil and natural gas in north-west Siberia, as well as a vast oil and gas pipeline construction programme, with some pipelines leading all the way into central Europe.

The new Baikel-Amur railway, soon to be completed, will open up some of the mineral riches of east Siberia. There have been many difficulties, not the least of them transport (the Trans-Siberian is heavily overloaded) but, bearing in mind the natural obstacles to be overcome, these are surely examples of the problems of success.

The worst problems arise in sectors which are not in the top priority category. They suffer because of the truly impossible scale of centralized planning: in principle every production unit must be told what to produce, where to deliver, and from whom to obtain the necessary inputs; it must be given targets for such factors as output, labour productivity, wages and profits.

But there are literally millions of different products so 'the plan' becomes a multitude of 'plan-instructions' issuing from numerous ministries, committees and departments. Coordination becomes a nightmare.

To enable the centre to cope with an impossible job it is necessary to aggregate the millions of products into a smaller number (for example 'footwear', 'ball-bearings', 'miscellaneous agricultural machinery'), with plan-targets expressed in millions of pairs, tons or roubles. The result is neglect of quality and of the customers' requirements, and also sheer waste; thus anyone whose plan is expressed in tons is penalized if a new design happens to weigh less.

Innovation, though genuinely desired, is in fact discouraged by the fact that management is judged above all by the fulfilment of plans, and because new materials or new designs usually require a change in planned inputs or additional investment, and these need permission from higher authority.

The more important enterprises usually obtain their more important supplies (for example, iron ore for metallurgical plants), but even they are often short of minor inputs of many kinds, and either have to make their own (for example, components and spares) or use the services of so-called tolkachi ('pushers', unofficial supply agents), whose methods include bribery. Non-delivery of planned supplies, is a constant source of complaint.

One cause of trouble is the division of products, and of delivery obligations, into 'most important' (vazhneishiye) and others, supposedly less important. But these are often complementary to one another: thus fertilizer supplies increased much faster than did the means to spread it in the fields, and Pravda noted the fact that, in the clothing industry, trousers are on the list of the 'most important', but zip fasteners are not.

Virtually all these weaknesses arise, directly or indirectly, from the impossibly large scale of central planning. The task is made more difficult by the lack of reliable information: management tends to understate its production potential — while overstating its needs for labour and materials — in the hope of obtaining a 'fulfillable' plan.

Harassed planners change plans frequently and workers can have little interest in decisions taken in remote planning offices, with the result that recent decrees have drawn attention to indiscipline, absenteeism and drunkenness.

Similar problems have been encountered in other East European countries. Their smaller size may seem to simplify the tasks of the planners but their much greater reliance on foreign trade calls for greater market-oriented flexibility.

In 1968 Hungary adopted a far-reaching reform, based on the principle that production should be determined by orders from the customers, not from planner-bureaucrats. Czechoslovakia would have adopted a similar system — but for the removal (for other reasons) of the reformers by Soviet troops.

Hungary has suffered from adverse terms of trade and has modified the reform, but none the less its economy seems to work more smoothly with supplies to the citizens more ample than in the Soviet Union. Likewise the East German economy seems more effective than the Russian, though not because of any move towards 'market socialism'. Its greater efficiency may be explained, in the words of a Polish colleague, 'because no system has yet been invented under which Germans can be prevented from working'.

Poland's troubles stem largely from the unsound and excessive investment boom of 1971-75; investment rose by 125 per cent in those five years, money wages by 60 per cent with large-scale borrowing from the West. The consequence was severe overstrain followed by deflationary measures. Half-hearted attempts to reform the planning system have been put into cold storage. Poland is perhaps the most vulnerable of the eastern economies.

In the Soviet Union, a few voices have been raised advocating a Hungarian style reform, with more reliance on the market mechanism, as an essential precondition for efficiency. Central planning would be confined to structurally significant investment decisions and to such key sectors as energy, metallurgy, transport, and, of course, armaments. Such proposals as these arouse strong opposition and will not be adopted by the present (septuagenarian) generation.

The present disarray of the western market economies, and the enhanced priority of the military-industrial sector strengthen the hand of the opponents of any effective decentralization. Yet, in the end, will there be any other way out of a situation of increasingly intolerable inefficiency?

---

1.   Outline the main differences between centrally planned economies and western market economies, taking examples and quotations from the article.
2.   Using examples and instances from the article, outline the advantages that central planning has over the market system.
3.   What are the problems that typically occur in a centrally planned economy?
4.   Explain what is meant by the term 'market socialism': in what way would it be an improvement or a worsening over the more usual centrally planned system of socialism?
5.   Explain some of the things that would happen if Britain moved towards a centrally planned economy.

ANSWERS TO SAQs

SAQ 1:   Scarcity exists because the total amount of commodities that people would like to have (were they free) exceeds our ability to produce because productive resources are limited.

SAQ 2:   right, rise, increase, above, normal; supernormal, enter, right, normal; profits, leave.

SAQ 3:   Consumers became anxious to buy cars that were economical on fuel, and so firms which could supply such cars prospered. As a result, design teams worked to bring out cars that were fuel-efficient. So, as a result of consumers attempting to keep down their motoring costs and firms attempting to maximise profits, the desired adjustment was made.

SAQ 4:   Because teachers will notice that a few students are trickling away to the rival establishment and will therefore be anxious to improve their school: it is argued that this will happen before all the students disappear, and so even though relatively few parents can afford private education, the existence of private education will be a spur.

SAQ 5:   By the price system: a surplus causes excess supply, which forces down price, so clearing the market and discouraging producers. High prices result from shortages, allocating scarce supplies and drawing in new producers.

SAQ 6: Because the target was expressed in weight, and so nail firms produced heavy nails that are simple to make rather than the fiddly small nails that make it more difficult to fulfil the quota.

SAQ 7: (a)   Producing less of something else — that is, producing less than the equilibrium quantity of another product. (b) This means that MU will be less than MC in the expanded market (i.e. the last few units produced will add more to costs than to satisfaction) but in the product that has been reduced in output, MU will exceed MC (i.e. additional units could be produced which add more to utility than to costs).

SAQ 8: Instead of providing free schooling and health care, and subsidised municipal housing, the government could add to the incomes of the poor with cash payments. This would allow the poor to choose a school or health insurance scheme of their choice. If the government was anxious to avoid this money being spent on 'beer and bingo', it could use vouchers rather than cash benefits.

SAQ 9: Small-ads give consumers information about prices in the market, and increase the numbers of buyers and sellers in contact; *Which* gives buyers information about products; the DGFT acts against uncompetitive practices; Job Centres improve the flow of information about vacancies and wage rates.

SAQ 10: (a)   Because for those units the true cost to society (private costs *plus* externalities) exceed the benefits, as true MC exceeds MU for this quantity.

(b)   No: pollution would be allowed providing it was part of a productive process that added more to utility than to costs. For further information, see Beckerman's book, *In Defence of Economic Growth* (Cape).

SAQ 11: Additional costs of medical care for addicts; crime control costs to prevent them robbing to gain money for their habit; support for their families as addicts become unable to maintain family living standards.

SAQ 12: Via the political system: voting for MPs and councillors, lobbying their representatives, setting up pressure groups, etc.

SAQ 13: If demand is more elastic than supply, the cobweb will return to equilibrium. In other cases, the market will 'oscillate' between good and bad years, or even get ever more wildly out of control (diverging cobweb).

SAQ 14: (a)   Unemployment, lost output and income, and slow economic growth are caused by too low a level of NI; when demand is too high, we experience inflation and balance of payments problems.

(b)   Fiscal policy.

19 Government spending

AIMS OF UNIT 19

When you have worked through this unit, you should be able to:
- explain why government intervenes in the economy
- define merit goods and collective goods
- explain what is meant by 'redistribution of income and wealth' and show three ways the government attempts to achieve this objective
- assess the size of the public sector, breaking this term down to its component parts
- list the main sources of government revenue, distinguishing between direct and indirect taxes, progressive and regressive ones
- evaluate the advantages of the UK tax system, and outline some proposed reforms to that system.

INTRODUCTION

This unit aims to discuss the role of government in the economy. It's therefore a very important part of your course, for the government now enters our lives at almost every point. Here's an SAO that will illustrate the point:

SAQ 1: *Jot down your normal daily routine; now list the ways that government action affects it.*

In the distant past, government was not as pervasive. A medieval peasant could go through life with no more contact with government than the sight of an occasional coin: as late as 1900, the government spent less than 15% of our national income. The picture today is very different: how the government collects its taxes, distributes its spending and plans its economic policies is crucial to the economy.

SAQ 2: *In 1986, government spending was £155 690m, and national income was £277 771m. The population was 56.7m. Work out (a) government spending per head and (b) the proportion of national income that passed through the hands of the government.*

Why should we have such massive government intervention, when the studies we have made of the workings of the market economy indicate that the forces of supply and demand can produce and distribute commodities to firms and consumers well enough unaided?

REASONS FOR GOVERNMENT INTERVENTION

Collective goods

In fact, even the most efficient market economy needs the firm hand of government. No economy could work if money could be stolen with impunity, if foreigners could plunder our wealth or if firms could welsh on their contracts. So, at the very least, government must assure national defence, and law and order. The important thing to note about the provision of these services is that they cannot be consumed individually. For example, a country is either adequately defended or it is not — one cannot defend 17 Acacia Avenue without defending No. 19 as well. Similarly, an orderly and law-abiding community confers benefits on all of its citizens indifferently. Economists call commodities that must be provided to all, or to nobody, 'collective goods' or 'public goods'.

SAQ 3: *Which of the following commodities are collective goods (that's to say, commodities that cannot be supplied to one individual without being supplied to everyone)? (a) clean air; (b) good housing; (c) street lighting; (d) lighthouses; (e) university education; (f) diplomatic representation abroad.*

As public goods must, by definition, be provided for all, they cannot be restricted only to those who have paid for them. To avoid the problem of the 'free-rider' who might be tempted to enjoy the benefits of such services without paying, it seems sensible that government should provide the services and pay for them from a compulsory payment levied on citizens. This is the origin of tax and of government; for the provision of defence, and law and order was the first responsibility of the king or tribal leader.

Merit goods

The government also supports the production of some services that are not truly collective or public goods. It would be quite easy to charge individual users for health care, education, library membership, for example. However, government wishes to encourage the consumption of these commodities as they are widely felt to encourage the development of a literate healthy community. That's why they are provided free, or at low cost, by the government.

SAQ 4: *(a) What is the essential difference between a merit good and a public good? (b) Jot down a couple of paragraphs about state subsidy of university education. In one paragraph, put forward the view that it should be continued as a merit good; in the second, the view that the individuals who receive university education should pay the full cost.*

Redistribution of income and wealth

Market economies often generate considerable differences in income and wealth between families and individuals. These disparities arise essentially from two sources — from the fact that individuals differ in the market value of their labour, and in their possession of wealth (land, shares, businesses, etc) due to inheritance or accumulation. Left alone, the differences in income and wealth would result in disparities of living standards that a civilised society would find hard to defend: 'the rich man has milk for his cat, the poor man none for his children'. A society anxious to even things out will use the government's ability to tax and spend to 'redistribute' that pattern of income and wealth that is the result of a market economy's workings. Three main ways are used.

1.   Progressive taxation
A tax system is said to be progressive when it takes a larger proportion of high incomes than of low ones. Recently, UK tax rates on income have been reduced to two bands only. A system which emphasised progressivity might look more like the previous system below:

		£
Basic rate	27%	0-17 900
Higher rates	40%	17 901-20 400
	45%	20 401-25 400
	50%	25 401-33 300
	55%	33 301-41 200
	60%	over 41 200

If the government pays for its services by the use of such a progressive tax system, then the distribution of after-tax incomes will be more equal than the distribution of before-tax incomes.

SAQ 5: *Look at the table below, which shows the shares of total incomes received by rich and poor before and after tax in a recent year.*

Group of taxpayers	Percentages of total income	
	before tax	after tax
Top 1%	5.5	3.9
2-5%	10.6	9.8
6-10%	10.0	9.7
Top 10%	26.2	23.3
11-20%	16.3	16.2
21-30%	13.4	13.4
31-40%	11.0	11.3
41-50%	9.1	9.3
51-60%	7.3	7.7
61-70%	5.9	6.2
71-80%	4.6	5.2
81-90%	3.6	4.4
91-100%	2.5	3.0

You may find it easier to refer to these ten per cent slices in the proper way as 'deciles' of the population. Thus the second richest ten per cent slice (the 11-20%) are called the second decile.

Now comment on this table briefly, paying particular attention to the progressiveness of the tax system.

We will look again later in this unit at the advantages and disadvantages of a progressive tax system. However, a tax system, no matter how progressive, cannot by itself help those who receive no income in a market system. So a second method of equalising incomes is used by modern governments.

2.   Transfers
The government can further even out market distribution of incomes by transfers: switching money raised from taxpayers to the old, the disabled, the unsupported family or the unemployed.

SAQ 6: *Should these pensions and benefits be counted in the National Income? Why, or why not are they so counted?*

3.   Free provision
The final way in which governments try to moderate the unequal living standards that households would enjoy under a pure market system is by the free or greatly subsidised provision of certain essential services. This includes health care and education in the UK.

SAQ 7: *What is meant in economics by the term 'free goods'? (If in doubt, flick through Unit 1). Is primary education a free good in this sense? What is meant by the economists' cliché 'there are no free school meals'?*

Economists differ about the extent to which governments should try to equalise incomes. Some feel that greater equality is a policy objective that should be pursued (a bit like lower inflation or unemployment): others are reluctant to go beyond providing a 'safety net' of basic living standards below which no family should fall. Economists also differ about how effective the government is in using the three ways we have outlined to equalise incomes. As we have seen in SAQ 5, the tax system as a whole is not fiercely redistributive. Further, many of the commodities provided at low cost by the government (higher education, motorways, opera houses, even health care) are consumed as much, or more, by the rich as by the poor. The problems that government encounters in helping low income groups have created the interest in new approaches to tax policy that we shall look at later in this unit.

But let's proceed. We've so far picked out three reasons why the government intervenes in the economy — to provide collective goods, to provide merit goods, and to redistribute incomes. There is a fourth reason —

Increasing our economic efficiency

The last reason for intervention in the economy is to improve its performance. For example, we saw earlier in the course that Keynesian economic theory advises governments to use their power to tax and spend to raise or lower the level of aggregate monetary demand.

SAQ 8: *What name is given to the idea of using the government budget to adjust the level of demand?*

But this is not the only way the government tries to make the economy more efficient. You've read in this course that government attempts to: spread economic activity around the country with the use of its regional policy; encourage firms to contribute to economic growth by favourable tax treatment for business investment; cut into distortions to the free market caused by large firms with its legislation against monopoly and restrictive practices. Government action against pollution and harmful development is intended to ensure that divergences between 'social cost' and 'private cost' are closed, and thus that business decisions take account of the true interests of the community.

SAQ 9: *Taking waste disposal from a chemical works as your example, and using the terms 'private cost' and 'social cost' explain why a market system might lead to a decision about production that was not in society's best interests.*

WHAT DOES THE GOVERNMENT SPEND OUR MONEY ON?

Types of spending

In order to achieve the four objectives that I've mentioned above, the government spends money on:

- current consumption
- transfers
- capital spending.

(Additionally, the nationalised industries buy the factors of production and produce goods and services for sale. Although the nationalised industries are publicly owned, their output is not considered as 'public spending' proper. It seems sensible to leave them out of a discussion on government spending by regarding them as independent business organisations. Curiously, though, their borrowing needs are included in the PSBR.)

Let's look at the three categories of government expenditure one by one:

1.   Current consumption

Current consumption means government purchase of commodities — ammunition for the army, fuel for police cars, beds and drugs for the NHS, streetlighting, school heating, etc. It also covers the wages and salaries of government employees. Central government consumption was £48 724m in 1986, and we must add to this the £30 699m of local authority consumption expenditure.

2.   Transfers

As we have seen earlier in this unit, the government doesn't just tax in order to spend: it uses some to finance transfers. For example, in 1986, over £17.7b was transferred from taxpayers to old people in the form of retirement pensions, £4.9b in child benefits, and £8.2b in supplementary benefits.

SAQ 10: *Name three other government transfers.*

Subsidies can also be looked upon as a transfer: the government programmes that are still large-scale receivers of subsidy include housing, transport undertakings, agriculture and the coal industry.

3.   Capital spending

Capital spending involves spending on major long-term improvements in our roads, prisons, schools and hospitals amongst others.

The table below shows the current and capital spending of central government.

	1986
Current spending, subsidies and transfers (£b)	140.4
Capital spending (£b)	6.6

Programmes

An alternative way of categorising the spending of government is to put it down to the various programmes of the government: education, housing, defence, the arts and so on.

SAQ 11: *How accurate an idea have you about the cost of the programmes of government? Check it out by placing the following in order of their cost to the country: military spending; external relations; roads; transport; employment services; fuel and energy; agriculture; housing; libraries, museums and the arts; education; the NHS; social security benefits.*

IS GOVERNMENT SPENDING TOO GREAT?

The 1979 Conservative Government's first *White Paper on Public Spending* opened as follows: 'public spending is at the heart of Britain's economic difficulties'. This stark judgement summed up a decade of worry at the size of government spending, which had been growing both absolutely and as a proportion of national income.

SAQ 12: *Look at these pie charts, which are from* Barclays Bank Review

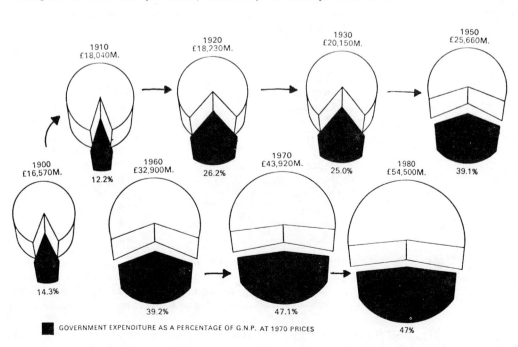

GOVERNMENT EXPENDITURE AS A PERCENTAGE OF G.N.P. AT 1970 PRICES

(a)   Which of the following statements are true?

(i)   Government spending is absolutely greater today than in 1930
(ii)   National product is absolutely greater now than in 1950
(iii) Private sector spending is absolutely smaller in 1980 than in 1960
(iv)   Private sector spending is relatively smaller in 1980 than in 1960
(v)   The public sector was larger in 1980 both absolutely and relatively, than in 1950.

(b)   In what way will a recession affect the ratio of government spending to national income? (Clue: What happens to government spending in a slump? And what happens to national income?)

Why the rise?

There are a number of factors that account for the rising spending of governments. Peacock and Wiseman have shown how wars have had the effect of raising government spending relative to national income: even after heavy wartime taxation is removed, public expenditure is left higher than in pre-war times. You can look at the pie charts in SAQ 13 to confirm this. The explanation is two-fold. On the one hand, the emergency levels of taxation get people used to the government taking a bigger slice of their incomes. On the other, war reveals social needs or creates new commitments (e.g. higher debt interest, replacing damaged houses and transport, extra pensions). Indeed, the Second World War created the climate within which it was possible to launch the welfare state. Investigation shows that it is the social services that have been responsible for most of the rise in government spending since the war. This can be traced to a number of factors:

1.   The population of dependent age has risen relative to the working population: there are, for example, more students and, particularly, old people than before. In 1950 there were less than six million school-children; in 1975, over nine million. In 1901, there were half a million people over 75; today, more than three million.

2.   The welfare services are better. Classes are smaller, pensions higher, health care and housing better and more widely available.

3.   More people are covered by the welfare measures. More people have become entitled to benefits, and new measures (like attendance allowance, Family Income Supplement (FIS), mobility allowances, redundancy pay) introduced. There has been a greater 'take-up' of social programmes – the numbers in higher education, for example, have increased dramatically.

4.   Government services, being very labour intensive, have become relatively more expensive than private sector commodities.

These factors have been international, and indeed the trend to higher government expenditures is seen in many countries.

SAQ 13:   *Look at the figures below and answer the questions that follow*

Tax and Social Security contributions as a percentage of gross national product

	1980
Australia	35
Belgium	48
Canada	36
France	48
FR Germany	44
Italy	38
Japan	28
Netherlands	52
Norway	59
Sweden	55
Switzerland	31
UK	42

(Source: *Social Trends*)

(a)   Which is the most heavily taxed country in the table?
Which is the least heavily taxed? Where is the UK?

(b)   What might account for the low position of countries in this table? Does it imply that the inhabitants of those countries enjoy a higher real income than inhabitants of countries higher up?

(c)   What is the justification for including social security contributions in the calculations?

The dangers of over-large government spending

So far we have seen that, although the UK is far from being the most heavily taxed country in the world, nevertheless government takes a very large share of our national resources. Whilst no-one likes paying taxes, most people welcome higher pensions, improved health care, more efficient transport and policing, better schools. Why then is there concern about the level of government spending that is necessary to achieve these things? To answer this questions, we have to pull together a number of ideas we've already encountered on this course:

— 'Government spending is inflationary'. You met this argument in the unit on inflation. The argument is twofold. Firstly, employees and firms resent the increases in taxation necessary to meet government spending plans, and seek to pass the burden of these taxes on. Employees do it with higher wage claims, employers in higher prices.

SAQ 14: *There is a second inflationary danger from higher public spending — which occurs if a government is not prepared to raise taxes enough to pay for its programmes of spending.*
(a)   How then is the money found to pay for them?
(b)   What inflationary dangers does this present?

— 'Government spending limits choice'. Taking money away from the taxpayer and spending it on his or her behalf is argued to be an interference with individual liberty. At the extreme, we might move to a Soviet-style economy in which the state is so dominant that liberal democracy cannot survive. But even in western countries, higher taxes mean replacing 'consumer sovereignty' with the decisions of civil servants. For example, citizens often have little choice as to when their operation is to be done, or where their children are to be educated. On the other hand, it can be argued that an electorate that has voted for a political party that promises a better health service *has* exercised choice about how its income is to be spent: and some forms of government spending (e.g. transfers) do not reduce choice, but transfer it between individuals.

— 'A large public sector decreases economic growth and efficiency'. It has long been the belief of some economists that the state is less likely to produce commodities efficiently than private enterprise. Private business, it is argued, faces the vigour of competition, and must pay attention to costs and efficiency to maximise profits. These views were given· added point by the work of Bacon and Eltis (*Too Few Producers*, Macmillan, 1975) who argued that the cause of the UK's slow economic growth was the large public 'non-market sector', which could neither generate exports nor investment for the economy.

— 'High taxation has a disincentive effect'. There is a danger — perhaps one that has been exaggerated — that high tax rates will reduce the will to work and thus reduce the output and efficiency of the economy (see page 299 of this unit).

WHERE DOES THE MONEY COME FROM?

The bulk of government income comes from taxation — £143 358m in 1986. Before we go into taxation in more detail, here's a way to review ho far you've got in this unit:

SAQ 15:   *Look at this question from the November 1981 AEB examination paper, and jot down an outline of your answer. What other information do you need to make a full answer?*

Taxation has several functions in addition to raising revenue. Discuss these additional functions with reference to the UK tax system.

Taxes on income

In 1986, the government raised £52 430m from taxes on income. In addition, £26 067m was raised from social security contributions to the national insurance fund, effectively an additional income tax. Income tax is a *direct tax* — that is to say, it is levied directly onto the individual who is intended to pay it.

Taxes on spending

Taxes on spending on the other hand are *indirect taxes* — levied on commodities like wine, petrol, clothes, cigarettes and so on. They are paid indirectly by the individuals and firms that buy these commodites. In 1986, we paid £62 273m in this way. Spending taxes fall into two categories:

— 'ad valorem' taxes that are charged as a percentage of the price of the commodity. An example is VAT, which (at the time of writing) is charged at a rate of 15%.
— 'specific' taxes, like the UK's excise taxes, which are charged at a fixed rate — like 50p on a pack of cigarettes, £5 on a bottle of spirits and so on.

SAQ 16: *(a)   How does inflation affect the amount of money raised by the government from indirect taxation if the tax is (i) ad valorem or (ii) specific?*
(b)   The tax on wine is a specific one: so much per litre. Which bottle is therefore proportionately most highly taxed — a bottle of cheap 'plonk', or vintage claret?

Taxes on wealth
The third way to raise money is to tax not income, or spending, but wealth.

SAQ 17: *What is someone's wealth? How does it differ from their income?*

The UK does not, in fact, have a wealth tax. However, transfers of wealth may be taxed under the provisions of the Inheritance Tax, although this has a number of allowances and loopholes that mean it yields less than the old 'death duty'. Local authority rates may be considered as a wealth tax, in that they are charged on the value of property — often a family's largest individual item of wealth. Wealth taxes are direct taxes, as the individual who is to pay them is charged.

Many European countries have wealth taxes, which differ in detail. Some take the form of an annual levy on capital: the aim is as much to equalise wealth as to raise revenue. Whilst such taxes pose formidable problems of implementation and evasion, the Labour Party is keen to introduce one to the UK.

SAQ 18: *We've now looked at the three forms of taxation. What is the major source of government income apart from taxes? (Clue: What does the government do when its tax revenues are not sufficient to meet spending?)*

HOW GOOD IS OUR TAX SYSTEM?

To answer this question, we must consider what factors make a good tax. It may be true (in the politicians' cliché that 'to tax and to please is not given to man', but some taxes are plainly more acceptable than others. Adam Smith picked out four 'canons of taxation'

1.   *Certainty* — the taxpayer should be clearly aware how much is due, and when and where.
2.   *Convenience* — taxes should be payable at a time and place that suits the taxpayer.
3.   *Economy* — taxes should be reasonably inexpensive to collect.
4.   *Equality* — taxes should relate to the taxpayer's ability to pay.

Progressive and regressive
This last point touches on an area of controversy: precisely how should taxation relate to a taxpayer's means? Economists use three terms to simplify discussion of this issue. A tax is 'progressive' if it takes a higher proportion of higher incomes than of lower ones; it is 'regressive' if it takes a higher proportion of low incomes than higher ones; and it is 'proportional' if it takes equal proportions of both high and low incomes. Look at this simplified example:

	Income (£ per annum)			
	2000	*4000*	*6000*	*8000*
Tax A	200	400	600	800
Tax B	100	100	100	100
Tax C	–	200	600	1600

Tax A is proportional – it takes one-tenth of all incomes, high or low. Tax B, however, is regressive: although the same money amount is paid at each level of income, £100 is a greater chunk of a low income than of a higher one. The progressive tax is C – taking 20% of £8000, 10% of £6000, 5% of £4000 and nothing from the lowest income shown.

SAQ 19: *You'll need a calculator now. The statistics below are real – they come from the Government's* Family Expenditure Survey, *and show taxes paid by two groups – the poorest ten per cent of the population, and the richest ten per cent of the population – in 1979.*

	Bottom decile	Top decile
Gross income including state benefits	*1730*	*14420*
Direct taxes paid	–	*3250*
Indirect taxes paid	*380*	*2320*

(a)   *What are direct and indirect taxes? Give examples.*

(b)   *Work out the proportion of income taken by each sort of tax. Which is regressive? Which is progressive?*

(c)   *Explain why the different taxes should have such different effects.*

Adam Smith's canons (or principles) of taxation indicate the basics that go to make a 'good tax'. Nowadays, though, we should ask more of a tax than that it should be convenient and economical to collect, certain and equitable in its impact. We would also wish that a tax should be:

1.   *flexible*   We have seen in our work on fiscal policy that, to make adjustments to the level of aggregate demand, the Chancellor must be able to alter tax rates on some taxes quickly.

SAQ 20:   *The Chancellor has the power to alter some tax rates without Parliamentary approval: what is this power called?*

2.   *free from distorting effects on the economy*   If we believe that a market system will allocate resources efficiently, we must strive not to muck things up with the tax system. An example of a tax that does distort output is UK road tax, which encourages the production of three-wheeled cars and vans by taxing them no more heavily than motorcycle sidecars. We shall look at more important distortions in a moment.

3.   *no disincentive to effort*   A tax that takes a disproportionately large share of additional income might act to reduce the supply of effort. Workers may thereby be discouraged from looking for promotion, moving to a better-paid job, seeking overtime or production bonuses. Where extremely high tax rates exist, a further rise in the tax rate may be so great a disincentive that the amount of tax received by government falls.

Economists have failed to find any convincing evidence of disincentive effects of high taxation. This is because a rise in taxation has two contrasting effects

(a)   Firstly, as the take home pay per hour is cut, it becomes less lucrative to work. The opportunity cost of leisure therefore falls; and with the fall in cost, more is consumed. In everyday language, less work is done.

(b)   Secondly, though, there is an income effect. As higher taxes cut into take-home pay, workers need to work more hours, or find a higher-paid position, to gain a given net 'target' income. This might cause a rise in taxes to raise the amount of effort rather than reduce it.

The actual effect of a rise in tax on the supply of effort will depend on which of these two effects – the substitution effect of cheaper leisure, or the income effect is the stronger.

SAQ 21:   *(a) President Reagan's economic policy rested on the idea that it was possible to reduce the government borrowing requirement whilst cutting taxes. Explain how this might make sense, even if government spending remains unchanged.*

(b) A primitive medieval form of tax was the Poll Tax – each member of society paying a fixed sum to the Exchequer. This form of tax has no disincentive effect, as increased work creates no increase in taxation: so why did it fall into disuse?

How does our tax system measure up to these principles?

The UK system has three major drawbacks when measured against our seven principles of taxation.

Distortion

The UK tax system does not treat all savings and income alike. Some forms of savings are subsidised, others heavily taxed. For example, saving in the form of buying a house attracts income tax relief. Saving to buy shares or invest in your own business doesn't: in fact it is double-taxed — when you first earn it, and when it yields a profit later. The result is predictable. Over ninety per cent of UK personal savings go into housing, pension contributions, and insurance/assurance policies. As a result, after-tax returns on savings depend on almost anything but the basic profitability of an investment.

A narrow tax base

A tax base is the amount of income or wealth that is to be taxed. Now, in the UK so many tax allowances are available that a substantial chunk of income goes untaxed. Additionally, incomes in kind are rarely included. As a result, 50% of UK personal income is reckoned to avoid income taxation; so income tax must be levied at a higher rate on what remains. This means that income tax starts at 25%. (Although the present government envisages an eventual rate of 20%.

The poverty trap

The poverty trap is the name given to the Catch 22 that affects poor families: they can earn more and be no better off. It works like this. In line with the government's aim of redistributing incomes, poorer families can claim a number of benefits that raise their living standards: FIS, rent and rate rebates, free school meals etc. These benefits are not available to middle income families. The result is that if the household income rises, so much is lost in income tax, social security contributions, and loss of welfare benefits that net income rises hardly at all. Look at this example from the *Economist* (13th November 1982); it refers to a household with two adults and two children.

			£
1.	*Original earnings £60*		
	take-home pay	=	50.86
	plus FIS		15.75
	free school meals		5.00
	rent rebate		12.59
	rate rebate		4.15
	child benefit		11.70
	net income		100.05
2.	*Original earnings £120*		
	take-home pay		87.91
	rent rebate		3.92
	rate rebate		1.21
	child benefit		11.70
	net income		104.44

SAQ 22: *Economists distinguish between the average tax rate (that is, total income divided by total tax paid) and the marginal tax rate (that is, the portion of an additional unit of income that is payable in tax). What is the marginal tax rate above? (Work out what addition to net income results from the addition of £60 to the household's original income, and express it as a percentage.)*

REFORMS FOR THE TAX SYSTEM

Avoiding distortions through an expenditure tax

James Meade (an economics Nobel Prizewinner) chaired an independent commission on the UK tax system that reported in 1978. His commission recommended that income tax be replaced with a tax on expenditure. A pure income tax is levied on all income: an expenditure tax only on the proportion of income that is spent. We've seen earlier in this unit that UK income tax does have concessions for some forms of savings.

SAQ 23: *Which forms of savings get tax concessions?*

Others, however, get no concessions: a tax based on expenditure only would avoid this discrimination and the consequent distortions. Such a tax system would make post-tax returns from savings

more close to the pre-tax returns

The obvious objection to such a change is that such a tax would appear to be regressive, but this can be avoided. An expenditure tax doesn't have to be levied at the point of sale in the same way as VAT. It could be levied at the year's end as a direct tax on the difference between household income and savings. Such an arrangement (which Meade called a Universal Expenditure Tax) would allow a range of progressively higher tax bands, which would not be possible under a VAT-type expenditure tax. Alternatively, an expenditure tax could use both a basic VAT for everybody, and a UET levied only on the higher incomes: this would 'soak the rich' whilst minimising paper-work by excluding the 85% of taxpayers who do not pay higher rate income tax. An additional advantage of such an expenditure-based tax is that it would tax people who gain income through chance – such as gambling wins or inheritance.

Out of the poverty trap with Negative Income Tax

Negative (or reverse) income tax is a very simple idea. At present, there is a level of income that attracts no tax. For a single person with no other allowances, this was £2 605 in 1988. Above this level, you start to pay tax, but you do not get anything back from the taxman if you fall below this level. With NIT, you would. If the NIT rate was 50%, you would get 50p for every £1 by which your income fell short of the 'break-even' level.

SAQ 24: *(a) Suppose the break-even level was £2000 and your original income was £1900. How much aid would you receive from the state if the NIT rate was 50%?*
(b) What would be the minimum income any individual would receive with such a break-even point and NIT rate?
(c) What are the advantages and disadvantages of a very high rate of NIT – say 80%?

NIT offers the opportunity of abolishing all means-tested benefits like free school meals or rent rebates: perhaps it would be more accurate to say that it offers the ability to amalgamate them into one rational scheme. In fact, if the minimum income could guarantee households enough money to buy adequate education and health insurance, it might not only replace the retirement pension and supplementary benefit systems, but also replace state-provided goods with greater consumer choice. No more NHS specs and dentures – buy privately instead. This is the attraction to those economists and politicians who wish to act against poverty without abandoning the market system.

There are a number of practical problems involved in bringing in a NIT scheme. Firstly, it is difficult to identify the income unit we should use – the individual or the family? If the individual, we might end up paying the minimum income to rich teenagers in a wealthy family home. Settling the NIT rate will involve a delicate judgement between disincentive and poverty relief: the higher the rate, the lower the incentive to get a job, for who wants to work for an additional £20 if it involves losing (say) £16 in NIT? Lastly, there is the problem of timing: whereas supplementary benefit is assessed weekly, tax assessments are annual and so use of the tax system would involve difficulties when people's circumstances change within the year.

We shall look again at schemes for the relief of poverty and equalisation of income and wealth later in the course, when we investigate earnings and wealth in the real world.

REVIEW SECTION

Further reading

On the role of government in a mixed economy, see *Current Issues in Economic Policy* by Grant and Shaw (Phillip Allan 1980) Chapter 1, or *Modern Economic Analysis 2* edited by David Gowland (Butterworth 1983) Chapter 8. Much recent ground is covered in *Public Finance* by George Stanlake (Longman Economic Studies): see also *The Guardian Guide to the Economy* by Cairncross and Keeley (Methuen 1981) – especially Chapters 2 and 3.

Taxation policy is covered in a number of books. Look in your library for *Taxation Policy* ed. Crick and Robson (Penguin – old but still useful); G. H. Peters *Public and Private Finance* Fontana), King and Kay *The British Tax System* (OUP). The Meade proposals are outlined in *The Structure and Reform of Direct Taxation* (Institute of Fiscal Studies) and *Tax Reform in the UK* Brown, Bird and King (Economics Association – try your tutor). *The Economist* carried a series of articles in autumn 1983 on tax reform and problems, summarised in the issue of 2 December 1983.

A useful source of information is *Public Finance* by M. Wilkinson (one of the Economics Briefs series). The first article in the *National Westminster Quarterly Review*, May 1987, looks at tax reform on an international basis.

An issue hotly debated at present is the replacement of local rates by a community charge (poll tax). *The Royal Bank of Scotland Review,* June 1987 contains an article which takes a critical look at the theoretical work available on rates. Try, also, to obtain some of the following articles: 'Government Policy, Taxation and Supply-Side Economics', *Economics*, Summer 1987; 'Taxation and Employment Policy, *Economic Review*, January 1986; 'Tax Reform', *Economic Review*, September 1986; 'Lower Taxes, Lower Borrowing, Higher Spending?', *Economic Review*, September 1987.

Examination questions

The importance of this topic in our society is reflected in the weight given to it by examiners. Look, for example, at the following as examples of the slant given to this subject by the examiners:

1. (a)   Distinguish between direct and indirect taxes.   [6]
    (b)   Distinguish between progressive and regressive taxes.   [6]
    (c)   Why do governments impose taxes?   [13]

    (University of Cambridge Local Examinations Syndicate November 1986)

2.   'Increases in public expenditure lead to lower unemployment and eventually to a reduction in public expenditure; public expenditure cuts lead to higher unemployment and to increased public expenditure.' Critically discuss this statement.

    (AEB June 1985)

3.   Examine the arguments for and against a shift from direct to indirect taxation.

    (London 'A' January 1987)

4.   What are the characteristics of a good tax? In 1986 the Government proposed to replace the domestic rates on property by a community charge (a poll tax) for local services, payable at the same rate by all the adult residents of a local authority. Explain whether or not you think that this will be an improvement.

    (JMB 'A' June 1987)

5.   Discuss the economic arguments for and against the imposition of high taxes to deter cigarette smoking.

    (AEB 'A' June 1987)

6.   The table below gives a forecast of income and expenditure of the United Kingdom public sector for 1984—85 figures in £ thousand millions).

Income		*Expenditure*	
Central Government Taxation			*(£ million)*
Income tax	33.8	Social security	37.2
Value added tax	18.0	Defence	17.0
Corporation tax	8.4	Health and personal social services	15.4
Oil duties	6.1	Education and science	13.1
Petroleum revenue tax	6.0	Scotland	6.9
Spirits, beer, wine, cider and perry	4.0	Industry, energy, trade and employment	5.6
Tobacco	4.1	Law, order and protective services	4.9
Vehicle excise duty	2.1	Transport	4.4
National insurance surcharge	0.9	Northern Ireland	4.0
Taxes on capital	1.7	Other environmental services	3.5
European Community duties	1.4	Housing	2.5
Other (including accruals adjustments)	2.9	Wales	2.6
Total	89.4	Overseas aid and other overseas services	2.3
		Agriculture, fisheries, food and forestry	2.0
National insurance, etc. contributions	23.0	Other public services	1.8
Local authorities rates	12.9	Common services	1.1
North Sea oil royalties, etc.	2.0	Arts and libraries	0.6
General government trading surplus and rent	3.0	Local authority current expenditure not allocated to programmes (England)	0.7
General government interest and dividend receipts	2.4		
		Adjustments	
Adjustments			
		Special sales of assets	−1.9
Accruals		Reserve	2.8
Public corporations transactions		General allowance for shortfall	—
Other	−1.8		
		Planning total in Cmnd 9143	126.4
Total receipts	135.1		
		Revisions since Cmnd 9143	−0.1

Public Sector Borrowing Requirement	7.2	Revised planning total	126.2
		Gross debt interest	16.0
Total receipts and borrowing	142.3	Planning total plus gross debt interest	142.3

(Source: *Economic Progress Report*, No. 166, March–April 1984)

(a)   Explain briefly the item 'gross debt interest'.

(2 marks)

(b)   (i)   If total public sector expenditure in 1984–85 turned out to be 5% *above* the forecast figure and total receipts were actually £5.1 thousand million *below* the forecast figure, by how much would the Public Sector Borrowing Requirement (PSBR) have differed from that forecast?

(2 marks)

(ii) Discuss the ways, other than by increasing tax rates, by which the government could meet this increased Public Sector Borrowing Requirement.

(4 marks)

(c)   With specific reference to the table, discuss the likely economic effects of each of the following. For each of your three answers, assume all other items in the table remain unchanged.

(i)   A 20% increase in expenditure on social security;

(5 marks)

(ii) a 30% reduction in defence spending;

(3 marks)

(iii) a reduction in the rate of Value Added Tax to 10%.

(4 marks)

(London 'A' January 1987)

ANSWERS TO SAQs

SAQ 1:   The answer will depend on your day: don't forget use of coinage, listening to BBC TV or radio, encounters with the law (if only zebra crossings and speed limits), taking the children to a state school, and so on.

SAQ 2:   My misbehaving calculator works it out at £2 745 per head, and government spending at 56% of national income. Do remember that this last figure is not a 'real' statistic, as government spending includes a lot of transfers – pensions etc. – that are not included in the national income calculations.

SAQ 3:   (a) (c) (d) and (f); (b) and (e) could be supplied individually.

SAQ 4:   (a) A public good is one that must be provided for all, or for no-one. A merit good is provided to individuals (or households) but has substantial external benefits. Merit goods reflect also the presence of ignorance – and where consumers are ignorant of all the benefits of a commodity and confer benefits on others in consuming it, the government has a case for expanding production beyond what would be bought in a free market.
(b) University education has substantial external benefit to third parties. It provides a supply of skilled professional labour to the community, and the society benefits from having a more educated population. On the other hand, many of the benefits of higher education come back to the individual who receives it in the form of higher income, and so one may argue that it should be financed by those individuals.

SAQ 5:   The message of the table is that the tax system has a substantial effect on the top 1% and the bottom twenty per cent or so – but doesn't seem to affect the vast bulk of tax-payers in between in a redistributive sense. For example the second and third deciles (11-20% and 21-30%) get virtually the same proportion of after-tax as pre-tax income.

SAQ 6:   We would be guilty of double counting if we put pensions into the national income, as they are obtained from taxing earnings that have already been counted once: that's why they are not included.

SAQ 7:   Free goods are goods which are not scarce in an economic sense – things like fresh air or sea-water. One consumer can therefore have as much as he or she likes without reducing the amount available to others. Primary education is not free in this sense, as it requires resources to be produced. The old cliché about 'free school meals' implies that everything has to be paid for, even if it is not charged at the point of use. Thus a desire that 'all bread should be free' simply means that it should be paid for in another way than at the bakers.

SAQ 8:   Fiscal policy

SAQ 9:   A private company tries to minimise private costs rather than total costs, and so might ignore the external cost of dumping waste in the air or fresh water. Society should try to take into account the social cost – that is the whole cost, including externalities as well as private costs – for dumping waste might cause a reduction in health, fishing, leisure areas etc. that the firm would not under a market system take into account.

SAQ 10:   Unemployment benefit, student grants, disablement pensions (etc. etc.)

SAQ 11:   The latest figures I have are:

UK National Accounts 1984

Defence	15 904	Agriculture	2 292
External relations	2 415	Housing subsidies	1 562
Roads	3 147	NHS	16 016
Transport	2 029	Social Security benefits	33 741
Employment services	2 917	Education (local councils)	15 583
Industry & trade	3 087	Museums etc.	798

How did you do?

SAQ 12:   (a) i, ii, iv and v are all true   (b) a recession will tend to increase the ratio of government spending to national income as receipts from taxation fall and payments for unemployment benefit and welfare payments rise.

SAQ 13:   (a) Norway is the most heavily taxed, Japan the lowest. The UK holds a mid-table position. (b) The low position is really a reflection of the political choices made in those societies – to rely more on the private sector than the public sector for living standards. It doesn't really tell us that those countries have got more efficient governments, or higher living standards. (c) Because they are effectively a tax – a compulsory deduction from pay. Leaving it out makes a very distorted figure, for some countries pay more in social security contributions than in tax.

SAQ 14:   (a) By borrowing (b) If the borrowing is not financed by the sales of government stock to the non-bank public, then the government deficit will be multiplied by the banking system causing a rise in the money supply. This might be reflected later in higher prices.

SAQ 15:   I think you have enough information to make a fair stab at this, bringing out the purpose of the tax system in equalising incomes and in regulating the economy. Perhaps you do need the information in the rest of this unit on the effectiveness of the UK tax system in meeting the objectives it sets itself.

SAQ 16:   (a) Inflation adds to 'ad valorem' duties, as it takes a percentage of the higher price. This isn't true of specific taxes, which have to be adjusted to ensure that the government gets the same real yield each year. (b) The cheap wine is most highly taxed – you pay proportionately less tax on a pricey bottle than on a cheap one.

SAQ 17:   Wealth is the stock of useful assets. Income is a flow – how much wealth you get per period.

SAQ 18:   Borrowing

SAQ 19:   (a) Direct taxes are paid directly by the taxpayer to the government – like income tax: indirect taxation is levied when you're doing something else, like drinking wine or buying a table, when you pay VAT. (b) In the example given, direct taxes take nothing from the bottom decile, but 22.5% of the income of the top decile – highly progressive. Indirect taxes take 25% of low incomes and just 16.1% of the top ones – rather regressive (c) The reason for the progressivity of income tax is that one is allowed to earn a given amount before tax is payable, and thereafter tax is levied at a rising percentage, but indirect taxes are levied on consumption, which tends to hit all groups – even hitting the poor the worst as their propensity to save is lower than the rich.

SAQ 20:   The regulator.

SAQ 21   (a) It can work if the cuts in taxation create such an increase in economic activity (as disincentives are reduced) that incomes and output rise substantially (b) Because it is so unfair – poor and rich pay exactly the same. This is the reason that a similar idea (a fixed tax on all electors) was rejected when governments in the seventies were looking for a replacement for local rates.

SAQ 22   The household receives an extra £4.49 from an increase of £60 in gross income – effectively a tax rate of 92%. This is the highest UK tax rate.

SAQ 23   House purchase and pension premiums.

SAQ 24   (a) £50 – 50% of the £100 shortfall. (b) The minimum income would be £1000 – if you receive no original income, you get 50% of the gap between zero and £2000. (c) The disadvantage of a high rate of NIT is the disincentive. At a rate of 80%, a wage earner would get just 20p of any additional £ earned in increased income, for 80p of NIT would be lost.

20 International trade

AIMS OF UNIT 20

At the end of this unit, you should be able to:
- give four reasons for international trade
- explain the idea of production according to comparative advantage
- distinguish between absolute and comparative advantage
- show why opportunity cost ratios will determine the prices between which commodities will be traded
- define and calculate the terms of trade, making clear the significance of such calculations
- explain the Heckscher-Ohlin principle
- list and evaluate five reasons for interference with international trade
- outline five ways in which governments intervene in international trade, explaining their advantages and disadvantages.

INTRODUCTION

Some questions keep recurring in economics. Topics like the causes of inflation, the proper level of profits, the rights and wrongs of trade union activity, have been discussed for at least the past hundred years. One of these perennial questions concerns international trade, and government attitude to it: it asks this vital question —

Should the government allow free international trade, or place restrictions on trade that aim to help home industries?

This unit looks at this topic, assesses the gains from trade and analyses the arguments against free trade. It also describes the ways governments control international trade. At the end of the unit you will find suggestions for further reading, and some past examination questions on the topic.

THE REASONS FOR TRADE

When the person in the street is asked why Britain engages in international trade, the reply usually runs along these lines: 'We need to trade with foreign countries because they have many things we need and can't produce'. Examples of such goods are easy to think of — mineral ores, for example, or tropical fruit. International trade started as a quest for rare commodities unobtainable in Britain

305

— spices, silks, fine wines. However, this is no longer a sound justification for trading with other countries, for two reasons. Firstly, it now technologically possible for an advanced country to produce almost anything it wants: oil from coal, tropical fruit in heated glasshouses, gold from sea-water. Secondly, a look at the wealth of imported goods in our shops — toys, cheeses, clothes, cars, calculators and so on — reveals that there are very few commodities that Britain could not produce quite easily.

The argument for international trade doesn't rest upon the idea that we are unable to produce these goods, but on the subtler idea of international specialisation. It was David Ricardo who, more than 150 years ago, first formulated the 'law of comparative costs' that revealed the advantages to be had from an international division of labour. The law says simply that if countries (or regions within a single country — all the same idea) specialise in the production of commodities in which they enjoy an advantage, world production (or the country's gross domestic product) will increase. This will make possible mutually advantageous trade in which each country (or region) ends up able to consume a greater quantity of commodities than before. There are no losers in the specialisation game, therefore free trade which will bring about maximum specialisation on the basis of comparative advantage can only raise world production and increase welfare.

SAQ 1: *So, in theory, regional specialisation leads to the highest level of national output. What are the real-world disadvantages of regional specialisation? In what crucial way does the real world differ from the textbook world to create this disadvantage?*

Comparative cost: an example

Some examples will make the idea of comparative advantage clearer. Imagine two countries, A and B, which can both produce rice and wheat. Suppose that with the same factors of production, they can produce as follows:

1. Country A   1000 tons of rice   *or*   200 tons of wheat
   Country B   200 tons of rice   *or*   1000 tons of wheat.

If these countries aimed at being self-sufficient, they might split their resources equally between rice and wheat production. If this happened, then

2. Country A produces   500 tons of rice   *and*   100 tons of wheat
   Country B produces   100 tons of rice   *and*   500 tons of wheat.

Total production between the two countries is, therefore, 600 tons of rice and 600 tons of wheat. Let's see what happens when the countries specialise according to their advantages. Country A is more efficient at producing rice, and should produce only rice: country B should stick to wheat. When this occurs, we find that

3. Country A produces   1000 tons of rice and no wheat
   Country B produces   no rice and 1000 tons of wheat.

World production has risen sharply — from 600 to 1000 tons in the case of each commodity.

SAQ 2: *How have the two countries contrived to increase their production by so much without using any more resources?*

However, the countries in question now have supplies of only one cereal each, and will wish to vary their diet through trade. Let's assume, for the same of simplicity, that one ton of rice trades for one ton of wheat, and that at this rate of exchange 300 tons of wheat are swapped for 300 tons of rice. After specialisation and trade, the picture looks like this:

4. Country A has 700 tons of rice   *and*   300 tons of wheat
   Country B has 300 tons of rice   *and*   700 tons of wheat.

Just compare this with the levels of output of the self-sufficient world shown at (2) above. Both countries are very much better off for having concentrated on their best product and traded it with the other.

SAQ 3: *Now work through this example as I have in the text so far. I've chosen the very examples that were used by Ricardo himself — woollen cloth from Britain and wine from Portugal. Assume that with given resources, Britain can produce 100 lengths of cloth or 50 barrels of wine, whereas Portugal can produce 50 lengths of cloth or 200 barrels of wine. Work out, then:*

(a) How much they would produce, acting as self-sufficient countries and dividing resources equally between wine and woollen cloth.
(b) How much they would produce specialising in their best product
(c) Assuming that 30 barrels of wine are exchanged for 30 lengths of cloth after specialisation, what is the final picture?

Comparative advantage

The examples that have been used so far in the text have been very straightforward. Countries, it appears, should concentrate on the commodities that they are best at. In our first example, one country was clearly superior in the production of rice, the other in the production of wheat. But what should happen when no such clear advantage exists – when, for example, one country is better than another at producing everything? Funnily enough, in these circumstances it still pays to specialise – in the products for which the country enjoys the greatest *comparative* advantage. For example, if the USA is ten times better than Taiwan at producing aircraft and twice as good at producing toys, then it would be best for the USA to concentrate on aircraft (where it enjoys the greatest comparative advantage) and leave toys to a less developed economy.

A worked example might make this surprising proposition clearer:

1. Country A can produce   500 tons of food or 1000 units of manufactures
   Country B can produce   400 tons of food or   50 units of manufactures.

You will see that country A is better both at producing food and at manufacturing. If, as in previous examples, the countries aimed at self sufficiency under the impression that no gains from trade could occur, their outputs would be (splitting resources equally again):

2. Country A has   250 tons of food   and   500 units of manufactures
   Country B has   200 tons of food   and   25 units of manufactures.

Now let's have some specialisation. The advantage that country A has is so great that probably only incomplete specialisation will take place: it will have to retain some resources in food production, for example, to actually feed its people. Nevertheless, let's go some of the way to specialisation, with country A putting 90 per cent of its resources in manufactures and country B putting all its resources into food. We now find:

3. Country A produces 50 tons of food   and   900 units of manufactures
   Country B produces 400 tons of food   and   no manufactures

Trading 200 tons of food for 200 units of manufactures, the final position is as follows:

Country A has 250 tons of food   and   700 units of manufactures
Country B has 200 tons of food   and   200 units of manufactures.

Compared to the position in 2. above, both sides have gained from a degree of specialisation and trade *even though* country A does everything better than country B. It is still efficient economics for the country to do the thing in which it enjoys the greatest *comparative* advantage.
Country A is 20 times better at manufacturing, but only 25 per cent better at food production, so it must favour manufacturing if it wishes for the highest living standards.

THE TERMS OF TRADE

At what prices will nations trade?

So far in this unit, our imaginary countries have swapped their output one-for-one. This has been a simplification that was aimed to keep the explanation uncluttered. However, it is unlikely that one-for-one trades will be a feature of the real world: international trade involves business deals not playground swaps. What prices will obtain in international trade?

Let's return to the very first example we looked at – the rice and wheat one. Country A produced rice five times as efficiently as Country B. If Country A had to produce wheat itself, it would have to sacrifice a considerable amount of rice – five tons for every ton of wheat produced. And so it benefits if it can obtain a ton of wheat for less than five tons of rice.

 SAQ 4: *What would be the final position in the rice/wheat example if country A traded 450 tons of rice for 100 tons of wheat? Are there still gains from trade when the country has to pay a price as high as 4.5 tons of rice for each ton of wheat: that is, is the country still better off than when it was self-sufficient?*

The same logic can be used to look at country B's position. The cost of rice to them is measured in the wheat they would have to forego if they had to put workers and land to producing rice.

SAQ 5: *What do we call cost measured this way?*

You can see that producing one ton of rice would involve giving up five tons of wheat. The price that country B would willingly pay for rice will reflect this opportunity cost. If, by trading, rice can be obtained at any price lower than five tons of wheat, country B benefits.

SAQ 6: *What would be the final position in the rice/wheat example if country B traded 480 tons of wheat for 100 tons of rice?*

Let's now compare the results we have got from SAQ 4 and from SAQ 6. In SAQ 4 country A gained a little from trade − it had as much wheat as if it had been self-sufficient, but more tons of rice. In SAQ 4, though, country B gained very considerably from trade, as its wheat was worth 4.5 times as much as country A's rice. Compared to the position when it was trying to be self-sufficient − with 100 tons of rice and 900 tons of wheat it now enjoys 450 tons of rice and 900 tons of wheat. In SAQ 6, by contrast, the boot is on the other foot: country A gains enormously, whilst B gets very little from international trade.

SAQ 7: *Look again at the example used in SAQ 3 − that is, the trade in wool and wine between Britain and Portugal.*
(a)   What is the greatest amount of woollen cloth that the British will be willing to exchange for one barrel of wine? Why?
(b)   What is the most, in barrels of wine, that Portugal will be prepared to pay for UK woollen cloth? Why?

So the gains from trade depend not just on specialisation, but also on the prices that countries obtain for the commodities they sell. In the example used in SAQ 7, cloth will be traded at a price between half a barrel of wine and four barrels of wine. However, Britain is better off if it can trade one length of cloth for four barrels of wine than if it can only get half a barrel of wine for its cloth. A fall in the amount of wine earned from producing and exchanging cloth means either that UK consumers can have less wine, or that they will have to give up more cloth to get the same amount of wine − in either case, a fall in their standard of living.

This is why economists are interested in the relationship between what we pay for our imports and what we earn from our exports. The ratio between export and import prices is called the 'terms of trade'.

Calculating the terms of trade

In the real world, countries export not just one commodity, but many: so a simple statement of how much wine can be exchanged for wool, or food for manufactures, is not much help. We need to measure how an average of *all* export prices varies in relation to *all* import prices. To help us do this, indices of export and import prices are constructed, using a base year as 100 and 'weighted' so that a change in the price of an important commodity (say, oil) has a greater effect on the index than a change in the price of a less significant commodity (say, brandy). Equipped with our indices, changes are measured as follows:

$$\frac{\text{Index of export prices}}{\text{Index of import prices}} \times 100 = \text{terms of trade}$$

Let's take an example. If, in a period of time, export prices increased by a half whilst import prices remained the same, it's

$$\frac{150}{100} \times 100 = 150$$

Such a movement is, on the face of things, very favourable to Britain. It means that we have to export fewer goods in order to afford a given amount of imports. An improvement in the terms of trade, then, is shown by a rise in the index. A fall in the terms of trade would show that prices had worsened against us, obliging us to export more goods in order to buy the same amount of imports.

For example, if import prices doubled whilst export prices remained unchanged, the calculation would be as follows:

$$\frac{100}{200} \times 100 = 50$$

SAQ 8: *Answer the following questions about the terms of trade.*
(a)   The text described an improvement in the terms of trade as, on the face of things, very favourable to Britain. What disadvantages might there be in a situation where our export prices are rising faster than the price of the goods we are importing?
(b) Work out the terms of trade in these examples:

	Index of import prices	Index of export prices	Terms of trade
(i)	120	120	–
(ii)	50	100	–
(iii)	120	100	–
(iv)	100	110	–
(v)	80	100	–
(vi)	80	60	–

(c) In which of the calculations above do the terms of trade worsen? What effect would this have on the UK standard of living? Why?
(d) Third-world countries export raw materials and tropical products and import oil and manufactures. Their terms of trade have greatly worsened in recent years – what does this tell you about:
 (i)   price changes of raw materials and tropical products as compared with oil and manufactures?
 (ii)   likely trends in living standards in the third world?

Summary of the unit so far
International trade takes place because output and   therefore living standards are improved by specialisation. There are gains from trade not only when different countries enjoy an absolute advantage in producing a product, but even when they enjoy just a comparative advantage. Goods so produced are then traded. Whilst trade at any set of prices between opportunity-cost ratios is worthwhile, the gains from trade accruing to an individual country will depend to some extent on the relationship between the prices it pays for its imports and those it gets for its exports – the terms of trade.

What commodities will a country specialise in?
According to the theory of comparative advantage, countries must choose to produce the products for which they enjoy the greatest comparative advantage – but what kinds of product will this include? This question was answered earlier this century by two Swedish economists, Eli Heckscher and Bertil Ohlin. They showed that specialisation will occur on the basis of each country's 'factor endowment' – their particular mix of land, labour and capital. A country well-endowed with abundant labour will export labour-intensive products; whilst a country with a large stock of capital will export capital-intensive commodities. This principle has become known as the **Heckscher-Ohlin** principle.

What reasons are there for trade apart from specialisation?
There are a number of justifications for international trade that do not depend on the law of comparative costs. For example, there is an additional source of gain from trade if an industry is in a position of decreasing costs.

SAQ 9: *Give another term that means 'decreasing costs'. In what unit did we learn about decreasing costs? List five sources of decreasing costs.*

In fact, some industries find that the size of the international market is essential for an efficient scale of production: the aircraft construction industry is an example. And even where the home market is big enough for all possible scale economies, international trade provides the chance for us to maintain competition in an industry where economies of scale mean we have only one or two British firms.

SAQ 10: *Name an industry where economies of scale exist but international trade ensures vigorous competition.*

A number of other justifications for international trade can be made. International trade can help when temporary shortages occur in one country — due, for example, to poor harvests. Finally, the links of trade can contribute to international understanding and friendship: two countries that depend on each other for prosperity, and whose citizens have frequent contact, are unlikely to go to war. Much of the original momentum behind European economic unity came from a desire to involve France and Germany in a cooperative endeavour that would eliminate the conflicts that led to three disastrous wars in a lifetime.

REASONS FOR PROTECTION

Having looked at the justifications for international trade, it seems inconceivable that we live in a world where numerous interventions are made to interfere with free international trade. Many barriers to trade still exist — import tariffs, quotas, regulations. This section covers some of the reasons for interference with free international trade, and outlines the methods used.

Strategic reasons

Military or strategic reasons may demand that a country preserve a particular industry against the advice of 'comparative cost'. For example, British agriculture has received much government subsidy and protection over the past forty years on the grounds that it is not wise to rely on foreign suppliers for all our food (as we discovered in the Second World War). In the same way, the USA subsidise and encourage their merchant shipping in order to retain a large seagoing transport capability, thought essential for the strategic needs of a great power. Much of Britain's traditional protection of the watchmaking and optical industries comes from a desire to retain crafts vital to armament manufacture.

To protect employment

Tariffs are often justified on the grounds that imported goods threaten jobs in Britain. For example, Britain imposed tariffs, so ending a century of free trade, during the interwar slump to cushion unemployment in many regions and industries; today there are controls on textile imports and on Japanese cars. Such protection is usually considered harmful, in that it hinders the reallocation of resources out of inefficient industries and into expanding and efficient ones. However, immobilities of labour and capital do exist.

SAQ 11: *What does this mean in plain English?*

Import controls may very well be justified to moderate what may otherwise be a brutal reallocation of resources for the people concerned. In addition, if there are no other jobs to go to, and the government is unable to restore full employment by expanding the economy and retraining redundant workers, it is not at all certain that protection leads to economic inefficiency.

SAQ 12: *Let's use the concept of opportunity cost that you learned in Unit 1 to illustrate this point. What is the cost to society (i.e. the opportunity cost) of keeping a worker in her job in the textile industry if:*
(a)   there is an alternative job to go to?
(b)   there is no alternative job to go to?

Related to the employment argument are *'anti-dumping'* measures. Dumping is the name given to the practice of monopolistic discrimination in which the price is raised in the protected home market, and part of the proceeds of the higher price are used to subsidise exports so that they can undercut competitors in other countries. This is an attractive policy where large scale economies exist, as a long production run can be sold partly at home (at high prices) and partly abroad (at low prices).

Where dumping occurs, government is clearly justified in protecting the home industry: indeed, international trade agreements specifically permit anti-dumping measures. In fact, however, we often hear allegations of 'dumping' and 'unfair competition' when all that is involved is competition on the basis of low wages. Whatever one may feel about the low wages paid in some poor countries, it is hypocritical to cry 'unfair competition!' when poor nations with abundant labour are only doing what the theory of comparative advantage says they should do.

To protect infant industry

Another important reason for protection is the infant industry argument. In developing countries tariffs are frequently imposed to protect new industries until they are strong enough to face foreign competition. The established industries of other countries already enjoy economies of scale and the technical knowledge that comes from 'learning by doing': their efficiency and monopoly power can prevent the development of new competitors. It is instructive to note that many of today's industrial powers — USA, Japan, Germany — had to protect their home industries from foreign competition (usually British) in order to help their development into industrial economies.

The infant industry argument is usually held to apply only to specific industries at specific times, but the implications of the argument are general. The basic idea is one of *altering* the existing pattern of comparative advantage to achieve strengths in new and more promising industries. The aim is to acquire new comparative advantages rather than submit to the existing pattern of international trade*.

One situation in which the protection and nurturing of new industry is very attractive occurs when a country is heavily dependent on one product, or a very few products, for export earnings. In this case, protection is essential for a programme of 'diversification' that reduces the country's dependence on the price or harvest of one product. Brazil, for example, has been anxious to reduce its reliance on coffee, and Cuba its reliance on sugar. Remember that there are a number of countries that rely on one product for more than 90 per cent of their exports (e.g. Mauritius and sugar).

To remedy a balance of payments crisis

The balance of payments is, as we shall see, a set of accounts that shows a record of the flow of money into and out of a country. Sometimes it happens that a country cannot earn enough from exports to pay for desired imports, and one solution is to restrict imports. We shall look in more detail at how to cure a payments crisis in a later unit, but the objections to import controls are clear: they may put off facing up to the underlying weakness (high costs, poor quality goods, excessive government spending abroad, or whatever) that caused the problem in the first place. In addition, it invites retaliation from countries whose exports are affected as happened when the UK in 1964 and the US in 1971 imposed surcharges on imports.

The terms of trade argument

This is one final, selfish, justification for taxing imports. If your market is sufficiently vital to a supplier, putting a tariff on imports may force the seller to lower prices in order to maintain sales. Clearly the success of such a policy relies on the importance of your market and the inability of the 'victim' to retaliate.

MEASURES USED TO CONTROL INTERNATIONAL TRADE

Governments have five main weapons for interfering with the flow of international trade: tariffs, subsidies, quantitative restrictions, non-tariff barriers and exchange controls.

Tariffs are taxes put on imported goods. They can be of two kinds, either specific (e.g. 50p per article imported), or, more commonly, *ad valorem* (e.g. 10 per cent of the price of the good). The general effect of tariffs is to raise the price of the imported commodity relative to home-produced goods, enabling home industries to compete more easily. Tariffs can also serve a purpose in raising revenue.

---

*One practical problem with the infant industry argument is that it requires the government to be a good judge of which industries should be promoted and developed, and which ignored. Such judgements are very difficult.

SAQ 13: *What aspect of the demand for imports will determine whether a rise in tariffs will raise money for the government, or deter consumers from buying and so reduce the receipts of the government?*

Subsidies have a similar effect to tariffs on imports, enabling the home producer to compete more easily – this time by lowering the market price with the help of money from the Government. There are, however, a number of important differences between protection by tariff and protection by subsidy:

1. Protection by subsidy makes clear the cost of a policy of interference with free trade. Protection by tariff doesn't show the cost so clearly.
2. With a tariff, the consumer pays the cost of protection through higher prices: with a subsidy, the taxpayer pays it through higher taxes.

SAQ 14: *Tariffs and subsidies also differ in their social impact. See if you can indicate how in this 'underline the right word' exercise:*
As taxpayers generally tend to have higher/lower incomes than consumers, subsidies funded from taxes will be more regressive/progressive than protection through tariffs.

Quantitative restrictions control the quantity of imports. A quota of a given amount of the product is set, and no more is allowed in once the quota has been reached. The limited amount let in finds its own price in the marketplace, and presumably earns a higher price than if a larger quantity was allowed in. The benefit of this higher price goes to the seller rather than to the government (as would be the case if government put on tariffs). One way round this is to auction import licences and give them to the highest bidder.

The significance of **non-tariff barriers to trade** has increased recently as tariffs have been reduced (e.g. by the Common Market, and other international negotiations). Non-tariff barriers take the form of discriminatory administrative practices, such as awarding government contracts to home companies even where their tenders are not as low as those from foreign rivals; insisting on individual technical standards; setting differing veterinary or hygiene regulations for foodstuffs and animal products, and so on. These barriers are very real, and are often called 'invisible tariffs'. Much of the effort that the European Commission continues to put into freer trade concentrates on the elimination of such barriers.

Finally, a government may reduce the flow of imports by **exchange controls**. The word exchange in this sentence refers to foreign exchange – that is, foreign currency that can be used to buy imported goods. A tight foreign exchange system would work like this:

All foreign currency earned by exports must be surrendered to the central bank, who exchange it for the home currency. Anyone wishing to import commodities can now only get the currency from one place – the central bank. If you want to import, you have to get approval before scarce foreign currency is granted. The government, through its central bank, can therefore deny permission (by denying currency) to import. Such a system is used in some third-world countries whose precious and scarce export earnings must be kept for such vital imports as medicines, machinery and fuel.

SAQ 15: *Read through the last section on 'Measures used to control international trade', and use the information there to answer these questions.*

(a)   Pick one advantage of using quotas, rather than tariffs, to restrict imports, and one disadvantage.

(b)   When the UK entered the European Economic Community, it abandoned its previous agricultural policy which involved supporting home agriculture by subsidies that enabled it to compete at world prices, and replaced it by the EEC policy involving tariffs on imported food. What are the advantages and disadvantages of such a change?

We shall return to the various ways of controlling international trade when we look at balance of payments policy later in the course. This is particularly relevant to the present debates about British economic policy, where some economists argue strongly that economic recovery demands import controls.

CRITICISMS OF FREE TRADE

This unit has outlined the advantages of free trade, and also given you a glimpse at some of the reasons — and ways — that governments interfere with trade. There are two main drawbacks to the theory.

1.   The theory of comparative costs is essentially a static theory. It takes no account of dynamic processes like economic growth, technical change and economies of scale. It tries to establish an international division of labour on the basis of present and existing comparative costs, rather than potential ones. This has the tendency to condemn many of today's poorer countries to the production of low-value commodities which will keep them poor forever.

2.   A further problem with the idea of international specialisation is that Ricardo's theory assumes full employment. When all resources can be fully employed, any diversification of the economy is always at the expense of specialisation. Yet the experience of most countries of the world at the moment is of much unemployment and underemployment.

REVIEW SECTION

Further reading

An account of the theory of comparative advantage (or 'the law of comparative costs') can be found in any textbook — have a look at one of the sources mentioned in your Study Guide for a 'second opinion'. Equally good as an introduction are the opening chapters of *The Economics of International Trade* by David Cobham. *The Guardian Guide to the Economy* by Frances Cairncross and Phil Keeley (Methuen) discusses the costs of protectionism for the UK.

For deviant views on the wonders of international specialisation, see the David Lomax article *International Trade and Industrial Policy* in the National Westminster Bank Review, May 1976; the most powerful and complete critique of the law of comparative costs from a radical standpoint is to be found in A. Emmanuel *Unequal Exchange* (New Left Books). Another assault on Ricardo is to be found in Chapter 9 of Thomas Balogh's *The Irrelevance of Conventional Economics*, Weidenfeld & Nicolson — see also his criticism of monetarism in Chapter 8.

A most important text that touches upon the place of the third world in the web of specialisation is the *Brandt Report*, published as *North-South* in Pan paperback — see especially p. 145.

International Trade by Andrew Leake (part of the series of Economics Briefs from *The Economist*) gives an applied view of this topic, look particularly at Units 2 and 9.

Examination questions

1.   Evaluate the case for free trade. Discuss the possible effects of the current spread of trade agreements among nations.

(JMB 'A' June 1986)

2.   Is the case for free trade weaker in a period of world recession and low growth of world trade?

(Oxford Local Examinations 'A' June 1985)

3.   (a)   What are a country's terms of trade?   [5]
     (b)   How are changes in the terms of trade measured?   [7]
     (c)   How, and why, may changes in the terms of trade affect domestic living standards [13]

(Cambridge Local Examinations Syndicate 'A' November/December 1985)

4.   Since economics demonstrates the beneficial nature of free trade, why do tariffs exist?

(Cambridge Local Examinations Syndicate 'A' November 1986)

5.   Explain what is meant by dumping in the context of international trade. Discuss whether or not dumping can or should be prevented.

(JMB 'A' June 1987)

ANSWERS TO SAQs

SAQ 1:   The disadvantage is that when the pattern of demand changes, regions are left with declining industries and unemployment: this is because resources are not perfectly mobile — shipbuilders and miners cannot instantly switch to take up newly demanded occupations.

SAQ 2:   Because they have specialised in what they do best: they are no longer wasting productive resources on the output of commodities they don't make very well.

SAQ 3:   (a)   Britain produces 50 lengths of cloth and 25 barrels of wine.
                 Portugal produces 25 lengths of cloth and 100 barrels of wine.

    (b)   Britain would produce 100 lengths of cloth and no wine.

            Portugal would produce no cloth and 200 barrels of wine.

    (c)   So, after trade, Britain has 100 lengths of cloth and 30 barrels of wine and Portugal has 30 lengths of cloth and 170 barrels of wine.

SAQ 4:   Country A would end up with 550 tons of rice and 100 tons of wheat. Country B would get 450 tons of rice and 900 tons of wheat. Country A has still benefited from trade — it is, for example, 50 tons of rice better off than in the example of self-sufficiency. However, the gain from trade has been dramatically reduced from example (4) on p. 16.

SAQ 5:   Opportunity cost.

SAQ 6:   Country B would have (after trade) 520 tons of wheat and 100 tons of rice — again, a very modest improvement over the self-sufficient position in (2) on p. 16.

SAQ 7:   (a)   Britain will not exchange if it has to give two bolts of cloth for one barrel of wine, for this is the opportunity cost of production in Britain: after all, we could get one barrel of wine in the UK by giving up two lengths of cloth.

    (b)   4 barrels per length of cloth — for at this cost they can produce the cloth themselves at less cost than importing from Britain.

SAQ 8:   (a) If our prices rise to a level where they are uncompetitive: if exports are too expensive, then they will not sell and therefore we shall not be able to earn to buy any imports! (b) (i) 100 (ii) 200 (iii) 83.3 (iv) 110 (v) 125 (vi) 75. (c) They worsen in (iii) and (vi) — wherever export prices fall below import prices and therefore the index goes below 100. The UK standard of living is adversely affected by this — see discussion in text. (d) (i) That raw materials and tropical products rose in price less than oil and manufactures. (ii) Other things being equal, this would worsen third-world living standards: a Jamaican Trade Minister remarked that, whereas they could once buy an Austin car for 3 tons of bananas, it nowadays took 11 tons.

SAQ 9:   Economies of scale — covered in Unit 14 on Big Business. The sources of scale economies are technical, financial, managerial, marketing and risk-bearing (remember?).

SAQ 10:   There are many: cars, chemicals, steel, pharmaceuticals, etc.

SAQ 11:   That labour and capital cannot be switched easily from one use (say, woollen textiles) to a new one (say, microelectronics).

SAQ 12:   The opportunity cost in case (a) is the output that would be added by that worker in the alternative job; in case (b) the opportunity cost is nil — we are not sacrificing anything by keeping her in her job. Complications to this view include the fact that it may cost the government something in subsidies (or the community something in tariffs) to keep the industry open; on the other hand, it would cost the community a lot to keep her unemployed.

SAQ 13:   The price elasticity of demand. A high degree of price elasticity will cause a tariff to reduce demand substantially, as consumers are deterred by the higher price. If the product has a low price elasticity of demand, consumers will keep on buying even though the price has risen.

SAQ 14:   Higher, progressive.

SAQ 15:   (a)   The main advantage of quotas is their certainty in impact — they allow the government to specify just how much of a product comes in. Without perfect information on demand elasticities, that isn't possible with tariffs. On the other hand, tariffs raise money for the government.

    (b)   The advantage of the EEC system is that it reduces the subsidy that tax-payers have to pay: the lower taxation that follows may create incentive effects. The disadvantages are (i) that we no longer know the full cost of the policy to consumers (ii) that the policy will be regressive, as taxpayers in effect get the money raised by higher food prices. Note that *both* policies may be criticised for interfering with international specialisation, although the tariff policy is more likely to create unsold surpluses as, with subsidies, consumers are encouraged to increase purchases.

21 Britain's trade and payments

AIMS OF UNIT 21

This unit moves on from the theory of international trade you met in Unit 20, and introduces you to Britain's trade — what we trade in, who we trade with, and how we measure our international payments. At the end of this unit, you should be able to:

- give an account of the pattern of UK exports and imports, both in terms of the commodities traded and the countries we trade with
- describe the changing trends in Britain's trade
- explain the reasons for the increasing share of manufactures in the UK import bill
- define the balance of trade
- explain what is meant by invisible trade, and account for the importance of invisibles to the UK balance of payments
- calculate the current balance from data on visible and invisible trade
- explain what is meant by the 'investment and other capital flows' on a balance of payments account
- define the balancing item, and use it in the calculation of a set of balance of payments accounts
- recognise and explain a set of balance of payments accounts, drawing attention to the balance for official financing and explaining its significance
- show how a balance of payments surplus or deficit is financed.

HOW IMPORTANT IS TRADE TO BRITAIN?

We have seen in the previous unit that it makes sense for all countries to engage in foreign trade. This not only allows us to enjoy a greater variety of goods, but will also ensure higher living standards because countries specialise in the products for which they enjoy the greatest comparative advantage, and exchange their surpluses.

International trade is important to Britain: with just one per cent of the world's population, the UK is a major trading nation. The British economy is strongly influenced by developments in international trade. One way to measure the importance of international trade to a country is to see what proportion foreign goods form of all the commodities traded in that country. In the UK, nearly 30 per cent of our national product is exported, making it a very 'open' economy.

315

SAQ 1: *The 'openness' of economies varies enormously from one country to another. Some countries are totally dependent on foreign trade: Malta exports more than 80 per cent of her national income, Belgium 46 per cent, Holland 55 per cent. Yet other countries trade proportionately less – for the USA, the USSR and India, the figure is less than ten per cent.*

(a)   Can you account for these differences from what you know of the nations mentioned?

(b)   Can you explain why, despite these figures, the US market is more important to the UK than Malta's?

(c)   The text says that 'the British economy is strongly influenced by developments in international trade'. Recalling what you learned of the effects of withdrawals and injections in Unit 5, explain the effects that foreign trade has upon employment.

THE COMMODITY STRUCTURE OF UK TRADE

What goods, then, do we trade in? Britain was traditionally regarded as the manufacturing centre of an Empire that supplied it with raw materials, food and fuel. In our days as 'workshop of the world' we would import wool and export clothes; import iron ore and export machinery; import rubber and export tyres. However, this picture has changed greatly in the past twenty years, and a more correct view would now be that our imports as well as our exports are predominantly finished or semi-finished manufactures.

Britain's exports

Here is the composition of our exports in 1986 (in percentages).

Food, beverages and tobacco	7.4
Basic materials	2.8
Oil	11.3
Other mineral fuels and lubricants	0.6
Semi-manufactures	28.8
Finished manufactures	46.0
Unclassified	3.0

This year is typical of UK exports: the only change in the picture has been the growing importance of North Sea oil exports since the mid-Seventies. Within the category of 'manufactures', UK textile exports have slumped.

Imports

As regards our imports, though, there has been a dramatic change in the postwar period. The traditional view I outlined above no longer holds, as you can see from these figures:

Commodity composition of UK imports, 1955–82 (percentages)

	1955	1965	1975	1986
Food, beverages and tobacco	36.2	29.7	17.7	11.3
Fuel	10.4	10.6	17.7	7.4
Industrial materials and semi-manufactures	47.9	43.0	34.1	32.0
Finished manufactures	5.2	15.3	28.3	47.3
Others	0.3	1.4	2.2	2.0

The most remarkable feature here is the growth in our imports of finished manufactures from 5 per cent of our import bill in 1955 to over 47 per cent in 1986; you may wish to bring this unit up-to-date by a look at the latest figures if your local library or college stocks the *Pink Book* of trade statistics. Semi-manufactures and finished manufactures now account for over-three-quarters of our total import bill. Economists have been able to account for this trend in the following ways:

(a)   Food, beverages and tobacco have a low income elasticity of demand.

SAQ 2: *Define income elasticity of demand. What is meant by an income elasticticity of demand of less than one? Why do you think that food, beverages and tobacco have a low income elasticity of demand?*

Rising living standards will therefore cause us to buy many more manufactured goods from abroad, but not much more food.

(b)   Trade liberalisation has occurred throughout the period, reducing tariffs, quotas and other barriers to trade. UK import duties are now less than half what they were in the mid-fifties.

(c)   Countries that have in the past supplied raw materials and ores to the UK now prefer to refine and process these materials themselves. The main reason for this preference is that primary industry (extracting minerals, growing crops) is much less lucrative than secondary industry.

(d)   There has been a decline in raw material imports due to both greater substitution (plastic and nylon instead of jute and sisal, for example) and to greater economy in the use of raw materials. Today's fridge or car uses much less metal than its fifties equivalent.

(e)   The use of import duties and subsidies as part of the EEC's agricultural policy has encouraged greater food production in Britain.

SAQ 3: *In the light of what you learned in the last unit, is this a good thing?*

(f)   International specialisation has proceeded apace in a number of manufactured products. Most of Europe's refrigerators, for example, come from Italy. Even within a given industry, such as aircraft or cars, individual components may be mass-produced in one country and exported to another for assembly.

(g)   After giving due weight to all these factors (which have caused the share of manufactures as a proportion of all imports to rise in a number of countries), the suspicion must remain that one of the reasons for increased import penetration must be the uncompetitive nature of UK manufacturing industry. Such suspicions gain credibility from (i) the persistent problems we had throughout the 50s, 60s and 70s in earning enough abroad to pay for our imports (ii) slower economic growth and lower investment.

SAQ 4:   *What is meant by 'economic growth'? What is meant by the term 'investment' here? What relationship is there between investment and economic growth?*

(iii) the decline in the UK's share of world trade in manufactures – 20 per cent in 1954, 9 per cent today. (N.B. Some economists feel the 1954 figure was artificially high.)

SAQ 5: *Why might the 1954 figure be so high?*

Point (g) is particularly troubling, as manufactured goods will surely be an area of the economy in which we should enjoy the greatest comparative advantage. If we are unable to compete there, what hope is there for employment and living standards in the UK?

How should we specialise?
One explanation for the failures of UK export performance concentrates attention on the type of products that the UK exports, and argues that we have stayed too long in old, basic industries rather than putting the emphasis on the advanced technical commodities that yield the best results. (There is a strong relationship between industries that undertake a lot of research, and industries which do well in export markets.) According to this argument, the UK's comparative advantage will not be in specific industries, because as technologies change, so does the pattern of comparative advantage. Remember that the 'law' of comparative costs depends on a comparison of one country's costs with another's – and so, as other countries catch up and learn how to do what was once Britain's speciality, we shall lose our comparative advantage and have to move onto new products. It is argued that all technologies start off being advanced and difficult – even the steam engine – and eventually become known and easy. When this happens, low-wage countries will enjoy an advantage in being able to underprice the UK and other advanced countries.

SAQ 6: *(a) Look at these industries. Which of them do you think are older technologies that are attracted to low-wage countries? Which of them are at present in advanced countries but will shortly transfer to less developed nations? Which are so advanced that they are likely to stay in advanced nations in the foreseeable future?*

Car making	Cotton textiles	Nuclear engineering
Shipbuilding	Computer design	Petrochemicals
Steel	Aircraft manufacture	Railways

(b) What type of unemployment will be caused by the decline of ageing industries, and how might government reduce such unemployment?

What else can explain our problem?

It may now be a good idea to review the elementary explanation of the UK's economic problems that you met in Unit 2. In addition, I'd like to mention one of the other factors that is brought into discussion – poor marketing. For a number of years, economists tried to explain the poor performance of UK exports by reference to high prices, caused by UK costs rising faster than those of foreign competitors. However, the UK's performance worsened even in those periods of time when its prices moved favourably in relation to those of its competitors. As a result, concern is now expressed about such non-price factors as:

- delivery delays
- quality control
- export marketing
- after-sales service
- ability to meet technical specifications
- adapting the product to local conditions.

THE AREA STRUCTURE OF UK TRADE

Changes in the sort of goods we have been importing and exporting have been reflected in changes in our trading relations with other countries. In particular, other developed countries are now by far our most important trading partners. Underdeveloped countries took nearly a third of all our exports in 1955 – now, less than one eighth. By contrast our trade with Western Europe has gone up from 25 per cent in 1955 to over 57 per cent today. Typical of this trend has been the increased importance of the EC, which provided 12 per cent of our imports in 1955, but accounted for over 50 per cent in 1986. Our trade with North America and the 'developed sterling area' (i.e. the white Commonwealth) has become less important as a result. These changes in economic relations have been reflected in political relations – a turning away from the Commonwealth and towards Europe.

Another new factor is the increased importance of the oil-producing nations for our traders. While the import bill for oil shot up following the mid-seventies 'oil shock', the increased earnings of the oil-exporters created new markets. In the late 70s, exports to oil-exporting countries were expanding at more than 20 per cent per year.

The much-publicised growth of Japan is less striking: from less than one per cent of our imports in 1955 to just over 3 per cent today. The impact of this comparatively small proportion is, however, exaggerated by the way it falls on a narrow range of commodities, particularly electrical goods and automobiles.

HOW DO WE MEASURE OVERSEAS TRADE?

Exporters and importers have to make returns to the Customs and Excise, and from the information gathered we compile our overseas trade statistics. However, the figures thus obtained are deceptive, for whilst exports would be valued as they went on to the ships or aircraft carrying them away (that is, without any allowance for transport and insurance costs), imports would include payment for credit, insurance and freight (prices c.i.f., we say). Adjustments are made to the import and export returns so that they are comparable, by valuing both on an 'f.o.b.' ('free on board') basis.

SAQ 7: *Which of the following adjustments have to be made to the export and import statistics to make them comparable?*
(a) allowance for insurance charges during transit;   (b) allowance for packaging and freight costs;
(c) allowance for goods sent back as faulty.

On this adjusted basis, we exported £73 099m of goods in 1986, and bought £86 066m of imports. Note that we have measured our trade in £s. This might be deceptive, for trade in fact goes on in barrels of oil, tonnes of steel and litres of wine. Measuring trade with the money yardstick enables us to reduce all the commodities to one valuation. However, it does make it difficult to distinguish between changes in the amount of goods traded and changes in the price they fetched. Changes in the actual amount traded are referred to as 'volume' changes, whereas a change caused by higher or lower prices is called a 'value' change.

SAQ 8: *Suppose that we increase our volume of exports by 25 per cent, but find that our export earnings have risen by only 20 per cent.*
(a)   What could explain this; (b) Assuming import prices have remained stable, what has happened to the terms of trade? (c) What effect will this have on UK living standards?

The balance of trade

Let's return to the trade figures. In 1982, we exported rather more than we imported. The home market was depressed, with unemployment reducing consumer spending: and, importantly, on the credit side, North Sea oil was selling in increasing amounts. The result was a positive trade balance — a *trade surplus*, as it is called.

UK visible trade, 1982 (£m)

Exports	55 565
Imports	53 234
Trade surplus	2 331

It is, of course, possible that a country can import more goods than it exports, as happened in the UK in 1983.

UK visible trade, 1986 (£m)

Exports	72 843
Imports	81 306
Trade deficit	8 463

So when the trade balance is negative, it is called a deficit; when positive, economists speak of a surplus.

SAQ 9: *What is the balance of trade in these circumstances?*
(a)   Visible exports 3400, visible imports 3600
(b)   Visible exports 3000, visible imports 2600
(c)   Visible exports 4500, visible imports 4500
(d)   Here are some statistics that show UK visible trade. Work out the trade balance for all of them, and state the years in which we earned a surplus.

	1981	1983	1985
Visible exports (£m)	50 977	60 776	78 111
Visible imports (£m)	47 617	61 611	80 289

So the difference between the goods we buy from abroad and the ones we sell to foreign customers is known as the visible trade balance, or often simply the *balance of trade*. It is this calculation that appears in news reports of the monthly 'trade figures'. Until North Sea oil started to be delivered, Britain was nearly always in deficit on visible trade. Indeed, in only three years between the end of the war and 1980 was there a visible trade surplus.

INVISIBLES

Stated like that, it sounds as if Britain has been sinking deeper and deeper into debt in its recent history. However, we must remember that we do not just trade in goods. Services like tourism, travel, insurance and banking are bought and sold internationally; UK residents receive interest and profits from their overseas investments; and people and governments transfer money to and from the country for various reasons. These transactions are all recorded in the 'invisibles' section of the balance of payments accounts: let's look at them one by one.

Services

A good idea of the contribution made by the services we sell abroad can be obtained from the table below:

Services account, 1986 (£b)		(details may not add up to totals because of rounding)	
	Credits	*Debits*	*Balance*
Government	0.5	1.9	−1.4
Sea transport	3.3	4.3	−1.0
Civil aviation	2.9	3.4	−0.5
Travel	5.4	6.1	−0.7
Finance and other services	12.8	4.4	8.4
Total	24.9	20.1	4.8

Sea transport is one of the largest single items — not surprisingly for an island nation like ours, though remember it also includes some earnings from British shipping carrying goods between third countries. Sea transport results in a slight deficit on the balance of payments, as does air transport. Travel is a term that covers spending by UK residents when abroad, and by overseas residents in the UK. This isn't just holiday spending, of course — a good half of our receipts come from business spending by foreigners in the UK. Financial services are a regular contributor to our invisible surplus: this includes the overseas earnings of the insurance companies, banks, commodity traders and brokers. Other services include royalties on works of art, inventions, TV and film programmes, earnings from construction work abroad, commission and consultancy fees. Government appears here because government services abroad (like embassies and armed forces) entail us spending money abroad, whilst foreign governments' expenditure here earns us money. So, in summary, the services section of our invisible account earns us a handsome surplus (nearly £5 billion in 1986, for example).

SAQ 10:   *The French government placed restrictions on the amount of money their holidaymakers could take abroad in 1983: explain which part of the UK balance of payments would be affected by this move, and what the effect would be.*

Interest, profit and dividends (IPD)

Britain has built up very large holdings of property abroad — and as a result earns a correspondingly large sum each year in profits, interest and dividends. The bulk of these earnings comes from the overseas branches and subsidiaries of British companies: additionally, a certain amount of earnings comes from 'portfolio investment' — that is, UK residents' ownership of the shares and bonds of foreign companies and governments. These earnings increase UK national income.

SAQ 11:   *How is property income from abroad treated in the national income calculations? Check back to Unit 3 if you can't remember.*

Earnings from interest, profits and dividends vary sharply from year to year, being particularly vulnerable to changes in the exchange rate. However, the trend of the net balance is downwards, reflecting the investments of overseas oil companies in the 70s and 80s being repaid in North Sea oil profits.

Transfers

By contrast, transfer have always been negative — that is, governments and individuals have always tended to transfer more money out of the country than foreigners and their governments have sent to us. Transfers can cover a variety of things — private gifts and transfers to dependants abroad, charities with overseas activities, government subscriptions to, and receipts from, the EC. In 1986, transfers caused over a £2 billion deficit to be added to our invisible account: approximately £700 million of this came from our European Community obligations.

The invisible balance

When added together, the balances from services, IPD and transfers form our invisible balance. Let's look at the 1986 figures together:

UK invisibles balance	(£m)
Services	+ 4 990
IPD	+ 4 686
Transfers	− 2 193
Total	+ 7 483

SAQ 12: *Here is a list of some transactions recorded in the UK balance of payments accounts. Beneath the list is a box showing various categories on the visible and invisible accounts. Write the appropriate letter in the right box — I've started you off with (a).*

(a)   Talbot cars sold in kit-form to Iran
(b)   the dividend to US shareholders in Ford UK
(c)   the England football team's expenses on a European tour
(d)   the salary of the UK ambassador in Paris
(e)   Canadian wheat carried to the UK in British ships (2 entries, please!)
(f)   royalties on the performance of an American film in the UK
(g)   profits from the subsidiary of a UK company in Venezuela
(h)   subsidies to UK farmers paid by the EEC
(i)   British engineer working in the USA sending money to family in Bristol
(j)   Save The Children Fund sending money to Eritrea
(k)   spending by USAF personnel in the UK
(l)   brokerage fees paid to a British agency by a Kenyan customer
(m)   greater profits for Brooke Bond on their Sri Lankan tea plantations

	Credit	Debit
Visible trade	(a)	
Invisible trade		
Services	....	
Interests, Profits and Dividends	....	
Transfers	....	

One fact stands out on the invisible trade figures — that the large surplus earned by private sector services is compensated for by a large deficit on government services and transfers. General government transactions in 1986 were over £3 billion in deficit.

The importance of invisible trade

As we have seen, Britain has only rarely been able to pay its way on visible trade alone. Throughout the last century, we have relied on an invisible surplus to pay for the goods we wish to import: nearly £1 in every £3 we earn abroad has come from invisibles. The traditional picture of the UK balance of payments has been a trade deficit, paid for by an invisible surplus.

However, like so much else, the picture is changing. In recent years we have begun to earn a trade surplus from our oil; yet that very development has obliged us to pay more out to overseas investors. EEC payments have also reduced our invisible balance. As a result, we can no longer rely on a massive invisible surplus to support our Balance of Payments.

THE CURRENT BALANCE

If we add together the visible balance and the invisible balance, we come to our current balance — an indication of whether we are earning enough to pay for the goods and services we wish to import. Let's take an example to illustrate this:

UK Current balance, 1986	(£m)
Visible exports	72 843
Visible imports	81 306
Balance of trade	−8 463
Invisible credits	76 202
Invisible debits	68 719
Invisible balance	+7 483
Current balance (i.e. visible balance + invisible balance)	−980

So in 1986, the large invisible surplus was not sufficient to pay for the £8 463m deficit on visible trade.

SAQ 13: *What is the current balance in these circumstances?*
(a)   Visible trade +30, invisible trade +80
(b)   Balance of trade +40, invisible balance +200
(c)   Balance of trade −70, invisible balance +100
(d)   Visible exports 2000, visible imports 3000, invisible balance +600
(e)   Visible imports 4000, invisible imports 2000
*   visible exports 4500, invisible exports 1500*

Now look at these figures from a recent year, and work out:
(f)   the balance of trade (i.e. the visible balance)
(g)   the invisible balance
(h)   the current balance.

	(£m)
Exports	78 111
Imports	80 289
Services balance	5 381
IPD balance	2 992
Transfers balance	−3 276

We haven't yet finished with the UK balance of payments accounts. Remember those profits, interest and dividends? To earn them, we must have made an investment abroad at some time in the past, paying for our acquisition of shares, property or companies with a matching outflow of funds. Similarly, when overseas residents wish to buy UK assets, there must be an inflow of funds. These movements of money are not for trade in goods and services, but are known as capital movements. We have not yet put these transfers of money into out balance of payments accounts, and we will now repair that omission.

THE CAPITAL ACCOUNT

If the current balance records money changing hands in exchange for goods and services, the capital account shows money being exchanged for assets — buying and selling firms, factories, shares and bonds, deposits in bank accounts. There are a number of ways that can be used to categorise capital flows.

Long-term v. short-term   Some capital flows have a very long 'time horizon': investment in a new car plant, for example, may not be expected to pay off for five or more years. On the other hand, there are some very short-term funds that flow swiftly from country to country, seeking the highest return in interest rates or currency appreciation. Such funds are sometimes called 'hot money' and cause enormous problems of control to governments trying to maintain a stable currency.

Public v. private   Alternatively, one can divide capital flows into those that come from government actions (like long-term overseas aid, or nationalised industry borrowing abroad), and those that arise from the private sector.

The official balance of payments figures analyse capital flows into many categories to get a clearer idea of what is happening. The investment and capital flows that make up the capital account make interesting reading for those concerned with the lack of investment in the UK:

Total investment and other capital transactions, 1983–86(£m)

1983	–4 742
1984	–6 916
1985	–7 421
1986	–10 747

(+ indicates an inflow of money to the UK; – shows an outflow)   (Source: CSO)

If we add the current balance to the capital account, we should arrive at a total that indicates how much the country has gained or lost in its transactions with foreign countries in a given year. However, accurate records of the gains or losses of foreign currency by the UK are kept by the Bank of England, and the figures of exports and imports kept by the government never seem to come to the same total as the record of our foreign currency holdings. It is inevitable that errors and omissions occur in any set of accounts, and the main source of the problem in the UK balance of payments is that payment for goods and services is often made at a different time from delivery of the commodities. The *balancing item* allows for such errors, and can be either positive (indicating that the UK received greater amounts of foreign currency than the figures at first showed) or negative (indicating a larger outflow of funds than the trade, invisible and capital figures give evidence for). The balancing item can reach quite enormous sizes — in 1986, for example, this record of unaccounted transactions reached –£11 727m!

THE BALANCE FOR OFFICIAL FINANCING

When we add together the current balance, plus the capital transactions, plus the balancing item, we come to the total flow of currency that has occurred as a result of our transactions with the rest of the world. This 'total currency flow' (TCF) can be either positive or negative.

SAQ 14: *Work out the answers to the following questions.*
(a)   The current balance is +100, the capital balance is +100, and the balancing item is +40. What is the TCF?
(b)   The capital balance is –50, the current balance is +50, and the balancing item is zero. What is the TCF?
(c)   The current balance is –300, investment and capital flows +100, the TCF is –250. What is the balancing item?
(d)   The current balance is +250, the balancing item is +50, and the TCF is +100. What is the value of investment and capital flows?
(e)   In which of the above examples do British residents acquire assets overseas. (Clue: in which of them are we paying capital sums to foreigners?)

When the TCF is positive, we can add to our reserves of foreign currency or repay debts to overseas residents or governments. If, on the other hand, it is negative (when, to use a common phrase, we have a 'balance of payments deficit') we must either use up our reserves to pay for our spending, or borrow the difference. The TCF must be financed somehow — the balance of payments always balances — and so the present term used to describe the total sum left after we have counted the visible balance, the invisible balance, the capital and investment flows and the balancing item is the *balance for official financing*. Let's take the figures from a past year to help our understanding.

UK balance of payments, 1980 (£m)

Visible trade	+1 233
Invisibles (balance)	+1 702
Current balance	2 935
Investment and other capital transactions	–1 593
Balancing item	+ 30
Balance for official financing	1 372
Financed as follows:	
Added to reserves	291
Repayments of debt	1 081

(adapted from *Economic Trends*)

So, to talk you through this table: the surplus in 1980 came from the usual invisibles surplus added to a newly acquired surplus on visibles. As a result, even a billion pound outflow of capital left the government with funds to add to reserves and money to repay overseas creditors.

SAQ 15: *Now write a brief paragraph explaining the following balance of payments table from 1976, a year when the overseas transactions were rather different:*

UK balance of payments, 1976 (£m)

Visible trade	*-3571*
Invisible trade	*+2344*
Current balance	*-1227*
Investment and other capital flows	*-2819*
Balancing item	*+ 418*
Balancing for official financing	*-3628*
Financed as follows:	
Borrowing from IMF	*1018*
Other borrowing	*1825*
Drawing on reserves	*853*

SUMMARY

You may have found the second half of this unit rather arid, dealing as it did with ways of reading official statistics. In fact, though, many of today's controversies are hidden within the balance of payments figures. Let's pick just two:

Should we control capital movements? You'll remember from Unit 2 that one of the major problems with the UK economy has been lack of investment to modernise industry: indeed, some commentators feel that this has been crucial in our disappointing performance in relation to our competitors. Does it make much sense to send large amounts of investment funds abroad to build up other country's industries – as much as £7 billion in 1981?

How will we best use our North Sea oil revenues? You'll have noticed in this unit how North Sea oil developments have transformed the UK balance of payments in the recent past. Yet this asset will not remain with us forever – what is the best way to use its earnings to safeguard our future? Some say that a good way would be to take the money earned from oil and invest it abroad – ensuring a steady flow of invisible earnings throughout future years. Others want to use the money in the UK to build up and modernise industry so that we can compete effectively when onve again we have to pay our way with services and manufactures.

One last note. There are constant revisions of the balance of payments. Firstly, the actual numbers themselves are changed as better information about our overseas transactions comes in. Secondly, there are often minor changes in the presentation of the figures: the 'bottom line' figure from the tables has been called the 'basic balance' and the 'total currency flow' and the 'balance for official financing' in the recent past. Don't worry: a sound understanding of current account (visible and invisible), capital account and how it is financed will see you through these revisions.

Footnote for cynics
If you add together all the balance of payments tables of the whole world, there is a substantial deficit. This doesn't make sense (unless someone's trading with Mars) but has yet to be explained: one guess might mention the fact that internationally, as well as nationally, there is a 'black economy' (*see* Unit 3, p. 46).

REVIEW SECTION

Further reading
The most up-to-date figures will be contained in the balance of payments figures published each year as the *Pink Book*.

SAQ 16: *What is the* Blue Book?

On the thorny topic of Britain's trade performance, journals and magazines might very well be more up-to-date than textbooks. Look, for example, at *Economic Review*, March 1984, 'Patterns of International Trade 1950-80' by Alan Winters, *Barclays Bank Review*, August 1982 ('The Changing Structure of UK Balance of Payments') and the *Economist*. The government publish *Economic Progress Report* monthly (available free from Publications Division, COI, Hercules Road, London SE1 7DU) which has up-to-date figures and articles on UK trade, employment, government spending and investment. Cobham *The Economics of International Trade* and Prest *The UK Economy* (get the latest edition) are useful. See if you can get hold of *The Guardian Guide to the Economy* by Cairncross and Keeley (Methuen) and *A Question of Economics* by Peter Donaldson (Penguin), for its chapter on 'De-industrialisation: have the jobs gone forever?', which deals with Britain's declining manufacturing base.

Examination questions

1.   What have been the reasons for the fluctuations in the Balance of Payments on current account in the past decade?

(Oxford and Cambridge 'A' 1984)

United Kingdom Balance of Payments

(figures in £ million)

	1973	1977	1978	1983
Exports (f.o.b)	11 937	31 728	35 063	60 625
(of which: oil exports)	(344)	(1 979)	(2 235)	(12 525)
Interest, Profits and Dividends (net)	1 257	97	623	1 948
Government Expenditure (net)	−409	−699	−732	−832
Total Investment and Other Capital Transactions (net)	178	4 169	−4 264	−3 648
Imports (f.o.b.)	−14 523	−34 012	−36 605	−61 341
(of which: oil imports)	(−1 285)	(−4 750)	(−4 219)	(−5 650)
Balancing Item	+30	+3 139	+1 976	−84
Foreign Currency Borrowing	999	2 227	−1 203	213
Financial Services (net)	601	1 409	1 575	2 745
Official Reserves (changes in)	−228	−9 588	2 329	603
Travel (net)	31	1 166	958	−399
Other Services (net)	563	1 480	2 057	2 388
Transfers (net)	−436	−1 116	−1 777	−2 218

(Adapted from: *United Kingdom Balance of Payments*, C.S.O., 1984.)

(a)   Can one infer from the above statistics that the United Kingdom exported approximately five times more goods in 1983 than in 1973? Explain your answer.

(2 marks)

(b)   Tabulate and calculate:
(i)   the Balance of Payments on current account for 1983;

(2 marks)

(ii)   the Balance for Total Official Financing for 1983.

(2 marks)

(c)   Examine the factors that might account for the changes in *three* of the following over the period 1973–1983:

(i)   Official Reserves (changes in);
(ii)   Travel (net);
(iii)   Total Investment and Other Transactions (net);
(iv)   Interest, Profits and Dividends (net).

(3 x 2 marks)

(d)   In the light of the data in the table, would you consider the U.K. Balance of Payments in 1983 to have been satisfactory? Give reasons for your answer.

(8 marks)

(London 'A' June 1986)

Your understanding of the workings of the figures within the balance of payments accounts will be tested in multiple-choice items rather than essays. You may, though, be interested in the following 'O' level questions.

3.   Read the tables below and then answer the following questions.

United Kingdom Tourist Expenditure. £ Billion at 1979 Prices

	1972	1974	1976	1978	1980
Expenditure by United Kingdom residents abroad	1.6	1.5	1.2	1.6	2.4
Expenditure by foreigners in the United Kingdom	1.6	1.9	2.7	3.0	2.6
Expenditure by United Kingdom residents in the United Kingdom	3.9	2.8	3.7	3.7	3.8

	1972	1974	1976	1978	1980
Average exchange rate of £ sterling	$2.40	$2.35	$2.00	$1.95	$2.30

Source: Lloyds Bank Economic Bulletin

(a)   Clearly showing your workings, calculate the net earnings of tourism on the invisible account in 1976.

(b)   Name the year and the amount when the total receipts of the United Kingdom tourist industry were greatest.

(c)   Describe the relationship between the exchange rate of sterling and the pattern of tourist expenditure.

(d)   What factors would promote an increase in foreign travel by United Kingdom residents?

or

Discuss the likely effect on the UK balance of payments of:

(a)   a decision to equip the Army with American tanks

(b)   a successful tourist promotion campaign in America entitled 'Visit Britain Now'

(c)   a complete stoppage of work by French dockers for 2 months

(d)   a refusal by Middle East states to allow UK banks to continue operations in their territories.

ANSWERS TO SAQs

SAQ 1:   (a)   Large, self-sufficient countries do not need to undertake international trade to gain the commodities they need, whereas small countries need to trade, not just to obtain commodities that cannot be produced internally but also to obtain the benefits of scale economies (see previous unit).

(b)   Because ten per cent of the vast US GNP is much more lucrative than 80 per cent of Malta's tiny market.

(c)   Increased imports cause an increase in withdrawals, raising unemployment: a rise in exports will raise the injections, increasing national income and jobs.

SAQ 2:   The responsiveness of demand for a good to changes in a buyer's income: it is measured as

$$\frac{\%\text{age change in quantity demanded}}{\%\text{ change in income}}$$

When income elasticity of demand is less than one, then expenditure on the good concerned rises by a smaller percentage than the rise in income. Food, beverages and tobacco have low income elasticities as increases in income will tend to be spent on 'luxury goods' rather than necessities. We would not double our bread consumption if our income doubled.

SAQ 3:   Not necessarily, if the import duties prevented countries that enjoyed a comparative advantage in the production of a product (say, butter) being able to sell it. See discussion later in this volume on EEC policy.

SAQ 4:   Economic growth refers to the increased productive potential of the economy caused by increases in the size and efficiency of the factors of production — it's crudely measured by increase in GNP. Investment in this context means new productive tools and machinery — computers, machine tools, factories, etc. Unit 2 showed a strong relation between investment rates and economic growth. Countries with high rates of investment appear to grow quicker.

SAQ 5:   Because some of our major competitors — Germany and Japan, France and Italy, etc. were still recovering from the war.

SAQ 6:   (a) This is a matter of judgement. My own idea would be that cotton textiles are already in low-wage countries; steel, shipbuilding and railway engineering are on their way; carmaking is showing signs of going (with Korean plants now outperforming Japanese ones). Petrochemicals are also becoming common in low-wage countries. In principle, there's no reason why any of the rest shouldn't go eventually, though the prospect is reasonably long-term in some cases. (b) Structural unemployment — best remedied by retraining programmes and (if necessary) regional policies.

SAQ 7:   All of them.

SAQ 8:   (a) A fall in the prices we are getting for our exports. (b) They have fallen (see previous unit). (c) Other things being equal, it will reduce them — but hold on until you've read the passage on the 'right' exchange rate in the next unit before finally condemning low export prices.

SAQ 9:   (a) −200; (b) +400; (c) balance of zero; (d) 1981 comes to +3 360, 1983 to −835 and 1985 −2 178. So there was a surplus in 1981 and a deficit in 1983 and 1985.

SAQ 10:   It would reduce our earnings under the 'travel' section of the invisibles account.

SAQ 11:   It is added on to the GDP calculations to reach the GNP figure.

SAQ 12:   Visible trade: credit (a); deficit (e); Invisibles: services, credits (e), (k), (l); debits (c), (d), (f); IPD credits (g), (m); debits (b); Transfers credits (h), (i); debits (j).

SAQ 13:   (a) +110; (b) +240; (c) +30; (d) −400; (e) 0; (f) −2 178; (g) 5 097; (h) 2 919.

SAQ 14:   (a) +240; (b) zero; (c) −50; (d) −200; (e): (b) and (d) — whenever capital flows are negative.

SAQ 15:   The deficit in 1976 came from a large visible trade deficit and a large outflow of capital, so substantial that even generous invisible earnings were unable to compensate. The £3.6b deficit was financed by borrowing from the IMF and elsewhere, and to a lesser extent by drawing on our reserves of foreign currency built up over previous years.

SAQ 16:   The book of National Income and Expenditure.

22 How to deal with a payments problem

AIMS OF UNIT 22

At the end of this unit you should be able to:

- define foreign exchange
- explain how international trade leads to the demand for and supply of foreign exchange
- list the ways in which foreign exchange markets resemble perfect markets
- define exchange rate, explain how it is measured, and show how its value is affected by the forces of supply and demand
- explain what is meant by a depreciation and appreciation of the exchange rate, and distinguish between a devaluation and a depreciation of the currency.
- show how the exchange rate of sterling is affected by the confidence of the international financial community
- explain what is meant by a 'purchasing power parity', and show why exchange rate values may differ from a purchasing power parity in the real world
- distinguish between fixed and floating exchange rate regimes, explaining how fixed exchange rates were maintained and why they collapsed
- show how changes in the exchange rate affect the balance of payments, drawing attention to problems of elasticities and time lags
- know and be able to apply the Marshall-Lerner criterion for a successful devaluation/depreciation
- explain the advantages of using exchange rate changes to remedy problems in foreign payments, and detail four major disadvantages of such an approach
- define deflation, explain how it works to cure a payments problem and identify the disadvantages of such a policy
- define and use the concept of the 'propensity to import'
- explain how direct controls may be used as part of a payments policy, outline and evaluate the objections to direct controls on international transactions.

INTRODUCTION

In our work on international trade so far, we have learned that countries trade with each other in order to obtain the higher living standards that can be achieved by international specialisation. The exchanges of goods, services and assets that take place between the UK and its trading partners are charted on the balance of payments accounts, which provide a record of the movements of money into and out of the country that result from these transactions. Specialisation and trade also occur between regions inside the UK: we have seen in our study of industrial location and regional policy that different parts of the country concentrate on producing different commodities. There are, however, a number of crucial differences between inter-regional trade and international trade — and the major one is that different currencies are involved. All international transactions (except a few inter-government deals that involve barter) involve a matching 'foreign exchange' transaction: **foreign exchange** is the term given to national currencies when they are used for international trade. Let's look at the way transactions involve foreign exchange with a simple example.

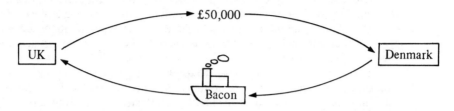

In this diagram, a UK foodstore is buying a shipment of bacon from a Danish farmer.* As far as the UK end is concerned, we receive £50 000 worth of food; to the Danish exporter, the transaction earns £50 000 in money. However, the Danish farmer wishes to use this remittance to meet payments that are due to Denmark — bills for animal feed, interest payments to the bank, wages, household expenses. He or she will therefore wish to be paid in kroner rather than in sterling. So when the payment is received, it will be taken to the bank and changed for kroner. As a result, an import from Denmark to the UK involves the sale of a certain amount of sterling and the purchase with it of a matching amount of foreign currency. The effect would be the same if the UK importers changed the money received for the bacon into kroner in the UK and paid the Danish producer in Danish currency.

Imports into the UK therefore involve the supply of sterling and the demand for a foreign currency, whereas exports from the UK involve foreigners demanding sterling in exchange for their own currencies.

SAQ 1: *To check your understanding of this principle, show the foreign currency sales and purchases that would be caused by:*
(a)   a UK clothing store chain buying US-made jeans
(b)   a UK wine shipper buying wine from Germany
(c)   a French company importing UK North Sea oil.

Demand and supply of sterling don't just originate from visible and invisible trade, of course. International transactions in capital assets will also lead to sales and purchases of foreign exchange. The demand and supply for foreign currencies for international transactions meet on the foreign exchange markets.

FOREIGN EXCHANGE MARKETS

The market for foreign exchange is worldwide. It consists of banks and dealers in all the world's major financial centres, buying and selling currencies via telephone or telex links. International trade, and the resulting need for foreign currency, is such an important feature of our modern way of life that the amount of foreign exchange business is vast. Hundreds of millions of pounds worth of foreign exchange are traded every day.

In many ways, the market for foreign exchange gets close to the textbook idea of a perfect market. There are many buyers and sellers, and few individual transactions are large enough to influence the market by themselves. Information is very nearly perfect — financial analysts watch movements and events in all the major economies, and money can swiftly be transferred when one currency offers greater interest rates or a likelihood of appreciation in value.

In such a market, price is determined by the forces of supply and demand. We have already seen where the supply of, and demand for, a currency originates — we demand a particular country's currency when we wish to buy the commodities it exports, or purchase assets in that country, and we offer in exchange (i.e. we supply) our own currency. But if we are clear what we mean by the supply and demand for a currency, how do we measure the price of a currency? By seeing how much of another currency we have to pay to obtain it. Economists have a term for the price a currency fetches in relation to another currency on the foreign exchange markets — they call it the exchange rate.

*For the sake of simplicity, we'll miss out the middlemen that would inevitably exist in the real world. It doesn't affect the illustration.

How do we measure the exchange rate?

It is common to express the exchange rate of sterling in terms of one other important currency, such as the US dollar. In this way, a deterioration in our exchange rate is shown by the fact that we can buy fewer US dollars with a given sum of sterling — as would happen when the exchange rate fell from £1 = $1.50 to £1 = $1.20, for example. Such a movement downwards is called a currency 'depreciation'. An appreciation would have occurred if we found ourselves able to buy more US dollars with a given sterling sum. Such a movement happened in the late 70s, when the £ recovered from £1 = $1.60 to over $2.00.

The danger of using just one other currency, however important, as a measuring rod is obvious. It might very well be that the currency chosen is itself moving against other currencies, distorting our view of the genuine sterling exchange rate. For example, if the £ and the $ were both falling against other currencies, the sterling exchange rate would appear stable when in fact it was depreciating, and we were able each year to buy fewer foreign goods with a given amount of sterling. That's why we have now moved to speaking of sterling's 'exchange rate index' (ERI); that is, its exchange rate in relation to a wide range of other currencies. To calculate this effective exchange rate, an index has to be constructed which reflects the importance of various currencies in world trade The dollar, for example, contributes just one-quarter to the index:

Currencies in sterling's trade-weighted index (as of January, 1981).

	% share
United States	24.6
West Germany	14.1
Japan	13.7
France	10.4
Italy	7.2
Holland	4.8
Ireland	4.1
Belgium	4.0
Sweden	3.7
Switzerland	3.0
Norway	2.1
Australia	2.0
Spain	1.9
Canada	1.5
Denmark	1.1
Austria	1.0
Finland	0.8

Source: Bank of England

The December 1975 value of sterling in relation to this index is taken as 100, and the present value compared with this. A movement above 100 would indicate that a given sum of sterling could buy more foreign currency than in that month: regrettably, this hasn't happened. By 1983, the effective sterling exchange rate was down to 83.3.

For simplicity of explanation, the rest of this unit takes a single currency exchange rate — often the $ — to indicate changes in the value of the £. Remember throughout, though, that other currencies besides sterling fluctuate in value, and so the true comparison is with the wider basket indicated by the sterling index.

SAQ 2: *Plot these supply and demand curves on the graph paper provided. They refer to the supply and demand for sterling on a particular day. Then answer these questions:*

(a)   What will be the equilibrium exchange rate on that day?
(b)   What will be the effect on the sterling exchange rate if bad economic news shifts the demand curve for sterling to the lower demand curve indicated by Qd_2?

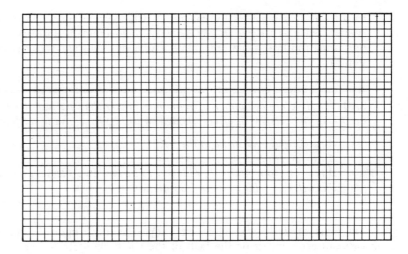

Price ($)	3	2.5	2.00	1.50
Qs	250	200	150	100
Qd_1	50	75	100	125
Qd_2	25	50	75	100

SAQ 3: *Look at these diagrams, which show demand and supply curves for sterling after a number of events, detailed below. SS and DD indicate the original curves, SS_1 and DD_1 indicate the new curves after the named event. See if you can match the event to the diagrams:*

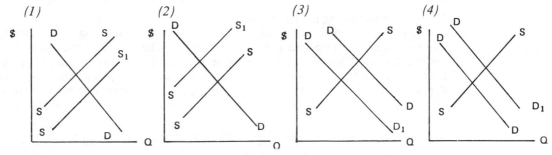

(a)   a rise in the value of the £ caused by increased demand for UK exports
(b)   a fall in that value caused by increased imports into the UK
(c)   the effects of government restrictions on holiday spending by Britons abroad.

SAQ 4: *This unit has so far referred to the value of the £ sterling in terms of its effective rate. What other meaning could be put to the term 'the value of £'?*

After those exercises, perhaps we need a summary to check how far we have come in this topic. The price of foreign exchange is determined, we've found, by supply and demand — forces that originate in international transactions like importing and exporting. We measure the value that is determined by these market forces by the currency's exchange rate against one other currency, or a basket of several other currencies. Changes in demand and supply will change the exchange rate of a currency.

It's important to grasp that foreign demand for a country's currency doesn't originate only from a desire to buy that country's exports. Individuals, banks, firms, even other governments are willing to hold stocks of foreign currency — for example sterling bank accounts — as a way of holding their wealth. In this way, foreign exchange is unlike other commodities whose value is determined by supply and demand. Once a supply of bacon is bought, it is consumed and disappears from the market: but when (for example) a foreigner buys sterling to hold as a store of wealth, that amount of money is not in any sense 'consumed'. It continues to exist, and may re-enter the market at any time, to be exchanged for another currency when the value of the £ sterling may be in doubt.

There are very substantial holdings of sterling by foreigners, and as a result changes in the sterling exchange rate may be caused by changes in the attitude of foreign holders of these sterling balances just as much as by changes in UK exports and imports. This explains why economic events – such as a strike in key industry, or government statistics showing money supply or inflation rising too fast – can precipitate a wave of selling and thus a sharp fall in the exchange rate of sterling.

SAQ 5: *Here are a number of economic events that are not strictly related to spending on UK exports or imports. What effect, though, will they have on the sterling exchange rate?*

(a)   A prolonged coal strike in the UK.
(b)   A new North Sea oil discovery.
(c)   A request from Arab oil producers to be paid in dollars rather than sterling as in the past.
(d)   Statistics showing a rise in US inflation.

The value of sterling, then, depends almost as much upon the confidence with which foreigners view our economy as on the facts of the UK trade performance. One complicating factor is that UK foreign exchange reserves are much less than foreigners' sterling balances, and so we cannot repay the sterling balance holders if they all demand other currencies at once. This has meant that the UK government has always been obliged to place a high – some would say too high – priority on maintaining the confidence of overseas sterling holders, perhaps at the expense of other desirable social and economic aims (like increased welfare spending, or faster economic growth). This is the origin of Harold Wilson's comment about the unfavourable influence of foreign financiers that he nicknamed 'the gnomes of Zurich'.

Sterling is not the only currency that suffers from uncertainty caused in this manner. The dollar, too, is widely held throughout the world, and the dollar balances that foreigners hold outside the USA have even got their own name – 'Eurodollars'. The large Eurodollar balances reflect not just past US balance of payments deficits: they also reflect the fact that foreigners have been willing to hold dollar balances rather than exchange their earnings into their own currencies.

What will determine the level of exchange rates?
Having seen the supply and demand factors that act upon our exchange rate, and mentioned the way that its value is measured against other currencies, let's ask the basic question – at what value will the £ settle? One answer to this question is to be found in the idea of 'purchasing power parity'. The word parity here means exchange rate, and so the idea of purchasing power parity (or PPP as we shall call it) is that exchange rates will tend towards a position where a given sum of money will buy the same amount of commodities, whatever the currency that amount of money is changed into.

Illustration: If £1 is equal to 2 US dollars, 4 deutschmarks or 10 French francs on the foreign exchanges, then, according to PPP ideas you would be able to buy an equivalent amount of commodities in the UK for £1000 as you can in the USA for $2000, or in Germany for DM4000 or in France for F10 000.

This seems to fit in with common sense. No currency, surely, can get too far out of line with living costs in its 'home country'. One might argue that if $2000 spent in the USA bought much more than £1000 spent in the UK, DM4000 spent in Germany or F10 000 spent in France, then US prices – and that includes export prices – would be so much lower than European ones that the US would enjoy a trade surplus, increasing the demand for dollars and the supply of European currencies so that £1, DM4 of F10 would come to equal (say) just $1.50.

However, if you travel abroad you may notice that there are some countries where we get much more, or much less, than the 'purchasing power parity' of our holiday £s. Why should this be?

Firstly, it may be that the average UK traveller doesn't experience the full range of prices when travelling abroad, and that this is causing us to get the wrong picture. For whilst most people will have bought a meal, a drink, or petrol when abroad, few will have bought consignments of chemicals, machine tools, or an insurance policy. Secondly, we must remember that many products are not traded internationally. For example, UK housing is, by international standards, good and cheap, and yet does not affect the exchange rate of the pound sterling. There is, as yet, no export trade in semi-detached houses. Thirdly, recall the passage we have just read in which it was pointed out that the value of currencies is determined not just by trade-related expenditure, but also by international capital movements. For example, London moved from being a cheap holiday spot for foreigners to a very expensive one when the exchange rate appreciated in the late 70s, an appreciation caused more by the prospect of tighter monetary policy and North Sea oil prospects than by any improvement in UK exports.

Finally, governments may intervene in foreign exchange markets to affect the exchange rate of their currencies. We will discuss this further in a moment.

SAQ 6: *(a) Explain what will happen to the sterling exchange rate under PPP, if the UK experiences a rate of inflation 5% higher than that of Germany.*
(b) Switzerland's stable government and sound monetary policies have attracted a considerable investment demand for Swiss francs. What effect will this have on the value of the Swiss franc? Will the Swiss franc have a purchasing power parity with other currencies? Will prices in Switzerland seem high or low to a tourist from the UK?

What exchange rate should we aim for?

Having an exchange rate which is higher than the purchasing power parity seems at first sight to be most attractive. Let's take an example. Suppose the £ were to be valued at 20 per cent above its PPP. This means that we can buy goods from abroad very cheaply — our terms of trade are very favourable — and UK tourists abroad will find their holiday money going that much further. The low import prices will mean that we can import raw materials, fuels and food inexpensively, contributing to a lower inflation rate in the UK. However, this advantage is not without cost elsewhere. Our exports will be 20 per cent dearer than those of our foreign competitors: unless we can somehow achieve cuts in costs to offset this penalty, export markets will be lost. This is what happened to Holland in the 1970s, when the high exchange rate that resulted from energy self-sufficiency (North Sea gas) handicapped Dutch exports. That's why the phenomenon of an overvalued exchange rate causing unemployment in export industries is called the 'Dutch disease'.

SAQ 7: *The Japanese government was accused by European governments in 1982 of holding its exchange rate down. What benefits might it expect to gain from such a manoeuvre? Are there any disadvantages?*

FIXED AND FLOATING EXCHANGE RATES

Floating exchange rates

The unit so far has talked of exchange rates moving up and down in response to changes in supply and demand. We have seen how an increased demand for sterling, whether it is due to greater sales of UK exports or due to an increase in foreigners' desire to hold their assets in sterling, will lead to an appreciation of the currency. A decline in demand for sterling will have the opposite effect. As a result, the value of the £ on the foreign exchanges will be subject to changes from day to day. This will come as no surprise to an alert reader of the newspapers — the effective exchange rate has varied very considerably over the past ten years. This 'floating exchange rate' system, though, was frowned on before 1972-3. In the years between 1945 and the early 70s exchange rates were agreed between governments, and kept fixed and stable. Under the Bretton Woods Agreement of 1944, governments were under an obligation to maintain their currency's 'par value'. For example, from 1949 to 1967, the par value of the £ sterling was maintained at $2.80.

Fixed exchange rates

How did governments maintain such stability during such a period of growth in international trade, when supply and demand for each currency must have fluctuated from day to day and from year to year? The answer is that governments intervened in foreign exchange markets to ensure that supply was always equal to demand at the par value exchange rate. When demand was too low, they increased demand for their currency; when the exchange rate looked like going too high, they increased the supply of the currency.

Look at the diagram below, which depicts an imaginary supply and demand situation for sterling on a given day. Let's suppose that the exchange rate fixed by the government is £ = $2.80, and that at this exchange rate demand for sterling is less than the amount supplied.

SAQ 8: *Why should this be?*

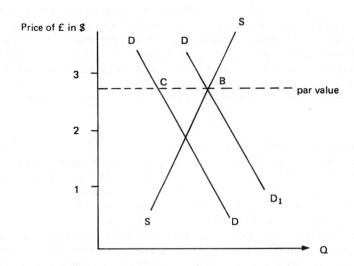

Unless the government intervenes, the rate will fall, and so the Bank of England steps in to buy up sterling. The important thing to grasp here is that the Bank must buy sterling with foreign currency — this is the only way to increase purchases of sterling, though other measures (like a rise in interest rates) might be used to persuade foreigners to hang onto their sterling balances. In the diagram used, the Bank will have to buy up CB of sterling, in order to shift the first demand curve (DD, representing the original demand for sterling) to DD_1 (private demand plus Bank of England demand).

Where does the Bank get this foreign currency from? There are a number of sources. The most important are the foreign currency reserves of the UK — a stock of gold, dollars and other currencies built up in order to meet those occasions when supply of sterling will exceed demand. However, as we shall see in the next unit, the Bank has a number of other sources from which to borrow foreign exchange: other central banks, for example, or private banks. One large and influential lender to governments needing foreign exchange is the International Monetary Fund, to which we shall return.

SAQ 9: *How might the Bank of England keep the exchange rate down when it moved above the par value? What effect will this have on:*
(a)   the level of foreign exchange reserves
(b)   the sterling money supply?

Under a fixed exchange rate regime, the government stabilises the par value of the £ by sales or purchases of foreign exchange. It may also wish to use these methods to affect its currency's exchange rate under a floating system. Floating exchange rates could be run as a 'hands-off' system, with no government intervention, though in practice this hasn't happened. A certain amount of government intervention may be justified as 'smoothing' operations to adjust day-to-day demand for the currency to ensure that there are no exaggerated drops or rises caused by one or two large and untypical transactions. However, in practice, today's foreign exchange system isn't just a slightly smoothed float, but a system of 'managed flexibility' where governments constantly intervene. Such a system has received a nickname that has stuck: 'dirty floating'.

However, no government can maintain its currency at an unrealistically high or low exchange rate forever. For example, the foreign currency reserves required to make the purchases needed to keep the exchange rate above the level indicated by market equilibrium will not be limitless. Foreign exchange reserves can run out, and no-one will be willing to lend to support a currency that is plainly overvalued. In this situation, the government must take action to increase earnings of foreign exchange or reduce foreign exchange expenditure. This unit now looks at the various ways that are open to a government intent on doing this.

HOW TO CURE A BALANCE OF PAYMENTS DEFICIT

Before proceeding to this section of the unit, make sure that you have covered and understood not just the work in the first few pages of this unit, but also the balance of payments accounting that was done in Unit 22..Remember that the balance of payments always balances, for a deficit that is the result of importing more than we are exporting (or of capital outflows) is met either from the country's reserves of foreign exchange or by borrowing from international monetary institutions or from foreign banks or governments.

However this is a relatively short-term answer to the problem. A family cannot endlessly live on savings or borrow from friends, and neither can a country. Measures must be taken to solve the problem. These policy measures may be divided into three basic types:

1.   changing the value of the currency (such as a devaluation or depreciation of sterling)
2.   lowering the level of economic activity – deflation
3.   direct controls on foreign trade.

We shall now look at each of these methods in turn, seeing how they work and contrasting their advantages and disadvantages. Be clear, though, that these methods are not exclusive alternatives. A government's foreign trade policy might incorporate two, or all of the methods. For example, the persistent UK balance of payments problems of the 60s were brought to an end by a combination of a lower exchange rate and deflationary monetary and fiscal policies.

Method 1: Devaluation/depreciation
One way that a government could act to remedy foreign payments problems might involve reducing the exchange rate of its currency. Under a fixed exchange rate system, this would involve 'devaluation' – announcing that the central bank will no longer support the former par value, but will support instead a lower par value. Under a floating exchange rate system, the changes are not as sudden or dramatic. The exchange rate would be allowed to depreciate, as the excess supply caused by low demand for the currency forced the rate down. The government might even give the exchange rate a push, with sales of currency or reductions in interest rates. The argument that follows is valid under both floating and fixed exchange rate regimes.

What effect will a fall in the exchange rate have?
A reduction in the sterling exchange rate will have two effects on the prices of the commodities in which the UK trades. Our exports will be cheaper when priced in foreign currencies, and the goods and services we import will be more expensive when priced in sterling. Let's take a couple of examples to illustrate this. Suppose that an item of UK machinery costs £10 000 to make. When the exchange rate is £1 = $2, the machine will market for $20 000 in the USA. But were the exchange rate to fall to £1 = $1.80, the dollar price of the machine is just $18 000. The lower price will increase sales and thus our dollar earnings. The increased export success will be matched by reduced imports. Again, let's explain this by working through an imaginary example. Suppose US coal costs $100 per ton. At an exchange rate of £1 = $2.00, the sterling price is £50. However, after a reduction in the sterling exchange rate to $1.80, the price will be £55. Such a rise in imported good prices will reduce sales, adding to improvement coming from the increased exports.

The diagram below illustrates the process.

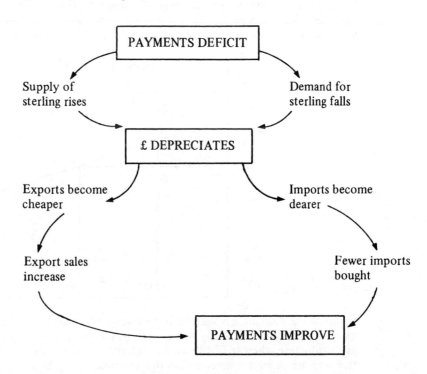

Several examples of this process can be observed – not just for Britain, but for a range of foreign countries. For example, the US dollar depreciated sharply in the late 70s, leading to a considerable improvement in the current account.

SAQ 10: *A change in the exchange rate can also adjust the payment position of a country with a large surplus. For example, Japan and Germany ran large current account surpluses in 1977-78 that were eliminated in the following years by movements in their exchange rates. Check your understanding of this by drawing a diagram similar to the one above starting with*

PAYMENTS SURPLUS

The conditions for a successful devaluation.
Lower export prices will only increase our foreign exchange earnings if the reduced amount of dollars (etc.) gained from each individual sale is outweighed by the increase in revenues coming in from a greater volume of sales. If a 10 per cent reduction in export prices results in only a 5 per cent increase in sales, the total amount of foreign exchange earned by exports will be less than before. A successful devaluation therefore requires that the rise in quantity of exports demanded must be greater than the fall in price resulting from the exchange rate fall.

Now you have already learned how to measure the response of quantity demanded to changes in price — the concept of price elasticity of demand introduced in the unit on Demand. Review your understanding of price elasticity of demand, if necessary, before going further by attempting this self-assessment question:

SAQ 11: *Calculate the price elasticity of demand in these cases.*

	%age change in price	%age change in quantity demanded
(a)	+10	-10
(b)	- 8	+ 4
(c)	+ 5	0
(d)	-15	+45

What terms are given to the elasticity values in each of these cases? (Remember, of course, that elasticity values are always negative, because they are reached by dividing a positive quantity by a negative one or vice versa. It is conventional to ignore the negative sign.)

If we are talking about exports alone, it's clear that a successful devaluation/depreciation requires that the price elasticity of demand for UK exports must be greater than unity. The increase in sales will then outweigh the drop in prices. This might be easier to illustrate on a diagram.

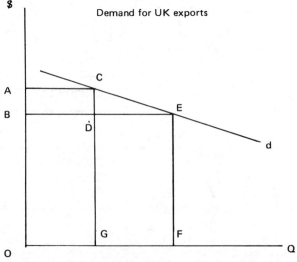

In the above diagram, a reduction in the foreign exchange price of UK exports from OA to OB has increased sales from quantity OG to OF. In the process, revenue of BACD has been lost by the price reduction whereas DEFG has been gained by the increased sales volume. Because the percentage increase in sales is greater than the percentage drop in price, the exchange rate depreciation has increased foreign exchange revenues.

SAQ 12: *In which of the following cases will a devaluation or depreciation of sterling increase UK export earnings of foreign exchange?*
(a)   If price elasticity of demand for UK exports was (i) 2   (ii) 1.3   (iii) 0.5   (iv) zero
(b)   If an exchange rate depreciation of 10 per cent was followed by a sales increase of 8 per cent
(c)   If a devaluation of 14 per cent raised export sales volume by 27 per cent.

Imports
Of course we can't ignore how a depreciation will affect our import bill in assessing the effects on the balance of payments. Again, for exchange rate changes to be helpful, price elasticity of demand must be high rather than low, choking off demand for imported goods as their sterling price rises. If price elasticity of demand for UK imports was very low, then a sterling depreciation would result in the UK paying almost as much as before in foreign exchange for fewer goods.

SAQ 13: *What will happen to the sterling value and volume of UK imports after a depreciation of the exchange rates if price elasticity of demand for those commodities were: (a) greater than one; (b) unity; (c) less than one?*

The Marshall-Lerner criterion
Taking the effects of a sterling depreciation it is clear that favourable elasticity conditions for one can outweigh unfavourable responses from the other. For example, a modest rise in export earnings can be supplemented by a large fall in imports. That's why the conditions of a successful devaluation require us to consider the price elasticities of demand for both exports and imports. The rule is this:

> A devaluation/depreciation of the currency will improve the balance of payments if the sum of the price elasticity of demand for exports and imports is greater than one.

This is named the Marshall-Lerner criterion after the economists who discovered it (Marshall) and refined it (Lerner).

SAQ 14: *Here is a table showing price elasticities for UK exports and imports. Select the sets of figures which would result in a depreciation which improved the UK balance of payments:*

	Price elasticity of demand for:	
	exports	imports
(a)	*0.5*	*0.6*
(b)	*0.8*	*0.4*
(c)	*0.3*	*0.4*

Are the elasticities likely to be right?
We have seen that if a change in the exchange rate is to be effective in correcting a balance of payments deficit, the elasticities must be right. The vital question is — will they be right in reality? To answer this question we must return to our knowledge of elasticity, and the factors that affect it. Remember how crucial *substitutes* were. If it is possible to switch expenditure between commodities — to economise by buying less of the commodity that has increased in price by purchasing a substitute, then price elasticity of demand will be high. If there are few substitutes, by contrast, elasticity of demand is likely to be low. That's why the elasticity of demand for soap is low, but the price elasticity of demand for one brand of soap is likely to be high. Now, are UK exports subject in this way to substitution? The answer is likely to be 'yes'. There is vigorous competition in many fields of industry — textiles, cars, aviation, banking, tourism — and in these areas and others, an attractive price cut will gain the uncommitted buyer.

Spare capacity
But the elasticity criteria alone are not enough to assure successful adjustment through exchange rates. Another concerns the presence of spare capacity in our export, or import-substitution, industries. It is, after all, no use creating increased demand for UK exports unless that demand can be satisfied. If unemployed resources are available to produce the additional exports, the problem disappears. But if not, action will have to be taken to direct resources into the production of additional exports or import substitutes.

The advantages of using exchange rate variations
The use of exchange rate variations to adjust imbalances in our international payments has a num-

ber of advantages. The outstanding one is that it is a more-or-less automatic way of redressing the problem (as long as the elasticity conditions are met). Suppose, for example, a balance of payments deficit is caused by an outflow of capital. A floating exchange rate will depreciate until the demand for sterling once again equals the supply. A moment's thought reveals that this will be where the surplus on trade is large enough to pay for the capital outflow.

SAQ 15:   *Work out for yourself what will happen to (a) the exchange rate and (b) the visible trade balance if there is a balance of payments surplus caused by large capital inflows and an invisible surplus.*

The 'automatic' nature of the floating exchange rate means that governments do not have to take actions that might impede international trade — import duties, for example, or capital flow restrictions. They may therefore concentrate on their desired domestic policies without being diverted by battles to defend the £ or launching 'export drives' to meet import bills.

The disadvantages of using exchange rate changes
But floating exchange rates are not the painless solution that some economists thought they were. We'll now go on to look at four major disadvantages of using exchange rate changes to solve payments problems.

(a)   *J-curve effects*
The J-curve is a device used to explain how a currency depreciation initially worsens a balance of payments deficit before improving it. Let me explain. We have seen that a successful devaluation/ depreciation of the exchange rate has two effects on exports. Firstly, it reduces their price to foreign markets; secondly, it increases their volume. It is important to grasp that these two effects may not happen simultaneously. It is likely that the price reductions will occur before the increases in sales volume are evident. Let's take the case of a sterling depreciation. It will take time for foreigners to learn of, and act on, the increased value-for-money represented by UK goods; time for UK stores and wholesalers to find alternative sources of supply in the UK for their high-priced imports; time for UK firms to exploit the new export opportunities. In the time-lag between the cut in prices and the increased sales, UK export earnings will fall. The hope is, of course, that ultimately the exchange rate depreciation will improve the payments position; that's where the idea of a J-shaped curve comes from. I've drawn an imaginary one below, showing that in year 1 (when the exchange rate depreciation occurred) the balance of payments went into a more acute deficit, and it was not until years 2 and 3 that the improved price structure paid off in improved payments performance.

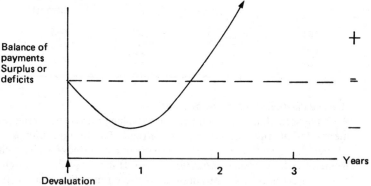

The danger with a freely floating exchange rate is that the time needed for the adjustment will not take place. The first deterioration will trigger further sales of the currency, which slips us down to a further J-curve, which causes less confidence and further reductions in the value of export earnings.

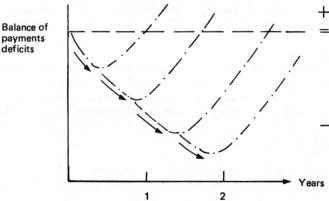

The path might very well take the form shown in the the previous diagram (bottom p. 49), where a country's payments performance gets cumulatively worse under successive depreciations. A halt will occur when the country's exports are plainly underpriced and extremely competitive, and imports to that country are extremely expensive. But this process might very well have coincided with a precipitous decline in the 'victim's' exchange rate.

(Important qualifications: this discussion (a) assumes that exporters reduce their prices in line with devaluation: i.e. if sterling depreciates by 10 per cent, UK export prices are reduced by a similar amount. There is a substantial amount of evidence that this is not the case. Exporters may prefer the additional profit that can be obtained by charging the pre-devaluation price at the post-devaluation exchange rate. Referring back for a moment to the example used on page 46, note how the exporter who is successfully selling a £10 000 machine for $20 000 might make an extra $2000 profit by maintaining the dollar price rather than reducing to $18 000 after a devaluation. Such behaviour would require us to modify our views about the way that a depreciation/devaluation works in improving the balance of payments. If after a devaluation UK exporters maintain their foreign exchange prices at the same level as before, foreign trade will be that much more profitable, and will thus attract more interest from UK firms. The larger profit margin also provides funds for aftersales service, advertising or other marketing advantages. But it is the higher profitability rather than the lower price that is raising sales).

(b)   *Effects on the domestic price level*
The second major disadvantage of using changes in the exchange rate to adjust balance of payments deficits is that, due to the way devaluation raises import prices, it can add to inflation. Remember that in the UK, 30 per cent or so of all goods traded are imported. So when sterling falls by 10 per cent, UK inflation goes up by 3 per cent. This means that a sharp depreciation of the currency can add significantly to inflation. What is worse, the inflationary impulse created by increased import prices might be passed on, as firms and wage-earners adjust prices and wages to match the increased inflation rate. Some economists are very pessimistic about the inflationary effects of a depreciation, believing that in a relatively short time – three or four years – the domestic inflation caused will wipe out the cost advantages conferred on exporters by the lower exchange rate.

SAQ 16: *Importers to the UK are sometimes observed to hold their sterling prices steady rather than adjust them in line with a sterling depreciation.*
(a)   Why might they do this?
(b)   If they do so, will the inflationary impact of currency depreciation be worsened or lessened?

If one believes in purchasing power parities, then the cause of a sterling depreciation might well be excessive UK inflation – inflation, that is, above the level experienced by competitors. To pluck numbers from the air, a UK inflation rate 5 per cent higher than the competition would precipitate a 5 per cent fall in the exchange rate. This will cause import prices to rise by the extra 5 per cent, bringing the effective inflation rate for imported goods into line with the inflation rate of UK goods. In this situation, it would be mistaken to blame import prices for contributing to inflation – they are being dragged along behind UK inflation.

(c)   *Uncertainty*
As a third disadvantage of exchange rate changes, it is argued that fluctuations in the rate of exchange will increase uncertainty about international dealings. Firms will be unable to estimate whether a commodity that they have contracted to supply will be profitable or not, because they do not know the rate of exchange that will prevail when they get paid.
Three examples:

● *Rolls Royce* tendered for a US aero-engine contract at a dollar price that would only allow them to break even if the sterling exchange rate stayed below $1.80. When the sterling exchange rate subsequently rose above $2.00, the contract became a loss maker.

● *Sir Freddie Laker* contracted some loans from banks in dollars when the sterling exchange rate was high: the rate of exchange had fallen by the time the loans fell due for repayment, with the result that his business collapsed.

● *J. Lyons and Co.*, the catering giant, were brought down by borrowing in Swiss francs. These cut their interest costs, but the debt soared in terms of the £ sterling when the pound went through one of its periodic crises.

If such uncertainties discourage firms from entering into international trade, then many of the advantages that are expected to result from international specialisation will be missing. Imagine the problems of trading with Italy when (as has happened) the lire falls by 30 per cent in six weeks.
But while it must be admitted that fluctuations in exchange rates do indeed cause headaches for international traders, firms have become wiser about the exchange rate changes and are able to

avoid many of the problems by the use of 'hedging'. Hedging a currency involves paying a small premium in order to secure delivery of a stated amount of that currency at some time in the future at present exchange rates: up to six months cover is common.

Plainly, the amount of the premium will vary according to the risk involved in promising to deliver the currency concerned in the future. The market in Swiss francs is likely to be less problematic than that in the Brazilian cruzeiro. Problems will exist. too, where the firm wishes to assure itself of foreign cover over a period longer than six months.

However, it would be foolish to compare the admitted fluctuations of a floating rate with some imaginary totally stable exchange rate, for no such rate has existed in recent times. Under the Bretton Woods Agreement from 1945 until 1972, countries were allowed to devalue their currencies when suffering from a 'fundamental disequilibrium' in their balance of payments. Although such devaluations were infrequent, they were large in size – dropping the £ by 14 per cent in one day in 1967, for example. It is at least arguable that the small daily movement under floating is less disturbing to traders than sharper but less frequent changes in value.

(d) Speculation

Finally, it is argued that permitting exchange rates to change from day to day opens the door to speculative activity – activity that will make the foreign exchange markets unstable and subject to sudden changes in values. Now, if speculators are regarded as people who buy and sell currency in order to profit from foreign exchange rather than in order to finance international trade, then they certainly are present in foreign exchange markets. What is at issue between economists is whether such speculative activity is a destabilising influence. Friedman believes that it is not. Speculators, he argues, make money by buying at a low price and selling at a higher one. The effect of buying at high prices and selling at low ones is to moderate the extremes of price movements.

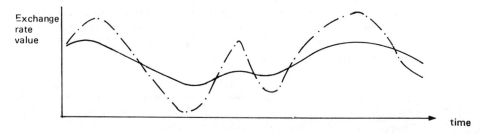

The diagram above shows the alleged effect – the bold line shows the path of the actual rate of exchange, the broken line showing what it might have been without speculative purchases and sales. Other economists, it must be said, are not so sure about this theory. Since the widespread adoption of floating exchange rates in the early 70s, fluctuations in exchange rates have been more pronounced than the advocates of floating expected. The ability to promise future deliveries of currency that you haven't got – possible where hedging is done – enables speculators to make a profit on a falling market. Where this happens, speculation can be destabilising – waves of selling forcing the price down, creating expectations of further falls and thus further sales.

It should be said that speculation also existed under the fixed-exchange-rate system of Bretton Woods. Speculative profits can be made from devaluations as follows.

> When the pound is being heavily sold and is only keeping to its par value because the Bank of England is intervening, a devaluation is rumoured. A speculator borrows £1 m and sells it for dollars at the existing exchange rate of $2.80, obtaining $2.8m in exchange. When the government can no longer hold the sterling exchange rate, and devalues to £1 = $2.40, the dollars are changed back into sterling. This yields £1,166,666. The £1 m may now be repaid and a profit of £166,666 retained.

One important factor about fixed-exchange-rate speculation is that it is a 'one-way option'. When sterling, for example, is under pressure, there are only two possibilities – it maintains its value, or the government devalues. It certainly will not rise in value, and so a speculator selling sterling will never make losses from having to buy back the currency at a price higher than when it was sold. At least under the floating exchange rate system, the possibility that sterling may rise as well as fall from its existing value may induce caution and prevent massive selling.

Summary

To summarise this section, we have seen that changes in exchange rates can help a country through a balance of payments problem by increasing export sales whilst restraining purchases of imports. Such a policy will work as long as the elasticities are right, and as long as spare capacity exists or can be created in export industries. However, using changes in exchange rates as a method of resolving payments problems has a number of disadvantages: time-lags causing J-curve effects, inflationary effects on the level of prices in the UK, uncertainty in international trade made worse by fluctuations caused by speculative activity. These disadvantages were compounded in the inter-war period by 'competitive devaluations' as countries sought advantages from undercutting their competitors. These disadvantages were what determined the wartime planners to choose a fixed-exchange-rate system for their postwar world, and more recently, what led some Common Market countries to seek to stabilise the relationship between their currencies in a mutually supporting European Monetary System. But if we decide to avoid flexible exchange rates, some alternative way must be found to adjust balance of payments problems, which leads us to deflation.

Method 2: Deflation
Deflation means a reduction of economic activity, and results in a lower level of national income, aggregate demand and employment. The government can bring about a deflation in the national income with either monetary or fiscal measures.

SAQ 17: *Look at the measures in the list below, and mark down: (i) in the first column, whether they are monetary or fiscal measures (M or F) and (ii) in the second column, whether they will tend to deflate (D) or reflate (R) the economy.*

(a)   income tax cuts   ...   ...

(b)   higher interest rates   ...   ...

(c)   open market purchases of government stock   ...   ...

(d)   reductions in government spending   ...   ...

(e)   raising VAT   ...   ...

(f)   a call for special deposits   ...   ...

How does deflation work?
Reducing, or merely slowing the growth of, the national income improves the balance of payments because imports are a function of national income. In other words, the total amount spent on imported commodities depends on the total incomes. The relationship between income and imports is measured in the propensity to import. For example, if we have a national income of £200 billion and import £40 billion, the average propensity to import is $\frac{40}{200}$ or 0.2. This is just the average, of course: in working out the changes in import spending that will result from changes in national income, we are more concerned with the marginal propensity to import – not $\frac{\text{imports}}{\text{N.I.}}$ but $\frac{\text{change in imports}}{\text{change in N.I.}}$. Numbers probably make it easier to explain how deflation works in improving the balance of payments. Let's take a country with a deficit of £1 b and a marginal propensity to import of 0.2. In this case a reduction of £5 b in total spending would reduce spending on imports by the required £1 b. Note that for expenditure on imports to fall by £1 b, expenditure on home-produced goods must go down by £4 b.

SAQ 18: *Work through this exercise to check your understanding of the relationship between spending on imports and the level of national income. Start from a position where the national income is 100 and spending on imports is 10.*
(a)   What is the average propensity to import?

If an increase of 50 in the national income increases spending on imports by 20:
(b)   What is the new level of national income and import spending?
(c)   (i)   What, at this new level, is the average propensity to import?
*   (ii) The marginal propensity to import?*
(d)   With the marginal propensity to import that you have discovered, calculate how much national income would have to fall to reduce spending on imports by 1. By how much will spending on domestically-produced goods fall as part of this process?
(e)   Using the marginal propensity to import you've calculated in question (c) above, work out the increase in import spending that would result from a rise in national income of 10.
(f)   An actual example: in 1976, the UK ran a payments deficit of £5 b. If the propensity to import was one-third, by how much would national income have to fall to cure the problem by deflation alone?

So far we have concentrated on the way that deflationary measures cure payments problems by reducing imports. You may think that deflation will leave export sales unaltered – after all, if UK imports depend on the UK national income, then UK exports will depend (as we learned in an earlier unit) on the world's income. However, it is sometimes observed that deflation improves export performance as well. Firms which find themselves unable to sell to the home market may look abroad for the sales they are unable to achieve at home. Monetary measures are thought to be more effective than fiscal in turning firms towards export markets, as they make it important for firms to maintain their cash balances with sales.

Advantages of using deflation as a method of curing payments problems

If a balance of payments problem results from a very high level of economic activity in the UK — with a full-employment level of spending that is sucking in excessive amounts of imports — deflation is a sensible response. In that situation, the reduction in demand brought about through fiscal or monetary policies would be likely to help the government achieve other desirable economic goals — such as the reduction of inflation. Deflation also means avoiding the disadvantages of the other means of repairing the balance of payments — the problems of fluctuating exchange rates and the inefficiency of import control.

The drawbacks of deflation

The problem with using deflation concerns the losses of output and wealth that result. Remember, it isn't just import spending that is reduced — it's domestic spending and output as well.

SAQ 19: *Which will result in the smallest loss of domestic output to achieve a given reduction in the value of imports — a low propensity to import, or a high one?*

Whilst the reduction in inflation will help exports by cutting UK costs, the longer-term influences of deflation may be less helpful. Fluctuations in sales and demand in the UK may make firms reluctant to expand and re-equip: why cater for increased sales when the government will shortly bring economic growth to an end with a harsh budget? Similarly, workers are unlikely to cooperate with new work practices that will raise productivity if the changes will result in fewer jobs rather than greater output. In the long run, UK export success depends on efficient, high-quality production, using up-to-date production methods that lead to low unit costs. Deflationary measures aimed at achieving a temporary balance of payments improvement might work against the forces that will assure long-run health.

Throughout the 50s and 60s, a series of payments crises induced governments to introduce deflationary measures. Amongst the measures aimed at reducing expenditure were limits on hire purchase and bank lending to consumers. This tended to create fluctuations in car sales: a boom of high sales when credit was easy to obtain, followed by a period where fewer cars were sold. UK manufacturers were content to supply the 'basic demand', leaving the extra boom-year sales to importers. As a result, foreign car firms gained a foothold in the UK car market, a foothold that was used to expand the level of sales until it exceeded UK production.

Method 3: Import controls

Bearing in mind the drawbacks of currency depreciation and deflation, it is not surprising that policy makers have started to look again at direct controls on foreign trade. It had become clear in the UK that a fundamental shift had occurred in trade performance, knocking firms out of a number of manufacturing industries where they had previously been dominant. This process of 'de-industrialisation' continued despite severe deflation (over 3 million unemployed in 1981-4) and depreciation of sterling. It was argued by a number of economists that a positive strategy of industrial renewal behind the protection of tariff walls was required. The arguments traditionally deployed against import controls were answered as follows:

'Import controls interfere with international specialisation'

But international specialisation is not a static, once-and-for all idea. The industries in which individual countries excel change through time, and can be developed and protected as part of a conscious government policy. Other countries protect and subsidise their vital industries: if we play according to the 'free-trade' rules and accept their imports, we will be left to produce what our competitors don't want to produce. In this way, foreign industries will decide our economic future.

'Import controls will reduce UK living standards'.

No. Certainly, they deny the UK consumer access to cheaper imported items, but this is a small loss beside the jobs and industries that have collapsed in the face of international competition. If import controls allow the expansion of the UK economy and the creation of more jobs, any loss of welfare from higher-cost imports will be far outweighed by the benefits of greater UK output and higher incomes. It must be realised that all methods of curing a payments surplus involve some theoretical losses in the UK standard of living. Devaluation worsens the terms of trade. and therefore reduces the amount of commodities available for our consumption because we have to export more to buy the same amount of imports. Deflation reduces living standards very directly – in its effect on economic activity, output and incomes.

'Import controls invite retaliation'

They may. But logically, they shouldn't. We must explain to our foreign trade partners that a high UK national income with import controls will be importing as much – maybe more – than a stagnant UK economy under free trade. All methods of curing a balance of payments problem involve reducing imports – whether deflation, devaluation or import controls. It is illogical of foreign governments to react to import controls that cut their sales to the UK when no such reaction results from a sterling depreciation or a tight monetary policy, which have broadly the same effect.

SAQ 20: *Is it true that all methods of curing a balance of payments problem involve reducing imports? Explain your answer with respect to: (i) deflation; (ii) devaluation/depreciation; (ii) import tariffs or quotas.*

One might say that a policy of import controls already exists. In many areas, agreements between producer and consumer countries exist which limit trade in certain commodities. The Multi-Fibre Agreement places limits on the amount of textile imports advanced countries will accept from less developed suppliers, and Japanese car exporters have had to accept 'voluntary' import quotas – such as 11 per cent of the UK market – in the knowledge that a failure to do so may bring in compulsory controls.

Other forms of direct control

So far, I've spoken about import controls as if they refer solely to measures designed to prevent the UK consumer buying foreign goods. But other methods of reducing expenditure by overseas UK residents will improve the balance of payments. For many years, for example, UK residents had difficulty buying property and shares overseas as the Bank of England enforced controls on their ability to purchase foreign exchange. Foreign exchange for investment purposes had to be purchased from a pool kept by the Bank – and as the funds available were rarely sufficient to satisfy demand, they commanded a higher price than free-market dollars – a difference known as the dollar premium.

SAQ 21: *What effect would successful controls on capital exports (that is, UK residents buying capital assets overseas) have on the exchange rate of sterling? What, therefore, would you expect to have been the effect on the exchange rate of sterling of the abolition of exchange controls by the Conservative Government in 1979-81?*

Controlling the access to the foreign currency needed to make purchases of foreign commodities or assets is known as 'exchange control': it's another form of direct control on imports. The advantage of such a policy is that, if the control of funds is centralised, then priorities in the use of foreign exchange may be established. A poor country with limited export earnings can therefore use exchange controls to limit imports in a more selective way than could be achieved by tariffs.

REVIEW SECTION

Further reading

You would do well to make use of your local library in order to undertake some back-reading on this important and contentious topic. If you have found my treatment difficult to follow, then a good idea is to look up a traditional textbook explanation for a different slant. Good supplementary reading is to be found in:

Cairncross and Keeley *The Guardian Guide to the Economy 2* (Methuen) Ch. 4
David Cobham *The Economics of International Trade* (Woodhead-Faulkner) Ch. 5 and 8
Barker *Case Studies in International Economics* (Heinemann Education) Case study 3
Gowland *Modern Economic Analysis* (Butterworth) Ch. 2 (difficult but worth the struggle)
Grant and Shaw *Current Issues in Economic Policy* (Phillip Allan) Ch. 13
Davies *The UK and the World Monetary System* (Heinemann) Ch. 1–3 especially.

Bear in mind when reading that so much has changed in the last few years that a book published more than, say, five years ago is useful only for the explanation of broad principles rather than detailed information. Your best chance of up-to-date material is in such journals as *The Economist* and in Bank Reviews, (see, for example, 'The World's Largest Creditor — How Long Can Japan's Surplus Last?'), *Economic Progress Reports* and the *Economic Review,* (e.g. 'The Political Economy Of Tariffs', May 1987).

Examination questions

Essay choices

1.   'An efficient international financial system, based upon either fixed or floating exchange rates, requires an adequate supply of liquidity and a mechanism for ensuring orderly balance of payments adjustments.' Discuss.

(AEB 'A' November 1986)

2.   'A lower exchange rate for sterling must improve the United Kingdom balance of payments and raise output because competitiveness improves'. Discuss.

(Oxford Local Delegacy 'A' June 1986)

3.   Why might a government wish to eliminate a surplus on its current account balance of payments? What measures could it use to achieve this end?

(London 'A' June 1987)

4.   Explain what is meant by saying that the Pound is 'weak' against the Dollar. Under a flexible exchange rate system should the Government be concerned about the value of the Pound against other currencies?

(JMB 'A' June 1985)

5.   An economy has a persistent deficit on the current account of its balance of payments.

    (a)   Explain carefully what is meant by, ' . . . a persistent deficit on the current account of its balance of payments'.
    (b)   What are the likely causes of such a deficit?
    (c)   Describe and explain the measures which a government may take to reduce this deficit.

(Cambridge Local Syndicate 'A' June 1987)

6.   How is the devaluation of the currency supposed to cure an economy's balance of payments current account deficit? Is it likely to do so? Explain your reasoning.

(Cambridge Local Syndicate 'A' November/December 1985)

7.   Analyse the probable consequences of an increase in import controls on prices, output and unemployment.

(London 'A' January 1987)

Multiple choice questions on balance of payments policy

Questions 1 to 4 use the following list of events in foreign exchange markets.

(i)   a rise in the demand for sterling
(ii)   a rise in the sterling exchange rate
(iii) a rise in the supply of sterling
(iv)   a fall in the demand for sterling

Using the answer codes shown in these boxes, indicate which of the above would follow from the event named in the question.

answer (a) if (iii)	answer (b) if (ii) and (iii) only	answer (c) if (i) and (ii) only	answer (d) if (iii) and (iv) only

1.   An increase in UK exports
2.   A fall in UK interest rates compared with overseas rates
3.   A rise in UK imports
4.   An announcement of encouraging economic news for the UK
5.   The idea of purchasing power parity states that the exchange rate of a currency will depend on:
    (a)   the relation between the value of imports and the value of exports
    (b)   the amount of commodities that can be bought with a given amount of a currency

      (c)   the amount of foreign currency that can be purchased per unit of domestic currency

      (d)   the supply and demand conditions in the market for that currency.

6.   Which of the following would be true if the £ sterling were valued below purchasing power parity?

      (a)   UK exports would be relatively more expensive than competing goods

      (b)   The terms of trade would be adverse, compared to what they would be if purchasing power parities prevailed.

      (c)   Imports into the UK would have a price advantage over competing UK goods when both were priced in sterling

      (d)   The balance of trade would be adverse, compared to what it would be under a purchasing power parity.

7.   If the Bank of England were entering the foreign exchange markets in order to support the value of the £ sterling, which of the following would be true?

      (a)   The Bank would be selling foreign exchange

      (b)   The Bank would be selling sterling

      (c)   The Exchange Equalisation Account would be rising

      (d)   The Bank would encourage the purchase of UK exports.

8.   In which of the following cases is a devaluation of the currency *least* likely to succeed?

      (a)   where elasticity of demand for both exports and imports was high

      (b)   where elasticity of demand for exports was high, but for imports was low

      (c)   where elasticity of demand for exports was low, but for imports was high

      (d)   where elasticity of demand for both exports and imports was low.

9.   Which of the following terms would most properly refer to the exchange rate regime at present in use in international trade?

      (a)   a free float

      (b)   the Bretton Woods system

      (c)   fixed exchange rates

      (d)   managed flexibility.

10.   By how much will the domestic price level rise following a 10 per cent depreciation of the exchange rate if imports form 50 per cent of all commodities traded in a country? (Assume importers change prices in line with the depreciation.)

      (a) 5%   (b) 10%   (c) 50%   (d) 60%

11.   Which of these considerations is *NOT* an argument against floating exchange rates?

      (a)   They may increase uncertainty and thereby inhibit beneficial international trade.

      (b)   They might give rise to destabilising speculation in foreign exchange markets.

      (c)   They mean that a deficit country has its balance of payments worsened in the long run as the exchange rate falls.

      (d)   They add to inflation by raising the cost of imports after a depreciation of the exchange rate.

Look at these definitions, and answer questions 12 and 13 from them:

(a) $\dfrac{\text{imports}}{\text{national income}}$

(b) $\dfrac{\text{price of exports}}{\text{price of imports}}$

(c) $\dfrac{\text{change in imports}}{\text{change in national income}}$

(d)   visible and invisible exports minus visible and invisible imports

Which of these refer to:

12.   The balance of payments on current account?

13.   The marginal propensity to import?

14.   If the marginal propensity to import is 0.2 and the national income is £150b, then a rise of £20b in national income will increase imports by   (a) £2b   (b) £4b   (c) £34b   (d) £40b

15.   Which of the following is an advantage of using deflation to remedy balance of payments problems?

      (a)   Firms will seek overseas markets and gain export sales, so employment will rise.

      (b)   There will be a need for greater efficiency, so firms will increase investment expenditure.

      (c)   There is a lower level of aggregate demand, so domestic inflation may be moderated.

      (d)   Imports will be reduced, so the exchange rate may be allowed to rise.

Here are a number of problems that are associated with particular approaches to balance of payments policy. Link the policies named in questions 16 and 17 with the relevant problem in the list on the right.

16. Devaluation

17. Import controls

(a) unlikely even in the short term to contribute to a reduction in imports
(b) liable to worsen the balance of payments in the short run
(c) liable to provoke retaliation from foreign governments
(d) prone to cause losses of output in the domestic economy.

18. Which of the following would contribute to a reduction in a Japanese payments surplus in transactions with the USA:
     (a) deflation of the Japanese economy
     (b) depreciation of the yen.
     (c) expansion of the US economy
     (d) depreciation of the US dollar?

19. In 1981 the UK enjoyed a substantial current account surplus while over 3 million people were unemployed. If the UK government had succeeded in expanding the economy to create jobs for the unemployed, the. (assuming no import controls and an unchanged exchange rate) the effect on the balance of payments would be:
     (a) positive — the increased workforce would increase the national product and therefore the amount of exports
     (b) positive at first, as government expenditure on UK-produced goods rose but later negative as exports are diverted to satisfy UK demand
     (c) negative at first, as raw materials are imported, then positive as the manufactured exports are sold
     (d) negative — the increased incomes would suck in more imports whilst export volume would change little.

20. Which of the following could properly be described as a 'smoothing' transaction?
     (a) intervening to keep the exchange rate down in order to promote exports
     (b) purchasing currency to compensate for a large and untypical currency sale
     (c) choosing an exchange rate policy that will minimise the risk of retaliation
     (d) intervening to keep the exchange rate up to moderate domestic inflation.

ANSWERS TO SAQs

SAQ 1: (a) The UK clothing store (or, more likely, its bank) would sell sterling and acquire dollars. (b) There would be an increased supply of sterling and demand for marks. (c) The French company would have to pay us in sterling, and so would offer francs for sterling.

SAQ 2: (a) $1.67 (b) $1.50.

SAQ 3: (a) 4, (b) 1, (c) 2.

SAQ 4: The value in terms of the goods it can buy in Britain: this could be measured through the Retail Price Index, and is affected by inflation.

SAQ 5: (a) Lost confidence in the UK may make foreigners switch out of sterling, causing the exchange rate to fall. (b) Promise of future export earnings (and government tax revenues) would raise confidence and boost sterling. (c) Sterling would fall, as oil companies that previously needed sterling no longer buy it. (d) If this meant that investors holding dollars were likely to lose out, they might very well switch to sterling, causing a rise in its exchange rate.

SAQ 6: (a) The £ will depreciate by 5 per cent relative to the mark, so that once again they can buy the same amount of commodities. (b) This will cause the Swiss franc to be higher than PPP as demand is high: thus, Swiss prices will seem relatively high to a UK (or French, or Italian) tourist.

SAQ 7: It gains greater export sales as Japanese goods seem cheaper. However, it does mean that Japanese inflation is higher (due to imports being more costly than necessary) and Japanese living standards are being lowered by adverse terms of trade.

SAQ 8: Perhaps because UK exports are uncompetitive, or a capital outflow.

SAQ 9: The Bank might do so by selling sterling and purchasing foreign currency. Alternatively, interest rates might be reduced in the UK to make holding sterling less attractive relative to other currencies. However, assuming that the bank is supplying sterling and in exchange acquiring foreign currency, then the level of our foreign exchange reserves will rise and the sterling money supply will also rise.

SAQ 10:

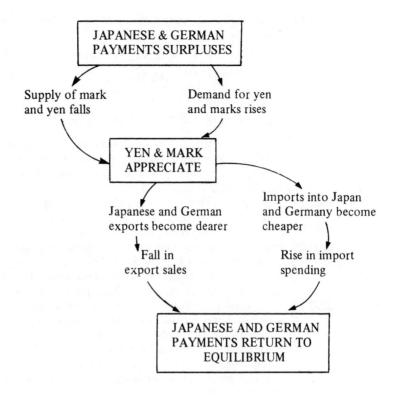

SAQ 11: Remember that the price elasticity of demand is calculated by the formula:

$$\frac{\% \text{ Change in quantity demanded}}{\% \text{ Change in price}}$$

So using the simple figures in the exercise, this works out to:

(a) 1   (b) 0.5   (c) 0   (d) 3.

Using words, we would describe these as respectively unit elastic, inelastic, perfectly inelastic and elastic with regard to price.

SAQ 12: (a) Devaluation will work where price elasticity of demand for UK exports is greater than one — that is, where increased sales will cancel out the lower price. This is true in (i) and (ii) but not in (iii) and (iv) where the response of sales to a price is sluggish. (b) Here, demand is price inelastic — sales rise by less than price is cut, so a depreciation/devaluation wouldn't work. (c) Here, demand is elastic with regard to price so that devaluation is successful.

SAQ 13: (a) Volume will fall by a greater percentage than the sterling price rises, so total spending will fall. (b) Volume will fall by the same percentage as price, so the amount spent on imports will remain unchanged. (c) Volume will fall by a smaller percentage than the change in price, so our sterling import bill will rise.

N.B. The amount we spend on imports *in foreign currency* will always be less, unless demand for imports is perfectly inelastic. Remember, devaluation/depreciation raises the sterling price in the UK of the commodities we are importing — it doesn't affect the dollar or franc price of those commodities in world markets. To take our earlier example: if we choose to buy less US coal because the $100 price is now £55 rather than £50, then we shall be demanding less US coal and therefore fewer dollars to pay for US coal imports even if demand is pretty elastic.

SAQ 14: The trick is to sum the two figures to see if they exceed the Marshall-Lerner rule of unit elasticity. I make (a) 1.1 and (b) 1.2 — devaluation/depreciation will improve the balance of payments here. This will not be true in (c) where the sum of the price elasticities is just 0.7.

SAQ 15: When the balance of payments is in surplus, demand for sterling to purchase UK goods, services and assets will exceed supply of sterling arising from a UK desire to buy overseas quantity supplied price rises — so the sterling exchange rate appreciates. At the higher exchange rate, the balance of payments will return to equilibrium, where the counterpart of the invisible surplus and capital inflows will be a visible deficit.

SAQ 16: (a) They do it to retain their 'market share' — that is, their sales in the UK. They prefer to earn lower profits rather than lose the sales and possibly their foothold in the UK market. (b) Because prices of imported goods are not being raised, the inflationary impact will be lessened.

SAQ 17:   Check through your units on monetary and fiscal policy if you haven't got the following:

(a) F, R   (b) M, D   (c) M, D   (d) F, R   (e) F, D   (f) M, D.

SAQ 18:   (a) 0.1 (i.e. $\frac{10}{100}$)   (b) The new NI is 150, the new level of imports is 30.   (c) (i) Average propensity to import is 0.2 (i.e. $\frac{30}{150}$), (ii) Marginal propensity is higher at 0.4, calculated from $\frac{20}{50}$.   (d) With an m.p.i. of 0.2, total spending will have to fall by an amount of which 1 is 0.2 — which is 2½. This implies that domestic spending falls by 1½ as well.   (e) If national income rose 10, then imports would rise by 0.2.   (f) By £15b: such a fall would involve a reduction of domestic production of £10b and a reduction in imports of £5b.

SAQ 19:   A high one. With a high propensity to import, a given increase in NI leads to a larger rise in import spending than with a smaller m.p.i. — so a given decrease in NI will achieve a larger reduction in imports.

SAQ 20:   It is true. A deflation reduces imports by reducing UK incomes, which leads to lower sales of imports in the UK. A devaluation cuts imports by raising their (sterling) price in relation to domestically-produced goods. Import quotas do so by placing an actual limit on imports, tariffs by raising prices with the addition of an import tax.

SAQ 21:   Successful controls on capital movements out of the UK will reduce the supply of sterling and the demand for foreign currencies, and so lead to the exchange rate being higher than would otherwise be the case. If this is sound, then the abolition of exchange controls on capital would have led to an increased demand for foreign assets (and therefore currency) and a supply of sterling to pay for this. So the exchange rate would move below the level that would have prevailed had the controls been maintained.

23 International economic institutions

AIMS OF UNIT 23

At the end of this unit, you should be able to:

- explain the need for international economic bodies
- outline the functions and working of the IMF
- show where the IMF obtains its funds
- account for the breakdown of the fixed parity system
- explain the aims of the World Bank and GATT
- list the common policies of the EEC
- outline the advantages and disadvantages of EEC membership to the UK
- explain and criticise the workings of the CAP
- describe the aims and workings of the EMS.

INTRODUCTION

In the last few units we have looked at the topic of international trade — how it may benefit countries that engage in it, how Britain's trade and payments have shaped up in the recent past, the ways that governments can tackle problems in the balance of payments. This unit looks at bodies that aim to help countries cooperate — gaining the benefits of trade without restrictions or payment problems. We'll look at a number of important, but differing institutions that crop up in the news — the IMF, the World Bank, GATT and the European Economic Community. International cooperation can be important, for international trends can affect the health of our own economy.

SAQ 1: *Explain how the following can be affected by international factors: the rate of inflation; unemployment; economic growth.*

THE BRETTON WOODS INSTITUTIONS

The way economies can be harmed by international events was evident to the statesmen and economists, including Keynes, who met in the New Hampshire resort of Bretton Woods in 1944 to plan

the postwar economic order

SAQ 2: *Where have you met Keynes before?*

They had lived through the 30s, when countries responded to the international slump with trade barriers and competitive devaluations; and they had witnessed the problems of poorer nations, restricted in their development because commercial banks were unable to see profitable outlets in lending for the roads, ports and school buildings that were needed. The Bretton Woods Conference, therefore, identified two needs.

Firstly, there was a need to help countries that had short-term problems with their balance of payments.

SAQ 3: *What is meant by the term 'balance of payments'? What is meant by a 'balance of payments problem', and what help is needed when such problems are encountered?*

Secondly, underdeveloped countries needed access to capital funds for the long-term projects essential to the development of their economies.

In answer to the second problem, the International Bank for Reconstruction and Development was established — more snappily known as the 'World Bank'. We'll come to it in a moment. But first let's look at the body that was set up to deal with the first problem — the International Monetary Fund (IMF).

THE IMF

The International Monetary Fund was set up in Washington in 1947. The Fund is required by its charter to take two main roles. Firstly, it has to set a code of international economic behaviour for its members, and try to ensure that it is respected. The second role is to act as a 'bank manager' for its members, lending money in support of their own gold and currency reserves when needed.

Where does the money come from?

The resources that the IMF has to achieve these ends are considerable: the fund started out in 1947 at $9 000m, and has been regularly revised — it now stands at $70 000m. This pool of money comes mainly from subscriptions paid in by members (supplemented by a little commercial borrowing). A nation that is a member of the IMF — and most are members, including every significant non-communist country except Switzerland — pays a subscription, called a 'quota'. A country's quota depends on its wealth — the US pays about 20 per cent of the total IMF quota, for example, the UK 7 per cent, and so on. The quota is payable 75 per cent in the member's own currency, and 25 per cent in gold, dollars or SDRs (the IMF's own currency — more about it later).

Putting together all the subscriptions of the 146 members creates a pool of many currencies — dollars and deutschmarks, sterling and yen, ryals and escudos, and so on. This is the Fund proper, and is available for members to borrow when required to meet payments deficits.

SAQ 4: *The system couldn't work if all nations wanted help at the same time. Think carefully — why won't this happen?*

How borrowing works

Members in trouble need foreign exchange. They have the right to 'purchase' it from the pool in exchange for their own currency. This facility is, naturally, subject to rules. The nation in question can draw out 25 per cent of its quota almost without question — it has, after all, paid this amount in foreign currency itself. This first slice of borrowing is called the 'gold tranche': 'gold' because until 1976 members paid this amount in gold, 'tranche' because that's the French word for 'slice'. Having drawn out this first slice, members can make four further drawings (the 'credit tranches') at increasing rates of interest, provided that the IMF believes that sensible economic policies are being used to correct the balance of payments problem.

The member is, therefore, initially entitled to draw 25 per cent more than it has subscribed — and, more importantly, the loan is in the form of the foreign currency it needs to pay its bills. Additional facilities have been created over the 70s and 80s to extend the help that the IMF can give in an increasingly turbulent world to those countries in the balance of payments convalescent ward: an oil fund to help countries hurt by higher oil prices; facilities for countries hit by sudden changes in commodity prices (see Unit 24); other funds for countries in need of extended help. It it now possible, by totalling all the special fund help, for a nation to borrow up to 450 per cent of quota.

Those IMF conditions

Above, we saw that the full extent of IMF help is available 'provided the IMF believes that sensible economic policies are being used'. What this means in practice is that an IMF team visits the country concerned, and looks at 'the books' — trends in imports and exports, output and tax revenues, money and incomes. To obtain a substantial loan, a country must accept targets for fiscal and monetary policies.

SAQ 5: *What is fiscal policy? How might it be used to improve a balance of payments deficit?*

A devaluation of the currency is also a usual feature of the IMF remedy, but import controls are generally avoided: remember, the whole point of IMF help is to prevent countries falling back on protectionism.

SAQ 6: *So devaluation and deflation are the preferred methods for restoring balance of payments equilibrium. What are the disadvantages of these policies?*

Some critics and governments — Jamaica and Turkey, for example — have felt that the IMF's terms for loans have been unnecessarily severe, putting financial orthodoxy before the living standards of the poor. It's claimed that the IMF often demands reduction in government spending (e.g. the abolition of food subsidies), even when that spending is important to the very poor.

Other sources of help

Commercial banks

Generally, the knowledge that a country has obtained the confidence and support of the IMF is enough to restore confidence to the foreign exchange markets. IMF approval makes it easier, too, for a government to borrow from commercial banks, whose resources in total far exceed the funds of the IMF. Commercial banks took a considerable role in lending in the 70s and 80s. They had received enormous deposits from the oil-rich, and lent them on, often to countries that, in the cold light of afterthought, could offer little prospect of repayment. This is the origin of the 'debt crisis' that flits onto and off our newspaper pages as various countries — Poland, Argentina, Brazil, Mexico and so on — find themselves unable to keep up repayments contracted in the 70s.

Swap facilities

A commonly used method by which governments obtain foreign currency is the 'swap facility'. After a meeting in Basle in 1961, the central banks of the major western countries agreed to supplement the help of IMF could give with this arrangement.

SAQ 7: *What's a central bank? Name one. How do they differ from commercial banks?*

A country in difficulties is able to swap its currency with that of another country. It works like this:

> Suppose on the foreign exchange markets there are substantial sales of sterling, with speculators buying DMs instead. If the Bank of England wishes to moderate the collapse in the £s value, it will buy up the £s that are being sold with DMs from its reserves. So it loses DMs and gains £s: without help, it will run out of DMs and be forced to let the £ fall. But if the Bundesbank is prepared to swap the excess £s the BoE has bought in for DMs, the Bank of England need never run out and will therefore always have enough funds to resist the speculators' attack.

The swapped money must be repaid later, at the exchange rate at which it was borrowed. This deters governments from using the facility to prop up an overvalued currency.

SAQ 8: *Why might they wish to keep the value of a currency up? What is the main disadvantage of such a policy?*

Stand-by credits

Often, the announcement of a sound programme of stabilisation and IMF support will reduce the need for money to meet panic sales of currency. When this happens, governments do not need to draw the full amount of IMF support, and so it makes sense to arrange a 'stand-by credit' — that is, the ability to draw money if needed. This plainly makes a more economical use of the IMF's funds, although a stand-by also requires IMF approval of government policies. Often this takes the form of a 'Letter of Intent' — the government writing to the IMF an open letter outlining the fiscal and monetary steps it will take to sort things out.

The General Agreement to Borrow

The GAB is a special fund created by the Group of Ten leading industrial nations, who have access to this additional pool of funds after the normal consultations.

Policing the system

But you'll remember that supplying loans to countries with balance of payments difficulties was just one part of the IMF's job. It was also required to supervise the system of international payments to avoid the damaging chaos of the 30s. In the years between the establishment of the Fund and 1973, it was felt that world trade would be best encouraged by fixed exchange rates.

SAQ 9: *How is it possible to keep a currency's exchange rate at a fixed level?*

As a result, under IMF rules, members were required to hold their exchange rates fixed in value, allowing only minor variations against a 'parity' fixed in terms of gold and dollars. To be sure, these parities were not immovable: from time to time, the economy of a member would move so decisively out-of-line with the others that there was a 'fundamental disequilibrium' in their international payments, and then a devaluation was required. The UK devalued, for example, in 1949 and 1967. But this was a rare occurrence that required IMF approval.

In the early 70s, though, the system of fixed parities that had worked so well until the 60s, and had at least coped after then, fell apart under the great pressure of economic events. There were a number of reasons for this collapse, which was a major event in the economic history of the post-war world.

1.   The main reason was the growth in size of capital flows. By the mid-seventies, the amount of money free to move from country to country and from currency to currency was much too large to be controlled by the central banks. The name given to the largest of these flows was 'Eurodollars'.

Eurodollars are dollars held outside the US both by Americans — originally attracted by higher interest rates abroad when there were limits on US rates — and by foreigners, content to hold the dollars that poured out of the US during the deficits of the 60s and 70s. These funds are held in banks through the world: and not only are Eurodollars no longer just 'Euro-', they are also other things besides dollars. Markets have grown up in the investment and lending of other currencies outside their 'home base' — the mark and the franc, even 'Eurosterling', though the dollar is still the major Eurocurrency. Indeed, it is common to refer to all currencies held in bank accounts outside their country of origin as 'Eurodollars'.

The size of the Eurocurrency funds is enormous. Any estimate made at the time of writing will quickly be out of date, but the *Economist* guessed $800 billion in 1979 — twice as large as the UK GNP, and probably larger than all the reserves of the IMF members added together. No government can defend a parity against capital flows of this size.

2.   The oil shock drastically altered the economic prospects of many nations whilst creating a pool of unspendable large wealth among the 'low absorbers' that fed into the world banking system.

3.   The 'asymmetry' of the old IMF system, which required countries with deficits to alter their policies without any such obligation on the surplus countries who also contributed to the problem. Debtor countries, because they had to go to the IMF and follow instructions, had to make changes: creditor nations were under no parallel obligation to revalue their currency or reflate their economies to reduce their surpluses.

SAQ 10: *What adjustment will occur to a surplus country under freely floating exchange rates?*

4.   Lastly, it must be admitted that countries who were in chronic deficit (like the UK in the 60s and the US in the early 70s) or in persistent surplus (like Germany and Japan throughout the 60s) did not make the exchange rate adjustments needed at the time, and of the magnitude, required. There was a tendency to cling to the old parity as a kind of badge of national pride.

The result of all these pressures was that governments were obliged to let their currency find its own value against other currencies.

SAQ 11: *What is this system called? Under it, what determines the external value of a currency?*

Originally, the IMF hoped that the period currencies spent unpegged would be brief, giving a useful indication of the level at which new fixed parities would be enforced. But the fixed-exchange-rate system never re-appeared. Instead, the IMF now presides over a floating-exchange-rate regime, establishing the ground rules and providing a forum for discussion. The IMF guidelines, for example, require members not to 'fiddle' their exchange rates to secure a competitive advantage and to avoid wild short-term movements in their exchange rate values. (For more details, *see* the latest edition of Prest and Coppock, *A Manual of Applied Economics*.)

Does floating work?
So floating was really forced on the international financial community. But, as we have seen in Unit 22, there are some cogent arguments in favour of floating anyway – indeed, a number of economists, like Friedman, feel that floating is the best mechanism for international payments.

SAQ 12: *Where have we met Friedman before?*

Run over the arguments in the last unit – and if you would like to place yourself in a position to evaluate the success of floating as compared with the years of fixed exchange rates look at 'Have Floating Rates Been a Success' by David Higham (*Economics*, Spring 1983).

More about SDRs
Many of the problems of the world's financial system can be attributed to the fact that there is no world currency. As a result, international transactions have to take place in someone's national currency. Further, countries have to hold their international reserves in someone else's currency, or gold. Currency is available only if the country concerned – usually the US for its dollars – is happy to allow large deposits of its currency to be held outside its control. Even then, problems are caused by fluctuations in the value of the dollar, and US economic policy is affected (as UK policy was in the high years when sterling was an international currency) by the central role of the dollar. No wonder countries like Germany, whose currency could become a reserve currency, have taken steps to avoid this happening.
    As far as gold goes, the supply depends on the output of mines in South Africa and the USSR – neither a sound economic base for a stable reserve unit, nor politically acceptable to the majority of nations.
    Now, if the expansion in world trade is not matched by an expansion in internationally usable money ('international liquidity') increasing payments crises will occur. Inside a country, after all, governments take great pains to achieve a stable and adequate supply of money.

SAQ 13: *What will happen if they do not?*

Yet there is no international agency assuring a stable and adequate supply of international liquidity to finance world trade. It's left to the lottery of gold and dollars.

The IMF has tried to meet this problem by inventing a form of paper money issued to all members — the SDR (Special Drawing Right). The SDR is a unit of currency based on a basket of five major currencies: at the time of writing it's worth about $1.26. It comes into existence in this way:

> The IMF adds a certain amount of SDRs to all member's quotas — a percentage of their quotas. If a country wishes to spend its SDRs, it informs the IMF. The IMF will know another country that has currency available — the first country can now use its SDRs to buy currency from the second country. In its books, the IMF reduces Country 1's SDR account and increases Country 2's. To compensate Country 2 for the fact that it has lost a well-established currency in exchange for a new and untried international money, it receives interest on its SDR holding.

SDRs have not taken a very great role in settling international debts, but are increasingly being used as a way of expressing the value of large contracts, international loans or foreign government statistics. Indeed, a number of international bond issues are now expressed in SDRs, for this avoids investors being exposed to the shifts and switches of value that might happen to one country's currency.

SAQ 14: *What are the three functions of money? Which function is the SDR fulfilling when loans, investments and contracts are denominated in SDR terms?*

Summary

The IMF, therefore, has a most important role in today's increasingly integrated world economy. It provides funds to tide members over their temporary balance of payments problems; it supervises the floating-exchange-rate system that covers the world's major currencies; it provides a forum for reforms in the international monetary system. The problem for students is that its workings change rapidly, and so the best source for further information is likely to be a Bank Review article or *Economist* piece rather than a textbook. *See* the Review Section at end for advice.

THE WORLD BANK

The other Bretton Woods institution, the International Bank for Reconstruction and Development (World Bank) was set up to answer the needs for funds for development in the third world. Like the IMF, the World Bank works on a subscription basis: members pay 2 per cent of quota in gold, dollars or SDRs, 18 per cent in their own currency, and hold the rest until the IBRD wants to use it. With this money, IBRD grants loans through its subsidiaries the IDA (International Development Association) — for public works like dams, roads and power supplies — and the International Finance Corporation, which can take holdings in private companies and invest in commercial enterprises.

Despite vigorous leadership, the IBRD has never had the massive resources to match its aims. The problem here is not only the immensity of the task of world development, but also the political realities of control. Remember that in the IMF and IBRD, nations get votes in line with subscription. Thus they are controlled by a small group of rich nations, with an effective veto by the USA.

GATT

The third international body, the *General Agreement on Tariffs and Trade* may best be thought of not as a fixed body but as a regular conference. Its aim is to reduce trade barriers between countries on a multilateral basis. There are several problems facing a single country trying to achieve freer trade, and so this task is best achieved by many countries meeting and agreeing to remove restrictions on an 'I-will-if-you-will' basis. The success of GATT in its progressive 'rounds' of negotiation has been considerable, particularly with respect to manufactures. It is a sign of this success that its discussions have moved on to non-tariff barriers to trade.

SAQ 15: *What nickname is given to non-tariff barriers to trade? Give some examples of such barriers.*

THE EUROPEAN COMMUNITY

What is the EC?

One of the trends in the postwar world has been the formation of a number of regional economic groupings. Countries have agreed that trade amongst members of their 'common market' should be free of normal restrictions. Examples include the Latin American Common Market, Comecon (in Eastern Europe) and the subject of this unit, the European Community.

The origins of the EC

'Europe will be united by money, or it will not be united at all' said Robert Schuman, one of the fathers of European unit. This certainly appears to have been the case with the EC. Its origins are to be found in the European Coal and Steel Community, an agreement for free trade in coal and steel products signed in 1951 between France, Germany, Italy and Benelux countries. The ECSC was a success. Trade barriers were removed as planned, trade thrived between members and living standards rose. The natural consequence was the extension of the provisions for free trade to a wider range of goods and services, and so the Treaty of Rome (1957) aimed at establishing a European Economic Community for all commodities. Full free trade was scheduled for 1970, but in fact was achieved in 1968.

The UK looked at these developments from outside. We had been approached at the time of the formation of the ECSC, but 1951 was a particularly unfortunate time for such a project so far as the UK was concerned. We were in the middle of an election campaign, and the steel industry had just been nationalised – hardly the right time to allow control to go to a supra-national High Authority. The structure of the EC was also unsuited to the UK: the common external tariff, together with the common agricultural policy, would have meant a break with the Commonwealth. Other countries found themselves unable to join the EC, either because they felt it compromised their neutrality (Sweden, Switzerland, Austria) or because they had fishing or agricultural sectors that needed special treatment (Norway and Portugal, plus Ireland and Denmark who depended so much on the UK food market): these countries banded into the European Free Trade Area (EFTA) which restricted free trade to manufactures.

During the 50s and 60s, however, the UK looked with increasing envy at the rapid economic growth of the EC, and several applications to join were made, both by Conservative (1962) and Labour (1967) Governments. After a couple of refusals, the Heath Government negotiated terms of admission and signed the Treaty of Accession in 1972: we eventually became members on 1st January 1973, and a five-year transition period ended in 1977. Ireland and Denmark joined at the same time as the UK; Greece joined in 1981, and Spain and Portugal in 1986.

EC common policies

The EC aims to form a single economic unit of its members by the adoption of the following common policies:

- *free trade among members* Tariffs between members have been completely abolished. An energetic campaign to remove non-tariff barriers to trade is under way (and is the source of all those stories about Eurobeer, Eurobread and the end of the British milkman).
- *common external tariff* This means that goods entering the EC from outside are treated the same, no matter which member's border they cross first. The import tax on an American machine or an Australian apple is the same in Genoa as in Grimsby, Bristol or Bremen.

SAQ 16: *What would happen if members offered differing tariffs to goods entering the Community from outside?*

- *free movement of labour* All citizens of the Community are free to seek work anywhere within the Community on equal terms with nationals of the home country. No work permits are needed, and social security rights are the same.
- *free movement of capital* The Community aims at a free movement of capital between members: this has been tougher to achieve than some of the other aims. The UK conformed to this in 1979, but more as an expression of the Thatcher Government's free-market philosophy than to fulfil EC policies.
- *common agricultural policy (CAP)* Farmers throughout the Community receive the same support for their products, and food policy is administered from Brussels rather than by member governments.
- *common policies of industrial support*; the aim being to ensure that struggling industries or regions receive comparable support, no matter where they are in the EC. This has two aims – to see that prosperity is spread more evenly, and to avoid member governments outbidding

each other with incentives to get new firms to come to their country or region.

- *a common voice in dealing with the rest of the world* The EC presents a united front in international economic negotiations, and also offers agreed concessions (outlined in the Lomé Convention) to third-world producers seeking access to Community markets.

How the EC works

The day-to-day running of the EC is supervised by the *European Commission*. The Commission is a body of full-time officials who got their jobs on the recommendation of member governments, but when appointed act as 'Europeans' – that is, they do not in any sense represent or argue for their own country. Each Commissioner is responsible for one area of Community policy – such as agriculture, energy, transport, industry, the environment, etc. The Commission can make regulations for the EC, and when a major policy change or initiative is planned, the Commission works on it before passing it on to member governments.

The governments are represented on the *Council of Ministers*: really big decisions will be made here, rather than by the Commission. The Council is made up of one minister from each member government – usually the Foreign Minister, although it might be another minister according to the topic under discussion – such as agriculture ministers when farm policy comes up. The thrice-yearly conferences of Heads of Government ('summits') are part of this series. For very important decisions, unanimity is essential, especially where a member feels essential interests are at stake: in theory, though, most decisions can be passed providing there is a substantial majority. Voting (as at the IMF) is weighted.

The *Court of Justice* settles legal disputes involving Community laws. There is one judge from each Community member, serving for six years. The judgements of the Court are binding on individuals, firms and governments within each member country.

The last Community body is the *European Parliament* of 410 members. Each country has a number of members proportionate to its size – 81 for Britain, 15 for Ireland, 25 for Holland, and so on. The Parliament can question the Commission and Council, debate their proposals and prepare reports on them: however, Parliamentary resolutions are not binding on the Commission, and so up until now the Parliament has remained something of a 'talking-shop'.

What were the advantages to the UK of EC membership?

We saw earlier that the UK's entry to the EC was the culmination of a considerable campaign. What advantages did those who worked so hard for entry foresee?

- *Faster growth*
  You will remember from Unit 3 that the UK has suffered from slower growth than its European competitors. The table below shows the comparison in the year of our signing the Treaty of Accession:

1962/72	EC members	UK
Rise in exports	142%	63%
Rise in investment	68%	12%
Rise in GNP	56%	26%
Rise in consumption	45%	19%

SAQ 17: *What is GNP? Does the table show that the EC had higher GNP than the UK in 1972?*

Of course, economic growth cannot be magicked up simply by signing a Treaty – it must be achieved by greater efficiency and higher investment. Nevertheless, the example of Belgium – a country whose dated economic structure (not unlike Britain's) was renovated in its years of EC membership – held out hope.

- *Greater international specialistion*
  We have met in Unit 20 the theory that the international division of labour results in better living standards and higher incomes for all countries. It follows logically that countries should gain from a reduction in trade barriers. Whether or not this argument can be simply applied to the EC is far from clear, however.

  The area of economics that concerns 'customs unions' (i.e. common markets) distinguishes between the 'trade-creating' and 'trade-diversion' effects. Trade-creation refers to the gains in trade resulting from the demolition of tariff walls, which allow efficient producers within a community to expand their production and sell in the markets of other member nations. However, let's remember that when the UK joined the EC it was obliged to place import duties on goods (especially food imports, and goods from the Commonwealth) that had previously been let in free. So there must be a 'trade-diversion' effect of EC membership as well (e.g. by making us replace cheap West Indian cane sugar with expensive European beet sugar, or NZ butter with more costly European butter). In the case of the EC, it is at least arguable that the trade-diversion effects are greater than the trade-creating effects. The barriers that existed between European nations were relatively low, and were getting lower.

SAQ 18: *Which international body was working to lower international tariffs?*

In exchange for removing these modest barriers, the EC has erected the external tariff, a protectionist agricultural policy and an often unhelpful attitude at international trade talks.

- *Scale economies*
  Scale economies formed another justification for market entry. Large firms can get lower costs with long production runs – but they can only produce as much as they can sell. As Adam Smith remarked 200 years ago, 'the division of labour is limited by the extent of the market': it is of little use for, say, a large chemical company to learn that the cheapest scale of fertiliser production is 5m tonnes a year if the home market can only absorb 2m tonnes. The advantage claimed for EC membership here is that it offers a home market of 260m, big enough for an efficient scale of production with almost any industry. International trade, too, offers us the opportunity for scale economies without monopoly.

    N.B. the last two arguments – scale economies and greater specialisation – rest on the assumption that EC markets were effectively closed to us before entry.

- *Trade trends*

SAQ 19: *Look back at page 318 of Unit 22, and write a brief paragraph arguing, with figures, that the prevailing trend in UK trade direction made it beneficial to join the EC.*

- *Negotiating strength* The EC acts together, as we've noted earlier, in its discussions with other groups on international issues – like Japanese imports, or fishing agreements with the USSR. Britain has also gained support in other areas (e.g. the Falklands embargo on Argentina). Probably just as important is the matter of technical specifications: as tariff barriers fall, the major barriers to international trade become those national technical and safety regulations and specifications. As a major EC member, Britain can take a part in framing those specifications rather than having to sit outside and accept what might be awkward decisions.

So what were the disadvantages?
But Britain's accession to the EC has not been a wholly happy affair. Many of the problems that have arisen during the period of membership – rapid inflation following the oil shocks of the 70s, then high unemployment during the world slump of the 80s – cannot be blamed on the EC. Other problems, however, are plainly related to EC membership.

- *The budget problem*
  The EC Budget, like all budgets, involves receipts and expenditure. We must look at both to understand the basis of the British belief that we have had a raw deal. Firstly, receipts. The EC gets money from two main sources – the yield of 1% VAT and the customs money from the import levies. Because we in the UK have a broad VAT base (with a high proportion of national income consumed, and a low proportion invested and exported) and import much of our food, we pay a disproportionately large part of the bill. On the spending side, let's note that three-quarters of the Budget is spent supporting farmers.

SAQ 20: *Look back at SAQ 18 of Unit 2, and explain why a policy which concentrates on supporting farmers works against the UK.*

The result of paying more in revenues and getting less in pay-outs is that the UK (together with Germany) is a large net contributor to the EC budget. Hence the acrimonious debate throughout the 70s and 80s about a UK 'refund'.

- *The common agricultural policy (CAP)*
  The EC operates, as we have noted, an agricultural policy for all its members. The CAP establishes a support price for most farm products, fixed at a level which, it is hoped, assures farmers of a decent income. These 'target prices' are high — between two and five times world levels. Now two things could imperil the fixed price — cheap imports, or overproduction within the EC. Imports are kept out with the use of a variable import levy that makes sure that low world prices are topped up to EC support levels. Overproduction is dealt with in a different way.

SAQ 21: *Check back to Unit 12, pp. 198–199 and explain (a) why the CAP results in surpluses and (b) how the EC prevents this surplus reducing the market price.*

The policy has a number of defects. Food costs more than it would do if we bought from world producers. The policy of purchase and storage is very costly and very wasteful (creating piles of unsold products to be destroyed, or sold outside the EC). Note also that the policy goes against the doctrine of international specialisation by preventing efficient food producers outside the EC having access to our markets (and earning money that might have been spent buying the exports of genuinely competitive EC industries); it even *competes* with efficient producers in export markets.

- *Sovereignty*
  For the first time, the UK Parliament and courts can be over-ruled by an international body. This means that the UK government is restricted in its economic policies. EC regulations forbid a number of options — import controls, restrictions on capital exports, job subsidies and food subsidies — that a radical government may wish to consider.

The European Monetary System: a note
Earlier in this unit, we noted that the fixed exchange rate system of the IMF broke down in the early 70s, and was replaced by a floating-exchange-rate regime. Whilst floating exchange rates have their advocates, many economists and businessmen feel that the daily fluctuation of exchange rates interferes with trade, creating an uncertainty that hits jobs and output. A UK exporter to Germany, for example, incurs costs in £s and receives revenues in DMs — the whole profitability of the enterprise could therefore depend on changes in exchange rates. Stability in exchange rates has, therefore, been a longstanding aim of the EC: in 1971 it adopted the aim of full monetary union by 1980. This never happened in the turmoil of that decade, but it led to an attempt at stability — the European Monetary System (EMS). The EMS was agreed at the July 1978 EC Summit at Bremen, and was born in March 1979.

The EMS has at its centre a newly created unti of currency, the Ecu (European Currency Unit). The Ecu is made up of all the European Currencies — 32% DM, 15% Sterling, 19% Franc etc. It is worth about 70 pence at the time of writing: changes in its value follow changes in the value of constituent currencies, and can be checked each day in the *Financial Times*. As with the SDR, the Ecu is used basically as a unit of account: some commercial deals are being expressed in Ecus even at the present early stage of development.

Members of EMS undertake to keep their currencies in line, by not varying against the Ecu by more than 2¼ per cent above or below the par. There are also cross-rates against the other member currencies — all very similar to the old Bretton Woods fixed-exchange-rate regime.

SAQ 22: *Look at the diagram below and say (a) what would a member of EMS do if their currency rose to the upper intervention point (b) or to the lower intervention point?*

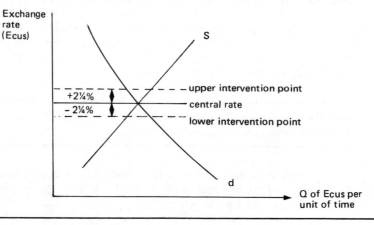

Another feature of the system is a partial pooling of foreign exchange reserves: members put 20 per cent of their reserves into a common pool (Fecom – the European Monetary Cooperation Fund) to help stabilise currencies.

Summary

The fact that, within a floating-exchange-rate regime, there are attempts to secure currency stability in the EMS shows the twin pressures working in the international money world. On the one hand, there is the desire to stabilise exchange rates so that trade can flourish in an attitude of certainty. But on the other hand, it must be recognised that when countries have different fiscal and monetary policies, inflation rates and changes in productivity, balance of payments deficits and surpluses will occur. This will make it difficult to align currencies. Italy, for example, works within a wider EMS band of plus or minus 6 per cent. The UK has not joined at all, because as sterling is a petrocurrency, it and other European currencies will tend to move in opposite directions.

SAQ 23: *The birth of the EMS coincided with a French attempt to expand their economy.*
(a)   What effect would this have on the French balance of payments?
(b)   What effect would this have on the value of the FFranc?
(c)   What action would therefore be required to keep the franc in the EMS?

REVIEW SECTION

Further reading

As I mentioned earlier in this unit, the picture of international organisations changes quickly – sometimes from week to week. Whilst there are some excellent basic books on the world's monetary system (like Pulay and Clarke *The World's Money* and Brinley Davies *The UK and the World Monetary System,* Heinemann), these quickly become dated. My advice would be to use the latest edition of A.R. Prest *The UK Economy* (Weidenfeld and Nicolson) as your starting point, following up with the readings from Bank Reviews recommended there. On Eurocurrency, see David Gowland *Modern Economic Analysis 1*, Macmillan. *The Economist*, as ever, is an excellent source as is the series of Economics Briefs published from articles in *The Economist;* once again look at the one titled *International Trade.*

Those wishing to gain a more political viewpoint will learn that many writers on the left regard the IMF/IBRD as institutions which are used to perpetuate capitalist control of the world economy: countries are denied funds unless they toe the orthodox financial line. If interested, read Theresa Hayter *Aid as Imperialism* or Cheryl Payer's *The Debt Trap,* both Pelican.

Barclays Bank Review, November 1987 looks at the role of the IMF and World Bank. For an article on GATT see the *Economic Review,* March 1987.

As far as the EC goes, much material (not very neutral, but colourful and free) is available from the Commission of the European Communities, 20 Kensington Place Gardens, London W8 4QQ. Unit 4 of *International Trade* (mentioned previously) looks at UK trade with the EC.

G. Dennis looks at the EMS in the *Economic Review,* March 1987. In *Economics,* Autumn 1987, J. Redmond discusses the merits (or otherwise) of the UK joining the EMS.

As far as the Common Agricultural Policy goes, see if you can lay hands on 'Down on the Farm' (*The Economist,* 23 October 1982, reprinted in their Schools Brief series) and also 'The Impact Of The Common Agricultural Policy on Agricultural Trade and Development' – *National Westminster Quarterly Review,* February 1987.

Examination questions

1.   Describe the main features of the European Monetary System. Assess the arguments for and against United Kingdom membership of the system.

(AEB 'A' June 1987)

2.   Assess the advantages and disadvantages for the United Kingdom of the Common Agricultural Policy of the European Communities.

(Oxford Local Delegacy 'A' June 1986)

3.   'The United Kingdom stands to gain more from participation in the European Monetary System than it obtains from its present participation in the Common Agricultural Policy of the EC.' Discuss.

(Oxford Local Delegacy 'S' June 1985)

ANSWERS TO SAQs

SAQ 1:   The rate of inflation can be worsened either by a fall in the exchange rate, or by a rise in the price of essential imports; unemployment is affected because nearly a third of everything produced in the UK is sold abroad; and economic growth for the same reason – if we expand the economy faster than that of our neighbours we will suck in imports.

SAQ 2:   His work on macroeconomics (*The General Theory of Employment*) formed the basis of Units 4, 5 and 6.

SAQ 3:   The balance of payments is a set of accounts detailing a country's financial transactions with the rest of the world. A balance of payments problem is generally understood to apply to the situation when the country's receipts (from exports and capital flows) are insufficient to meet expenditure (on imports and capital outflows): when this occurs the country will aim to cure the problem, but in the short term it needs foreign exchange to meet the bills.

SAQ 4:   Because it is logically impossible for all members to have a deficit at once – for every deficit is someone else's surplus.

SAQ 5:   The use of taxation and spending policy by the government to alter the level of aggregate demand. By raising taxes and cutting public spending, the level of aggregate demand will be reduced, thus reducing spending on imports.

SAQ 6:   The disadvantage of devaluation is twofold – firstly, it worsens the terms of trade, making imports cost more in terms of the exports that have to be sold to pay for them. Secondly, it adds to inflation by making imported goods dearer. Deflation reduces economic activity, increasing unemployment and reducing incomes.

SAQ 7:   Central Banks are the publicly owned banks that control the money supply – in the UK, the Bank of England. Commercial banks, like the National Westminster, are privately owned profit-making institutions that take deposits from the public with the aim of lending them on to borrowers profitably.

SAQ 8:   To reduce the cost of living (see answer to SAQ 6): the main disadvantage of this is that it makes exports expensive, reducing their sales and thus employment.

SAQ 9:   By purchases and sales from its reserves: when a currency rises in value above parity, the Central Bank sells it, driving the price back down: when the value falls below parity, the Central Bank purchases its own currency with its foreign exchange reserves (or increases the private demand for it with higher interest rates or forward purchases).

SAQ 10:   Its currency will float upwards in value, because demand for its currency will exceed supply. As a result the country's exports will be dearer and imports cheaper, bringing into play forces that will (given the right elasticities) bring the balance of payments back to equilibrium.

SAQ 11:   Floating. Supply and demand for a currency.

SAQ 12:   As the arch-monetarist and free-marketeer.

SAQ 13:   A matter of great controversy, this: the safe answer is to use the Fisher equation and say that inflation will occur unless the money supply is controlled: too sharp a reduction in money will cause a slump.

SAQ 14:   As a means of exchange, store of value and unit of account. The SDR is being used as a unit of account in these cases.

SAQ 15:   Invisible tariffs, such as scientific and technical specifications, hygiene regulations (remember the UHT milk?), discriminatory tendering procedures for government contracts, etc.

SAQ 16:   Traders would import the goods through the cheapest import country, and transport them across the unrestricted borders of member countries to their market: the alternative to this is a cumbersome documentation of origin, which would impose the need for customs between members as (say) tea from Ceylon was taxed between Britain and France.

SAQ 17:   GNP is a measure of the amount of commodities produced in a country in a given year (including property income from abroad). The table does not show that EC members had a higher GNP, merely that the GNP they had was growing faster than the UK's.

SAQ 18:   GATT

SAQ 19:   My attempt goes like this:
    Throughout the postwar period, the advanced industrial markets of Europe were becoming more important to the UK, and the importance of the underdeveloped markets of the Commonwealth was declining. The third world took one-third of our exports in 1955, now less than one-eighth: Western Europe went up in the same period from 25 per cent to 57 per cent. It makes sense to go where your markets are.

Incidentally, I find this curious: doesn't the idea of international specialisation say that countries with differing opportunity-cost ratios should trade advantageously, not countries with similar opportunity-cost ratios?

SAQ 20: Because the UK has a very small proportion of its population in agriculture compared with other EC members.

SAQ 21: (a) The surpluses are a straight result of fixing the price above equilibrium: it is a text-book example of excess supply (b) the surplus is bought up and stored — or destroyed.

SAQ 22: (a) It would sell its own currency and purchase the currency of other members of the system to bring the rates back in line (b) the reverse — buying the endangered currency and selling other currencies.

SAQ 23: (a) It would worsen, as a rising national income would involve more imports, (b) It would fall, as demand for francs would fall whilst demand for foreign currency (to purchase the imports) would rise. (c) Either defence of the existing parity, involving the purchase of francs with guilders, DMs, lire etc., or a revision of the parity — effectively, a devaluation. Restrictive economic policies and higher interest rates would also work.

24 The Third World

AIMS OF UNIT 24

At the end of this unit, you should be able to:
- explain what is meant by a less developed country
- list the essential problems common to LDCs
- outline W. W. Rostow's theory of economic development, using the terms 'take-off, 'maturity' and 'high mass consumption'
- explain and criticise Arthur Lewis' dual economy theory
- describe the barriers to growth that exist in third-world economies
- outline the debt problem
- explain how overseas aid might be used to help LDCs.

INTRODUCTION

In the course so far, we have looked at the problems of an industrial economy, very often in a British context. We have looked at how a £200 billion GNP is measured; how consumers choose between various commodities; discussed whether welfare can be best served by large or small firms. In this unit we will be looking at economies with an altogether tougher problem: simply providing enough to keep their people alive. The conditions of social and economic underdevelopment and poverty in which four-fifths of the world's population now live, and the ever growing gap between rich and poor nations are often passed by in economics textbooks with the briefest of comments. Yet, as Peter Donaldson argues in *Economics of the Real World* (p. 231):

> The continued existence of poverty and world inequality on the present scale represents *the* most pressing economic problem of our times.

And inside the poverty of most of the world's countries, there is a more profound misery:

> . . . about 800m people in the developing world still live in absolute poverty, with incomes too low to ensure adequate nutrition, and without access to essential public services. Many of these people have experienced no improvement in their living standards; and in countries where economic growth has been slow, the living standards of the poor may even have deteriorated.

> (*World Development Report*: IBRD)

WHAT IS A LESS DEVELOPED COUNTRY?

Terminology changes fast in this area of economics: what were once 'backward countries' spent a brief period of time being 'underdeveloped', became 'developing' and were then elevated to the status of 'less developed countries', or LDCs. Words are easier to change than facts. Whatever the terms used, LDCs suffer in the following ways:

Poverty

The North, including Eastern Europe, has a quarter of the world's population and four-fifths of its income: the South, including China, has three billion people — three-quarters of the world's population, but living on one-fifth of the world's income (*Brandt Report*).

The following table illustrates the disparity between rich and poor countries:

Income (US $ per head, 1979)

Switzerland	13 987
West Germany	11 080
USA	9 637
UK	6 372
India	185
Ethiopia	118
Bangladesh	109
Cambodia	50

SAQ 1: *A first reading of the above figures indicates that citizens of Switzerland are nearly three hundred times richer, on average, than Cambodians. What precautions should be taken before accepting a comparison of dollars-per-head like this? What is the particular problem with comparisons of advanced and less developed economies? (See Unit 3 p. 44-47).*

The World Bank in its 1979 *World Development Report* assessed the gap between rich and poor at a ratio of 40:1 — and felt that it would widen to 47:1 by 1990 unless aid and development policies changed.

But inequality isn't simply a problem of the division of income and wealth *between* rich and poor countries. The distribution of income *within* most LDCs is usually more unequal than in the rich countries. In Western countries, the richest 10 per cent of households typically receive 25 to 30 per cent of the income. But Griffin points out that in Latin America, generally the richest 10 per cent get 40 per cent of the income. World Bank figures (1980) show that in Brazil and Honduras the richest 10 per cent receive half the national income. This means that the per capita figures quoted above do not tell the whole story. Concealed behind the average figure lies in a far more crushing poverty for the majority of the population of most LDCs.

Agricultural dominance

The second major characteristic of LDCs is the high proportion of the workforce still working on the land. It is rare for manufacturing to contribute more than 10 per cent to GNP. In the poorest countries, 85 per cent or more of the population live off the land: in middle-income LDCs the proportion is nearer 50 per cent. The agriculture is often backward, peasant farming, with low productivity, threatened by drought and other natural or man-made disasters.

SAQ 2: *What proportion of the UK workforce are in agriculture? (Try to do this without checking back to Unit 2!)*

The LDCs, then, are poor and heavily dependent on subsistence farming. But they have a number of other problems in common, the most widely publicised being that of population growth.

Population

Population in the poor countries is growing much more rapidly than in rich countries largely because a lower death rate, brought about by improvements in disease control and public health, has not yet been matched by a lower birth rate. Many people see the 'population explosion' as *the* key problem of the third world. Although this view is probably over-simple (the answer to lower population growth lies in economic and social development itself), population growth rates are without doubt one of the problems facing the LDCs. A country like Mexico with a population growth rate of 3 per cent per year requires 3 per cent extra GNP simply to maintain living standards. GNP in the third world grew at an encouraging 4 per cent per year throughout the 50s and 60s — but population trends meant that GNP per capita went up just 1½ per cent per year. Between 1960 and 1975, the figures were less happy: population up by 2.4 per cent compared with increased food output of 2.1 per cent.

In fact, the world population is growing more slowly now, due to slowing birth rates in the third world: nevertheless, no-one anticipates a stable world population before 2100. There will be a fuller discussion of the nature and effects of population economics in the next unit: but besides the problem of standards of living, population pressure creates problems in finding jobs for all the new entrants to the labour force.

Unemployment and underemployment

Many LDCs have massive urban unemployment — because towns offer higher wages than the country, just an outside chance of a job in industry is worth a life in the slums. But in the country there is very substantial underemployment. This is caused by the seasonal nature of traditional agriculture — outside the growing season, there is little to do, with the result that up to a third of the population is underoccupied for nearly half the year.

SAQ 3: *List the types of unemployment (if in doubt, see Unit 5, pp. 84-5); which are the two major types of unemployment evident in LDCs?*

These are the basic facts of underdevelopment — poverty, inequality, high population growth rates, unemployment and underemployment. Other important problems include:

Poor health and lack of health and welfare facilities

In the North the average person can expect to live for more than seventy years; he or she will rarely be hungry, and will be educated at least to secondary level. In the countries of the South the great majority of people have a life expectancy of closer to fifty years; in the poorest countries, one child in four dies before the age of five; one fifth or more of all the people in the South suffer from hunger and malnutrition; fifty per cent have no chance to become literate. (*Brandt Report* p. 32).

The example of Zambia is striking: at independence in 1964, a population of 3½ million had just 100 university graduates, and only 1200 had finished secondary schooling.

Lack of economic infrastructure

Unit 1 introduced you to the idea of social capital — facilities like ports, roads, railways, postal services, electric power, schools, sewage disposal and so on. These investments are in many ways just as vital to economic development as items of business investment, such as power tools, steel mills or textile factories.

SAQ 4: *Which Bretton Woods institution was established to provide finance for public investment projects of the sort outlined above?*

HOW DO NATIONS DEVELOP?

How did it happen that the world became divided into different sorts of country — some enormously rich by history's standards, others barely able to feed their peoples? What are the causes of underdevelopment and poverty? How can today's LDCs escape from their problems, and manage to feed, enjoy, clothe and house their millions? That is what concerns the remainder of this unit. Firstly, I shall briefly review two influential theories of economic development; then I shall take a down-to-earth look at the barriers that seem to stand between less developed economies and their progress to prosperity.

Theory 1: 'The Stages of Economic Growth'

One well-known theory of economic development was outlined by the American economic historian W. W. Rostow in *The stages of Economic Growth*, CUP 1960. Rostow admits that his theory is a very generalised conception of the process of development — which is inevitable, given the varied societies one considers in attempting a world-wide theory of development. But, despite that he sees each industrialising society going through a series of similar stages of growth.

They start in a 'traditional society', based economically on agriculture and socially on the family or clan. Life in the traditional society remains much the same for generations — 'the range of possibilities open to one's grandchildren would be just about what it had been for one's grandparents'. But new technology and new markets create the 'preconditions for take-off', and when these forces of economic advance gain in strength, then 'take-off' occurs. New industries expand, towns grow, investment and savings rise to historically high levels. The change is so great that a steady rate of economic growth becomes assured, and the economy passes through a 'drive to maturity' until it attains 'high mass-consumption'.

How convincing is Rostow's model?

Rostow's book is easy for the non-specialist to read, and you may wish to get hold of a copy yourself to assess the weight of his arguments. His model starts all countries from more or less the same base: the answer for those countries who have not 'taken-off' is to discover what it was that enabled today's rich countries to become 'mature'. Various authors cite an increase in the capital stock (i.e. investment), a more efficient use of the existing capital stock, increased education, an increased rate of technical change — even a burst of population growth — as the crucial factor. Many nations have, in fact, taken the path to development since the emergence of the first industrial nations like the USA, Britain and Germany. Japan, Sweden and Canada have caught up, and other countries like Mexico, Iran, South Korea, Taiwan, Brazil and Singapore form a group of 'newly industrialised countries' (NICs).

Yet the drawback of Rostow's theory is just that — in the way it sees the growth of today's LDCs mirroring that of today's developed countries. Even if we ignore the turbulent international relationships that have existed between industrialised countries and the LDCs — plunder, colonialism and the rest — we cannot ignore the fact that the LDCs are growing in a modern world, where modern techniques already exist and large international companies provide vigorous competitors or dominant partners. Even the entrepreneurs of the British industrial revolution — the Watts and Boultons, Owens and Stephensons — would have been inhibited if faced with foreigners who owned much of manufacturing industry and always had first access to new techniques.

Theory 2: the 'dual economy'

Attempts to take into account the simultaneous presence of both modern and traditional elements in LDC economies are known as 'dual economy' theories. Dual economy theorists (like Jorgensen or, more famously, Sir Arthur Lewis) divide the economy of an LDC into two largely independent sectors. On the one hand is a modern industrial sector which is dynamic and responsive to market signals.

SAQ 5: *What are 'market signals' and why might modern firms respond to them?*

But on the other hand, there is a traditional agricultural sector with much disguised unemployment and a subsistence level of income. The process of growth takes place through a flow of labour from agriculture to expanding industry.

Now, as agriculture is typified by widespread underemployment, farm output and incomes are not affected by shedding surplus labour to the developing manufacturers in the towns. Only when agricultural labour becomes scarce does that sector start to modernise itself.

A development plan based on Lewis' theory notes that wages will be kept very low by the existence of the pool of labour from the country. Not until that reserve is exhausted will wages have to rise much above subsistence levels: as a result, there will be opportunities for entrepreneurs to earn large profits that can be reinvested to raise the capital stock. In the long run, this will boost growth and national income, and thus 'trickle down' to improve the living standards of the average family.

What's wrong with Lewis' model?

It should be noted that in Lewis' model, development is an urban process that results, at least initially, in little improvement in worker incomes. In fact, urban wages are often substantially higher than those in the countryside, which contributes to the attraction of towns and consequent unemployment. Other criticisms concentrate on the drawbacks of using Lewis' ideas as a basis for development plans. Specifically:

- the failure to raise agricultural incomes means that the market for manufactures inside the country remains small, and so industrial production has to cater for export or for the luxurious tastes of the rich.
- it is implied in the 'dual economy theory' that peasants do not respond to economic incentives, and do not save. But they do: the example of Kenya, which now produces an exportable surplus of maize, shows that given the land and decent prices, peasant farmers can produce the food.
- development plans which neglect the countryside in favour of industry increase urban unemployment and slums: what is worse, in those countries with a majority of the population in farming, it will also direct funds away from those most in need of help.

It is this last criticism which has hit home with most force. Aid programmes have swung in recent years to help agriculture and the rural poor. The IBRD, which in the 60s devoted ten per cent or less of its funds to rural programmes, now gives a third or more. In the UK, the 1975 White Paper on development policy (titled *More Help for the Poorest*) announced a switch to helping the majority in the fields – and at the extreme became a 'basic needs' strategy aimed at providing the most basic needs of the very poor.

SAQ 6: *In the last few pages I've described two modern theories of economic development. Yet one of the most famous I've ignored – that is to say, Karl Marx's theory of capitalist development. See if you can look out some reference books to write down a paragraph or so on Marx's theory of development. Don't try to summarise Das Kapital – there are plenty of brief and readable summaries around: start maybe with a good encyclopaedia, or the first chapter of the* Communist Manifesto.

A comment

Perhaps theories which look to LDCs for development mask the nature and depth of the problem. Given a high rate of population growth, even the highest of possible growth rates will not dramatically raise living standards near those in the rich North. What is more, the LDCs start from a low base: a five per cent growth is less impressive when you realise that it's five per cent of not very much. If a rich and a poor country are both growing at a given percentage, the real living standards of the two are moving sharply apart for this very reason. In fact, rich countries grow faster than poor ones in per capita income. The low-income LDCs raised their per capita standard of living by 0.6 per cent per year 1960-76; the middle-income countries by 2.8 per cent, and the rich industrialised countries by 3.4 per cent.

Let's now move away from theory into a look at the factors that appear to hold back the development of LDCs at the moment. I have divided the barriers to growth into two categories:
- internal barriers: factors within the countries themselves that impede economic progress
- external barriers – those features of international relations that contribute to the underdevelopment of nations.

INTERNAL BARRIERS TO GROWTH

Problems with investment

It is common ground between most economists that high rates of growth require high levels of investment.

> The central problem of the theory of economic development is to understand the process by which a community which was previously saving and investing 4 or 5 per cent of its national income or less, converts itself into an economy where voluntary saving is running at about 12 to 15 per cent of national income or more.   (Arthur Lewis)

The disagreements begin over:
- how the savings and investment are to be generated
- how they are to be used.

Priorities in the use of investment funds have to be decided between industry and agriculture; physical capital and human capital; heavy industry v. light industry; manufacturing v. social capital; modern technology v. low-cost technology of a more environmentally sound nature ('alternative technology') and so on.

SAQ 7: *What might be meant by the phrase 'human capital'?*

The sources of capital raise as many questions: high levels of investment require high levels of domestic saving, or taxation, or borrowing from abroad in the form of aid or commercial investment. In most LDCs the proportion of investment and saving in the national income is low, as is the proportion of taxation. The poverty of the majority of the population is such that they can save little, even if efficient savings institutions exist to channel savings to potential investors. The great inequality of incomes inside LDCs is often justified on the grounds that the rich save more than the poor:

'if you gave a poor Indian an extra rupee he would be likely to spend it on consumption; if you gave a rich Indian a rupee, he might well invest it, adding to future income' (Michael Parkin).

Thus, a more equal distribution of income would lower savings.

SAQ 8: *What is meant by the abbreviations MPS and APS? If a more equal income distribution would reduce total savings, which is larger – the MPS or the APS?*

If true, this creates quite a problem (the 'growth/distribution problem') – fairness now, or growth in the future? In fact, though, there is little evidence that the rich *are* good savers – often they spend their money extravagantly on luxury imported goods or invest their money more safely abroad. Clearly a successful development strategy must raise the domestic rate of saving somehow, if the country is not to become increasingly dependent on foreign funds. This is one of the great attractions of planning in the third world, allowing vigorous government action to force higher levels of savings and investment.

One important by-product of an unequal distribution of a small national income is the resultingly small internal market for the mass consumption goods that could be produced profitably by domestic industry. This weakness of the internal market limits investment opportunities generally, and the pattern of effective demand determined by the distribution of income diverts much investment into relatively non-productive luxury areas like the construction of up-to-the-minute flats. Thus the problem of investment concerns the size of the internal market as much as the low level of savings.

In considering the question of 'what investment?', we must stress the importance of investment in human capital and the infrastructure. Investment in human capital includes any investment which improves the productivity of human labour without providing better tools or machines. A well-fed, healthy person is much more productive than someone who is weak from malnutrition, often ill, and illiterate. Infrastructural investment similarly creates the economic and social environment within which economic growth is possible. It's no use increasing the production of rice to feed urban workers if there is no road or railway to transport the rice from the countryside to the town.

Land-tenure

We've seen earlier that plans which place too great an emphasis on urban growth and jobs lead to a lopsided development that neglects the countryside.

SAQ 9: *What theories were those plans based upon?*

But the development of agriculture in many LDCs is often not a simple problem of increased investment or better incentives for peasant farmers. In many parts of the world – particularly Latin America – the key problem is the ownership and division of the land. For historical reasons, the best land in many LDCs is monopolised by a rich group of landlords who farm only a small part of that land. The mass of peasants are squeezed onto small plots of land, often on stony hillsides. Such is the latifundia/minifundia system in many Latin American countries.

Problems with land-tenure: a case study.

A *Financial Times* report on Brazil's north-east (25th Oct 1977) pointed out that the land distribution was becoming more, not less unequal, with land concentrated in large underused estates. The last census showed that two-thirds of farm properties were of less than 24 acres and occupied 6% of all farmland, while there were many estates of 2,000 acres where only 50 or 100 acres are in use. Meanwhile the smaller farms, many of them less than 2½ acres, are too small for efficient agriculture.

Land reform and an attack on the monopoly power of landowners are basic and highly political issues in agricultural development for many LDCs.

Other, less politically sensitive agricultural problems include the importance of irrigation and flood control (especially in India and China), the provision of effective credit and marketing services for smaller farmers and the availability of tools and seeds at prices that peasant farmers can afford.

The 'green revolution'
Publicity has recently been attracted to the introduction of new techniques — modern strains of seed, fertilisers, irrigation, multiple cropping — that have enabled farmers to increase yields by 50 per cent or more. Technical advance in farming is, of course, an essential: yet such change often has undesired side effects. The new machinery and fertilisers can only be bought by the richest farmers: the new crops need expensive irrigation, good soils, pesticides. As a result, the introduction of 'green revolution' techniques can increase inequality, and even worsen the welfare of small farmers because of increased competition.

Inefficient industry

The problem of monopoly power in agriculture is often mirrored by a similar situation in industry, with attendant inefficiency and high prices. One strategy of industrialisation stresses a process of import substitution whereby domestic industries, sheltered by tariffs, are protected so that they may grow to replace imported goods.

SAQ 10: *Check back to Unit 20 p. 311 to see the name economists give to such industries.*

Such policies often have the effect of creating and then protecting monopolies in industry, monopolies which intertwine with political forces to make a corrupt barrier to growth.

SAQ 11: *Give three major criticisms of monopoly. What advantages might be offered by a monopoly firm? Why are these advantages unlikely to be present in such a situation as mentioned above?*

Population growth

Population growth can also form a barrier to growth. The initial effect of a surge in population is to worsen the dependency ratio (*see* Unit 2, p. 19): many more children have to be supported by the existing workforce. Valuable funds are necessarily diverted into education and training together with increased housing and other welfare investments — resources that might well be more usefully invested in productive industry. And in some countries, though by no means all, the additional population will increase pressure on the land. The actual effect of population growth on economic prosperity is something we shall have to consider more fully in the next unit, and it is by no means a one-way argument: additional people increase the size of the internal market and provide a boost to the workforce. Research does not establish any simple connection between population control and economic prosperity. Keith Griffin, an economist who has worked in Chile and Pakistan as well as teaching at Oxford, noted that, if anything, the countries with fast population growth seem to do rather better.

EXTERNAL BARRIERS TO GROWTH

Unstable export earnings

The need to import machinery for development programmes — and often also to buy food, fuel and consumer goods, and repay debts — makes LDCs anxious to sell abroad to earn foreign exchange. Yet export earnings of LDCs are often very unstable. This is due to three interconnected factors.

- LDCs typically depend on one or two commodities to earn the bulk of their foreign exchange. 94 per cent of Zambia's export earnings come from copper; Mauritius relies on sugar for 90 per cent of export earnings, Cuba 84 per cent; the Gambia 85 per cent from groundnuts; and so on. These figures are from the *Brandt Report*, which goes on to say that between 1970 and 1972, over half the non-oil developing countries obtained more than fifty per cent of their export earnings from one or two crops or minerals.
- Demand for these commodities is stagnant. Income elasticity of demand for primary products is low and in many cases synthetic substitutes are available.

SAQ 12: *How do we measure income elasticity of demand? Why is it likely to be low for nut-oil, sugar etc?*

Yet the price of manufactures continues to creep upwards. As a result, the cost of LDC exports tends to fall relative to the cost of imports.

SAQ 13: *What is our measure of the relationship between export prices and import prices? If in doubt, check back to Unit 20, pp. 307-9.*

- The prices for primary products fluctuates enormously. Supply is inelastic with respect to price, and so is demand. As a result, minor shifts in supply and demand can cause very substantial changes in price.

When you combine the price shifts with the importance of primary commodities to LDCs, the effect is to create a startling instability in export earnings. Few countries can develop when subject to falls of thirty or forty per cent in their export earnings.

There have been a number of proposals aimed at moderating the effects of these swings in export earnings. We've seen that the IMF has arranged special finance for countries trapped by collapsing commodity prices. Yet the best way seems to be to eliminate the vast swings in prices with the use of a buffer stock scheme.

SAQ 14: *Briefly explain how a buffer scheme works to moderate changes in the prices of agricultural goods. Why are such schemes particularly needed in agriculture, rather than industry? (If in doubt, see Unit 12, pp. 206-8.)*

It's interesting to look back into history and note that an original part of the Bretton Woods proposals — never adopted — was for an International Trade Organisation to stabilise commodity prices. Proposals for International Commodity Agreements (ICAs) to help were made in the 70s, without success, although the EEC's Stabex scheme does provide a modest start.

An alternative way to stabilise earnings is to form a cartel: producers combining to restrict output and sales. A number of such cartels have been tried and failed, due to 'back-door' sales outside the schemes which have undermined the official intervention price.

Tariffs and protection in rich countries

These problems with fluctuations in the earnings of primary commodities, the problem of the small internal market and the long-term decline in the prices of primary products have made LDCs keen to diversify their exports, and in particular to increase their sales of semi- and fully-manufactured goods. Some of the middle-income LDCs have made strides in this direction — manufactures rising from 5% of exports in 1960 to 17% in 1975. However, such attempts have been hindered by the protectionism of the advanced countries. The tariffs of rich countries generally favour unprocessed raw materials over processed materials or manufactured goods. What the LDCs need is access to the markets of rich countries for their manufactures. Yet, despite some protestations of belief in free-trade, rich countries have become increasingly protectionist (tariffs on third-world manufactures are twice those on industrial nations' goods) and have increased their surpluses in trade in manufactured goods with LDCs.

The recession of the 70s and 80s has worsened the protectionism of the richer countries. The effect has been redoubled, for when unemployment and low output are present in industrial countries,

- the richer countries will tend to import less (for imports are a function of national income: *see* Unit 5, p. 77).
- the richer countries will be more reluctant to extend overseas aid and concessions on trade
- migrants will be less welcome; indeed, a number of the richer countries took steps to expel migrants from the third world.

SAQ 15: *Explain precisely how the existence of migrant workers might improve the balance of payments of an LDC.*

It is not just in manufactured trade that the protectionism of the advanced North of the globe matters. It is true increasingly in the area of agricultural goods: Europe, once a major market for food, is now a net food exporter — and some of these food exports are subsidised, placing primary producers at an even greater disadvantage.

Problems with financial flows

The other external barriers to growth concern the problems caused by foreign aid, investment and borrowing. Undoubtedly, aid with no 'strings' — on generous terms and earmarked for useful development projects — can be of help to a developing country. Unfortunately, much aid is not of this kind. Firstly, many countries use the meagre aid they give — or lend — as a means of boosting their own exports. This is the practice of giving 'tied aid', where the funds must be spent on goods produced by the donor country. This will often reduce the value of the aid, because the donor country's goods are unsuitable or uncompetitive in terms of price or quality, and create a future dependence on spare parts, etc. Secondly, aid has been used, often cynically, as a political bargaining counter — to support friendly and compliant third-world governments, however corrupt, and bring the defiant to their knees.

Official government aid has not, in any case, been big enough to match the problem. It falls far short of the UN aim of 0.7% of GNP in almost every advanced nation — coming out at about 0.3% of GNP. Official aid is actually a declining proportion of the financial flows from rich to poor nations, falling from 60 per cent of all flows in 1960 to less than one-third today. With the failure of official aid to match the scale of the problem, many LDCs turned to commercial loans, usually arranged by banks from the Eurocurrency markets. Because loans from these private sources have higher interest rates and need to be repaid more quickly than official development funds, the cost of debt to LDCs is rising sharply. By 1982, the debt of non-OPEC developing countries amounted to $540 000m, and the cost of debt servicing (interest charges and repayments) was taking up to a quarter of all the export earnings of some LDCs. Problems in servicing the debt burden leads to new borrowing and a worsening debt service problem — what Cheryl Payer (see sources at end) has called 'the debt trap'.

This is not the only financial problem. Trans-national companies who invest in LDCs are able to repatriate profits to such an extent that money is in many cases being transferred from poor to rich rather than vice versa. Further, the extent to which overseas aid and commercially borrowed funds — or even domestic savings — are used to purchase advanced capital equipment from richer countries, creating income and jobs there rather than in the LDCs, is also an indication of the complexity of the problem.

Balance of payments deficits

We've already noted a number of factors that will create payments deficits: falling terms of trade, imports of capital goods, debt servicing, remittances to multinational companies. One more must be mentioned — and that is the consequence of the rising oil prices in the 70s.

> To take three countries in three separate continents and all with stable governments, between 1972 and 1979 the cost of fuel imports into Costa Rica rose ninefold from $20m to $190m. The figures for Fiji show a rise from $16m in 1972 to $87m in 1979. In Malawi, fuel imports in 1972 cost $12m and in 1979 $58m.There were comparable rises in the cost of chemicals, basic manufactured goods and transport equipment.
>
> (Lord Walston in *The Guardian*)

Where does aid fit in?

We have seen the practical problems with aid, but in theory it can still be most valuable, both in supplementing domestic savings and in relieving the crushing balance of payments problems we've just looked at. Aid, though, is subject to two sorts of criticisms.

Criticism from the right

Peter Bauer — now Lord Bauer — is known as the most severe critic of overseas aid: he simply advocates ending all aid programmes. The main drift of his argument is that aid encourages the idea that development can be painlessly brought in from abroad, whereas in fact it needs sacrifice and social change within the LDC itself. In addition, aid fortifies the power of central government (usually dictatorial) and often skews development in inappropriate directions.

Criticism from the left

We have already quoted Cheryl Payer's comments on the debt trap. Teresa Hayter has published a book — *Aid as Imperialism*, Pelican — which attacks current aid policies because they create and sustain a class in LDCs which is subservient to the interests and ideas of the rich nations. The promise of aid keeps LDCs within the capitalist world order, paying dividends to multinational companies and interest on past loans.

SUMMARY

This unit has ranged over a number of facts and theories, and discussed the problems that face LDCs in their drive for social and economic development. Inevitably, the treatment of these issues has been superficial and sometimes one-sided: further reading will be particularly useful if you wish to develop this topic into one of your examination strengths. The main argument I have put forward is that the economic development of most third-world countries requires a series of major reforms or structural changes both within themselves and in their situation in the world economy. In this sense, the problems of the third world are very different from the problems of growth in the developed countries.

REVIEW SECTION

Further reading

Introductory: Look first at Lipsey's chapter on development — chapter number varies according to edition. Other useful sources include Peter Donaldson's *Worlds Apart* (and a good chapter in *Economics of the Real World.*) There's a (perhaps surprisingly) excellent introduction on LDC problems in *Pears Cyclopaedia*, full of facts and case studies. Gunnar Myrdal's classic *Challenge of World Poverty* is available in Penguin paperback. The *Brandt Report* is also readable and cheap — published as a paperback by Pan as *North-South: A Programme for Survival*: a follow-up survey was published in 1983.

Useful: Development in a Divided World ed. Seers and Joy, Penguin. *Two Views on Development* — a debate between Barbara Ward and Peter Bauer published by the IEA. For a good survey of the idea of 'intermediate technology', see *Small Is Beautiful* (Abacus) by E.F. Schumacher, Chapter 14.'

Radical: Various books exist to put forward the radical, anti-imperialist view — that is, the idea that many of the problems of the poorer countries originate in a systematic mechanism of oppression of LDCs by rich nations. An early one was, of course, Lenin's *Imperialism, the final stage of capitalism*. Other books taking the argument into our own day are:

Michael Barratt Brown *The Economics of Imperialism*, Pelican
Teresa Hayter *Aid As Imperialism*, Pelican
Cheryl Payer *The Debt Trap*, Pelican
Paul Baran *The Political Economy of Growth*, Pelican

The view is by no means established, and you may read dissenting views expressed by Bauer (see above) and in *Dissent on Development* and *Equality, the Third World and Economic Delusion*, Weidenfeld and Nicolson, by Revel in *The Totalitarian Temptation*, Penguin and (a balanced and typically thoughtful approach) in George Lichtheim's *Imperialism*, Penguin.

Sound and basic: I've already mentioned *Economics*, the economics teachers' journal: the Spring 1983 edition has an excellent article on theories of development by Stephen Hurd. See also 'Unemployment and Poverty' by G.P. Marshall in the *Economic Review*, September 1987 and 'Oil Prices and Debt' by Professor G. Bird in the *Royal Bank of Scotland Review*, June 1987.

Examination questions

1.   What is the term 'less developed' intended to convey about an economy? Evaluate the following methods of assisting less developed economies: charitable gifts of goods and services (e.g. 'Live Aid'); official aid from governments; credit from the international financial institutions.

(JMB 'A' June 1986)

2.   Examine the advantages and disadvantages of overseas aid for (a) donor countries and (b) recipient countries.

(AEB 'A' November 1986)

3.   How would you distinguish between the terms 'economic growth' and 'economic development'? Compare the possible effects of a policy of population control with either investment in manufacturing, or improvements in agriculture on the standard of living in a less developed economy.

(JMB 'A' June 1987)

4.   Three decades of progress in market economies (1950–1980): income, education and health.

Table 1: Income

	GNP per person (1980 US dollars)	
	1950	*1980*
low income countries	170	250
middle income countries	640	1 580
industrial countries	4 130	10 660

Table 2: Education

	adult literacy rate (percentage)	
	1950	*1980*
low income countries	22	42
middle income countries	48	78
industrial countries	95	99

Table 3: Health

	life expectancy at birth (years)	
	1950	*1980*
low income countries	37	52
middle income countries	48	61
industrial countries	67	74

Source: *World Development Report*   published by the World Bank, 1984.

(a)   With reference to the three broad divisions of market economies in Table 1, what assessment could be made of the relative levels **and** rates of change in GNP per person 1950–80?

(2 marks)

(b)   (i)   Given the data in Table 2, suggest **two** possible economic advantages of rising literacy rates.

(2 marks)

(ii)   Suggest **one** economic disadvantage of rising literacy rates.

(1 mark)

(c)   (i)   What are the main trends in the life expectancy data in Table 3?

(2 marks)

(ii)   Suggest **two** factors which might explain these trends.

(2 marks)

(iii)   Analyse the *economic* consequences of the trend in life expectancy.

(3 marks)

(Total 12 marks)

(Cambridge Local Examinations Syndicate 'A' November/December 1985)

ANSWERS TO SAQs

SAQ 1:   There are a number of problems to be tackled before accepting a simple 'dollars-per-head' figure as indicating real differences in living standards. These qualifications include:
(a)   If production is made up of investment goods, or arms, a high GNP per head may not indicate high levels of consumption.
(b)   GNP per head is an average only: if there is considerable inequality of income (as there is in many LDCs) it tells us little of the life of the typical citizen.
(c)   GNP per head shows us income, but takes no account of wealth: the income of the US or UK household adds to a considerable pre-existing store of wealth.

(d)   Unmarketed goods are difficult to account — but unless we make an allowance for all the commodities made and consumed within a household, we will under-estimate the living standards of the subsistence farmer.

(e)   The standard of living is a narrower idea than the standard of life, which must also take account of pollution, leisure, crime, life expectancy, and a million other things.

(f)   International comparisons have to use rates of exchange, which can be very deceptive. (b),(c) and (d) are particular problems when comparing 3rd world countries with the rich countries.

Follow up the reference in the SAQ to Unit 3 for fuller explanations.

SAQ 2:   Just about two per cent.

SAQ 3:   Cyclical, structural, seasonal, frictional. The two types evident in the LDCs are seasonal (see text) and structural (because workers do not have the right skills, experience, etc.), though the world recession must add some cyclical unemployment on top of this.

SAQ 4.   The IBRD (World Bank).

SAQ 5:   The market signals through price: when there is a shortage, prices rise causing a wind-fall profit to producers, and encouraging other firms to enter and existing firms to expand. Falling prices reverse the effect. As a footnote, we should notice that in some LDCs food prices are fixed at a low level in order to maintain urban living standards — with the predictable effects on agricultural output and incomes.

SAQ 6:   Marx started, as Rostow did later, from a traditional society in which power was based on the ownership of land. This feudal society disappeared with the growth of towns, new technologies, new discoveries: the dominant class of the new society (called capitalism, because within it power came from the ownership of capital) was the bourgeoisie. They became the masters of the new society by supplanting the aristocracy which was based on land: Marx viewed history as a succession of class struggles and the final triumph of the new capitalist order is signalled by the dominance of the bourgeoisie. However, history does not stop with industrialisation: the constant need to expand trade and output to gain profits hits a ceiling because low wages limit the size of the market. Profit rates suffer, and workers' incomes are so low that the industrial working class ultimately revolt and take over power. The means of production — factories, tools, machinery, ships and railways, banks and ports — are taken over by the proletariat and a society based upon common ownership of the means of production — socialism — dawns.

SAQ 7:   See last paragraph under the heading **Problems with investment** (middle of p. 367).

SAQ 8:   The marginal propensity to save and the average propensity to save — check back to Unit 4, pages 57-8 for revision. If the APS was equal to the MPS, then no matter how a given GNP was distributed, the total amount of savings would be the same. But in the case mentioned, the MPS exceeds the APS.

SAQ 9:   Dual economy theories, like that of Lewis.

SAQ 10:   Infant industry.

SAQ 11:   Monopoly results in higher prices, inefficient production and possibly x-inefficiency (*see* Unit on monopoly): the advantages of monopoly concern scale economies and innovation — although it is unlikely that a firm which enjoys such advantages would require the protection of a tariff barrier.

SAQ 12:   By dividing the percentage change in expenditure on the goods concerned by the percentage change in income — when the figure comes out at less than one, we speak of demand for a product being inelastic with respect to income. Commodities like cooking oil and sugar will have a low income elasticity of demand as the amount we can consume is limited, and as the cost is low we have already bought what we need: as a result, very little — if any — of any increase in income will be spent on them.

SAQ 13:   The terms of trade.

SAQ 14:   A buffer scheme works as follows: when supply exceeds demand, and so there is downward pressure on price, the purchasing board enters the market to buy up and store the surplus. But when prices shoot up during a shortage, the authorities enter the market to sell from the buffer stock, moderating the rise in prices. Such schemes are needed in agriculture because prices are more unstable than industrial commodities for all the reasons shown in Unit 12, pp. 206-8.

SAQ 15:   Migrants typically remit funds home, thus increasing the invisible earnings of their country of origin.

25 The economics of population

AIMS OF UNIT 25

What are the causes of growth in the world's population — and what are the economic effects? Should we try to reduce the UK's population to ease pressure on our land, or be more worried that present low birth rates would reduce our future workforce? These are the questions this unit aims to consider, and at the end of it you should be able to:

- explain the term 'demographic transition'
- define the terms 'birth rate' and 'death rate'
- explain and criticise the idea of 'optimum population'
- show what is meant by the 'structure of population' and interpret the population pyramids that illustrate population structure
- discuss the economic effects of changes in both population size and structure.

INTRODUCTION

In 1066 there were about 1¾m Britons: that number had crept up to 10½m or so by the time of the first census in 1801. Yet in the nineteenth century, the population grew explosively to 28m; and by the end of 1986, the British population stood at 56.7m. To understand how this happened, we have to consider both the changes in the birth rate and the death rate. Let's start with some definitions:

The birth rate is measured as the number of live births per thousand of the population in a given period — usually a year. This can be simply calculated as follows:

$$\frac{\text{Total births}}{\text{Total population}} \times 1000$$

The death rate is expressed as the number of deaths per thousand of the population in a given period, and is calculated in a similar way.

Now, think of population as the water in a bath. The size of the population is shown by the level of water in the bath — a level which will rise if the amount of water coming through the taps (the birth rate) goes up. But it will also go up if the amount of water going out of the plughole (the death rate) falls. So changes in the size of population are caused by changes in the relationship between birth and death rates.

The birth rate in Western Europe at the moment is about 12: the death rate about 11.

SAQ 1: *Will this cause a rise or fall in population – and by what percentage ?*

But during economic development, this rough balance between births and deaths is very different. Let's start by considering an under-developed economy. Here, birth and death rates are high, and as a result, although the rate of infant mortality (the number of deaths of infants under the age of one, expressed as a ratio of 1000 live births) is high, population remains stable. Yet one of the first effects of economic advance is a decline in the death rate. This is attributable to a number of factors:

- higher incomes, leading to better nutrition and housing
- improved public health services – water and sewage
- scientific and medical advances.

There follows a period when this sharp fall in the death rate is not matched by any fall in the birth rate. This results in a fast growth in size of the population.

SAQ 2: *Look at these statistics and select the country with the fastest rate of population growth. Unit 24 warned that some third-world countries have a growth of population as fast as their economic growth rates. What's wrong with that? Is there any evidence of this in the table?*

	Population (mid-1980 est.)	Birth rate	Death rate
W. Europe	*153m*	*12*	*11*
China	*975m*	*20*	*8*
India	*676m*	*34*	*15*
Malaysia	*14m*	*31*	*6*
Kenya	*16m*	*55*	*14*
Nigeria	*77m*	*50*	*17*
Ethopia	*33m*	*50*	*25*

What happens next, though, is that birth rates fall. As the size of families gets smaller, the population growth slows. This is due to:

- the spread of contraceptive knowledge
- the realisation that children will survive to adulthood
- the changing role of women
- the increasing cost of raising children in a society where years of education are expected, and child labour is discouraged
- the fact that children cannot work as effectively in towns as perhaps they could on farms.

Ultimately, then, we arrive at a society in which both birth and death rates are low. The process has come full circle in a sense, for we are now back once again to a stable population size. This change, called the **demographic transition**, is the long-term hope in concern for world population size – that ultimately birth rates will come down, stopping the present increases in world population. However, the size of the population is now much bigger than at the start of the process – just look at the British figures I quoted at the beginning of this unit for an example.

SAQ 3: *Fill out the gaps in this diagram, which illustrates the process of 'demographic transition' that we've just described.*

	Stage 1	Stage 2	Stage 3
Birth rate	*High*		
Death rate			*Low*
Population size	*Stable but small*		

THE RESULTS OF CHANGING POPULATION SIZE

Malthus

How will such explosive increases in population affect living standards? The prospect of overpopulation has been a worry for hundreds of years. When, in the sixteenth century, a succession of bad harvests caused starving country people to descend on towns as gangs of beggars, there were suggestions that the problem was one of too many people, and could best be solved by migration to the colonies across the Atlantic. But overpopulation fears were put in a more rigorous form in Thomas Malthus' *First Essay on Population*, 1798. Malthus constructed his theory from two tendencies. On the one hand, population would tend to grow geometrically (that is – 2, 4, 8, 16, 32, 64, 128: constantly doubling). By contrast, food supplies could never be expanded this fast – at the very best they would increase at an arithmetical rate (1, 2, 3, 4 etc.). As population growth outstripped the supply of food, living standards would fall to a bare subsistence level. At this point. population growth would be checked by disease and famine.

This is a dismal forecast, and Malthus could only see it being avoided by later marriages and general sexual restraint. He was personally opposed to contraception (which he included under those 'preventive checks that clearly come under the head of vice') but his predictions lent strength to early birth-control pioneers. Indeed, one of the first birth-control clinics in London was opened by a group of pioneers calling themselves the Malthusian League.

There is undoubtedly much force in Malthus' argument. We learned in Unit 13 that if we add more and more of a variable factor (i.e. labour) to a fixed factor (such as land), productivity will ultimately fall.

SAQ 4: *What did we call that mix of productive factors that ensures lowest costs?*

In Unit 13 this principle – known as 'diminishing returns' – was used to derive a firm's cost curves, but it can equally be applied on a larger scale when considering population problems. Adding more and more people to a small planet must, it seems, drive down productivity per head and therefore living standards. However, we also learned when looking at theories of the firm, that costs can fall and productivity rise when the scale of production is increased. How can these countervailing tendencies be incorporated into out ideas about population?

'Optimum population'

It was the Victorian economist Edwin Cannan who incorporated such ideas. He realised that there would be some tendencies that would actually make a rising population increase living standards. The logic goes like this:

In a small population, everyone has to be self-sufficient. We all have to grow food, tailor clothes, make carts and so on, whatever our preferences and skills. As society grows bigger, specialisation can take place, and thus we achieve higher living standards. This process was described in Unit 2 – you may remember the gains achieved when Howard and Neil concentrated on what they were best at. Further gains are possible as population grows, for now mass-production is possible with all the attendant economies of large-scale production. Economies can also result from spreading the cost of large, indivisible items (like dams, rail links, defence forces, broadcasting etc.) across more consumers and taxpayers. In other words, there are reasons to believe that a rising population will make production cheaper and more efficient, raising living standards.

There is, however, a countervailing tendency – the one spotted by Malthus. As more and more people are added to a fixed quantity of land, they each add successively less to output (diminishing returns again). A Simple example of this might make the principle clearer. If you take a farm and keep adding labourers, whereas the addition of the second or third worker will help to expand output considerably, there is little to be gained from the employment of the fortieth or fiftieth person.

Adding these two tendencies together – the increasing returns gained from a larger market, and the diminishing returns caused by changing the factor mix – leads us to the diagram below. At first, as population rises, living standards grow: but ultimately a point is reached where diminishing returns set in, and from that point on extra population will lower living standards.

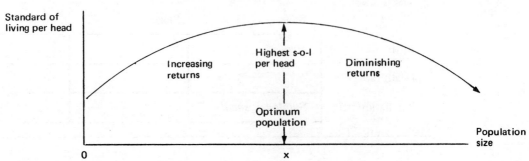

Note that there is a peak where living standards are at their highest — where the advantages of large size are not yet weighed down by diminishing returns. Cannan named this the point of 'optimum population'. It is useful, for it gives us a neat idea of 'over population' and 'underpopulation'. The country shown in the diagram can be considered underpopulated if its population is less than OX, for increasing population may be expected to raise living standards.

SAQ 5: *Where in this diagram do dangers of overpopulation exist?*

Criticisms of optimum population

At first sight this seems a very powerful idea. It is attractive in that it alerts us to the idea that rising population may have different effects on different countries: we might well be more concerned at population growth on Mauritius (429 people per km^2) than in Cameroon (13 people per km^2). However, the theory of optimum population can be criticised on a number of grounds.

- it is very indefinite. Whilst admitting that the logic seems sound enough, you'll note that it isn't possible to name the right population for any given country.
- the concept of diminishing returns depends on adding successive units of a variable factor (in this case labour) to a fixed factor (presumably land and capital): so population could grow as long as new reserves of raw materials were exploited and capital accumulated.
- no account is taken of the technical and scientific progress that enables us today to support a population five times as large as in Malthus' day at a vastly higher standard of life.

Other effects of changes in population size

Before leaving this discussion about the 'right' size of population, I should like to mention two other effects of population growth. Firstly, there will be an effect on the balance of payments if our population grows faster than the rest of the world. Other things being equal, it will add to the demand for imports without increasing the demand for UK exports.

SAQ 6: *So how did the slowdown of population growth in the mid-seventies affect the balance of payments?*

Secondly, there will be environmental effects. Additional population and output will cause raw materials to be consumed more quickly, greater pressure on food supplies, and perhaps more pollution as industrial production expands. I discussed this briefly in Unit 2 (p. 25 and references at the Unit end), and examined whether the market system could cope with externalities like pollution in Unit 18. However, these were a necessarily brief look at the modern revival of interest in the Malthusian balance between population and resources.

THE STRUCTURE OF POPULATION

In practice, changes in the size of population are rarely as important as changes in *population structure*: that is, how the population is distributed in terms of age, sex and occupation. At this point, you should re-read the section on labour in Unit 2, pp. 18-19, where the terms 'activity rate' and 'dependency ratio' are introduced. These terms allow you to determine whether or not the addition to a population will add to the workforce, or not: this will be crucially important in deciding the effects on living standards of a given change in the population size.

SAQ 7: *Now go back a couple of paragraphs to my list of criticisms of the theory of optimum population, and add a new one incorporating this point.*

Population pyramids

Changes in the sex and age structure of a population can be neatly illustrated with the aid of population pyramids. I've illustrated one below. This technique builds up a diagram of the population by giving each age range its 'slice': typically the pyramid divides men and women, enabling us also to read off changes in sex structure. You can read off the scale at the bottom what proportion of the population (or, sometimes, how many individuals) are in each age group.

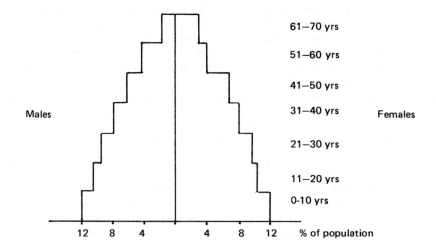

The shape of the population pyramid will give us a number of clues about the history and level of economic development in a country. The population pyramid for an LDC will be squat – broad at the base, narrowing quickly towards the top, showing fast population growth, large numbers of young people and relatively few in the older age ranges. For contrasting reasons, the population pyramid of a European country will look like an artillery shell on end, indicating lower birth rates and more people surviving to old age. This can be modified by historical factors – wars will tend to thin out the male members of a generation more than the female – and by demographic factors, such as the fact that females live longer than males and so are more heavily represented in the older age groups.

Population pyramids need not refer to entire populations, of course – you could construct one from census information to illustrate your own town or city. An expanding industrial town would show a young population; indeed, a booming third-world town might bow out on the male side showing the influx of young men from country districts. By contrast, some towns and regions are ageing: the population pyramid for a popular retirement location might be cylindrical rather than a pyramid.

SAQ 8: *Look at the following population pyramids, and explain which ones might represent the structure of population in (i) Colwyn Bay, a North Wales town with a high proportion of retired folk (ii) Lagos, a booming port in Nigeria (iii) Milton Keynes, a newly built industrial new town in the South Midlands of the UK. Explain your answers.*

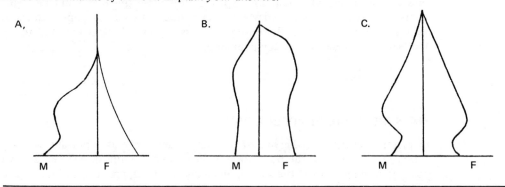

THE EFFECTS OF A CHANGE IN POPULATION STRUCTURE

Changes in the age structure will be represented as either a younger population, or an ageing population. Let's look for a moment at the economics of such changes.

An ageing population
A population with a rising average age will experience a number of effects.

SAQ 9: *What factors might cause rising average age?*

Perhaps these would be best represented in the form of a list.

- There would be a change in the pattern of demand, in that maturer age groups buy different commodities than younger age groups: as one commentator put it, 'more walking sticks, fewer hockey sticks'.
- There will be a decline in occupational and geographical mobility of labour. Young people are considered more willing to move to jobs, and to undergo training than the older worker: this effect could of course be moderated with appropriate government policies.
- The sociology of the workplace will reflect the lower mobility of the ageing workforce, perhaps creating fewer promotion opportunities and increased frustration for younger workers.
- Ultimately the dependent population will rise as the older age groups enter retirement, without being balanced by increased entrants into the workforce. This will, other things being equal, reduce living standards as a larger population has to live off the efforts and output of fewer people.
- An additional factor reducing living standards will be the increased call on welfare services: the older person makes a much heavier call on these (particularly health care) than the younger. The worrying trend here is the increased proportion of the very old, who take a disproportionately large amount of health-care spending. The fact that between now and the end of the century the numbers over 75 will go up 13 per cent (whereas the numbers between 65 and 74 will actually fall by a similar amount) will raise health-care costs.

The last two factors will combine to increase the tax burden on the working population. Whether this will markedly affect their living standards depends on the growth of incomes and productivity. Certainly slow growth plus an ageing population seems to combine the worst of both worlds.

SAQ 10: *Now write a section on the economic effects of a drop in the average age of the population. Concentrate on the effects such a change would have with respect to:*
- *the pattern of consumer demand*
- *the quality and mobility of labour*
- *opportunities for the young*
- *the dependency ratio*
- *public spending and taxation.*

Looking at the answers to SAQ 10, one might believe that a population would gain from a fall in its average age. However, such a shift could realistically only be achieved by an ever-expanding population, which would be open to all the problems of diminishing returns and increased competition for food and raw materials that we discussed earlier.

What are the economic effects of immigration ?
One way that a population can change size without reference to birth or death rates is by migration. An analysis of the economic effects of migration must take into account both the factors we have already discussed — that is, both changes in the size of the population and in its structure. What I'll now do is run through the outline you might give to an essay question such as 'Discuss the economic effects of immigration' (AEB June 1978). If we use a list, we might lay it out like this:

Effects on living standards Taking simply the effect on population size, we must use the concept of 'optimum population': for the effect will vary according to where we find ourselves on the optimum population diagram. Whereas one country might be overcrowded in relation to its land and other natural resources (in which case additional population might reduce living standards), it is possible to think of areas of the world (perhaps Australia or Brazil) which have not yet attained a large enough population for an efficient internal market or full exploitation of natural resources.

On the dependency ratio As migrants are usually of working age, an inflow benefits the dependency ratio, adding more to the working age groups without a matching addition of children or old people. Surveys of the UK reveal that migrants make a lesser call on social services than the domestic population because of the lack of very old people in their community: this effect will, of course, be moderated in the longer view.

On wage rates and inflation Applying simple supply and demand ideas to wages, we might think that additional labour supplies will keep wages lower (and therefore profits higher) than would otherwise be true. This will contribute to a lower inflation rate. As a historical sidelight, the depressing effect of immigration on wages was one reason why US unions opposed greater immigration in the past.

On the balance of payments As we saw earlier, increasing the home population will tend to raise the demand for imports: this is unlikely, however, to be an important effect in reality.

On the pattern of demand If the migrant community have different tastes to the host' community, the pattern of demand will change – which may be confirmed by a visit to a grocer or vegetable stall in an area of migrant settlement.

Perhaps one should add at this point that the UK is a net emigrant country – except for a brief interlude between 1930 and 1960, more people have left Britain than entered it.

What's been happening to the British population?

Predicting population trends has been a rather hazardous business this century. During the 20s and 30s, the worry was that the UK population would fall sharply.

> The long period of increasing population that has lasted since the eighteenth century, if not longer, has come to an end; and there is every sign that the population of Great Britain will fall in the near future. Moreover, . . . the fall, once it begins, will continue at a rapidly increasing rate.
>
> (GDH Cole, 1947)

This discussion was followed by a Leargue of Nations Table that estimated the UK population in 1970 as just 43.6m. It turned out to be 55.7m following the postwar population growth. That in turn led forecasters to quite the opposite mistake – the belief that the population would go on growing fast. In fact, the birth rate started to fall in 1963 and has never reached the level of the postwar years since. As a result, population estimates have had to be drastically revised downwards;

Estimate of the size of the UK poulation in 1991

1971 estimate	1976 estimate	1983 estimate	1985 estimate
62.3m	57.3m	56.4m	57.5m

As a consequence, the government has had to revise a number of social programmes. New town plans have been shelved, and some teacher-training colleges phased out. But though distant forecasts can be inaccurate, the immediate prospects based on people who have already been born can be seen with greater clarity.

The dependency ratio peaked in 1974 and is now falling. This is due to two factors – the declining numbers of dependent children, and the small numbers of people in the age group coming up to retirement.

The average age of the population will not rise: the number of old people will not expand greatly, partly due to the factor just mentioned (a small age group born in the 20s and 30s) and partly because it would be unwise to assume that the mortality rate will fall any more unless radical breakthroughs in heart disease and cancer occur.

REVIEW SECTION

Further reading

Examiners (perhaps wrongly) seem to be more interested in the economic theory of population (optimum population and so on) than in the facts of UK population. The outline of British population is best given in *Social Trends*, a publication brought out every year by the government, and available in most libraries. On the historical side, Carlo Cipolla's *Economic History of World Population*, Penguin, is a marvellous sweeping view of population change, and *Population* by Richard Powell (Longman Economic Studies) goes into the facts of the British experience in much more detail than I have been able to.

Examination questions

1.   Discuss the economic consequences of an ageing population.

(London 'A' January 1987)

2.   'The size of a nation's population is not as important as its age, sex and geographical distribution.' Discuss.

(AEB 'A' June 1986)

3.   The table below shows the age distribution of the United Kingdom's population based on census data for 1931 to 1981.

*Table A: Age distribution of the enumerated population in the United Kingdom
(figures in thousands)*

	1931	1951	1961	1971	1981
Persons (all ages)	46 038	50 225	52 709	55 515	55 039
Under 5	3 531	4 326	4 213	4 505	3 337
Under 18	–	13 248	14 631	15 705	14 241
Under 21	–	15 162	16 667	17 993	16 899
5 – 14	7 643	6 999	8 123	8 882	8 088
15 – 29	11 853	10 328	10 258	11 678	12 402
30 – 44	9 717	11 125	10 526	9 759	10 755
45 – 64	9 877	11 980	13 400	13 384	12 294
65 – 74	2 461	3 689	3 971	4 713	5 045
75 and over	957	1 777	2 218	2 594	3 118

(Source: *Annual Abstract of Statistics*, H.M.S.O., 1984.)

(a)   Outline the main population trends apparent in Table A.

(b)   Discuss the economic implications of these trends.

(London 'A' June 1986, (part))

ANSWERS TO SAQs

SAQ 1:   It will cause a very slow rise in population of 1 per thousand – which is 0.1%.

SAQ 2:   You can pick the country with the fastest rate of growth of population by seeing who has the biggest gap between birth and death rates: it's Kenya, with a 41 per thousand growth rate – 4.1 per cent. This is indeed pretty high for an economic growth rate, and you'll notice that some of the other nations have comparable population growth. This is indeed a problem, for it means that economic development will not actually improve living standards (= National Income per head).

SAQ 3:   The birth rate boxes should read *High, High, Low;* the death rate boxes should read *High, Low, Low:* and the population size is *Stable but small, Growing fast, Stable but large.*

SAQ 4:   Optimum factor combination.

SAQ 5:   To the right of point OX, where additional people reduce the standard of living.

SAQ 6:   It would have improved the balance of payments by causing demand for imports to rise more slowly: I confess to thinking this effect pretty trivial.

SAQ 7:   My paragraph would go as follows.

No account is taken of population structure. It will make a great difference to living standards whether the additional population is in the working age groups, well-qualified and skilled, or whether it is an addition to the dependent age groups or unskilled.

SAQ 8:   (i) is B, with its preponderance of old people, bowed out on the female side to represent the lower mortality of women (ii) is A, a squat pyramid with the addition of young male migrants. (iii) is C, showing a preponderance of young workpeople, and families just starting up (giving a gap in the teenage groups).

SAQ 9:   A falling birth rate or a falling death rate.

SAQ 10:   This a pretty straightforward. Consumer demand would be biassed in favour of younger age group products (indeed, the pop boom of the sixties was attributed to demographic change!); the mobility of labour would be higher both occupationally and geographically; a younger workforce would find advancement more easy; the dependency ratio would fall (although the large number of children might stop this happening immediately); public spending and taxation would be reduced by a larger number of workers, although in the short term health and education for youngsters might be expensive. Certainly a population with a large workforce and small retired population would find it easier to pay for welfare for that older age group.

26 The theory of earnings

AIMS OF UNIT 26

Having completed this unit, you should be able to:
- explain what is meant by derived demand
- outline the idea of diminishing returns, and show how it relates to a downward-sloping marginal productivity curve
- define marginal revenue, and show how a marginal-revenue-product curve relates to the demand for a factor of production
- show how the wage rate is equal to the MRP of the last worker employed
- distinguish between the whole-economy supply curve for labour and the supply curve of labour to individual industries
- derive an equilibrium wage from the supply and demand curves for labour, and show how differences in the supply elasticities of labour will affect wages as demand shifts
- define transfer earnings and economic rent
- show how differentials in earnings can exist in competitive factor markets
- list the drawbacks to MRP theory.

INTRODUCTION

The question 'for whom?' is one of the central economic questions that was introduced in the first unit of the course. David Ricardo regarded it as the most crucial issue in economics: 'to determine the laws which regulate this distribution is the principal problem in political economy'. Indeed, an economist's views on the distribution of national income between rents, profits and wages is a pretty good test of political viewpoint.

The neo-classical view is to see earnings as just one area in which the theory of equilibrium price can be used. In working out the earnings of any particular factor (we'll use labour in this unit, but the analysis is good for capital and land) one draws the supply-and-demand curves for the factor in question on a diagram.

The price at which the factor will be bought and sold is indicated by the intersection of the supply-and-demand curves: it's OA here. With an equilibrium quantity of OB being traded, the total income of the factor concerned is OB times OA, shown by rectangle OAEB. Thus, the share of the national income going to this particular factor is $\frac{\text{OAEB}}{\text{N.I.}}$

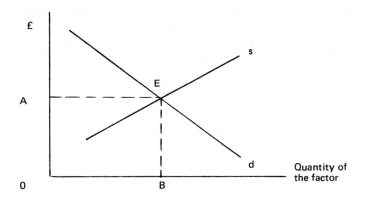

Fig. 26.1 Supply and demand for a factor

We will need to have a clearer idea, though, of the shapes and origins of the supply and demand curves before we can make accurate assessments and predictions.

THE DEMAND FOR A FACTOR OF PRODUCTION

The first thing to say about the demand for a factor of production is that it is *derived demand*. No-one wants a blast-furnace or a cornfield or a mine for itself; we demand the services of these factors of production because we want steel or bread or coal. The demand for coalminers' services is therefore derived from the demand for coal. If the demand for coal falls, so will the demand for miners.

Having understood this, you'll see why the elasticity of demand for a factor is connected to the elasticity of demand for the final product. If a worker makes a product with a low price elasticity of demand, then a rise in pay can be passed on to the consumer in the form of a higher price without a fall in quantity demanded; so few workers will lose their jobs. The elasticity of demand for a factor will also be connected to the technical conditions of production. If a factor's earnings are a small part of the final price, then demand for that factor will be price-inelastic. On the other hand, we may expect the demand for a factor of production to be more elastic when it becomes possible to substitute some other factor in production.

SAQ 1: *Which of the factors just mentioned are relevant to the case of Fleet Street print workers? They have traditionally enjoyed very high earnings – why? And the introduction of new technology threatens to lower those earnings – why?*

Marginal productivity

But mere knowledge of the derived nature of factor demand doesn't allow us to explain why the demand curve for a factor of production is one shape or another. This element of the theory was added by the American economist, John Bates Clark. He introduced the idea of the marginal producitivity of a factor.

> The marginal productivity of a factor is the extra output added by one unit of that factor, while other factors are held constant.

So, for example, the MP of labour is the extra output obtained by adding one unit of labour, holding the capital and land inputs constant. Let's look at this in practice. We'll take labour on a simple textbook farm as an example. If one man works the farm, we imagine that he will do the essential work on the very best field. The employment of a second man will raise output, as he can do a variety of other necessary (but maybe less urgent) work and help the first man with his tasks. A degree of specialisation might even help output. Adding a third employee to the same amount of land and tools will raise total output still further. But the addition of each man will raise output by successively smaller amounts.

SAQ 2: *Distinguish between total output, average output and marginal productivity in this case. What will happen to them as more labour is added to fixed amounts of land and capital? Where have you met this idea before?*

Diminishing returns

What we are meeting here is the old idea of diminishing returns. In fact, we might even consider the possibility that the addition of extra workers might at some point actually reduce *total* output due to overcrowding and mismanagement — 'too many cooks spoil the broth'. The diagram below shows the additional output on the vertical axis plotted against the extra workers on the horizontal axis.

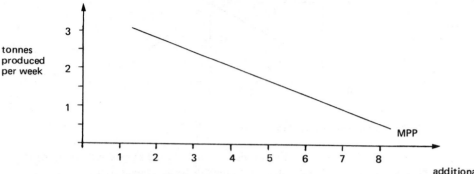

Fig. 26.2   The marginal-physical-product curve

I've titled the curve above 'the marginal-physical-product curve', because it measures the physical increase in output — so many extra tonnes of wheat or gallons of milk. Mind you, the firm and the worker are interested not so much in the physical increase in output — the extra tonnes of wheat or coal — as in the extra money that is brought in by producing additional units of output. In a competitive market, we can arrive at this figure by multiplying the marginal physical product by the price. For example, if the MPP is 1 tonne of coal, and the price of coal is £50 per tonne, then the addition to total revenues gained from employing one additional unit of labour is £50. Economists have a name for this: the marginal revenue product. Below is the MRP curve derived from the MPP curve above, with a price of £50 per tonne of coal.

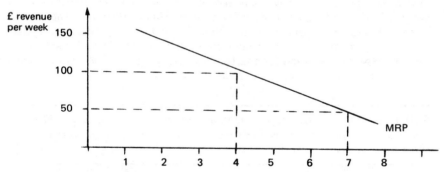

Fig. 26.3   The marginal-revenue-product curve

The interesting thing is that we read off from this diagram how many workers will be demanded at various wages. Look first of all at the fourth worker, who adds just over £100 to output. Plainly it will be worth employing this person at a wage of £100: but not the fifth worker. This fifth worker adds less than £100 to revenue.

SAQ 3: *How do you know this?*

He, therefore, would not be employed at a £100 wage. If the wage fell to £50, it would be profitable for the firm to employ seven workers.

Important point: A profit-maximising firm will employ labour right up to the point where MRP is equal to the market wage. As a result, the wage rate is equal to the MRP of the last worker.

This conclusion reveals that the demand for labour is shown on the MRP curve; in fact *the demand curve for all factors is shown by that factor's MRP curve*. This MRP curve, as we have seen, depends essentially on two considerations.

- the technical conditions of production, which means the marginal physical productivity of the factor and the ease with which we can replace that factor with another
- the derived demand for the product coming through in the price of the commodity.

SAQ 4: *Use the two rules above to show what determines the demand for farm workers.*

THE SUPPLY OF LABOUR

The supply of labour can be roughly measured in hours worked.

SAQ 5: *Why is this just a rough measure of the supply of labour?*

The amount of hours offered derives from three factors:

- the size of the population, which is determined by social factors more than economic ones
- the proportion of the population at work, which depends to a large extent on the dependency ratio of the population, and to a lesser extent on social factors such as attitudes to women (and children) working. The proportion of the population working also varies with aggregate demand.
- the number of hours worked by each worker

SAQ 6: *(a) What is the measure of the proportion of the population of working age who are working (or seeking work)?*
(b) In a recession, numbers employed fall faster than numbers unemployed rise. Why does this happen, and does it confirm that 'the proportion of the population working . . . varies with aggregate demand'?

In assessing the effect on hours of labour supplied at each wage rate we must be careful to distinguish between the position of the economy as a whole and the situation in particular industries. If one industry raised its wages above that of others, it would obtain additional labour from other industries. For example, an increase in the wages of dustmen would attract workers away from other unskilled manual trades. However, the position of the whole economy is probably different.

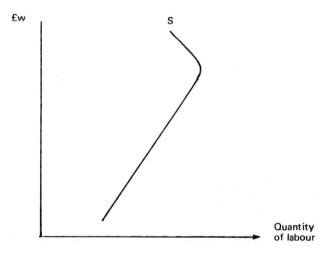

Fig. 26.4 The whole-economy supply of labour

A backward-sloping supply curve for labour?

An increase in pay throughout the whole economy may not raise the amount of hours worked at all. While the higher pay might make it more attractive to go to work rather than take time off, it might, by contrast, be true that workers would enjoy their higher real income by taking increased leisure. They can now, after all, earn the same income with less effort.

Some interesting light was shed on this question in the work of Layard, Piachaud and Stewart in their *NWBR* article on 'The Causes of Poverty'. They estimate that a ten per cent *fall* in a man's wages causes a one per cent increase in hours worked, whereas for women a ten per cent *rise* increases the participation rate by some four per cent.

SAQ 7: *So which sex feels an incentive effect from changes in wages? Can you suggest why?*

The elasticity of supply of productive factors

This measures the responsiveness of quantity of factors supplied to changes in price. So the elasticity of supply of labour would indicate whether an increase in wage rates would bring forth a substantial increase in labour supplied.

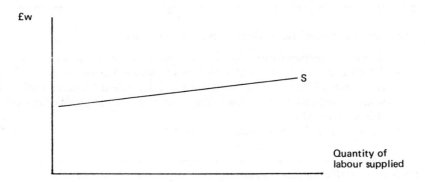

Fig. 26.5 An elastic labour supply curve.

The diagram above indicates a situation where labour supply is very elastic with respect to changes in wage rates. A modest increase in pay would bring forth a large increase in labour. This would be true of industries where no great skill or training was required, nor were any barriers to entry present: waitresses, barmen, unskilled labour generally. A steeply-sloping supply curve would indicate an industry in which the supply of labour was not responsive to price, either due to barriers to entry caused artificially or through the need for long training or special skill. The contrasting effects on earnings of shifts in demand are shown in the diagram below.

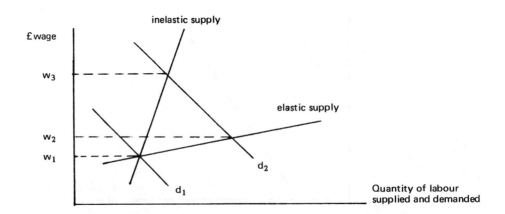

Fig. 26.6 Effects on wage/rates of shifts in demand

When the demand curve shifts rightwards (from d_1 to d_2) earnings are raised very much less steeply in the case of the elastic supply of labour than where supply is inelastic. Remember, though, that supply elasticities depend very much on time-periods.

SAQ 8: *What will be the effect of an expansion in the demand for air travel on the wages of: (a) airline pilots, (b) airport baggage handlers?*

The logic works both for an increase and a decrease in demand, of course. If the pace of development in the North Sea oil fields slackens, then divers' wages fall more sharply than the wages of general labourers in Aberdeen.

SAQ 9: *What will happen in this case to employment for divers and general labourers? (Draw a diagram and find out.)*

PUTTING SUPPLY AND DEMAND FOR FACTORS BACK TOGETHER

Having looked in turn at the supply and demand for productive factors, let's place them together again on a supply-and-demand diagram, for it offers us the prospect of an answer to the who-gets-what problem.

Below we have the MRP (=demand) curve for the factor under consideration – say, labour. If we take the equilibrium wage to be £100, then four workers will be employed: the share of labour in output will be four times £100 = £400. But because only the final worker employed actually gets the full value of his/her MRP, the MRP of earlier workers is available as a surplus for the payment of other factors of production. This area is shaded on the diagram.

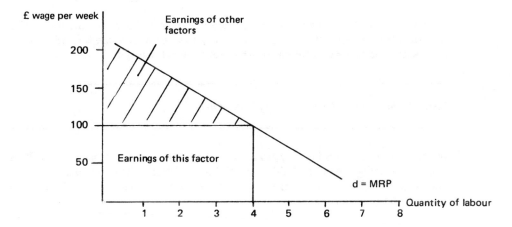

Fig. 26.7 The earnings of a productive factor

Shifts in supply and demand

You will probably be able to work out for yourself the effect of shifts in the supply and demand for labour on wages and numbers employed in a particular industry. The analysis is similar to that used in the unit on equilibrium price. Remember, though, that reasons for shifts in labour supply and demand will involve the concepts of derived demand, participation/activity rates, education and training and so on.

SAQ 10: *The 'A' level examiners once asked this essay question: 'If there were fewer doctors, doctors would be better off; if there were fewer of all of us, we would all be better off'. Discuss.*
Briefly sketch your outline answer to this question, bringing in concepts from this unit and from the previous unit on population.

ECONOMIC RENT AND TRANSFER EARNINGS

In discussions of the earnings of the factors of production, economists distinguish between economic rent and transfer earnings.

- The payment needed to keep a factor in its present use and prevent its transfer elsewhere is a 'transfer earning'.
- Any earnings on top of this are known as 'economic rent'.

Sometimes the word 'rent' is used in this very specialised sense, creating some confusion with the other use of the word to describe payment for the use of land. I'll try to write 'economic rent' in full to avoid this confusion. We'll now illustrate the idea of economic rent and transfer earnings in diagrams, and then try to explain the significance of the distinction.

Earnings all economic rent

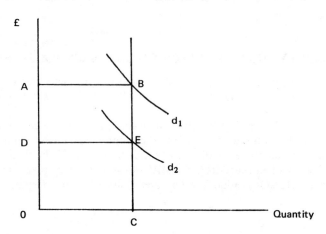

Fig. 26.8 Economic rent

In this diagram, the supply curve for the factor is vertical. The same amount is offered at all prices. An example might be a piece of land in   a busy town centre, which is fixed in supply and (as it has no cost of production) is offered for whatever return it may get.

SAQ 11: *So what is the elasticity of supply here?*

In this case, price is entirely determined by the position of the demand curve. If demand were d_1, earnings would be OABC; but if demand fell to d_2, exactly the same quantity would be offered for sale despite a collapse in the price to OD. As nothing is needed to keep this factor in use, the earnings here are pure 'economic rent'.

Earnings partially economic rent

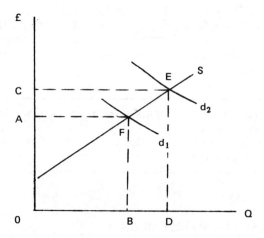

Fig. 26.9 Partially economic rent

In Fig. 26.9, we can see that at least some economic rent is involved whenever the SS curve slopes up. Let's take this as a diagram showing labour supply and demand: the original equilibrium point gives a wage of OA to OB workers.

If there is an increase in the demand for labour then we see a shift to d_2, raising the wage to OC.

SAQ 12: *What might cause an increase in the demand for labour?*

Of course, all workers in the industry now get OC, despite the fact that previously OB of them were content to stay for a wage of OA. A wage of OC is a transfer earning for the very last worker recruited, but involves an element of economic rent for all previous workers, who had been content to work for less than OC.

Figure 26.10 shows the extent of economic rent in a competitive market for any factor: the economic rent is the shaded area.

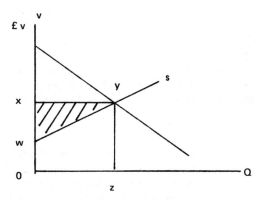

Fig. 26.10 Economic rent in a competitive market

SAQ 13: *If the shaded area shows the economic rent earned by the factor concerned, what is the rest of earnings made up of? How can you find it in the diagram? Indicate and label this area with dots.*

Earnings all transfer earnings

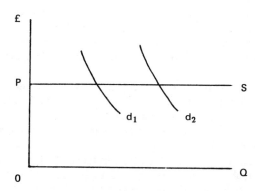

Fig. 26.11 Transfer earnings

If the supply of a factor is perfectly elastic – as in Fig. 26.11 – it implies that at the going market price (OP), firms can employ as much of the factor as they want, but at any lower price nothing at all will be supplied. As a result, there is no element of economic rent here at all – it's all transfer earnings.

The significance of economic rent

The concept of economic rent was first used in the context of returns to the factor of land, and it is still in this area that the idea is of most interest. As we saw in Fig. 26.8, the value of land in a valuable site is entirely demand-related. As the community's wealth grows – through savings and capital accumulation, through advances in technology and work practices, through greater skill and energy from the workforce — the demand for land will grow. Demand for town-centre land is, after all, a derived demand coming from our need for shops, offices and places of entertainment. So the owners of the land will be sitting on a rising value. The idea of economic rent shows us that the rising profits of the landowner can be taxed away without either diminishing the supply of that factor, or raising the price to the consumer.

SAQ 14: *City-centre restaurants say their prices are high to cover their high rents. Landlords say the rents are high to reflect the profitability of the desirable site. Who is right?*

N.B. The original debate about 'economic rent' derives from the vital Victorian question — are land rents high because corn is dear, or is corn dear because the farmers have to pay high rents?

The concept can also be used to look at the costs of various ways of increasing the supplies of a productive factor. Take the present desire to increase the number of maths teachers in schools as an example. A look at Fig. 26.10 will show that simply increasing the salaries of maths teachers will be wasteful, as it involves unnecessary payments of economic rent to those already in the teaching workforce. A better idea would be to shift the supply of maths teachers rightwards — perhaps by means of better grants of maths/science teacher-training courses.

Quasi-rents

One sometimes finds the word 'quasi-rent' used in economic discussion. When a factor has a fixed and unchangeable use (like a bubble-gum dispenser or a motorway) all its earnings are in a sense economic rent: no matter how low the returns to that factor fall, it will remain in its present use. However, in the longer term low earnings will switch resources away from that use: an unused road will not be repaired, an unprofitable machine will not be replaced. In the longer view, then, the earnings of such fixed-use factors are not quite economic rent: they are quasi-rents.

SAQ 15: *Recall now what you learned of the perfectly competitive firm. What part of the earnings of such a firm could be considered 'economic rent': which could be 'transfer earnings'?*

CAN MARGINAL PRODUCTIVITY THEORY EXPLAIN DIFFERENTIALS?

One of the characteristics of a perfect market is that there is a single equilibrium price for the product under consideration. It is clear that there is no such unique price for labour: surgeons earn more than park-keepers, chefs earn more than waiters, pilots earn more than poets. How can we adapt our theory to account for differentials in earnings?

The best way to approach this would be to start with the very simplest of markets for labour, and gradually add complications. So, for a start, we would imagine that wages in all occupations would be alike if:

1. there was perfect competition between those who buy and sell labour (i.e. no-one able to influence the going rate for labour, which employer has to offer and employee is in no position to alter, perfect information; absence of risk; etc.)
2. there was perfect mobility of labour (geographical and occupational: anyone could take up any job anywhere)
3. labour was homogenous (all workers alike in talents and competence, energy and skill)
4. all work was equal in its non-money advantages and disadvantages (i.e. all jobs were as interesting, prestigious, dangerous, risky, dirty, etc. as each other).

If all four of these assumptions were true, wages would be equal.

SAQ 16: *Why?*

However, they are not true, and so earnings between occupations and individuals differ. Let's remove the simplifications one by one to return to the real world.

If jobs differ. . .

Let's first of all dismiss (4). Some jobs are more pleasant than others. Now, the assumption made in economic theory about the owners of the factors of production is that they seek, not the greatest sum of money for their factor services, but the greatest 'net advantage'. The net advantage of a factor employment is defined as the sum of all the money and non-money advantages minus the sum of all the money and non-money disadvantages. It would therefore seem likely that jobs with substantial non-money advantages would be worse-paid than jobs with considerable non-money disadvantages. Because the supply of labour to the pleasant job would be more abundant than to the unpleasant one, differentials may very well exist between the occupations: such differentials are called 'compensating differentials' (Prest) or 'equalising differentials' (Samuelson). They are necessary to ensure an adequate supply of labour to each market.

Ceteris paribus we would expect workers to require compensation for entering occupations which:

- require long periods of education and training
- are dangerous or dirty
- lack job security
- lack prestige, social status or fringe benefits
- involve shiftwork or time away from home in uncongenial places
- require high levels of expense to keep equipment, uniforms, etc. in order.

SAQ 17: *Select examples of all the above from the real world.*

If people differ. . .

Thus, even if labour was homogenous we would expect some wage differentials to exist. However, we know that labour is not homogenous, so let's strip away simplification (3). Many individuals do not have the talent to fill some high-paid jobs, and some workers are more productive than others. We would therefore expect wage levels to differ between individuals on the basis of ability to work.

At the extreme, there are exceptionally gifted people in areas like sport and entertainment who will receive very high earnings. An international-class footballer may earn £50,000 per year for playing football — something he enjoys doing anyway. Outside sport, he could probably earn no more than (say) £5,000. Between these limits, his 'supply curve' is completely inelastic. Hence economists can term the excess of his income above the alternative wage pure 'economic rent'. This is known as the 'rent of ability'. We know, though, that for many occupations differentials are explained neither by superior job performance nor by compensating differentials. A further education teacher's job is not only better paid than a local authority manual worker's: it is nicer. Why then don't dustmen and road gangs move into teaching and bring their earnings more into line?

If labour is immobile. . .

The answer is that they can't. We have to dismantle simplification (2) from page 390 now, and realise that labour is immobile. This immobility may be occupational (i.e. people cannot switch from one job to another— or geographical (people cannot switch from one location to another). Immobility between occupational groups is so pronounced that many labour markets may be considered as totally separate from other ones. There are hundreds of labour markets: for electricians, welders, teachers of maths, disc-jockeys, divers, hairdressers, occupational therapists, etc. In the short term, such groups are not in competition with one another: they are, in the jargon, 'non-competing groups'.

In the longer view, of course, differences in earnings between groups will attract new entrants to those professions. Even mature workers may retrain, given sufficient motivation. Nevertheless, immobility of labour means that changes in demand for workers may result in differences in earnings rather than a reallocation of the labour force.

SAQ 18: *Look back at the last 5 or 6 paragraphs and suggest why jobs of great responsibility offer high wages.*

Having stripped away three of our initial assumptions we are left with this table:

Situation	Result
1. People are all alike and jobs are all alike	No differentials at all
2. People are all alike, but jobs differ in their advantages	Compensating differentials
3. People differ and labour is in 'non-competing groups'	Wage differentials that are pure economic rents
4. People differ, jobs differ, and there is some mobility between groups	Wage differentials that reflect differences in the supply and demand for labour ('equilibrium differentials')

Thus, in a competitive set of markets, there will be a tendency towards what is known as an 'equilibrium pattern of differentials' — a pattern of wage differentials at which total demand for each category of labour matches exactly its total supply. When this happens, there will be no need for further narrowing or widening of differentials.

As a result, enthusiasts of the market are opposed to attempts to interfere with market differentials in pay, whether through prices and incomes policies designed to defeat inflation, or through minimum-wage legislation that attempts to lift the earnings of low-paid employees. It is argued that the forces of the market cannot be restrained forever, and ultimately market forces will precipitate a 'wages explosion' or 'winter of discontent'.

DOES MARGINAL PRODUCTIVITY EXPLAIN REAL-WORLD DIFFERENCES IN EARNINGS?

No. I'll move in a moment to discussing the problems of the theory, but even those economists who keep faith with MRP theory would agree that the pattern of individual earnings is also affected by monopoly and monopsony, and ownership of wealth.

Monopoly and monopsony

We now have to strip away simplification (1) from page 101. Both monopoly (one seller of labour — typically workers co-operating in one large union) and monopsony (one buyer of labour — a large firm, perhaps, or single government agency like the NHS) elements exist in factor markets.

> Metcalf (1977) has argued that membership of a trade union will typically increase the earnings of an individual by 20%. This analysis is restricted to formal trade unions and ignores the effects of professional trade unions such as the British Medical Association and the professional groups of lawyers, accountants, estate agents and dentists . . . . such evidence as there is . . . . suggests that professional control of the supply of skilled labour can influence lifetime earnings' patterns significantly.
>
> (Prest and Coppock *A Manual of Applied Economics* (Weidenfeld and Nicolson))

> The effect of monopsony, or oligopsony, can be discussed in theory but the evidence has not been collected in a systematic manner. Johnson (1969) has argued that about 70% of those with higher education qualifications in the UK are employed, in one way or another, by the State. The state thus has considerable buying power, and Johnson argued that it has used this power to pay wages less than the marginal product of these skilled workers . . . .
>
> (Gowland *Modern Economic Analysis 1* (Butterworth), pp. 215-6)

We shall look at the activities of trade unions in Unit 27, and that seems to be the appropriate place to consider the theoretical fun and games that take place when monopoly and monopsony are present in labour markets.

Ownership of wealth

The other factor that MRP theory does not take into account is an individual's holdings of wealth. Individual 1 may have a much higher income than the more talented and hardworking individual 2 due to holdings of income-yielding wealth (land, shares, etc.). For example, the Sixth Duke of Westminster left Harrow with two 'O' levels, yet earns an estimated £10 800 an hour (*Sunday Times* 20 February 1983). Unit 28 looks more closely at issues of wealth and income in the real world.

OTHER PROBLEMS OF THE THEORY

Because of the weaknesses of MRP theory, and possibly also because of the political and social controversy that surrounds the question of earnings and fair shares, there is considerable criticism of the neo-classical view on factor earnings. The next section of the unit attempts to list some of the most commonly-heard objections to the theory. To be fair, there are more profound criticisms of its methodology that I cannot fully cover here: if you're interested, look for *The Dilemma of Distribution Theory*, an Economist Association pamphlet by Professor Nevin of the University of Swansea. Let's run through our objections.

1. *The theory is unrealistic* It is not in practice possible to pick out the MRP of any individual in any but the most simple of industries: what is the MRP of London's 247th bus driver, or of BSC's 10 000 steelworker? Further, the theory assumes that factors of production are infinitely divisible so that small amounts can be added to other factors: this is false — you can't add a tiny amount of lorry or oil tanker or welding robot ('the problem of indivisibility').
2. *It pays too little attention to social power* It is argues that the high earnings of professional workers like lawyers or company directors are due not to superior MRP but to their holding

positions of social power. Even if it was possible to calculate a high MRP for (say) one additional lawyer to a practice, would this not reflect the fact that society allows lawyers to charge fat fees? If this is true then the worker's desired income is reflected in the market price of his/her services, rather than vice versa.

3. *It ignores collective bargaining*
4. *It ignores private wealth*
5. *Many workers do not work for profit-maximising entrepreneurs* The whole concent of equalising MRP and factor earnings rests on profit-maximising behaviour by producers. However relevant this was when Clark wrote at the turn of the century (when 90 per cent plus of the labour force were in private employment), it isn't true today, when a third or more of the labour force in most western countries are in non-profit/government employment. It is, in any case, difficult to calculate the MRP of a social worker, history professor, etc.
6. *The theory should take note of government intervention* We have already noted that the theory warns government against intervention in labour markets to upset the 'equilibrium pattern of differentials'. Yet governments do so, and a theory which ignores the incomes policies and minimum-wage legislation of any countries is seriously deficient.
7. *Tax and social security contributions* mean that for almost every worker in a modern industrial economy, the wage paid is not the same as the take-home pay upon which decisions about job selection are made.

Nevertheless, it can be argued that the market will out. Unskilled workers are much more prone to unemployment than skilled ones; individuals of high ability or educational attainment typically earn higher incomes than individuals of lesser ability or training; phenomena like the 'brain drain' and 'tax exiles' indicate that high earners can still command a pre-eminent position in the market despite high taxes or monopsonistic employers. So perhaps there's life in the old theory yet.

REVIEW SECTION

Further reading
First of all, have a look at the basic theory of earnings in a standard textbook, such as Lipsey or Livesey (mentioned in your Study Guide): for a lively alternative, see if your local library has Paul Samuelson's *Economics* (Chapters 27 and 28 in my edition – may be different in yours). Other books that I have found useful in preparing this unit are:

Frances Cairncross and Phil Keeley *Guardian Guide to the Economy 2*, Methuen (Chapter 2)
Jan Pen *Income Distribution*, Allen Lane
Peter Donaldson *Economics of the Real World*, Penguin
B. J. McCormick *Wages,* Penguin Economics (quite advanced)
A.R. Prest *The UK Economy*, Weidenfeld and Nicolson (Chapter 5)

I can also recommend Ralph Turvey's *Supply and Demand*, Allen and Unwin, for its chapter on labour markets (Chapter 7), which deftly combines theory and real-world examples. See also 'Rigor Mortis In The Labour Market', Chapter 4 of the *Schools Briefs on Markets* published by the Economics Association.

Examination questions
1. What is the marginal productivity theory of wages? Assess the validity of this theory in explaining wage levels in a developed economy.

(London 'A' June 1986)

2. Why do differences in wages exist? Do such differences have any economic purpose?

(Cambridge Local Examinations Syndicate 'A' November/December 1985)

3. What determines the total supply of labour in the United Kingdom, and the supply of a particular type of skilled labour?

(Oxford Local Examinations 'A' June 1985)

4. Outline the theory of relative pay determination in a freely competitive market. How far is it possible to explain salary differentials within the teaching profession and between teaching and other professions in terms of labour supply and demand analysis?

(JMB 'A' June 1986)

5. Give examples of low-paid workers in Britain and suggest reasons why they are low-paid. Would a national minimum wage improve the position of the low-paid in Britain?

(JMB 'A' June 1985)

6. To what extent can minimum wage legislation solve the problem of low pay?

(London 'A' June 19

7. Discuss the relationship between economic rent and the elasticity of supply of the factors of production.

(A

Multiple choice questions

1.   The population is at an optimum when
   (a)   the dependency ratio is highest
   (b)   the ageing index is stable
   (c)   all the population can be employed
   (d)   national product per head is maximised.

2.   The elasticity of demand for a productive factor might be low if
   (a)   a rise in the factor price will do little to increase the quantity supplied in the short run
   (b)   the factor forms a large part of total costs
   (c)   it is difficult to use other productive factors in its place
   (d)   the elasticity of demand for the final product is high.

3.   In the long run, a quasi-rent must be considered
   (a)   economic rent
   (b)   a minimum wage
   (c)   a transfer payment
   (d)   earnings for a factor other than land.

4.   This curve shows the MRP of labour. What additional information is needed to determine the quantity of labour that would be earned by a profit-maximising firm?

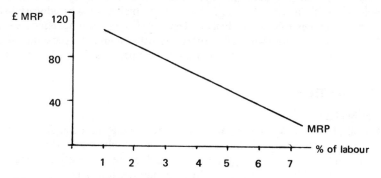

   (a)   the value of the marginal physical product
   (b)   the price of the final product
   (c)   the supply curve of labour
   (d)   the wage rate.

5.   Transfer earnings will form the major part of the earnings of a factor if
   (a)   the demand for the finished product is highly elastic
   (b)   economic rent is high as a proportion of earnings
   (c)   the supply of the factor is perfectly elastic
   (d)   entry to the market is restricted.

6.   The 'law' of diminishing returns assumes that
   (a)   all units of the variable factor are different
   (b)   production can take place in various factor combinations
   (c)   scale economies are not present
   (d)   additional units of a factor reduce total output.

The following questions 7–10 use this diagram and answer code

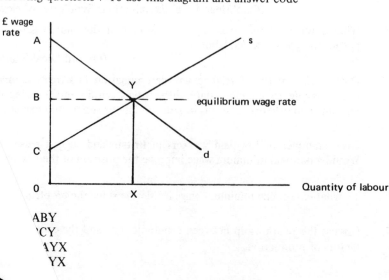

ABY
'CY
AYX
YX

Which of these areas indicates:

7. transfer earnings of the factor?

8. total earnings of the factor?

9. the earnings of other productive factors in this industry?

10. the economic rent accruing to the factor in the diagram?

Questions 11-13 use the figures below, which show the output of a good which sells for £3 per ib.

Workers employed	1	2	3	4	5
Total product (lbs)	50	70	90	108	120

11. What assumptions are needed before we can use these figures to calculate the marginal physical product of labour?

    (a) all workers are identical in ability
    (b) all factors are increased in proportion with labour
    (c) the presence of a perfect market
    (d) all factors but labour must be held constant.

12. At which point do diminishing returns set in? With the addition of the

    (a) 2nd worker
    (b) 3rd worker
    (c) 4th worker
    (d) 5th worker.

13. How many workers would be employed at a wage of £54?
    (a) 2 (b) 3 (c) 4 (d) 5

14. A doctor earns £300 per week, but she would still remain in that job for £100 per week. This implies that
    (a) the bulk of her earnings are economic rent
    (b) she does not work for a profit-maximising employer
    (c) her MRP is between £50 and £500
    (d) transfer earnings are a high proportion of her earnings.

15. The following diagrams show the age distribution in four economies.

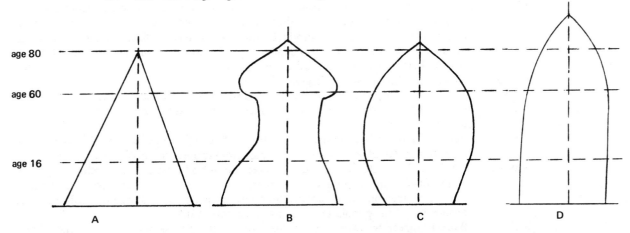

    In which economy is there likely to be the highest level of taxation on the working population?

16. Occupation A earns twice as much as Occupation B. Which of the following would *NOT* form a satisfactory explanation of this differential?
    (a) despite unequal money pay, they are equal in non-money advantages
    (b) one job requires much greater ability than the other
    (c) significant barriers to mobility between the jobs exists
    (d) one of the labour markets involved was imperfect.

Questions 17-20 use this answer code.

use (a)   if you think only option i is correct
use (b)   if you think only options i and ii are correct
use (c)   if you think only options i and iii are correct
use (d)   if you think all three options are correct.

17.   Demand for a factor depends upon
       (i)   that factor's MPP
       (ii)   the price of the final product
       (iii)   how easy it is to replace the factor in the productive process with a substitute.

18.   Which of the following factors would make a labour market more perfect in an economic
       sense?
       (i)   speedy notification of vacancies
       (ii)   anti-union legislation
       (iii)   powerful employer organisations.

19.   Which of the following is true?
       (i)   Transfer earnings show what a factor could earn in its next best alternative use.
       (ii)   Transfer payments are deducted from the national income calculations to avoid double
               counting errors.
       (iii)   Transfer payments and transfer earnings are very much the same thing.

20.   Which of the following might be considered a labour monopsonist?
       (i)   the government in establishing national pay scales for teachers
       (ii)   the BBC in the employment of television presenters
       (iii)   ICI in the employment of industrial chemists.

ANSWERS TO SAQs

SAQ 1:   Two really — the fact that printworkers' wages are a small element of the cost of a
          newspaper (making management reluctant to make a firm stand against a high wage
          claim) and the fact that until recently it was difficult to substitute capital for labour.
          A factor not mentioned here, but mentioned later in the unit, is the trade union power.
          New technology threatens the present position by altering the technical conditions of
          production in a way that opens the possibility of substituting capital for labour if
          labour rises too much in cost.

SAQ 2:   As labour is added, total output will rise with each additional worker (unless we take
          it to extremes): however that addition to output coming from the addition of one
          more worker (the marginal product) will progressively decline, pulling down average
          product per worker. This is very similar to the behaviour of the cost curves of the com-
          petitive firm that we met in Unit 13, pp. 214-5.

SAQ 3:   You can read it off on the diagram.

SAQ 4:   The demand for farmworkers will therefore depend on the technical conditions of
          production of agricultural products (such as the possibility of substitution) and the
          demand for food.

SAQ 5:   Because labour differs wildly in quality. An hour of one person's work may be worth
          more than a day of someone else's — apart from differences in skill and training.

SAQ 6:   (a) the activity rate. (b) Because workers do not all register as unemployed (see Unit
          5, pp. 86-7), and because some workers drop out of the labour force — particularly
          married women and those approaching retirement. This does indeed confirm that the
          proportion of the population working varies with AMD.

SAQ 7:   Women appear to have an incentive, whereas the reverse appears to be true of men.
          Suggestion: men have to work to get money for the household, but for some women
          work is discretionary, and they can decide at low wage rates that they prefer to spend
          time on other activities, such as housekeeping and looking after children. This is just
          my explanation.

SAQ 8:   (a) As the supply of air pilots is inelastic, because it takes a while to train and requires
          great ability and fitness, we might expect a shift of demand to raise their wages con-
          siderably, but (b) the supply of baggage handlers is probably more elastic, meaning
          that no great increase in wages will occur as a result of a shift in demand.

SAQ 9:   If you draw a diagram like 26.6, you'll notice that the effect of a fall in demand on
          employment is much less with an inelastic demand curve than with an elastic one.
          Look at 26.6, moving back from d_2 to d_1.

SAQ 10:   The answer to this question needs to be in two parts. One will deal with the effects on a single labour market of a lower supply: a relatively simple supply-and-demand treatment can show why this would indeed make doctors better off. Yet the second part of the question requires you to deal with the topic of population size, using many of the ideas in the previous unit — such as optimum population. You'll have to make clear that there are times when the theory of optimum population will suggest that a fall in population will make us worse off, due to losing scale economies and specialisation.

SAQ 11:   Zero — totally inelastic (*see* Unit 10, p. 19).

SAQ 12:   Two things — a change in the derived demand (i.e. more of the final commodity itself being demanded, causing a price rise) or a change in the technical conditions of production (a new process that needs more labour, for example). I suppose you must also enter the possibility of a change in other factor prices having an effect.

SAQ 13:   Transfer earnings — OWYZ.

SAQ 14:   The landlords. Just draw a diagram to check. If supply is inelastic, the level of price is entirely due to demand — which must reflect the earning potential of the site.

SAQ 15:   Supernormal profit is not required for continued production, so it's a sort of economic rent. However, if normal profit is not earned, the firm closes down or switches to other commodities: so it must be thought of as the transfer earning.

SAQ 16:   Because any tendency for a wage in one occupation to get out of line would be stopped by labour movement. A fall in a job wage would result in all the workers switching to other jobs, which now have more to offer; similarly, any rise in one occupation's earnings would immediately attract an influx of labour.

SAQ 17:   Doctors and lawyers require long training; mining and deep-sea trawling are dangerous and dirty, creating a differential in pay over similar skilled manual jobs with less problems; economics teachers have more job security than economists in private firms, and earn less; debt collecting and striptease dancing involves low social status; jobs in the Persian Gulf have to pay a premium to persuade Britons to spend time away from home; workers as diverse as dancers and chefs have to keep expensive dress and tools in order. Your own list may be different: lists that use real-world examples are to be found in Prest and in Turvey (see refs at the end of the unit). Turvey, for example, compares the pay of temporary secretaries with permanent staff and sees their slightly higher pay reflecting lack of holiday and pension entitlement; Prest shows that firemen earn more than comparable workers, which is attributed to the risk of their job.

SAQ 18:   Well, if you've followed the unit so far, I've given two reasons — because they have substantial non-money disadvantages (i.e. long training, tossing and turning at night worrying about that vital export order) and the need to recruit applicants of above-average ability. I should add that if you find these reasons unconvincing, you are not alone: many economists would attribute the high earnings of influential decision makers to their social power.

27 Trade unions and the economy

AIMS OF UNIT 27

At the end of this unit, you should be able to:

- define a trade union and collective bargaining, and distinguish between different types of trade union
- outline recent trends in trade union membership
- explain how, in theory, a trade union may increase the earnings of its membership, and list the factors that might help a union in this task
- explain and evaluate criticisms of trade unions based on their effects on output, prices and employment
- distinguish between competitive and imperfect labour markets, and show how the distinction leads to differing results in wages and employment
- describe and evaluate the UK strike pattern.

INTRODUCTION

Unit 26 started our look at earnings from the viewpoint of pure economic theory, and whilst it offered insights into the causes of differentials and changes in wages, it concluded with a number of criticisms of MRP theory. One way in which we found the simple use of supply-and-demand analysis deficient was in the way it ignored the monopoly elements that are often present in factor (especially labour) markets. This unit attempts to fill that gap by considering the economic effects of trade unions.

WHAT IS A TRADE UNION?

A trade union was defined by the social historians Beatrice and Sidney Webb as

a continuous association of wage earners for the purpose of maintaining and improving the conditions of their working lives

and in the cooler prose of the Department of Employment as

all organisations of employees — including salaried and professional workers, as well as manual wage-earners — which are known to include among their functions that of negotiating with employers with the object of regulating conditions of employment.

Trade unions have existed in Britain for more than 150 years. They have four main purposes:
- negotiation of wages and conditions of employment
- welfare functions, such as legal help for members and education in industrial relations, strike and sickness funds
- trying to increase the power of the workforce in decision-making at work
- representing the interests of their members at a national level in the formation of economic and social policy, and the enactment of legislation that will be helpful to members.

The history of trade unions has been marked by many changes in their power and position, by successes and failures. In 1984, 11.08m people belonged to trade unions — about 40% of the working population. Trade unions exist in almost all trades and industries, although the extent of unionisation varies considerably: to contrast two extremes, 100% of coal miners are unionised, but just 5% of those in the hotel and catering trade. Unions tend to be strong among manual workers, skilled and semi-skilled workers, and those with manufacturing or public sector jobs. Despite a recent growth in female unionism, a trade-union member is still more likely to be male than female.

Unions started among skilled manual workers, who formed unions that united workers who shared the same craft or skill. Many present day unions reflect these origins and are thus called 'craft unions': they recruit all the carpenters and joiners, or boilermakers, or engineers, whatever the industry in which they work. For example, an electrician would belong to the EEPTU whether he worked in a shipyard, a car factory or in local government maintenance. This is in contrast with the 'industrial unions' which may be found abroad, where all the employees of one industry would belong to the same union. In Germany, for example, all the workers in a car factory would belong to the same union, be they welder, electrician, administrator, transport driver or assembly-line operative. The significance of this difference in organisation will be discussed later.

A third type of union is becoming increasingly important in the UK — the 'general union' which joins together workers from a variety of trades and industries. One such is Britain's biggest union, the Transport and General Workers' Union.

SAQ 1: *Place the following unions in their correct category:*
(a) the General, Municipal and Boilermakers' Trade Union, which recruits from a wide range of industries
(b) the National Union of Railwaymen, which includes nearly all the workers in the railways
(c) the Post Office Engineers Union, which recruits those with telecommunications engineering skills.

RECENT TRENDS IN UNIONISM

I've noted above that unions tend to be male and manual. This is less true now than in the past, under the influence of the following trends.
- The growth of 'white-collar unionism'. One of the fastest-growing areas of unionism has been in clerical, administrative and professional jobs — teachers, bank employees, local government administrators. This reflects the considerable growth in the white-collar labour force, and also perhaps changes in the attitudes of professional and administrative workers about their position in society.
- Many more women belong to trade unions today than formerly: this reflects the increased importance of women in the labour force, and the penetration of unions into areas (like clerical employment) which were previously only weakly unionised.
- Union membership in the craft unions has been falling under the influence of the recession. Although unemployed workers retain membership in theory, in practice many lose touch with their union, with the curious consequence that in the early 1980s some unions had a block vote at Labour Party and TUC conferences rather larger than their paid-up membership.
- The number of unions is falling, and the dominance of the largest is increasing. At the turn of the century, there were more than 1300 unions; at the end of 1984, just 371. And whilst 80% of unionists are in the largest 22, less than 1% are in the smallest 250. Every year, some of the smaller trade unions decide to forgo their independence in a merger with one of their larger brethren. So the plumbers are now in with the electricians; the teacher-training lecturers in with technical-college teachers, and technicians and draughtsmen with the engineers.

SAQ 2: *What does this information suggest about scale economies in union organisation? Which scale economies do you feel might be most important here? Are there any other advantages in belonging to a very large union, apart from lower organisational costs?*

DANGERS OF BIAS

Having had a brief look at the nature and trends of trade unionism, I'll move on to analyse the effects unions have on the economy. It's worth pointing out the problems of objectivity and bias that are bound to creep in here. I would like to make two points.

Firstly, trade unions arouse strong emotions. Even avoiding the emotive language habitually used by the press ('wildcat', 'bully-boys', 'above the law', etc.), it is possible to bring in bias simply in the topics and terminology used. Economists, for example, measure the damage caused by strikes in 'working days lost', but not the damage caused through unemployment. Similarly, they concentrate their attention on the effects of trade unions on inflation and industrial efficiency, where it can be argued that trade unions have a harmful effect. But if we looked instead at how trade unions work to create a fairer balance of power in the workplace, or work for safer factories and offices, or fight for better pensions and welfare for employees, we might get a much more positive view.

Secondly, there is a temptation to look at the extremes of industrial relations, to talk, for example, about strikes even though 95 per cent of firms haven't had a strike for years. A firm working cordially together is not news: an angry walk out is.

Nevertheless, for most of the past twenty years or so there has been continued public concern – and government action – about our system of industrial relations.

> The incidence of strikes and other forms of industrial action in this country is the most evident manifestation of the inadequacy of our industrial relations, but it is by no means the only one. The persistence of restrictive practices, of outdated working methods and of over-manning have contributed just as powerfully, if more insidiously, to our economic problems.
>
> (*1981 Green Paper on Trade Union Immunities*, Cmnd 8128 para. 2)

The concern has been two-fold. Firstly, there has been the belief that trade unions have worsened inflation by being able to insist on increases in money wages greater than increases in productivity, causing a rise in prices.

SAQ 3: *What is this form of inflation called?*

Secondly, there has been the worry that the UK's industrial efficiency, and therefore economic growth, has been harmed by trade union insistence on demarcation and overmanning (see Unit 2 p. 29). What I shall do in the remainder of this unit is discuss how unions might affect wages and employment in theory, and then use that analysis to evaluate the complaints that have been made against the union movement.

UNIONS AND WAGES: THE THEORY

In Unit 26 we used the framework of supply and demand to analyse wage levels. The demand curve for labour was, we found, its MRP curve. MRP depends on two things, the physical productivity of a factor (very much a question of the techniques of production), and the price at which the final product is sold (which depends on the supply and demand for that product). The demand curve is downward sloping, showing that fewer units of labour are employed at a higher wage. This is because higher wages will cause higher product prices, reducing sales; factor substitution will also take place, with entrepreneurs selecting a factor combination that uses less labour.

The supply of labour to an industry was upward-sloping, the elasticity of supply depending on how easy it was for an employee to enter and leave the industry. Having found the supply and demand curves for labour, we could derive an equilibrium wage at which the supply of labour to a market was exactly matched by the demand. This equilibrium wage would be affected by shifts in supply and demand in much the same way as equilibrium price in Unit 12.

SAQ 4: *Look at these two examples of changing earnings and answer the questions, using the knowledge you've gained in Unit 26.*
(a)   In 1976 the Equal Pay Act came into force, making it illegal to pay women lower wages than men for similar work. The effect was initially to raise women's wages relative to men's What would you expect to happen to female unemployment as a result of this Act?
(b)   In Unit 26 we learned that the demand for miners was a derived demand. From what is it derived? What would be the effect on miners' wages of:
(i)   a long-run fall in the price of competitive fuels?
(ii)   a long-term rise in the price of competitive fuels?

If wages are influenced by the supply and demand for labour, then a union wishing to raise the wage of its membership has three options:
- it can try to shift the supply curve leftwards
- it can attempt to shift the demand curve rightwards
- it can work for a stated minimum wage for its members.

Let's look at these three strategies in turn.

Method 1: shifting the supply curve

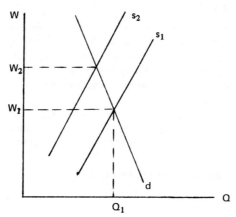

Fig. 27.1 Leftward shift of supply curve

Figure 27.1 refers to a labour market. The vertical axis shows the wage rate W, and the horizontal axis the numbers employed. In a competitive market, the wage would be W_1 and the numbers employed Q_1. If, however, the supply of labour can be restricted (to S_2 in the diagram), then the wage rate will rise to W_2.

This restriction in supply can be achieved in a number of ways. Informal barriers to entry exist in some skilled manual trades (printers, dockworkers) where it's difficult to find a job unless you've a relation already employed in the industry. More common is an exaggerated stress on entry qualifications. In many jobs, the length of apprenticeships and professional training is much greater than is needed to acquire the necessary job skills. But whether formal or informal, the effect is the same — the supply curve shifts to the left, raising wages.

Notice that in Fig. 27.1, the numbers employed fall as a result of the restriction of labour supply. In a competitive market with a downward-sloping demand curve for labour, increased wages are bound to mean fewer jobs. The union must, therefore, think of the consequences of a wage rise on employment. This leads us to the view that unions will be most likely to be successful in obtaining large wages with relatively minor rises in unemployment when the demand for labour is price-inelastic.

SAQ 5: *(a) Draw a diagram with two demand-for-labour curves of differing elasticity. Show how restricting labour supply is more effective in its effects on wages and employment in the case of the price-inelastic curve.*
(b) Check back to Unit 26 and list the factors that affect the price elasticity of demand for labour. Which type of union will therefore be most effective in raising wages without employment costs?

Method 2: shifting the demand for labour

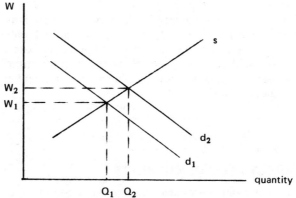

Fig. 27.2 Rightward shift of demand curve

The second way of raising wages is to act on the demand side. Figure 27.2 shows the effect of an increase in demand on the level of wages in an industry. Demand for a factor derives, you'll remember, from the MPP and from the demand for the final product; and so an increase in the demand for labour can be brought about either by raising MPP (by improved productivity and skill) or by raising demand for the final product. Demand for a particular sort of labour can be increased artificially by restrictive practices like insisting on an unnecessary plumber's mate, junior barrister, or train guard. Political campaigns to ensure contracts for expensive projects, or to reduce foreign competition by either a 'Buy British' campaign or tariffs would achieve a similar end by increasing demand for UK goods and therefore UK workers. Note that in Fig. 27.2, increased demand raises wages and employment.

SAQ 6: *The National Union of Teachers has been campaigning for many years in favour of an all-graduate teaching profession. The National Union of Mineworkers has expressed fierce opposition to the expansion of the nuclear power programme.*
(a) Explain, with the use of diagrams, why the success of these two policies might benefit the respective union membership.
(b) If these campaigns are successful in raising wage levels in mining and education, what will be true of the 'economic rent' element in the earnings of those already employed in those industries?

Method 3: increasing the wage by direct means

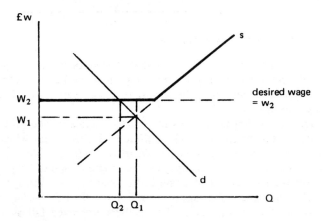

Fig. 27.3 Insistence on minimum wage

So trade unions could try to manipulate the market for labour by shifting the supply and demand to achieve higher earnings for their members. Alternatively, a union could be sufficiently confident of its strength to demand a wage rise of a given amount. In Fig. 27.3, the union has held out for a rise from W_1 to W_2 by the threat of withdrawing labour. No labour will be supplied at all below the desired wage level of W_2; effectively, the union has created a new supply curve, which I have marked in boldly. This requires cohesive and organised action on the part of the union membership. Such solidarity is, sociologists believe, easier to achieve in workforces that:
- are concentrated geographically, often being the dominant group in their own communities
- face closely similar employment situations
- share (perhaps for historical reasons) militant and class-conscious values and attitudes.

Research has shown that miners, seamen and dockers, for example, have a high propensity to strike in a number of different countries.

Note that, just like labour supply restriction, direct wage rises reduce the numbers employed in an industry – from Q_1 to Q_2 in Fig. 27.3. This will concern unions, who wish to preserve jobs (and maintain numbers in membership). As a result, unions may seek 'manning agreements' to preserve employment – say at Q_1 in Fig. 27.3. This will only be possible if the union has sufficient power to enforce its wishes, and if the employer has excess profits (or is able to obtain subsidy) to finance the excess employees. However, the problems of maintaining employment in the longer view remain, because an unrealistic manning agreement will raise unit costs and reduce profits and competitiveness.

MONOPOLY IN LABOUR MARKETS

So far in this unit we've used the traditional tools of the economist: supply and demand curves intersecting to reach a competitive equilibrium. In order to do so, I have made two unstated assumptions. Firstly, that the market is competitive, so that using supply-and-demand is appropriate to the cases we've been analysing. Secondly, I've maintained a 'ceteris paribus' assumption

SAQ 7:   *Check back to Unit 26, p. 102 and say what this means.*

In fact, there are good reasons to believe that neither assumption is warranted.

Labour markets are imperfect   Trade unions owe their formation to the perception that employers are not 'perfect competitors', but in fact have considerable power: to, as the *1981 Green Paper* put it, 'the inherent imbalance of power between the employer and the employee'. By their very nature, unions cannot exist in a competitive market, for they represent combinations — cartels — of working people. And we saw in Unit 15 that firms are growing in size. So labour markets which are truly competitive — that is, which feature many unorganised workers and many competing employers — are the exception rather than the rule.

SAQ 8:   *Can you think of any examples of such a truly competitive labour market?*

In most labour markets there are large employers and large unions: wages are not flexible like equilibrium prices, but 'sticky' like the oligopolistic prices we met in Unit 15. In these imperfect market conditions, we need to draw upon the ideas we met in the units on monopoly and oligopoly.

Other things aren't equal   When unions succeeded in raising wages in the examples we have considered so far, employment fell as a new equilibrium was reached at a point further up an unmoving demand curve. But if wages are rising in a number of industries at the same time, isn't it likely that the demand curve for any individual commodity will shift rightwards?

I'll try now to look anew at trade-union action using a more sophisticated model.

Monopsony in labour markets

I shall look first at monopsony — one buyer of labour. Here there is just one employer, who can offer any wage rate he chooses. Workers are unorganised, and must work for this form or be unemployed. Such a situation isn't common, but does exist, particularly in local labour markets: the phenomenon of the 'company town' might serve as an example. Figure 27.4 illustrates the situation: the supply curve shows the amounts of labour that would be supplied at various wage rates. However, the demand for labour is rather more complicated, for here the marginal cost of employing one additional worker is greater than the average cost. If our hypothetical employer offers a higher wage to attract one more worker, he has to pay his existing workforce the new high rate.

If, for example, 100 units are employed at 50p per hour, then total cost is £50 and average cost per unit is 50p. If 101 units are employed and the hourly rate goes up 1p, total cost becomes £51.51 and total cost has risen £1.51 as a result. The marginal cost thus exceeds the wage paid.

(Lipsey, *Introduction to Positive Economics*).

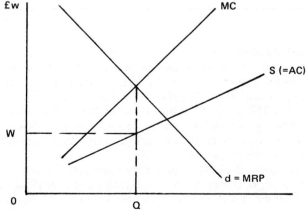

Fig. 27.4 One employer

I've shown this in Fig. 27.4. Note that the MC curve rises faster than the supply curve. Now, a profit-maximising monopsonist will equate the marginal cost of labour with its marginal product: he will, in other words, go on hiring labour until the last unit increases total costs by as much as it increases total revenue.

This is where the marginal cost curve cuts the demand (= marginal revenue product, remember?) curve. Equilibrium, then, is at point OQ, and there the employer can get all the workers he wants for wage OW.

SAQ 9: *Compare the result of the monopsonist's equilibrium above with what would happen in a competitive market. What is the effect of monopsony on (a) the wage rate and (b) employment?*

Monopoly in labour markets: one union

Suppose that, by contrast, there is not monopsony but monopoly in the labour market: that is, one seller (say, a massive union that controls the supply of labour) and many buyers — weak, small firms who have to accept the union-dictated wage. The analysis that follows (see Fig. 27.5) is precisely the same as in the normal monopoly case (*see* Unit 14, p. 233). By supplying more of his commodity — in this case labour — the monopolist drives down the price and thus lowers the earnings of those already in the industry. To resume our numerical example: if there has to be a 1p reduction in wage-rates per hour to get one more person employed, then the total earnings of labour will fall by 1p times all the hours worked. Thus MR falls more steeply than the demand curve.

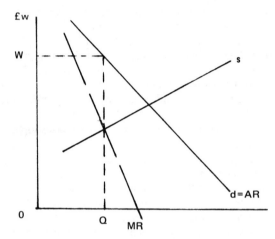

Fig. 27.5 A labour market monopoly

A rational labour organiser will limit the labour supply to the point where the additional revenue from one more worker employed is equal to the cost of supplying that additional worker — shown on the supply curve.

SAQ 10: *Contrast the equilibrium wage and numbers employed under a competitive market with that under a labour monopoly. Looking back at SAQ 9, what seems to be true of departures from competition in labour markets?*

Collective bargaining

Now, one-sided monopsonistic and monopolistic labour markets certainly exist, but in reality the most common form of labour market contains elements of both. Well-organised and stable unions face large powerful firms. This is called 'bilateral monopoly', and can be seen in the matching of Ford and the TGWU, the Coal Board and the National Union of Mineworkers. In such a situation, where conditions of employment are decided, not by individual agreement between worker and boss, but on behalf of groups of employees after negotiations between union and employer, we speak of 'collective bargaining'.

The last figure, 27.6 puts together the monopoly elements of 27.5 and the monopsony of 27.4 to see if economic theory can tell us anything about bilateral monopoly. Superimposing the two diagrams, we see that there is a region of indeterminacy. We cannot predict what the wage will be. It will be somewhere between the low monopsony wage W_1 that would be paid by an unopposed firm to powerless workers, and the monopoly wage W_2 that would be forced on weak employers

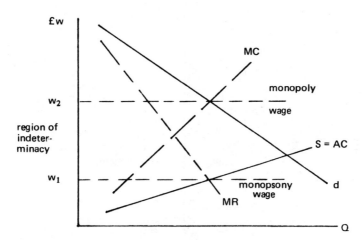

Fig. 27.6 Bilateral monopoly

by a dominant union. 'The outcome is in principle as indeterminate as two millionaires haggling over an oil painting' (Paul Samuelson).

This must be a disappointing conclusion for a student entering the theory of wages looking for an answer about the influence of unions on wage rates. The fact is that the actual wage will be settled between W_1 and W_2 according to the bargaining strength of the union and employer. There have been a number of interesting attempts to analyse the bargaining process, and if you would like to look more closely at them I can recommend Jennett's article in Gowland (ed) *Modern Economic Analysis 2*, Butterworth, 1982, which explains and tests Hicks' model of bargaining power (see especially pp. 144-9).

ECONOMIC EFFECTS OF TRADE UNIONS: THE REAL WORLD

What follows is my attempt to supplement the rather disappointing results of the economic theory we've surveyed up to this point. I've broken the topic down into a series of allegations, and will attempt to deal with them by reference to a mixture of economics, sociology and common sense. Please be aware that the problems of bias are as present in my comments as in other people's — though the facts presented are all genuine.

Charge No. 1: trade unions reduce output and growth

The first version of this argument asserts that strikes reduce output and place Britain at a disadvantage in relation to foreign competition. Now, the statistics that I'll use to judge this matter aren't completely reliable: it's unlikely that the Department of Employment gets to hear of every strike. Anyway, a low strike rate isn't necessarily a sign of industrial health. Conceding excessive wage claims or exaggerated manning levels is probably as bad as resisting them at the cost of a strike: at the extreme, a firm which always gave in to every demand would have a strike-free record in its brief life before bankruptcy. Nevertheless, a number of points can be made about the productive loss caused by strikes.

1. What matters in deciding whether strikes handicap us in relation to our industrial rivals is not whether we have strikes, but whether our record is worse than theirs. In fact, it isn't:

> ... Britain's record is very far from being the worst among industrial countries. In fact ... we are placed sixth or seventh among the 15 countries for which adequate information is available ... International statistics can thus be used to demonstrate that the 'British disease' is neither peculiar to this country nor apparently present in its most virulent form ...
>
> (*Strikes In Britain*, Department of Employment Manpower Paper No. 15)

The strike thermometer (Fig. 27.7, from the *Economist* 27 August 1983) shows the average annual loss of days per thousand workers in a number of comparable industrial countries. You'll see that the UK has a position in mid-table.

2. Loss of output due to strikes is often exaggerated — or made up later. Production can only be considered truly 'lost' if the firms concerned have a full order book and are working at full capacity. In any other situation, firms can quickly make up for the lost production when work resumes. Another exaggeration of strike-loss comes from believing that the full value of the firm's output is lost: that, for instance, a failure to produce 1000 cars valued at £5000 is a £5m loss. In fact, we should only count the value added by that

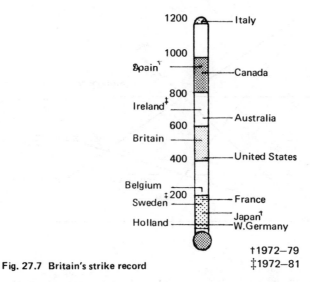

Fig. 27.7 **Britain's strike record**

†1972—79
‡1972—81

firm as loss. Yet the savings in wages, components, fuel and energy are rarely deducted from the news media's accounting of the 'cost' of the strike. (For further explanation of the over-valuation of strike losses, see Hyman *Strikes* pp. 34-6.)

3. As a cause of working days lost, strikes are relatively unimportant. The annual average for the years 1973-82 (quite a bad period for British industrial relations) was less than 500 days lost per 1000 workers — say, ½ a day a year for the average worker.

SAQ 11: *This exercise shows you how important time lost in strikes is in relation to other causes of lost working time. For comparison, bear in mind that there were 5.3m working days lost in strikes in 1982.*
(a)   How many working days are lost each year in total due to the unemployment of 1m people? (Assume a working year of 220 days.)
(b)   How many working days are lost each year as a result of the decision to add a May Day Bank Holiday to the calendar? (Assume a workforce of about 26m.)

Other causes of lost industrial time exist that we haven't mentioned in SAQ 11. Industrial accidents are responsible for the loss of about 20m days, sickness and absenteeism for more than 200m working days. One sociologist put it like this:

> ... it is clear that the loss of working time from other causes has hitherto been very much greater than the loss from strikes. Again, loss of time and output through man-agerial inefficiency, for example, may sometimes be considerable; but while time lost by workers is measurable, that lost by management is not.
>
> (Knowles *Strikes: a study in industrial conflict*)

4. There is some evidence that strikes are a problem of inadequate management rather than of irresponsible unions. Strikes are much more likely to occur in large plants than in small ones; and half of British strikes are found in just 100 firms. The finding that the majority of Brit-ish strikes are unofficial, short and small is thought to be a sign that the procedures in UK industry are inadequate, that sometimes the only way to bring a grievance forcefully to the attention of managers is in a walk-out.

All of this is not to say that we should be complacent about UK strikes. They plainly don't help the economy, and there is the worry that they fall disproportionately on vital industries — engin-eering, so important to our exports, and the public utilities like refuse collection and power gen-eration. Nevertheless, Whittingham and Towers comment made in their *National Westminster Bank Review* article more than ten years ago is still valid: 'if there is a British strike problem, it is sectoral rather than national'.

Hampering management
So the charge that strikes seriously affect UK prosperity appears weak. However, the trade union system affects efficiency and output in other ways. One accusation is that unions 'reduce the ability of managers to manage': that is, interfere with the authority of managers in their task of adjusting output and work practices in an attempt to lower costs and meet demand. Of course, one of the functions of a trade union is precisely this — to increase the power of the workforce relative to management. But the evidence of many well-managed and strike-free firms in the UK —

and the speedy 'turning round' of ailing companies by vigorous new management – suggest that it is possible to achieve the firm's objectives whilst retaining the support and loyalty of the work-force.

Reducing productivity with outdated practices

We've already spoken of demarcation disputes and overmanning (*see* Unit 2, p. 29). It is argued that such problems are worsened by the UK union structure, with its emphasis on craft unions.

SAQ 12: *What is a craft union? Why would demarcation problems be less acute under a system of industrial unions?*

The 1968 Royal Commission on Trade Unions (chaired by Lord Donovan, and therefore called the Donovan Commission) considered recommending a change from the craft union structure to industrial unions. They looked at it this way:

Advantages of such a change:	1. Sectional claims on behalf of different occupational groups within a particular factory could be more easily harmonised. 2. It would end many demarcation disputes.
Drawbacks of such a change:	1. It would interfere with the transfer of craftsmen from industry to industry. 2. 'The really decisive objection is a practical one. However defined, industrial unionism would involve a drastic upheaval in the structure of almost every major union in the country.'

(Donovan Report para. 677)

It was this final, practical objection that swayed the balance against a recommendation of wider industrial unionism.

Charge No. 2: trade unions cause inflation

The accusation
The idea that trade unions are the cause of the regular annual inflation of prices that has been a feature of the post-war years involves rejecting alternative explanations of inflation in favour of a cost-push explanation.

SAQ 13: *What are the alternative explanations of inflation?*

The cost-push explanation goes like this:

> Like any monopoly (*see* Unit 14) trade unions can raise prices above the free-market level. As wages are pushed up, industrial costs rise and so prices are adjusted upwards by a cost-plus method. Other unions react by pushing up wages in their sectors because of the need to stay level with the cost-of living, and the desire to maintain 'comparability' with the group that have received a rise.

Problems with this theory of inflation have been briefly discussed in Unit 9. Let's divide them here into theoretical and empirical objections.

Theoretical objections
Firstly, let's refer back to Fig. 27.4 on p. 403 of this unit, where we say that under monopsony, wages are kept below free-market levels. Whilst it may be true in the purest theory that a union entering a perfectly competitive market will drive up wages and reduce employment (*see* Fig. 27.5 and SAQ 10), this is an unrealistic scenario. In imperfect markets where employers have some monopsony power, unions are as likely to push wages towards equilibrium as away from it.

Secondly, theory suggests that the monopolisation of a market will cause just one jump in price – when it moves from a competitive to a monopoly price. Monopoly cannot therefore account for continuing inflation unless markets throughout the economy are gradually becoming monopolised: yet the proportion of the population unionised hasn't varied a great deal in recent years, and unions which have been monopolies for years (e.g. NUM) seem no less successful than newly-important unions.

Thirdly, the increases in wages forced by union action would have to be accompanied by increases in the money supply, otherwise wage rises would cause unemployment. To check why, do this SAQ.

SAQ 14: *(a) Write out Fisher's equation involving P, M, V and T.*
(b) What would happen to T if P rose without any compensating rise in V or M? Does this matter?
(c) Is it likely that V will rise to compensate?

Of course, it may well be that a government concerned to maintain full employment *will* expand the money supply to allow full employment at the higher price level — indeed, this is a modern version of the cost-push theory that has the advantage of explaining the apparently telling relation between expansions in the money supply and inflation.

> It does appear that a strong association exists between rising prices and increases in the stock of money. What many Keynesians object to is the interpretation in monetarist terms of what is merely a statistical association. Many Keynesians — for example Kaldor (1970), Robinson (1973) — argue that prices rise for reasons other than excess demand produced by prior monetary expansion. They maintain that, in economies where the government is pledged to a policy of full employment, the trade union movement may take advantage of this commitment and press for ever higher wage increases. In the absence of monetary expansion, such wage increases will raise the unemployment rate . . . in the light of the full employment commitment of most governments since the Second World War, sustained trade union pressure for higher wages will *produce* expansions in the supply of money.
>
> (Trevithick *Inflation*, Penguin 1977)

SAQ 15: *How might economic researchers discover which of these two theories best fits the evidence?*
1.   Rises in the money supply cause inflation.
2.   Trade unions push up wages and prices, and so governments are forced to expand the money supply to avoid unemployment.

Empirical objections
Just as there are theoretical problems with the idea that prices are pushed up by trade-union wage inflation, there are a number of empirical problems — that is to say, it's difficult to make the theory sensibly fit the facts.

Firstly, inflation varies considerably from year to year — from 30 per cent in 1975 to 4 per cent in 1987 — with a very similar degree of unionisation. Secondly, no impressive research has ever connected union militancy with the inflation rate, although many attempts have been made (see Prest and Coppock's *The UK Economy: A Manual of Applied Economics* 11th edition, p. 328). Lastly, countries without unions, or with very weak unions, suffer from inflation at least as bad as unionised countries, and in the UK, some non-unionised labour markets (e.g. office skills) have seen rises in wages at least as great as elsewhere.

Charge No. 3: trade unions reduce employment

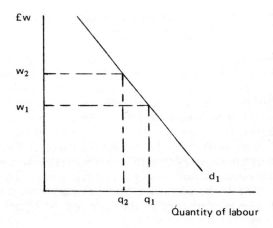

Fig. 27.8 'Pricing yourself out of a job'

A third criticism of trade-union actions is based upon the idea that they are responsible for unemployment. The most common version of this idea is based on the downward-sloping demand curve shown in Fig. 27.8 as d_1. It is argued that raising wages can only occur at the expense of employment – for example, a rise from w_1 to w_2 implies a fall in jobs from q_1 to q_2. The union has succeeded in 'pricing its members out of a job'. However, this can only be true in the simplest 'ceteris paribus' case. As we noted earlier in this unit, if wages were rising generally throughout this economy, the ceteris paribus assumption could not remain valid. For increases in income increase demand for products, and with rising incomes, the firm will not be too concerned about raising their product prices. The effect of these two factors will be to shift the demand curve for labour – which, remember, is derived from the final demand for the product – to the right. This is illustrated in Fig. 27.9. As in Fig. 27.8, the wage rate has been raised at the insistence of the unionised workforce, but as similar rises have been granted in other occupations, employment remains unchanged at q_1.

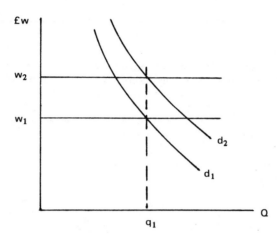

Fig. 27.9 Rightward shift of demand curve

It's important to realise that, though the union's members have not suffered from increased unemployment, neither have they increased their living standards. For although they are receiving a higher money wage, they are no better off as prices have risen throughout the economy. The only way that the membership can gain increased purchasing power is if their increase is greater than the general rise in prices and wages – that is to say, if they get a rise in *real* wages. But if that were to be true, the analysis of Fig. 27.8 would become valid again.

(This is a very similar point to that made by Keynes in the 20s and 30s. It was argued then by many economists that wage cuts would increase employment – that by accepting reduced earnings (from w_2 to w_1 in Fig. 27.8) workers could 'price themselves back into jobs'. What Keynes saw was that the wage cuts would be matched by cuts in prices, and in the wages of other industries, which would shift the demand for commodities and therefore the derived demand curve for labour leftwards. It would be like moving from w_2 and d_2 in Fig. 27.9 to w_1 and d_1. Employment could not be increased by 'balanced deflation' when price cuts and wage cuts matched each other. Only a cut in the real wage would raise employment: and this would be almost impossible to achieve without great social conflict and cost.)

So it's unlikely that the union in Fig. 27.9 will lose or gain much from its wage rise. Yet it cannot afford to stay out of the wages race. For other unions would continue to press their claims, causing our membership to lose their places in the wages league. Thus, unions may be thought of as competing with each other, rather than with employers: and the individual union is on something of a treadmill. The only way off would appear to be some form of incomes policy.

The pushing of unions to keep abreast of one another raises a fascinating thought. We've seen in Unit 26 that wages in unionised trades are 20 per cent or so higher than outside; yet we shall review arguments in the next unit that the share of national income going to labour has remained reasonably stable. So it appears that unions have gained not at the expense of employers, but at the expense of the non-unionised.

Hayek's theory of how unions cause unemployment
The analysis above suggested that changes in the general level of money wages cannot be blamed for unemployment. But Friedrich von Hayek, the distinguished Austrian economist, suggested that unions might raise unemployment through their effect on relative wage rates. The argument follows from the idea of an equilibrium pattern of differentials, described in p. 391 of Unit 26.

SAQ 16: *What essential function is performed by wage differentials in a market economy? What is meant by 'an equilibrium set of differentials'?*

Hayek noted that there is a rigid and inflexible set of relativities in the wages of various industries. 'Comparability' is a union watchword, and no group likes to fall out of its place in the wages league table. As a result, wage differentials are extremely difficult to adjust.

Now, consider for a moment if occupation A grew in demand, and occupation B suffered a fall in demand. If wage differentials were flexible, then wage B would fall relative to wage A. If this cannot happen because wage differentials are fossilised, there will be a much higher unemployment rate in B than in A. The result is curious: it is relative unemployment rates, rather than relative wages, that act to allocate labour to different industries and occupations. What we see is not an equilibrium pattern of differentials, but an equilibrium pattern of unemployment rates.

SAQ 17: *In the UK, unemployment rates are much higher amongst the unskilled than amongst skilled workers. What would be Hayek's analysis of the reason for the difference in unemployment rates?*

Cost-push and jobs
One last point. Unions can increase unemployment if we believe in the cost-push theory of inflation, because in an open economy export sales may be lost if costs rise faster than competitors' costs.

SAQ 18: *What policy could the government adopt to compensate for this upward pressure on our export prices?*

SUMMARY

This unit has tried to think clearly about how trade unions affect our economy. Look back at the aims of the unit to check that you've grasped the important ideas. I've tried to keep a rational view throughout, bringing in theory and evidence as appropriate. To read the popular press, one might think that trade unions were something that has happened to our economy from outside — almost like an industrial disease. Yet trade unions represent their members, who make up almost half the UK workforce: and, being democratic bodies, they must represent at least to some degree the wishes of their members. If we have complaints about what trade unions do, perhaps we should remember that in many ways union actions reflect our own ambitions, wishes and fears.

REVIEW SECTION

Further reading
The main omission from this unit is details of trade-union legislation, although page 155 has a brief review of the situation to date. This is because at the time of writing there are a number of changes proposed: you can check for yourself the most recent trends in *Keesing's Contemporary Archives* in your library (a publication which builds up a list of all the events and personalities too recent to make the textbooks), or by finding the latest copy of Prest and Coppock *A Manual of Applied Economics*. *Trade Unions*, edited by McCarthy, is a reader in the Penguin Economics series that has a number of interesting articles and extracts, including the relevant sections of the Donovan Report. The Heinemann Studies book *Trade Unions* by Williamson has suffered more than most in the series from getting quickly out-of-date, but still has some useful sections. On strikes, see Hyman *Strikes*, Fontana or *Strike Activity in the UK* by Evans and Creigh (Economics Association Occasional Paper). Each January, the 'Employment Gazette' publishes facts and figures of Trade Union membership.

Some sound basic thinking is to be found in Peter Donaldson's *A Question of Economics* (Pelican — see especially Ch. 3, 17 and 19). On the question of whether higher wages cause unemployment, see 'Do Higher Real Wages Cause Unemployment?' by Richard Layard and James Symons (*Economic Review*, January 1984) and 'Unions and Pay', *Economic Review*, September 1984.

The textbooks are useful in dealing with the idea of monopoly and monopsony in labour markets — Lipsey and Samuelson, as usual, thorough and clear. Jennett's article in *Modern Economic Analysis 2 ed*. Gowland (Butterworths) has been recommended in the unit, and I'd repeat that here.

For more punchy and controversial stuff, see *The Union Makes Us Strong* by Tony Lane (Arrow) and *British Trade Unionism* by Allen Hutt (Lawrence and Wishart), both very class-conscious trade-union supporters, or on the other side *Inflation and the Unions*, an IEA reader available from the Institute of Economic Affairs, and available in many college and public libraries.

Examination questions
Examiners can use a variety of ways to test your knowledge of this topic — multiple-choice questions on your understanding of monopolistic labour markets, data response to check on your knowledge of trade-union structures.

1. How, if at all, is it possible to estimate the cost of strikes to the economy? Consider and say whether you agree with the view that ultimately all strikes are about pay.

(JMB 1981)

2. 'Congress emphatically refutes the assertion that wage increases are a source of inflation and unemployment.'

(Resolution, TUC Conference 1981)

Explain the basis of the view that wage increases cause both inflation and unemployment. Discuss whether on the basis of theory and the experience of recent years you agree with the resolution quoted.

(Joint Matriculation Board 'A' June 1982)

3. What effect do trade unions have on the rate of inflation?

(University of London June 1983)

4. 'Higher wages, fewer jobs.' Discuss with reference to particular industries in the United Kingdom.

(Oxford Local Delegacy 'A' June 1983)

5.

Union Membership ('000s)	1972	1979	1982
Transport and General Workers' Union	1640	2070	1700
National and Local Government Officers' Association	463	729	796
Association of Scientific, Technical & Managerial Staffs	250	471	428
National Union of Mineworkers	276	255	250
Confederation of Health Services Employees	102	215	231

Source: *The Economist*

Outline and account for the trends evident in the table. How is the trade union movement reacting to these trends?

(Oxford and Cambridge 'A' July 1984)

ANSWERS TO SAQs

SAQ 1: (a) the GMBTU is a general union (b) the NUR very nearly an industrial union and (c) the POEU is a craft union.

SAQ 2: If unions are growing larger, then it suggests scale economies exist in the organisation of labour. Technical economies might exist — for example, in the computerised processing of membership that would not be worthwhile in a small union; managerial economies would be present if, as seems likely, a large union could employ specialist economists, lawyers and accountants; marketing economies if it found it cheaper to print newsletters and circulars, and was able to spread the cost of advertising over more members; financial economies if it was better known to banks — maybe even risk-bearing economies, in that union funds and power would not be adversely affected by a slump in one trade if it has members across the industrial landscape. Apart from lower costs, a union might be more powerful in its united action.

SAQ 3: Cost-push inflation.

SAQ 4: (a) Economic theory would predict that female unemployment rose: and that's what happened.   (b) Judging from shifts in the demand from workers derived from (i) a fall and (ii) a rise in the demand for coal, one would expect (i) to reduce miners wages' and (ii) to raise them. Between 1947 and 1956, when demand for coal was strong, miners' wages rose swiftly in relation to other wages. From 1957 to 1973, miners' wages fell back relative to other workers in the face of cheap oil prices; but the increased price of energy from 1974 onwards boosted miners' pay. Supply and demand accounts for these changes much better than 'union cost-push' appears to.

SAQ 5:   (a)

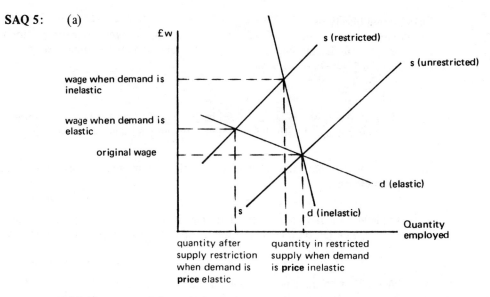

(b) Elasticity of demand for a factor will be low if demand elasticity for the final product is low, if it is difficult to substitute other factors for it, or if it forms a small part of final production costs. This implies that unions representing workers with an important skill but without being a major part of production costs will be able to secure substantial rises without too much unemployment.

SAQ 6:   (a) The NUT wishes to restrict entry to the profession in order to drive up teachers' salaries (your diagram should therefore look like 27.1); the NUM are raising the demand for coal and thus improving miners' prospects in the field of wages and job security: Fig. 27.2 is the relevant one. Of course, there are sound reasons for both policies unconnected with cynical considerations of earnings and jobs. (b) The economic rent element will rise, as people who are already in the industry (and presumably content to work for existing wage levels) receive additional pay.

SAQ 7:   Other things being equal.

SAQ 8:   There are some — perhaps the biggest in Britain is the market for office workers in London, in which many employers seek workers in a field where unions are far from strong. Another example: the market for barstaff.

SAQ 9:   (a) The wage rate is lower and (b) employment lower also. You can read off the competitive equilibrium in Fig. 27.4 where the supply and demand curves cross (of course).

SAQ 10:   Again, contrast with the supply-and-demand equilibrium; you'll see that wages are higher and quantity lower than under competitive conditions. SAQs 9 and 10 show that employment is lower under monopolistic conditions than under competitive ones.

SAQ 11:   (a) 220m — so the 3m or so unemployed in that year caused the loss of nearly 700 working days, or a loss of hours nearly 140 times more serious than that caused by strikes. (b) 26m working days — so a Bank Holiday (or Royal Wedding, or whatever you please) caused as much lost production in one day as strikes do in five years.

SAQ 12:   See the beginning of the unit for a definition of a craft union; demarcation disputes would be less under industrial unionism, it's claimed, as members moving from one job to the next would all be members of the same union.

SAQ 13:   Excess demand and monetary explanations.

SAQ 14:   (a) $P = \dfrac{MV}{T}$ (b) T would fall; this does matter, for T is the number of transactions — that is, the real output of the economy. A fall in T implies a fall in employment and living standards. (c) Probably not. Whilst V is reasonably elastic in the short term, it tends to be stable over the longer term (*see* Unit 8 p. 140).

SAQ 15:   By seeing whether the expansion of the money supply precedes (monetary) or follows (cost-push) the inflationary surge. Of course, in a time of constant inflation, this is easier said than done.

SAQ 16:   They ensure that supply and demand for labour is matched in each labour market — that is, that the unpleasantness of a job or the special demands of an occupation are reflected in the money wages so that there is neither excess nor shortage of labour. An equilibrium set of differentials will exist when supply and demand are matched in all labour markets, giving no need for any change in the existing differentials.

SAQ 17;   He would presumably say that the unskilled were paid too much in relation to other workers, and that a restoration of a wider differential would bring the relative unemployment rates more closely into line.

SAQ 18:   Well, several: a devaluation of the currency seems the obvious one, but incomes policy or deflationary fiscal policy would also be the basis of correct answers to this SAQ.

28 Problems of income and wealth

AIMS OF UNIT 28

At the end of this unit, you should be able to:
- distinguish between inequalities of income and wealth
- use the Gini coefficient and the Lorenz diagram as indicators of economic inequalities
- outline the facts and trends in income and wealth distribution in the UK
- define decile, quartile, quintile and percentile
- contrast the ideas of absolute and relative poverty and suggest measures of relative poverty
- list and evaluate six anti-poverty measures
- know the importance of women in the workforce, and indicate how their earnings fall short of men's
- explain why women earn less than men.

INTRODUCTION

Over the past two units, we've looked at the factors that affect earnings. Unit 26 used a market approach, speaking of an equilibrium wage determined by supply and demand in a competitive market. In Unit 27, we investigated how unions might cause us to modify that first look at wages. In this unit, I shall try to shed light on three major problems in the topic of earnings:
- inequalities of income and wealth
- poverty
- women's earnings.

The unit covers as much of the ground as you'll need to tackle the exam, but it can only be a relatively quick skim over three very controversial and complex subjects. If you wish to take your study further, then have a look at the recommended reading I've given you at the back of the unit. The linking factor between the three topics is, of course, the problems caused by differences — sometimes very large differences — in earnings.

SAQ 1: *How does the conventional theory of economics account for differences in earnings? What other factors have we studied in the past two units that might be important in establishing differences in earnings between individuals?*

Inequality

HOW DO WE MEASURE INEQUALITIES OF INCOME AND WEALTH?

By using the national income figures
In Unit 3, I showed you how the national income is calculated. Although there were a large number of complications, in essence there are just three ways of working out the figure, one of which entails adding up all the productive incomes earned by UK residents.

SAQ 2: *What are the other two ways?*

The figure is presented like this:

	£m	%age
Income from employment	209 445	63.8
Income from self-employment	34 340	10.5
Gross trading profits of companies	50 785	15.5
Gross trading surpluses of public corporations	8 126	2.5
Rent	22 497	6.8
Others	3 187	.9
Total domestic income	328 380	

Fig. 28.1 United Kingdom GNP 1986   (Source: Blue Book 1987)

One trend that caused considerable interest in the past was the observation that in many countries and through many periods, labour maintained a constant share of the national income. Keynes himself remarked that the stability of the proportion of the national income going to labour was one of the 'best established facts in the whole range of economic statistics'. Some diverting theories were put forward to explain this*, but recent research has cast great doubt on the theory of constant shares. For whilst the figures that Keynes looked at showed an unchanging wage share, that of salaries was rising sharply. The increased number of salaried workers can be attributed to the growth of the tertiary, service, sector of the economy.

If we add together the share of wages and salaries to reach a sum which may be called 'labour's share', we see no constancy at all:

> One thing that emerges quite clearly from the best recent work on economic history is a trend toward labour taking a growing share of the national income.
>
> (Glyn and Sutcliffe, 1972)

> In broad terms it appears that there has been a rise in the share of earned income and a fall in the share of profits and rents.
>
> (Atkinson, 1983)

> For employment incomes as a whole the trend since 1914 has been so unmistakably upwards as to suggest to those who see little difference in the distinction between wages and salaries a strong presumption in favour of an increase in the share of labour.
>
> (Deane and Cole, 1969)

This trend has been greeted with great interest by two groups. The political right attribute the poor performance of the British economy to the declining share of profits, and look for action by governments that will redress the balance in favour of capital. Leftists see the rising share of labour and the falling share of profits as confirmation of Marx's belief in the declining rate of profit: they expect vigorous class struggle as capitalists try to wrest back their share of national income. For more information, see *British Capitalism, Workers and the Profits Squeeze* by Glyn and Sutcliffe, Penguin, 1972, or (more balanced) A. B. Atkinson *The Economics of Inequality*, Clarendon, 1983, pp. 200-222.

*Accounts of them may be found in J. Pen *Income Distribution*, Allen Lane, 1971 or B. J. McCormick *Wages*, Penguin, 1969.

SAQ 3: *In what way might a decline in profits damage a market economy?*

National income shares do not, though, give us much information on inequality. The share of labour rises in a slump, because industrial profits fall faster than wages and salaries. But few would see a deep recession as actually working to raise living standards of the poor. However, the major reason that we cannot use shares in national income as a genuine indicator of greater or lesser equality is due to the enormous variety of today's workforce. Society is no longer divided simply into workers, landlords and capitalists. There are a number of highly paid professional employees who receive wages and salaries. Most people would regard an increase in the incomes of the highly paid — doctors, accountants, airline pilots, top managers — at the expense of low-paid workers as a significant change in income distribution, yet it would not show up by the income share method. By contrast, profits might very well swell the pension fund of a low-paid group, for we have learned that many shares are now owned by institutional investors like pension funds and insurance companies (*see* Unit 15 p. 248).

By using the tax figures
If we are interested in the distribution of income between people, as opposed to factor shares, then we must find a source of information. The obvious place to start is the tax returns submitted to the Inland Revenue. Before we look at these figures, though, I'd like to mention two sets of problems that arise.

- *Are the tax figures correct?* The first problem arises because tax figures are not a complete statement about personal incomes. For example, most married couples are assessed together and appear as one high-paid 'tax unit'; on the other hand, about 6m tax units don't earn enough to be taxed at all. Then we must recognise that tax evasion will mean that some incomes are unreported (*see* Unit 3 p. 46); and it is difficult to make complete allowance for income in kind — the rep's company car, a manager's generous expense account, the schoolteacher's free meal and the bus driver's free ride to work.
- *What do we mean by equality?* The second problem is tougher. The income tax figures of one year cannot tell us everything about inequality between individuals for two reasons. Firstly, people's earnings vary though their life — a highly-paid surgeon may well have spent a number of years as a poor medical student. Similarly, a person will tend to be poorer as a student or a pensioner than when in employment, and this will create the appearance of inequality in one year's figures that isn't there in people's lifetime income. Secondly, people's needs vary. An income that might be generous for a single person would be inadequate for a family with children. When we are concerned with notions of fairness through people's life-cycle, we speak of 'vertical equity': and when considering fairness between people at the same stage of life or with similar responsibilities, or 'horizontal equity'.

Having made those qualifications, let's look at a table prepared from the Inland Revenue survey of personal incomes: it shows how personal income was distributed amongst the 23m tax units reporting in 1979-80.

The table is arranged in 'quantiles' — that is, percentage slices of the population. A one-per-cent slice is called a 'percentile', a ten-per-cent slice a 'decile' and a twenty-per-cent slice a 'quintile'.

United Kingdom

	Income before tax		Average income before tax (£s)	Income after tax		Average income after tax (£s)
	(£s million)	(percentages)		(£s million)	(percentages)	
Quantile groups						
Top 1%	6 410	*5.2*	27 800	4.140	*4.1*	18 000
2–5%	12 600	*10.2*	13 600	9 600	*9.5*	10 400
6–10%	11 600	*9.4*	10 100	9 240	*9.2*	8 060
Top 10%	30 600	*24.8*	13 300	23 000	*22.8*	10 000
11–20%	19 200	*15.6*	8 340	15 700	*15.5*	6 790
21–30%	15 800	*12.6*	6 850	12 900	*12.8*	5 610
31–40%	13 600	*11.0*	5 880	11 200	*11.1*	4 860
41–50%	11 300	*9.2*	4 920	9 490	*9.4*	4 120
51–60%	9 620	*7.8*	4 170	8 080	*8.0*	3 510
61–70%	8 140	*6.6*	3 530	6 870	*6.8*	2 980
71–70%	6 530	*5.3*	2 840	5 860	*5.8*	2 540
80–90%	4 930	*4.0*	2 140	4 440	*4.4*	1 930
Bottom 10%	3 580	*2.9*	1 550	3 430	*3.4*	1 490

(source: Social Trends 1983)

Fig. 28.2 Distribution of total income before and after tax, 1979–80

The figures reveal a substantial degree of inequality between individuals. Before tax, the poorest half of the population receive just about one quarter of the income. The top ten per cent have an average pretax income 8½ times bigger than that of the bottom ten per cent. Even after tax, the ratio is nearly 7:1.

SAQ 4: *(a) What share of pretax incomes went to the top percentile?*
(b) What share went to the top quintile?
(c) What share of pretax incomes went to the bottom decile?
(d) What evidence is there in the tables of the progressivity of the tax system?
(e) What will the effect of these two factors be on any estimate of inequality we make from the above tables:
(i)   the omission of 6m low-earning tax units
(ii)   the combination of a married couple into a single tax unit?

By using the Lorenz curve and the Gini coefficient

Inequality statistics like the income tax figures above can look pretty formidable in a table, but it's possible to convert them into an easily-understood diagram. It's called the Lorenz diagram, and uses a box. On the vertical axis, we plot the cumulative percentage of income; and on the horizontal axis, the cumulative percentage of income units (i.e. households).

If there was complete equality of income, then 1% of the income units would receive 1% of the income, 5% would earn 5% of the income, 10% receive 10%, and so on. If we plotted this 'line of equality' on the Lorenz diagram, then we should arrive at a 45° line — which I've marked as OY in Fig. 28.3. By contrast, complete inequality would exist where one person takes all the national

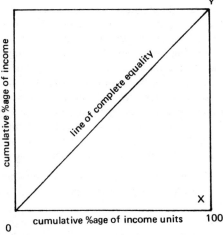

Fig. 28.3 The Lorenz diagram

income, leaving the remaining 99.9999% of the population with nothing. In this case, 1% of the population would get 0% of the income, 5% would 0%, 10% would get 0%, and so on until we came upon our Croesus in the last percentile. So this would be plotted by a line around the edge of the box, OXY. Neither of these curves, of course, exists in real life. Let's plot the data from Fig. 28.2 to see what shape the Lorenz diagram will give to a real-life example. I've plotted the income units against income shares: if you look at Fig. 28.2, you'll note that the bottom decile got 2.9% of the pretax income, the bottom quintile got 4.0 + 2.9 = 6.9% of the income, the bottom thirty per cent got 2.9 + 4.0 + 5.3 = 12.2%, and so on. These are the points I've plotted, right up to the top right where the bottom 95% of the income units got 84.6% of the income. Of course, the curve must touch the top right corner of the box, for in all societies 100% of the population get 100% of the income.

The Lorenz curve — for that's what we've drawn in Fig. 28.4 — indicates the degree of inequality in a society. The nearer it is to the 45° line, the more equal is that society's income distribution; the further away (i.e. the nearer to the edges that show inequality) the more unequal is the distribution of income. So we can see the degree of inequality in that gap between the actual line of incomes, and the 45° line.

We can use this information to express the amount of inequality in a number. Look at the Lorenz curve in Fig. 28.5. Here, the line of total equality is 45°, as you know, and the actual distribution of income is shown by the Lorenz curve to its right. I've labelled two areas in the diagram — A and B. The bigger A is, the greater the inequality shown by the diagram. The Italian statistician Gini used this knowledge to construct a coefficient of inequality. Its calculated as:

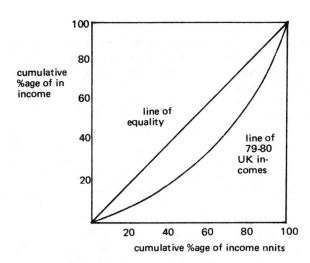

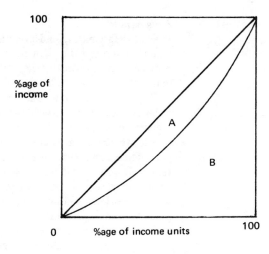

Fig. 28.4 The distribution of pretax UK incomes 1979-80

Fig. 28.5 Constructing the Gini coefficient

$$\frac{\text{Area A}}{\text{Areas A + B}} \times 100$$

Thus, if there was perfect equality, the Gini coefficient would be zero; area A does not exist. If there was complete inequality, it would be 100; area A takes up the whole of A + B. So we could measure changes in inequality by looking at changes in this figure. If inequality increased, the Lorenz line would move to the right, increasing the size of area A and thus raising the Gini number; but if the Gini number went down, then it would indicate greater equality.

SAQ 5: *Look at this table, and answer the questions underneath it.*

Gini coefficient:	original income	final income (inc. taxes and benefits)
1961	*38.4*	*33.5*
1973	*39.7*	*31.7*

(Semple, quoted in Atkinson *The Economics of Inequality*)

(a)   Is the distribution of original incomes more or less equal in 1973 than it was in 1961?

(b)   Is the distribution of final income, after taking account of taxes and benefits, more or less equal in 1973 than in 1961?

SAQ 6: *Look at the Lorenz diagram below, which depicts hypothetical Lorenz curves for an LDC and an advanced industrial nation. Which belongs to which? Explain your answer, with reference to Unit 24, p. 363.*

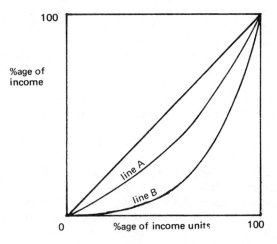

Fig. 28.6

Pen's parade

The most fascinating and graphic description of the distribution of incomes was presented by the Dutch economist Jan Pen in his 1971 book *Income Distribution* (Allen Lane). In many ways it provides a more forceful exposition of the topic than all the Lorenz curves in the world, so (like many other authors) I'll quote from it at length.

Pen describes a grand parade, in which the whole British population walks past our gaze in sixty minutes. The special touch about this parade is that everyone has a height corresponding to their income. We, the observers, earn average incomes, so we're about 5 ft 10 in. in height. The first people we see are actually walking upside down — small businessmen who've made a loss on the year. Then come tiny gnomes, the size of a matchstick ('housewives who have worked for a short time, schoolboys with a paper round'). These take five minutes or so to pass. In the next five or six minutes we see an increase in height. We see 3 ft tall people passing — some young people, women workers, old age pensioners, divorced women and the unemployed. Next come the lower-paid workers — dustmen, underground ticket collectors, unskilled manual and clerical workers, including a large number of black people. 'It takes almost fifteen minutes before the passing marchers reach a height of substantially more than four feet. For you and me this is a disturbing sight: fifteen minutes is a long time to keep seeing small people pass who barely reach our midriff.'

The parade continues. We are looking at skilled industrial workers, office workers: yet thirty minutes have passed and we are still looking down at the passing marchers. 'The height is growing with tantalising slowness, and forty-five minutes have gone by before we see people of our own size arriving.' This is because the few very high incomes distort the average: most people earn less than the average wage. The people coming by now are teachers, foremen, a few farmers. But as we move into that last quarter of an hour the height begins to shoot up. Headmasters, managers of small departments reach up to 6 ft 6 in.; police inspectors are 11 ft tall. 'Giants suddenly loom up. A lawyer, not exceptionally successful: eighteen feet tall; the first doctors come into sight, seven or eight yards tall, the first accountants.'

We are now into the last minute, watching the most prosperous sixtieth of our citizens. 'University professors nine yards, senior officers of large concerns ten yards, a Permanent Secretary from the Civil Service thirteen yards tall.' The highest-paid directors of Shell and Lonrho are over 70 yards tall. During the last few seconds of the parade we see the ankles of people whose 'heads disappear into the clouds, and probably they themselves do not know how tall they are . . . Tom Jones, nearly a mile high . . . John Paul Getty. His height is inconceivable: at least ten miles, and probably twice as much.'

The really gigantic figures at the end of the parade are made of two groups. At the beginning of the last minute are the exceptionally gifted managers, sports people, pop stars; but as we move into those with enormous incomes we see the people who are living off their wealth rather than their earnings. Differences in incomes reflect, then, not just differences in earnings but also differences in wealth and thus property income from shares, land, etc. Because wealth is much less equally distributed than income, its effect is to make the unequal distribution of income more pronounced.

THE DISTRIBUTION OF WEALTH

What is wealth?

Wealth may be broadly thought of as an individual's total stock of useful assets: this, however, is rather a broad idea and it is conventional in estimates of the distribution of wealth in the UK to deal with marketable wealth — that is, assets that can be sold. We shall consider whether this distorts the picture in a moment. In 1980, the Inland Revenue estimated that there was £566 000m of marketable wealth in the UK. It was made up of two categories: actual physical assets like cars, land and houses, and financial assets such as shares, cash and bank deposits. Figure 28.7 shows the composition of personal wealth in the UK. Notice the growing proportion of houses as a component of personal wealth.

SAQ 7: *Look back to Unit 19 p. 300 and suggest reasons for the growth of wealth in the form of houses.*

The precise figure I've given to the total amount of wealth, and the neat diagram showing its composition are deceptive. It is in practice very difficult to assess the size and ownership of wealth in this country: there is no regular taxation of wealth to provide data, and subjects are reluctant to cooperate in surveys into the topic. However, estimates of ownership may be made from two methods.

Every year people die and thus have to be assessed for *Capital Transfer Tax*. We can regard those who die as a cross-section of the population if we make adjustments for the fact that more

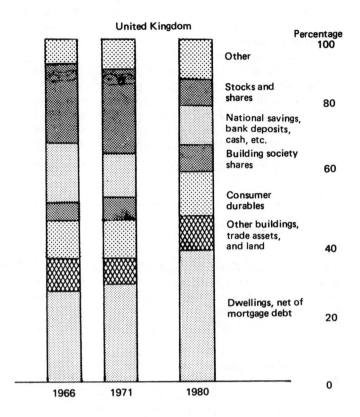

(*source:* Inland Revenue, from Sector Balance Sheets, Central Statistical Office)

Fig. 28.7 Composition of marketable wealth of individuals

old people die than young (by multiplying each generation's deaths by the appropriate mortality rate). The CTT returns thus give us a 'snapshot' of the wealth held by a sample of the population in a given year. Alternatively, we can look at people's *investment income*. If someone gets an investment income of (say) £50 000 per year at a time when the average yield on investments is (say) 10%, then it is likely that the principal off which they are living is around the £500 000 mark. Wealth calculated this way turns out to be more unequally distributed than if calculated from the CTT returns.

Who owns the wealth?

In the years just before the First World War, it has been estimated that the top 1% of the population held nearly 70% of the nation's wealth, and the top 5%, 87%. This stunning level of inequality has been moderated as the century passes. By the eve of the Second World War, the share of the top 1% had fallen to 56%, of the top 5% to 75%. The trend continued in the post-war years of economic growth and wider home ownership, so that by 1964 the top 1% were estimated to own 35% of the wealth, and the top 5% to own 61%. Despite these trends, wealth in Britain is still very much more unequally distributed than income. Whereas the top 1% of income units receive about 5% of total income, the top 1% of wealth owners hold 23% of all wealth.

SAQ 8: *So will the Gini coefficient for wealth be higher or lower than that for income?*

The table below shows the trends in wealth ownership over the past decade. You'll notice that the share of the top percentile fell sharply between 1971 and 1974. This was probably a result of falling share prices and rising property prices, for shares and land take up a higher proportion of larger fortunes, whereas houses and insurance policies are more important in smaller estates. Since then, the figures have moved very little. Note that such moves towards equality that have happened have occurred *within* the top 25% (who owned 86% of the wealth in 1971 and still owned 84% in 1981).

	United Kingdom			*Percentages and £s billion*			
	1971	1976	1977	1978	1979	1980	1981

Marketable wealth
Percentage of wealth owned by:

		1971	1976	1977	1978	1979	1980	1981
Most wealthy	1 per cent of population[1]	31	24	23	23	24	23	23
Most wealthy	2 per cent of population	39	32	30	30	32	30	31
Most wealthy	5 per cent of population	52	46	44	44	45	43	45
Most wealthy	10 per cent of population	65	61	58	58	59	58	60
Most wealthy	25 per cent of population	86	84	82	83	82	81	84
Most wealthy	50 per cent of population	97	95	95	95	95	94	94
Total marketable wealth (£s billion)		140	259	300	360	438	508	535

[1] aged over 18

(*source:* Social Trends 1984)

Fig. 28.8 Distribution of wealth

The share of the second to twenty-fifth percentiles (that is, the top quarter of the population minus the top 1%) actually rose − from 55% in 1971 (86% minus 31%) to 61% in 1981 (84% minus 23%). This might even be caused by richer families spreading their wealth more widely to avoid capital taxes. The bottom 75% of the population thus own just 16% of the wealth; the poorest half, who started in 1971 with just 3% have struggled up to 6%.

Problems of measurement
We meet a number of problems when we try to draw firm conclusions from wealth distribution data. Some of these problems we've met before in our discussion of inequalities of income: the influence of tax evasion on the data, the problem of variations in wealth-holding according to age, the aggregation of married couples into single tax units. There is, however, a special problem that concerns our very definition of wealth. We have so far concentrated on marketable wealth. However, many people have assets that are plainly valuable without being marketable. Chief amongst these assets are pension rights and education.

Pension rights
Why should we include pension rights in estimates of wealth? Well let's compare two men on the verge of retirement at 65. Mr A has worked as a self-employed accountant all his adult life, and he has saved £50 000. He has invested this amount, and aims to live off the investment earnings and interest − which he expects to be about £5000 p.a. − in his retirement. His neighbour, Mr B, has worked as a local government officer and although he has no visible savings, he has contributed all his working life to a pension scheme, and will receive half-pay − about £5000 − until he dies. Now, common sense suggests that both men are equally well set up for their retirement; indeed, as Mr B's pension is index-linked, he might be considered the better off. Yet his right to a local government pension cannot be sold, and so in a simple count of marketable wealth, Mr A will appear much more wealthy than him. This absurdity can be avoided if we include pension rights in our calculation of personal wealth: such an adjustment is made in each year's figures.

SAQ 9: *Compare the table below, which includes an allowance for occupational pension rights, with Fig. 28.8. What is the effect on inequality of wealth of including pension rights: (a) on the share of the top 1%; (b) on the share of the top 50%?*

		1971	1976	1977	1978	1979	1980	1981
(Marketable wealth plus occupational pension rights)								
Percentage of wealth owned by:								
Most wealthy	*1 per cent of population[1]*	*27*	*21*	*19*	*19*	*20*	*19*	*19*
Most wealthy	*2 per cent of population*	*34*	*27*	*25*	*26*	*26*	*25*	*25*
Most wealthy	*5 per cent of population*	*46*	*40*	*38*	*39*	*38*	*37*	*37*
Most wealthy	*10 per cent of population*	*59*	*53*	*51*	*52*	*51*	*50*	*50*
Most wealthy	*25[2] per cent of population*	*78-83*	*75-81*	*74-78*	*75-79*	*75-79*	*73-77*	*73-77*
Most wealthy	*50[2] per cent of population*	*90-96*	*89-93*	*88-92*	*89-93*	*89-93*	*89-93*	*89-93*

[1] aged 18+ over   [2] varies according to assumptions

(*source: Social Trends 1984)*

Fig. 28.9 Distribution of wealth

Human capital
The other unmarketable but economically valuable asset which people possess is education. It has been estimated that each additional year of education consumed adds, on average, 9% to annual earnings. Two people of the same age cannot be considered to be in an economically equal position if one of them has much higher educational qualifications even if they hold similar amounts of marketable assets. It is exceptionally difficult to reach genuine valuations of the wealth embodied in qualified people because of the extremely wide variation in their earnings. Some highly qualified workers earn very little.

DOES INEQUALITY MATTER?

Some economists consider that the present degree of inequality is not a problem*. They think that we should allow energetic and enterprising individuals to build up their wealth. In any case, it's argued, the distribution is not unreasonably wide when measured fairly, and is becoming more equal as time passes. I would argue that this is a complacent view as:

- economic inequalities are accompanied by other forms of disadvantage. Frank Field's book *Unequal Britain*, Arrow, 1974, documents this starkly. The poor have worse health and die younger; work longer hours and have fewer holidays; enjoy less job satisfaction and security; receive fewer fringe benefits. Crucially, economic inequality goes with political inequality: those without wealth have little power.
- wealth inequalities are rarely the product of 'saving' or enterprise. If wealth reflected human differences, disparities in its distribution would be similar in scale to other human differences. But in fact income and wealth are very much more unequally distributed than other human qualities such as height (remember Pen's parade) or intelligence. Perhaps Frank Knight got it about right — the possession of wealth depends on 'inheritance, luck and effort, probably in that order of importance'.
- inequality may always have to exist, it's true. In this case, the policy debate on wealth and income distribution will concern how much inequality is acceptable. But few will be content with the present allocation if it allows the simultaneous existence of great wealth and degrading poverty. It is to the problem of poverty that we now turn.

Poverty

WHAT IS POVERTY?

There are two ways to define poverty. One is to measure in terms of some absolute standard, such as the basic minimum needed to maintain life and health. This approach, defining what is called *absolute poverty* is difficult to justify. It would imply that a family unable to afford Christmas presents or a TV, a holiday or sweets for the children, was not poor. It is surely more sensible to consider poverty as a relative condition — relative, that is, to the general standard of living. The normal way of defining this idea of *relative poverty* is to create a poverty line below which people have an income barely adequate to meet their needs and participate in the relatively wealthy society that is modern Britain.

Where is the poverty line?
We now have to choose where to draw the poverty line. Draw it too low, and poverty appears to be a minor problem that can be cured by minor adjustments in the welfare machinery; draw it higher, and it becomes a massive social problem of general inequality requiring radical remedies. A convenient way to avoid this controversy would be to take the level of Supplementary Benefit (SB): this is, after all, an indication of what government and society see as a basic minimum. SB has a number of advantages — it is adjusted in line with inflation, and (because payment varies according to circumstances) represents a poverty line that is adjusted to each household's needs. SB is about half the average income.

Mind you, the SB level is not without drawbacks. The obvious one is that a generous rise in SB will make more people fall below the poverty line: contrariwise, an attempt to depress SB will apparently take people out of poverty. Furthermore, a line drawn in simple money terms will not tell us of the households kept out of poverty by excessive overtime, shift work, working mothers with young children, and similarly disruptive and exhausting styles of coping.

*See, for example, Polanyi and Wood *How Much Inequality*, IEA, 1974.

How serious is the problem?

Measured in absolute terms, poverty in Britain has declined in the past twenty years – from about a fifth of the population in 1953 to about a fortieth in 1973*. Yet this improvement was entirely the product of economic growth, which increased all incomes at roughly the same rate. In relative terms, the picture hardly changed at all. For my information on this, and much of what follows, I am using *The Causes of Poverty*, a fascinating and important research paper produced for the (now defunct) Royal Commission on the Distribution of Income and Wealth by Richard Layard, David Piachaud and Mark Stewart. They analysed 1975 data, but there is no reason to suppose that the broad picture is inaccurate today: with higher unemployment, it's probably worse.

They estimated that 4½m people live at, or below, SB level; another 4½m are below 120% of SB, and 5m more below 140% of SB. So if we consider people are poor if they don't have an income more than 40% above SB level, we have nearly 14 million people – more than a quarter of the population – living in poverty.

WHO ARE THE POOR?

Of those at or below SB level, about half are pensioners and about a quarter are children (one-third of them in single-parent households). The majority of the poor – about 60 per cent – are dependent on state benefits. Their poverty is the result of the social security payments being lower than average earnings. About a quarter of the poor are working, and their poverty is due to having incomes too low to meet needs. This may be caused by low pay, though poverty is much commoner where children and a non-working wife swell the household's needs.

SAQ 10: *Look at this diagram, which is reprinted from Layard, Piachaud and Stewart's article in the* National Westminster Bank Review. *Check through it, and answer the questions below:*

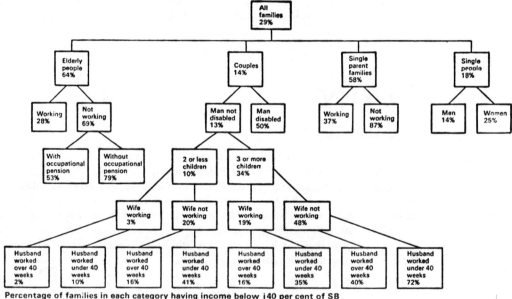

Percentage of families in each category having income below 140 per cent of SB
Note:
The number given in each box gives the percentage of that group of families defined by the corresponding 'branch' of the tree who have an income of below 140 per cent of SB.

(a)   *What proportion of elderly people are poor?*
(b)   *What proportion of single-parent families are poor? What difference does it make if the single parent is working?*
(c)   *How common is poverty in small families where both husband and wife work?*
(d)   *In which three groups do we find the highest proportion of low-income households?*
(e)   *What is the relationship between family size and poverty?*

*Prest *The UK Economy* 9th Edn p. 286, quoting Feighan, Lansley and Smith *Poverty and Progress in Britain*, CUP, 1977.

REMEDIES FOR POVERTY

What then can be done to improve the position of those whose incomes are too low to assure decent living standards? What I'll do now is go through a number of possible anti-poverty policies, looking at their advantages and disadvantages.

A national minimum wage

A minimum wage raises the incomes of workers by making it illegal to pay less than a stated minimum-wage rate. At first it seems an attractive proposal, until we realise that:

- the low-paid and the poor are not the same people. The poor are made up overwhelmingly of the retired, the unemployed, and the single parent: only 26% of 1971 poor households had the head of household at work. What appears to matter is the presence or absence of earnings, not the level. The low paid tend to be women and young people providing second incomes: only a fifth of low-paid workers are in low-income households. There may be other reasons to raise low pay, but it would be an inefficient way to relieve poverty.
- because of rigid differentials in the labour market (*see* Unit 27, p. 407), attempts to establish minimum wages often lead to wage demands by middle-income workers whose relative lead is threatened. As a result, incomes policies that have attempted to equalise incomes (both in the UK and Sweden) have been thwarted by a rapid restoration of differentials.
- minimum-wage laws can result in unemployment.

SAQ 11: *(a) Jot down a diagram showing why a minimum wage might be responsible for a rise in unemployment in that industry. If this baffles you, look back to Unit 12, pp. 199-200.*
(b) Under what circumstances could a minimum-wage law raise earnings without causing unemployment? If in doubt here, check back to Unit 27 pp. 403-5.

Using the tax system

One way of altering the distribution of income would be to use a 'progressive' tax system (*see* Unit 19, p. 298-9). It is widely believed that the British tax system is highly progressive: indeed, concern is expressed that it is so progressive that it diminishes effort amongst the highly skilled, and encourages the gifted to move abroad to keep more of their earnings. The evidence, on the other hand, indicates that the British tax system is not very progressive at all (*see* Unit 19, p. 293 and SAQ 4 of this unit). There are a number of reasons for this.

Firstly, the tax system contains elements which are regressive.

SAQ 12: *What is a regressive tax?*

For a start, there is VAT, a tax on consumption. As the rich have a lower-than-average APC, they pay proportionately less VAT. Excise duties are also regressive: your capacity for beer or tobacco does not increase with income.

Then again, one doesn't pay income tax on total income, only on taxable income. The difference between the two is made up by allowances — not just the personal allowance, but allowances for mortgage interest, assurance policies, trading losses, children's private school fees, business expenses, and so on. These concessions help the rich most of all: few poor people have a mortgage, let alone children at private school or a cooperative accountant to classify the family car as a business expense. The result of allowances is to reduce the quantity of income upon which the government can levy tax. Therefore, we have to tax more people, and at a higher rate, than otherwise. In 1947, a married man with two children did not pay income tax until his earnings were higher than average: today, he can be paying tax at half average earnings. Indeed, he can be paying income tax at the same time as he receives welfare benefits like free school meals — an absurd situation.

To summarise: the tax system could be used to redistribute income boldly: but it isn't. For a longer look at this, see *To Him Who Hath* by Frank Field, Molly Meacher and Chris Pond, Penguin, 1977.

SAQ 13: *Explain the following table as if to a lay person.*

	Change in Gini coefficient
Direct taxes	*-2.23*
Indirect taxes	*+1.77*
All taxes	*-0.46*

(source: *Report of Royal Commission on Distribution of Income and Wealth, Table 25)*

Comprehensive benefits

The use of minimum-wage legislation and tax systems misses the heart of the poverty problem — the 75% of the poor dependent wholly on state benefits. When the framework of the 'welfare state' was outlined in the 1942 *Beveridge Report*, the intention was that poverty would be eliminated by full employment and comprehensive benefits: benefits that would be available to all as of right. Education and health care are provided free to all; and the intention was that the government should pay a level of unemployment benefit, child allowance and retirement pension that would keep everyone out of poverty. But benefits have never been high enough to achieve this aim, with the result that many pensioners and unemployed have to top up their income with SB. This could be avoided if the level of state benefits were dramatically raised: indeed, this 'New Beveridge' proposal is supported by a number of economists researching the topic of poverty. The plan has two main advantages:

- it will work
- it avoids the form-filling and social stigma that put so many people off SB and Family Income Supplement.

However, it has a number of drawbacks:

- it would be wasteful, as rich pensioners and children would receive extra money as well as the poor
- it would be expensive, for providing *all* children, pensioners and unemployed people with a rise costs a great deal. According to the generosity of the scheme, it would add between 4p and 7p per £ to income tax.
- comprehensive benefits may help the rich more than the poor: research shows that more is spent by government on the education, health care and transport of the middle and upper income groups than is spent on the poor
- compulsory state schemes remove the element of choice. Left to ourselves, we might prefer to invest our money in a different pension scheme, use our income to buy independent education or subscribe to a private health insurance scheme.

Selective benefits

Because of the drawbacks of comprehensive provision (mostly the cost), there has been a growth in selective benefits. A benefit is said to be selective when it is not available as of right, but only on proof of need.

SAQ 14: *So which of the following are selective, and which comprehensive benefits?*
(a) Unemployment benefit   (b) Mobility allowance   (c) Student grants   (d) Family Income Supplement   (e) Supplementary Benefit   (f) Retirement pensions   (g) Free school meals

The obvious advantage of selective benefits is their cheapness: because money is only paid to those in need, it achieves maximum relief for minimum payment. There are, however, three outstanding and unsolved disadvantages.

- Because it requires the claimant to prove need, it requires a 'means test'. This prevents many people from claiming because of a belief that social security is charity, and therefore shaming; others never find out that they are entitled, or are deterred by the form-filling. Only half the families entitled to Family Income Supplement are reckoned to get it; it's even estimated that a quarter of those entitled to SB don't claim.
- If you receive means-tested benefits, and your earnings rise, you lose benefit. This is the poverty trap we met in Unit 19: a family can lose its rate and rent relief, free school meals, free NHS drugs, its FIS and many other benefits by passing through a narrow band of earnings. There are, after all, forty or so means-tested benefits. The effect is to create a very high marginal tax rate: and there are more families in the poverty trap than on the top tax rate.
- The widespread adoption of a selective approach would involve provision for the poor alone. When this occurs, the provision is usually bad. NHS spectacles and dentures are avoided by those able to afford better, and American 'free' hospitals are notorious.

In practice our social security system is a combination of using the tax system and benefits, comprehensive and selective. Despite its clumsiness, it achieves a great deal. The effect of the comprehensive and selective cash benefits is to reduce the numbers of those below the poverty line from 7.6m to 1.1m (Lansley, 'What Hope For The Poor' *Lloyds Bank Review*, April 1979). To put it another way, the gap between the poor's actual incomes and the poverty line was about 6 per cent of GDP before the social security system benefits were paid, but just ¼% of GDP afterwards.

It is possible to consider two other ways of tackling poverty and inequality.

Negative income tax

SAQ 15: *What is negative income tax? How might it work? What are its advantages and disadvantages? (If in doubt, consult Unit 19, p. 301.)*

Labour market policies

We might also reduce poverty and inequality by affecting the supply and demand for labour. On the demand side, the problem could be alleviated by government policies that reduce unemployment either nationally (through fiscal policy) or locally (with regional policy). Job subsidies for troubled industries — like the Temporary Employment Subsidy — will help, too. Studies have established a strong link between unemployment and poverty.

There are also a number of possible measures that would help the poor on the supply side of the labour market. Adult vocational retraining, and schemes that compensate for poor secondary school achievement (like the US Head Start programme) have been shown to be effective in raising the earnings of the low paid. Remember too that poverty is rare when wives or single parents are working (*see* SAQ 10 for evidence), and so good day-care facilities for children will help.

Women's wages

INTRODUCTION

The number of women in paid employment has risen steadily since the 1920s. This increase has been almost entirely due to a rise in the number of married women working*. In the 1930s, only one wife in ten went out to work; now more than half do so. Women form 41% of the workforce. It is difficult to be sure of the causes of this very significant social change, but undoubtedly some weight must be given to:

- smaller families
- labour-saving technology in the home
- full employment in the years after the Second World War
- changing social attitudes towards working women.

Yet despite the growing importance of women to the labour force, and even equal-pay laws, women continue to be paid less than men. Women's pay is on average just 75% of men's pay, and women are very much more likely to be low-paid, and less likely to be highly-paid than men. In 1981, men were 25 times more likely than women to be earning £300 per week. The reasons for the disparity in earnings may be simply reduced to three: lower productivity, prejudice, and the way women are concentrated disproportionately in a small number of occupations. Let's look at these explanations in turn.

Lower productivity

In Unit 26 we used supply-and-demand curves to look at earnings. We discovered that the demand for a factor was affected by that factor's marginal productivity: the higher the productivity of a factor, the more it was demanded. If women are less productive than men, the demand curve for their services will be to the left of that for men, reducing their earnings. The lower productivity of women might have a number of causes:

- lesser physical strength than men. However, the number of occupations where sheer physical power is important are few and (with the growth of service industry) getting fewer.
- poorer qualifications. Women tend to be less well-qualified than men: 8% of men are graduates but only 3% of women. Similarly, boys are about five times more likely than girls to enter an apprenticeship on leaving school.
- higher labour turnover and absenteeism. Statistics show that women are slightly more likely to change jobs and to be absent from work than men.
- lower mobility. Women tend to be less free to move to a new job, or a promotion in the existing firm, than men.
- less experience. Years of experience in a job are an important factor in pay differentials: this is particularly true in professional and administrative jobs. Because of the tradition of women dropping out of the labour force to care for children, a women of a given age tends to have less experience than a man of the same age.

It is important to point out that hardly any of the above characteristics are inherently female.

*In fact, the activity rate of young single women has actually fallen.

There is no fundamental reason why a woman should not be as well-qualified as a man; should always be the one to stay at home when the children are young or ill, should have to follow her husband's job rather than expect her husband to follow her. In other words, the low MRP of women is socially-determined.

Further, the characteristics may be mutually reinforcing. If women have low pay, there seems little point in investing in an expensive education; if men earn more than women, it makes sense for women to be the ones to give up work when children come along. Economic and social factors are interacting to reinforce the low earnings of women.

Prejudice

The factors I've just listed plainly do not apply to all women. There are well-qualified women who have the same amount of experience as their male colleagues, yet who earn less. Common sense would put this down to discrimination based on prejudice. This is hard to handle in economic theory, for, faced with women workers who were equally as productive as men but cheaper, a profit-maximising employer would recruit women rather than men.

SAQ 16: *What would this do to the differential between male and female earnings?*

So one of the following must be true: either women are less productive than men (for the reasons we've just looked at), or employers aren't profit maximisers. This second possibility would imply that (predominantly male) managers prefer males in senior positions and are prepared to pay a little extra to have them there. A final possibility is that employers simply don't have accurate information about female job performance and take their decisions on the basis of prejudice.

Concentration in a narrow range of occupations

The final reason for women's low earnings is that they are crowded into a narrow range of industries and occupations. In 1979 three-quarters of all women worked in service industry, and 59% of women were in just three service industries – professional and scientific services (26.7%), distributive trades (16.5%), and miscellaneous, which includes hairdressing, laundries, catering, etc. (15.4%). A similar picture appears when we look at women in manufacturing industry, with over half the women employed in four industries (textiles; clothing and footwear; electrical engineering; food, drink and tobacco). The result is 'occupational segregation': and the use of the word segregation is interesting. Sexual segregation at work is now more pronounced in the USA than racial segregation.

SAQ 17: *Look at the diagram below, which is taken from* Social Trends, *depicting the percentages of white men and women, and coloured men and women, in various occupational groups. Comment on the position of women in this table.*

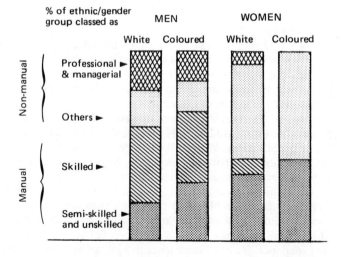

In Britain, the annual *New Earnings Survey* lists 396 occupations; a full sample of both male and female earnings could be found in only one-tenth of them. Women find themselves in semi- and unskilled manual and clerical jobs – as typists, secretaries, nurses, canteen assistants, hairdressers, assembly workers. They are more likely than men to work for small employers, and less likely to be unionised.

The effect of the growth in numbers of working women, and the way they have crowded into relatively few occupations has been to increase the supply of labour selectively.

SAQ 18: *What will be the effect on the wage levels of the occupations which women enter of an increase in labour supply? Draw a diagram to illustrate your answer. What will be the effect of a liberation of women that opens up all occupations to them on (a) the wage levels in previously all-male jobs and (b) the wage levels in what had previously been considered 'women's work'?*

POLICIES FOR WOMEN'S EQUALITY

Equal Pay

The Equal Pay Act of 1970 made it illegal to pay women less than men for the same, or broadly comparable work. The provisions of the Act were phased in, and became operative, in the mid-seventies. It has been fairly effective: average hourly wage rates for women rose 15% relative to men between 1973 and 1976. Equal pay legislation, though, doesn't really get to the heart of the problem, which concerns the lower commitment of women to the workforce (reflected in low qualifications and more time off) and the concentration of women in a limited range of low-paid industries.

So *equal opportunities legislation* also has a role, to open up professions and occupations which formally or informally exclude women and to provide job security to women who wish for maternity leave. A major component of an equal opportunities approach would be the positive encouragement of women to enter fresh occupational fields — engineering, accountancy, management, the higher professions.

SUMMARY

Although this has been a very discursive unit, I hope you can see that economics is able to make quite a contribution to the discussion of social issues. We've used concepts like progressivity, disincentives, supply and demand, marginal productivity to shed light on some controversial topics. I hope you've also felt that you've put to work skills such as analysing diagrams and tables to get closer to the reality of these issues. Most important of all, you may feel that your own view on these topics is now sufficiently well-informed to make a judgement on policies that might reduce poverty and inequality.

REVIEW SECTION

Further reading

I've named a number of sources in the text for students who wish to take their study of this topic a little further. For the basic information, look at the most easily available reprint of the Layard, Piachaud and Stewart research in *Nat West Bank Review* (Feb 79), and consult the latest edition of Prest *The British Economy*. The basic book on inequality is A. B. Atkinson *The Economics of Inequality*, Clarendon Oxford, 1983, 2nd Edn; you may find it easier to lay hands on the same author's *Unequal Shares*, Penguin, 1974. An interesting article on women's earnings is 'Female Discrimination in the Labour Market' by Maureen Pike (*Economic Review*, May 1984). On the broader question of inequalities, you might take a dip into Christopher Jencks *Inequality*, Peregrine, 1975, an American study which tests a wide range of theories on inequality. I've mentioned Frank Fields's book in the text: a worldwide view of poverty may be found in Jack and Janet Roach's *Poverty*, Penguin Modern Sociology Reader.

On the non-redistributive nature of the UK tax system, see *Poverty and Equality* by Jim Kincaid (Penguin, old but good) or *To Him Who Hath*, Field, Meacher and Pond, Penguin, 1977. Further information on negative income tax may be found in Friedman's chapter in Gill *Economics*, Prentice-Hall; a British advocate is Michael Beenstock (in 'Poverty, Taxation and the Welfare State' *Nat West Bank Review* Aug. 1980). The disadvantages are discussed in *Taxation Policy* ed. Crick and Robson, Penguin (see especially Piachaud's chapter).

The classic study of poverty is Peter Townsend *Poverty in the United Kingdom*, Allen Lane, 1979. Useful summaries on poverty and social policy may be found in Grant and Shaw *Current Issues in Economic Policy*, Phillip Allan, 1980 pp. 187-209 and David Gowland *Modern Economic Analysis 1*, Butterworth, 1979 — Chapter 12. The Penguin *Introducing Economics* Chapter 42 deals with poverty policy at some length. See also 'The Poverty Trap', *Economic Review*, May 1985.

Examination questions

The real distribution of income is quite a newcomer to economics examinations. The inclusion of the subject allows examiners to ask you to relate theory to reality:

1. How does economic theory account for differences in wages? Discuss briefly whether the theory adequately accounts for the difference between male and female wages.

(AEB June 1981)

and to assess government policies in the light of the comments I've made on comprehensive and selective benefits:

2. Outline and evaluate the economic arguments for subsidising the price of school meals provided by local authorities.

(AEB June 1981)

3. 'Equal pay for equal work'. Discuss the effects which the implementation of this policy could have on the employment of both men and women.

(University of London 'A' June 1980)

4. 'A minimum wage would not really help the poorest families because, of those in the bottom 10% of the earnings distribution, only 20% are in the bottom 10% of the household income distribution.' Discuss the factors that might explain this result.

(University of London 'A' January 1982)

5. To what extent are the problems of urban poverty the results of economic forces? Discuss the types of economic measure which might contribute to the alleviation of urban poverty in (i) Britain and (ii) a developing country such as India.

(Joint Matriculation Board 'A' 1982)

The topic also lends itself to data response questions:

6. Table 1. Distribution of income before and after tax in the United Kingdom.

		1972/3		1977/8	
		Income before tax (percentages)	*Income after tax (percentages)*	*Income before tax (percentages)*	*Income after tax (percentages)*
Top	10%	26.9	23.6	26.1	23.4
Next	11-20%	15.8	15.8	16.3	16.2
Next	21-50%	33.3	33.9	33.5	34.0
Bottom	50%	24.0	26.7	24.1	26.4

Table 2. Distribution of wealth in the United Kingdom

		1978	
		Marketable Wealth (percentages)	Marketable Wealth plus occupational and state pension rights (percentages)
Most wealthy	1% of population	23	13
Next	2-5% of population	21	12
Next	6-10% of population	14	11
Next	11-25% of population	25	21
Next	26-50% of population	12	22
Bottom	50% of population	5	21

Source: *Social Trends*

(a) Distinguish between income and wealth.   *(2 marks)*

(b) Describe the distribution of
    (i)   income before tax in 1972/3 and 1977/8;   *(2 marks)*
    (ii)   marketable wealth in 1978   *(2 marks)*

(c)   Account for the differences between
  (i)   the distribution of income before and after tax in 1977/8;   *(4 marks)*
  (ii)   the distribution of income before tax in 1977/8 and marketable wealth in 1978;
  (4 marks)
  (iii)   the distribution of wealth before and after pension rights are included in the definition of wealth.   *(4 marks)*

(Associated Examining Board 'A' June 1983)

ANSWERS TO SAQs

SAQ 1:   In conventional theory, differences in earnings reflect differences in supply and demand for labour. If a particular sort of labour is in short supply — due to high levels of skill, or the unpleasantness of the job, for example — wages will be higher than in the case of abundant labour — where a job is unskilled or especially pleasant. Similarly, demand for labour will vary with marginal productivity and with demand for the final product. We later modified this simple market explanation of differences in earnings by mentioning factors like monopoly and monopsony (including unionisation) and the possession of wealth (which yields additional income).

SAQ 2:   The output method (the value of all commodities produced) and the expenditure method (the total of spending on final commodities): *see* Unit 3.

SAQ 3:   By reducing the level of private business investment, which would have adverse effects on employment, efficiency and economic growth.

SAQ 4:   (a) 5.2%   (b) This means the top 20%, so it's the share of the top 10% (24.8) plus the next 10% (15.6), or 40.4. (c) Just 2.9% (d) The evidence is there in the way the share of the top 10% is reduced from 24.8% of the pretax income to 22.8% of the posttax income, and the bottom decile improves from 2.9% of income to 3.4% of post tax. But it doesn't seem to affect the middle-income groups much in terms of their share of total income. (e) (i) will make us underestimate income inequality: adding 6m poor units to the table would make the very-high-income groups stand out more sharply. But (ii) makes us exaggerate the inequality. What appears to be a £20000 a year income could be a husband on £12000 and wife £8000 (or vice versa).

SAQ 5:   (a) Less equal — remember, the higher the Gini coefficient, the more unequal the income distribution   (b) More equal — the Gini coefficient fell from 33.5 to 31.7.

SAQ 6:   Line B is the LDC income distribution. Being to the right of line A, it shows a more unequal distribution of income than in an advanced industrial country — as explained in the reference in Unit 24.

SAQ 7:   The major reason is the tax incentive to buy houses via mortgage tax relief. Also important has been the growth in incomes (bringing more people to a level where they can take on house purchase) and the collapse of the market for rented housing (under the influence of Fair Rent legislation).

SAQ 8:   Higher. The Gini coefficient for income is about 25; for wealth, about 75. This shows greater inequality, of course.

SAQ 9:   (a) It reduces the share of the top 1% from 23% to 19% but the share of (b) the top 50%, goes from 94% to 89-93% — no great change. This is because occupational pensions are unequally distributed, and tend to be earned by people in better-paid jobs. Adding state pension right is also done — this achieves a greater reduction in equality, the share of the top percentile coming down to 12% and the top 50% to 79-83%. Even this, the broadest definition of wealth, leaves half the population with little but their state retirement pension.

SAQ 10:   (a) 64%   (b) 58% in all — but this drops to 36% if the single parent is working. 87% of non-working single parents are in poverty, which indicates how important being in work is (and what a difference creches could make?)   (c) Very uncommon — just 2% of families where wife works and husband works a full year. (d) Non-working elderly people without an occupational pension; large families where neither the husband nor wife work; and non-working single-parent families. Notice the importance of having an income — this will crop up later in our discussions of remedies to poverty. (e) There is a connection: 10% of small families are in poverty, but 34% of larger ones.

SAQ 11:   (a) The diagram is in Unit 12, and rests on simple equilibrium price theory: when price (i.e. wage) is fixed above equilibrium, excess supply exists. (b) In cases of monopsony, where the employer is paying an exploitative low wage, it can be shown that minimum wages do not cause unemployment.

SAQ 12:   One that takes a greater *proportion* of low incomes than of high ones: remember, it's the proportion, not the absolute amount that matters.

SAQ 13:   Here goes my attempt: 'The Gini coefficient is a measure of inequality: the higher it is, the more unequal is the distribution of (say) income or wealth. Total equality is 0, total inequality is 100. Now, the table shows that direct taxes reduce inequality, as its effect is to reduce the Gini coefficient by 2¼ points; but indirect taxes increase inequality (see how it adds 1¾ points to the Gini coefficient), and so the overall effect of the tax system is only slightly progressive.'

SAQ 14:   Only (f) and (a) are comprehensive. All the others require you to prove need in some way — by a test of parental income (student grant), of disability (mobility allowance), of need (SB), etc.

SAQ 15:   This is all discussed in the unit referred to.

SAQ 16:   Close it. The increased demand for women would pull up their wages and depress men's wages until they were the same and there was no further cost advantage in recruiting women.

SAQ 17:   It shows that the group with the largest share of skilled manual and professional/managerial jobs are white males. Coloured males do less well, with more unskilled jobs and fewer professional/managerial, but they do better than women, who are concentrated in unskilled manual and non-manual jobs. The position of black women is the worst of all — they have no significant numbers in professional/managerial or skilled managerial jobs.

SAQ 18:

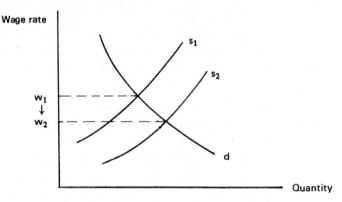

The effect will be as shown on this supply and demand diagram. The increased supply has led to increased employment by the classic mechanism of the market economy — a lower price, or wage rate. So the effect will be to depress earnings in the occupations which women enter below the level at which they would otherwise be. The effect of a 'post-liberation' economy will be (a) a relative fall in the wage rates in previously male-dominated jobs and (b) a rise in earnings in the previously overcrowded occupations as women cease to dominate (e.g. nursing, clerical jobs, hairdressing, catering).

29 Study Guide

AIMS OF UNIT 29

This unit is rather different to the previous twenty-eight. In Unit 29, we're trying to improve your effectiveness as a learner. When you've finished it, I hope you'll be a little better at:

- organising time and space for study
- preparing an essay answer
- finding supporting reading material
- understanding economic language and explanation
- organising an efficient system of notes
- comparing revision styles, developing one that works for you and using it to construct a revision programme
- understanding and tackling the examination

INTRODUCTION

At the start of this book, I wrote a brief section on 'How to use this book'. This section aims to build on the ideas I introduced there and help you study economics successfully. You can think of this unit as falling into two halves: the first section looks at the factors that are important in your study of the subject, and the second section helps you face up to the examination.

ORGANISING FOR STUDY

You'll have realised by now that to do well on this course you will have to put in a great deal of hard work. The course material, and your teacher, will try to help you through any study problems that may crop up, but the motivation and graft will have to come from you. You will have to plan how best to create the free time that the course demands amid the other commitments that you have got. But as well as needing time, you'll need *space*: unless you have remarkable powers of concentration and endurance you will need somewhere quiet, warm and free from distractions to work in. You may be lucky enough to have a spare room, but if not your local library will almost certainly offer quiet study accommodation — with the advantage of a lack of distractions.

ECONOMICS EXAMINATIONS

Most economic examinations these days test your understanding of the subject with three different sorts of question:

Multiple choice questions (MCQs) give you a choice of responses — usually four or five, marked 'a' to 'e' — from which you must choose the best answer. Here's an example:

> Jaguar Cars report an increase in the sales of their most expensive model. Which of the following is most likely to have been the cause of this?
> (a)   a rise in the price of petrol
> (b)   a rise in income tax
> (c)   the introduction of stricter hire-purchase regulations
> (d)   a reduction in the special purchase tax on cars
> (e)   a fall in the price of the competing Mercedes model.

If you look through the responses, you'll see five factors that could supposedly cause the sales of Jaguar Cars to fall; but only one response, (d), makes sense. Such questions are used to find out whether you have understood simple relationships or the meaning of technical terms. There will be examples of multiple choice questions throughout the course, and from time to time I will ask you to complete some MCQs for your tutor-marked assignment. This will not only check your learning, but give you practice in this type of testing.

Data response questions aim to see whether you can apply your learning to real situations. They present you with some 'data' — a chart, a table of figures, perhaps an article from a newspaper — and use this material to probe your comprehension of economic principles by asking a number of questions related to the data.

You'll find quite a lot of data-response work in this course. Throughout the text there will be diagrams, charts and quotations for you to analyse and comment upon.

Free-response or essay questions test your ability to discuss economic issues and give the right weight and importance to various parts of a topic. While essays are the form of answer with which you're probably most familar — perhaps from homework essays — they are often the most difficult to do really well.

WRITING ESSAYS

Preparation

My first piece of advice is: give yourself time to do the work. If you aim to complete an assignment with a couple of days to spare, then you'll have the time to deal with unforeseen difficulties that might require extra study or perhaps contact with your tutor.

When attempting an essay question, you must start by studying the actual question asked. You're rarely asked to write all you know about some part of the syllabus. Although essays aim to make you review and come to a better understanding of key sections of the course, most questions will focus on a particular aspect of a topic or problem. So the problem is: what is the question asking me to do? Look in the working for clues: key words such as *discuss, list, evaluate, explain,* and *compare.*

Getting it together

Next, decide what information you need to answer the question. If all the information is in the course units, then reread the relevant sections. If, on the other hand, you feel that a full answer will require a little supplementary research outside the text, then look up the suggested further reading (or look for some useful sources of your own in a local library). Then take brief notes from the course unit and from any further reading you may have done: a series of headings or key-words is often enough unless you wish to use quotations or close paraphrase (in which case you'll need to give the author's name, the book title and the page reference). Write your preliminary notes on one side of paper only to make them easier to review spread out on a table — and maybe rearrange their sequence using paste-and-scissors before you start your essay proper.

Down to work

Now that you have collected the material, you will have to decide the pattern of your answer: that is, the order in which you'll take the points, and the importance you'll give to each. Some people like to have rigid 'essay-plans', while others have a looser approach which leaves space for inspiration. You must, though, cover a number of points: a good 'A' level essay will deal with a topic from more than one angle, and, while it's dangerous to generalise, it's unlikely that you'll be able to cover all the necessary ground in less than three to four sides of A4 paper.

Although you should certainly start the essay by outlining the points made in the question, it's possible to overdo the *introduction.* You will be short of time in the examination and will have to get to the meat of the essay pretty quickly. One important feature of any introduction however is a definition of the terms used. Some words (unemployment, prices, firms) are straight-forward and don't need further clarification. Others, though, (free enterprise, full employment, competition) could mean one of a number of things and so are worth accurate definition. This is all the more true when you are using a common word – say, money – in its precise technical sense.

Once you are into the *main body* of the essay, try to make the argument 'flow': conclude each paragraph with a sentence or phrase that leads on to the next point. This flow will not just make the essay more pleasant to read; it will also show your mastery of the topic. You may well find that there is a particular way of structuring the essay that will minimize flow problems and cut out any need for résumés.

When you've come to the end of the main points, come to a *conclusion* – not a limp summary, but a statement of your own viewpoint. Examiners won't deduct marks for views they disagree with as long as your case is well argued.

The finished article

Write neatly, separating paragraphs and leaving a wide margin for comments: remember that on every exam paper it says 'careless and untidy work will be penalised'. Use diagrams where they help, labelling them and making clear in the text how they relate to your main points. Put your name on the essay, and (important when you've been given a choice of essays) write out the title of the essay in full at the head of the first page.

An essay isn't completed until it's been reviewed. First compare it with your original plan to make sure you haven't left out any of the points you intended to include. Then, if you can, put the essay away for a day or two before rereading it – this is a marvellous way of allowing your brain to unclog itself and look more objectively at its own work. Of course, if you want a truly independent view, ask someone else to read it through and comment upon it: get them to tell you the bits they found interesting, and the bits they found difficult to follow. Remember, your essay should make sense to the non-economist: the examiner should be treated as if he or she is an interested non-specialist wanting to know more about a particular topic.

FURTHER READING

Much of the material that you put into an essay will come from your teacher or from this book. I'm aiming, after all, to provide you with most of the material you'll need to pass a GCE or professional body's economics examination. However, there are times when you'll find it worthwhile to do some further reading about a topic. You may wish to find out more to complete an essay or other assignment, or just because the topic interests you. In this case, refer to books on that topic – trade unions, perhaps, or international trade, or unemployment – that are mentioned in the Review Section of each unit. Don't feel restricted to them, of course: you'll need plenty of other excellent sources, particularly where it's important to be up-to-date. Although you may wish from time to time to invest in an inexpensive paperback, your main help with further reading will be your local public, school or college library. Find out where the economics section is, and don't be afraid to ask for help from the library staff.

Another reason for seeking further reading would be because you found the topic difficult, and would like, as it were, a 'second opinion'. In this case, there are a number of general economics textbooks that you may find useful. Here's my shopping list, with comments:

Philip Hardwick, Bahadur Khan and John Langmead *An Introduction to Modern Economics*, Longman, is a recent publication that is available in paperback. Well-written, modern and broad in scope, it would be my first choice when double-checking on a topic. It is written, I suspect, for students setting out on a degree course, but isn't too difficult despite that.

Richard Lipsey *Introduction to Positive Economics*, Weidenfeld and Nicolson, is a classic textbook: again, written with the first-year university student in mind. It is written at quite a high level, so though it is an excellent and rigorous outline of economic theory, students at a lower level than that often find it a little difficult.

Frank Livesey *A Textbook of Economics*, Polytech Press, covers less ground than any of the above two books, but it has a directness and clarity of style that you might prefer – together with helpful exercises and examples.

G.F. Stanlake Introductory Economics, Longman, is a poular textbook. It is clearly and simply written, although macroeconomics is not as well covered as I would like it to be in a basic textbook (the author has also published a textbook called *Macroeconomics*). Stanlake has also published workbooks to go with his textbooks – these are particularly useful.

I can also recommend some paperbacks. Peter Donaldson's *A Question of Economics* and *Introduction to the British Economy*, Penguin, form lively and readable introductions to our economic problems. Slightly more advanced is *The Guardian Guide to the Economy (Vols 1 and 2)*, by Frances Cairncross and Phil Keeley, Methuen, which reprint and update a series of splendid articles published in *The Guardian*. Mention of *The Guardian* reminds me that reading a good daily paper will help you on the course. The business sections will be useful – finding an example of a principle or problem you've just learned in the pages of the *Times, Guardian* or *Telegraph* is always a plus

— and the political and social reporting will also raise topics and up-date information you'll meet on the course. The quality Sunday papers provide summary and background on the week's news.

Economic magazines will also be helpful. *The Economist* (despite its title) is basically a business journal, but it contains many stories that will illustrate economic ideas and problems; you'll have found diagrams, references and quotations from it throughout this book. A decent library should hold back copies for the past three or four years to allow you to follow up references. Other important sources are *Economics*, the journal of the Economics Association, and a new publication, useful for applying the theory you'll learn to the real world of today and full of exam tips, *The Economic Review*, published by Phillip Allan Publishers, Oxford OX5 4SE.

EXPLAINING ECONOMICS

Economic language

You'll sometimes find that this book uses technical language — economic jargon. These might be words that are unfamiliar to you — *oligopoly, dissaving, fiscal* — or familiar words given a special (and sometimes distinctive) meaning — *investment, demand, scarcity*. Technical terms are useful, since they enable us to be quite clear about what we're discussing and so to avoid long and cumbersome explanations. I'll try to keep the jargon to a minimum, but when a new term does seem appropriate it will be introduced — in heavy type — and defined. Some units will have a glossary of terms in the review section, but you may still find it useful to buy a specialised economic dictionary which defines economic terms and gives brief outlines of economic ideas and institutions. I use, and heartily recommend, *The Penguin Dictionary of Economics* by Graham Bannock, R.E. Baxter and Ray Rees.

Diagrams and maths

Economics is a social *science*. Let's look for a moment at that word 'science'. It means that we should be dealing not with personal opinions but with ideas that can be tested against the facts. Of course, we may find that it's more difficult to test economic ideas than ideas in physics or chemistry, because we are dealing with the behaviour of human beings rather than with lumps of matter. What's more, we can't create 'laboratory conditions' to test our theories: we are dealing with the real world where events are changing the conditions the whole time. A simple prediction (such as the proposition that cutting the price of UK cars will increase sales) may be knocked right off course by one of a number of factors (like more unemployment, higher taxes, dearer HP, more imports, and so on). That's why, in framing their theories, economists often say that one thing will affect another 'other things being equal' (or, in Latin, *ceteris paribus*).

Even though economic relationships are never going to be exact, economists often find it helpful to express their ideas in a mathematical form. Now, studying economics to degree-level requires good maths. Many colleges, for example, put on a compulsory course of 'Mathematics for Economists' for first-year degree course students: and for some of the more mathematical economics courses, you'll need 'A' level Maths to actually gain admission. You'll not need anything like that level of mathematical ability to succeed on this course, but there will be times when I'll be using simple mathematical techniques. As long as you're not scared stiff of maths, you should have no problems.

Graphs

Economic ideas concern the relationships between two, or more, factors. For example, I said above that if we cut the price of cars, more of them will be bought; and another example can be found in the simple idea that as one's income rises, more will be saved. Propositions of this sort are often easiest to illustrate on a graph. We start the construction of a graph by selecting a horizontal axis (the line going across the page) and a vertical axis (the line going up the page). These *axes* (the plural for axis) can now be used to *plot* points on the diagram — that is, place them accurately to show the relationship between the two factors. The way the axes are marked off depends on what we are illustrating. Let's take the example we've dealt with already — the idea that when price is cut there is a rise in the quantity sold. There are two factors here — the price, which I'll plot on the vertical axis, and the quantity sold, which will go on the horizontal axis. If the relationship between price and sales is as follows:

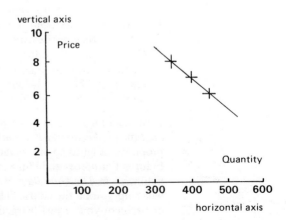

if the price were £8000, 350 would be sold
if the price were £7000, 400 would be sold
if the price were £6000, 450 would be sold

then the relationship would be that shown on the diagram above. You'll see that the diagonal line links all the combinations of price and sales — 350 at £8000, 400 at £7000 and so on. The word used to describe the steepness of the slope of the line is *gradient*. The gradient shows how the relationship between the two factors is changing, and there will be times during this course when we'll wish to measure the gradient. (You can probably see even now that a car manufacturer would wish to know not just that more cars would be sold by cutting prices, but how many more would be sold.)

Finally, you should note that the relationship plotted on the graph above is 'linear' — in other words, it creates a straight line. You'll also meet some curved relationships in the course, of course — life is rarely kind to students!

Further help with maths

If you're having a real struggle with a particular diagram then the best person to help you will be your teacher. However, there are a number of books on the market that take you through a very thorough course in mathematics for economists. You'll find that either of these paperbacks:

> J.M. Pearson *Mathematics for Economists*, Longman
> R. Morley *Mathematics for Modern Economists*, Fontana
> A.J. Mabbett *Work Out Mathematics for Economists*, Macmillan

are very helpful and cover much more ground than would be needed for this course. Use them, if you wish, for a second look at any particularly mathematical part of the course.

A note on calculators

From time to time during the course material, you'll be asked to do simple calculations. There will be nothing that can't be done on the back of an envelope, but you will probably find a cheap calculator quicker and more accurate.

APPROACHING THE EXAMINATION

We're now moving into the second part of Unit 29 — concerned with examination preparation. Many people, of course, have their own systems of exam preparation; but this unit will help those who haven't, and maybe give food for thought to those who have. I'm going to suggest how you might improve your chance of a good result by sound preparation and improved examination technique.

There is, of course, no easy route to success. You will not achieve the result you're looking for unless you have a solid basis of understanding of the factual and conceptual side of economics. No box-of-tricks can replace hard work and intelligence. But many examination failures can be put down to carelessness and poor preparation rather than laziness or stupidity.

SAQ 1: *Think about previous exams you have taken. Why did you pass some and do less well in others? Lack of work? Poor teaching? Overconfidence? Lack of revision? Failure to answer the questions fully?*

Stage 1: the continuous learning process

Too many students leave revision far too late. If you are one of those who rarely look back at the coursework you've done until the course is finished and 'it's time for revision', you are already reducing your chances of success. I've encouraged you to make outline notes on each unit as you went through the course. This should have contributed to the 'continuous learning approach'. Remember, too, that the time to undertake the 'reading around' a topic is when you are covering the material for the first time, not a few weeks before the examination. This enables you to check over the parts of the unit you found difficult: I once had a student who, when troubled by a hard part of the syllabus, would go to a library and swear not to come out until she understood it. Background reading isn't just for confirming the basic ideas, though: it's also to acquire extra information and ideas. You'll lose these unless you jot them down — either on your unit outline, or in this course book itself.

Finally, it's a good idea, when you reach the end of a unit — or major section of a unit — to take stock. The idea is to spend some time reviewing your notes, consolidating your knowledge and understanding, and raising any troublesome points with your teacher. Use the 'learning aims' that are printed in list form at the very start of every unit as a checklist of your understanding: are you able to do all the things set out there?

If you study like this – continuously – then, when examinations approach, you will be in a much stronger position than if you try to cover the whole syllabus at once.

Stage 2: planning your revision

Before you begin revising, it is essential that you devise a planned revision programme. Although you may feel that this is a waste of time – you want to get down to revision straight away – it is in fact time well spent. In order that you plan your revision effectively, take note of the following tips.

1. *Leave yourself plenty of time* for revision before the examination. Plan to finish the syllabus four to six weeks before the examination, and start your final 'run-in' then.

2. *Make out a revision programme* This will require you to:
   (a)   decide how much time you have available until the examination (remembering that you will still have other subjects to study and domestic and social commitments)
   (b)   break the subject down into topics. Topics, I said, not units, for an examination topic might come up in more than one unit (e.g. employment), be one section of a single unit (e.g. monopoly theory, the balance of payments accounts), or pop up in a number of places through the course (e.g. taxation). You have three aids in deciding which topics to choose: the syllabus, the past papers, and the examiners' reports. The syllabus is published by the examining board to explain all the skills and topics to be examined: it also outlines how the papers are divided up, and the allocation of marks within the papers. The best place to get hold of a syllabus is the school, college or public library: most exam boards bring out an annual book full of all the syllabuses they offer. Make sure you have the right year, as details do change. Just as important as the syllabus are the past papers, which show you how the skills and knowledge are to be tested and which areas of the subject are the most crucial. I've included a number of essay and data response questions throughout the text of the course, but they can't give you the full flavour of the actual paper. Lastly, the examiners report each year on the performance of the candidates (that's you) in their exam. If you can find the past paper and the examiners' report together, you'll have the marker's eye view of the right answers – what should have been said, what people left out, what were the common mistakes.

SAQ 2:   *Take an early unit – say, 4, 5 or 6 – and break it down into a number of component topics (about three or four per unit).*

   (e)   decide how much of the available time you need to devote to each topic or subject. On the whole, it is a good rule to devote equal time to equally important sections: don't concentrate overmuch on your favourite topic, nor ignore it in a desperate bid to bring your weaknesses up to scratch.
   (d)   divide the topics into the available time in the form of a timetable. Don't be overambitious and set yourself unrealistic targets: you will fail to keep up with the pace and this will cause you frustration, anxiety and guilt. Do leave yourself some time free from study or work to cater for unexpected emergencies and to keep a portion of your social life going. It's a question of balance: you'll get nowhere without intensive study, but a sports match or night off won't do much harm if you've got an adequate revision plan.

3. *Keep to the timetable* If you have problems disciplining yourself, get some help. Stick the timetable somewhere where your parents, flatmates or friends can see it and nag. If it does prove unworkable, reshape it – maybe in consultation with your teacher.

SAQ 3:   *Get out a diary and a side of A4 paper (i.e. paper the size of this page). Make a plan of the weeks between now and the examination. How many are there? When do your examinations fall (remember, they may be a week or more apart)?*

4. *Consider your revision technique* The reading and rereading of course units is a common but not particularly effective method, being both time-consuming and boring. You should certainly start revision with a survey of your course material, reading through carefully to pick out areas of difficulty or misunderstanding. Mark these areas, and do so more work on

them: a good way is to discuss them either with your teacher, or with a non-economist. Make clear what the particular part of the course is trying to explain, and outline your difficulty: often simply putting it like that clears the fog. Don't gloss over problem areas with the hope that 'I'll do something about it later'. Now is later.

Whilst reading your course units, make notes on them. I've recommended this more than once through the course text. It is an active as opposed to a passive revision method, and it slims down the material. no-one can remember 450 pages of text (not even me, and I wrote it). Notes on notes are meant to be brief, so be unashamed in your abbreviation, T↓ is much snappier than 'a reduction in taxation', even if you're the only person who can translate it.

There are basically two ways to construct outline notes. One is the traditional way, using numerals and letters to arrange the headings you've selected. An example might be.

Monetary Policy Measures

Define monetary policy – contrast with fiscal, prices and incomes – mention monetarist revival, then

1. Control on the PSBR (i.e. T↑ G↓; n.b. Keynesians would see this worsening a slump)
2. Interest rates
   (a)   Increase sales of govt debt to non bank public
   (b)   Reduce demand for loans & reduce credit creation multiplier
           (n.b. problems with Investment, home loans, cost of national debt servicing, inflows of hot money)
3. Acting on a bank's reserve assets
   (a)   Open market operations – explain
   (b)   Special Deposits
   (c)   (Funding)
4. Direct controls
   (a)   quantitative (e.g. corset – does it work?)
   (b)   qualitative (e.g. 60s exhortation to lend to exporters, mfrs etc.)

Another method uses this diagram – not arranging the material in sequence, but in a pattern. This way of taking notes and remembering ideas was pioneered by psychologist Tony Buzan from Sussex University.

SAQ 4: *Here is an example of the pattern-style summary of a topic. It's looking at the slow growth of the UK economy, and tries to relate the various factors.*

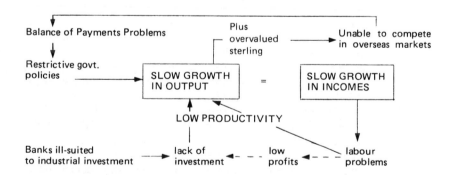

(a)   Jot down on a scrap of paper how the various factors inter-relate.
(b)   One factor that has been alleged to hold back the British economy is the lack of trained engineers: where would you put that in this diagram?
(c)   Spend a moment or so learning this diagram. Now, shut this booklet and try to reproduce it. Was it easier to do than learning a page of traditional notes?

When you feel confident about a topic, attempt to answer questions from a past paper, or from the units of this course. It isn't always necessary to write full answers, but try to jot down the main points that form the basis for a complete answer. It may be useful at this stage to dig out old homework or essays and analyse how you could have improved on them. Another help will be the examiners' reports: if you read them after attempting an essay answer, you can see whether you've grounds for confidence or panic!

4. *Learn effectively* You can learn facts by simply memorising them, by saying them out loud, or by writing them down again with your books closed. There are some facts, equations and lists that just have to be learned – don't be afraid to use mnemonics (i.e. memory aids).

SAQ 5: *Think up an easy-to-remember mnemonic for:*
(a)   the factors that affect demand
(b)   the internal economies of scale.

Having said all this, however, it's much, much easier to remember things if you know the reasoning behind the facts. Remember how you learned the three injections and the three withdrawals in Unit 5, without having to make a big effort? That was because you could see that savings, taxes and imports prevented money flowing on to UK firms. It made sense: the basis of sound learning is *understanding*.

Having said that, there are some important points to bear in mind. The brain absorbs information best in short doses. It's better, then, to work for four half-hours than in a solid two-hour stretch. Information and ideas generally 'stick' better at the beginning and the end of a revision session, so it's a good idea to change the order in which you tackle the same piece of material. Why not start that problem unit in the middle, rather than always at the start?

And there are some common-sense pieces of advice that are ignored too often. Don't revise when you are tired – the early part of the day is often best. Above all, find a place that is free of distractions. Background music and TV don't usually help. If you can't find a congenial study area at home, try the local library facilities. They also have the advantage of cutting out tea-making, table-clearing and other work-avoidance rituals.

It may be that you'll have to be pretty frank with parents and friends: you've got an important date coming up, and they can show their support for your efforts by helping you in your study arrangements. It's only for a short while, and you owe it to yourself to make the best effort you can. If you weaken, think of that result slip coming through the post in August.

Stage 3: the exam approaches

You need to have certain information about the exam well before you sit it.

1. *The date of the examination* This is important for two reasons. Firstly, if you are unsure of the date you will miss the examination: don't laugh, thousands (yes, thousands) do it every year. Secondly, knowledge of the dates well in advance will enable you to plan your revision effectively.
2. *The style of the examination* You'll need to know how many papers there are to each examination subject, and how the papers divide up the subject. In economics, it's common to have three papers – the multiple choice and data response in the same session, and the essay paper in addition. Which order are they in this year? Once you have obtained your past papers (checking once again it's the same syllabus) you can see if you get a choice of questions, and how many questions you must answer within the time limit (enabling you to calculate your time-per-question).
3. *The time and place of the examination* There are few things worse than turning up in the afternoon for an examination that was held in the morning, or having to search for a room or run through town because you weren't quite clear where the exam was to be held.
4. *The night before* A long revision session the night before is likely to do more harm than good. By all means run fairly quickly through your revision notes early in the evening, but after that try to relax. A good night's sleep will be of more benefit than trying to cram your mind at the last minute. Similarly, reading through your notes just before you enter the room is more likely to increase your anxiety than contribute to greater knowledge and understanding.

When you've got these four parts of your preparation right, you are ready to face the day itself with calmness and confidence. This take us right up to the examination hall.

Arrive on time. It isn't a good idea to arrive just in time but breathless, and arriving late puts you at a clear disadvantage. On the other hand, if you arrive too early and have to hang around this can increase anxiety. It helps if you can arrive calm and collected.

When you go into the room, find your place as quickly as possible and check that you have everything that you need – question paper, answer sheet or book, pen, pencil, ruler. If something is missing, tell the invigilators straight away: they're there to help you.

Stage 4: the question paper

When you are told to begin working, I suggest.

1. You check the 'rubric' – that is, the instructions at the start of the paper – and ensure that you have understood them. Always turn over the pages so that no questions are missed.

2. You answer multiple-choice questions by working through the questions quickly and care-fully, leaving out any to which you are not sure of the answers. Having answered the certain-ties within the allotted time, you should be able to go back to those that you have missed out. Remember *never* to leave an objective test item unanswered. Even with a total guess, you have a 25% chance of getting the answer right (better than 0% by leaving it blank); by eliminating those answers which you know to be wrong, you can improve the odds in your favour even further.

If you wish to gain practice with multiple-choice tests, look at a past paper book (remem-ber, it's half the size there that it'll be in reality). Alternatively, there are a number of economics multiple-choice booklets available from bookshops — they might make a worth-while investment if you wish to gain revision practice.

3. You answer data-response questions in a similar manner: here again, it's best to answer the one you can do best first. This will build your confidence, prevent you wasting time strug-gling over different questions and allow your mind to lay back and remember what you thought it had forgotten.

Look for economic principles in the DRQ paper: certainly explain your view of a situa-tion or table, but 'paraphrase' — that is, simple repeating what the passage or table says in other words — is a waste of your time and the examiner's. If the question has mark alloca-tions (like the assignment that you did for Unit 28), respect them — the part that is awarded 8 marks is more important than that with just 2 marks.

4. For essay questions, start by looking through the questions and ticking those you feel you can make a decent attempt at. After a little (not too much!) selection time, make your choice of a first question; again, attempt your best one first. When doing essay-style questions, work out a plan first and don't just plunge in. This preparation should take no longer than 5-6 minutes, and should include at least 5 or 6 main ideas. It is not worthwhile doing the question and then copying up — you just don't have the time. In most exam boards, you must leave all your rough work in the booklet after crossing it through.

Make sure you have answered the question that was asked. This normally means noting the key words in the question: 'discuss', 'list', 'explain', 'compare' and then doing as you are told. Remember, too, to answer all the question: often the second part of the question scores much more than the first, simple, half. For example, in these two questions:

What is the National Debt? Critically evaluate the argument that the size of the national debt is unimportant.

and

What are the functions of money? Outline the origins of a rise in the money supply.

I suspect that at least three-quarters of the marks will be awarded to the meaty second half of the question. The clue is not difficult to see: if the first half of the question can be covered in five minutes, then there's thirty minutes of real meat in the ending.

Look back to my earlier advice about introductions and paragraphs: remember too to include all relevant diagrams, labelled and clearly-related to the written text.

By the time you have reached the end of your main content, you should have developed your argument fully. The final touch is to sum up briefly your position in a concluding para-graph.

5. Make sure that you answer all the questions you are asked to within the time you have allotted yourself in your calculations before the great day. Spending only a few extra minutes on each section or question will eat into the safety net of ten minutes that you have prudently left yourself at the end. You must *never* leave a question unanswered — it is rela-tively easy to pick up the first few marks on a question and fiendishly difficult to write an answer that will result in your getting all the available marks. In examination answering as in economic theory, diminishing returns are present.

6. Leave yourself time at the end to review your work, so that you can make any adjustments or minor alterations that you think necessary.

7. You must write legibly. Examiners will always make an effort to understand your work, but being very busy people working through several hundred scripts, they will not feel favour-ably inclined to a candidate who makes their job needlessly difficult.

8. If you find yourself desperately short of time, then make the best of a bad job by answering questions in brief note form rather than full sentences. This stratagem should only be used as a last resort. As far as abbreviations go, you may use recognised abbreviations (e.g. GNP, PSBR, MRP, ATC) as long as you make clear what they mean at the first usage — as in 'aver-age variable cost (AVC)'. Do not use the abbreviations that you have developed for your note-taking, like BoP for Balance of Payments, gvt for government or mfg for manufacturing. Keynesian symbols like C, I, G and so on are acceptable as long as they are explained at first usage: the same is true of the components of the quantity theory.

CONCLUSION

This unit has been a list of suggestions for tackling examinations that have generally been success-ful. They are not an infallible guide to approaching study and success. No amount of skill in the exam hall can compensate for deficiences such as those caused by inadequate preparations during the progress of your course. Nevertheless, very few students can honestly say that they haven't squandered a few marks in an examination by carelessness or poor technique.

REVIEW SECTION

Further reading

There are a large number of data-response and multiple-choice workbooks on the market for you to use to test yourself in the run-up to the exam. On the MCQ side, try J. Harvey *Multiple Choice Questions for Intermediate Economics*, Macmillan Education or (more basic) *Basic Economics Objective and multiple completion tests* by Ernest Clarke (John Murray). As I said in the text, the best policy is to get some JMB back-papers and check your responses against the examiners' reports.

For data response, see *Worked Examples in Data Response Questions for 'A'-level Economics* by Watts and Glew (Heinemann Educational) or *Data Response Questions in 'A'-level Economics* by J. M. Oliver (Heinemann Educational). The ever-reliable *Economist* publishes booklets to test its articles on the economy – such as *Questioning the British Economy* by Peter Maunder (Econo-mist Publications, from Collins Educational) or *The UnCommon Market* by Peter Maunder (from Economics Assn., Hamilton House, Mabledon Place, London WC1 9BH): perhaps your tutor might have either. Also recommended are the 'Case Studies' series from Heinemann Educational and the 'Casebooks on Economic Principles' by Andrew Leake (on, e.g., macroeconomics, factor markets, market analysis) from Macmillan Educational. Frank Livesey publishes a Data Response Questions book to accompany his textbook (Polytech Publishers).

ANSWERS TO SAQs

SAQ 1:   Only you can answer this. One way might be to dig out an old exam paper and go through it, trying to determine how many marks you lost due to poor technique, (e.g. misreading or failing to answer questions) and how many because you simply didn't know (due to poor preparation of some sort – what sort?).

SAQ 2:   There is no right or wrong summary. Note the headings we've used, though. Capitals usually mark major sections; bold headings mark out the major divisions in those sections, bold writing at a paragraph's start marks an important subsidiary point. You could do worse than simply start with these as your skeleton outline.

SAQ 4:   (a) The UK's slow growth is due to a complexity of causes. Low productivity is one reason, caused by low investment and labour problems (which themselves diminish in-vestment by lowering profits). Investment is also limited by the UK banks' desire to lend over a short term and avoid taking shareholdings in firms. The poor record in productivity growth, combined with an overvalued exchange rate, make export sales difficult and allow import penetration; these combine to cause balance of payments problems that inhibit government reflation. (b) I'd put it somewhere around the 'low productivity' slogan – it's another contributor to that problem. (c) Well, did you find it easier? Some people do, others don't.

SAQ 5:   (a) Well, it's the Price of the good, the Income of households, the Tastes of households, the price of Substitutes and Complements, the Distribution of income and the Popu-lation size. Now, PITSCDP – how about 'People in tight skirts can't drive properly'? (b) Technical, Managerial, Financial, Marketing, Risk-bearing: can we link in with the way scale economies lower costs in some way? Internal scale economies allow us 'To Make Fings More Reasonably'?

APPENDIX A: CONSUMPTION AND INVESTMENT

Theories on the determination of investment spending

Throughout Unit 5 (pp. 75-95), a straight line investment demand has been drawn across the diagrams. I simply explained in the text that this was determined by businessmen's profit expectations. Of course, at any one time businessmen will have a number of investment ideas on their minds, and each of these projects will be more or less promising. A very few projects might be expected to make a high profit: one thinks at the moment of North Sea oil developments, for example. Other projects will make a more modest return, and there are many projects that might just pay for themselves. I have put this idea on the graph on the left: the horizontal axis shows the amount of investment, and the vertical axis plots the returns from those investment projects. You'll see that only OA investments will earn r_2%: but if we are content to earn just r_1%, then OB investments are worthwhile. This curve was called the 'marginal efficiency of capital' by Keynes, and in his book he goes into the reasons it slopes down in some detail (that we don't need here).

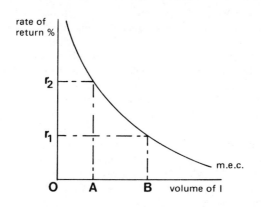

Now, what will decide the rate of return that we hope a project will make before it is undertaken? Plainly, we will not start any project that is not going to earn enough to pay the interest on the money we have borrowed. So, for example, if firms have to pay r_2% interest, only OA will be invested. However, if the rate of interest falls to r_1%, it will be worthwhile undertaking extra investment projects that are now profitable. Keynes' idea about the volume of investment, then, was that it was determined by the interaction of the marginal efficiency of capital (that is, the expected rate of return of one additional unit of investment) and the rate of interest.

The crucial thing to realise here is that we are talking about expectations, and this is affected by the mood of the business community. Keynes felt that the vigour and optimism of the business community (their 'animal spirits' as he put it) was at least as important as any careful mathematical calculation. A sudden shift in business confidence can shift the m.e.c. curve rightwards or leftwards, accounting for the sharp changes in investment behaviour that economists have noticed for many years.

Of course, simply saying that investment depends on the animal spirits of the business community doesn't get you very far, and so economists have developed another idea that is a little easier to pin down and test.

The accelerator

This theory is called the accelerator, and says that investment will be affected by the rate at which national income is changing. If, for example, total demand and therefore national income start to rise faster than expected, businessmen will realise that they don't have enough capital equipment to meet future demand. They will therefore increase their investment plans, so as not to be caught out. Investment spending will rise sharply — maybe even more sharply than the rise in the national income.

If national income slumped, and orders were hard to come by, the reverse would happen — businessmen would not replace machinery at all. Now, when you remember the multiplier effect, you can see that we have developed a theory that might explain trade cycles. A rise in national income is exaggerated by the accelerator effect, which (via the multiplier) adds further to demand; and when businessmen stop investing, the multiplier again combines with the accelerator to cause a sharp drop in national income. After all, the accelerator theory is about a rise in national income causing a burst of investment spending, and the multiplier says that a burst of investment spending causes a rise in national income bigger than itself.

What's wrong with these theories?

There are a number of holes that can be picked in these theories of investment — most firms, for example, have capacity to spare and can produce extra output by overtime working and taking up slack. New machines are not needed. What is more, much investment is by the government, and for residential housing, neither of which can look to a theory based on profit as their main motive.

The consumption function

But it isn't just the level of investment that determines national income — the level of consumption is also crucial. Governments will therefore wish to know the factors that determine the level of consumption expenditure. It is this (including the a.p.c. and the m.p.c.) that we are investigating when we are looking at the **consumption function**.

To say that something is a 'function' of something else is a mathematical expression: if X is a function of Y, then the amount of X depends on the amount of Y. For example, road accidents are a function of the number of cars and lorries on the road and also of the training and attitudes of drivers; the sales of raincoats are a function of consumer incomes and the weather. So the consumption function relates the level of consumption spending to the things it depends on.

Many factors affect consumption, as we have noted in this unit — advertising, social attitudes to thrift, tastes, the ease with which we can get credit, wars (consumption spending fell during the Second World War as there was nothing worth buying in the shops!), the prevalence of pension schemes, expectations about future inflation, uncertainty about job prospects, changes in the distribution of the national income between different social classes, and so on. However, we have learned in this unit that the main factor is income.

The generalisation we have come to is that consumption is a function of income. We developed two measures in the text — the average propensity to consume (that is, total consumption spending divided by total income) and the marginal propensity to consume (that is, the relationship between changes in income and changes in consumption). Keynes viewed the marginal propensity to consume as one of the great constants of economics — it would be less than one but more than zero. If you chew this over for a moment, you'll realise that this is not a remarkably astute insight — all it says is that people will spend some of an increase in income, but not all of it. What have economists found to confirm, or deny, the ideas about consumption that we have used in the text?

In the very short run, there appears to be little relation between income and consumption. If next week, for example, I were to lose my job and earn nothing, I would not spend much less than I did this week. After all, I'm used to my present standard of living, and find the process of adjust-

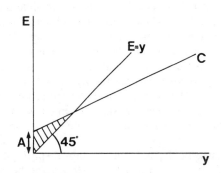

ing it painful — and I can use my savings as a cushion. After a while, however, we must relate our consumption to our income, and so we see the traditional Keynesian consumption line coming through (see left). Here, there is a certain amount of dissaving at low income levels (shown by the shaded area), and as the level of income rises, the average propensity to consume falls.

Indeed, it may even be true that the m.p.c. falls, causing the C line to bend a little at the top, as shown on this diagram on the right here.

We can express the consumption spending in the diagram above in an equation. The amount of consumption will be equal to A (the amount of dissaving, or consumption spending when income is zero) *plus* a proportion (the m.p.c.) of whatever the level of income may be. So

$$C = A + bY \text{ (where } b \text{ is the m.p.c.)}$$

This equation does in fact fit the consumption spending in the British economy.

In the long run, that is to say if we look at

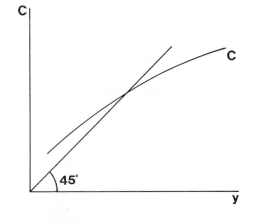

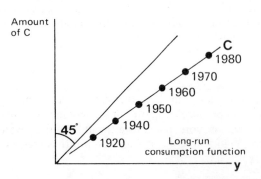

consumer spending through the years, we find a consumption like the one on the left. Consumption is very strongly related to income, and the a.p.c. becomes almost equal to the m.p.c. When income rises, we spend it; when income falls we reduce our consumer spending in line. There are two contrasting explanations for this. Economic historians believe that it shows a number of C lines, gradually shifting upwards. The reasons given for the drift upwards in the consumption function are social and historical. As farmers save more than towns-people generally, a move from farms to towns will reduce the savings propensity and therefore increase consumption. What is more, consumption will be affected by how families see themselves

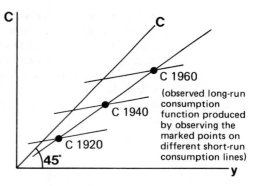

in the social class system. A certain income which was high in 1920 would be low in 1980: so a family on that income would consume more in 1980 than in 1920. A more likely explanation is Milton Friedman's 'permanent income' idea. He points out that people will spend a proportion of what they see as their *permanent* income. So if their income rises, they won't spend it all until they become used to earning a higher income — at which point they will spend as much as the next person. If income falls, then savings can be spent for a short while but in the long run expenditure must be fitted within income: when it is realised that income has permanently fallen, then, consumption spending falls to being a proportion of it. I find this appealing, for it actually fits what we see of human behaviour — that spending expands to fit any income.

APPENDIX B: CAN WE RECONCILE KEYNESIAN AND MONETARIST VIEWS?

This unit has so far introduced you to two differing explanations of how money affects the economy — the 'monetarist' and the Keynesian. The popular view of these two groups of economists sees them in two opposing armies, throwing research evidence and abuse at each other in almost equal measure. And yet, from the moment that Keynes published his 'General Theory of Employment, Interest and Money' in the 1930s, economists have worked to reconcile the two viewpoints. The concluding part of this unit explains one such attempt, named after the two economists — Sir John Hicks and Alvin Hansen — who developed it. The 'Hicks-Hansen diagram' relates an equilibrium level of national income to the rate of interest and the supply of money in the following way:

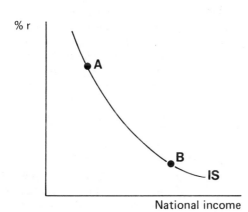

Firstly, one constructs a diagram that relates the amount of investment (and therefore savings — remember that S = I) that happens at various rates of interest to the size of the national income. This is done on the left here — high interest rates discourage investment, and are thus associated with a lower national income. At point A, for example, interest rates are high and national income is low. If interest rates were lower, the amount of investment and therefore (via the multiplier) the national income is higher. Position B shows a point of lower interest rates and higher national income. The curve that shows this changing relationship between interest rates and national income is labelled IS.

(In an article entitled 'Mr Keynes and the Classics', Hicks explained the IS curve this way: as the national income rises, more and more savings occur — for savings are a function of income. In order to absorb all the extra savings into investment, and even lower interest rate must exist.)

The second curve used in the Hicks-Hansen diagram traces what would happen to interest rates if the money supply were to be held fixed whilst the national income varied. At a low level of national income, the demand for money will be low: there will be fewer transactions, and the prices at which those transactions will be taking place will be low. The supply of money will appear generous in relation to the national income, and the spare cash will bid down interest rates.

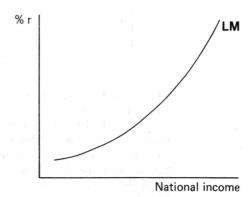

But as the size of the national income rises, more and more money will be needed simply to finance the day-to-day trade of the community. Money will prove scarce and high rates of interest will be needed to persuade money-holders to part with their spare balances. Thus, the LM curve (liquidity/money) rises very sharply indeed when we come to high levels of national income.

Now let's put the two diagrams together. Firstly, you will notice that there is only one point — where the national income is OB and the rate of interest is OA — consistent with equilibrium between interest rates and national income.

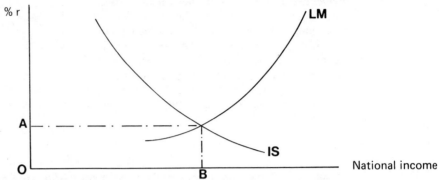

This diagram combines a little of both the contrasting approaches to macroeconomics that we have seen in the last few units. It incorporates a monetary view in the LM curve, which takes into account the demand for money; and it also uses a Keynesian approach in the IS curve. One use of this diagram is to inform us as to the effectiveness of monetary and fiscal policy. Look for a moment at the diagram below at the lower end of the LM curve. I have drawn in an IS curve there.

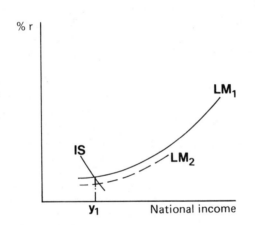

would be shown by a shift to the right of the IS curve.

If this were really to be the case, the economy would be in a deep depression. How might we raise the level of economic activity — output and jobs? An increase in the supply of money would shift the LM curve to the right (more money would mean lower interest rates at any given national income size). The lower LM curve has been drawn in (LM$_2$ — the dashed line). The new equilibrium shows no great improvement in the level of national income. This illustrates something that has been observed in the past — that monetary policy is not effective in dragging an economy out of a slump. Expanding the money supply won't help anywhere near as much as an expansion of aggregate demand — which in this diagram

The reverse can be found at the 'boom end' of the diagram. In the diagram on the left, we concentrate on the upper end of the LM curve, where there is a high level of national income. Variations in the IS curve (that is, changes in business expenditure or, if you like, of government spending) will not have much effect on the size of the national income. A rise in business investment, as shown by the shift from IS$_1$ to IS$_2$ that I have illustrated on the diagram, would tend to raise interest rates as more borrowers scrambled to get their hands on a limited supply of funds; but it doesn't raise the total level of national income appreciably.

At the high level of activity depicted, though, monetary policy would be effective. Shifting the LM curve to the right (i.e. expanding the money supply) would cause a rise in national income, and a restriction of money supply would reduce national income.

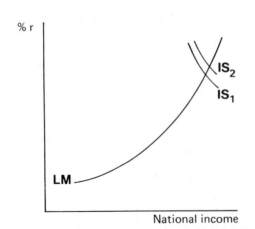

Perhaps the Hicks-Hansen approach offers us a reconciliation of monetary and Keynesian ideas. It isn't that monetary policy is always effective, or never works. What appears to be true is that monetary measures are ineffective in pulling an economy out of a slump, but that they have their uses in controlling the economy when there is a high level of activity. To use a favourite economists' cliché about monetary policy in boom and slump — 'you can pull on a string, but you can't push on a string'.

Index

Index